M000111553

The 80x86 Family

Design, Programming, and Interfacing

Second Edition

JOHN UFFENBECK
Wisconsin Indianhead Technical College

Prentice Hall
Upper Saddle River, New Jersey   *Columbus, Ohio*

Library of Congress Cataloging-in-Publication Data

Uffenbeck, John E.
    The 80x86 Family : design, programming, and interfacing / John
Uffenbeck. — 2nd ed.
      p.   cm.
    Rev. ed. of: The 8086/8088 Family : design, programming, and interfacing. c1987.
    Includes index.
    ISBN 0-13-362955-4
    1. Intel 80x86 series microprocessor. I. Title.
QA76.8.I29U34   1998
004.165—dc21
                                                  97-3741
                                                CIP

Editor: Charles E. Stewart, Jr.
Production Editor: Rex Davidson
Design Coordinator: Julia Zonneveld Van Hook
Cover Designer: Julia Zonneveld Van Hook
Cover Art: © Frank Shirley/SuperStock
Production Manager: Deidra M. Schwartz
Marketing Manager: Debbie Yarnell
Production Supervision: Custom Editorial Productions, Inc.

This book was set in Times Roman and Helvetica by Custom Editorial Productions, Inc., and was
printed and bound by R.R.Donnelley & Sons. The cover was printed by Phoenix Color Corp.

© 1998, 1987 by Prentice-Hall, Inc.
Simon & Schuster/A Viacom Company
Upper Saddle River, New Jersey 07458

All rights reserved. No part of this book may be reproduced, in any form or by any means, without
permission in writing from the publisher.

Printed in the United States of America

10 9 8 7 6 5 4 3 2 1

ISBN   0-13-362955-4

Prentice-Hall International (UK) Limited, *London*
Prentice-Hall of Australia Pty. Limited, *Sydney*
Prentice-Hall Canada Inc., *Toronto*
Prentice-Hall Hispanoamericana, S. A., *Mexico*
Prentice-Hall of India Private Limited, *New Delhi*
Prentice-Hall of Japan, Inc., *Tokyo*
Simon & Schuster Asia Pte. Ltd., *Singapore*
Editora Prentice-Hall do Brasil, Ltda., *Rio de Janeiro*

Preface

This is the second edition of a book previously titled *The 8086/8088 Family: Design, Programming, and Interfacing.* As the new title suggests, it has been expanded to include coverage of all of the 80x86 processors, from the 8-bit 8088 to the 16-bit 8086 and 80286 and the 32-bit 80386, 80486, Pentium, and Pentium Pro processors.

As in the first edition, this edition is more than a survey of Intel microprocessor chips. Think of these processors as the *vehicles* that will allow you to explore the real world of microcomputer technology. To appreciate the trip, you should be familiar with digital logic circuits and the binary and hexadecimal numbers systems. In addition, a familiarity with DOS and Windows will come in handy when the software features of the processors are explored.

Philosophy

If this book has an underlying philosophy, it is to stand back and observe the microprocessor as one component in a *microcomputer system.* In the case of the 80x86 processors, that system—thanks to IBM—has become known as the *PC* or *Personal Computer.* This philosophy is embedded throughout the book. Particular attention has been paid to developing examples based on the PC architecture. The software chapters, for example, use DEBUG, a utility commonly available with MS-DOS for program development. The program examples are all designed to run on a PC and utilize calls to the BIOS services and MS-DOS functions of the PC.

The hardware chapters focus on chips and circuits used in the PC. Chapter 8, for example, describes the PC's parallel printer interface. Software drivers for this circuit using programmed I/O and interrupt-driven I/O are also included. Chapter 9 includes a detailed description of the 8259A PIC (Programmable Interrupt Controller) still used by the PC today (in integrated form). Chapter 10 focuses on serial I/O and provides detailed coverage of the 16550 UART (Universal Asynchronous Receiver/Transmitter). Also included in this chapter is a description of the popular modem standards and the Hayes AT command set. Chapter 11 describes the architecture of the PC and the different bus systems, including ISA, EISA, MCA, VESA, PCI, SCSI, and USB.

Organization

Each chapter presents a consistent interface to the reader. The *Outline* lists the major sections of the chapter, followed by a list of *Objectives*. The chapter *Overview* gives a quick look at the chapter and tries to answer the question, "Why is this chapter important?" Each section is numbered (1.1, 1.2, 1.3, and so on) and includes a brief introduction that reiterates the objectives to be covered. To measure your understanding, a set of *Self-Review* questions (with answers) is also provided.

Each chapter ends with a *Self-Test,* typically twenty questions requiring short answers readily found in the text. More thought-provoking questions are included in a separate section entitled *Analysis and Design Questions*. These are keyed to the appropriate section in the chapter.

Changes from the Previous Edition

This new edition represents a major redesign of the original textbook. A brief summary of these changes follows.

- Chapter 1 has been split into two chapters. The first provides a history of computing from ENIAC to the present day. Also included is an overview of each processor in the 80x86 family. The second chapter provides a review of the binary and hexadecimal number systems and a description of various computer codes. Computer programming is also explained as well as computer operating systems (updated to include Windows).
- Chapter 2 of the first edition has also been split into two new chapters. One focuses on the specific architecture of each 80x86 processor, the other provides an overview of the 80x86 processor instruction sets. New in this chapter is a description of the MS-DOS BIOS services and function calls.
- The software chapters of the first edition have been completely redone. Two chapters are now provided. Chapter 5 illustrates 80x86 programming techniques. Seven program examples are provided in that chapter, each developed using a unique outline approach and coded using DEBUG. Chapter 6 explains 80x86 assembly language using Microsoft's Programmer's Workbench. Techniques for creating COM and EXE files are provided as well as the complete design of a simple game program.
- Chapter 7 on memory has been updated to include flash memory, SIMMs and DIMMs, EDO RAM, synchronous DRAMs and SRAMs, and PAL address decoders.
- The input/output coverage has been expanded to two chapters. Chapter 8 covers parallel I/O and programmed I/O techniques. Chapter 9 covers interrupt driven I/O and the 8259A PIC. DMA techniques are also included in this chapter.
- Chapter 10 on data communications now includes coverage of the 16550 UART and common modem standards. The AT command set is also covered.
- Chapter 11 of the first edition has been replaced with a new chapter that describes the architecture of the PC and the common bus systems. This includes the ISA and extended ISA buses, the microchannel architecture, and the EISA, VESA, and PCI buses. Two I/O buses are also covered, SCSI and USB.

Included Disk

In your book you will find a diskette that includes the assembly listings for all of the programs in the book. These are organized by chapter, with the figure name used as the program name. In addition, you will also find a copy of *DEBUG32* on this disk. This is an enhanced version of the popular DEBUG utility supplied with MS-DOS. It allows full access to the 32-bit registers and addressing capabilities of the 80x86 processors. In addition, it can also be used for debugging protected-mode programs. A special thanks to Rob Larson and Michael Schmit of Quantasm Corporation for their permission to include this program.

Acknowledgments

I would like to thank Charles Stewart and Kim Gundling of Prentice Hall, Inc., who encouraged me to resurrect this book nearly ten years after the first edition appeared. I would also like to thank Rex Davidson, also of Prentice Hall, and Jim Reidel of Custom Editorial Productions, Inc., the two editors who assisted me with the final production of this book. These are the people I spent the most time with, especially Jim, who had to put up with my last minute changes!

I am grateful to Intel Corp., Texas Instruments, Inc., Advanced Micro Devices, National Semiconductor Corp., Quantasm Corp., BYTE Publications, Hitachi America Ltd., and Addison Wesley Longman Ltd. for permission to include many of the data sheets and technical drawings presented throughout the book. I would also like to thank Al Subera of ADS Photography for many of the photographs that illustrate the book—and the Smithsonian Institution for the chapter-opening photographs that highlight significant computers from the past.

Finally, I want to give my special thanks to my students at Wisconsin Indianhead Technical College. Instead of using a "real" book, these folks have had to lug around a manuscript for the last several years. Their questions and comments have been available to me as I prepared this new edition.

Final Thoughts

I first started teaching microprocessors at Hartnell College in 1976. We used a "briefcase" computer-trainer based on the 8080, called the MST-80. Microcomputer technology has come a long way since those days. To compare the Pentium Pro with the 8080 is to compare the Space Shuttle with the Wright Brothers' first powered airplane. Yet somehow we must come to grips with this incredible, rapidly accelerating technology. It is exciting, but frightening. Take a summer off and you may find yourself hopelessly behind. I hope you find this book useful as you attempt to hang on to the fast-moving technology train.

John Uffenbeck
Wisconsin Indianhead Technical College

Contents

1 Microcomputers and Microprocessors

One of the first practical computers was ENIAC (Electronic Numerical Integrator and Computer). Built in 1945, it contained nearly 17,000 vacuum tubes, weighed more than 30 tons, and required 1500 square feet of floor space. It is interesting to note that in 1949, *Popular Mechanics* magazine predicted that "computers in the future may perhaps only weigh 1.5 tons!" (Photo courtesy of Smithsonian)

Outline

Objectives

After completing this chapter you should be able to:

1. Draw a block diagram of a stored program computer.
2. Explain the fetch and execute processing cycle of a stored program computer.
3. Define the role of the data, address, and control buses in a stored program computer.

4. Trace the evolution of the computer from the vacuum tube era to the microprocessor.
5. Identify significant computers that have been built over the years.
6. Explain the difference between a microprocessor, a microcomputer, and a micro-controller.
7. Compare digital signal processors (DSPs) with conventional microprocessors.
8. Trace the evolution of Intel microprocessors from the 8086 through the Pentium Pro.
9. Compare the bus widths and internal register sizes for all of the processors in the 80x86 family.
10. Explain the difference between the 80x86 processor's Real, Protected, and Virtual 8086 modes of operation.
11. Explain the difference between a microprocessor second source and a clone.

Overview

This chapter presents a core of digital computer principles upon which the following chapters can build. In it you will find a brief introduction to much of the terminology you will be reading about in the later chapters. You will also learn about the evolution of the computer from the vacuum tube-based ENIAC to Cray supercomputers. The chapter concludes with brief descriptions of the microprocessors in the Intel 80x86 family. These descriptions will be expanded upon in later chapters.

1.1   The Stored Program Concept

Introduction

As complex as today's computer systems are, most are still based on a design principle first proposed by Dr. John Von Neumann in 1946. Now taken for granted by most computer users, Von Neumann's idea defined the architecture to be used by all computers for the next 50 years.

In this section we:

• Draw a block diagram of a stored program computer
• Explain the fetch and execute processing cycle of a stored program computer
• Define the role of the data, address, and control buses in a stored program computer

The Stored Program Concept Is Born

ENIAC.   One of the first digital computers was a machine called ENIAC (Electronic Numerical Integrator and Computer). It was designed and built in 1946 at the Moore School of Electrical Engineering at the University of Pennsylvania. ENIAC measured over 18 ft. high and was 80 ft. long. It contained nearly 18,000 vacuum tubes, weighed more than 30 tons, and required 1500 square feet of floor space. More than 200,000 man-hours went into its construction (500,000 solder connections alone were required). It was programmed by setting up to 6000 switches and connecting cables between the various units of the computer.

While ENIAC was under construction, Dr. John von Neumann, also of the Moore School of Electrical Engineering, wrote a paper in collaboration with A.W. Burks and H.H. Goldstein that would define the architecture to be used by nearly all computers from that day on.[1] Now called the *stored program concept,* von Neumann suggested that rather than rewire the computer for each new task, the program instructions should be stored in a memory unit, just like the data. The resulting computer would then be *software programmable* rather than *hardware programmable.*

One of the first stored program computers to be built was called EDVAC (Electronic Discrete Variable Automatic Computer). Completed in 1952, it had a memory capacity of 1000 words of 10 decimal digits each. EDVAC was superior to ENIAC because it could be programmed much more efficiently and used a paper tape input device. At about this same time, the first random access core memory appeared. The first generation of computers was now well under way.

The Stored Program Processing Cycle

Fetch and Execute.   Figure 1.1 is a block diagram of a basic stored program computer. There are three major parts to this system: (1) The *central processing unit (CPU),* which acts as the "brain" coordinating all activities within the computer; (2) the *memory unit,* where the program instructions and data are temporarily stored; and (3) the *input/output (I/O) devices,* which allow the computer to input information for processing and then output the result.

At one time, the CPU of a computer was constructed using many different logic circuits and several circuit boards. Today, all of this circuitry has been reduced to a tiny (typically 1/4 inch on a side) silicon chip, or integrated circuit (IC), called the *microprocessor.* The entire computer, including microprocessor, memory, and I/O, is called a *microcomputer.* The Intel microprocessors studied in this book derive their heritage from a chip whose part number was 8086. Subsequent versions of this chip have been numbered 80286, 80386, and 80486. The term *80x86* is therefore used to describe the *family* of compatible Intel microprocessors. (Section 1.2 describes the evolution of the microprocessor and microcomputer in more detail.)

The basic timing of the computer is controlled by a square wave oscillator, or clock generator circuit. This signal is used to synchronize all activities within the computer, and determines how fast the program instructions can be fetched from memory and executed.

As shown in Figure 1.1, the CPU contains several *data registers* (flip-flops wired in series with each other). Some are general purpose and are used for storing temporary information. Others are special purpose. The accumulator, for example, is reserved for performing complex math operations such as multiply and divide. On 80x86 microprocessors, all data intended for the I/O devices must pass through this register.

The basic processing cycle begins with a memory fetch or read cycle. The *instruction pointer (IP)* register (also called the *program counter*) holds the address of the memory cell to be selected. In computerese, it "points" at the program instruction to be fetched. In this example, IP is storing the address 672,356, and the binary equivalent of this address is output onto the system address bus lines and routed to the memory unit.

---

[1]In Section 1.2 we discuss *parallel processors,* which offer an alternative to the von Neumann architecture.

Figure 1.1   The stored program computer consists of three units: the CPU, memory, and I/O devices.

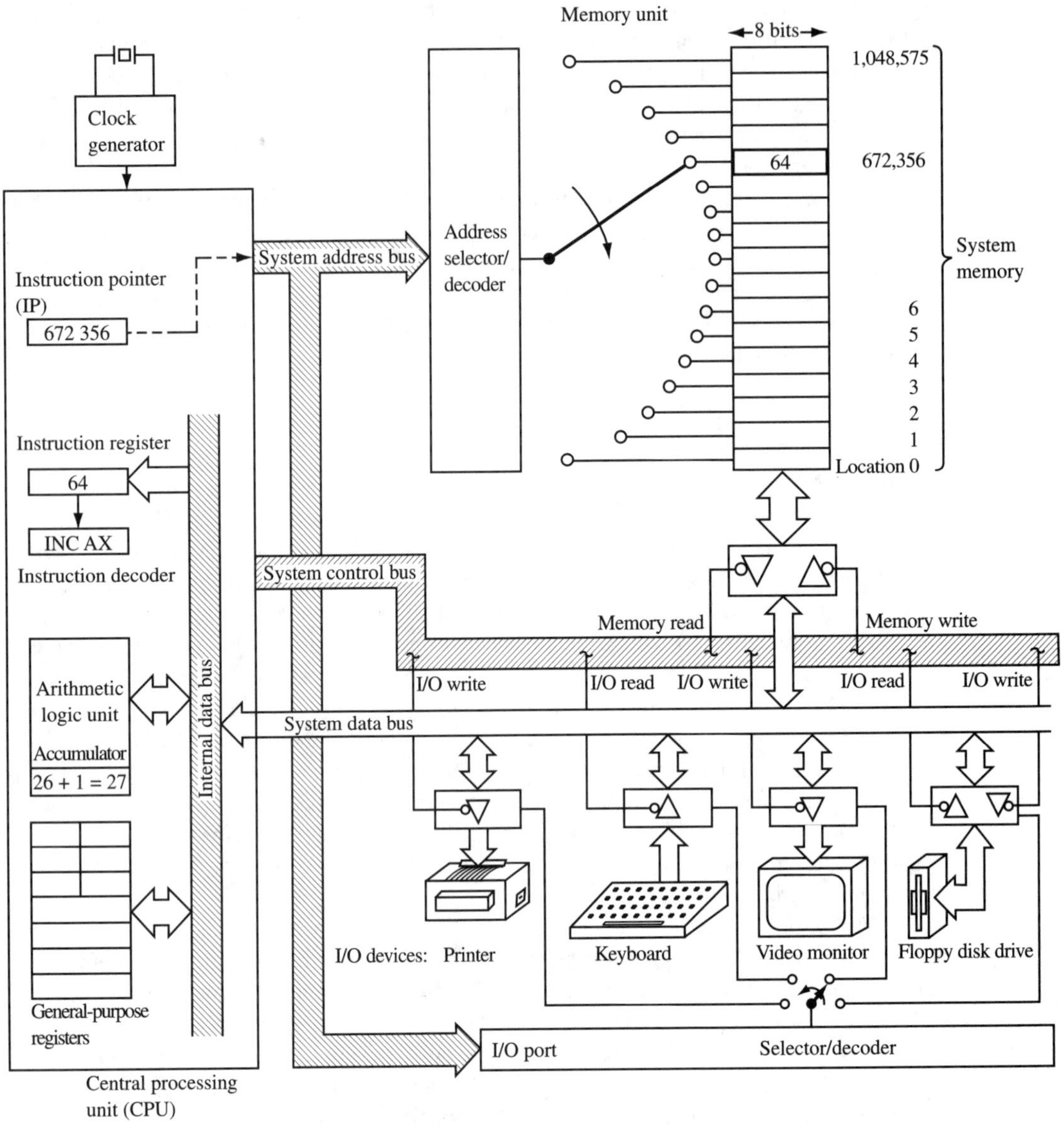

The memory unit consists of a large number of storage locations, each with its own unique *address*. Because the CPU can randomly access any location in memory, the term *random access memory (RAM)* is often used. In this example, we assume each memory location is 8 bits wide, referred to as a *byte*. This memory organization is typical for most microprocessors today.[2]

---

[2]16-, 32-, and 64-bit microprocessors can fetch 2, 4, and 8 bytes, respectively, in one cycle. We still describe the memory capacity of these processors in bytes, however.

An important characteristic of RAM is its *volatility*. This means its contents will be lost when power is turned off. Because of this, a portion of the memory unit is often built using *read-only memory (ROM)* chips. The program stored by a ROM is permanent, and therefore not lost when power is removed. As the name implies, the data stored by a ROM can only be read, not written. A special program is required to write data into a ROM. (Chapter 2 explains the role of the boot ROM in a typical computer; Chapter 7 provides more detail on ROM programming.)

The memory unit's address selector/decoder circuit examines the binary number on the address lines and selects the proper memory location to be accessed. In this example, because the CPU is reading from memory, it activates its **MEMORY READ** control signal. This causes the selected data byte in memory to be placed onto the data lines and routed to the *instruction register* within the CPU.

Once in the CPU, the instruction is decoded and executed. In this example, the instruction has the decimal code 64, which (for an 80x86 microprocessor) is decoded to be INC AX—increment the accumulator register. The *arithmetic logic unit (ALU)* is therefore instructed to add 1 to the contents of the accumulator where the new result will be stored. In general, the ALU portion of the CPU performs all mathematical and Boolean logic functions.

With the instruction complete, the cycle repeats, beginning with a new instruction fetch cycle. The control logic in the CPU is wired so that register IP is always incremented after an instruction fetch; thus the next sequential instruction in memory will normally be accessed. The entire process of reading memory, incrementing the instruction pointer, and decoding the instruction is known as the *fetch and execute* principle of the stored program computer.

The Instruction Set.   It is the job of the instruction decoder to recognize and activate the appropriate circuits in the CPU needed to carry out each new instruction as it is fetched from memory. The list of all such instructions recognizable by the decoder is called the *instruction set*. Microprocessors in the 80x86 family are known as *complex instruction set computers (CISC)* because of the large number of instructions in their instruction set (more than 3000 different forms). Some recent microprocessors have been designed to have only a small number of very fast executing instructions. Computers based on this concept are called *reduced instruction set computers (RISC)*. (RISC and CISC are discussed in more detail in Section 1.2.)

Modern CPUs.   Most microprocessor chips today are designed to allow the fetch and execute cycles to overlap. This is done by dividing the CPU into an *execution unit (EU)* and a *bus interface unit (BIU)*. The BIU's job is to fetch instructions from memory as quickly as possible and store them in a special instruction *queue*. The EU then fetches instructions from this queue, not from memory. Because the fetch and execute cycles are allowed to overlap, the total processing time is reduced.

Some processors have a *pipelined* execution unit that allows the decoding and execution of instructions to be overlapped, further increasing processing performance. Intel's latest processor, the Pentium Pro, has a 12-stage pipeline with three engines: the Fetch/Decode unit, the Dispatch/Execution unit, and the Retire unit. This architecture is referred to as *superscaler*. Superscaler microprocessors can process more than one instruction per clock cycle. (Chapter 3 discusses the architecture of the 80x86 family of processors in detail.)

Three-Bus System Architecture

8-, 16-, 32-, and 64-Bit Buses.   A collection of electronic signal lines all dedicated to a particular task is called a *bus*. In Figure 1.1 there are three such buses: the *address, data,* and *control* buses. This three-bus system architecture is common to nearly all microcomputer systems.

The Data Bus.   The width of the internal data bus in bits is usually used to classify a microprocessor. Thus, an 8-bit microprocessor has an 8-bit data bus, a 16-bit processor has a 16-bit data bus, etc. The width of the data bus determines how much data the processor can read or write in one memory, or I/O, cycle.

The width of the *internal* data bus (see Figure 1.1) is usually the same as the external bus—but not always. The 80386SX processor, for example, has a 32-bit internal data bus, but externally the bus is only 16 bits wide. This means the 80386SX will require two memory read operations to input the same information that the 80386 (with matching 32-bit internal and external data buses) inputs in one memory read cycle. The result is that the 80386SX operates less efficiently than the 80386.

The Pentium and Pentium Pro processors, on the other hand, have an external data bus width of 64 bits, but a 32-bit internal data bus. These chips are *data processing engines,* capable of executing two or three instructions per clock cycle, with clock rates greater than 200 MHz. The expanded data bus width is needed to keep these chips supplied with data.

Memory Banks.   You may be wondering how a 64-bit (or 32-bit or 16-bit) processor can access an 8-bit-wide memory. The "trick" is to divide the memory into *banks*. The 64-bit Pentium and Pentium Pro, for example, require eight banks of memory, with each bank organized as one byte wide.[3] *Bank enable* signals are output by the processor to specify which bank (or banks) are to be accessed. (Chapter 7 discusses memory interfacing in detail.)

Example 1.1

An 80486 processor has its memory organized as shown in Figure 1.2. Determine the total amount of memory available to this processor.

Solution
The 80486 has a 32-bit data bus, and therefore requires four banks of memory as shown. Note that each bank is organized as 1,048,576 8-bit bytes (1 megabyte or 1 MB). Four bank enable signals (BE0–BE3) are required to allow selection of each individual bank. The total amount of memory is:

$$4 \text{ banks} \times 1 \text{ MB/bank} = 4 \text{ MB}$$

The Address Bus.   The *address bus* is used to identify the memory location or I/O device (also called I/O *port*) the processor intends to communicate with. For the 80x86 family of processors, the width of this bus ranges from 20 bits for the 8086 and 8088, to 32 bits for the 80386/486 and Pentium, and 36 bits for the Pentium Pro.

---

[3]These memory banks usually consist of memory chips soldered to small circuit boards called *SIMMs (single in-line memory modules)* or *DIMMs (dual in-line memory modules).* Thirty-pin SIMMs are 8 bits wide; 72-pin SIMMs are 32 bits wide. DIMMs are 64 bits wide.

Figure 1.2 Memory organization for the 80486 microprocessor. Four 8-bit (one-byte) banks are required. In this example, each bank stores 1 MB, thus providing a total of 4 MB of memory to the processor. Bank enable signals are used to select each memory bank.

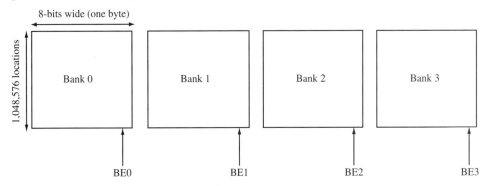

Example 1.2

How many different memory addresses can an 8086 output? Repeat for a Pentium processor.

Solution
The 8086 has a 20-bit address bus and can therefore output all combinations of addresses from 0000 0000 0000 0000 0000 to 1111 1111 1111 1111 1111. This corresponds to 1,048,576 different addresses (2^{20}) or 1 MB (one megabyte).

The Pentium has a 32-bit address bus and can therefore access

$$2^{12} \times 2^{20} = 4096 \times 1 \text{ MB or } 4096 \text{ MB (four gigabytes)}$$

The Control Bus.   How can we tell if the address on the bus is a memory address or an I/O port address? This is where the *control bus* comes in. Each time the processor outputs an address, it also activates one of four control bus signals. These are:

1. **MEMORY READ**
2. **MEMORY WRITE**
3. **I/O READ**
4. **I/O WRITE**

Thus, if the 8086 address bus holds 1010 0100 0010 0110 0100 ($672,356_{10}$) *and* the **MEMORY READ** signal is active, the data byte in memory location 672,356 will be selected to be read. The memory unit responds by outputting the contents of this location onto the data bus.

The control bus also identifies the *direction* of data flow on the data bus. When **MEMORY READ** or **I/O READ** is active, data is *input* to the processor. When **MEMORY WRITE** or **I/O WRITE** is active, data is *output* by the processor; that is, the control bus signals are defined from the processor's point of view.

Summary.   The microprocessor manages the flow of data between itself, memory, and the I/O ports via the address, data, and control buses. The control and address buses are output lines (only) but the data bus is *bidirectional*.

Self Review 1.1 (Answers on page 32)

1.1.1   The three major blocks of a stored program computer are the _____, _____, and the _____.

1.1.2   The instruction pointer:
(a) Holds the address of the next memory location to be fetched into the instruction register.
(b) Is located within the processor.
(c) Is automatically incremented as part of the basic fetch and execute cycle.
(d) All of the above.

1.1.3   Complex arithmetic operations are performed in the _____ _____ _____, with results stored in the _____.

1.1.4   A microcomputer system with a 24-bit address bus could potentially access _____ memory locations.

1.1.5   The memory unit for an 80486 microprocessor requires _____ banks of memory.

1.1.6   When the processor writes data to the video terminal in Figure 1.1 the _____-_____ control bus signal will be activated.

1.1.7   Of the three system buses, only the _____ bus is bidirectional.

1.2   Types of Computers

Introduction

The first generation of computers were described in terms of hundreds of feet of floor space, tons of weight, and thousands of vacuum tubes. Reliability was often measured in hours or even minutes. Loading a new program required tens of man-hours to rewire the computer, and could only be done by trained engineers and technicians. Today we have *desktop* computers, *laptop* computers, and even *notebook* computers. We describe the processor in terms of submicron line spacings, millions of transistors, and onboard floating-point processors. Indeed, the *evolution* of the computer has occurred so rapidly that it is sometimes called a *revolution*.

In this section we:

- Trace the evolution of the computer from the vacuum tube era to the microprocessor.
- Identify significant computers that have been built over the years.
- Explain the difference between a microprocessor, a microcomputer, and a microcontroller.
- Compare digital signal processors (DSPs) with conventional microprocessors.

The Vacuum Tube Era

IBM Emerges.   *First-generation computers* were massive machines based on vacuum tube technology. They occupied entire rooms and required an air-conditioned environment to operate reliably. In fact, because the average life of a vacuum tube was 3000 hours, and several thousand tubes were required to build a machine, some predicted that no useful work could ever be done—technicians would constantly be tracking down and replacing bad tubes! Nevertheless, in 1951, Remington-Rand delivered the first Univac I (UNIVersal Automatic Computer) to the Bureau of the Census. In 1952, CBS used a Univac I to predict the defeat of Adlai E. Stevenson by Dwight D. Eisenhower in the presidential election.

International Business Machines (IBM) reluctantly entered the computer field in 1952 with its Model 701 Data Processing System. IBM's founder, Thomas Watson, Sr., had to be convinced by his son, Watson, Jr., of the importance of these machines. Indeed, Watson, Sr., is reported to have said that he could imagine a need for no more than eight to ten of the large "brains" for the entire scientific and business community!

The Transistor Is Born

Mainframe Computers. In 1956, three Bell Laboratory scientists, Drs. William Shockley, John Bardeen, and Walter H. Brattain, received the Nobel physics award for their invention, in 1948, of the bipolar transistor. In 1954, another Bell Labs team demonstrated the significance of this invention with the first all-transistorized computer (TRADIC). The 800-transistor machine generated much less heat than its vacuum tube counterpart, making it more reliable and less costly.

IBM's first transistorized computer was the 7070/7090, announced in 1958. It was followed by another all-transistorized computer, the business-oriented 1401, in 1959. Computers of this era were called *second-generation machines,* and because of their reduced size and cost, they became popular with business and industry. Machines of this era were built on circuit boards mounted into rack panels, or frames. The term *mainframe* was applied to describe the central processing unit portion of the computer (the *main* frame). Today we think of a mainframe computer as one designed to handle large volumes of data while serving hundreds of users simultaneously.

Integrated Circuits

A New Way of Thinking. Certainly one of the most significant scientific developments of the twentieth century has been the invention of the integrated circuit (IC), in 1959, by Dr. Robert Noyce at Fairchild Semiconductor Corporation and Jack Kilby at Texas Instruments. Their invention was more a triumph of creative thinking than it was a technological breakthrough. After all, the invention of the transistor at Bell Laboratories had ushered in the solid-state era 11 years previously. In fact, the concept of a solid-logic module (all circuit components fabricated from one piece of semiconductor material) was well known. What was not known was how to do it. The following quote from Noyce voices this frustration:

> With the advent of diffusion the industry was able to make hundreds of transistors in a slice of silicon. But then people cut these beautifully arranged things into little pieces and had girls hunt for them with tweezers in order to put leads on and wire them all back together again; then we would sell them to our customers, who would plug all these separate packages into a printed circuit board.

Kilby's invention, patented early in 1959, involved fabricating resistors, capacitors, and transistors on a germanium wafer and then connecting these parts with fine gold wires. Later that year, Noyce, working independently of Kilby, suggested isolating the individual components with reverse-biased diodes and depositing an adherent metal film over the circuit, thus connecting the components (and avoiding the connecting wires in Kilby's design). Noyce filed his patent six months after Kilby's.

Third-Generation Computers. The first integrated circuit contained only a handful of components, enough to construct a simple two-transistor multivibrator (oscillator). However, manufacturers were soon producing ICs with several hundred components; by the mid 1960s, memory chips with 1000 components were common. In 1964, IBM announced one of the most famous computers ever to be built, and the first to use integrated circuit (third-generation) technology, the 32-bit 360 series. The IBM 360 was actually a family of six compatible computers with 40 different input/output and auxiliary storage devices. Memory capacity varied from 16K words to over 1 MB. Internally the processor contained sixteen 32-bit registers, a 24-bit address bus, and a 128-bit data bus. It could perform 375,000 computations per second.[4] IBM reportedly spent nearly $5 billion developing this computer, and its success gave them the lead in the (mainframe) computer business it would never relinquish.

Minicomputers.   With the advent of the transistor and the integrated circuit, the electronics industry began to boom in the 1960s. The United States was engaged in a "space race" with the Soviet Union and President Kennedy had challenged the nation to put a man on the moon by the end of the decade. There was accordingly a tremendous demand by scientists and engineers for an inexpensive computer that they could operate themselves. A young engineer named Edson de Castro, working for Digital Equipment Corporation (DEC), was put in charge of designing such a computer. The result, in 1965, was a landmark machine called the PDP-8 (Programmed Data Processor). Using integrated circuits, de Castro's group constructed a low-cost ($25,000) *minicomputer* (scaled-down mainframe). The 12-bit PDP-8 became an immediate hit and was soon followed by the 16-bit PDP-11.

Today the distinction between minicomputer and mainframe computer (or even microcomputer) is not so clear. The so-called *supermini* has capabilities rivaling those of the mainframe. And top-of-the-line microcomputers (discussed in the next section) are challenging minicomputers. Today minicomputers are primarily used by small organizations in a time-shared environment with 50–100 users.[5] With the advent of local- and wide-area microcomputer networks, even this distinction is fading.

Microprocessors

CPU on a Chip.   In 1968, Robert Noyce and Gordon Moore, two of the original founders of Fairchild, started a new company called Intel (Integrated Electronics). Their intention was to exploit the then-expanding semiconductor memory market. However, in 1969 the Japanese calculator company Busicom approached them to fabricate a custom set of ICs for a new calculator design. Two engineers, Ted Hoff and Stan Mazor, were assigned to the project and came up with the idea of fabricating a 4-bit central processing unit on a single chip, supported by separate read-only memory (ROM) and random access memory (RAM) chips. Fredrico Faggin, a process engineer for Intel, took these ideas and converted them into a chip set that became known as the *4000 family*. It consisted of four chips:

1. The 4001, a 2K ROM with 4-bit I/O port
2. The 4002, a 320-bit RAM with 4-bit output port
3. The 4003, a 10-bit serial-in parallel-out shift register
4. The 4004, a 4-bit processor

Never before had the entire central processing unit of a computer been constructed on a single piece of silicon. The trade journals soon began describing this processor-on-a-chip as

---

[4]A 100 MHz Pentium can perform 150 million instructions per second!

[5]For a fascinating insider's view of the minicomputer world in the 1970s, read the book *The Soul of a New Machine* by Tracy Kidder (Boston: Little Brown, 1981).

a *micro-processor*. The 4004 was followed by the 8-bit 8008 in 1972, and an improved version called the 8080 in 1974. At this same time, several other companies began to introduce competitive microprocessor chips. Motorola had the MC6800, MOS Technology (a spin-off from Motorola) the 6502, and Zilog (a spin-off from Intel) the Z-80. These chips all had 8-bit data bus widths and 16-bit address buses. The addressable memory space was 64K.

In the late 1970s, several 16-bit microprocessors began to appear. The two most popular were Intel's 8086 and Motorola's MC68000. These processors introduced new 16-bit instructions, including hardware multiply and divide, and with 20-bit address buses could access up to 1 MB of memory.

The evolution continues to this day with 32-bit (the 80386, 80486, MC68020, MC68030) and 64-bit (Pentium and Pentium Pro) CPUs. Table 1.1 charts the astonishing growth of microprocessors from the 2250-transistor 4004 to the 5.5 million-transistor Pentium Pro. Considering Figure 1.3, that's quite an achievement for a little man with a jackhammer!

Figure 1.3 Microprocessor chips began to flourish in the late 1970s. The January 1979 issue of *BYTE* magazine illustrates one point of view on how these chips are made. (Reprinted courtesy of Robert Tinney Graphics and BYTE Publications, Peterborough, N.H.)

Table 1.1 The Evolution of Intel Microprocessors[1]

Microprocessor	Year Introduced	Number of Transistors	Minimum Feature Size (microns)	External Data Bus Width	Internal Register Widths	Address Bus Width/ Memory Space	Estimated Processing Rate (MIPs)[2]	Onboard Coprocessor	Internal Cache Memory	V_{CC} (volts)	P_D (watts)
4004	1971	2,250	10.0	4	4	10/1K	.06 (.108MHz)	no	no	±5, 12	1.2
8080	1974	6,000	6.0	8	8	16/64K	.2 (2 MHz)	no	no	5	1.7
8086	1978	29,000	3.0	16	16	20/1 MB	.47 (4.77 MHz)	no	no	5	1.7
8088	1979	29,000	3.0	8	16	20/1 MB	.33 (4.77 MHz)	no	no	5	1.7
80286	1982	134,000	1.5	16	16	24/16 MB	2 (8 MHz)	no	no	5	3
80386DX	1985	275,000	1.5	32	32	32/4 GB	5.5 (16 MHz)	no	no	5	1.95
80386SX	1988	275,000	1.5	16	32	24/16 MB	3.9 (16 MHz)	no	no	5	1.9
80486DX	1989	1.2 million	0.8	32	32	32/4 GB	20 (25 MHz)	yes	8K	5	5
80486SX	1991	1.2 million	0.8	32	32	32/4 GB	13 (16 MHz)	no	8K	5	3.4
80486DX2	1992	1.2 million	0.6	32	32	32/4 GB	41 (50 MHz)	yes	8K	5	4.8
80486DX4	1994	1.2 million	0.6	32	32	32/4 GB	60 (75 MHz)	yes	16K	3.3	
Pentium P60	1993	3.1 million	0.8	64	32	32/4 GB	100 (60 MHz)	yes	16K	5	14.6
Pentium P100	1994	3.1 million	0.6	64	32	32/4 GB	150 (100 MHz)	yes	16K	3.3	10.1
Pentium P120	1995	3.1 million	0.35	64	32	32/4 GB	185 (120 MHz)	yes	16K	3.3	12.8
Pentium Pro 150	1995	5.5 million[3]	0.6	64	32	36/64 GB	350 (150 MHz)	yes	16K/256K[4]	3.3	29.2
Pentium Pro 200	1996	5.5 million	0.35	64	32	36/64 GB	475 (200 MHz)	yes	16k/512K	3.3	35
P7[5]	1997–8	12 million	0.2	—	—	—	750	yes	—	—	—

[1]Specifications shown are for initial introduction of part.
[2]Millions of instructions per second (internal clock rate shown in parentheses).
[3]256K level two cache (separate die in same package) has 15.5 million transistors.
[4]16K data/code level one cache plus 256K level two cache.
[5]Best guess.

The Personal Computer. Once the processor-on-a-chip (the *microprocessor*) became a reality, *microcomputer* systems began to appear. These were complete computers based on a particular microprocessor chip. One of the first was the MITS Altair 8800. Announced in 1975, it cost $399 in kit form and featured the 8-bit Intel 8080 microprocessor. Figure 1.4 shows an ad for the Altair taken from the October 1976 issue of *BYTE* magazine. In its simplest form, the Altair was programmed by depositing 1s and 0s into memory via a set of front panel switches. LED indicators provided a view of the contents of memory.

New microcomputer companies began to spring up almost overnight, each based on a particular microprocessor chip. Using Intel's 8080 were MITS, Imsai, HAL Communications, E&L Instruments, and Processor Technology. Motorola's 6800 was used in Southwest Technical Products' SWTPC 6800 computer, and the Z-80 was used by North Star Computers, Cromemco, and Radio Shack/Tandy (the latter in its TRS-80 model computer). At about this same time, two college dropouts, Steve Jobs and Steve Wozniak, began showing off a new computer they had designed called the Apple I. It was based on the MOS Technology 6502 microprocessor, featured 8K of memory, and could be programmed in BASIC. The rest of the story, as they say, is history, as Jobs and Wozniak went on to become multimillionaires and Apple became the fastest-growing computer company of all time.

Many of the early microcomputers were offered in kit form and required expertise in machine language programming to do useful work (hardly machines for the masses). In 1982, IBM began selling the idea of a *personal computer* (see Figure 1.5).[6] It featured a system board designed around the Intel 8088 8-bit microprocessor, 16K of memory, and five expansion slots. This latter feature was probably the most significant, as it opened the door for third-party vendors to supply video, printers, modems, disk drives, and RS-232 serial adapter cards. Indeed, the open architecture of the original IBM PC led to the development of the *generic PC*. This is a computer with interchangeable components manufactured by a variety of companies.

Today, most users describe their computer in terms of its microprocessor chip. For example:

> "What kind of computer do you have?"
> "I've got a 16 MB Pentium 166 with a 1.6 GB SCSI drive."

Translation: The user has a computer based on the 64-bit 166 MHz Pentium microprocessor chip, 16 million bytes of user memory, and a 1.66-gigabyte hard drive with an SCSI (Small Computer Systems Interface) controller.

Microcontrollers

Hidden Computers. Microcomputers get all of the headlines, but *microcontrollers* are far more popular. Dataquest, a San Jose, California, based semiconductor market research firm, reported that for 1995, microcontrollers outsold microprocessors ten to one. But little is heard of these workhorse chips. Study Figure 1.6 and see if you can spot the *14* microcontrollers in this scene.

---

[6]IBM's apparent strategy was to get people thinking about owning their own computers (count the number of times the phrase "Personal Computer" appears in the ad in Figure 1.5). The strategy apparently worked: To this day we speak of a microcomputer as a *PC*.

Figure 1.4   The MITS Altair is often credited with starting the microcomputer revolution. This ad ran in the October 1976 issue of *BYTE* magazine. (Reprinted courtesy of BYTE Publications, Peterborough, N.H.)

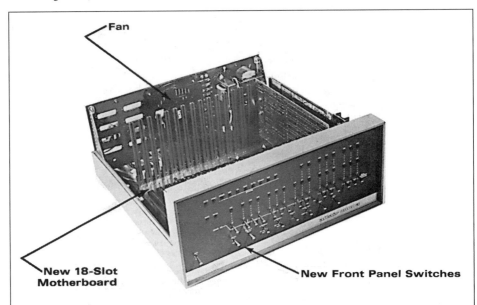

Fan

New 18-Slot Motherboard

New Front Panel Switches

The four boards, along with the power supply, mount in an 18" deep x 17" wide x 7" high (45.7 x 43.2 x 17.7-cm) metal cabinet.

SPECIFICATIONS

Number of Boards	Up to 18
Microprocessor	
Model	8080A
Technology	NMOS
Data Word Size, Bits	8
Instruction Word Size, Bits	8
Clock Frequency,	2MHz
Add Time, Register to	
Register, Microsec.	
Per Data Word	2
Number of Instructions	78
Input/Output Control	
I/O Word Size, Bits	8
Number of I/O Channels	256
Direct Memory Access	Optional
Interrupt Capability	Std. one level
Vectored Interrupt (8 priority levels)	Optional
Software	
Resident Assembler	Yes
Cross Assembler	No
Simulator	No
Higher-level Language	BASIC
Monitor or Executive	Sys. mon.; text edit.
Software Separately Priced	Yes

mits

2450 Alamo S.E. Albuquerque, New Mexico 87106

Figure 1.5   In 1982, using ads such as this, IBM began selling the idea of a *personal computer* or *PC*. (Reprinted courtesy of BYTE Publications, Peterborough, N.H.)

"My own IBM computer. Imagine that."

One nice thing about having your own IBM Personal Computer is that it's *yours*. For your business, your project, your department, your class, your family and, indeed, for yourself.

Of course, you might have thought owning a computer was too expensive. But now you can relax.

The IBM Personal Computer starts at less than $1,600† for a system that, with the addition of one simple device, hooks up to your home TV and uses your audio cassette recorder.

You might also have thought running a computer was too difficult. But you can relax again.

Getting started is easier than you might think, because IBM has structured the learning process for you. Our literature is in *your* language, not in "computerese." Our software *involves* you, the system *interacts* with you as if it was made to—and it was.

That's why you can be running programs in just one day. Maybe even writing your *own* programs in a matter of weeks.

For ease of use, flexibility and performance, no other personal computer offers as many advanced capabilities. (See the box.)

But what makes the IBM Personal Computer a truly useful tool are software programs selected by IBM's Personal Computer Software Publishing Department. You can have programs in business, professional, word processing, computer language, personal and entertainment categories.

You can see the system and the software in action at any ComputerLand® store or Sears Business Systems Center. Or try it out at one of our IBM Product Centers. The IBM Data Processing Division will serve those customers who want to purchase in quantity.

Your IBM Personal Computer. Once you start working with it, you'll discover more than the answers and solutions you seek: you'll discover that getting there is half the fun. Imagine that. **IBM**

IBM PERSONAL COMPUTER SPECIFICATIONS
ADVANCED FEATURES FOR PERSONAL COMPUTERS

User Memory	Display Screen	Color/Graphics
16K - 256K bytes*	High-resolution (720h x 350v)*	*Text mode:* 16 colors*
Permanent Memory (ROM) 40K bytes*	80 characters x 25 lines Upper and lower case	256 characters and symbols in ROM*
Microprocessor High speed, 8088*	Green phosphor screen*	*Graphics mode:* 4-color resolution:
Auxiliary Memory 2 optional internal diskette drives, 5¼", 160K bytes per diskette	**Diagnostics** Power-on self testing* Parity checking*	320h x 200v* Black & white resolution: 640h x 200v*
Keyboard 83 keys, 6 ft. cord attaches to	**Languages** BASIC, Pascal **Printer**	Simultaneous graphics & text capability* **Communications** RS-232-C interface
system unit* 10 function keys* 10-key numeric pad Tactile feedback*	Bidirectional* 80 characters/second 12 character styles, up to 132 characters/line* 9 x 9 character matrix*	Asynchronous (start/stop) protocol Up to 9600 bits per second

The IBM Personal Computer   and me.

†This price applies to IBM Product Centers. Prices may vary at other stores.

For the IBM Personal Computer dealer nearest you, call (800) 447-4700. In Illinois, (800) 322-4400. In Alaska or Hawaii, (800) 447-0890.

Figure 1.6   Microcontrollers are often called "hidden computers." In this picture there are 14 different microcontrollers. (Reprinted courtesy of Intel Corporation and Microcomputer Solutions)

A microcontroller is an entire computer on a chip; that is, a microprocessor with on-chip memory and input/output (I/O). Typically these parts are designed into (embedded within) a product and run a "canned" program that never changes. For example, an electronic thermostat is controlled by a microcontroller. It inputs an analog temperature signal, converts this to digital via its internal analog-to-digital converter (ADC), reads the time and date from its internal clock, compares this with its programmed limits, and activates the furnace or air conditioner via an output control signal.

As Figure 1.6 suggests, there are numerous applications for embedded controllers. In addition to the home, there are industrial applications (machine tools, programmable logic controllers), telecommunications applications (modems), and automotive applications. Indeed, the modern automobile has several "hidden" controllers. They are used for engine control, antilock braking systems (ABS), heat, venting, and air-conditioning control (HVAC), navigation systems, and multiplex wiring (several devices connected via a single wire) control.

Microcontrollers have evolved somewhat differently than microprocessors. While the latter are continually being upgraded to higher speeds and greater bus widths, the newer microcontrollers have greater *I/O* capabilities. Intel's MCS-51 family, for example, is based on an 8-bit processor, but features up to 32K of onboard ROM, 32 individually programmable digital input/output lines, a serial communications channel, and three 16-bit timers. The MCS-96 family is similar but is based on a 16-bit processor and includes an onboard 10-bit analog-to-digital converter.

High-Performance Processors

Supercomputers.   One definition for a *supercomputer* is "the most powerful computer available at any given time." These machines are used to solve complex problems such as the design of a supersonic aircraft, modeling of global climates, the structure of oil-bearing formations within the Earth, the molecular design of new drugs, or the prediction of complex financial behavior in securities markets. Two of the first supercomputers were the Control Data Corporation CDC 6600 and CDC 7600. Both were developed by Seymour Cray, one of the founders of CDC. In 1972, Cray left to found Cray Research, Inc., and in 1976 developed the Cray-1, generally acknowledged to be the first true supercomputer.

The Cray-1 used high-speed emitter coupled logic (ECL), the fastest (and most power hungry) logic circuits available at the time. The computer was packaged as a 6.5 ft. high cylinder surrounded by a circular seat (see Figure 1.7). Each circuit board was mounted on a copper heat exchanger through which liquid freon was circulated. The total power consumption of the computer was 128 KW! Processing speed was 130 MFLOPS (millions of floating-point operations per second).[7] In all, 63 Cray-1 computers were sold (at a cost of $5.1 million each).

Parallel Processors.   Computers like the Cray-1 were single processor, sequential machines. This means the processor handles one instruction at a time, in sequence. In the 1980s, the performance (measured in MFLOPS) of such machines began to level off. This was due to the finite length of time required for an electrical signal to propagate through a piece of wire. Researchers began looking for a new computer architecture that could achieve performance levels measured in tens of *gigaflops* (billions of floating-point operations per second).

---

[7] A 100 MHz Pentium can achieve 150 MFLOPS.

Figure 1.7   The CRAY-1 supercomputer. (Photo courtesy of Smithsonian)

One of the answers was *parallel processing*. This is a scheme in which multiple processors are wired together via a common bus, and each is given a portion of the problem to solve. The *hypercube*, shown in Figure 1.8, was initially thought to provide the optimum architecture for supercomputers. It consists of a set of interconnected processors called *nodes*. Figure 1.8 shows examples of 1-, 2-, 4-, 8-, 16-, and 32-node hypercubes. The first hypercube computer was the Cosmic Cube, developed at the California Institute of Technology in the early 1980s. The supercomputer division of Intel Corp. (now called the Scaled Systems Division or SSD) developed the iPSC hypercube based on the i860 (RISC) microprocessor.

More recently, supercomputer designers have opted for a *two-dimensional* rectangular mesh architecture with multiple processors at each connecting node. Nodes communicate over a high-speed internal interconnect network. Intel, for example, is developing a *teraflops* (1000 GFLOPS) computer with 4500 nodes. Each node will be powered by two 200 MHz Pentium Pro processors. Total memory is expected to exceed 600 gigabytes, with over two trillion bytes of disk storage! The projected processing performance is 1.8 teraflops.

Cray Research is offering a similar computer, called the T3E. With liquid cooling, it supports up to 2048 DEC Alpha EV5 RISC processors, 1 to 4 terabytes of memory, and a processing rate as high as 1.2 teraflops.

Figure 1.8 A hypercube is an arrangement of processors in the form of an *n*-dimensional cube each connected by a high-speed data channel.

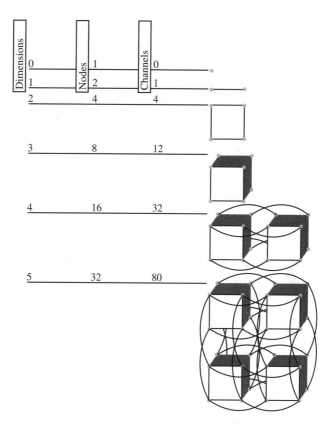

RISC Processors.   In the early 1980s, a new trend in computer design began to appear called *RISC*—reduced instruction set computer. Taken literally, this means a computer with a small (less than 128) number of instructions. The opposite of RISC is *CISC*—complex instruction set computer. A CISC is characterized by:

1. A large number of variable length instructions.
2. Multiple addressing modes (these are different methods of specifying the memory address).
3. A small number of internal processor registers.
4. Instructions that require multiple numbers of clock cycles to execute.

The 8086 microprocessor fits the definition for a CISC exactly. It has over 3000 different instruction forms, each requiring anywhere from one to six bytes. Nine different addressing modes are supported, but internally the processor has only eight general-purpose registers. Instruction execution times vary from 2 clock cycles to more than 80 cycles for the complex ASCII adjust for multiplication instruction.

Compare the CISC to Intel's i860 RISC processor (sometimes called a "Cray on a Chip"):

1. 82 instructions, each 32 bits in length
2. Four addressing modes

3. 32 general-purpose registers
4. All instructions execute in one clock cycle

Because all of the instructions in a RISC are of the same length and require only a single clock cycle, the control unit is much simpler that that of a CISC. This allows the instructions to be executed faster with less total on-chip logic. In fact, studies have shown that in a CISC, the control unit accounts for 50 percent of the chip area compared to only 10 percent in a RISC. This means there is more area available in a RISC for other features such as an expanded register file, data and instruction caches (onboard memory for storing the most recent instructions and data), and a floating-point unit or coprocessor.[8]

In 1993, the industry alliance of IBM, Apple, and Motorola announced a new 32-bit RISC processor called the *PowerPC*. Designed to combat Intel's 80x86 family of processors, the PowerPC supports several different operating systems, including MS-DOS (via emulation) , IBM's OS/2, Apple's System 7, Windows NT, and UNIX.[9] The advantage to users is the ability to run and exchange data between programs that were heretofore limited to a specific processor (for example, Apple programs required a Motorola 680x0 processor; MS-DOS programs required an 80x86 processor).

Application-Specific Microprocessors

Digital Signal Processors.   As the microprocessor has continued to evolve, many application-specific processors have been developed. We have already seen the example of the *microcontroller*, which includes onboard memory and I/O functions. Other examples include video and graphics processors, printer coprocessors, local-area network (LAN) coprocessors, and communications processors.

Note that all of the computers in the above list are designed for processing digital (on and off) signals. Analog signals, which can take on an infinite set of values over time, have had to be processed with discrete circuits; typically op-amps (operational amplifiers) supported with capacitors, inductors, and resistors to form filters, amplifiers, and other frequency-selective circuits. However, as IC technology has advanced, low-cost analog-to-digital and digital-to-analog converters have become available. This, in turn, has led to the development of the *digital signal processing system*. As shown in Figure 1.9, this is a specialized computer system that inputs an analog signal, converts it to digital form, performs specialized arithmetic operations on the data, and then converts this data back to analog form via a digital-to-analog converter.

The key element in this system is a new type of microprocessor called the *digital signal processor (DSP)*. DSPs are used to perform complex mathematical computations on the converted analog data; for example, a digital filter can be constructed by sampling the input data and then transforming each of the data points according to a mathematical formula. One computation can require as many as 500,000 add-multiply operations. To enhance this

---

[8]Typically the coprocessor "watches" the instruction stream of the CPU looking for special floating-point instructions. These might be transcendental functions like tangent, sine, and cosine, basic math operations like add, subtract, divide, and multiply, or more complex operations such as computing the logarithm of a number. When such an instruction is spotted, the floating-point unit takes over, generating the result for the main CPU.

[9]An operating system is a control program that manages the resources of the computer. Chapter 2 discusses operating systems in more detail.

Figure 1.9 In a digital signal processing system, analog input signals are converted to digital form, processed by the DSP, and then converted back to analog form.

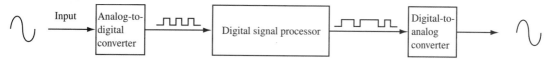

process, the architecture of a DSP differs from that of a conventional microprocessor in several ways:

1. The data and program instructions are stored in two different memory areas, each with its own buses. This is called Harvard Architecture.
2. Hardware multipliers and adders are built into the processor and optimized to perform a calculation in a single clock cycle.
3. Arithmetic pipelining is used so that several instructions can be operated on at once. For example, two numbers may be multiplied in one part of the processor while two other numbers are being added in another part.
4. Hardware DO loops are provided to speed up repetitive operations.
5. Multiple (serial) I/O ports are provided for communication with other processors.

DSPs are in widespread use today. Multimedia sound cards, for example, typically employ DSPs to compress speech and music signals so that they can be stored as (reasonable size) data files. Because the DSP can be reprogrammed, some sound cards can be altered to also function as modems, thereby combining the functions of two typical microcomputer peripherals on one adapter card.[10] Other applications include cellular phones, speech and image compression, optical character recognition, and video conferencing.

Self-Review 1.2 (Answers on page 32–33)

1.2.1 The first and second generations of computers are generally associated with the _____ _____ and _____.
1.2.2 The first computer to use integrated circuit technology was the _____.
1.2.3 How does a minicomputer differ from a mainframe computer?
1.2.4 What is the difference between a microcomputer and a microprocessor?
1.2.5 Why are microcontrollers called "hidden computers"?
1.2.6 What is a parallel processor?
1.2.7 Why are RISC processors more efficient than CISC processors?
1.2.8 How does a DSP differ from a conventional microprocessor?

1.3   The 80x86 Family of Microprocessors

Introduction

Intel Corporation, founded by Robert Noyce and Gordon Moore in 1972, has become the leading manufacturer of microprocessor chips in the world. Indeed, the "Intel architecture,"

---

[10]A modem is a device that converts the 1s and 0s of a digital signal into audio tones that can be transmitted over conventional telephone lines. Modems are discussed in detail in Chapter 10.

begun with the 8008 in 1972, has become the de facto industry standard. Today, more than 90 percent of the personal computers in use feature an Intel (or Intel-compatible) microprocessor.

In this section we:

- Trace the evolution of Intel processors from the 8086 through the Pentium Pro.
- Compare the bus widths and internal register sizes for all of the processors in the 80x86 family.
- Explain the difference between the 80x86 processor's Real, Protected, and Virtual 8086 modes of operation.
- Explain the difference between a microprocessor second source and a clone.

The 8086 Microprocessor

The 80x86 Architecture Is Defined.   In 1978, Intel announced the 16-bit 8086 microprocessor. It featured several improvements over the previous generation's 8-bit chips. Among these were:

- A 20-bit address bus, compared to 16 bits for the 8-bit chips. This allowed access to 1 MB of memory, 16 times the 64K limit of previous 8-bit microprocessors.
- Reorganization of the processor into a separate bus interface unit (BIU) and execution unit (EU). This allowed the 8086 to fetch and execute instructions simultaneously.
- Internal processor registers expanded from 8 to 16 bits wide, but with the ability to access the high or low 8 bits separately if desired.
- Hardware multiply and divide instructions built into the processor.
- Support for an external math coprocessor that could perform floating-point math operations in hardware as much as 100 times faster than the processor alone via software emulation.

The instruction set of the 8086 was designed to be compatible with the older 8-bit 8080 and 8085 microprocessors popular at the time. Intel even provided a program that could input 8080/8085 programs and output an 8086 equivalent.

The 8088 Microprocessor

The PC Standard Is Defined.   After its introduction, the 8086 languished for several years without much interest from the industry. This was due partly to its requirement of two separate 8-bit memory banks to supply its 16-bit data bus. Memory chips were quite expensive at the time, and designers were reluctant to select a processor that required twice as many chips as the current 8-bit systems.

For this reason, Intel announced, in 1979, the 8088 microprocessor. This chip is identical to the 8086 except that it features an *external* 8-bit data bus. Internally, the data bus (and all registers) remains 16 bits and the address bus is still 20 bits wide. This was accomplished by redesigning the BIU to access memory 8 bits at a time. The result is a less efficient chip (two memory accesses are required to input or output 16 bits of data, compared to one access for the 8086) but one that requires a less expensive memory interface—only a single 8-bit bank.

In 1982, IBM announced the *personal computer,* or PC. It used the 8088 microprocessor and had 16K of memory (expandable to 64K). The clock speed was 4.77 MHz. The PC standard was now established.

The 80186 and 80188 Microprocessors

High-Integration CPUs.   If you were to study the schematic diagram for IBM's original PC, you would see that besides the 8088 microprocessor, several additional chips are required to construct a practical computer. Among these are a clock generator, a programmable timer, a programmable interrupt controller, a direct memory access controller, and circuitry to select the I/O devices. To simplify the design of such systems, Intel introduced the 80186 and 80188 microprocessors. These chips have at their core an 8086 (or 8088) processor, but include all of the above functions onboard. For this reason the 80186 and 80188 are often referred to as *high-integration* processors. The instruction set of these chips is 100 percent compatible with the 8086 and 8088, but includes nine new instructions.

Although neither chip has achieved the success of the 8086 or 8088, they have been used as the basis for several IBM-compatible computers. And because of their high integration, some manufacturers have used them as embedded controllers.

The 80286 Microprocessor

A "Fatal Flaw"?   The 80286 is a more powerful version of the 8086 and was used by IBM in its AT (advanced technology) computer in 1984. Like the 8086, it has a 16-bit data bus, but its address bus has been expanded to 24 bits. Two programming modes are provided: *Real Mode* and *Protected Mode.* When first powered on, the 80286 (or 286) comes up in Real Mode. In this mode the chip functions exactly like an 8086. That is, any 8086 program can be run on a Real Mode 286 without change. In this mode the 286 uses only its 20 least significant address lines, so memory space is limited to 1 MB, just like the 8086.

Intel designed the 286 to be software-compatible with the 8086 and 80186. Thus all of the existing software designed to run on these processors will run on the 286 without change. Sixteen new instructions were added, but these were all intended for managing the Protected Mode of the processor. When operated in Real Mode, the only significant difference between the 286 and the 8086 is that most of the 286 instructions execute faster due to a redesigned processor and a higher maximum clock speed (6 or 8 MHz).

When switched to Protected Mode, the 286 supports a *multiprogram* environment. It does this by giving each program a predetermined amount of memory. In this scheme, programs no longer have physical addresses, but rather are addressed via a segment selector. On the 286 this allows a program to "see" as much as 16 MB of memory. Protected Mode is so called because several programs can be loaded into memory at once (each in its own segment), but are protected from each other; that is, a program running in one segment cannot read or write data from another segment.

When the 80286 was designed, it was decided that once switched to Protected Mode, the chip should not be able to switch back to Real Mode. This was to prevent a clever programmer from accessing data in another segment by switching the chip back and forth between the two modes. This has turned out to be a *fatal flaw,* as the MS-DOS operating system (the dominant microcomputer operating system for 80x86 processors) requires that all programs be run in 8086 (Real) mode. As a result, most, if not all, 286 chips are operated in Real Mode and thus function only as fast 8086s.

The 80386 Microprocessor

Setting a New Standard.   When Intel announced the 80386 (the 386) microprocessor in 1985, they made a commitment that through the year 2000, each successive microprocessor generation would remain compatible with this chip. The 386 represents a major redesign of the older 8086 and 80286 processors. The data bus width and internal processor registers are all 32 bits wide, as is the address bus, thus allowing the chip to access 4 GB (4096 MB) of physical memory.[11]

Like the 286, the 386 supports two different operating modes. These are called *Real Address Mode* and *Protected Virtual Address Mode* (Protected Mode). Real Address Mode is identical to the 80286's Real Mode and limits the processor to 1 MB of memory. In effect, the 386 becomes a (very) fast 8086 processor. This is the mode used by MS-DOS.[12]

The true power of the 386 is revealed when switched to Protected Mode. In this mode the onboard memory management unit (MMU) manages the 4 GB of memory in a way similar to that of the 286 Protected Mode; that is, tasks are given a segment of memory in which to run, governed by a descriptor register. This register defines the segment base address, the segment limit, and the *attributes* for that segment (execute code, program data, read-only, etc.). These segments can be as large as 4 GB, or as small as a single byte. In addition, using a technique called *paging,* 4K pages can be swapped in and out of memory (using a hard disk drive) to allow a task to have a virtual memory space as large as 64 terabytes (64 million megabytes!).

The Protected Mode features of the 386 can only be taken advantage of by an operating system that is aware of these features. Common examples are Microsoft Windows, IBM's OS/2, and UNIX. Windows and OS/2 use another Protected Mode feature of the 386 called *Virtual 8086 Mode*. This mode is similar to Real Mode, except that multiple 8086 machines can be run simultaneously, protected from each other. Windows uses this technique to launch multiple DOS programs, each in its own window.

The 386 requires just two clock pulses per (memory read or write) bus cycle and is available with clock speeds as high as 40 MHz. Because of this, an external memory *cache* is required to prevent the processor from entering long wait cycles while data is read from or written to (slow) conventional main memory. A cache is a relatively small amount of very fast memory located between the microprocessor and main memory. Cache memory typically uses fast static RAM (SRAM) chips, while main memory is based on slower dynamic RAM (DRAM) technology. The cache is designed to hold information that the processor will likely require in the near future. If the desired information is indeed in the cache when needed, a *hit* is said to occur. If not, the processor must wait while the desired

---

[11]Assuming you could afford to buy it!

[12]You might wonder why DOS would force the 386 to operate in such a limited mode. The answer is *compatibility.* If DOS was written to require the 386's Protected Mode, all users of 80286 and 8086 machines would be left out.

data is transferred to the cache. When operated with a 64K cache, the 386 achieves a hit rate of 93 percent. This means the processor operates at full speed 93 percent of the time.

The instruction set of the 386 is again 100 percent compatible with the older processors in the family (the 8086, 80186, and 80286). Fourteen new instructions have been added and several others have been modified. For example, data can now be moved between the internal processor registers 8, 16, or 32 bits at a time. (Chapters 3–6 provide more detail on the 386 architecture, instruction set, and programming.)

The 386SX.   Just as the 8088 helped designers make the transition from 8-bit microprocessors to 16-bit processors, the 80386SX is designed to ease the transition from 16- to 32-bit microprocessors. This is done by providing a 16-bit external data bus width and reducing the address bus to 24 bits. In all other ways the 386SX is identical to the 386 (now called 386DX to differentiate the two chips).

The 80486DX

Maintaining Compatibility.   In 1989, IBM's PC was seven years old, and the Intel microprocessor architecture (8086, 80286, 80386) was solidly entrenched as the de facto standard. Accordingly, Intel realized that new processors in the family would have to maintain compatibility with the past generations. The 80486 therefore represents a more polished and refined 386. Only six new instructions have been added, and these are intended primarily for use by operating system software, not by applications programs. The data bus, address bus, and internal registers all remain 32 bits wide. The core of the chip has been redesigned using RISC concepts, allowing frequently used instructions to execute in a single clock cycle. Chips with clock speeds as high as 50 MHz are available. A new five-stage execution pipeline allows portions of five instructions to be executing at once.

The 486 is also highly integrated. Included on board is an 8K memory cache and a floating-point processor that is the equivalent of the (external) 80387 coprocessor chip popular in 386 systems. The result is a processor that operates about twice as fast as a 386 for any given clock speed; that is, a 20 MHz 486 gives performance equivalent to a 40 MHz 386.

The 486SX.   Based on its numerical designation, you might expect the 486SX to be a 16-bit version of the 486DX. However, that is not the case. Instead, Intel has designated this chip for low-end applications that do not require a coprocessor or internal cache. Therefore, these functions have been disabled. In addition, clock speeds for the 486SX are limited to 33 MHz.

The 486DX2 and DX4.   As microprocessor system clock speeds have increased, the job of designing a compatible microcomputer around these chips has become increasingly difficult. A 50 MHz clock signal, for example, provides only 20 ns between clock "ticks." This means the time required for a signal to travel from point A to point B on the system board becomes significant (about 6 in. per nanosecond). A buffer that introduces 5–10 ns of delay may cause the entire system to shut down.

Once again, a new way of thinking was required. The result was a new breed of microprocessors that operate with an *internal* clock rate that is twice (DX2) or three times (DX4) the *external* clock rate. This allows the computer system board to be designed using less expensive components while still allowing the processor to operate at its maximum data rate (internally). Of course, operations that require access to data outside of the processor will have to be slowed down to the system-board rate. The internal cache of the 486 helps offset this loss, so that a DX2 chip achieves about 80 percent of the performance of a DX chip.

DX2 and DX4 chips are usually described in terms of their internal clock rate. Thus, the description 486DX2 66 is interpreted to mean a 486 microprocessor with an internal clock rate of 66 MHz and an external clock rate of 33 MHz. A DX4 100, with the same external clock, operates internally at 100 MHz.

The Overdrive Processors.   Many 486 system boards are designed to include an *overdrive socket*. These sockets are intended to allow users to upgrade their (low-speed) 486DX or (no coprocessor) 486SX CPUs with 486DX2 or DX4 style processors. The overdrive chips are thus 486DX2 and DX4 chips with overdrive socket pin-outs.

The Pentium

Superscaler Processor.   One method of increasing the complexity of an integrated circuit is simply to *scale* the chip down. For example, if every line etched into the silicon die could be shrunk in half, the same circuit could be built in one-fourth the area. The evolution of dynamic memory chips (DRAMs) follows this rule exactly. The original IBM PC used 16K DRAMs. These were soon replaced with 64K chips, then 256K chips, and now 1 MB, 4 MB, and 16 MB chips. 64 MB chips are in development.

The trick, of course, is being able to improve your skills sufficiently to allow this scaling to continue. Table 1.1 shows that the minimum feature size (the smallest detail that can be etched into a chip) has shrunk from 10 microns (10×10^{-6} meters) in 1969 to 0.35 microns in 1995.

The Pentium uses a *superscaler* architecture. This means that its capabilities go beyond those achieved by simply scaling down the size of the chip. In particular, the Pentium is the first microprocessor in the Intel family to support two instruction pipelines, each with its own arithmetic logic unit, address generation circuitry, and data cache interface. The result is a processor that can actually execute two different instructions simultaneously.

Like the 486, the Pentium incorporates an onboard cache and floating-point processor. However, to avoid bottlenecks when accessing program instructions and data, separate 8K code and data caches are provided. The 486's coprocessor has been completely redesigned and now includes an eight-stage instruction pipeline. In addition, many of the floating-point functions have been optimized. As a result, the Pentium achieves five to ten times the floating-point performance of the 486.

The internal architecture of the chip presented to the programmer remains compatible with the 386 and 486. That is, all registers are 32 bits wide, as is the address bus. The external data bus, however, has been expanded to 64 bits to allow higher data transfer rates.[13] Six new instructions have been added, but again these are primarily for use by the operating system, not the applications programmer. In all other ways, the Pentium remains compatible with the 386 and 486.

---

[13]Note that this approach is *opposite* to that taken with the 8088 and 80386SX. These chips have external data buses smaller than the internal register sizes.

Performance tests have shown the Pentium to be about twice as fast as the 486 at any given clock speed. The entry level P66, for example, operates at 66 MHz and provides twice the performance of the 486DX2 66.

The Pentium Pro

Two Chips in One.   Perhaps the most striking feature of the Pentium Pro is the package itself. As shown in Figure 1.10, the Pentium Pro consists of two separate silicon die. The largest is the processor: Fabricated with 0.35 micron design rules, it incorporates 5.5 million transistors. The smaller die beside it is a 256K *level two cache*.[14] Oddly enough, the cache has three times as many transistors as the processor (15.5 million) but, because of its uniformity, less silicon area is required. Versions of the Pentium Pro with a 512K (31 million transistor) cache are also available.

The Pentium Pro retains all of the architectural features of the Pentium that preceded it. That is, internally all registers are 32 bits, while the external data bus is 64 bits wide. Four additional address lines have been added, allowing 64 GB of physical memory to be accessed. From a software point of view, the Pentium Pro remains 100 percent compatible with previous-generation 80x86 processors. Three new processor instructions have been added (see Chapter 4), as well as two new floating-point unit instructions.

Dynamic Execution.   The most touted feature of the Pentium Pro is what Intel calls *Dynamic Execution*. This is a new approach to processing software instructions that reduces idle processor time to an absolute minimum. It consists of the following three techniques:

1. *Multiple Branch Prediction.* Conventional processors "blindly" fetch instructions without regard to program branches. If a conditional jump instruction is fetched, subsequent instructions may have to be discarded if the jump is taken. Using a technique called *multiple branch prediction,* the Pentium Pro can look as far as 30 instructions ahead to anticipate these program branches.
2. *Data Flow Analysis.* Using this technique, the Pentium Pro looks at upcoming software instructions and determines if they are available for processing, dependent on other instructions. The Pentium Pro then determines the optimal sequence for processing and begins executing them.
3. *Speculative Execution.* This is a technique that allows the Pentium Pro to execute instructions in a different order from which they entered the processor. This "out-of-order" execution allows the Pentium Pro processor to execute instructions with optimum efficiency. The results of these instructions are stored as speculative results until their final states can be determined.

Superscaler Processor of Degree Three.   Like the Pentium processor before it, the Pentium Pro is superscaler. However, where the Pentium was able to execute two instructions per clock cycle, the Pentium Pro, with three instruction decoders, can execute three simultaneous instructions.

---

[14]A level two cache is a cache that interfaces to the *external* address, data, and control lines of the processor. Because of this, it operates at a lower speed than a level one cache, which is built into the architecture of the processor. Prior to the Pentium Pro, level two caches were implemented with discrete chips on the system board. The Pentium Pro also includes a (16K) level one cache internal to the processor.

Figure 1.10   The P6 is two chips in one. The larger die is the processor, the smaller a 256K level two cache. (Courtesy of Intel Corporation)

Internal Cache.   The onboard (level one) 8K data and instruction cache of the Pentium was described previously. As you will learn in Chapter 3, most microcomputer systems include an *external* cache of 64K to 256K. The Pentium Pro incorporates a 256K (or 512K) level two cache *onboard*. This simplifies system board design, requires less space and, because the processor and cache are wired in the same package, allows the CPU core to communicate with the cache at full (core) speed.

The 133 MHz version of the Pentium Pro provides twice the performance of a 66 MHz Pentium and four times that of a 486DX2 66. Compared to a 100 MHz Pentium, the Pentium Pro offers a 70 percent performance boost.

Intel-Compatible Microprocessors

Second Sources.   In the early 1980s, many computer vendors felt uneasy "throwing all of their eggs in one (Intel) basket." After all, Intel was a relatively small chip manufacturer at the time and the microprocessor market was as yet untested. Vendors were concerned that labor problems or part shortages could prevent them from getting their chips. For this reason, Intel licensed other companies to produce 80x86 chips in competition with themselves. This may seem odd, but second sources help legitimize and secure a wider market acceptance for a new product. In addition, a royalty agreement ensures that a portion of each sale is returned to the original designer.

Clones.   To help gain market acceptance, Intel licensed several companies to produce 8086, 8088, and 80286 chips. Their strategy worked, and by the time the 386 came along, the Intel architecture had become the de facto PC standard. Consequently, beginning with the 80386, Intel no longer second-sourced their products (except to IBM). This did not stop the competition from producing Intel-compatible processors, however.

These chips, called *clones* or *look-alikes*, are a redesigned version of the 386 and 486 series of microprocessors. They (usually) have pin-outs identical to the corresponding Intel part, and are fully hardware and software compatible. In some cases, the clone part may even offer superior performance. The Advanced Micro Devices AMD 386DX, for example, operates at 40 MHz, about 20 percent faster than Intel's 33 MHz part, and consumes less power. Several clones of the 486 are available: The most notable are the Cyrix 486SLC and SLD chips, and IBM's 486SLC2.

Because the name *Pentium* is copyrighted by Intel, clones of this chip are typically referred to as the 586. AMD, for example, offers the 133 MHz Am5x86. It features a Pentium-like architecture, including 16K onboard cache. Cyrix offers a similar chip called the Cyrix 5x86. It operates at 100 or 120 MHz. Unlike Intel's Pentium, however, it retains the 32-bit data bus of the 486. Internally the data bus width is 64 bits. Cyrix is also offering a Pentium Pro equivalent called the Cyrix 6x86. It features a 64-bit data bus and clock speeds to 150 MHz. It does not include the onboard level two cache found in the Pentium Pro, however.

Self-Review 1.3 (Answers on page 33)

1.3.1 Compare the 8086 and 8088 microprocessors. In what ways are they similar? In what ways do they differ?

1.3.2 Which of the microprocessors listed below have 16-bit internal data registers?
   (a) 8086
   (b) 8088
   (c) 80286
   (d) 80386
   (e) 80386SX
   (f) 80486DX

1.3.3 The 386 introduced a new Protected Mode feature called _____ _____ Mode.

1.3.4 When using MS-DOS, the 386 is operated in _____ Mode.

1.3.5 To speed up memory accesses, the 386 uses an external _____. On the 486, Pentium, and Pentium Pro the _____ is internal.

1.3.6 The Pentium has _____K of cache memory, _____ instruction pipelines, and an onboard _____ _____ _____.

1.3.7 Using _____ _____ _____, the Pentium Pro is able to look ahead as many as 30 instructions.

1.3.8 The Pentium can execute _____ instructions simultaneously. The Pentium Pro can execute _____instructions simultaneously.

1.3.9 Companies licensed by the parent company to produce compatible microprocessor chips are called _____ _____.

Chapter 1 Self-Test

1. The three main parts of a stored program computer are _____, _____, and _____.
2. Stored program computers repeatedly follow the sequence _____ and _____.
3. When data flows from memory into the processor, a _____ _____ cycle is said to occur.
4. Under what conditions can the fetch and execute cycle of a computer *overlap*?
5. Under what conditions can the instruction decode and execute cycles of a computer overlap?

6. List the three buses of a stored program computer.
7. 80x86 processors organize their memory into banks, with each bank _____ bits wide.
8. An 80x86 processor with a 20-bit address bus could access _____ bytes of memory.
9. The IBM 360 is an example of a _____-generation computer.
10. The first microprocessor chip was based on a _____-bit processor.
11. A microprocessor with built-in I/O and memory is called a _____.
12. How does the architecture of a supercomputer differ from that of a desktop microcomputer?
13. Which of the following are characteristic of a CISC? List all that apply:
    (a) All instructions execute in a single clock cycle.
    (b) A small number of general-purpose processor registers.
    (c) A large number of instructions with many different addressing modes.
    (d) Each instruction has the same length.
14. A DSP is:
    (a) An analog microprocessor.
    (b) A microprocessor optimized to perform repetitive math operations.
    (c) A microprocessor designed to process analog signals that have been converted to digital form.
    (d) (b) and (c).
15. Which of the following 80x86 microprocessors have internal data bus widths that *do not* match their external data bus widths?
    (a) 8086
    (b) 8088
    (c) 80386
    (d) 80386SX
    (e) 80486
    (f) 80486SX
    (g) Pentium
    (h) Pentium Pro
16. When operated in Real Mode, an 80x86 microprocessor appears to be a _____ processor.
17. Which of the 80x86 microprocessor chips listed below have 32-bit internal processor data registers?
    (a) 8086
    (b) 8088
    (c) 80386
    (d) 80386SX
    (e) 80486
    (f) 80486SX
    (g) Pentium
    (h) Pentium Pro
18. When using a cache memory, the processor first searches the cache for necessary data or the next program instruction; if found, a _____ is said to occur.
19. Which of the following 80x86 microprocessors have more than one instruction decoder?
    (a) 8086
    (b) 8088
    (c) 80386
    (d) 80386SX
    (e) 80486
    (f) 80486SX
    (g) Pentium
    (h) Pentium Pro

20. We would expect a chip numbered 486DX4 100 to operate with an internal clock rate of _____ MHz and an external clock rate of _____ MHz.

Analysis and Design Questions

Section 1.1

1.1 Compare the architecture of a modern stored program computer with that of ENIAC.

1.2 The 8086 microprocessor has a 16-bit data bus. Its memory is organized into _____ banks, each _____ bits wide.

1.3 A microprocessor with a 24-bit address bus could access _____ MB of memory.

1.4 Explain the difference between a memory read cycle and an I/O read cycle. In which *direction* does data flow for these cycles?

Section 1.2

1.5 Number the following events in time order (1 = oldest).
- _____ (a) The first minicomputer (the PDP-8) is announced.
- _____ (b) Intel introduces one of the first 32-bit microprocessors, the 80386.
- _____ (c) The transistor is invented at Bell Laboratories.
- _____ (d) IBM begins selling a personal computer based on the 8088 microprocessor.
- _____ (e) IBM announces the first IC-based computer, the model 360.
- _____ (f) The integrated circuit is independently invented at Texas Instruments and Fairchild.
- _____ (g) IBM announces its first electronic computer, the vacuum tube-based model 701.
- _____ (h) The first processor-on-a-chip, the 4004, is announced by Intel.
- _____ (i) Cray Research announces its first supercomputer, the Cray-1.
- _____ (j) Apple, IBM, and Motorola announce the PowerPC RISC.
- _____ (k) ENIAC is designed and built at the University of Pennsylvania.

1.6 Use a spreadsheet to create a bar graph comparing the number of transistors in micro-processor chips from the 4004 to the Pentium Pro. Refer to Table 1.1 for your data. *Hint: Use a log scale for the y-axis (number of transistors).*

Section 1.3

1.7 Use a spreadsheet to create a *scatter graph* (data points only) comparing the processing rate in MIPs (y axis) of 80x86 microprocessors with the corresponding minimum feature size (x-axis). Refer to Table 1.1 for your data. *Hint: Use a log scale for the y-axis.*

1.8 Intel microprocessors organize their memory into 8-bit-wide banks. The 16-bit 80286, for example, requires two such banks. Typically these banks are built using 1 MB or 4 MB SIMMs (single in-line memory modules). For each of the following processors, determine the *minimum* number of 1 MB SIMMs required, the resulting amount of memory, and the maximum amount of memory possible. The 80286 case is given as an example (assume byte-wide SIMMs).

Microprocessor	Minimum number of SIMMs	Total memory capacity for these SIMMs (at 1 MB each)	Maximum memory capacity for this processor
80286	2	2 MB	16 MB
80386DX			
80386SX			
80486DX			
Pentium			

1.9   Explain why each of the following microprocessor features affect (or *do not affect*) the processing rate of the chip.
(a) clock frequency
(b) data bus width
(c) address bus width
(d) internal cache memory
(e) coprocessor (internal or external)

1.10   Beginning with the 386, the 80x86 processors supported three different operating modes. List these modes and give a brief explanation of each.

1.11   For each of the following, indicate if the feature is the same or different for the Pentium and Pentium Pro processors. If different, explain the difference.

Feature	Same/Different	Explanation (if different)
Data bus width		
Address bus width		
General-purpose registers		
Execute simultaneous instructions		
Cache		
Instruction Set		
Package		
Dynamic execution		

1.12   Why might it be advantageous for a chip manufacturer to *second-source* its products to another vendor?

Self-Review Answers

1.1.1   CPU, memory, I/O
1.1.2   (d)
1.1.3   arithmetic logic unit, accumulator
1.1.4   16,777,216 (16 MB)
1.1.5   4
1.1.6   I/O WRITE
1.1.7   data
1.2.1   vacuum tube, transistor
1.2.2   IBM 360
1.2.3   A minicomputer is a scaled down mainframe. Typically much less costly than a mainframe.
1.2.4   A microcomputer is a computer system built using a microprocessor as the processor.
1.2.5   They are embedded within a product and therefore not visible as a computer.
1.2.6   Multiple CPUs wired in parallel, each processing a portion of the program simultaneously.
1.2.7   A RISC has a simpler control unit because all instructions are of the same length and execute in a single clock cycle. The simplified control logic can operate faster than that of a CISC and requires less space on the chip.

1.2.8   A DSP has separate data and instruction memory, onboard hardware multipliers and adders optimized for one clock cycle execution rates, arithmetic pipelines to perform simultaneous math operations, hardware optimized for repetitive operations such as DO loops, and multiple serial I/O ports for communicating with a host processor.

1.3.1   Internally, the 8086 and 8088 are essentially the same. Both have 16-bit registers and execute the same instruction set. Externally, the 8086 has a 16-bit data bus while the 8088 has an 8-bit bus.

1.3.2   (a), (b), and (c)

1.3.3   virtual 8086

1.3.4   Real

1.3.5   cache, cache

1.3.6   16K, two, floating-point unit

1.3.7   multiple branch prediction

1.3.8   two, three

1.3.9   second sources

2 Computer Codes, Programming, and Operating Systems

In 1964, IBM released the 360 series of computers. Using solid-state devices integrated on small ceramic substrates, ten different models were offered, allowing the 360 series to be adapted to a wide range of applications. IBM is said to have "bet the company" on the 360 series, investing nearly $5 billion. The bet paid off—more than 30,000 System 360s were eventually sold. (Photo courtesy of Smithsonian)

Outline

Objectives

After completing this chapter you should be able to:

1. Compare and contrast the decimal and binary number systems.
2. Show how a binary number is converted to decimal and vice versa.
3. Show how a binary number is converted to hexadecimal and vice versa.

4. Show how a hexadecimal number is converted to decimal and vice versa.
5. Show how letters of the alphabet are represented in ASCII.
6. Explain the parity and checksum methods of error detection.
7. Demonstrate how positive and negative numbers are represented in the two's complement code.
8. Show how decimal numbers are represented in BCD.
9. Compare and contrast programming in machine language, assembly language, and a high level language.
10. List the steps required to develop an assembly language program.
11. Explain why programming with a high level language is (usually) preferred over machine or assembly language programming.
12. Explain the role of the operating system software in a typical microcomputer.
13. List the sequence of events that occur when an 80x86 computer is booted up with MS-DOS.
14. Draw the memory map for an 80x86 computer running MS-DOS.
15. Explain how to access the BIOS services and functions of MS-DOS.

Overview

Think of this chapter as a review of the software side of digital electronics. If you are already familiar with this material, move on to Chapter 3, but if you need a quick refresher, read on. You will find a review of the binary and hexadecimal number systems, and several important codes including ASCII, two's complement, and BCD. We also compare machine and assembly language programming and contrast these low level languages with two high level languages—BASIC and C. The chapter concludes with a discussion of computer operating systems. Particular attention is paid here to MS-DOS and Windows, the dominant control programs for 80x86 computers.

2.1 The Binary and Hexadecimal Number Systems: A Quick Review

Introduction

In the following chapters we will use the *binary* number system—the "native" language of digital circuits—extensively. Because binary numbers can be quite awkward to use, it is advantageous to express these numbers in *hexadecimal* format. This section provides a brief review of these number systems.

In this section we:

- Compare and contrast the decimal and binary number systems.
- Show how a binary number is converted to decimal and vice versa.
- Show how a binary number is converted to hexadecimal and vice versa.
- Show how a hexadecimal number is converted to decimal and vice versa.

Comparing Binary and Decimal Numbers

Converting from Binary to Decimal. Table 2.1 compares decimal and binary numbers. Decimal has a base, or *radix,* of 10, meaning that there are ten unique symbols in this

Table 2.1 Comparing the Decimal and Binary Number Systems

	Decimal	Binary
Basic or radix	10	2
Number of unique digits	10 (0–9)	2 (0, 1)
Weighting of digits (right to left)	1	1
	10	2
	100	4
	1000	8
	10,000	16
	.	.
	.	.
	.	.
Example	367	1101
	$7 \times 10^0 = 7$	$1 \times 2^0 =$ 1
	$+ 6 \times 10^1 =$ 60	$+ 0 \times 2^1 =$ 0
	$+ 3 \times 10^2 = \underline{300}$	$+ 1 \times 2^2 =$ 4
	367	$+ 1 \times 2^3 = \underline{\ 8}$
		13

number system. The binary number system has only two symbols, 0 and 1. We refer to these binary digits as *bits*. The base of the number system also identifies the *weighting* of each digit position. In decimal, the rightmost digit counts units, the digit to its left tens, the digit to its left hundreds, and so on. Another way of saying this is that the digits are weighted in the order 10^0, 10^1, 10^2, etc. Thus, the number 367 can be thought of as three one hundreds, six tens, and seven ones.

The binary number system works in exactly the same way, except that the digit weightings are in the sequence 2^0, 2^1, 2^2, etc. Table 2.2 lists these powers of two through 2^{24}. Since a binary digit can only be a 1 or a 0, all binary numbers are formed from the various powers of two shown in Table 2.2. The binary number 1101 is the sum of 2^3 plus 2^2 plus 2^0; that is, $8 + 4 + 1$. You will probably find it easier to count from right to left in the sequence 1-2-4-8-16-32, etc., summing those digits that are a 1.

Example 2.1

Convert the binary number 101001 to decimal by adding the appropriate powers of two.

Solution

Starting from the rightmost bit and counting in the sequence 1-2-4-8-16-32:

$$101001 =$$

$$1 \times 1 = 1$$
$$+ 0 \times 2 = 0$$
$$+ 0 \times 4 = 0$$
$$+ 1 \times 8 = 8$$
$$+ 0 \times 16 = 0$$
$$+ 1 \times 32 = \underline{32}$$
$$41$$

Thus, 101001_2 (binary) = 41_{10} (decimal).

Table 2.2   Powers of Two

n	2^n	Binary Ks
0	1	—
1	2	—
2	4	—
3	8	—
4	16	—
5	32	—
6	64	—
7	128	—
8	256	—
9	512	—
10	1024	1K
11	2048	2K
12	4096	4K
13	8192	8K
14	16,384	16K
15	32,768	32K
16	65,536	64K
17	131,072	128K
18	262,144	256K
19	524,288	512K
20	1,048,576	1024K (1M)
21	2,097,152	2048K (2M)
22	4,194,304	4096K (4M)
23	8,388,608	8192K (8M)
24	16,777,216	16384K (16M)

Example 2.2

Determine the decimal equivalent of the following binary numbers:

(a) 1001   (b) 1111   (c) 11000101   (d) 1100011101101001

Solution
Counting from right to left in the sequence shown in Table 2.2:

(a) $1001 = 1 + 8 = 9$
(b) $1111 = 1 + 2 + 4 + 8 = 15$
(c) $11000101 = 1 + 4 + 64 + 128 = 197$
(d) $1100011101101001 = 1 + 8 + 32 + 64 + 256 + 512 + 1024 + 16,384 + 32,768 = 51,049$

Large binary numbers are more easily converted to decimal by converting them to *hexadecimal* first, and then to decimal. This technique will be explained later in this section.

Converting from Decimal to Binary.   Decimal numbers can be converted to binary by finding the appropriate powers of two in the decimal number. Two methods can be used.

Repeated Subtraction. In this method, the highest power of two is first subtracted from the number. The process is then repeated, subtracting the next highest power of two from the remainder. For example, to convert 49 to binary:

$$
\begin{array}{rl}
49 & \\
\underline{-32} & 2^5 \text{ (highest power of two in 49)} \\
17 & \\
\underline{-16} & 2^4 \text{ (highest power of two in 16)} \\
1 & \\
\underline{-1} & 2^0 \text{ (highest power of two in 1)} \\
0 & \text{done!}
\end{array}
$$

The answer is formed by writing a 1 for each power of two that is present and a 0 for those powers not present. Starting from the left, we can say:

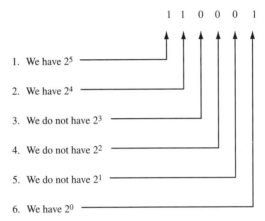

Thus, $49_{10} = 110001_2$.

Example 2.3

Convert the number 483 to binary using the repeated-subtraction method.

Solution

$$
\begin{array}{rl}
483 & \\
\underline{-256} & 2^8 \text{ (highest power of two in 483)} \\
227 & \\
\underline{-128} & 2^7 \text{ (highest power of two in 227)} \\
99 & \\
\underline{-64} & 2^6 \text{ (highest power of two in 99)} \\
35 & \\
\underline{-32} & 2^5 \text{ (highest power of two in 35)} \\
3 & \\
\underline{-2} & 2^1 \text{ (highest power of two in 3)} \\
1 & \\
\underline{-1} & 2^0 \text{ (highest power of two in 1)} \\
0 &
\end{array}
$$

Assembling the bits from highest power of two to lowest and writing the result from left to right, we have: $483_{10} = 111100011_2$.

Repeated Division.   In this method, the decimal number is repeatedly divided by two. The remainder, always a 1 or 0, becomes the binary result. For example, again converting 49 to binary:

$$49/2 = 24 \quad \text{remainder} = 1 \text{ (least significant bit)}$$
$$24/2 = 12 \quad \text{remainder} = 0$$
$$12/2 = 6 \quad \text{remainder} = 0$$
$$6/2 = 3 \quad \text{remainder} = 0$$
$$3/2 = 1 \quad \text{remainder} = 1$$
$$1/2 = 0 \quad \text{remainder} = 1 \text{ (most significant bit)}$$

Now, working from *bottom to top* (and left to right), we can assemble the result as:

$$1\ 1\ 0\ 0\ 0\ 1$$

The advantage of this method is that the 1s and 0s "emerge" as the calculations progress: The result can then be recorded directly. The disadvantage is that it requires one calculation for each bit of the result. The number 483, for example, will require nine separate divisions.

Example 2.4

Show the steps required to convert 483_{10} to binary using the repeated-division-by-two method.

Solution
Using R for remainder:

1. $483/2 = 241$ R1 (least significant bit)
2. $241/2 = 120$ R1
3. $120/2 = 60$ R0
4. $60/2 = 30$ R0
5. $30/2 = 15$ R0
6. $15/2 = 7$ R1
7. $7/2 = 3$ R1
8. $3/2 = 1$ R1
9. $1/2 = 0$ R1 (most significant bit)

The result is thus 1 1 1 1 0 0 0 1 1.

Combinations of Bits

The 2^n Rule.   One binary digit allows *two* different numbers to be defined (0 and 1). However, when two bits are used, *four* different combinations or numbers result. These are 00, 01, 10, and 11, corresponding to the decimal numbers 0 through 3. In general there will be 2^n different combinations of an *n*-bit binary number.

This result is a very important one to remember when working with digital circuits. It tells how much information can be distributed over *n* binary lines. For example, the 8086 microprocessor with 20 address lines will be able to output 2^{20}, or 1,048,576, different address combinations. This is referred to as 1M (see sidebar).

Bytes, Kilobytes, Megabytes, and Gigabytes

The following definitions are often applied to measure the size of a binary number:

Width (bits)	Description
4	nibble
8	byte
16	word
32	double-word
64	quad-word

The size of a computer's memory is usually measured in *kilobytes* (K) or *megabytes* (MB). Oddly enough, a 1K memory does *not* store 1000 bytes, nor does a 1 MB memory store 1,000,000 bytes. The reason can be seen in Table 2.2. A 1K memory requires 10 address lines. When all 2^{10} combinations of these lines are accounted for, 1024 will be found. Similarly, a 1 MB memory requires 20 address lines and thus provides 2^{20} or 1,048,576 memory locations. These differences are simply due to the fact that there are no integer powers of two that come out exactly to 1000 or 1,000,000.

It is convenient to remember that $2^{10} = 1K$ and $2^{20} = 1M$. For example, the capacity of a memory chip with 16 address lines can quickly be computed as:

$$2^{16} = 2^6 \times 2^{10} = 64 \times 1K = 64K$$

Similarly, the memory capacity of a microprocessor like the 80286 with its 24-bit address bus can be computed as:

$$2^{24} = 2^4 \times 2^{20} = 16 \times 1 \text{ MB} = 16 \text{ MB}$$

Several microprocessors today have 32-bit address buses. This memory capacity can be calculated as:

$$2^{32} = 2^2 \times 2^{10} \times 2^{20} = 4 \times 1K \times 1 \text{ MB} = 4K \times 1 \text{ MB} = 4096 \text{ MB}$$

Noting that $2^{30} = 2^{10} \times 2^{20} = 1024$ MB, and defining this to be 1 GB (gigabyte), the 32-bit calculation becomes:

$$2^{32} = 2^2 \times 2^{30} = 4 \times 1 \text{ GB} = 4 \text{ GB}$$

Example 2.5

List all possible combinations of five binary digits and determine the decimal value of the largest combination. State a general rule to find the value of the largest binary number, given n bits.

Solution

With $n = 5$, there are 2^5 possible binary combinations. These are listed in Table 2.3. The largest number is $11111 = 16 + 8 + 4 + 2 + 1 = 31$. In general, for an n-bit binary number, there will be 2^n different combinations and the value of the largest number will be $2^n - 1$.

Table 2.3   Counting in Decimal, Binary, and Hexadecimal

Decimal	Binary	Hexadecimal
0	0 0 0 0 0	0
1	0 0 0 0 1	1
2	0 0 0 1 0	2
3	0 0 0 1 1	3
4	0 0 1 0 0	4
5	0 0 1 0 1	5
6	0 0 1 1 0	6
7	0 0 1 1 1	7
8	0 1 0 0 0	8
9	0 1 0 0 1	9
10	0 1 0 1 0	A
11	0 1 0 1 1	B
12	0 1 1 0 0	C
13	0 1 1 0 1	D
14	0 1 1 1 0	E
15	0 1 1 1 1	F
16	1 0 0 0 0	10
17	1 0 0 0 1	11
18	1 0 0 1 0	12
19	1 0 0 1 1	13
20	1 0 1 0 0	14
21	1 0 1 0 1	15
22	1 0 1 1 0	16
23	1 0 1 1 1	17
24	1 1 0 0 0	18
25	1 1 0 0 1	19
26	1 1 0 1 0	1A
27	1 1 0 1 1	1B
28	1 1 1 0 0	1C
29	1 1 1 0 1	1D
30	1 1 1 1 0	1E
31	1 1 1 1 1	1F

Example 2.6

Determine the number of bits required to represent the decimal number 837.

Solution

We could answer this by converting 837 to binary. However, there is an easier way. Referring to Table 2.2, note that 837 falls between 512 (2^9) and 1024 (2^{10}). This means 9 binary digits will not be enough. With 10 digits, however, we can represent all numbers from 512 to 1023. Thus, 10 digits are required. As a check, 837, when converted to binary, becomes the 10-digit number 1101000101.

Hexadecimal Numbers

The Rule of Fours.   Hexadecimal is a popular number system used with microcomputers. Hex numbers are formed by grouping the binary digits four at a time, beginning on the right (the *Rule of Fours*). Each resulting number group has 16 possible bit combinations from 0000 to 1111, as shown in Table 2.3. The first ten can be represented by their decimal equivalents. But what of the combinations 1010 through 1111 (decimal 10–15)? Although these cannot be represented by a single decimal digit, we can "create" new symbols for these combinations. By tradition, the first six letters of the alphabet are chosen. This is also shown in Table 2.3.

Consider the 8-bit binary number 11010101. To convert this number to hex, group the bits four at a time, beginning on the right. The result is:

$$11010101 = 1101\ 0101 = D5_{16}$$
$$\text{D}\quad\ \ 5$$

The hexadecimal number system takes some getting used to—especially the letter combinations A through F. For example, it is now possible to have a "BAD" number![1]

$$1011\ 1010\ 1101$$
$$\text{B}\quad\ \text{A}\quad\ \text{D}$$

Example 2.7

Convert the following hex numbers to binary:

(a) 20   (b) 3C   (c) FFFF

Solution
Writing the binary results in groups of four bits:

(a) $2\ 0_{16} = 0010\ 0000$
$$2\quad\ \ 0$$
(b) $3C_{16} = 0011\ 1100$
$$3\quad\ \ \text{C}$$
(c) $FFFF_{16} = 1111\ 1111\ 1111\ 1111$
$$\text{F}\quad\ \text{F}\quad\ \text{F}\quad\ \text{F}$$

Counting in Hexadecimal.   Note that hexadecimal and decimal are identical for the first ten numbers (Table 2.3). Hex then continues in the sequence A through F. Following the number F, hex starts again with 10 and continues through 1F.

Example 2.8

Determine the next number in the count sequence for each of the following hexadecimal numbers:

(a) 2E   (b) 9F   (c) 7CBF   (d) CFFFF

Solution
Noting the sequence in Table 2.3:

(a) 2E + 1 = 2F
(b) 9F + 1 = A0
(c) 7CBF + 1 = 7CC0
(d) CFFFF + 1 = D0000

---

[1]It is common practice to write binary numbers in groups of 4 bits each. This makes it easier to recognize the hexadecimal digits. Thus, 101110101101 is more often written 1011 1010 1101. We will follow this practice throughout this book.

Decimal Conversions.   Each digit in a hexadecimal number has a weight given by 16^n, where n is the digit position ($n = 0$ for the rightmost bit). The first four hex digits are thus worth 16^0, 16^1, 16^2, and 16^3. To convert a hex number to decimal, calculate the sum of the digits making up that number.

Example 2.9

Convert the following hexadecimal numbers to decimal:

(a) 2C   (b) A09   (c) FFFF

Solution

Remembering that each digit position is weighted 16^n:

(a) $2C_{16} = 2 \times 16^1 + 12 \times 16^0 = 32 + 12 = 44$
(b) $A09_{16} = 10 \times 16^2 + 0 \times 16^1 + 9 \times 16^0 = 2560 + 9 = 2569$
(c) $FFFF_{16} = 15 \times 16^3 + 15 \times 16^2 + 15 \times 16^1 + 15 \times 16^0$
$\qquad\qquad = 61{,}440 + 3840 + 240 + 15 = 65{,}535$

Decimal numbers can be converted to hexadecimal by applying the *repeated-division-by-16* method.

Example 2.10

Convert the following decimal numbers to hexadecimal:

(a) 39   (b) 94   (c) 418

Solution

(a) 39/16 = 2 remainder 7

    2/16 = 0 remainder 2

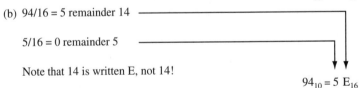

$39_{10} = 2\ 7_{16}$

(b) 94/16 = 5 remainder 14

    5/16 = 0 remainder 5

    Note that 14 is written E, not 14!

$94_{10} = 5\ E_{16}$

(c) 418/16 = 26 remainder 2

    26/16 = 1 remainder 10

    1/16 = 0 remainder 1

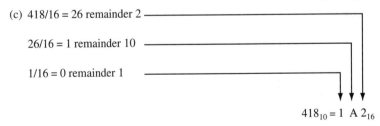

$418_{10} = 1\ A\ 2_{16}$

Note that, for large decimal numbers, first converting the decimal number to hexadecimal, and *then* to binary, may be easier than converting the number directly to binary.

Table 2.4 Numeric Notation

Radix	Notation	Example
Binary	B	11000B
Decimal	D or none	24 or 24D
Hexadecimal	H	18H

Numeric Notation.   In the previous sections we have used subscripts to indicate the base of a particular number. For example, 37 hex is written 37_{16}, while 37 decimal is written 37_{10}. Computer programmers use a different method of indicating the intended number base. This is to append the letters *B, D,* or *H* to the end of the number. Table 2.4 shows how the decimal number 24 is represented in each number system. Most computer programs assume decimal, and the letter *D* need not be appended when working with such programs. We will follow the convention in Table 2.4 for the remainder of this book.[2]

Data Sizes.   A *byte* (8 bits) is the smallest amount of data stored by a computer. Computers with a 16-bit-wide data bus can access two bytes simultaneously: This is referred to as a *word*. The 80386 and 80486 microprocessors each have 32-bit-wide data buses: This amount of data is called a *doubleword* or *dword*. Finally, the Pentium and Pentium Pro processors have 64-bit-wide data buses: This amount of data is referred to as a *quad word*.

Self-Review 2.1 (Answers on page 67–68)

2.1.1   Convert the following binary numbers to decimal:
  (a) 0010
  (b) 1111
  (c) 101010
  (d) 11111111

2.1.2   Convert the following decimal numbers to binary using the repeated-subtraction or repeated-division method:
  (a) 13
  (b) 75
  (c) 187
  (d) 47,629

2.1.3   When counting in binary, what binary number follows 11011?

2.1.4   How many binary digits will be required to represent the decimal number 2467?

2.1.5   There are _____ different combinations of 10 binary bits.

2.1.6   Convert the following binary numbers to hexadecimal and then to decimal:
  (a) 111001
  (b) 11010100
  (c) 100000110101

2.1.7   Convert the following hexadecimal numbers to binary:
  (a) E9H
  (b) FC3H
  (c) FFFFH

---

[2]Another method for representing hexadecimal numbers that is becoming popular is to precede the number with *0×*. For example, 24 becomes 0×18.

2.1.8   Using the repeated-division-by-16 method, convert the following decimal numbers to hex:
   (a) 90
   (b) 328

2.1.9   Classify each of the following hexadecimal numbers as a byte, word, dword, or quad word:
   (a) 3C00H
   (b) 27H
   (c) 1A29E47AH
   (d) 123456789ABCDEF0H

2.2   Computer Codes

Introduction

Information is stored and processed by a computer in binary form. In fact, the power of the computer lies in its ability to process binary numbers extremely fast. Therefore, if the computer is to do useful work, some method must be found for representing everyday information (text and numbers, for example) in binary form. The most common way of doing this is to devise a *standard code* for this information. In this section we:

- Show how letters of the alphabet are represented in ASCII.
- Explain the parity and checksum methods of error detection.
- Demonstrate how positive and negative numbers are represented in the two's complement code.
- Show how decimal numbers are represented in BCD.

ASCII

The Standard for Text.   ASCII (American Standard Code for Information Interchange) was first defined by the American National Standards Institute in 1968. In this code, each letter of the alphabet, punctuation mark, and decimal number is assigned a unique 7-bit code number. With 7 bits, 128 unique symbols can be coded: These are shown in Table 2.5.

To determine the ASCII code for a particular letter, find that letter's *column* and then its *row*. For example, the letter Q is in column 5, row 1. Its code is thus 51H, or 0101 0001. Note that all of the entries in Table 2.5 are written in byte (8-bit) form with the eighth (most significant) bit a 0, as is common practice.

The first two columns in the table list ASCII *mnemonics* (abbreviations) for special control codes. **LF,** for example, stands for *line feed* and will cause the carriage on a printer to roll up one line. Similarly, **BEL** will cause the "bell" to ring.[3] In 1968, when ASCII was first introduced, mechanical teletypes were popular input/output devices, and many of the control codes are defined with this in mind. Today, the codes **SOH** to **SUB**—corresponding to the *control-A* through *control-Z* keys on a computer keyboard—will have varied meanings. **SUB,** for example, may be interpreted as "end of text" by one program, but "scroll the video screen" by another.

ASCII is a very important code because it has become the standard code for conveying text information electronically. Indeed, most computers input ASCII characters from

---

[3]Of course we don't have "bells" anymore. Nowadays, this code causes an electronic "beep."

Table 2.5   American Standard Code for Information Interchange (ASCII)*

Least Significant Bit	Most Significant Bit							
	0 **0000**	**1** **0001**	**2** **0010**	**3** **0011**	**4** **0100**	**5** **0101**	**6** **0110**	**7** **0111**
0 0000	NUL	DLE	SP	0	@	P	'	p
1 0001	SOH	DCI	!	1	A	Q	a	q
2 0010	STX	DC2	"	2	B	R	b	r
3 0011	ETX	DC3	#	3	C	S	c	s
4 0100	EOT	DC4	$	4	D	T	d	t
5 0101	ENQ	NAK	%	5	E	U	e	u
6 0110	ACK	SYN	&	6	F	V	f	v
7 0111	BEL	ETB	'	7	G	W	g	w
8 1000	BS	CAN	(	8	H	X	h	x
9 1001	HT	EM	)	9	I	Y	i	y
A 1010	LF	SUB	*	:	J	Z	j	z
B 1011	VT	ESC	+	;	K	[	k	{
C 1100	FF	FS	,	<	L	\	l		
D 1101	CR	GS	–	=	M	]	m	}
E 1110	SO	RS	.	>	N	^	n	~
F 1111	SI	US	/	?	O	—	o	DEL

*Bit 7 of the code is assumed to be 0.

Source: J. Uffenbeck, *Microcomputers and Microprocessors: The 8080, 8085, and Z-80,* Prentice Hall, Englewood Cliffs, N.J., 1985.

their keyboards, display ASCII characters on their video screens, and output ASCII characters to their printers. This standardization is truly the most important aspect of the code.

Error Detection Codes

Parity.   One of the advantages of ASCII is that it allows text information to be transmitted between computers over long distances. This is done by converting the seven parallel ASCII data bits to bit-by-bit serial form. Using a device called a *modem,* the serial data are converted to audio tones, allowing computer-to-computer communication through the telephone network.[4]

Whenever data is sent from a transmitter to a receiver, data errors can occur. This may be due to high current or voltage switching in nearby equipment, lightning, signal distortion due to long cable lengths, or inductive coupling (cross-talk) between adjacent conductors. To protect against these errors, redundant checking bits are often sent along with the data. The simplest scheme is to append a *parity* bit to each character being transmitted. This bit is chosen such that the total number of 1s in each transmitted character is even or odd. The choice of even or odd parity must, of course, be decided upon before transmission begins. Figure 2.1 outlines the method for including parity bits in a serial transmission.

---

[4]Serial communications and modems are discussed in detail in Chapter 10.

Figure 2.1   A parity generator circuit is used to add a parity bit to a 7-bit ASCII character before it is transmitted. The parity checker on the receiving end indicates an error if the received parity does not agree with the transmitted parity. (From J. Uffenbeck, *Digital Electronics: A Modern Approach,* Prentice Hall, Englewood Cliffs, N.J., 1994)

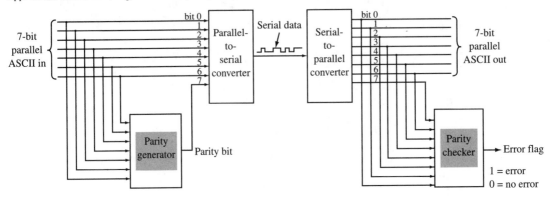

As an example, assume the letter *F* is to be encoded in ASCII with even parity. Referring to Table 2.5, *F* has the ASCII code 46H, or 100 0110. Noting the odd number of 1s in this character, the parity bit must be a logic 1 to produce even parity. Appending this bit in the leftmost position, the even parity-encoded *F* becomes **1**100 0110. In a similar fashion, the letter *A,* when encoded for even parity, has the 8-bit binary code **0**100 0001. In this case the parity bit is a 0.

Example 2.11

Assume the following bytes have been received over a serial data line: E1H, 20H, 72H. If these bytes were encoded using even parity, which, if any, are in error?

Solution
Begin by converting each byte to binary:

$$E1H = 1110\ 0001$$
$$20H = 0010\ 0000$$
$$72H = 0111\ 0010$$

By inspection, only the byte 20H has an odd number of 1s and must therefore be in error. The actual bit in error, however, is unknown.

As you may have noted, the parity method of error detection can only be used to detect *odd* numbers of errors. For example, consider what will happen if the data byte 72H in the example is changed to 77H:

$$72H = 0111\ 0010$$
$$77H = 0111\ 0111$$

Bits 0 and 2 are now in error. The parity, however, is still even, and the error goes undetected.

In many cases, the likelihood of even single bit errors is very small, and the addition of a single parity bit is a very effective error detection method. Many microcomputer systems use this technique to protect data bytes fetched from memory by the processor. Looking inside these computers, you will often see *nine* memory chips per memory bank. The ninth chip stores a parity bit used to protect the data in the other eight bits.[5]

Checksum.   When data is to be transmitted over long distances via the telephone network, single parity bits are less effective. This is because the data is subject to *burst* noise sources that may persist for several milliseconds, changing the value of many data bits in the process. This is the case for a lightning strike. For this type of noise, data is often protected by sending a *checksum* character following the transmission of a large block of characters (typically 512 or 1024 bytes). The checksum is computed by adding the numeric values of all bytes in the block. If the received checksum does not match the computed checksum byte, the receiver requests that the entire data block be retransmitted.[6]

Two's Complement

The two's complement code provides a way to represent positive and negative binary numbers—*signed binary numbers*—in a form that can be processed by a computer. A binary number can be converted to signed two's complement form as follows:

1. If the number is positive, make no changes.
2. If the number is negative, *invert,* or *complement,* all bits and then add 1.

For example, assume the number –6 is to be expressed in byte form as a two's complement signed binary number:

$$-6 => \overline{0000\ 0110} + 1 = 1111\ 1001 + 1 = 1111\ 1010 = \text{FAH}^{[7]}$$

Thus –6 when written as a signed number becomes FAH. Table 2.6 shows the range of signed numbers for 8 bits. Note that the rules for two's complement numbers cause negative numbers to always have the leftmost bit—the *most significant bit (MSB)*—set. Studying Table 2.6, you can see that the MSB actually functions as a *sign bit.* As shown in this table, numbers from 0 to 7FH are positive and their MSB is a 0; numbers from 80H to FFH are negative and their MSB is a 1.

Signed numbers can be extended to any number of bits. Using 16 bits, –6 becomes:

$$-6 => \overline{0000\ 0000\ 0000\ 0110} + 1 = 1111\ 1111\ 1111\ 0110 + 1 = 1111\ 1111\ 1111\ 1010$$
$$= \text{FFFAH}$$

Again, note that the MSB—bit 15 in this case—indicates the sign of the number. Figure 2.2 compares 8- and 16-bit signed binary numbers.

---

[5]The trend with newer computers is to accept memory modules with or without parity bits. As memory technologies improve, the need for parity protection is decreasing.

[6]Chapter 10 provides additional information about the checksum method of error detection and a related code called the CRC. Also covered in this chapter is the *Hamming code,* which can be used to detect all multi-bit errors and correct any single bit errors.

[7]The overbar is used to indicate that all bits are to be inverted to the opposite logic value. In this example, 0000 0110 becomes 1111 1001 when inverted. This operation is also called forming the *one's complement.*

Table 2.6 Two's Complement Signed Binary Numbers*

Decimal	Binary	Hexadecimal
–128	10000000	80
–127	10000001	81
–126	10000010	82
–125	10000011	83
–124	10000100	84
.	.	.
.	.	.
.	.	.
–3	11111101	FD
–2	11111110	FE
–1	11111111	FF
0	00000000	0
+1	00000001	1
+2	00000010	2
.	.	.
.	.	.
.	.	.
+125	01111101	7D
+126	01111110	7E
+127	01111111	7F

*Positive numbers are formed without change. Negative numbers
are formed by inverting all bits and adding 1. Thus –6 becomes
$00000110 \rightarrow 11111001 + 1 = 11111010$.

Example 2.12

Convert the following signed binary numbers to their decimal equivalent:

(a) 1101 0001   (b) 0101 0000   (c) 1000 1111 0101 1101

Solution
When the MSB is set, a negative number is indicated and its decimal value can be found by inverting
all bits and adding 1. Positive numbers can be converted directly.

(a) $\overline{1101\ 0001} + 1 = 0010\ 1110 + 1 = 0010\ 1111 = 2FH => -47$
(b) $0101\ 0000 = 50H = +80$
(c) $\overline{1000\ 1111\ 0101\ 1101} + 1 = 0111\ 0000\ 1010\ 0010 + 1$
$$= 0111\ 0000\ 1010\ 0011 = 70A3H => -28,835$$

Two's Complement Arithmetic.   The two's complement coding of negative numbers may
at first seem complicated, but it is actually a very clever code. Consider the subtraction problem 14–20. Coding these numbers in signed binary, we can view the problem as +14 + –20:

$$
\begin{array}{rl}
+14 = & \quad\quad\quad\quad\quad\quad\quad\quad\quad\quad\quad 0000\ 1110 \quad (0EH) \\
+-20 = \overline{0001\ 0100} + 1 = 1110\ 1011 + 1 = & +1110\ 1100 \quad (ECH) \\
\hline
-6 & \quad\quad\quad\quad\quad\quad\quad\quad\quad\quad 1111\ 1010 = FAH
\end{array}
$$

Figure 2.2 Comparing (a) 8-bit and (b) 16-bit signed binary numbers. (From J. Uffenbeck, *Digital Electronics: A Modern Approach,* Prentice Hall, Englewood Cliffs, N.J., 1994)

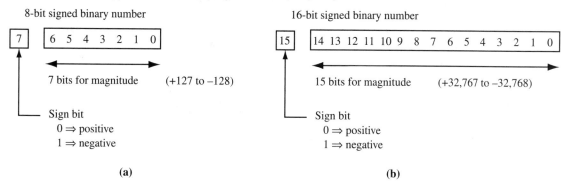

The result, FAH, has its MSB set, indicating a negative number. Converting this to its decimal equivalent:

$$1111\ 1010 => \overline{1111\ 1010} + 1 = 0000\ 0101 + 1 = 0000\ 0110 => -6$$

Note that the result, FAH (250 decimal), also corresponds to the *unsigned* addition of 0EH + ECH (14 + 236). A digital circuit designed to add binary numbers can't tell the difference between the addition and subtraction problems (because there is no difference!). It is up to the programmer to interpret the result based on his intent.

Example 2.13

Show that the subtraction problem 13 – 9 results in the answer +4 when 13 and 9 are encoded as two's complement binary numbers. Show that the result also corresponds to the unsigned addition of 13 plus 247.

Solution

Converting –9 to its two's complement equivalent:

$$
\begin{array}{rll}
+13 = & & 0000\ 1101 \quad (0DH)\\
\underline{-9} = \overline{0000\ 1001} + 1 = 1111\ 0110 + 1 = & \underline{+1111\ 0111} \quad (F7H)\\
+4 & & 0000\ 0100 = +4
\end{array}
$$

Note that the carry (if present) is ignored. The unsigned result corresponds to 0DH + F7H (13 + 247) = 104H = 260. Note that the carry *cannot* be ignored for the unsigned result.

Overflow. Whenever two signed numbers are added or subtracted, the possibility exists that the result may be too large for the number of bits allocated. For example, assume we want to add +64 and +96 using 8-bit signed numbers for each:

$$
\begin{array}{rl}
+64 = & 0100\ 0000\\
\underline{+96} = & \underline{0110\ 0000}\\
+160 & 1010\ 0000\ ????
\end{array}
$$

Note that the sign bit has changed and is indicating a *negative* result. This is because +160 cannot be represented in signed form with only 8 bits (see Table 2.6—the limit is +127). In this case we say that an *overflow* has occurred. Computers have overflow flags (flip-flops) that can be tested under program control to determine if this error has occurred. In this example, we can solve the problem by expressing +64 and +96 as *16-bit* signed numbers.

$$
\begin{array}{rl}
+64 = & 0000\ 0000\ 0100\ 0000 \\
+96 = & 0000\ 0000\ 0110\ 0000 \\
\hline
+160 & 0000\ 0000\ 1010\ 0000
\end{array}
$$

Note that the sign bit (bit 15) in this number is a 0, indicating a positive result, as expected.

Binary Coded Decimal (BCD)

The BCD code provides a way for decimal numbers to be encoded in a binary form that is easily converted back to decimal. Following a "Rule of Fours" similar to that for hexadecimal, each decimal digit is written as a 4-bit binary number. For example, 367 becomes 0011 0110 0111. Similarly, the 8-bit BCD number 1001 0101 is interpreted as decimal 95.

Table 2.7 lists all ten BCD numbers and their hexadecimal counterparts. Note that the combinations 1010 through 1111 are considered *invalid* BCD numbers, because each of these numbers requires two decimal digits. For example, 15 is written as 0001 0101 in BCD—not 1111. Coding a number in BCD is *not* the same as expressing that number in binary. In fact, as the following example illustrates, more binary digits will be required to represent a number in BCD than in unsigned binary.

Table 2.7 Comparing Binary, Hexadecimal, and BCD

Binary	Hexadecimal	BCD
0 0 0 0	0	0
0 0 0 1	1	1
0 0 1 0	2	2
0 0 1 1	3	3
0 1 0 0	4	4
0 1 0 1	5	5
0 1 1 0	6	6
0 1 1 1	7	7
1 0 0 0	8	8
1 0 0 1	9	9
1 0 1 0	A	Invalid
1 0 1 1	B	Invalid
1 1 0 0	C	Invalid
1 1 0 1	D	Invalid
1 1 1 0	E	Invalid
1 1 1 1	F	Invalid

Example 2.14

Convert the following decimal numbers to unsigned binary form and to BCD form:

(a) 9   (b) 26   (c) 243

Solution

The unsigned binary forms can be found in several ways: summing the highest powers of two, re-peated-division-by-two, or conversion to hexadecimal and then to binary. The BCD forms are found by simply writing the 4-bit binary equivalents of each decimal digit. The results are:

Decimal	Unsigned Binary	BCD
(a) 9	1001	1001
(b) 26	11010	0010 0110
(c) 243	1111 0011	0010 0100 0011

The most common application of BCD is with *seven-segment displays*. As shown in Figure 2.3(a), such displays have seven segments (typically light-emitting diodes or liquid crystals) arranged in a figure-eight pattern. By turning selected segments on, the numbers 0–9 can be displayed. This is shown in Figure 2.3(b). In practice, a *BCD to seven-segment decoder* inputs one 4-bit BCD number and outputs a segment pattern-code corresponding to that number. Figure 2.3(c) shows the number 0100 (4) being input, causing segments b, c, f, and g to turn on.

Figure 2.3   (a) A seven-segment display is used to display (b) the BCD numbers 0 through 9; (c) a BCD to seven-segment decoder converts the BCD number into a code that activates the proper segments for that digit.

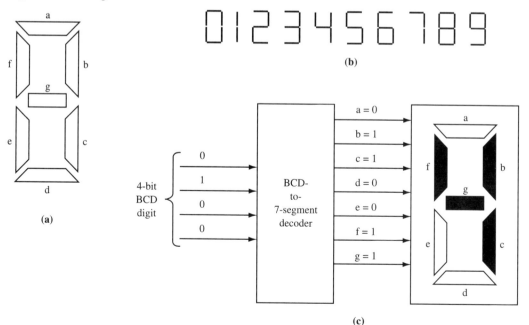

(c)

Self-Review 2.2 (Answers on page 68)

2.2.1   What is the 8-bit ASCII code corresponding to the letter M? Assume the character uses even parity.

2.2.2   What ASCII character is represented by the hex number F8? Assume the character uses odd parity.

2.2.3   Express –47 as a signed 8-bit binary number.

2.2.4   Convert the two's complement signed binary number 1011 0101 to its decimal equivalent.

2.2.5   Under what conditions will an *overflow* occur when performing signed arithmetic?

2.2.6   The BCD equivalent of 84 is _____. The decimal equivalent of BCD 1001 0111 is _____.

2.3   Computer Programming

Introduction

A computer is usually described by its *hardware*—the number of bits used by its data and address buses, the amount of RAM and ROM memory, the type of processor chip, etc. But to do useful work, it is the *software* that is important; that is, the programs that can be run on that computer. And although there are literally thousands of different computer programs, there are only three different ways of writing these programs.

In this section we:

- Compare and contrast programming in machine language, assembly language, and a high level language.
- List the steps required to develop an assembly language program.
- Explain why programming with a high level language is (usually) preferred over machine or assembly language programming.

Machine Language vs. Assembly Language

Object Code.   The instruction set of a computer is a list of the operations that can be performed by the processor; for example, *move data from memory into one of the general-purpose storage registers*, or *add one to the contents of the accumulator*. Each of these instructions has its own unique binary code. Consider the following 80x86 microprocessor program that adds two numbers input from a keyboard:

```
11100100
00100111
10001000
11000011
11100100
00100111
00000000
11011000
11100110
00110000
11110100
```

Not too clear, is it? Of course it is crystal clear to an 80x86 processor. This type of program is referred to as *machine language* or *object code* and is the only code a computer can execute. However, it is nearly impossible for a human to work with.

Object code is machine-dependent; that is, object code written for an 80x86 processor will only work with processors in the 80x86 family. Similarly, object code written for a Motorola 68000 will only run on that processor. Of course, you can "feed" 80x86 object code to a 68000, but it will interpret the binary codes as if they were 68000 instructions, leading to unpredictable results. It's as if you were speaking English to a person who understands only German: They would hear what you are saying, but the words would make no sense.

Object code is usually written in hexadecimal form. The previous program written in hex becomes: E4 27 88 C3 E4 27 00 D8 E6 30 F4. Certainly this is more readable than the binary version, but the *function* of the program is still hidden.

Assembly Language.   When programming a microprocessor, programmers often use *assembly language*. This involves using 3–5 letter abbreviations for the instruction operation codes (*mnemonics*) rather than the binary or hex object codes. Figure 2.4 shows the previous program written in mnemonic form. The hexadecimal object code is shown for each instruction. The comment field further clarifies the purpose of each instruction. The address column identifies the memory locations occupied by each instruction.

The function of the program now becomes clear. The two numbers to be added are first input from port 27H (where the keyboard is assumed to be connected). The first number is temporarily saved in one of the 80x86's general-purpose registers—register BL—so the second input operation won't overwrite it. The ADD AL,BL instruction adds the contents of registers AL and BL, leaving the result in register AL (the accumulator). This value is then output to port 30H (where the video display is assumed to be connected). Finally, the computer is instructed to halt.

Studying Figure 2.4, we can make a number of observations:

1. When written in mnemonic form, the function of the program becomes clear (especially when comments are added).

Figure 2.4   80x86 assembly language program written to input two numbers, compute their sum, and output the result. Shown are the instruction object codes, instruction mnemonics (operation codes and operands), and program comments.

Address	Hex Object Code				Mnemonics		Comment
					Op-Code	Operand	
0100	E4	27			IN	AL,27H	Input first number from port 27H and store in AL
0102	88	C3			MOV	BL,AL	Save a copy of register AL in register BL
0104	E4	27			IN	AL,27H	Input second number to AL
0106	00	D8			ADD	AL,BL	Add contents of BL to AL and store the sum in AL
0107	E6	30			OUT	30H,AL	Output AL to port 30H
0109	F4				HLT		Halt the computer

2. Each instruction has its own unique object code, and most require two bytes (two hex digits[8]).

3. Most instructions are made up of an *op-code* that defines the operation that is to occur, and an *operand* that defines the registers, memory locations, or I/O ports that are to be operated on.

4. The programmer must be (very) familiar with the architecture of the processor and the computer's hardware. For example, he must know the I/O port address of the keyboard and video display and the names and functions of the processor registers.

Source Code.   The assembly language program in Figure 2.4 is said to be in *source-code* form. As its name implies, the source code is the original source of the program. More than just a list of the program instructions, the source code typically includes the programmer's line-by-line comments that annotate program operation. When testing a program, the source code is invaluable, as it explains how the program works.

The Edit, Assemble, Test, and Debug Cycle.   You may be wondering how a program in source-code form can be executed by the computer. After all, the processor is designed to read binary object codes, not instruction mnemonics/comments.

   The development of a modern computer program actually requires four separate steps:

1. Using an *editor,* the source code of the program is created.[9] For an assembly language program, this means selecting the appropriate instruction mnemonics to accomplish the task.

2. A *compiler* program, which examines the source-code file created by the editor and determines the object codes for each instruction in the program, is then run. When compiling assembly language programs, the compiler is often referred to as an *assembler.*

3. The object code produced by the compiler is loaded into the target computer's memory and run.

4. Usually the program does not work correctly on the first try, and changes must be made. This involves reinvoking the editor to modify the source-code file, recompiling, loading the modified program back into memory, and retesting. Locating and fixing the source of errors is called *debugging.*

   In Chapters 4–6 we will provide several examples of 80x86 program development. These vary from simple machine code programs written with DEBUG (an MS-DOS utility program that can be used to develop 80x86 programs) to more complex assembly language programs written and debugged with Microsoft's macro assembler.

High Level Languages

Too Much Power?   Assembly language is very powerful. The complete resources of the processor and computer are available to the programmer, with no restrictions. And because the instructions created are native to the processor, assembly language programs run faster

---

[8]Some 80x86 instructions require as many as 10 bytes.

[9]An editor is a word processing program. A common example is EDIT, available with the MS-DOS operating system.

than any other type of program. Yet many programmers shy away from assembly language. Why is that?

It's sort of like trying to drive a car with a 500 HP engine. "It goes extremely fast, but if you're not careful, you will end up in the ditch!" Because assembly language programs work directly with the processor, it is possible to write programs that "crash" the computer.[10] For example, a program error might cause the processor to endlessly loop through a sequence of instructions, with no means for the programmer to halt the process. Another common error is to miscalculate a transfer of control address, causing the processor to begin executing random instructions with disastrous results.[11]

BASIC.   Many programmers opt to work in a safer environment. They choose a *high level language* that offers an easier to comprehend syntax together with a built-in "safety net" that will (usually) prevent their programs from crashing. One of the best-known examples is *BASIC* (*B*eginners *A*ll-Purpose *S*ymbolic *I*nstruction *C*ode). When written in BASIC, the previous program to input and add two numbers becomes:

```
10 INPUT N1,N2
20 PRINT "SUM = ";N1+N2
30 END
```

A comparison with the original binary program is striking. Even without a background in BASIC you can probably understand the program's function. Of course one of the main goals of a high level language, is to let the programmer communicate in a language that is similar to his own.

Notice how the BASIC programmer need not be concerned with I/O port addresses or processor registers. In fact, because the BASIC program does not refer to specific system resources, it will run on any computer—not just an 80x86 processor. This is another reason high level languages are so attractive to programmers—the resulting code can be transported to almost any computer, regardless of its processor.

Programming in BASIC requires a BASIC *interpreter,* or *compiler.* When using interpreted BASIC, the application program may be entered to memory without an editor. The command **RUN** is then given, causing the interpreter to examine each BASIC statement and execute a sequence of machine code instructions equivalent to that statement.

The use of an interpreter usually results in very slow program execution speeds compared to the assembly language version. For example, if the computer is in a loop, the interpreter will (needlessly) reinterpret the instructions in that loop over and over. Because the computer is so fast, we don't usually notice (or care about) this delay.

The BASIC program given previously to add two numbers might require 1 ms to calculate the sum and print the result. The machine language version could do it in less than 1 µs. That's 1000 times faster, but in our human time frame, unnoticeable.

This time delay can become very noticeable, however, when the operation must be repeated a number of times. For example, let's say we had to perform the addition problem one million times. This would require $1{,}000{,}000 \times 1$ ms = 1000s, or 16.7 minutes, with the BASIC program. The machine language version would require $1{,}000{,}000 \times 1\mu s$ = 1s!

---

[10]To "crash" a computer means to lose control. That is, the computer no longer responds to its keyboard (or any other input device). To recover, the machine must usually be reset, thus losing any data in memory.

[11]I have seen some programs write over the top of themselves so that there is no program left to debug!

High Level Language Compilers.   A *compiler* is a computer program used to convert a high level language program to object code form. Using a compiler is similar to using an assembler, because an editor must be used to create the application program file. When the compiler is run, it compiles the high level language program into a binary machine code file. This has several advantages over the interpreter. For one, the code does not have to be reinterpreted over and over when loops are encountered. In addition, the resulting object code file will run all by itself, without the need for the compiler to be resident in memory. This saves memory space and allows for larger programs to be written.

The main disadvantage to using a compiler is that errors require reinvoking the editor, correcting the errors with the editor, and recompiling the program. Like assembly language programming, this can be frustrating when simple syntax errors—missing commas, for example—appear.

C.   In recent years, C has become the high level language of choice for most program developers. Many of the C compilers on the market have been developed for specific environments—particularly Microsoft Windows, Windows NT, and UNIX. As such, compilers provide libraries of common functions that are useful in a particular environment. For example, Borland's C++ provides the capabilities to develop 16- and 32-bit code for Microsoft Windows and DOS.

C is a *structured* high level language. Figure 2.5 shows the C version of the previous input and add program. Unlike the three-line BASIC version, the C programmer is required to perform several "housekeeping" chores to set up the program. The *include* statement tells the compiler to load the *stdio.h* file. This file provides a set of functions for input and output. The *main* statement follows and tells the C compiler where execution begins.

Figure 2.5   C verison of the input and add program.

```
#include <stdio.h>

main ()
{
      int        N1;
      int        N2;
      int        Sum;

      printf("\nEnter the first number to add    :");
      scanf("%d,&N1);

      printf("\nEnter the second number to add   :");
      scanf("%d,&N2);

      sum = N1 + N2;

      printf("%d + %d = %d\n", N1, N2, Sum);

}
```

Finally, three *declaration* statements are required to define the type of variable for the two numbers to be added and their sum. This is important because the computer stores integers in a different format than floating-point numbers or text.

Following these header lines, the actual program statements begin. The first line prints a message on the screen prompting the user to input the first number. The *scanf* statement retrieves this number. The next two lines are similar and cause the second number to be input. Finally, the sum is computed and printed. The }, or brace symbol, ends the program.

All of the structure associated with a C program can seem a bother. However, it allows the programmer to include only necessary features. In addition, the declaration statements ensure that all variables used in the program are accounted for. This, is turn, allows the compiler to produce efficient (fast-executing) machine code.

Self-Review 2.3 (Answers on pages 68–69)

2.3.1   A mnemonic is:
    (a) An operation code written in binary form.
    (b) An operation code written in hex form.
    (c) A computer instruction written in abbreviated form.
    (d) A special command written in BASIC.

2.3.2   Most instruction mnemonics have two parts, called the _____ and _____.

2.3.3   To write a computer program in machine language requires:
    (a) An interpreter or compiler to generate the object code.
    (b) The hexadecimal codes for each instruction.
    (c) A text editor for creation of the source code.
    (d) An assembler program.

2.3.4   *(True/False)* Programs written in a high level language are easier to write but execute more slowly than corresponding machine language programs.

2.3.5   A computer program in binary or hexadecimal form is also said to be in _____ code form.

2.3.6   A(n) _____ is used to convert a high level language program into machine code.

2.3.7   C is a _____ high level programming language.

2.4   Computer Operating Systems

Introduction

In Section 2.3 we learned different ways of creating application program software. There is, however, one piece of the puzzle still missing. That is the control software that is used to start (or boot) the computer and then manage all of the various system I/O devices. This software is typically referred to as the *operating system.* In this section we:

- Explain the role of operating system software in a typical microcomputer.
- List the sequence of events that occur when an 80x86 computer is booted up with MS-DOS.
- Draw the memory map for an 80x86 computer running MS-DOS.
- Explain how to access the BIOS services and functions of MS-DOS.

What Is an Operating System?

Booting Up.   In Chapter 1 we noted that stored program computers are wired to repeatedly fetch instructions from memory and execute those instructions. However, you might wonder how that "first" program gets loaded into memory when power is applied initially. What is needed is a special type of *permanent memory* that can be used to hold a *start-up* program. On most computers this problem is solved by installing a ROM chip at the reset, or start-up, address. In this way, whenever the computer is reset or powered on, the program in this ROM (often called the *boot* program) will be run.

On most PCs, the boot ROM takes control of the machine when power is first applied and initiates a complex sequence of events that has become known as *booting up* (or simply *booting*) the computer. Figure 2.6 provides an example of booting for a computer running MS-DOS.

Some computers (microcontrollers, for example) are not designed to run user programs. Instead, they are locked into running the programs stored in their boot ROM. This would be the case for a microprocessor-controlled microwave oven, for example. For such systems, the software can only be changed by installing a new ROM chip.[12]

PC-DOS and MS-DOS

The Standard for 80x86 Processors.   In Figure 2.6 we see that one of the last things the boot ROM does is load the *operating system* software into RAM. It is the job of this program to manage the system resources. This involves reading and inputting data from the keyboard, outputting data to the printer and video display, and controlling the storage and retrieval of data and program files from the floppy and hard disks. In fact, because the latter tasks are such an important part of the operating system, the term *DOS* (*D*isk *O*perating *S*ystem) is often applied to describe the entire operating system software.

The first commercial microcomputer operating system was CP/M (control program for microcomputers), written by Gary Kildall in 1978. Marketed by his company, Digital Research, CP/M was designed to run on 8080 and Z-80 based computers with 64K of memory and floppy disk drives for mass storage.

Shortly after the 8086 was announced, Seattle Computer Products began selling a CP/M workalike called 86-DOS. At the same time, a small software company called Microsoft was enjoying some success selling a version of BASIC for the Altair computer. Microsoft decided to expand its product line by purchasing 86-DOS from Seattle Computer. In 1981, IBM, looking for an operating system for their soon to be announced PC, licensed 86-DOS from Microsoft and renamed it PC-DOS 1.0. Under the license agreement, Microsoft retained the right to market its version of the program, which it called MS-DOS 1.0. The two were virtually identical (most PCs would boot up with either program). Over the years DOS has been updated many times, but the two companies—Microsoft and IBM—continue to market their own versions.

Today, several different operating systems are available for 80x86 computers. Of these, MS-DOS and PC-DOS are still the leaders. However, operating systems like IBM's OS/2 and Microsoft's Windows are becoming increasingly popular. PC-DOS and MS-DOS offer

---

[12]In Chapter 7 we study *flash* memory. This is a type of ROM that can be reprogrammed without removing the chip from the system.

Figure 2.6 Booting up an 80x86 computer with the MS-DOS operating system.

Boot Sequence—MS-DOS-Based Computer

1. Read master boot record from drive C to determine the location of each partition and which partition is active.

2. Read DOS boot record to determine sector size, the total number of sectors, and the number of sectors per track.

3. Load and transfer control to the bootstrap loader.

4. Bootstrap loader loads the hidden file IO.SYS, which contains extensions to the routines in the BIOS ROMs.

5. IO.SYS starts SYSINIT, which initializes the system and loads the hidden file MSDOS.SYS. This file contains the DOS system services available to applications programs (read the keyboard, write a file, send data to the screen, etc.).

6. SYSINIT examines the configuration file CONFIG.SYS, loading all drivers specified in this file.

7. SYSINIT loads and transfers control to the file COMMAND.COM. This file provides all of the built-in DOS commands such as COPY, CLS, and DIR.

8. COMMAND.COM searches the root directory for the file AUTOEXEC.BAT and executes the DOS commands in this file.

---

a *command line interface (CLI)* that requires the user to give commands using a particular syntax. For example, to copy a file named TEST.TXT from drive A (the system floppy drive) to a directory named TEMP on drive C (the system hard drive), the following command is required:

```
A:\>copy test.txt c:\temp\test.txt
```

Windows and OS/2, on the other hand, offer a *graphical user interface (GUI)*. As shown in Figure 2.7, Windows displays the files as *icons* that can be dragged from one location to another as required to move or copy a selected file. For most users this metaphor is more intuitive than the CLI of DOS.

MS-DOS Memory Map

The 640K Barrier.   DOS was designed to run on the original IBM PC. This computer used the 8088 microprocessor, which had a 20-bit address bus and therefore was limited to 1 MB of memory. For compatibility reasons, IBM divided this 1 MB address space up into specific blocks, as shown in Figure 2.8. Note that 640K of RAM (user memory) is provided, with the remaining 384K reserved for ROM functions [control programs for the video system, hard drive controller, and the basic input/output system (BIOS)].

In 1981, 640K of user RAM must have seemed enormous. After all, 8-bit computers of this era had 16-bit address buses and thus were limited to 64K of memory. However, as we have seen, the following generations of processors (the 386, 486, Pentium, and Pentium Pro) have increased the address bus width to 32 bits (and most recently to 36 bits). This is 65,536 times the capacity of the 8088! Nevertheless, to maintain compatibility with previous versions of DOS, these more powerful processors are forced to operate in Real Mode, which limits their address space to 1 MB. As fewer and fewer 8088 PCs are now in

How to Read a Memory Map

Think of the hex digits in the memory address as *counters*. For example, the 80386, 80486, and Pentium all have a 32-bit address bus that can be described with 8 hex digits (call them H7 to H0).

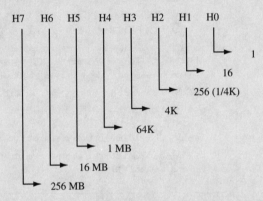

Thus, if we see a block of memory beginning at address A0000H and ending at address BFFFFH, we can calculate that this block contains two 64K "pages;" that is, all of page A0000H and all of page B0000H. The total size of the block is therefore 128K. Study the examples below and see if you agree with the calculations.

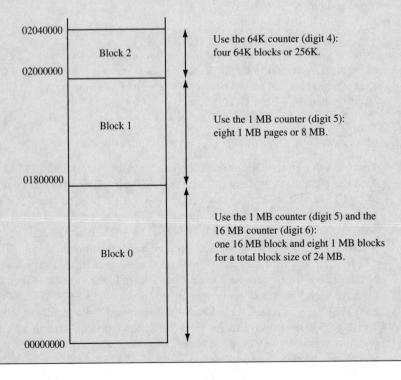

Figure 2.7 Windows Explorer with the Chap1 folder highlighted. The folder (and all of its files) can be copied to drive A by simply dragging and dropping its icon on the 3½ Floppy icon in the top window.

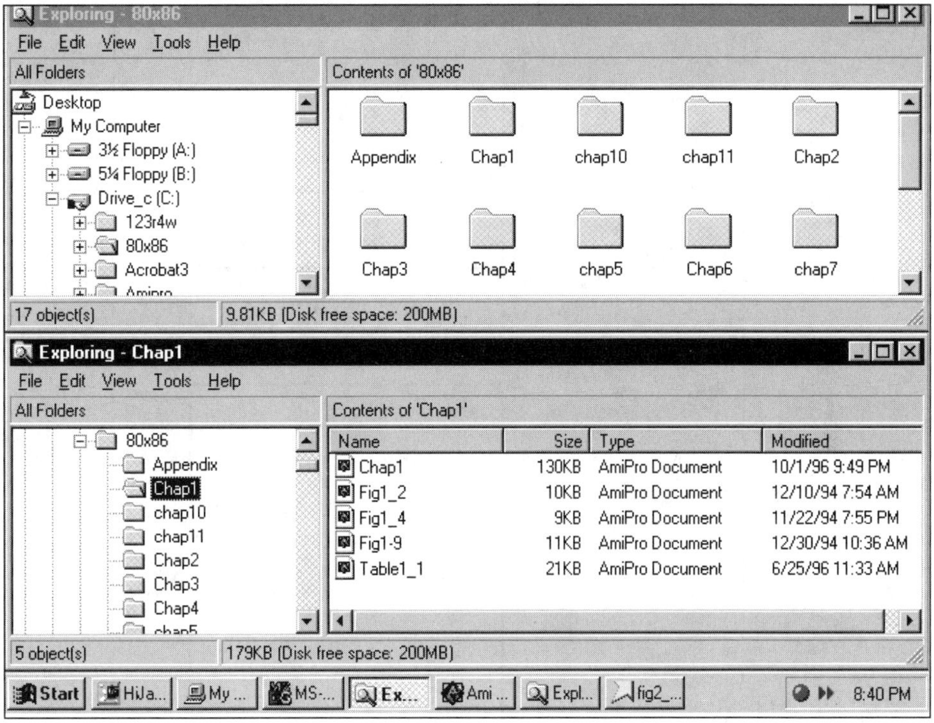

use, we can expect (and hope) that future versions of DOS will eventually break this 640K barrier.[13]

MS-DOS Functions and BIOS Services

Program Support.   One of the most important features of any operating system is the software support it offers to program developers. For example, almost all programs that run on the PC require user input from the keyboard. One way of getting this input would be for the developer to look up the I/O port address of the keyboard and then write a routine to access the data at that port address. Since every developer will most likely have to write such a program, why not build that routine into DOS itself? This is the idea behind the BIOS (basic input/output aystem) services. Usually stored in ROM, these routines provide primitive access to the hardware of the PC.

Access to the BIOS is done using the software interrupt instruction **INT** n, where n is a number that defines the particular service desired. The BIOS keyboard services, for example, are accessed using the instruction **INT** 16H. To read the next keyboard character, the high 8 bits of register AX (AH) should all be 0. The ASCII code for the key pressed will then be returned in the low 8 bits (AL) of this same register.

---

[13]Operating systems like OS/2 and Windows (which require at least a 386 processor) have already done so. These programs are referred to as *32-bit operating systems*.

Figure 2.8 Memory map for an 80x86 computer running MS-DOS. One MB of memory is required—640K of user memory and 384K of reserved memory should be special memory.

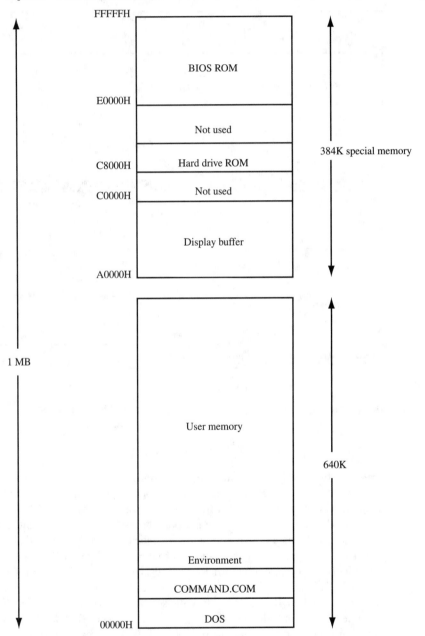

In addition to the BIOS services, DOS also provides higher level functions. These are accessed in the same way (via a software interrupt), but perform more complex tasks. For example, using the **INT** 21H instruction and specifying function 01H will cause the keyboard to be read and the character typed echoed to the screen. Chapters 4 and 5 provide specific program examples using the BIOS services and DOS functions available in MS-DOS.

Self-Review 2.4 (Answers on page 69)

2.4.1   The _____-_____ causes the operating system software to be loaded into the computer.

2.4.2   MS-DOS uses:
  (a) CLI
  (b) GUI

2.4.3   When running MS-DOS, 80x86 processors are limited to _____K of RAM and _____ K of reserved memory.

2.4.4   The _____ _____ provide primitive access to the hardware in the PC for user programs.

Chapter 2 Self-Test

1. The binary number 1101 0111 can be written as _____ in hexadecimal and _____ in decimal.
2. The decimal number 109 can be written as _____ in hexadecimal and _____ in binary.
3. There are _____ different combinations of 8 binary bits. The largest number occurs when all 8 bits are a 1 and this number equals _____ decimal.
4. The next number in the count sequence following D3CFH is _____.
5. A byte-wide memory chip with 18 address lines can store _____K.
6. The number 6AH, when interpreted as an 8-bit even parity ASCII character, corresponds to _____.
7. When expressed as an 8-bit signed binary number, $-25 =$ _____
8. Which of the following addition problems will result in an *overflow* condition when performed with 8-bit two's complement binary numbers?
  (a) $117 + 8$
  (b) $56 + 84$
  (c) $45 + 10$
9. When written in BCD, the decimal number $47 =$ _____.
10. Give an example of an 80x86 mnemonic.
11. Identify the op-code and operand for the 80x86 instruction ADD AX,BX.
12. List the four steps required to create an assembly language program.
13. When writing assembly language programs, the output of the editor is called the _____ code, and the output of the compiler is called the _____ code.
14. Give two advantages of programming in a high level language vs. in an assembly language.
15. What is the purpose of a *boot ROM*?
16. Two types of operating system user interfaces are _____ and _____.
17. When running MS-DOS, 80x86 processors are limited to _____K of user RAM.
18. MS-DOS reserves _____K of memory for the BIOS ROM(s).
19. What special type of instruction is used to access the BIOS services and DOS functions?
20. Besides the BIOS services, DOS provides _____ _____ functions via the INT 21H instruction.

Analysis and Design Questions

Section 2.1

2.1   Convert each of the following binary numbers to hexadecimal and then to decimal:
       (a) 1100
       (b) 10 0001
       (c) 1011 1101
       (d) 1111 1111 1111 1111

2.2   Determine the binary and hexadecimal values of each of the following decimal numbers:
       (a) 9
       (b) 26
       (c) 256
       (d) 31,274
       (e) 2,056,792

2.3   Write the hexadecimal equivalents of the decimal numbers 60 through 80.

2.4   Fill in the blanks in the table below regarding the capacity in bytes of a computer's memory. The first line is given as an example.

Address Lines	Capacity	Unit
10	1	K
14		K
	256	K
20		MB
28		MB
36		GB
	512	GB

Section 2.2

2.5   For each binary number shown in the table below, give its equivalent value, assuming the number is represented in the code indicated. The first row is given as an example.

| Binary Number | Code | | | |
	Unsigned Binary	8-Bit Signed Binary	Odd Parity ASCII	BCD
1001 1000	152	−104	CAN	98
0110 0001				
0111 0011				
1000 0101				
1001 0110				

2.6 Determine the largest and smallest (most negative) decimal numbers that can be represented using 16-bit signed binary numbers.

2.7 Determine the largest decimal number that can be represented with:
(a) 8-bit unsigned binary
(b) Positive 8-bit signed binary
(c) 8-bit BCD

2.8 The checksum byte is computed by calculating the sum of the other bytes in a data block and then forming the two's complement of that sum. Assume the four-byte block 10H, 23H, 45H, and 04H is to be transmitted. Calculate the value of the checksum character. Check your result by showing that the sum of the four bytes plus the checksum byte is 00 (ignoring any carries).

Section 2.3

2.9 Match the terms in the list below (a–i) with the specified phrases (1–9).
(a) op-code   (b) source code   (c) mnemonic
(d) assembler   (e) high level language (f) operand
(g) object code   (h) compiler   (i) editor

Matching phrases:
1. used to create source code
2. abbreviation for an assembly language instruction
3. convert instruction mnemonics to machine code
4. machine instructions in binary or hexadecimal form
5. instruction operation
6. data source/destination that is to be operated on by an instruction
7. convert high level language instructions to machine code
8. computer program in mnemonic form with comments
9. BASIC

2.10 For each of the following answer HLL (high level language) or AL (assembly language).
(a) Offers fastest program execution speed
(b) Requires that the programmer be familiar with the internal registers of the processor
(c) Programs are *not* processor-dependent
(d) Offers a protected environment to the programmer so that program crashes are unlikely

Section 2.4

2.11 A PC has 4 MB of RAM beginning at address 00000000H. Calculate the very last address (in hex) of this 4 MB block.

2.12 Figure 2.9 shows the memory map for a computer with the starting address for each memory block shown in hex.
(a) Calculate the size of the two ROM blocks in K.
(b) Calculate the size of the open area in K.
(c) Calculate the size of the RAM block in M.

Self-Review Answers

2.1.1 (a) 2 (b) 15 (c) 42 (d) 255
2.1.2 (a) 1101 (b) 100 1011 (c) 1011 1011 (d) 1011 1010 0000 1101
2.1.3 11100

Figure 2.9   Memory Map

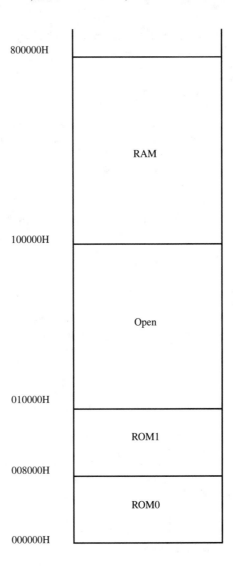

2.3.2   op-code, operand
2.3.3   (b)
2.3.4   true
2.3.5   object
2.3.6   interpreter or compiler
2.3.7   structured
2.4.1   boot ROM
2.4.2   (a)
2.4.3   640, 384
2.4.4   BIOS services

3 80x86 Processor Architecture

Minicomputers were used by a single researcher or as a laboratory controller. The PDP-8 (Programmed Data Processor) was first offered in 1965. It featured a 12-bit word size and sold for $18,000—still too expensive for most individuals, but cheaper than mainframes of this era. (Photo courtesy of Smithsonian)

Outline

Objectives

After completing this chapter you should be able to:

1. Identify the major components of the 8086 processor, including the bus interface unit and the execution unit.

2. Explain how the 8086's pipelined architecture allows the fetch and execute cycles to overlap.
3. List and identify the function of the internal 8086 CPU data registers and flags.
4. Explain the concept of even and odd memory banks as used by the 8086.
5. List the 8086 segment registers and show how to calculate a segment's base address.
6. Explain how to determine the default 8086 segment assignment associated with each instruction that accesses memory.
7. Show how to translate an 8086 offset, or logical, address into a physical address.
8. Compare and contrast the Real and Protected operating modes of the 80386.
9. Identify the major components of the 80386 processor, including the bus interface unit, central processing unit, and memory management unit.
10. List and identify the function of the 80386 general- and special-purpose data registers.
11. Explain the Protected Mode addressing mechanism of the 80386.
12. List the "rules of privilege" of the 80386 processor.
13. List those factors that make the 486 faster than the 386 for a given clock speed.
14. Explain the operation of a direct mapped cache.
15. Draw a block diagram of the 486 cache and explain the role of the cache SRAM, TAG SRAM, and the LRU SRAM.
16. List and identify the function of the data and control registers within the 486 floating-point unit.
17. Draw a block diagram of the Pentium processor, highlighting the bus interface, central processing, floating-point, memory management, and cache units.
18. Explain the operation of the Pentium's u and v pipelines.
19. Compare the various Pentium processor versions for speed, power consumption, and operating features.
20. Compare the processing cycle of the Pentium Pro with traditional sequential fetch and execute processors.
21. Draw a block diagram of the Pentium Pro processor and explain the role of the bus interface, central processing, memory management, floating-point, cache, and APIC units.
22. Compare the performance of the Pentium Pro with the other processors in the 80x86 family.

Overview

Today's microprocessor chips are extremely complex devices. The Pentium, for example, has over three million transistors; the Pentium Pro has more than five million! One way of coming to grips with such complex components is to create a model (block diagram) of the chip. In this diagram we can highlight the important features of the processor and learn how these individual blocks work together.

In this chapter we do exactly that for the 8086, 80386, 80486, Pentium, and Pentium Pro microprocessors. Although the 8086 is now obsolete, many of its features have been carried over to the more advanced processors, which makes this chip a good starting point for our journey.

3.1   The 8086 and 8088

Introduction

The 8086 microprocessor represents the foundation upon which all of the 80x86 family of processors have been built. Indeed, Intel has made the commitment that as new generations of microprocessors are developed, each will maintain software compatibility with this first-generation part. Thus, a good understanding of the 8086 is important if the more advanced processors in the family are to be mastered.

In this section we:

- Identify the major components of the 8086 processor, including the bus interface unit and the execution unit.
- Explain how the 8086's pipelined architecture allows the fetch and execute cycles to overlap.
- List and identify the function of the internal 8086 CPU data registers and flags.

Processor Model

The BIU and EU.   Figure 3.1 is a model for the 8086 microprocessor. It is organized as two separate processors, the *bus interface unit (BIU)* and the *execution unit (EU)*. The BIU provides hardware functions, including generation of the memory and I/O addresses for the transfer of data between itself and the outside world.

The EU receives program instruction codes and data from the BIU, executes these instructions, and stores the results in the general registers. By passing the data back to the BIU, data can also be stored in a memory location or written to an output device. Note that the EU has no connection to the system buses. It receives and outputs all of its data through the BIU.

The Fetch and Execute Cycle.   Although the 8086 functions as a stored program computer (described in Chapter 1), the organization of the processor into a separate BIU and EU allows the fetch and execute cycles to *overlap*. To see this, consider what happens when the 8086 is first started.

1. The BIU outputs the contents of the instruction pointer register (IP) onto the address bus, causing the selected byte or word in memory to be read into the BIU.
2. Register IP is incremented by one to prepare for the next instruction fetch.[1]
3. Once inside the BIU, the instruction is passed to the *queue*; a first-in/first-out storage register sometimes likened to a *pipeline*.
4. Assuming that the queue is initially empty, the EU immediately draws this instruction from the queue and begins execution.
5. While the EU is executing this instruction, the BIU proceeds to fetch a new instruction. Depending on the execution time of the first instruction, the BIU may fill the queue with several new instructions before the EU is ready to draw its next instruction.
6. The cycle continues, with the BIU filling the queue with instructions and the EU fetching and executing these instructions.

---

[1]It may actually be incremented by more than one, depending on the number of bytes in the instruction.

Figure 3.1   Processor model for the 8086 microprocessor. A separate execution unit (EU) and bus interface unit (BIU) are provided.

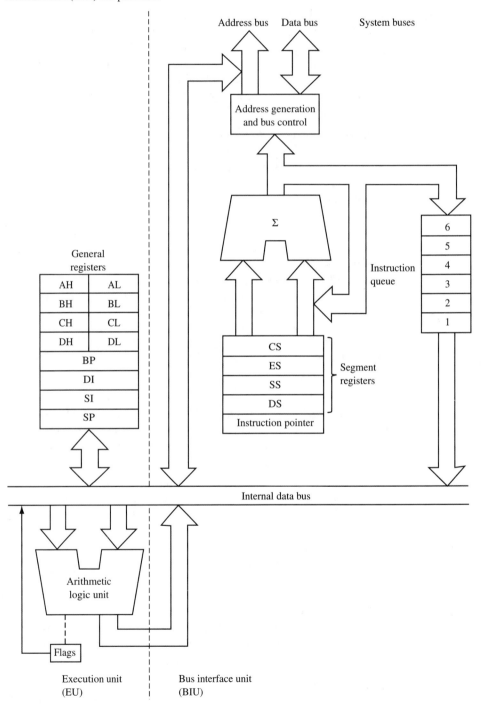

The BIU is programmed to fetch a new instruction whenever the queue has room for two additional bytes. The advantage to this pipelined architecture is that the EU can execute instructions (almost) continually instead of having to wait for the BIU to fetch a new instruction. This is shown schematically in Figure 3.2.

There are three conditions that will cause the EU to enter a "wait" mode. The first occurs when an instruction requires access to a memory location not in the queue. The BIU must suspend fetching instructions and output the address of this memory location. After waiting for the memory access, the EU can resume executing instruction codes from the queue, and the BIU can resume filling the queue.

The second condition occurs when the instruction to be executed is a *jump* instruction. In this case, control is to be transferred to a new (nonsequential) address. The queue, however, assumes instructions will always be executed in sequence and thus will hold the "wrong" instruction codes. The EU must wait while the instruction at the jump address is fetched. Note that any bytes presently in the queue must be discarded (they are overwritten).

One other condition can cause the BIU to suspend fetching instructions. This occurs during the execution of slow-executing instructions. For example, the instruction AAM (ASCII adjust for multiplication) requires 83 clock cycles to complete (for an 8086). At four clock cycles per instruction fetch, the queue will be completely filled during the execution of this single instruction. The BIU will thus have to wait for the EU to pull one or two bytes from the queue before resuming the fetch cycle.

A subtle advantage to the pipelined architecture should be mentioned. Because the next several instructions are usually in the queue, the BIU can access memory at a somewhat "leisurely" pace. This means slow memory parts can be used without affecting overall system performance. (Chapter 7 discusses memory access times in more detail.)

What About the 8088?   The only significant difference between the 8088 microprocessor and the 8086 microprocessor is the BIU. In the 8088, the BIU data bus path is 8 bits

Figure 3.2   (a) The nonpipelined microprocessor follows a sequential fetch and execute cycle. (b) The 8086's pipelined architecture allows the EU to execute instructions without the delays associated with instruction fetching.

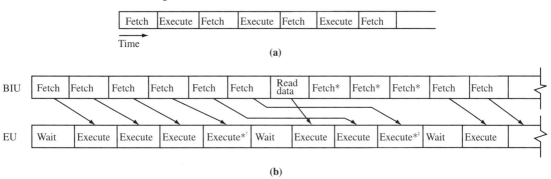

* These bytes are discarded.
† This instruction requires a request for data not in the queue.
‡ Jump instruction occurs.

wide vs. the 8086's 16-bit data bus. Another difference is that the 8088 instruction queue is four bytes long instead of six.

At first, you might be tempted to predict that the 8088 would offer only half the performance of the 8086. After all, the latter processor, with its 16-bit data bus, can input and output twice as much data per bus cycle. In practice, however, the 8088 is found to only be about 30 percent slower than an 8086. The reason? As long as the 8088's BIU keeps the queue full, instructions are executed without interruption. Depending on the nature of those instructions (long instructions provide more time for the BIU to fill the queue), the 8088 may well be able to keep up with the EU.

Programming Model

For Programmers Only.   The programming model for a microprocessor shows the various internal registers that are accessible to the programmer. Figure 3.3 is a model for the 8086. In general, each register has a special function that must be clearly understood if you are to write assembly language programs. In the following paragraphs we provide a brief description of each register group. (Chapters 4–6 will provide more detail on assembly language programming and the specific function of each of these registers.)

Note that because the 8086 and 8088 have identical EUs, the model in Figure 3.3 applies to both of these processors. Indeed, any program written for the 8086 will run without change on the 8088.

Figure 3.3   8086 programming model.

AX	AH	AL	Accumulator	Data group
BX	BH	BL	Base	
CX	CH	CL	Count	
DX	DH	DL	Data	

SP	Stack pointer	Pointer and index group
BP	Base pointer	
SI	Source index	
DI	Destination index	
IP	Instruction pointer	

| Flags_H | Flags_L | Status and control flags |

ES	Extra	Segment group
CS	Code	
DS	Data	
SS	Stack	

Data Registers.   The *data group* consists of the accumulator (register AX) and the BX, CX, and DX registers. Note that each of these is 16 bits wide but can be accessed as a byte or a word. Thus, BX refers to the 16-bit base register, while BH refers to the high order 8 bits only of this same register. The data registers are normally used for storing temporary results that will be acted upon by subsequent instructions.

Pointer and Index Registers.   The registers in this group are all 16 bits wide and, unlike the data registers, cannot be accessed as a low or high byte. These registers are used as memory *pointers*. For example, the instruction **MOV AH,[SI]** has the word interpretation "Move the byte whose address is contained in register SI to register AH." SI is thus interpreted as "pointing" to the desired memory location. The brackets around SI are used to indicate *the contents of memory pointed to by SI* and not the value of SI itself.

Example 3.1

Referring to Figure. 3.4, if SI=1000H, what is the contents of register AH after the instruction **MOV AH,[SI]** is executed?

Solution
Studying Figure 3.4, you can see SI pointing at the byte 26H in memory location 1000H. Thus, AH will store 26H.

Register IP is included in the pointer and index group, but this register has only one function—to point to the next instruction to be fetched to the BIU. Register IP is physically part of the BIU and not under direct control of the programmer, as are the other pointer registers (see Figure. 3.1).

Status and Control Flags.   Figure 3.5 shows the bit definitions for the 16-bit flag register. Six of the flags are *status indicators* reflecting properties of the result of the last arithmetic

Figure 3.4   Register SI is "pointing at" memory location 1000H.

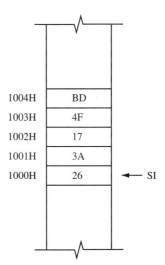

Figure 3.5 8086 flag word. DF, IF, and TF can be set or reset to control the operation of the processor. The remaining flags are status indicators. Bits marked X are undefined.

Flags$_H$ Flags$_L$

| X | X | X | X | OF | DF | IF | TF | SF | ZF | X | AF | X | PF | X* | CF |

Bit Position	Name	Function
0	CF	Carry flag: Set on high-order bit carry or borrow; cleared otherwise
2	PF	Parity flag: Set if low-order 8 bits of result contain an even number of 1 bits; cleared otherwise
4	AF	Set on carry from or borrow to the low-order 4 bits of AL; cleared otherwise
6	ZF	Zero flag: Set if result is zero; cleared otherwise
7	SF	Sign flag: Set equal to high-order bit of result (0 is positive, 1 is negative)
8	TF	Single-step flag: Once set, a single-step interrupt occurs after the next instruction executes; TF is cleared by the single-step interrupt
9	IF	Interrupt-enable flag: When set, maskable interrupts will cause the CPU to transfer control to an interrupt vector-specified location
10	DF	Direction flag: Causes string instructions to auto-decrement the appropriate index register when set; clearing DF causes auto-increment
11	OF	Overflow flag: Set if the signed result cannot be expressed within the number of bits in the destination operand; cleared otherwise

or logical instruction. For example, if register AL=7FH and the instruction **ADD AL, 1** is given (add one to the contents of register AL), the following results:

```
AL=80H ;7FH + 1 = 80H
CF=0    ;there is no carry out of bit 7
PF=0    ;80H has an odd number of logic ones
AF=1    ;there is a carry out of bit 3 into bit 4
ZF=0    ;the result is not 0
SF=1    ;bit seven is a 1
OF=1    ;the sign bit has changed
```

The 8086 has several instructions that can be used to transfer program control to a new memory location, based on the state of these flags. For example, the instruction sequence:

```
ADD AL, 1 ;Add 1 to register AL
JNZ 0100H ;Jump to location 0100H if the result is not zero (ZF=0)
```

will transfer control to location 0100H if the result of the **ADD AL,1** instruction is *not zero*. If it is desired to test for the zero condition, the **JZ** (jump if zero) instruction can be used. (Chapters 4–6 cover these transfer of control instructions in more detail.)

Three of the flags can be set or reset directly by the programmer and are used to control the operation of the processor: TF, IF, and DF.

When TF (the trap flag) is set, control is passed to a special address (previously defined by the programmer) after each instruction is executed. Normally, a program to display all of the registers and flags is stored there. Thus, setting TF causes the processor to operate in a software *single-stepping* mode, pausing after each instruction is executed. This is very useful for program debugging.

When IF (the interrupt flag) is set, external interrupt requests on the 8086's INTR input line will be enabled. When INTR is driven high (that is, an interrupt occurs), control is transferred to an *interrupt service routine (ISR)*. When this routine has finished, it normally executes an IRET (interrupt return) instruction and control is transferred back to the instruction in the main program that was executing when the interrupt occurred. (Software interrupts are discussed in Chapters 4–6; hardware interrupts are discussed in Chapter 9.)

The last control flag is DF (the direction flag). This flag is used with the block move (also called *string*) instructions. When DF is set, the block memory pointer will automatically decrement; if reset, the pointer will increment. (The block instructions are discussed in Chapter 4.)

You have probably noticed that some of the flags are marked with an *X*. These flags are undefined in the 8086 and 8088. However, most of these are defined in the more advanced processors—the 80386, 80486, Pentium, and Pentium Pro.

Segment Registers.   The final group of registers in Figure 3.3 are called the *segment group*. These registers are used by the BIU to determine the memory address output by the processor when it is reading or writing from the memory unit. In order to fully understand these registers, we must first study the way the 8086 divides its memory into *segments*. This is done in the next section.

Self-Review 3.1 (Answers on page 125)

3.1.1   The 8086 and 8088 microprocessors are divided into an _____ unit and a _____ _____ unit.

3.1.2   The pipelined architecture of the 8086 allows the fetch and execute cycles to _____.

3.1.3   What conditions will cause the BIU to suspend fetching instructions?

3.1.4   What is the word interpretation of the 8086 instruction **MOV CH,[DI]**?

3.1.5   What two 8-bit registers are the equivalent of register DX?

3.1.6   The 8086 can be single-stepped if the _____ flag is set.

3.1.7   If register AL=FFH and the instruction **ADD AL,1** is given, specify the new contents of register AL and the six status flags.

3.2   Segmented Memory

Introduction

Two types of memory organization are in popular use. Processors in the Motorola MC68000 family use *linear addressing*. This is a scheme in which the entire memory is available to the processor at all times. The second method, used by Intel with its 80x86 processors, is called *segmented addressing*. In this scheme, the memory space is divided into several segments and the processor is limited to accessing program instructions and data from only these segments. There are advantages and disadvantages to both techniques.

In this section we:

- Explain the concept of even and odd memory banks as used by the 8086.
- List the 8086 segment registers and show how to calculate a segment's base address.
- Explain how to determine the default 8086 segment assignment associated with each instruction that accesses memory.
- Show how to translate an 8086 offset, or logical, address into a physical address.

8086 Memory Organization

Even and Odd Memory Banks.   Even though the 8086 is considered a 16-bit microprocessor (it has a 16-bit data bus width), its memory is still thought of in bytes. At first this might seem a disadvantage—why saddle a 16-bit microprocessor with an 8-bit memory? Actually, there are a couple of good reasons. For one, it allows the processor to work on bytes as well as words. This is especially important with I/O devices like printers, terminals, and modems, all of which are designed to transfer ASCII-encoded (7- or 8-bit) data.

Second, many of the 8086's operation codes are single bytes. Other instructions may require anywhere from two to seven bytes. By being able to access individual bytes, these odd-length instructions can be handled.

We have already seen that the 8086 has a 20-bit address bus, allowing it to output 2^{20}, or 1,048,576, different memory addresses. Figure 3.6 shows how this memory space is typically drawn on paper. As you can see, 524,288 16-bit words can also be visualized.

As mentioned in Chapter 1, the 8086 reads 16 bits from memory by simultaneously reading an odd-addressed byte and an even-addressed byte. For this reason the 8086 organizes its memory into even-addressed and odd-addressed *banks,* as shown in Figure 3.7(a). If you are curious about how this works, note that the 8086 provides control bus signals that can be decoded by the memory to determine if a byte or a word is to be accessed. (Chapter 7 provides the details.)

Studying Figure 3.7(a) you might wonder if all words must begin at an even address. For example, is it possible to read the word stored in bytes 5 and 6? The answer is yes, as you can see in Figure 3.7(b). However, there is a penalty to be paid. The processor must perform two memory read cycles—one to fetch the low order byte, and a second to fetch the high order byte. This slows the processor down but is transparent to the programmer.

The last few paragraphs apply only to the 8086. The 8088, with its 8-bit data bus, interfaces to the 1 MB of memory as a single bank. When it is necessary to access a word (whether on an even- or an odd-addressed boundary), two memory read (or write) cycles are performed. In effect, the 8088 pays the performance penalty with every word access. Fortunately for the programmer, except for the slightly slower performance of the 8088, all of this is transparent.

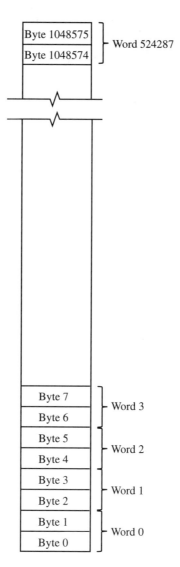

Figure 3.6 The memory space of the 8086 consists of 1,048,576 bytes or 524,288 16-bit words.

8086 Memory Map

Reserved and Dedicated Memory.   Still another view of the 8086's memory space is illustrated in Figure 3.8. Shown are 16 64K blocks of memory beginning at hex address 00000 and ending at address FFFFFH. This division into 64K blocks is an arbitrary but convenient choice, because the most significant hex digit increments by one with each additional block; that is, address 20000H is 65,536 bytes higher in memory than address 10000H.

The diagram in Figure 3.8 is also called a *memory map* because, like a road map, it is a guide showing how the system memory is allocated. For example, it might show RAM from 00000 to 3FFFFH, ROM from F0000H to FFFFFH, and the remainder of the

Figure 3.7   (a) By reading from an even-addressed bank and an odd-addressed bank the 8086 can read two bytes from memory simultaneously. (b) If the 16-bit word begins at an odd address, the 8086 will require two memory read or write cycles.

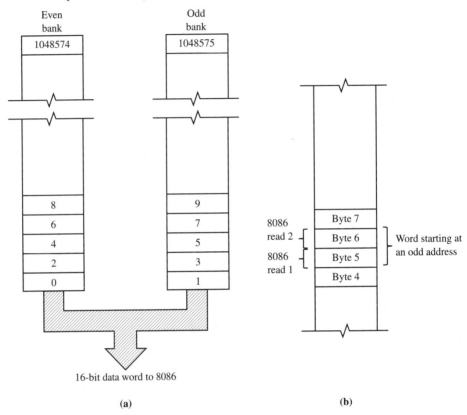

memory space unused. This kind of information is vital to the programmer who must know exactly where programs can be safely loaded.

Studying Figure 3.8, note that some memory locations are marked *reserved* and others *dedicated*. The dedicated locations are used for processing specific system interrupts and the reset function. Intel has also reserved several locations for future hardware and software products.[2]

Segment Registers

Code, Data, Stack, and Extra.   Within the 1 MB of memory space, the 8086 defines four 64K memory blocks: the *code* segment, *stack* segment, *data* segment, and *extra* segment. Each of these blocks of memory is used differently by the processor.

The code segment holds the program instruction codes. The data segment stores data for the program. The extra segment is an extra data segment (often used for shared data).

---

[2]These will be identified when the 386, 486, Pentium, and Pentium Pro processors are covered later in this chapter.

Figure 3.8 Memory map for the 8086 microprocessor. Some memory locations are *dedicated* or *reserved*.

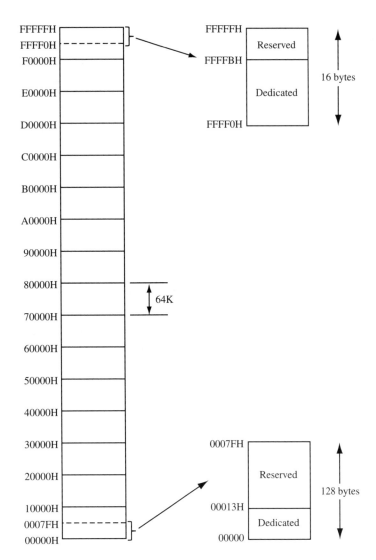

The stack segment is used to store interrupt and subroutine return addresses (explained more fully in Chapter 4).

You should realize that the concept of *segmented* memory is a unique one. Older generation microprocessors such as the 8-bit 8085 or Z-80 could access only one 64K segment. This meant that the program instructions, data, and subroutine stack all shared the same memory. This limited the amount of memory available for the program itself and led to disaster if the stack should overwrite the data or program areas.

The four segment registers shown in Figures 3.1 and 3.3 (CS, DS, ES, and SS) are used to "point" at location 0 (the base address) of each segment. This is a little tricky because the segment registers are only 16 bits wide; the memory address is 20 bits wide. The BIU takes care of this problem by appending four 0s to the low order bits of the segment register. In effect this multiplies the segment register contents by 16. Figure 3.9 shows an example.

Figure 3.9 The 8086 divides its 1 MB of memory address space into four segments, the data, code, stack, and extra segments. The four segment registers DS, CS, SS, and ES point to location 0 of the current segment. In this example, the stack and extra segments are partially overlapped. (From J. Uffenbeck, *Microcomputers and Microprocessors: The 8080, 8085 and Z-80,* Prentice-Hall, Englewood Cliffs, N.J., 1985)

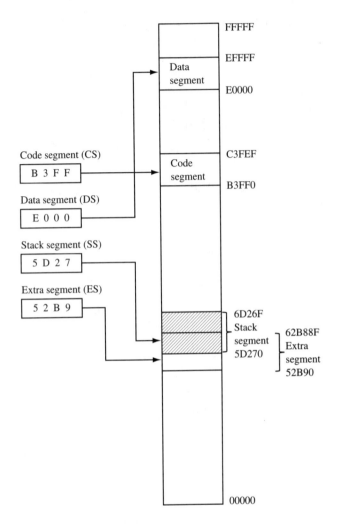

The CS register contains B3FFH but is interpreted as pointing to address B3FF0H. The point to note is that the beginning segment address is not arbitrary—*it must begin at an address divisible by 16.* Another way of saying this is that the low order hex digit must be 0.

Also note that the four segments need not be defined separately. In Figure 3.9 the stack and extra segments are *partially overlapped.* Indeed, it is allowable for all four segments to completely overlap (CS=DS=ES=SS).

Example 3.2

Calculate the beginning and ending addresses for the data segment, assuming register DS=E000H.

Solution.
The base address is found by appending four 0s. Therefore, the base address is E0000H. The ending address is found by adding FFFFH (64K); that is, E0000H + FFFFH = EFFFFH.

Memory locations not defined to be within one of the current segments cannot be accessed by the 8086 without first redefining one of the segment registers to include that location. Thus, at any given instant a maximum of 256K (64K × 4) of memory can be utilized. As we will see, the contents of the segment registers can only be specified via software. As you might imagine, instructions to load these registers should be among the first given in any 8086 program.

Logical and Physical Addresses

Do You Know Where Your Memory Bytes Are?   Addresses within a segment can range from address 0 to address FFFFH. This corresponds to the 64K length of the segment. An address within a segment is called an *offset,* or *logical,* address. For example, logical address 0005H in the code segment shown in Figure 3.9 actually corresponds to the real address B3FF0H + 5 = B3FF5H. This "real" address is called the *physical* address.

What is the difference between the physical and logical addresses? The physical address is 20 bits long and corresponds to the actual binary code output by the BIU on the address bus lines; the logical address is an offset from location 0 of a given segment.

Example 3.3

Calculate the physical address corresponding to logical address D470H in the extra segment. Repeat for logical address 2D90H in the stack segment. Assume the segment definitions shown in Figure 3.9.

Solution
For the extra segment:

$$
\begin{array}{ll}
52B90H & \text{(base address)} \\
+\ D470H & \text{(offset)} \\
\hline
60000H &
\end{array}
$$

and for the stack segment:

$$
\begin{array}{ll}
5D270H & \text{(base address)} \\
+\ 2D90H & \text{(offset)} \\
\hline
60000H &
\end{array}
$$

The result of this example might be surprising. However, when two segments overlap it is certainly possible for two *different logical addresses* to map to the *same physical address*. This can have disastrous results when the data begins to overwrite the subroutine stack area or vice versa. For this reason, be very careful when segments are allowed to overlap. (Chapters 4–6 provide more detail on how these segments are defined in a program.)

Also be careful when writing addresses on paper to do so clearly. To specify the logical address 2D90H in the stack segment, use the convention: **SS:2D90H.** Similarly, the logical address D470H in the extra segment is written **ES:D470H.** As we have just seen, both addresses map to physical address 60000H. There should be no ambiguity here, as five hex digits are required to specify a physical address.

Who's Who Here?   Now that we have seen the differences between physical and logical addresses, we must dig a little deeper and see how the instruction set uses each of the four

Table 3.1 Segment Register Assignments

Type of Memory Reference	Default Segment	Alternate Segment	Offset (Logical Address)
Instruction fetch	CS	None	IP
Stack operation	SS	None	SP
General data	DS	CS, ES, SS	Effective address
String source	DS	CS, ES, SS	SI
String destination	ES	None	DI
BX used as pointer	DS	CS, ES, SS	Effective address
BP used as pointer	SS	CS, ES, DS	Effective address

segments. For example, if register IP=1000H, where exactly is the next instruction fetch going to come from? Or where will the instruction **MOV [BP],AL**—*move a copy of register AL to the memory location pointed to by register BP*—store register AL?

The answer is contained in Table 3.1.[3] Every instruction that references memory has a *default* segment register, as shown. Instruction fetches occur only from the code segment with IP supplying the offset, or logical, address. Similarly, register BP used as a pointer defaults to the stack segment.

Table 3.1 is programmed into the BIU. If IP=1000H and CS=B3FFH the BIU will form the physical address B3FF0H + 1000H = B4FF0H and fetch the byte stored at this physical address for its next instruction.

Example 3.4

What physical memory location is accessed by the instruction **MOV [BP],AL** if BP=2C30H? Assume the segment definitions shown in Figure 3.9.

Solution
Table 3.1 indicates that when register BP is used as a memory pointer, the stack segment will be used. The physical address is:

$$\begin{array}{r} 5D270H \\ +\ 2C30H \\ \hline 5FEA0H \end{array}$$

Table 3.1 indicates that some memory references can have their segment definitions changed (note the *alternate* segment column in the table). For example, using a segment override, BP can also be used as a pointer into the code, data, or extra segments. On the other hand, instruction codes can only be stored in the code segment with IP used as the offset: similarly, string destinations always use the extra segment. The segment override operator is discussed further in Chapter 6.

---

[3]Believe it or not, this is one of the most important tables in this book. Later, when you are writing assembly language programs, you may find that your programs are not finding their data as expected. The usual cause of this problem is that you have forgotten the default segment assignments in this table.

Advantages and Disadvantages of Segmented Memory

Not Everyone Likes Segmented Memory.   Segmented memory can seem confusing at first. What you must remember is that the program op-codes will be fetched from the code segment; program data variables will be stored in the data and extra segments. Stack operations use registers BP or SP as pointers into the stack segment. As we begin writing programs, the consequences of these definitions will become clearer.

One advantage to having separate data and code segments is that one program can work on several different *sets* of data. This is done by reloading register DS to point to the new data. Another advantage of segmented memory is that programs that reference logical addresses can be loaded and run anywhere in memory, because the logical address always ranges from 0000 to FFFFH, independent of the code segment base.

Consider a *multitasking* environment in which the 8086 is running several different programs at once. An inactive program can be temporarily saved on a magnetic disk and a new program brought in to take its place—without concern for the physical location of this new program. Such programs are said to be *relocatable,* meaning they will run at any location in memory. The requirements for writing relocatable programs are that no references be made to physical addresses, and no changes to the segments' registers are allowed.

Despite these advantages, the 8086 has been criticized for its segmented memory. Why? Segmented memory introduces extra complexity in both hardware (memory addresses require two registers—an offset register and a segment register) and software (programs are limited to the segment size). The latter is especially frustrating, as the 8086 limits segments to 64K.[4]

Self-Review 3.2 (Answers on page 125)

3.2.1   *(True/False)* The 8086 and 8088 can read or write a byte or word in a single memory access.

3.2.2   To maximize 8086 processor performance, a data word should be stored beginning at an _____ memory address.

3.2.3   Each 8086 memory segment is _____ bytes long, and addresses within a segment are referred to as _____ or _____ addresses.

3.2.4   *(True/False)* The four memory segments can be located anywhere within the 1 MB of address space of the 8086.

3.2.5   What is the *physical address* corresponding to DS:103FH if DS=94D0H?

3.2.6   Assuming the default assignment (see Table 3.1), which 8086 memory segment will be accessed for the instruction **MOV [BX],AH** *(move a copy of register AH to the memory location whose offset is stored in register BX)*?

3.3   The 80386

Introduction

As mentioned in Chapter 1, the 8086 and 8088 were followed by the 80286, the first Intel processor to offer Protected Mode. The 80386 refined the Protected Mode features of the

---

[4]Programs greater than 64K can be run on the 8086, but the software needed is more complex, as it must switch to a new segment. Beginning with the 80386, segments can be as large as 4 GB—the total memory capacity of this chip. In effect, this disables segmented memory.

286 and expanded the data registers to 32 bits. In addition, a new feature called Virtual 8086 Mode was made available. As you will see, the 386 architecture has become the foundation for the 80486, Pentium, and Pentium Pro processors that followed.

In this section we:

- Compare and contrast the Real and Protected operating modes of the 80386.
- Identify the major components of the 80386 processor, including the bus interface unit, central processing unit, and memory management unit.
- List and identify the function of the 80386 general- and special-purpose data registers.
- Explain the Protected Mode addressing mechanism of the 80386.
- List the "rules of privilege" of the 80386 processor.

Operating Modes

Real Mode.   Following a system reset, the 386 is initialized in Real Mode. In this mode the chip looks virtually identical to an 8086; that is, it has the following features:

1. The address space is limited to 1 MB using the 20 low order address lines A0–A19 (the high address lines A20–A31 are inactive).
2. The segmented memory addressing mechanism of the 8086 is retained, with each segment limited to 64K.

Two new features are available to the programmer in Real Mode—access to the 32-bit register set of the 386 and the addition of two new segments called *F* and *G*. (This will be explained in more detail when the programming model is introduced later in this chapter.)

Protected Mode.   The primary difference between Real Mode and Protected Mode is the latter's new addressing mechanism and protection levels. Although memory segments are still retained, each segment may range from a single byte to 4 GB (the full physical address space of the 386). The addresses stored in the segment registers are now interpreted as *pointers* into a *descriptor table*. Each segment's entry in this table is 8 bytes long and identifies the 32-bit base address of the segment, the segment size, and the access rights. Memory addresses are computed by adding the offset specified by the instruction to the segment base address.

A *paging* mechanism can be used to translate the 32-bit linear address (segment base plus offset) into a physical address within a 4K page frame. The paging unit can manage multiple frames, even swapping these out to disk, such that 64 TB (65,536 GB) of *virtual memory* is available. (Protected Mode memory management is discussed in more detail later in this section.)

Finally, the 386 offers a protection mechanism in which tasks (programs) are run in a particular segment and assigned a *privilege level*. Tasks of a lower privilege level cannot access programs or data in a segment with a higher privilege level. Using this scheme, the operating system can run multiple programs, each protected from the others. (The "rules of privilege" are covered later in this section.)

Virtual 8086 Mode.   The 80386 offers two ways of running 8086 programs: The first, Real Mode, was covered previously; the second method, called *Virtual 8086 Mode*, allows multiple 8086 programs (or other 386 applications) to be run independent of each other. Each Virtual 8086 Mode task "sees" a 1 MB address space, which, via paging, may be mapped anywhere in the 4 GB physical address space of the 386.

Compared to Real Mode, which limits the 386 to 1 MB of physical memory and one 8086 task, Virtual 8086 Mode allows many such tasks, as well as other 386-style (Protected Mode addressing) programs, to run simultaneously. That is, the 386 can be operated in Protected Mode and Virtual 8086 Mode at the same time. Note that because each 8086 task is assigned the *lowest* privilege level, access to programs or data in other segments is not allowed, thus protecting each such task.

Processor Model

The 80386 processor is divided into three main units called the *bus interface unit (BIU),* the *central processing unit (CPU),* and the *memory management unit (MMU).* These are shown in block diagram form in Figure 3.10.

The BIU. This unit manages the 32-bit address and data buses of the 386, as well as the various control signals. Like the 8086's BIU, its job is to keep the instruction queue (now expended to 16 bytes) full so that the processor never has to wait for an instruction fetch.

Figure 3.10   The processor model for the 80386 microprocessor consists of the bus interface unit (BIU), central processing unit (CPU), and the memory management unit (MMU).

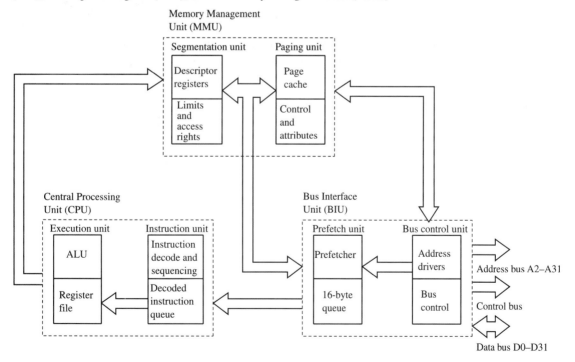

Two new features have been added. The first is called *address pipelining*. This is a technique in which the address of the next memory location to be accessed is output by the 386 halfway through the current bus cycle. In effect, this gives the external memory more address decode time and makes it easier for the memory to keep up with the two-clock-pulses-per-bus-cycle processor.[5]

The second feature is called *dynamic data bus sizing*. This allows the 386 to switch between a 32-bit and 16-bit data bus width "on the fly." In this way the chip can accommodate an external 16-bit memory card or I/O device. When 16-bit mode is selected, the BIU automatically adjusts bus cycle timing to use only the low 16 bits of the data bus.

Like the 8086, the 386 organizes its memory into *banks*. When the bus size is set to 32 bits, four banks are required. This arrangement is the same as that used by the 486 (shown previously in Figure 1.2.) With its 32-bit data bus, the 386 is able to access four bytes or a double word (dword) in one bus cycle. Note, however, that the dword must begin at an address *divisible by four*. If this is not the case, two bus cycles will be required to access the four bytes.[6]

The Central Processing Unit.   The CPU consists of an *instruction unit (IU)* and an *execution unit (EU)*. The IU retrieves instructions from the queue, decodes them, and stores them in the decoded instruction queue. The EU contains the ALU (arithmetic logic unit) and the same eight general-purpose data registers as in the 8086, now expanded to 32 bits each. Like the 8086, this architecture allows the fetching and executing of instructions to *overlap,* optimizing system performance.

The MMU.   This unit has two parts. The *segmentation unit* generates 8086-style (20-bit) physical addresses when the 386 is operated in Real Mode; when operated in Protected Mode, the *descriptor* registers store the base address, size, and attributes of the various segments. In effect, these registers cache the descriptor tables stored in RAM, allowing the processor to switch between tasks more quickly.

The second part of the MMU is the *paging unit*. This unit determines the physical addresses associated with each active segment and allows segments to be divided into 4K pages. Typically only the most current pages are kept in memory, with the others swapped out to disk. In this way, programs that actually require more memory than is physically present can be run. This is called *virtual memory*.

Programming Model

The 80386 programming model has two parts: the *general-purpose registers* used by applications programs and the *special-purpose registers* used by the operating system. The registers making up these two groups are shown in Figure 3.11(a) and (b).

General-Purpose Registers—The Data and Address Group.   These are the data, pointer, and index registers from the 8086. Note that each has been expanded from 16 to 32 bits. To reference the 32-bit register, the letter *E* (for extended) is added to the 16-bit register

---

[5]Recall that a bus cycle requires the output of a memory or I/O address and the activation of the appropriate control signals. Four bus cycle types are possible: I/O read, I/O write, memory read, and memory write. The 8086 requires four clock pulses per bus cycle, compared to only two for the 386.

[6]This is similar to the 8086 accessing a 16-bit word that begins at an *odd* address.

name. For example, when extended to 32 bits, register AX becomes EAX. Note that each of the registers EAX, EBX, ECX, and EDX can now be accessed in four ways. Using EAX as an example:

1. **AL,** the low 8 bits of register AX D0–D7 (data bits 0–7)
2. **AH,** the high 8 bits of register AX D8–D15
3. **AX,** the low 16 bits of register EAX D0–D15
4. **EAX,** the full 32 bits D0–D31

Figure 3.11 Programming model for the 80386. The general-purpose registers (a) are used by applications programmers. The special-purpose registers (b) are intended to be used by the operating system software.

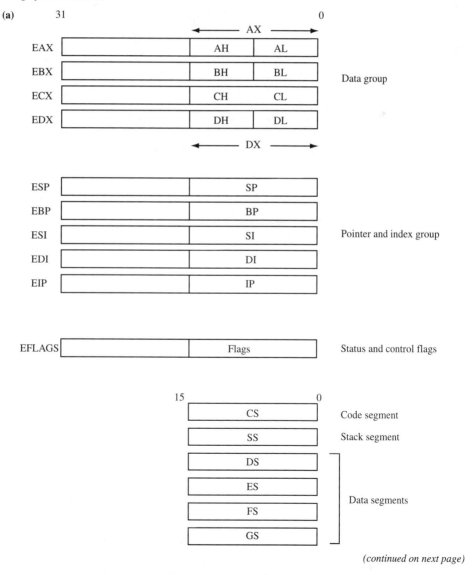

(continued on next page)

Figure 3.11   *(continued)*

(b)

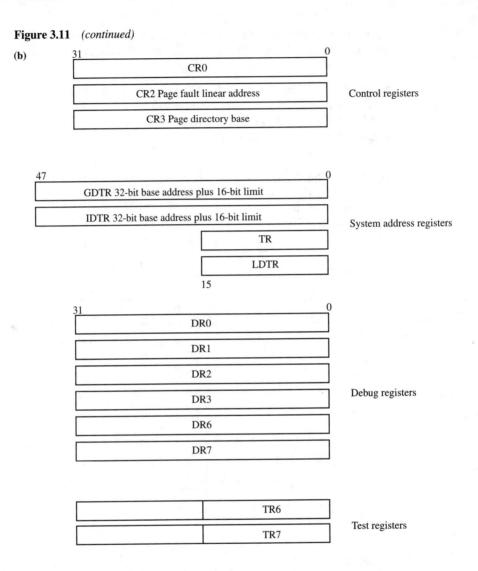

General-Purpose Registers—The Status and Control Flags.   The 8086 status and control flags have been retained, but have been extended to 32 bits, as shown in Figure 3.12. In addition, four new flags have been added.

VM   Virtual Mode. This is a Protected Mode control flag used to switch the processor to Virtual 8086 Mode.

RF   Resume Flag. This control flag is used with the debug registers (discussed in the next section). When set, the debug fault is ignored and the next instruction is executed normally.

NT   Nested Task. This status flag is used in Protected Mode to indicate that the current task was called from another task. This affects the type of return instruction to be executed when the nested task completes.

IOPL   Input/Output Privilege Level. These two Protected Mode control bits identify the current privilege level (0–3) required to execute I/O instructions. They allow the operating system to restrict the I/O privileges of a task.

General-Purpose Registers—The Segment Group.   Two new segment registers—FS and GS—have been added, so that six different segments can now be active at a time. All registers remain 16 bits wide, as in the 8086. Because no instructions default to the new FS and GS segments, the 8086 segment register assignments shown previously (Table 3.1) still apply.

In Real Mode, the segment registers hold the base address of the segment. As we learned in Section 3.2, physical addresses are computed by shifting the segment address four bits left and adding the offset. This is referred to as the *8086 addressing mechanism.*

When the 386 is switched to Protected Mode, the segment registers no longer hold segment base addresses. Instead, their contents are thought of as *pointers* into a *descriptor* table. The entries in this table then determine the base address of the segment, its size and its attributes. (This is covered in more detail in the next section.)

Special-Purpose Registers.   The registers in this group are shown in Figure 3.11(b). These registers are not normally used by the applications programmer, as they are intended to control the processor in Protected Mode and for testing.

Three 32-bit control registers are provided—CR0, CR2, and CR3. CR0 is used to enable the paging mechanism, monitor task switching, enable coprocessor emulation, and select Protected Mode. CR2 holds the address of the last instruction to cause a page fault—a reference to a page or segment that is not in memory (and therefore must be loaded from disk). CR3 holds the base address of the page table. This is a table that holds the starting address of each page frame and access information about that frame.

Four *system address registers* are provided to hold information about the descriptor tables used in Protected Mode. (These are described in more detail in the next section.)

Figure 3.12   The 80386 flag word is 32 bits long. Four new flags have been added compared to the 8086: VM, RF, NT, and IOPL. (Courtesy of Intel Corporation)

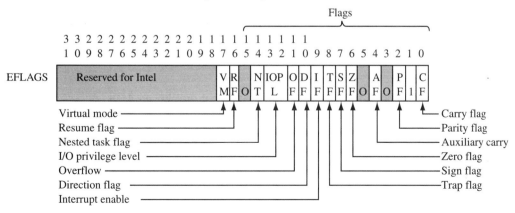

Note: ◻ indicates Intel reserved; Do not define.

There are six debugging registers—DR0–3 and DR6–7. They are used to set program *breakpoints*. Breakpoints are addresses where the program should *break* (pause) and pass control to a debugging routine. This allows the programmer to inspect the state of the registers and thereby debug his program. With older processors (the 8086), this debugging capability had to be supplied via external software.

Finally, two test registers, TR6 and TR7, are provided. They are used to test the RAM in the Translation Lookaside Buffer (TLB). The TLB is used by the paging unit to translate virtual memory addresses into physical addresses. (Paging is discussed later in this section.)

Memory Management in Protected Mode

Segment Descriptors.   A program on the 386 may have several different functions, or *tasks*. Each task, in turn, may require several different memory segments (for example, a code segment, a stack segment, and several data segments). Because these segments may be located anywhere in memory and may or may not be accessible to a given task, *descriptor tables* are used to identify the segment base address, segment size, and access rights. The 386 contains three types of descriptor tables.

1. *The Global Descriptor Table (GDT)*. Entries in this table describe segments that may be available to all tasks in the system.
2. *The Local Descriptor Table (LDT)*. Entries in this table describe segments associated with a given task. Each task may have a separate LDT.
3. *The Interrupt Descriptor Table (IDT)*. Entries in this table point to the starting address of up to 256 different interrupt service routines.[7]

Figure 3.13 illustrates how the GDT and LDT are used to compute the physical address of a memory operand in Protected Mode. The upper 13 bits of a segment register (CS, SS, DS, ES, FS, or GS) are used as an *index* into an 8-byte to 64K descriptor table (these bits are shown shaded in the figure). If bit 2 of this register is a 0, the GDT is used, if a 1, the LDT is used. Each entry in this table is 8 bytes long and specifies the base address, segment limit (up to 4 GB), and the access rights.

Assuming the requesting and current privilege levels (RPL and CPL—bits 0–1 of the data and code segment registers) allow access to this segment, the 32-bit base address stored in the descriptor table is added to the 32-bit instruction offset to form the physical memory address as shown. With a 13-bit index, as many as 8192 different descriptors can be stored in each descriptor table. The base address and limit of the descriptor tables is stored in the *system address registers* GDTR and LDTR.

Paging.   The local and global descriptor tables of the 386 can each be as large as 64K. Each descriptor, in turn, requires 8 bytes. Thus, a total of 16K (8K global and 8K local) descriptors can be defined. As each descriptor points to a segment, and each segment can be as large as 4 GB, the 386 can potentially support a program requiring 64 TB (16K segments × 4 GB/segment) of memory. To accomplish this feat with only (*only?*) 4 GB of physical memory available, the 386 employs a *paging* mechanism.

---

[7]Interrupts may be generated internally by the processor when a fault occurs, by external hardware, or by a software interrupt instruction. In all cases, the interrupt causes the processor to suspend the current task and switch to a new program—the interrupt service routine. (Interrupts are discussed in detail in later chapters.)

Figure 3.13   80386 Protected Mode addressing. Physical addresses are computed by adding the instruction offset to the segment base address stored in a descriptor table. The upper 13 bits of the segment register are used to point to a specific descriptor. The base address and limit of the descriptor tables are stored in the global and local descriptor table registers (GDTR and LDTR).

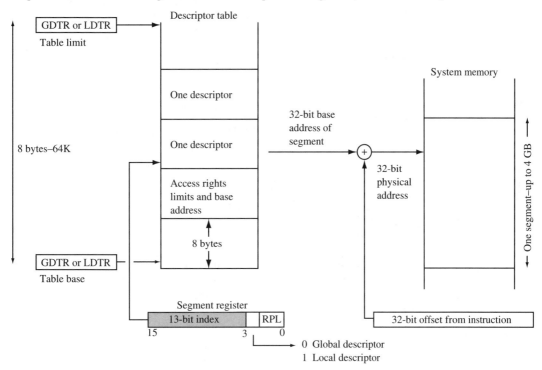

Paging is enabled by setting bit 31 of control register 0 (CR0). The Protected Mode addressing mechanism of the 386 is then modified from that shown in Figure 3.13 to include a paging unit, as shown in Figure 3.14. This unit inputs the 32-bit (linear) memory address (the sum of the segment base plus instruction offset) and, via a page directory and page table, computes a new physical address within a 4K *page frame*. By swapping these page frames out to disk, the full 64 TB of (virtual) memory can be realized.

Control logic within the paging unit keeps track of the pages so that a request for a page not currently in memory (a page fault) does not cause an error. It is up to the operating system to decide which pages to swap out to disk in this situation (typically a Least Recently Used algorithm is employed). To speed up the page look-up process, the paging unit incorporates a *Translation Lookaside Buffer (TLB)*, which stores the address of the 32 most recently accessed page frames. At 4K per page frame, this allows coverage of 128K of memory addresses. Intel reports that, via the TLB, the likelihood of a *hit* (a memory request for an address in the TLB) is approximately 98 percent.

Protection

The Rules of Privilege.   It is imperative that programs running in a multitasking operating system not be allowed to access privileged data or programs. If this is not the case,

Figure 3.14   When paging is enabled, the 32-bit linear address is first computed as the sum of the instruction offset and segment base address. The paging unit then translates this into a new physical address somewhere within a 4K page frame.

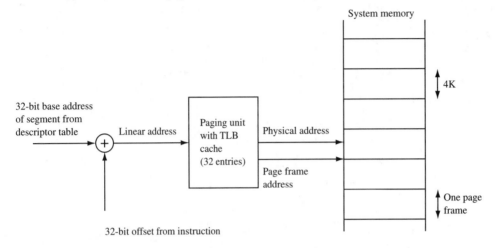

one failing task could bring down all of the others (including the operating system itself). As part of its memory management unit, the 386 incorporates *four levels* of protection optimized to isolate and protect user programs from each other and the operating system. The privilege levels (PL) are numbered 0 through 3, with level 0 the most privileged and level 3 the least privileged. The latter is typically assigned to user applications, and the former to the operating system kernel (core routines). (This is shown in Figure 3.15.)

Figure 3.15   The 80386 provides four levels of protection to programs and data. Level 0 is the most trusted; level 3 is the least trusted. (Courtesy of Intel Corporation)

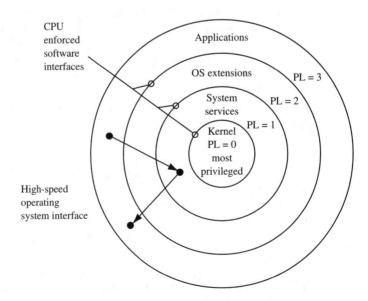

Figure 3.16   Protection validation check mechanism of the 80386. For the memory access to succeed, EPL (the effective privilege level of the task) must be (numerically) less than or equal to the DPL (descriptor privilege level) of the segment to be accessed.

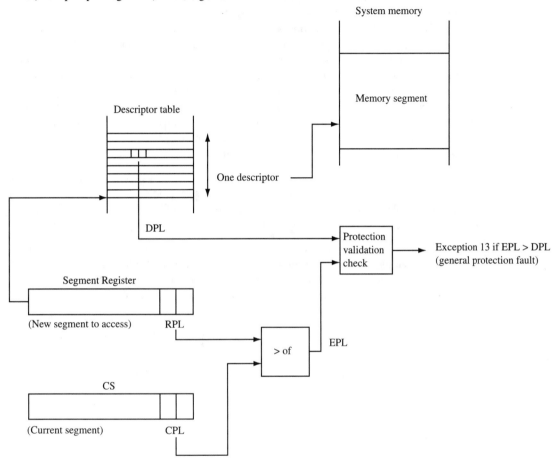

When operated in Protected Mode, the 386 applies the following two rules (*the rules of privilege*) each time a memory segment is accessed for data, or a code segment for a control transfer to run a new procedure.

1. Data stored in a segment with privilege level **p** can only be accessed by a program executing at a privilege level ≤ **p**.[8]
2. A program executing at privilege level **p** can only be called by a task executing at a privilege level ≤ **p**.

Figure 3.16 illustrates the protection validation check mechanism of the 386. The privilege level of the current program is stored in the two least significant bits of the code

---

[8]Recall that the lower the *numeric* privilege level, the more trusted is that level.

segment register and is referred to as the *Current Privilege Level (CPL)*. When access to a new memory segment is desired, an *Effective Privilege Level (EPL)* is computed. This is the greater of CPL and the *Requester Privilege Level (RPL)*. Note that RPL is stored in the two least significant bits of the segment register.

In Protected Mode, the segment register is interpreted as a pointer to an 8-byte descriptor associated with a particular memory segment. Among other things, the descriptor stores the Privilege Level of the segment. This is called the *Descriptor Privilege Level (DPL)*. Before the 386 allows a memory segment to be accessed, it compares the DPL and EPL, as shown in Figure 3.16. If the EPL is greater than the DPL (meaning the requester is less privileged than the segment to be accessed), an exception (interrupt) is generated by the processor and access to the segment is blocked.[9] Finally, note that because access to the DPL bits of the descriptor is restricted to tasks running at PL = 0, the operating system controls the accessibility of all memory segments.

Gates.   A gate is a special type of descriptor that provides a way for the operating system to allow less privileged programs to access data, other programs, and interrupt service routines, all at a higher privilege level. There are four types of gates:

1. *Call gates.* This gate allows access to code segments at different privilege levels.
2. *Task gates.* This gate is used to perform task switches (covered in the next section).
3. *Interrupt gates.* This gate is used to specify interrupt service routines.
4. *Trap gates.* This gate is used to specify trap handling routines. These are programs activated when an error occurs (for example, an attempt to divide by zero).

To access a gate, the rules of privilege are followed such that the EPL of the requester must be less than or equal to the DPL of the gate. Figure 3.17 shows an example of a call

Figure 3.17   Call gates are used to allow programs at a lower privilege level to access more privileged programs and data. (From D. Tabak, *Advanced Microprocessors*, McGraw Hill, New York, N.Y., 1991)

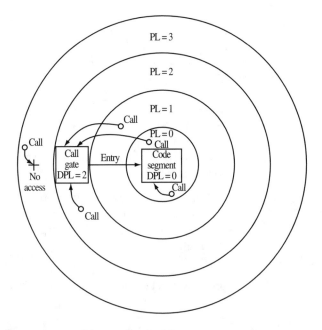

---

[9]This is called a *general protection fault.*

gate with DPL = 2. In this example, the call gate is assumed to point to a memory segment at PL = 0 (the most privileged level). Because this call gate's DPL = 2, any program whose EPL is less than or equal to 2 can access this gate. In particular, note that via this gate, programs at PL = 1 or 2 can access programs at PL = 0. Note, however, that the call gate restricts this access to the single memory segment pointed to by the call gate.

Task Switching.   The 386 has been specially designed to support a *multitasking* operating system—multiple independent programs all sharing access to the processor in a protected environment. A task switch differs from a subroutine call or jump instruction in that the entire state of the machine must be saved; that is, the contents of all the processor registers, the address space, and any links to previous tasks. The 386 accomplishes this through another special type of descriptor called a *task gate*.

Again following the rules of privilege, a call or jump to the task gate will cause protection checks to be performed, the current state of the machine to be saved, and a new machine state to be restored. On the 386, the entire task switch takes place in about 17µs.

Self-Review 3.3 (Answers on page 125)

3.3.1   When the 386 is operated in Real Mode, memory segments are limited to _____. However, when operated in Protected Mode, memory segments may be as large as _____.
3.3.2   List the three main units of the 386 processor.
3.3.3   List the four different ways in which the components of register EBX can be accessed.
3.3.4   What data is stored in a 386 descriptor table?
3.3.5   The 386 rules of privilege dictate that a code or data segment at PL = 2 can only be accessed by a task executing at PL = _____, _____, or _____.

3.4   The 80486

Introduction

The 80486 retains all of the operating modes and features of the 80386 but includes several enhancements to improve performance. The core features of the 386—Real and Protected modes, memory management, protection levels, register and bus sizes—all remain unchanged. Six new instructions have been added, but these are primarily intended for operating system software. The most significant changes are the inclusion of an onboard 8K cache memory (16K in the DX4 version of the chip) and floating-point unit. Although both of these could be had with 386 systems, external hardware was required. In this section we:

- List those factors that make the 486 faster than the 386 for a given clock speed.
- Explain the operation of a direct mapped cache.
- Draw a block diagram of the 486 cache and explain the role of the cache SRAM, TAG SRAM, and the LRU SRAM.
- List and identify the function of the data and control registers within the 486 floating-point unit.

A "Better" 386

Five-Stage Instruction Pipeline.   The classical description of the stored program computer is a machine that fetches instructions from memory, decodes those instructions, and then executes them. In today's modern microprocessors such as the 80486, however, even Dr. John von Neumann himself might have trouble recognizing these pieces.

On the 486, the fetch and execute cycle is implemented via a *five-stage pipeline*. The sequence begins with the prefetch (PF) stage, in which raw instructions are placed in one of two 16-byte buffers *(queues)*. Next, the instruction op-codes are determined by the Decode1 (D1) stage. A second decode stage, Decode2 (D2) then determines the memory address of the instruction operand (the data operated on by the instruction). The execution stage (EX) is used by the ALU to perform the indicated operation. Finally, the writeback stage (WB) updates the internal registers with the instruction results.

Reduced Instruction Cycle Times.   Like a carwash, several instructions may be in the 486's pipeline at a given time. Figure 3.18 shows an example with four instructions (I1-4) moving through the pipeline. As I1 moves from PF to WB, instructions I2–I4 move in behind it. When I1 is being executed, I2 is in the second decode phase, I3 is in the first decode phase, and I4 is being prefetched. Since most instructions can move from stage to stage in a single clock cycle, the 486 can effectively execute a new instruction every clock cycle. Compare this to the 8086, which requires four clock cycles per instruction, and the 80386, which requires two clock cycles per instruction.

The result is a microprocessor that more closely resembles a RISC processor; that is, a machine in which all instructions require a uniform number of clock pulses. Tests have shown that, when operated at the same clock speeds, the 486 is about twice as fast as the 386.

Processor Model

Figure 3.19 shows the processor model for the 80486. It includes the now-familiar bus interface, central processing, and memory management units from the 80386. In addition, two new units have been added: a floating-point unit and a cache memory unit.

Integrated Coprocessor.   When announced, the 80486 incorporated the tightest silicon design rules of any Intel microprocessor to date (0.8 micron minimum feature size). This allowed the 486 designers to build a chip with over one million transistors (the 386 has *only* 275,000 transistors). With this new capability, it became possible to incorporate the entire 80387 floating-point unit (coprocessor) onboard. This helps simplify system board

Figure 3.18   The 486's five-stage instruction pipeline allows several instructions to be processed at the same time. (Courtesy of Intel Corporation)

PF	11	12	13	14			
D1		11	12	13	14		
D2			11	12	13	14	
EX				11	12	13	14
WB					11	12	13	14

Figure 3.19 The processor model for the 80486 microprocessor is the same as that for the 80386 except for the on-board cache and floating-point unit.

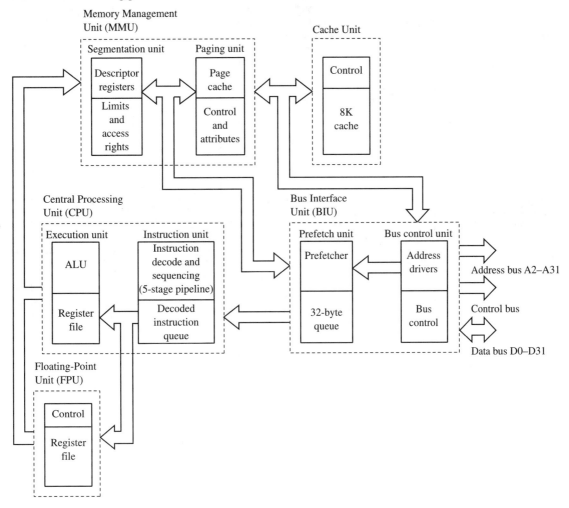

design (no coprocessor socket is required) and speeds up floating-point calculations, as these signals are now confined within the processor.

Onboard 8K Cache.[10]   With each new generation of microprocessors, system clock speeds have increased. The 8088 (announced in 1979) operated at 4.77 MHz; ten years later, the 80486 was announced with a clock speed of 50 MHz. Versions of the Pentium are available with clock speeds greater than 100 MHz, and the first version of the Pentium Pro operates at 133 MHz. Unfortunately, the access times of dynamic memory chips (the "core" memory of all modern microcomputer systems) have not been able to keep up with these clock speed increments. Today, the relatively slow response of these chips has become one of the major bottlenecks in most systems.

----

[10]The DX4 version of the 486 has a 16K cache.

Figure 3.20   The 486 cache is organized as four 2K caches. Each RAM location is mapped to a specific line in each 2K cache. Each cache location has a 21-bit TAG field that is compared with address lines A10–A31 to determine if that memory location is in the cache. Each line also has a *valid bit* that indicates if that line is holding data. If all four lines are full, the *least recently used* (LRU) bits are tested to determine which line to replace.

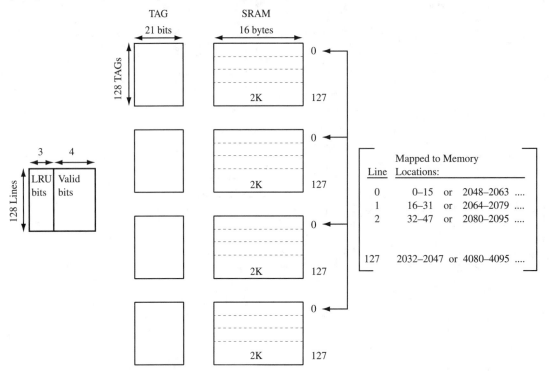

For these reasons, external *cache memories,* using fast static RAM, have become the norm. With the 486, Intel has moved the cache onboard to further decrease memory access times.[11] Intel's literature describes the 486's cache as a *write-through 8K code and data cache set up as four-way set-associative.* This means:

1. The cache stores both data and program instructions.
2. The size of the cache is 8K.
3. When data is written to the cache, it is also written to memory (*write-through*). This is to ensure that the contents of external memory match the contents of the cache.
4. The cache is organized as four direct mapped caches wired in parallel (see the sidebar What Is a Cache?).

Because the 486 accesses memory 32 bits at a time, it would be logical to design the cache to have this same width. However, since most programs access locations near those accessed recently, an even wider arrangement, 64 or even 128 bits, will increase the probability that future accesses will be found in the cache. As shown in Figure 3.20, this is the

---

[11]Most 486 systems still include an external cache of 128K to 256K to ensure optimum system performance.

What Is a Cache?

Cache memory is typically built using fast-responding static RAM (SRAM) chips located between the processor and main (DRAM) memory. The intent is to have the processor perform most of its memory accesses from these high-speed SRAM chips, thereby allowing the system to operate at its highest speed. However, because the cache is much smaller than main memory (typically 64K to 512K), it should be designed to hold only program code and data that the processor will likely require in the near future.

When a memory location is first accessed, the processor will have to wait while that data is fetched from the slower DRAMs. While this is occurring, the data will also be placed in the cache. The next time this location needs to be read, it can be read directly from the high-speed cache. After a period of time, the cache will fill with the most recently accessed data. The cache is designed so that subsequent memory reads will replace the *oldest* data in the cache. A hit is said to occur when the required data is found in the cache, a miss when it is not. The cache hit rate depends on the size of the cache. With a 64K cache, hit rates greater than 90 percent can be achieved.

The simplest type of cache is called *direct mapped.* In this scheme, each main memory location has a specific cache address to which it can be mapped. For example, assume the entire 4 GB memory space of the 486 processor is to be cached using 256K of cache memory. Each location in the cache will be mapped to 16,384 different locations in main memory (4 GB/256K). Cache location 0, for example, would map to main memory locations 0, 262,144, 524,288, 786,432 . . . etc. (16K locations in all). To keep track of which location is currently in the cache, TAG SRAMs are used. In this example, 256K TAG locations are required (one for each cache byte). Furthermore, each TAG location must be 14 bits wide in order to track the 16K possible addresses associated with each cache byte.

When a memory location is to be accessed, the processor outputs a 32-bit memory address. This address is interpreted by the caching hardware as follows:

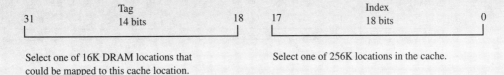

Select one of 16K DRAM locations that could be mapped to this cache location.   Select one of 256K locations in the cache.

The index bits are used to select one of 256K locations in the cache. Bits 18–31 of the memory address are then compared to the TAG bits stored in the TAG SRAM. If they compare, a hit occurs. If not, a DRAM access must be performed. In addition, the data at that location is copied to the cache and the TAG SRAM is updated.

The advantage of the direct mapped cache is simple hardware. If the processor wants to access memory location 262,144, the hardware need only check cache location 0: No other cache location can be mapped to this address. This advantage is also a disadvantage. Although other data in the cache may be "older" and less likely to be needed, memory location 262,144 can only be mapped to cache location 0. This is shown below.

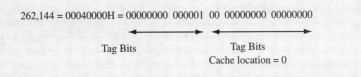

262,144 = 00040000H = 00000000 000001 00 00000000 00000000

Tag Bits   Tag Bits
Cache location = 0

(continued on next page)

It is also possible for a program to repeatedly access memory locations that map to the same cache address (0 and 262,144, for example). In this case the cache will actually *increase* memory access time, as the contents of these two DRAM locations will be repeatedly swapped in and out of the cache. This is called *thrashing*.

One way of eliminating this problem is to wire two direct mapped caches in parallel. This is called a *two-way associative cache.* Each DRAM location can then be mapped to *two* different cache locations (one in each direct mapped cache). Of course, the hardware complexity will double as two comparators and two sets of TAG SRAM and data SRAM will be required. A four-way cache provides even more flexibility, as each DRAM location can be mapped to four different cache locations.

scheme used by the 486. Four direct mapped caches are provided, each with 128 sets of 128-bit- (16-byte-) wide lines. The size of each cache is thus:

$$16 \text{ bytes/line} \times 128 \text{ lines} = 2048 \text{ bytes} = 2K$$

The total cache measures 8K.

The advantage of this organization is that each memory location can be cached to four different cache locations. Memory locations 0–15 (and 2048–2063, 4096–4111, etc.), for example, map to cache line 0 (in any of the four 2K caches). Similarly, memory locations 16–31 map to line 1, 32–47 to line 2, etc. When the 486 issues a 32-bit memory address, it is interpreted by the caching hardware as follows:

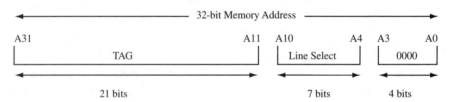

Because each line stores 16 bytes, A0–A3 are assumed 0 and ignored. Address lines A4–A10 are then used to select one of 128 lines in the cache. The four comparators associated with the four 2K SRAMs then compare the TAG bits at each matching line with A11–A31 of the memory address. If a match is found, a *hit* occurs and the memory read occurs from the cache and not the external RAM.

If the TAG bits *do not match* bits A11–A31, the memory access is made from RAM. In addition, the RAM data is copied to the cache. To decide which of the four lines in the cache to replace, the caching hardware first checks the four *valid bits*—one for each 2K SRAM block—associated with that line. If all four bits are valid—meaning that all four lines are already in use—the three *LRU (least recently used)* bits are examined to determine which line to replace.[12]

Burst Bus Mode.   When selected data is not in the cache, the 486 can use a special burst bus mode to quickly fill the cache line. Using this mode, 4 bytes of data can be input to the microprocessor in a single clock cycle (vs. two clock cycles for normal bus transfers).

---

[12]See Analysis and Design Problem 3.14.

Typically, 16 bytes of data (one cache line) are input in one burst cycle, with the addresses of these bytes aligned the same as those input by the cache; that is, bytes 0–15 are input in one burst cycle, bytes 16–31 in another, etc. Burst bus cycles are not restricted to cache fills. Any multicycle read request can be converted into a burst cycle. (Chapter 7 provides more detail on memory access times in burst mode.)

Programming Model

No Changes for the Applications Programmer.   Figure 3.21(a) illustrates the data register set of the 486 processor. The general-purpose registers, segment registers, and instruction

Figure 3.21   Programming model for the 80486. The general-purpose registers (a) are the same as those in the 80386. (b) The onboard floating-point unit includes eight 80-bit data registers.

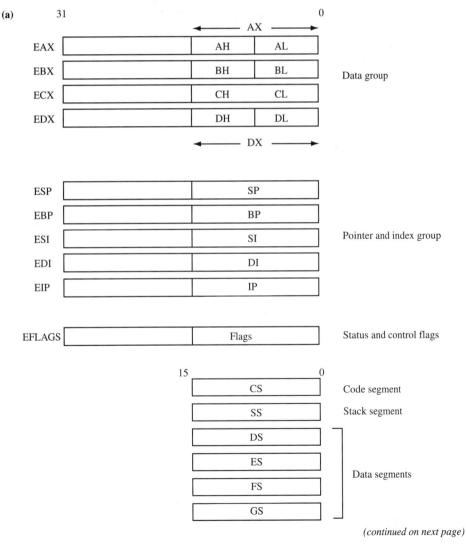

(continued on next page)

Figure 3.21 *(continued)*   **(b)**

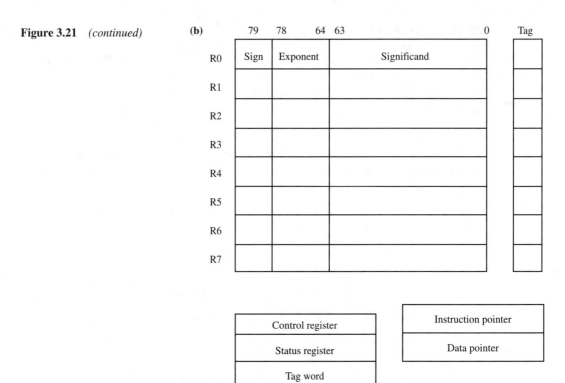

pointer all remain unchanged from the 386. This means the 486 is simply a faster 386 as far as the applications programmer is concerned. One new control flag, called *alignment check,* has been added (bit 18).When set, this flag will cause a software interrupt if a memory address is misaligned (a 16-bit word beginning at an odd address or a double word beginning at an address not divisible by four, for example).

With its onboard coprocessor, the programming model can be expanded to include the floating-point registers shown in Figure 3.21(b). Eight 80-bit registers are provided, allowing data to be stored and processed in any one of seven different data type formats. These formats are listed in Table 3.2.

The coprocessor's instruction and data pointers are intended primarily for troubleshooting, as they store the memory address of the last instruction and memory operand. The control register is used to set the numeric precision (24, 53, or 64 bits), the rounding (up, down, or truncate), and error detection (divide by zero, integer overflow). The tag bits are used to mark a data register as empty or non-empty.

Special-Purpose Registers.   The 486's special-purpose registers are shown in Figure 3.22. They remain unchanged from the 386, except for the following:

1. Five new bits have been added to CR0, primarily to allow control of the on-chip cache and coprocessor.
2. Two new bits have been added to CR3, again to allow control of the on-chip cache.
3. Three new test registers have been added for testing the cache.

Table 3.2 80387 Data Types (Courtesy of Intel Corporation)

Data Range	Precision	Formats	Most Significant Byte = Highest Addressed Byte
Word integer	$\pm10^4$	16 bits	(TWO'S COMPLEMENT) — 15 … 0
Short integer	$\pm10^9$	32 bits	(TWO'S COMPLEMENT) — 31 … 0
Long integer	$\pm10^{18}$	64 bits	(TWO'S COMPLEMENT) — 63 … 0
Packed BCD	$\pm10^{\pm18}$	18 digits	S, X, MAGNITUDE $d_{17}\ d_{16}\ d_{15}\ d_{14}\ d_{13}\ d_{12}\ d_{11}\ d_{10}\ d_9\ d_8\ d_7\ d_6\ d_5\ d_4\ d_3\ d_2\ d_1\ d_0$ — 79, 72 … 0
Single precision	$\pm10^{\pm38}$	24 bits	S, BIASED EXPONENT, SIGNIFICAND — 31, 23 … 0
Double precision	$\pm10^{\pm308}$	53 bits	S, BIASED EXPONENT, SIGNIFICAND — 63, 52 … 0
Extended precision	$\pm10^{\pm4932}$	64 bits	S, BIASED EXPONENT, I, SIGNIFICAND — 79, 64, 63 … 0

Notes:

1. S = Sign bit (0 = positive, 1 = negative)
2. d_n = Decimal digit (two per byte)
3. X = Bits have no significance; Intel387™ DX MCP ignores when loading, zeros when storing
4. ▲ = Position of implicit binary point
5. I = Integer bit of significand; stored in temporary real, implicit in single and double precision
6. Exponent Bias (normalized values):
    Single: 127 (7FH)
    Double: 1023 (3FFH)
    Extended Real: 16383 (3FFFH)
7. Packed BCD: $(-1)^s\,(D_{17}...D_0)$
8. Real: $(-1)^s(2^{E\text{-BIAS}})(F_0F_1...)$

Chip Versions

Over the years, Intel has offered five different versions of the 80486. Table 3.3 lists the distinguishing features of these chips. The DX2 and SX2 use clock *doubling* technology, in which the microprocessor core operates twice as fast as the external buses. A 486DX2 66, for example, operates internally at 66 MHz but externally at 33 MHz. The DX4 chips *triple* the bus frequency. A DX4 75 thus operates internally at 75 MHz but externally at 25 MHz.

Cyrix, AMD, and Texas Instruments also offer versions of the 486. Some of these have internal clock frequencies as high as 120 MHz.

Figure 3.22 The 80486 special-purpose registers. Three new test registers (TR3–5) have been added to allow cache testing.

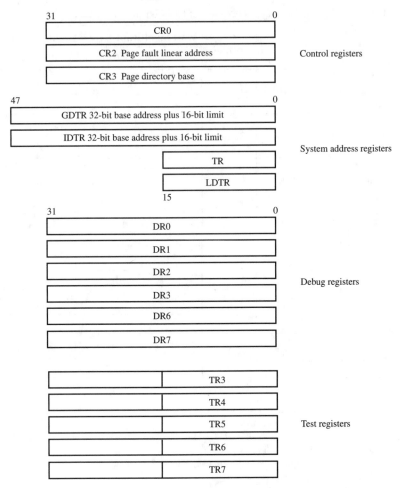

Table 3.3 80486 Processor Reference

Processor:	486DX4	486DX2	486SX2	486DX	486SX
Core Clock Frequency(MHz)	75,100	66, 50	50.00	25, 33, 50	16, 20, 25, 33
Bus Clock Frequency (MHz)	33, 25	33, 25	25.00	25, 33, 50	16, 20, 25, 33
External data bus width	32.00	32.00	32.00	32.00	32.00
Coprocessor	Builtin	Builtin	Overdrive processor required	Builtin	None
Level-1 Cache	16K	8K	8K	8K	None
V_{cc}	3.3V	5V or 3.3V	5V or 3.3V	5V or 3.3V	5V or 3.3V
iCOMP*	319, 435	231, 297	180	122, 166, 249	63, 78, 100, 136
Process (microns)	0.60	0.60	0.60	1, 0.8, 0.6	0.8, 0.6

*iCOMP stands for Intel Comparative Microprocessor Performance Index. The iCOMP Index is a weighted average of several industry-standard benchmarks.

Self-Review 3.4 (Answers on page 125)

3.4.1   Because of its _____ _____ _____ _____, the 486 is able to execute more than one instruction at a time.

3.4.2   Compared to the 386, the 486 is similar but adds two new units. These are the _____ _____ unit and the _____ _____ unit.

3.4.3   *(True/False)* In a direct mapped cache, each memory location can be stored in any cache location.

3.4.4   To determine if a memory location is stored in the cache, the _____ bits are compared with the high order memory address bits.

3.4.5   The data registers in the floating-point unit are _____ bits wide.

3.5   The Pentium

Introduction

The next step in the 80x86 microprocessor evolution is the Pentium processor. Several versions are available, including the original P60 and P66, which operate at 5V and achieve clock speeds of 60 and 66 MHz, respectively. Newer versions operate at 3.3V and achieve speeds as high as 200 MHz. While maintaining full compatibility with the 386 and 486, the Pentium offers significant enhancements over the 486. These include dual instruction pipelines, a 64-bit data bus, and separate 8K code and data caches.

In this section we:

- Draw a block diagram of the Pentium processor highlighting the bus interface, central processing, floating-point, memory management, and cache units.
- Explain the operation of the Pentium's *u* and *v* pipelines.
- Compare the various Pentium processor versions for speed, power consumption, and operating features.

Processor Model

Figure 3.23 shows the Pentium processor model. It contains the same five units shown for the 486. However, except for the memory management unit, each of these has undergone an extensive redesign.

Bus Interface Unit (BIU).   To increase the amount of data moved in a single bus cycle, the BIU's data bus width has been expanded from 32 to 64 bits. This allows 8 bytes to be read or written in one bus cycle. Special *burst bus cycles* can be run that allow four sequential read and write cycles to be performed with only a single system clock pulse per cycle. This is particularly useful for rapidly filling the cache whose line size has been expanded to 32 bytes (to accommodate these burst cycles). Like the 486, the Pentium also allows bus cycles to be *pipelined* so that the address for a new cycle can be output before the current cycle has completed.

The prefetcher now includes two separate prefetch buffers (queues). One is linked to a *branch target buffer (BTB)* that monitors the incoming instruction stream for transfer of control instructions (jumps). When such an instruction is found, the BTB predicts whether or not the branch will be taken and prefetches the instructions at that address.

Figure 3.23   Processor model for the Pentium. The BIU suplies instructions to the CPU via two pipelines called the *u* and *v* pipes. In addition, two separate 8K data and code caches are provided.

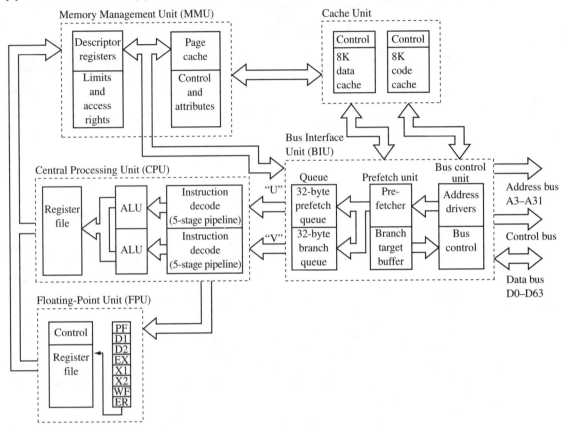

The* u *and* v *Pipes. The prefetch and queue units work together to pair instructions for the dual five-stage pipelines called the *u* and *v* pipes. The *u* pipe is capable of executing all instructions in the Pentium's processor set; the *v* pipe is restricted to simple integer instructions. It is the job of the prefetcher to sort the incoming instructions accordingly.

The two pipelines (and two ALUs) suggest that the Pentium can execute two instructions simultaneously. This is true only if special conditions are met. The primary consideration is that the two instructions must be *simple*.[13] If this condition is met, the two instructions are "paired" and move through the two pipelines in synchronism. When paired in this way, the Pentium can execute two instructions in one clock cycle. Note, however, that it is up to the programmer to arrange the instructions of the program in such a way that pairing can take place. This has become known as Pentium processor optimization.

---

[13]Simple instructions are those that move data between the various CPU registers and memory, and those that perform simple math operations such as increment and decrement.

Floating-Point Unit.   The onboard floating-point unit of the 486 has been completely redesigned for the Pentium and now includes an eight-stage pipeline. As shown in Figure 3.23, these stages are:

1. PF   Prefetch
2. D1   Instruction decode
3. D2   Address generation
4. EX   Memory and register read
5. X1   Floating-point execute stage one
6. X2   Floating-point execute stage two
7. WF   Write result to register file
8. ER   Error reporting

Tests have shown that the Pentium's FPU is as much as ten times faster than that of the 486.

Cache Unit.   The Pentium improves upon the 486's cache unit in several ways. Foremost is the organization into separate 8K data and code caches. This avoids bottlenecks within the BIU, as instructions will always be fetched from the code cache, and the data operated on by these instructions from the data cache (i.e., the data segments are cached separately from the code segments).

Each of the two caches is organized as *two-way set-associative,* with each set made up of 128 32-byte lines. This provides a higher hit rate than the 486's cache, which was organized as four-way set-associative but with just 16 bytes per line.[14] The one drawback is that each memory location maps to just two cache locations (the 486 provides four cache locations for each memory byte). This increases the probability of *thrashing.*

Programming Model

Maintaining Compatibility.   The 486's programming model presented in Figure 3.19 applies equally well to the Pentium. No new general-purpose registers have been added to the CPU or FPU. Of course this is by design, as it is in Intel's best interest to continue to support the huge software base that exists for the 80x86 processors.

Three new flags have been added:

- VIF (bit 19) *Virtual interrupt flag*
- VIP (bit 20) *Virtual interrupt pending*
- ID (bit 21) The ability to set and clear this flag indicates that the processor supports the CPUID instruction (a new Pentium instruction)

One new control register has been added (CR4). Bits in this register are very specialized and not normally used by the applications programmer. Similarly, five new bits have been added to CR0 and two new bits to CR3. These again have specialized functions such as controlling the cache and FPU.

---

[14]Using burst bus cycles, the Pentium (and 486) fill four lines of the cache in one (burst) cycle. However, with 32 bytes/line, the odds of the Pentium prefetching the next desired instruction are greater than the 486, with 16 bytes/line.

A new concept introduced with the Pentium is that of *model-specific registers (MSRs)* used to control hardware functions or monitor processor activity. The Pentium has three such registers. Two new instructions, **RDMSR** and **WRMSR** (read/write model-specific registers), are used to access these registers.

In addition to **RDMSR** and **WRMSR,** four other new instructions have been added to the Pentium, but these are intended primarily for system-level programmers. (These instructions are listed in Chapter 4.)

The Pentium Evolves

Higher Speed with Less Power.   Since the original P60 and P66 were announced in 1993, several higher speed versions of the Pentium processor have become available. In 1994, Intel offered 0.6 micron versions (the P60/66 use 0.8 micron feature sizes) with core clock frequencies of 75, 90, and 100 MHz. The corresponding bus frequencies are 50, 60, and 66 MHz, respectively.[15] These chips became known as the P75, P90, and P100.

In 1995 and 1996, 0.35 micron chips became available. This allowed core frequencies to rise to 133, 150, and 166 MHz (bus frequencies are 66, 60, and 66 MHz, respectively). Intel expects the Pentium to top out at 200 MHz.

Beginning with the P75, all of the Pentium processors use a 3.3V supply voltage. This, combined with the smaller die size due to the reduced feature sizes, allows the higher speed processors to run cooler than their (low-frequency) predecessors. The P66, for example, operates at 66 MHz and requires 3.2A of supply current (16W of power). The P100 operates at 100 MHz and draws 3.1A of supply current. However, the power required is only 10.1W because of the 3.3V power source.

Voltage Reduction Technology.   Laptop and notebook computers do not usually contain a cooling fan for internal components. As a result, significant thermal design (heat pipes, thermal sensors, heat vents) is required by system manufacturers. To help solve these problems, special versions of the Pentium are available with *voltage reduction technology (VRT)*. This is a scheme in which the external pins of the processor operate at 3.3V while the internal core operates at 2.9V. A power reduction of up to 40 percent can thus be achieved. For example, the VRT version of the P100 dissipates 5.9W maximum compared to 10.1W for the conventional part.

Dual Processors.   The newest Pentium processors are not just higher speed versions of the P60 and P66. Several new features have been added, including support for a *dual processor* system. In this mode, one chip acts as the *primary* processor and the second as the *dual* processor. The chips have been designed to share system resources (I/O and memory) in a "glueless" manner; that is, the chips are simply wired in parallel with no additional system wiring required (a *private* bus is required between the two processors to help arbitrate access to the common system buses). In fact, to the applications programmer, the two Pentiums appear as a single processor. Note, however, that it is up to the operating system to properly schedule computing tasks between the two chips. Currently the Windows NT and SCO UNIX operating systems provide this support.

---

[15]The core/bus frequency ratio is 1.5:1.

MMX. In 1997, Intel began delivering versions of the Pentium with *multimedia extensions (MMX)*. These processors have three architectural enhancements over non-MMX processors:

1. Fifty-seven new instructions have been added specifically designed for multimedia (audio, video, and graphical data) applications. Like DSPs, many of these instructions have been optimized for repetitive operations.
2. A process called *Single Instruction Multiple Data (SIMD)* allows the same function to be performed on multiple pieces of data. Because multimedia applications often require large blocks of data to be manipulated, SIMD provides a significant performance enhancement.
3. The internal cache size has been increased from 16K to 32K, increasing the likelihood that program instructions and data will be stored in the cache.

For general applications, benchmark tests show a 10–20 percent improvement over Pentium processors without MMX technology. This increases to a nearly 70 percent improvement when multimedia specific applications are considered.

Applications for MMX processors include decompression of audio and video files. Indeed, software video players may become a reality. Some vendors are looking into replacing conventional modems and sound cards with MMX-driven software equivalents.

Self-Review 3.5 (Answers on page 125)

3.5.1 The width of the Pentium's address bus is _____ bits; its data bus width is _____.

3.5.2 Two instructions can be executed simultaneously by the Pentium, but only if they are _____.

3.5.3 Each line in the Pentium's code and data caches is _____ bytes wide.

3.5.4 *(True/False)* When operated at 100 MHz, the P100 consumes less power than the 60 MHz P60.

3.6   The Pentium Pro

Introduction

There are three ways to build a faster microprocessor: (1) Increase the number of transistors; (2) increase the clock speed; or (3) increase the number of instructions executed per clock cycle. With the Pentium Pro processor (previously code-named *P6*), Intel has accomplished all three. Incorporating separate processor and level-two cache chips in the same (dual-cavity) package, the Pentium Pro processor chip incorporates over 5.5 million transistors. The 256K level-two cache chip requires an additional 15.5 million transistors (31 million in the 512K version). With 0.35 micron minimum feature sizes, clock speeds greater than 200 MHz can be achieved. Finally, using a totally redesigned central processing unit with twelve-stage pipeline and three separate processing engines, the Pentium Pro can execute as many as three instructions per single clock cycle. In this section we will:

• Compare the processing cycle of the Pentium Pro with traditional sequential fetch and execute processors.

- Draw a block diagram of the Pentium Pro processor and explain the role of the bus interface, central processing, memory management, floating-point, cache, and APIC units.
- Compare the performance of the Pentium Pro with the other processors in the 80x86 family.

Overview

Dual-Cavity Design.   The Pentium Pro is the first Intel processor to incorporate two silicon die in the same package. (A photograph of the "chip" is shown in Figure 1.10.) The larger die is the processor, the smaller a level-two cache. Two cache sizes are available: 256K and 512K. The multimodule chip arrangement not only simplifies system design, but also allows the processor core to communicate with the level-two cache at full speed.

Dynamic Execution.   Table 3.4 traces the evolution of the various 80x86 processors and shows the "tricks" the Intel designers have employed to offset the so-called *"von Neumann bottleneck."*[16] The techniques used in the Pentium Pro are called *dynamic execution* and represent the most radical departure from the classic von Neumann architecture to date. Three techniques are involved.

The first is *multiple branch prediction*. This technology attacks the problem of predicting the address of the next instruction when a conditional branch occurs (jump if not zero, for example). Using a 512 entry branch target buffer and a two-level adaptive algorithm, the Pentium Pro is able to predict this address with 90 percent accuracy.

The second and third techniques are called *data flow analysis with speculative execution*. To understand this concept, consider the following program segment:

```
mov    ax,[memory_location_1]
add    cx,ax
add    dx,ax
dec    si,di
```

Assume the first instruction causes a cache miss. A traditional processor will be *stalled* as it waits for its bus interface unit to access the data and return. The Pentium Pro, however, looks *ahead* into the instruction stream in search of a new instruction to execute. In this example, the second and third instructions depend on the outcome of the first and thus are not executable at this time. The fourth instruction, however, is executable. The Pentium Pro thus executes this instruction but does *not* commit the result to permanent machine state (i.e., the programmer-visible registers). Instead, the results are stored back in the instruction pool awaiting in-order retirement.

The Pentium Pro processor thus executes instructions *speculatively,* depending on their *readiness to execute*—not their program order. Using data flow analysis, the processor is able to look 20–30 instructions ahead of the current instruction pointer. The final result is a CPU that is seldom, if ever, stalled for instructions to execute.

---

[16]As discussed in Chapter 1, von Neumann developed the concept of the stored program computer. The basic processing cycle consists of fetching an instruction from memory and then executing that instruction. Because the program instructions must be executed one by one in sequence, a bottleneck occurs when the processor must wait while new instructions and data are fetched from memory.

Table 3.4 80x86 Processor Evolution

Processor	External Data Bus Width	Architecture	Processing Cycle	Instructions/ Clock Cycle	Maximum* Clock Speed
8086	16 bits	CISC with separate bus interface and execution units. Six-byte instruction queue.	Fetch and execute cycles overlap.	1:4	10 MHz
80386	32 bits	Real and Protected modes with 32-bit memory management.	Reduced instruction cycle times.	1:2	33 MHz
80486	32 bits	RISC like with 5-stage pipeline and onboard 8K cache and floating-point unit.	Parts of five instructions move through the pipeline at once.	1:1	100 MHz
Pentium	64 bits	Two five stage pipelines with branch prediction logic. Redesigned FPU with 8-stage pipeline. Separate 8K code and data caches.	Dual pipelines allow two instructions to be executed simultaneously.	2:1	166 MHz
Pentium Pro	64 bits	Three instruction decoders with 12-stage pipeline. Out of order execution. Onboard level-one and -two cache.	Instructions broken into micro-ops that move through the pipeline in a fetch/ decode; dispatch/execute; retire sequence.	3:1	200 MHz

*Higher speed versions of the Pentium and Pentium Pro processors will likely be introduced.

Table 3.5   Processor Performance

Processor	SPECint92 Benchmark
Pentium Pro 150 MHz	276
Pentium Pro 133 MHz	200
Pentium 100 MHz	122
80486 DX4 100 MHz	55
80486 DX 33 MHz	22
80386 DX 33 MHz	9

High Integration.   The Pentium Pro sets new standards of integration for the 80x86 processors. In addition to the floating-point unit and level-one cache previously included with the 80486 and later processors, the Pentium Pro includes a level-two cache controller and *Advanced Programmable Interrupt Controller (APIC).* The latter replaces the 8259A chips typically required in previous-generation chip sets.[17]

Performance.   With on-chip level-one and level-two caches, dynamic execution, and high integration, we expect the Pentium Pro processor to offer the highest performance of any 80x86 processor to date. This is borne out in Table 3.5, which compares various 80x86 processors using the SPECint92 benchmark (a benchmark that measures system performance using real applications).

Power Consumption.   The Pentium Pro operates at 3.1V V_{CC} (150 MHz version) and 3.3V for all other versions. The power consumption varies accordingly—29.2W maximum for the 150 MHz part to 35W maximum for the 200 MHz part.

Processor Model

Superpipelined.   Figure 3.24(a) shows the processor model for the Pentium Pro. Compared to the Pentium, only two new units have been added—the level-two cache and APIC. However, the central processing unit (CPU) has been extensively redesigned and now consists of the Fetch/Decode Unit, the Instruction Pool, the Dispatch/Execute Unit, and the Retire Unit. In addition, the five-stage pipeline of the Pentium has been replaced with a twelve-stage unit in the Pentium Pro.

Instructions begin their journey through the pipeline via the BIU and level-one cache [see Figure 3.24(b)]. The Branch Target Buffer stages (BTB0 and BTB1) continually examine the instruction stream and advise the BIU to fetch *out-of-order* instructions, as described previously. The Instruction Fetch Units (IF0, IF1, and IF2) assembles a line's worth of information for the decoders.

The three decoders break the instructions into uniform (RISC-like) *micro-ops,* each with two source operands and one destination operand. Like the Pentium before it, one of these decoders is designed to handle complex instructions; the others handle simple instructions. Three micro-ops are output to the instruction pool per clock cycle.

---

[17]Interrupts and the 8259A are discussed in detail in Chapter 9.

What Is a Benchmark?

Computer manufacturers use benchmark programs to measure the performance of a computer system (System Benchmarks) or of a component in that system (Component Benchmarks) such as the processor, disk subsystem, video card, or main memory.

The performance of large computers has traditionally been measured in MIPs (millions of instructions executed per second). However, this can be unreliable due to the dissimilar architecture of the processors in the machines being compared. As a result, many *synthetic* benchmarks have been developed to approximate the behavior of typical applications. Two popular tests are the Whetstone benchmark and the Dhrystone benchmark.

Whetstone. This benchmark was published in 1976 by Curnow and Wichmann from the National Physical laboratory in Britain. Originally released in ALGOL 60—an early block-structured programming language—it measures the time to execute integer and floating-point arithmetic instructions as well as the time to evaluate "if" statements. The name Whetstone is derived from the name of the ALGOL compiler used by the authors. As a high percentage of floating-point operations are included, it is most often used to represent numerical programs.

Dhrystone. This benchmark was released in 1984 by R.P. Weicker. It was originally coded in ADA, but PASCAL and C versions are also available. The Dhrystone is a synthetic benchmark consisting of 12 procedures with 94 statements. Much of the execution time is spent in string functions, and no floating-point operations are included.

Microcomputer Benchmarks. Many different microcomputer benchmarks have been developed. Some, such as Ziff-Davis' CPUmark and Symantec's Norton SI, measure processor performance only. Others, SYSmark/NT, for example, measure entire system performance when running real applications (Microsoft Office, Lotus Smart Suite, Borland Paradox, etc.).

SPEC. Standard Performace Evaluation Corporation has published a widely accepted CPU, memory system, and compiler code generation benchmark called SPECXX (a recent version is SPEC95). It is composed of two collections: CINT95 and CFP95. The first measures integer performance using eight different benchmarks. The latter measures floating-point performance using ten different benchmarks.

iCOMP. Many users believe that the speed of their processor in megahertz is a linear measure of that processor's performance. Certainly this number is important, but it is not necessarily a good measure of CPU performance. A 100 MHz 486 will provide inferior performance to a 100 MHz Pentium due to the latter's dual pipelines. Intel developed the iCOMP index in an attempt to come up with a single number that could be used to compare the various 80x86 processors. Four separate industry standard benchmarks are included: CPUmark32, Norton SI32, SPEC95, and the Intel Media Benchmark (a collection of multimedia benchmarks including audio and video playback, image processing, wave sample rate conversion, and 3-D geometry). The iCOMP ratings for several versions of the Pentium and Pentium Pro processors are shown below.

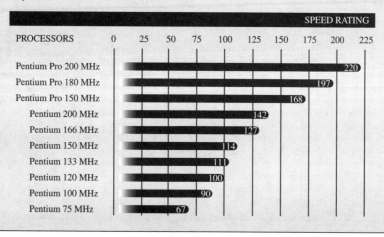

The Dispatch/Execute unit selects micro-ops from the instruction pool depending on their *readiness* for execution; that is, are the operands and execution resources needed by that micro-op available? If so, the Reservation Station sends that micro-op to the resource, where it is executed. As shown in Figure 3.24, there are five ports on the Reservation Station, allowing access to the integer and floating-point execution units and to the load and store Address Generation Units.

The Retirement Unit puts the original program back together by examining the instruction pool for *completed* micro-ops. These are then *retired,* in the order of the original program, thus committing their results to permanent machine state.

Fetch and Execute?   Traditional processors *sequentially* fetch instructions from memory and then execute those instructions. Based on the above, the Pentium Pro is *nontraditional.* The fetch and execute cycle becomes:

1. Fetch and decode the instructions into micro-ops.
2. Dispatch and execute the micro-ops *out-of-order,* depending on their readiness for execution.
3. Retire and commit the results to permanent machine state when all resources become available.

Figure 3.24   (a) Processor model for the Pentium Pro. The CPU has been totally redesigned and features three processing "engines" and an instruction pool. (b) Detail of CPU model.

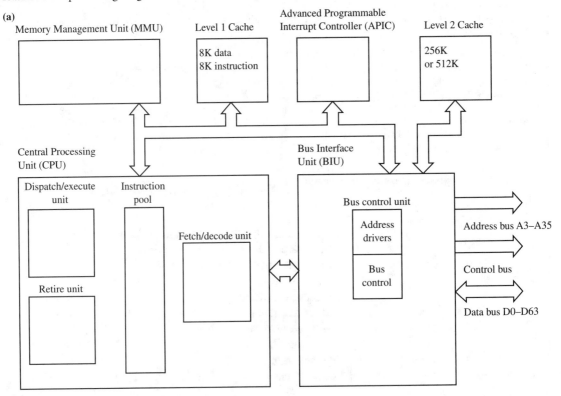

Figure 3.24   *(continued)*

(b)

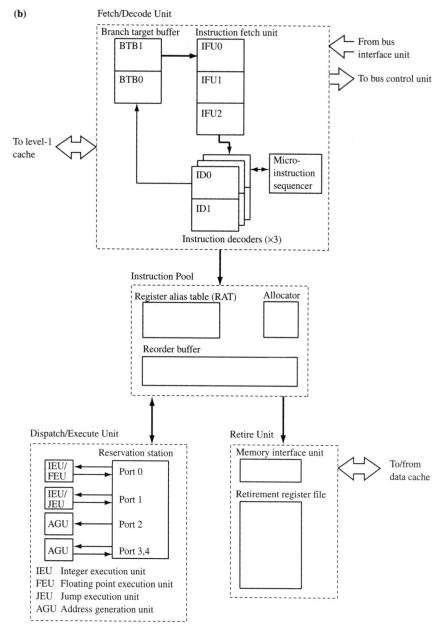

With its nontraditional architecture, the Pentium Pro becomes more of a *data flow machine,* continually processing instructions regardless of their original program order.

Level-One and Level-Two Caches.   The level-one cache remains 16K—8K for data and 8K for program instructions. However, like the level-two cache, the level-one cache is *nonblocking*. This means the processor will not be stalled by a cache miss. When a miss occurs, the processor continues executing other instructions while the new data is read into the cache.

With previous-generation processors the level-two cache has been included on the system board and operates at the bus speed of the processor. With the Pentium Pro, the cache is connected internally to the processor via a 64-bit bus. In this design, the cache operates at the core speed of the processor.

New Architectural Features

New Instructions.   The Pentium Pro offers several new architectural features not present in the Pentium processor. Although there are no new general-purpose flags or registers, five new (but highly specialized) instructions have been added. Three are specific to the CPU and two are used by the floating-point unit. (Chapter 4 provides the details.)

New Registers.   The Pentium first introduced the concept of *model-specific registers* used to control and monitor unique processor hardware functions. The Pentium Pro increases the number of these registers from three, with the Pentium, to well over 100. The **RDMSR** and **WRMSR** instructions are used to access these registers.

The Pentium Pro also introduces *memory-type range registers (MTRRs)*. These are used to optimize memory operations by allowing the processor to create an internal memory map describing the cacheability of various physical memory locations. For example, if the processor "knows" that a certain block of memory is specified as *write-through,* all writes to that block of memory will automatically be directed to the bus and the cache updated accordingly. The MTRR registers thus simplify hardware designs.

The Pentium Pro also includes two *performance-monitoring counters* that can be used to monitor over 100 different types of events, such as the number of instructions decoded, number of interrupts received, or number of cache loads. Two MSRs are used to store this information, which can then be read or written using the **RDMSR** and **WRMSR** instructions, respectively.

New Memory Management Features.   Finally, three new memory management features have been added. All are dependent on the processor operating with paging enabled. The first is called *physical memory address extension*. When enabled, the amount of physical memory within which pages may be mapped is increased from 4 GB to 64 GB. This is done by adding four additional address lines, thus creating a 36-bit address bus. Pentium Pro programs are still restricted to 32-bit addresses (the internal register sizes have not changed), but with the larger physical memory space, more programs can be kept in memory (via pages) than before.[18]

The second feature is support for larger page sizes. Previous 80x86 processors were limited to 4K pages. The Pentium Pro supports 4K, 2 MB, and 4 MB page sizes. By placing the operating system kernel in a 2 or 4 MB page, for example, the likelihood of a page miss is reduced and the system performance is improved.

---

[18]Assuming you can afford to purchase 64 GB of memory!

The final new feature is the *Page Global Enable flag*. When this flag is set, frequently used pages can be marked *global*. Global pages are not normally *flushed* (written to disk when a new task requires memory space). This again improves system performance by avoiding the reloading of these pages.

Glueless Four-Way Symmetric Processing. The Pentium Pro is designed with scalability in mind. Up to four processors can be interconnected *gluelessly*; that is, no additional logic is required other than the sockets for the additional processors. This makes the Pentium Pro a popular choice for high-performance file servers.

As mentioned in Chapter. 1 Intel's Scaled Systems Division is developing a teraflops supercomputer that will incorporate two Pentium Pro processors at each of 4500 system nodes. Projected performance is expected to exceed 1.8 teraflops.

Native Signal Processing (NSP). The floating-point unit of the Pentium Pro is designed to accelerate multiply-accumulate sequences typically associated with digital signal processing chips used in multimedia computers. By incorporating this capability onboard (natively), the design of dedicated multimedia subsystems (modems and sound cards) is greatly simplified.

Self-Review 3.6 (Answers on page 125)

3.6.1 The term _____ _____ is applied to describe the Pentium Pro's use of multiple branch prediction, data flow analysis, and speculative execution.

3.6.2 Unlike conventional processors, the Pentium Pro is able to execute instructions _____-of-_____.

3.6.3 The Pentium Pro can execute _____ instructions per clock cycle.

3.6.4 The Pentium uses a _____-stage pipeline. The Pentium Pro uses a _____-stage pipeline.

3.6.5 The Pentium Pro processor is *scaleable*. What does this mean?

Chapter 3 Self-Test

1. Under what conditions will the contents of the 8086's queue hold the "wrong" op-codes?
2. *(True/False)* Because of its pipelined architecture, the 8086 can execute several instructions at the same time.
3. List all 8086 registers that can be accessed as bytes or as words.
4. The 8086 instruction **MOV [BP], CX** transfers a copy of the *(byte/word)* in register CX to the memory location whose address is stored in register BP.
5. *(True/False)* Because of its segmented memory, the 8086 requires a minimum of 4 segments × 64K/segment, or 256K of memory.
6. Which of the following are valid 8086 segment base addresses?
   (a) FFFFFH
   (b) A0FF0H
   (c) 90000H
   (d) 10008H
7. If CS = 2DF6H and IP = 0A43H, compute the *physical* address of the next 8086 instruction fetch.

8. In question 4, the memory address stored in register BP will be interpreted as coming from the _____ segment.

9. Which of the following 386 features are available only when the processor is operating in Protected Mode?

  (a) Memory segments as small as 1 byte or as large as 4 GB.

  (b) Six different active memory segments.

  (c) Multiple 8086 programs running together in memory, each limited to 1 MB of address space.

  (d) General-purpose data registers as wide as 32 bits.

  (e) Virtual memory to support programs as large as 64 TB.

10. When operated in Protected Mode, physical addresses are computed by adding the 32-bit _____ from the instruction to the 32-bit base address of the segment stored in a _____ table.

11. A 386 program with PL = 3 can access a program at PL = 0 by using a _____ _____.

12. List four factors that make the 486 faster than the 386 for a given clock speed.

13. The 486 cache is organized as _____ 2K caches, each with _____ lines and _____ bytes per line.

14. *(True/False)* Each external memory location can be cached to any one of four locations in the 486 cache.

15. How does the 486 cache decide which line to replace when all lines are storing valid data?

16. List four factors that make the Pentium faster than the 486 for a given clock speed.

17. What does it mean when Pentium instructions are *paired*? What types of instructions can be paired?

18. The code and data caches in the Pentium are both two-way set-associative. This means that each DRAM memory location maps to _____ different cache locations.

19. List two new *units* available in the Pentium Pro processor but not available in the Pentium processor.

20. Traditional processors fetch and execute instructions *sequentially.* How does the Pentium Pro differ from this?

Analysis and Design Questions

Section 3.1

3.1   The Intel manual for the 8086 indicates that "a series of fast executing instructions can drain the queue and increase instruction execution time." Explain this statement.

3.2   Assume the 16-bit 8086 flag word = 0AC5H. Determine the values of the six status flags and the three control flags.

3.3   Determine the contents of register AL and the six status flags after the following 8086 instructions are executed:

```
MOV AL,4CH   ;Load register AL with 4CH
ADD AL,3EH   ;Add 3EH to the contents of register AL leaving the result in AL.
```

3.4   Refer to Figure 3.4. If register SI is pointing to memory location 1003H, determine the value of the following:

  (a) SI

  (b) [SI]

Section 3.2

3.5   What is the *logical* code segment address corresponding to *physical* address 5A3F7H? Assume CS=5822H.

3.6   Which 8086 registers, when used as memory pointers, cannot have their default memory segment assignments overridden? *Hint:* Refer to Table 3.1.

3.7   Assuming CS=0000, DS=2E98H, SS=A010H, and ES=B000H, draw an 8086 memory map similar to Figure 3.9 showing the starting and ending addresses of each memory segment.

Section 3.3

3.8   Match the expression in Column I with the term inColumn II. No letter is used more than once.

	Column I	*Column II*
3.8.1	_____ 1 MB address space	a. FS and GS
3.8.2	_____ Next memory address output during current bus cycle.	b. TLB
		c. Protected Mode
3.8.3	_____ 64 TB address space	d. Real Mode
3.8.4	_____ Bits 0–15 of ECX	e. CX
3.8.5	_____ Data segments	f. CPL
3.8.6	_____ Base address of descriptor tables	g. GDTR and LDTR
3.8.7	_____ 13-bit index to a descriptor	h. Instruction queue
3.8.8	_____ Speeds up page look-up process	i. Address pipelining
3.8.9	_____ Privilege level of the current program	j. Protected Mode Segment register
3.8.10	_____ Used by less trusted programs to access more trusted programs register	k. Virtual memory
		l. Call gate

3.9   At any given time, the 80386 has _____ active segments; however, when operated in Protected Mode, _____ different segments can be defined. (*Hint:* Think about the size of the descriptor tables GDT and LDT.)

3.10   In Figure 3.13, assume register DS points to a descriptor that in turn points to a segment base of 4EF82C90H. Calculate the physical address of the memory operand accessed by the instruction:

```
MOV AL,[09F04D3AH]   ;Move a copy of memory location 09F04D3AH to register AL
```

3.11   Assume segment register FS is to be pointed at global descriptor number 17. If the RPL = 2, determine the necessary contents of this register in hex.

Section 3.4

3.12   Calculate the total number of bits of SRAM storage required to implement the 80486 internal cache. Don't forget the TAG and LRU SRAM.

3.13   Draw the block diagram for an external 256K one-way direct mapped cache for the 80486. In your diagram, show the width of the data and TAG SRAMs. Specify the number of index and TAG bits required. Assume the full (32-bit) address space of the 486 is to be cached.

3.14   The 486 uses three LRU bits (B0–B2) to determine which line (L0–L3) of the cache to replace when all lines are full. B0–B3 are set as follows:
        (a) If the most recent access was to L0 or L1, B0=1, else B0=0
        (b) If the most recent access to L0:L1 was L0, B1=1, else B1=0.
        (c) If the most recent access to L2:L3 was L2, B2=1, else B2=0.
        Draw a flowchart showing how to test B0–B2 to determine which line of the cache should be replaced. Your test should begin with bit B0. If the LRU bits = 010 (B0–B2), which line of the cache was least recently used?

Section 3.5

3.15   Complete the following table by placing an X in the appropriate column if that processor meets the specified condition.

	Condition	Processor				
		8086	**80386**	**80486DX4**	**P60/66**	**P90/100**
(a)	20-bit address bus					
(b)	Separate code and data caches					
(c)	16-byte prefetch queue					
(d)	General-purpose registers are 32 bits wide					
(e)	Onboard floating-point unit					
(f)	Real Mode operation only					
(g)	Segments may be as large as 4 GB					
(h)	32-bit data bus width					
(i)	3.3V supply voltage					
(j)	Internal cache					
(k)	Five-stage execution pipeline					

3.16   Draw a diagram of the Pentium's data or code cache similar to Figure 3.20. Be sure your diagram shows the width of the cache (in bytes), the width of the TAG address (in bits), and the number of lines per cache set. The LRU and valid bits need not be shown.

Section 3.6

3.17   One way of improving a microprocessor's performance is to increase the number of instructions executed per clock cycle. Complete the table below, indicating the number of instructions executed per clock cycle and the architectural feature of the processors that permits this. The first entry is given as an example.

Processor	Instructions/Clock Cycle	Architecture
80486	1	Five-stage pipeline (one stage per clock pulse)
Pentium		
Pentium Pro		

3.18   The Pentium Pro processor can execute instructions out of order. Assume the first instruction in the 80x86 program shown below causes a cache miss. Which of the remaining instructions could be executed (out of order) by this processor?

```
mov    al,[1000]
inc    al
sub    bx,ax
add    cl,dl
mov    [si],b
```

Self-Review Answers

3.1.1   execution, bus interface

3.1.2   overlap

3.1.3   The instruction requires a memory operand not in the queue, or the queue is full.

3.1.4   The contents of memory pointed to by register DI is moved to register CH.

3.1.5   DL and DH

3.1.6   trap

3.1.7   AL=00; CF=1; PF=1 (0 is considered even parity); AF=1; ZF=1; SF=0; OF=0 ($-1 + 1 = 0$)

3.2.1   False—The 8088 can only access memory bytes.

3.2.2   even

3.2.3   64K, offsets, logical

3.2.4   False—The segment address must be divisible by 16.

3.2.5   95D3FH

3.2.6   Data

3.3.1   64K, 4 GB

3.3.2   Bus interface unit, central processing unit, memory management unit

3.3.3   EBX (full 32 bits), BX (low 16 bits), BL (low 8 bits), BH (bits 8–15)

3.3.4   segment base address, segment limit, and access rights

3.3.5   0, 1, or 2

3.4.1   Five-stage instruction pipeline

3.4.2   Floating-point unit and cache memory

3.4.3   False. Each memory location is mapped to one specific cache location.

3.4.4   TAG

3.4.5   80

3.5.1   32, 64

3.5.2   simple

3.5.3   32

3.5.4   True

3.6.1   dynamic execution

3.6.2   out-of-order

3.6.3   3

3.6.4   5, 12

3.6.5   As many as four processors can be wired together to form a multiprocessing system.

4   Introduction to 80x86 Programming

According to the cover of the 1975 issue of *Popular Electronics* magazine, the MITS (Micro Instrumentation and Telemetry Systems) Altair was "The World's First Minicomputer Kit to Rival Commercial Models." Designed around Intel's 8-bit 8080 microprocessor, it came with 256 bytes of memory, but no input or output devices besides front-panel switches and LEDs. The cost was $398 for a kit version and $498 for an assembled model. The machine was an immediate success: Hobbyists lined up for the opportunity to purchase their own personal computers. Within three months, MITS had a backlog of 4000 orders—not bad, considering the company hoped to break even by selling 200 units. (Photo courtesy of Smithsonian)

Outline

Objectives

After completing this chapter you should be able to:

1. Explain the difference between an instruction op-code and an operand.
2. List the different ways the 80x86 processors access memory operands.

3. Compare 80x86 16- and 32-bit instructions.
4. List the major instruction groups of the 80x86 processors.
5. Create an 8086 machine language program in COM format using DEBUG.
6. Use DEBUG to examine and change the contents of a CPU register or memory location.
7. Trace the execution of an 8086 program line by line using DEBUG.
8. Show the structure of MS-DOS and explain the roles of the BIOS and the MS-DOS kernel.
9. Explain the difference between hardware and software interrupts.
10. Provide a list of standard interrupt vectors for an 80x86 computer running MS-DOS.
11. Use DEBUG to write a program that accesses the BIOS services and MS-DOS functions.

Overview

This chapter introduces the software side of the 80x86 processors. We begin by identifying the op-code and operand forms of an instruction. The different ways of accessing memory—the addressing modes—are covered next. Finally, a table listing all of the instructions available with the 80x86 processors is given.

To avoid the feeling that you are simply "reading the dictionary," we introduce DEBUG as a tool for writing machine language programs. A simple multiplication program is developed as an example. The chapter concludes by examining the MS-DOS and PC-DOS operating systems. In this section you will learn how to access the BIOS services and DOS functions to control the hardware of the PC.

4.1   80x86 Instruction Set

Introduction

The instruction set of a microprocessor is a list of all of the software instructions the processor can execute. The 80x86 processors have been designed to be *backwards compatible*. This means that each new generation of microprocessors can execute all of the instructions of its predecessor. In this way, users can be assured that their existing software will continue to run, even as new microprocessors are developed.

In this section we:

• Explain the difference between an instruction op-code and an operand.
• List the different ways the 80x86 processors access memory operands.
• Compare 80x86 16- and 32-bit instructions.
• List the major instruction groups of the 80x86 processors.

Instruction Forms

Op-Codes and Operands.   Computer instructions are made up of an *operation code (op-code)* and a set of *operands*. The op-code identifies the action to be taken; the operands identify the source and destination of the data operated on. Op-codes are usually written in an abbreviated form called a *mnemonic*. Move, for example, becomes MOV, increment is INC, jump becomes JMP, and so on. The operands identify CPU registers, memory locations, or I/O ports. The complete form of an instruction is:

```
op-code    destination operand, source operand
```

The instruction MOV AL,BL is thus interpreted as moving a copy of register BL into register AL.[1] 80x86 processors may have as few as zero operands, and as many as three. Here are a few examples and their word descriptions.

```
HLT               ;zero operands (halt the processor)
INC  AX           ;one operand (add 1 register AX)
MOV  AX,100       ;two operands (store 100 in register AX)
SHLD DX,AX,4      ;three operands (shift register AX four bits
                   left into register DX)
```

Note that each instruction has an op-code that indicates the action to be taken (halt, increment, move, or shift left) and a set of operands that identifies the source of the data operated on and its destination. Sometimes there is no data to operate on (HLT), and sometimes the source and destination are the same (INC AX).

Immediate Addressing Mode. The 80x86 processors have several different ways of identifying the operands. The most straightforward is to supply the data as part of the instruction. This is called the *immediate* addressing mode.

```
ADD AL,3CH    ;Add 3CH to register AL[2]
```

Register Addressing Mode. Often the source and destination are separate CPU registers. This is called the *register* addressing mode.

```
MOV AL,BL     ;Move a copy of register BL into register AL
```

When using this mode, the size of the operands must *match.* The following instructions are all *invalid.*

```
MOV CH,100H   ;Data too large for an 8-bit register
MOV AL,BX     ;Can't move 16 bits into an 8-bit register
MOV BX,AL     ;Can't move 8 bits into a 16-bit register
MOV CX,EAX    ;Can't move 32 bits into a 16-bit register
```

Direct Addressing Mode.   When a memory location is to be referenced, its *offset* address must be specified. One way of doing this is to supply the address as part of the instruction. This is called the *direct* addressing mode.

```
MOV CL,[20H]    ;Move the contents of memory location 20H
                 into register CL
```

Note the brackets around 20h. These are used to show that we mean the contents of memory location 20H and not the immediate data 20H.[3] Contrast this with the immediate

---

[1]Looking at the instruction, it is tempting to describe it as "Move AL to BL." However, this is backwards. Instead, visualize an equal sign between the two operands and view the instruction as an assignment operation in BASIC; that is, AL = BL.

[2]The letter *H* is used to make it clear that 3C should be interpreted as a hexadecimal number.

[3]Recall that when general data is accessed, the data segment is used. Therefore, in this example, 20H is interpreted as the offset address in the data segment.

mode instruction MOV CL,20H, which loads register CL with 20H, *not* the contents of memory location 20H.

8-, 16-, and 32-Bit Memory Operands.   Just as the size of the *register operands* must match, so too the *memory operand* sizes must match. In the previous example, because register CL is 8 bits wide, we interpret the memory address 20H as representing the *byte* at this location. However, when used with the instruction MOV CX,[20H], the address is interpreted as the *word* beginning at address 20H (because the destination operand, register CX, is a word). Similarly, the instruction MOV ECX, [20H] accesses the doubleword beginning at address 20H. Figure 4.1 diagrams these three instructions. Note that, in all cases, the least significant byte of the data is always stored in the starting memory address. This is called *little endian* format: The "little" end of the number is stored first.

For some instructions, the size of the memory operand is not clear.

```
INC [20H]    ;Byte, word, or doubleword at 20H?
```

For this instruction, there is no CPU register the size of the memory operand can be inferred from. In this case, the BYTE PTR, WORD PTR, and DWORD PTR operators must be specified.

```
INC BYTE PTR[20H]     ;Increment the byte at 20H
INC WORD PTR[20H]     ;Increment the word at 20H
INC DWORD PTR[20H]    ;Increment the doubleword at 20H
```

Register Indirect Addressing Modes.   The direct addressing mode has the disadvantage of "locking" the memory address into the instruction. A more flexible scheme is to let a CPU register store the (offset) memory address. This is called the *register indirect* addressing mode.

```
MOV SI,20H    ;First point register SI at memory location 20H
MOV CL,[SI]   ;Move the contents of memory pointed to by
               register SI into register CL
```

The brackets are used to indicate that register SI should be interpreted as a memory pointer. Figure 4.2 diagrams this instruction. One caution: When registers are used as memory pointers, the 8086 is restricted to using registers BX, BP, SI, and DI. This restriction does not apply to the 386 and later processors.[4]

Figure 4.1 The memory operand size must match the CPU register size. In this example, all three instructions reference memory location 20H, but different data is accessed for each.

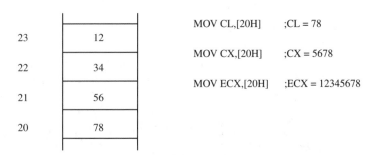

------

[4]When they are operated in Real Mode, this restriction applies to these processors as well.

Figure 4.2   The register indirect addressing mode uses a CPU register to specify the address of the memory operand. This example diagrams the instruction MOV AL,[SI].

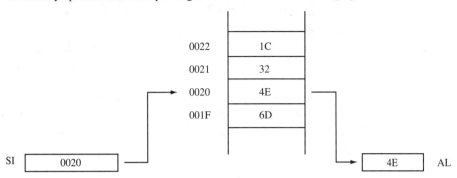

The Default Memory Segment.   Recall that the 80x86 processors partition memory into six segments, called the code, data, stack, extra, F, and G segments. Every instruction that references memory defaults to one of these six segments. (This was shown previously in Table 3.1.) The instruction MOV CL,[SI], for example, accesses the data byte pointed to by register SI in the *data* segment. However, the similar instruction MOV CL,[SP] accesses the data byte pointed to by register SP in the *stack* segment.

Example 4.1

Assume an 8086 processor executes the instructions (a) MOV CL,[SI] and (b) MOV CL,[SP]. Compute the physical address of the memory operands, asuming SI = 0100H, SS = E010H, and DS = 1A00H.

Solution
(a) The default segment is DS. The physical address can therefore be written as DS:[SI] = 1A000H + 0100H = 1A100H.
(b) The default segment is SS. The physical address can therefore be written as SS:[SI] = E0100H + 0100H = E0200H.

16-Bit vs. 32-Bit Instructions.   In Chapter 2 we learned that the 80286 and above processors can be operated in Real or Protected Mode. Real Mode restricts the processor to 64K memory segments, while Protected Mode allows segments as large as 4 GB. Accordingly, 80x86 processors can accommodate two types of program instructions: those that use 16-bit memory addresses *(16-bit instructions)* and those that use 32-bit memory addresses *(32-bit instructions)*. The first step in writing an 80x86 program, therefore, is to decide if the code is to be placed in a 16- or 32-bit memory segment. In assembly language this is done via the pseudo-op USE16 or USE32. This parameter tells the assembler to generate 16-bit (or 32-bit) instruction codes as the *default*.[5]

---

[5]For example, in a 16-bit segment, the instruction MOV BX,CX has the hex instruction codes 89 CB, and the instruction MOV EBX,ECX the codes 66 89 CB. 66 is called the *operand-size prefix*. It is required to override the (16-bit) default. If placed in a 32-bit segment, the MOV BX,CX instruction will require the override. The assembler generates this prefix automatically.

The above paragraph might lead you to believe that none of the 32-bit registers are accessible in a 16-bit segment (Real Mode). This is not the case. Consider the following instructions, which are all valid in Real or Protected Mode:

```
INC ECX              ;Add 1 to the contents of register ECX
SUB EDX,EBX          ;Subtract the contents of register EBX from
                      the contents of register EDX
MOV ESI,12345678H    ;Load register ESI with the 32-bit number 12345678H
```

The reason? Although each instruction accesses one or two 32-bit CPU registers, none of the instructions reference actual memory locations. The following instruction is *invalid* in a 16-bit memory segment because it uses a 32-bit memory address.

```
MOV AL,[20000000H]    ;Memory address cannot exceed 16 bits
                       in a (Real Mode) 64K segment
```

32-bit registers can be used as memory pointers in a 64K segment, but they must store a number less than or equal to FFFFH (the maximum for a 16-bit number).

```
MOV AL,[ESI]    ;Valid in a 64K segment only if ESI <= FFFFH
```

Similarly, in a 4 GB segment, 32-bit memory offset addresses are required. The following instruction is therefore *invalid* in such a segment:

```
MOV AL,[SI]    ;Memory pointer must be 32 bits long to
                access data in a (Protected Mode) 4 GB segment.
```

Instead, register SI should be replaced with ESI to allow a 32-bit memory address.

```
MOV AL,[ESI]    ;ESI allows access to all locations
                 in a 4 GB segment
```

Data Arrays.   High-level languages often store data in *arrays*. A variation of the register indirect addressing mode can be used to access individual elements in such arrays. Figure 4.3 illustrates an array beginning at address 0600H. Assume element four in the array (at address 0604H) is to be accessed;[6] the following code can be used:

```
MOV BX,0600H     ;BX points to array starting address
MOV AL,[BX+4]    ;Retrieve array element four
```

For 32-bit instructions, any CPU register can be used to point to the array starting address. The displacement value (four in the above example) is a 32-bit two's complement number and ranges from –2,147,483,648 to +2,147,483,647. If 16-bit instructions are used, only registers BX, BP, SI, and DI are allowed, and the displacement (limited to a 16-bit two's complement number) ranges from –32,768 to +32,767. This is called the *base plus displacement addressing mode.*

Often the data in an array is organized into *records,* with several data elements per record. Figure 4.4 shows an example where element three of record four is to be accessed. The following code can be used.

```
MOV BX,0600H        ;BX points to array starting address
MOV SI,0010H        ;SI points to record four
MOV AL,[BX+SI+3]    ;Retrieve element three
```

---

[6]Note that because the array begins with element 0, element four corresponds to the fifth location in the array.

Figure 4.3 The instruction MOV AL,[BX+4] can be used to access element four in a data array whose base address is stored in register BX.

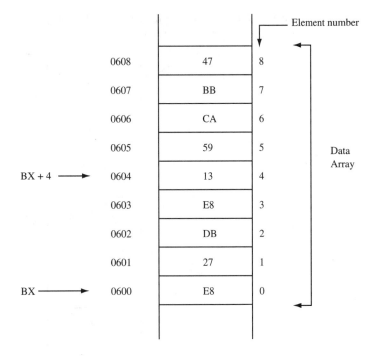

In this example, register BX is considered the *base* address, register SI the *index* address, and three is the *displacement*. The sum of the three address components is:

$$base + index + displacement = 0600H + 0010H + 0003H = 0613H$$

The same 16- and 32-bit restrictions apply as given in the previous example, with the addition that register ESP is not allowed for the index address.

Scaling.   Often the data stored in an array is organized as a byte, word (two bytes), doubleword (four bytes) or quad word (eight bytes). The index address of a particular record in such an array can be computed by multiplying the record number by the record size. For example, in Figure 4.4 each record stores a doubleword. The index address of record four is therefore 4 bytes/record × 4 (record number) = 16 = 10H. To access element three in record four, the following code can be used:

```
MOV BX,0600H       ;BX points to array starting address
MOV SI,0004H       ;SI points to record four
MOV AL,[BX+SI*4+3] ;Retrieve element three
```

The number four in the last instruction is called the *scale factor*. Allowable values are 1, 2, 4, or 8, corresponding to a byte, word, doubleword or quad word size record. Four components now make up the address:

$$base + index \times scaling\ factor + displacement$$

For the previous example we have: 0600H + 10H + 3 = 0613H, which does indeed correspond with the address of element three, record four in Figure 4.4.

Figure 4.4   The base + index + displacement addressing mode can be used to access a particular element in a particular record of an array.

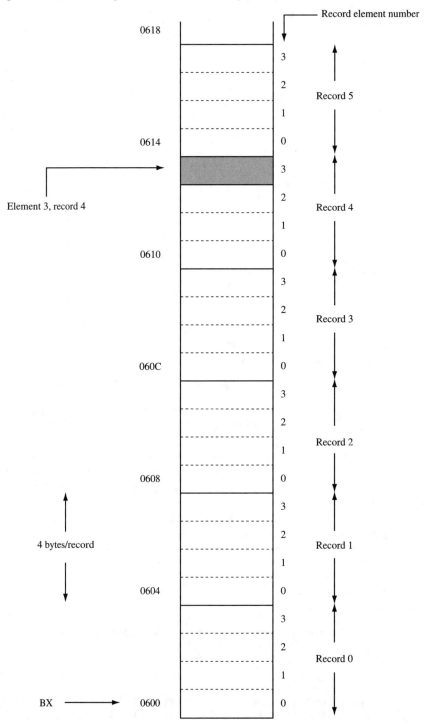

Table 4.1   Comparing 16- and 32-Bit Instructions

	16-Bit Instructions	**32-Bit Instructions**
Base Register	BX or BP	Any 32-bit general purpose register except
Index Register	SI or DI	Any 32-bit general purpose register except ESP
Scale Factor	none	1, 2, 4, or 8
Displacement*	0, 8, or 16 bits	0, 8, or 32 bits

*Interpreted as a two's complement number.

Table 4.1 summarizes the 16- and 32-bit instruction restrictions that apply when using the register indirect and array addressing modes.

Example 4.2

For each instruction below, determine the memory segment (CS, DS, ES, SS, FS, or GS) and offset address of the memory operand. Assume the CPU registers are as follows: BX = 0100H, BP = 2010H, and SI = 003AH.

(a) MOV AX,[1000H]
(b) INC [BX]
(c) MOV DL,[BX+SI]
(d) MOV CX,[BP+SI–20H]

Solution
(a) 1000H in the data segment
(b) 0100H in the data segment
(c) 013AH in the data segment
(d) 202AH in the stack segment

80x86 Instruction Set Overview

The instruction set of a microprocessor is a list of the various software commands that can be run by that processor. Table 4.2 lists the instructions available with the 80x86 processors.[7] Note that these tables are arranged by major instruction group and instruction type. Table 4.2(a), for example, lists the instructions in the *Data Transfer* group. There are five types of instructions in this group: *general-purpose, conversion, input/output, address object,* and *flag manipulation.* Finally, some of the instructions in these tables are not available with all of the processors. The five right-most columns indicate this information.

In the following sections, we provide a brief description of each of these instruction groups and types. This information is provided primarily to give you an *overview* of the instruction set. In practice, most programs use only a small subset of these instructions. The best way to learn the 80x86 instruction set is to practice writing your own programs. We will do this in Chapters 5 and 6.

---

[7]Only the instruction op-codes are shown. Most of the instructions require that a set of operands, whose form depends on the addressing mode, be specified.

Table 4.2(a)   Data Transfer Instructions

		8086	80386	80486	Pentium	Pentium Pro
General Purpose						
MOV	Move operand	X	X	X	X	X
PUSH	Push operand onto stack	X	X	X	X	X
POP	Pop operand off stack	X	X	X	X	X
XCHG	Exchange operand, register	X	X	X	X	X
XLAT/B	Translate using DS:BX or DS:EBX	X	X	X	X	X
PUSHA/D	Push all 16/32-bit registers on stack		X	X	X	X
POPA/D	Pop all 16/32-bit registers off stack		X	X	X	X
BSWAP	Byte swap			X	X	X
CMOVcc	Conditional move					X
Conversion						
CBW	Convert byte to word	X	X	X	X	X
CWD	Convert Word to Dword	X	X	X	X	X
MOVZX	Move byte or word, to word or Dword, with zero extension		X	X	X	X
MOVSX	Move byte or word, toward or Dword, sign extended		X	X	X	X
CWDE	Convert Word to Dword extended		X	X	X	X
CDQ	Convert Dword to Qword		X	X	X	X
Input/Output						
IN	Input operand from I/O space	X	X	X	X	X
OUT	Output operand to I/O space	X	X	X	X	X
Address Object						
LEA	Load effective address	X	X	X	X	X
LDS	Load pointer into D segment register	X	X	X	X	X
LES	Load pointer into E segment register	X	X	X	X	X
LFS	Load pointer into F segment register		X	X	X	X
LGS	Load pointer into G segment register		X	X	X	X
LSS	Load pointer into stack segment (SS)		X	X	X	X
Flag Manipulation						
LAHF	Load A register from flags	X	X	X	X	X
SAHF	Store A register in flags	X	X	X	X	X
PUSHF	Push flags onto stack	X	X	X	X	X
POPF	Pop flags off stack	X	X	X	X	X
CLC	Clear carry flag	X	X	X	X	X
CLD	Clear direction flag	X	X	X	X	X
CMC	Complement carry flag	X	X	X	X	X
STC	Set carry flag	X	X	X	X	X
STD	Set direction flag	X	X	X	X	X
PUSHFD	Push Eflags onto stack		X	X	X	X
POPFD	Pop Eflags off stack		X	X	X	X

Note: Due to space restrictions a complete description of each 80x86 instruction mnemonic cannot be provided. This information is available by writing to Intel Corporation, Literature Sales, P.O. Box 7641, Mt. Prospect, IL 60056-7641 or calling 1-800-879-4683. Documents may also be downloaded from Intel's World Wide Web site at http://www.intel.com.

Table 4.2(b)   Arithmetic Instructions

		8086	80386	80486	Pentium	Pentium Pro
	Addition					
ADD	Add operands	X	X	X	X	X
ADC	Add with carry	X	X	X	X	X
INC	Increment operand by 1	X	X	X	X	X
AAA	ASCII adjust for addition	X	X	X	X	X
DAA	Decimal adjust for addition	X	X	X	X	X
XADD	Exchange and add			X	X	X
	Subtraction					
SUB	Subtract operands	X	X	X	X	X
SBB	Subtract with borrow	X	X	X	X	X
DEC	Decrement operand by 1	X	X	X	X	X
NEG	Negate operand	X	X	X	X	X
CMP	Compare operands	X	X	X	X	X
DAS	Decimal adjust for subtraction	X	X	X	X	X
AAS	ASCII adjust for subtraction	X	X	X	X	X
CMPXCHG	Compare and exchange			X	X	X
CMPXCHG8B	Compare and exchange 8 bytes				X	X
	Multiplication					
MUL	Multiply double/single precision	X	X	X	X	X
IMUL	Integer multiply	X	X	X	X	X
AAM	ASCII adjust after multiply	X	X	X	X	X
	Division					
DIV	Divide unsigned	X	X	X	X	X
IDIV	Integer divide	X	X	X	X	X
AAD	ASCII adjust before division	X	X	X	X	X

Table 4.2(c)   String Instructions

		8086	80386	80486	Pentium	Pentium Pro
MOVS	Move byte, word, or Dword string	X	X	X	X	X
CMPS	Compare byte, word, or Dword string	X	X	X	X	X
SCAS	Scan byte, word, or Dword string	X	X	X	X	X
LODS	Load byte, word, or Dword string	X	X	X	X	X
STOS	Store byte, word, or Dword string	X	X	X	X	X
REP	Repeat	X	X	X	X	X
REPE/Z	Repeat while equal/zero	X	X	X	X	X
REPNE/Z	Repeat while not equal/zero	X	X	X	X	X
INS	Input string from I/O space		X	X	X	X
OUTS	Output string to I/O space		X	X	X	X

Table 4.2(d)   Logical Instructions

		8086	80386	80486	Pentium	Pentium Pro
Logicals						
NOT	"Not" operands	X	X	X	X	X
AND	"AND" operands	X	X	X	X	X
OR	"Inclusive-OR" operand	X	X	X	X	X
XOR	"Exclusive-OR" operands	X	X	X	X	X
TEST	"Test" operands	X	X	X	X	X
Shifts						
SHL/SHR	Shift logical left or right	X	X	X	X	X
SAL/SAR	Shift arithmetic left or right	X	X	X	X	X
SHLD/SHRD	Double shift left or right		X	X	X	X
Rotates						
ROL/ROR	Rotate left or right	X	X	X	X	X
RCL/RCR	Rotate left or right through carry	X	X	X	X	X

Table 4.2(e)   Bit Manipulation Instructions

		8086	80386	80486	Pentium	Pentium Pro
Single Bit Instructions						
BT	Bit test		X	X	X	X
BTS	Bit test and set		X	X	X	X
BTR	Bit test and reset		X	X	X	X
BTC	Bit test and complement		X	X	X	X
BSF	Bit scan forward		X	X	X	X
BSR	Bit scan reverse		X	X	X	X
Byte Set Instructions						
SETCC	Set byte equal to condition code		X	X	X	X

Table 4.2(f)   Program Control Instructions

		8086	80386	80486	Pentium	Pentium Pro
Conditional Transfers						
JA/JNBE	Jump if above/not below or equal	X	X	X	X	X
JAE/JNB	Jump if above or equal/not below	X	X	X	X	X
JB/JNAE	Jump if below/not above or equal	X	X	X	X	X
JBE/JNA	Jump if below or equal/not above	X	X	X	X	X
JC	Jump if carry	X	X	X	X	X

Table 4.2(f)   (continued)

		8086	80386	80486	Pentium	Pentium Pro
Conditional Transfers						
JE/JZ	Jump if equal/zero	X	X	X	X	X
JG/JNLE	Jump if greater/not less or equal	X	X	X	X	X
JGE/JNL	Jump if greater or equal/not less	X	X	X	X	X
JL/JNGE	Jump if less/not greater or equal	X	X	X	X	X
JLE/JNG	Jump if less or equal/not greater	X	X	X	X	X
JNC	Jump if not carry	X	X	X	X	X
JNE/JNZ	Jump if not equal/not zero	X	X	X	X	X
JNO	Jump if not overflow	X	X	X	X	X
JNP/JPO	Jump if not parity/parity odd	X	X	X	X	X
JNS	Jump if not sign	X	X	X	X	X
JO	Jump if overflow	X	X	X	X	X
JP/JPE	Jump if parity/parity even	X	X	X	X	X
JS	Jump if sign	X	X	X	X	X
Unconditional Transfers						
CALL	Call procedure/task	X	X	X	X	X
RET	Return from procedure	X	X	X	X	X
JMP	Jump	X	X	X	X	X
Iteration Controls						
LOOP	Loop	X	X	X	X	X
LOOPE/LOOPZ	Loop if equal/zero	X	X	X	X	X
LOOPNE/ LOOPNZ	Loop if not equal/not zero	X	X	X	X	X
JCXZ	Jump if register CX = 0	X	X	X	X	X
JECXZ	Jump if register ECX = 0		X	X	X	X
Interrupts						
INT	Interrupt	X	X	X	X	X
INTO	Interrupt if overflow	X	X	X	X	X
IRET	Return from interrupt/task	X	X	X	X	X
CLI	Clear interrupt enable	X	X	X	X	X
STI	Set interrupt enable	X	X	X	X	X

Table 4.2(g)   High-Level Language Instructions

		8086	80386	80486	Pentium	Pentium Pro
BOUND	Check array bounds		X	X	X	X
ENTER	Set up parameter block for entering procedure		X	X	X	X
LEAVE	Leave procedure		X	X	X	X

Table 4.2(h)   Operating System

		8086	80386	80486	Pentium	Pentium Pro
SGDT	Store global descriptor table		X	X	X	X
SIDT	Store interrupt descriptor table		X	X	X	X
SLDT	Store local descriptor table		X	X	X	X
STR	Store task register		X	X	X	X
LGDT	Load global descriptor table		X	X	X	X
LIDT	Load interrupt descriptor table		X	X	X	X
LTR	Load task register		X	X	X	X
LLDT	Load local descriptor table		X	X	X	X
ARPL	Adjust requested privilege level		X	X	X	X
LAR	Load access rights		X	X	X	X
LSL	Load segment limit		X	X	X	X
VERR/VERW	Verify segment for reading or writing		X	X	X	X
LMSW	Load machine status word		X	X	X	X
SMSW	Store machine status word		X	X	X	X
RDMSR	Read from model-specific register				X	X
WRMSR	Write to model-specific register				X	X
RSM	Resume from system management mode				X	X

Table 4.2(i)   Cache Control

		8086	80386	80486	Pentium	Pentium Pro
INVD	Invalidate cache			X	X	X
WBINVD	Write-back and invalidate cache			X	X	X
INVLPG	Invalidate TLB entry			X	X	X

Table 4.2(j)   Processor Control

		8086	80386	80486	Pentium	Pentium Pro
NOP	No operation	X		X	X	X
HLT	Halt	X		X	X	X
WAIT	Wait until BUSY inactive	X		X	X	X
ESC	Escape	X		X	X	X
LOCK	Lock bus	X		X	X	X
CPUID	CPU indentification				X	X
RDTSC	Read time-stamp counter				X	X
RDPMC	Read performance-monitoring counters					X
UD2	Undefined instruction					X

Data Transfer Instructions [Table 4.2(a)].   Instructions in this group provide a way for data to be moved between internal CPU registers, between memory and a CPU register, and between a CPU register and an I/O port. For example, the instruction MOV AL,BL moves a copy of register BL into register AL. The PUSH and POP instructions provide a quick way of saving a CPU register in memory and then restoring it later (see *Using the Stack*). The XCHG, XLAT, and BSWAP instructions provide specialized data transfer functions.

The CMOVcc instruction is available only with the Pentium Pro processor. It allows data to be moved between CPU registers or between memory and a CPU register. The data is moved, however, only if the condition is met. Table 4.2(f)—*Conditional Transfers*—lists the possible conditions. As an example, the instruction CMOVNZ AX,BX copies the 16-bit number in register BX to register AX if the result of the previous instruction affecting the flags was *not zero*.

The Conversion instructions provide a way to expand byte, word, and doubleword size two's complement numbers into word, doubleword, and quad size numbers maintaining the sign of the original number. The IN and OUT instructions move data between the accumulator and an I/O port. Rather than move the actual data, the Address Object instructions load the *memory address* of the data into a CPU register. Finally, the Flag Manipulation instructions allow the flags to be saved and restored, and each individual flag bit to be set or reset.

Arithmetic Instructions [Table 4.2(b)].   Instructions in this group provide the basic math operations of add, subtract, multiply, and divide. For example, the instruction ADD AL,BL adds the contents of register BL to register AL, storing the result in AL. Note that these instructions apply to the internal CPU of the processor, not the onboard floating-point unit (if present).[8]

String Instructions [Table 4.2(c)].   A string is a consecutive block of data bytes stored in memory. Instructions in this group allow bytes, words, or doublewords to be added to or retrieved from a string. The string scan instruction can be used to search a string for a particular byte, word, or doubleword. The REP instruction can be used to access multiple string elements. This is done by adding this instruction as a *prefix* to one of the string instructions, thereby allowing large blocks of data to be moved or searched. The INS and OUTS instructions allow large blocks of data to be moved through an I/O port at high speed.

Logical Instructions [Table 4.2(d)].   Instructions in this group mimic the operation of the basic logic gates (AND, OR, exclusive-OR, and invert).

Example 4.3

Determine the contents of register AL and the state of the flags after the following instructions are executed:

```
MOV AL,6DH    ;Load AL with 6DH
MOV BL,47H    ;Load BH with 47H
AND AL,BL     ;AND AL with BL bit by bit
```

Solution

Writing the register contents in binary and performing a bit-by-bit AND:

$$
\begin{array}{rl}
0110\ 1101 & (AL) \\
\times\ 0100\ 0111 & (BL) \\
\hline
0100\ 0101 = 45H = AL &
\end{array}
$$

---

[8]The floating-point unit has its own instruction set.

The flags are affected as follows:

```
CF = 0    ;CF is always reset by the AND instruction
PF = 0    ;45H has an odd number of 1s
AF = X    ;AF is undefined
ZF = 0    ;The result is not zero
SF = 0    ;The MSB (bit 7) of the result is zero
OF = 0    ;OF is always reset by an AND instruction
```

Using the Stack

The stack is a special area of memory designated for quick, temporary storage of program data and subroutine return addresses. What makes the stack unique is that it is a *last-in first-out* type of memory. Just as plates are pushed into a spring-loaded dispenser in a cafeteria, data is pushed onto the stack by the PUSH *source* instruction. The POP *destination* instruction causes the data currently on top of the stack to be popped into the destination operand.

To avoid overwriting program data or code, the stack is placed in its own segment with register SP (or ESP) used to identify the offset. The figure below shows an example with SP pointing to location 1000H—currently the top of the stack. Now assume the instruction PUSH CX is given. SP is decremented by two and CL and CH are pushed onto the stack. The new stack top is address 0FFEH (SP'). As you can see, the stack actually grows downward with each successive PUSH instruction. The stack top moves to 0FFCH (SP") after the instruction PUSH BX is executed.

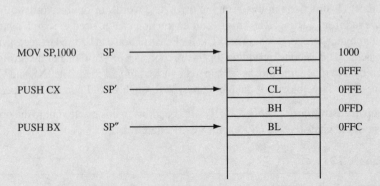

Once BX and CX have been saved on the stack, these registers can be used for other purposes. To restore these registers to their original values, the POP instruction is used. Registers should always be "popped" in the *reverse order* in which they were pushed. In this example:

```
POP BX    ;BL=[0FFC], BH=[0FFD], SP = SP+2 = 0FFE
POP CX    ;CL=[0FFE], CH=[0FFF], SP = SP+2 = 1000
```

The stack is used by other instructions as well. For example, the CALL instruction pushes a return address onto the stack. When the subroutine executes an RET instruction, this address is popped back into register IP, and the program resumes where it left off before the call. In a similar manner, software interrupts (INT *n*) push the return address and the flags onto the stack. An IRET instruction is then used to recover these values when the software interrupt has finished.

The TEST instruction works exactly the same as the AND instruction, but does not change the operands. That is, TEST AL,BL sets the flags, but does not change the contents of register AL.

Also included in this group are the shift and rotate instructions. These are diagrammed in Figure 4.5. Notice that the shifted or rotated quantity can be an 8-, 16-, or 32-bit CPU register or memory location. The main difference between a shift and a rotate is that the shifted bits "fall off" the end of the register, whereas the rotated bits "wrap around." The arithmetic shifts (SAL and SAR) operate so that the sign bit (bit 7, 15, or 31) does not change when the shift occurs. The shift or rotate is repeated the number of times indicated

Figure 4.5 The 80x86 (a) shift and (b) rotate instructions.

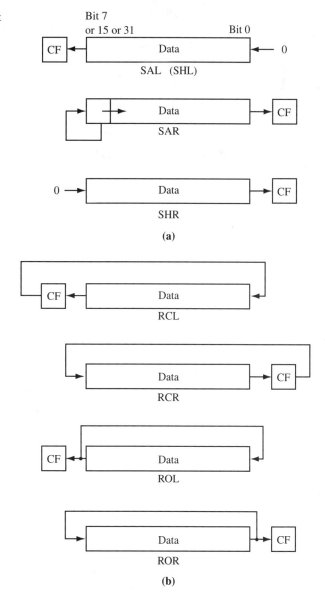

by the second operand, which is either an immediate number or the contents of the CL register. For example,

```
MOV AL,F0H    ;Initial value in AL = 1111 0000
SHR AL,3      ;After 3 right shifts, AL = 0001 1110
```

Bit Manipulation Instructions [Table 4.2(e)].   These instructions allow a single bit to be tested by copying it to the carry flag. The same bit can then be set or reset. For example, the instruction BTC AX,4 copies bit 4 of register AX into the carry flag and then clears (resets) this same bit. The bit scan instructions scan the operand to find the *first* bit that is set. For example, if register AX = 0470H, the instruction BSF AX,BX loads register BX with 0004H because bit four is the first bit in register AX (starting from 0) that is set.

Instructions in the byte set group store a byte value of 1 in the specified register or memory location if the condition is true: otherwise, a 0 byte is stored in that location. For example, the instruction sequence:

```
INC    AL    ;Add 1 to register AL
SETNZ BH     ;If AL is not zero, BH = 1, else BH = 0
```

increments register AL and, if the result is not zero, stores 0000 0001 in register BH. If the result in AL is zero, register BH stores 0000 0000. Several different conditions can be tested [see Table 4.2(f)].

Program Control Instructions [Table 4.2(f)].   Instructions in this group allow a program to make decisions based on the outcome of a test. Consider the following program, which inputs a number and then transfers control to a new program, depending on the value of that number.

```
MOV BL,47H   ;Load register BL with 47H
IN  AL,36H   ;Input a byte from I/O port 36H to register AL
CMP AL,BL    ;Compare register AL with register BL
JE  300H     ;If equal, execute the program starting in
               location 300H
JA  500H     ;If AL > BL, execute the program starting in location 500H
JMP 700H     ;Else, execute the program starting in location 700H
```

In this program, the CMP instruction serves as the test. The first two jump instructions (JE and JA) are *conditional*: The jump is taken only if the condition is met. The last jump (JMP) is *unconditional*: The jump is taken regardless.[9]

Most of the conditional jump instructions have two (equivalent) mnemonics; for example, JA (jump if above) and JNBE (jump if not equal or below). The two forms are the same, but one mnemonic may be more descriptive than the other, depending on the circumstances (this is shown in Table 4.3, along with the corresponding flag conditions required to take the jump).

Another common program structure is the *loop*; that is, a sequence of instructions that must be repeated several times. For example, the following program waits for a carriage return character (0DH) to be input from port 36H:

```
A1:  IN     AL,36H    ;Input a byte from I/O port 36H to register AL
     CMP    AL,0DH    ;Compare register AL with 0DH
     LOOPNE A1        ;If not equal, transfer control to memory
                        location A1
```

---

[9]Of course, within the context of this program, JMP 700H will be taken only if the first two jumps fail, meaning AL < BL.

Table 4.3 Conditional Jump Instructions

Mnemonic	Condition
	Signed Operations
JG/JNLE	Greater/not less or equal ((SF $\oplus$ OF) + ZF) = 0
JGE/JNL	Greater or equal/not less (SF $\oplus$ OF) = 0
JL/JNGE	Less/not greater or equal (SF $\oplus$ OF) = 1
JLE/JNG	Less or equal/not greater ((SF $\oplus$ OF) + ZF) = 1
JO	Overflow (OF = 1)
JS	Sign (SF = 1)
JNO	Not overflow (OF = 0)
JNS	Not sign (SF = 0)
	Unsigned Operations
JA/JNBE	Above/not below or equal (CF $\oplus$ ZF) = 0
JAE/JNB	Above or equal/not below (CF = 0)
JB/JNAE	Below/not above or equal (CF = 1)
JBE/JNA	Below or equal/not above (CF $\oplus$ ZF) = 1
	Either
JC	Carry (CF = 1)
JE/JZ	Equal/zero (ZF = 1)
JP/JPE	Parity/parity even (PF = 1)
JNC	Not carry (CF = 0)
JNE/JNZ	Not equal/not zero (ZF = 0)
JNP/JPO	Not parity/parity odd (PF = 0)

Note that in this program we have used the name A1 to represent the memory location in which the IN instruction is stored.

Large programs are often made up of many smaller *subprograms* (subroutines) or *procedures*. When it is desired to execute one of these procedures, the CALL instruction is used. The CALL transfers control to the subprogram but also saves the return address on the stack.[10] When the procedure finishes, it executes an RET instruction. This recovers the return address from the stack, allowing the calling program to resume from where it left off. (Chapters 4, 5, and 6 explore this programming concept in more detail.)

Finally, the *interrupt* instructions transfer control to an *interrupt service routine (ISR)* whose address is set up in a special interrupt vector table in low memory. (These instructions are covered in Section 4.3.)

High-Level Language Instructions [Table 4.2(g)]. These instructions assist in the development of high-level languages. BOUND, for example, checks that the specified register is pointing within a predefined range of memory addresses. If not, an interrupt is generated. ENTER and LEAVE are used to allow variables to be passed to a subroutine via the stack.

---

[10]The stack is a special area of memory used for storing temporary values and memory addresses. The stack operates in a *last-in first-out* manner; that is, the last item written to the stack becomes the first item read from the stack. For more details, see *Using the Stack* on page 142.

Operating System [Table 4.2(h)].   Instructions in this group control the operation of the processor in Protected Mode. As such, they are intended for use by operating system software only, and not applications programs.

Cache Control [Table 4.2(i)].   The three instructions in this group control the internal and external caches of the 486 and later processors.

Processor Control Instructions [Table 4.2(j)].   Several miscellaneous instructions are included in this group. The NOP instruction, for example, is often used to "rem" out another instruction for testing purposes. As such, it acts like a placeholder, reserving a program line for later substitution. The HLT instruction is seldom used, because once halted, the CPU cannot be restarted except via an interrupt. The WAIT instruction is used with the floating-point unit, as it forces the CPU to wait for a floating-point unit result before proceeding. The ESC instruction is used as a prefix to indicate that a floating-point instruction follows: The main processor then ignores the following instruction. The LOCK instruction locks the buses during execution of the following instruction. This instruction is intended for use in a multiprocessor environment where another processor might access shared memory and modify its contents between instructions.

Two instructions are available only with the Pentium and Pentium Pro. CPUID sets bits that identify the processor model and family in register EAX. Until this instruction was introduced, programmers had to write elaborate routines to determine which processor their program was running on. Finally, RDTSC returns the value of a 64-bit counter in the EDX:EAX register pair. This counter is incremented each CPU cycle.

The last two instructions in this group are available only with the Pentium Pro processor. RDPMC loads the 40-bit contents of the specified performance-monitoring counter into the register pair EDX:EAX. Two such counters are available and can be selected by placing a 0 or a 1 in register ECX. The performance-monitoring counters are event counters that can be programmed to count events such as the number of instructions decoded, number of interrupts received, or number of cache loads.

The instruction UD2 is provided to test the *invalid op-code* exception; that is, it does nothing except generate an invalid op-code. In this way, the exception handler can be tested.

Self-Review 4.1 (Answers on page 172)

4.1.1   Identify the op-code and operand for the instruction CMP CX,DX.

4.1.2   Which instruction below loads register BX with the data 1000H?

    (a) MOV [1000H],BX

    (b) MOV BX,1000H

    (c) MOV BX,[1000H]

    (d) ADD BX,1000H

4.1.3   In Question 4.1.2, which instruction loads register BX with the contents of memory location 1000H?

4.1.4   The instruction MOV AX,[BP] moves the _____ (byte, word, dword, qword) in the _____ segment, whose offset address is stored in register _____, to register _____.

4.1.5   In Figure 4.3, what is the instruction to copy array element six to register AL? Assume register BX = 0600H.

4.1.6   Determine the contents of register AL after the following instructions have executed:

```
MOV    BL,8CH
MOV    AL,7EH
AND    AL,BL
```

4.1.7   The instruction sequence

```
CMP    BL,AL
JA     100H
```

will transfer control to memory location 100H if BL _____ AL.

4.2   Machine Code Programming with DEBUG

Introduction

DEBUG, supplied with MS-DOS, is a program that "knows about" 8086 instructions. Using DEBUG, you can easily enter an 8086 machine code program into memory and save it as an executable MS-DOS file (in COM format). As its name implies, DEBUG can also be used to test and debug 8086 programs. Features include the ability to examine and change the contents of a memory location or CPU register. In addition, programs can be *single-stepped* or run at full speed to a break point.

Unfortunately, DEBUG supports only the 8086 and 8088 processors. And although it will run on 386 and above processors, you will be unable to access any of the 32-bit registers or use any of the newer (286 and above) instructions—even though your processor may support them. Nevertheless, DEBUG is a handy tool for creating and testing simple machine code programs, and it is available for free with all MS-DOS computers.

More advanced tools are commercially available. DEBUG32 from Larson Computing is a 32-bit debugger (included on a disk supplied with this book). It is similar to DEBUG but offers full support for 32-bit instructions and addressing. This program is discussed in Chapter 5. Microsoft's MASM (Macro Assembler) and Borland's TASM (Turbo Assembler) both provide integrated development systems that include editors, assemblers, and debuggers. Assembly language programming is discussed in Chapter 6.

In this section we:

- Create an 8086 machine language program in COM format using DEBUG.
- Use DEBUG to examine and change the contents of a CPU register or memory location.
- Trace the execution of an 8086 program line by line using DEBUG.

A Program Example

In the following paragraphs we provide an example that traces the steps necessary to create, test, and save an 8086 machine code program using DEBUG.

Problem Statement.   Write an 8086 program that accesses two 8-bit numbers stored in memory, computes their 16-bit product, and stores the result in two consecutive memory locations.

Understanding the Problem.   There are three different forms of the 80x86 multiply instruction, depending on the size of the numbers to be multiplied (byte, word, or double-

Figure 4.6 Three forms of the 80x86 multiply instruction: (a) byte operands, (b) word operands, and (c) doubleword operands.

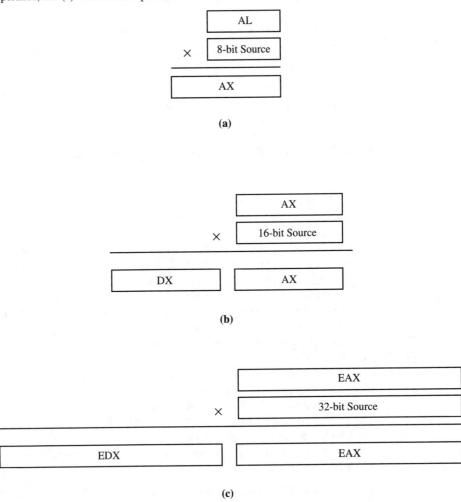

(a)

(b)

(c)

word). This is shown in Figure 4.6. Notice that in all three cases, register A, the accumulator, must be used for one of the numbers. Depending on the size of the operands, the result is returned in AX, DX:AX, or EDX:EAX.

Program Analysis. Keeping the above paragraph in mind, the following steps can be offered as a way to solve this problem:

1. Fetch the first number from memory to register AL.
2. Multiply AL times the second number in memory.
3. Store the 16-bit product (in register AX) back to memory.

Figure 4.7 shows one way of organizing memory to solve this problem. The program begins in memory offset address 0100H. This is the standard starting location for COM

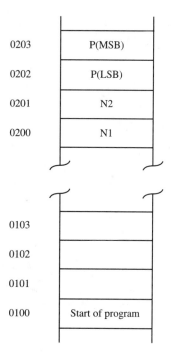

Figure 4.7 Memory organization for the multiplication program.

0203	P(MSB)
0202	P(LSB)
0201	N2
0200	N1
0103	
0102	
0101	
0100	Start of program

programs.[11] The two numbers to be multiplied, N1 and N2, are arbitrarily assumed to be stored in memory locations 200H and 201H. Finally, the product of N1 × N2 will be stored in the next two locations, 202H (least significant byte—LSB) and 203H (most significant byte—MSB).

Solving the Problem with DEBUG

Starting DEBUG. At the DOS prompt type *debug*. DEBUG's prompt is a dash (-) so nothing much appears to happen. Type a question mark (?) to get a list of available commands.

Entering and Displaying the Program Lines. Figure 4.8(a) shows how the program lines are entered (text entered by the user is shown in boldface). We begin by typing A100—this tells DEBUG that we want to begin **a**ssembling (entering) machine instructions at offset address 0100H (DEBUG only accepts hexadecimal numbers, so there is no need to type the H. In fact, you will receive an error message if you do). DEBUG responds by displaying the physical address in *segment:offset* format—1415:0100 in this example.[12]

The program instructions are entered next. Note the following:

1. Comments can be added to each program line by preceding them with a semicolon (DEBUG ignores all text following this character).

---

[11]Executable files in MS-DOS have the extension COM or EXE. COM files are limited to a single 64K segment; EXE files may contain multiple segments.

[12]When DEBUG is loaded, DOS picks a memory segment based on available memory. In this example, that segment is 1415. A different computer or a different memory configuration would cause this number to change. As our program uses only offset addresses, the segment address is unimportant.

Figure 4.8   (a) The A command is used to assemble the program instructions. (b) The U command unassembles memory and verifies program entry. (c) The E command is used to enter N1 and N2 into memory. The D command displays this data in hexadecimal and ASCII form.

```
-a100
1415:0100 mov    al,[200]                  ;Get first number
1415:0103 mul    byte ptr [201]            ;Multiply times second number
1415:0107 mov    [202],ax                  ;Store result
1415:010A int    20                        ;Return control to DEBUG
1415:010C
-
```

(a)

```
-u100 Lc
1415:0100 A00002          MOV     AL,[0200]
1415:0103 F6260102        MUL     BYTE PTR [0201]
1415:0107 A30202          MOV     [0202],AX
1415:010A CD20            INT     20
-
```

(b)

```
-e200
1415:0200   4D.10    E2.32    4D.0     ED.0
-d200 L10
1415:0200   10 32 00 00 4D F8 4D 03-4E 0E 4E 19 4E 24 4E 2F   .2..M.M.N.N.N$N/
-
```

(c)

2. Because we want to access the *contents* of memory locations 200 and 201, brackets are used around each address.
3. The BYTE PTR operator is required to make it clear that we want to multiply the *byte* in location 201 times the contents of register AL.
4. Because the product is stored in register AX, this register is moved to memory following the multiply instruction (AL to location 202, and AH to location 203).
5. To be sure that control returns to DEBUG when the program has finished, we use the software interrupt instruction INT 20. This calls a program built into DOS which simply returns control to the operating system (DEBUG in this example). This is preferable to halting the computer (HLT), which would also halt DEBUG, making it impossible to test the program to see if it worked (software interrupts are covered in detail in Section 4.3).
6. When no instructions remain to be entered, the ENTER key is pushed one last time. DEBUG's "-" prompt then returns.

In Figure 4.8(b), we type U100 LC to Unassemble 12 bytes (**L**ength = C) of memory beginning at address 100. Examining these lines, we see that DEBUG has "looked up" the hexadecimal object code required for each instruction and inserted these codes into memory. For example, the first instruction, MOV AL, [0200], requires three bytes; A0 00 02, and is stored in locations 100, 101, and 102. The next instruction thus begins in memory location 103. Examining the address of the last line of the program in Figure 4.8(a) (010C), you can see that a total of 12 bytes (010C–0100) are required for this program.

Entering and Displaying Data. Before the program is run, the two numbers to be multiplied should be entered into memory. This is shown in Figure 4.8(c). The command E200 tells DEBUG that we want to begin **E**ntering data at address 200. DEBUG responds by displaying the data currently in that location, 4D in this example. We type 10 (decimal 16) and press the *space bar*. The content of the next memory location is shown (E2). We override this and enter 32 (decimal 50). The next two locations will store the result. For now we put 0s in these cells.

To confirm that the data has been entered correctly, we type D200 L10—**D**isplay 10H (decimal 16) bytes of memory beginning at address 200H. DEBUG displays this data, first in hexadecimal and then as its ASCII equivalent.[13]

Checking the CPU Registers. Before running the program, make sure that register IP is pointing at memory location 0100, the start of the program. In Figure 4.9 we type **R** (for **R**egister). DEBUG displays the contents of all of the CPU registers and indeed shows that IP = 0100. The instruction at this location has also been unassembled and confirms that IP is positioned correctly.[14]

Figure 4.9 The R command is used to examine the CPU registers and verify that register IP points to the start of the program. Typing G runs the program. The D command is then used to observe the result in memory locations 202 and 203.

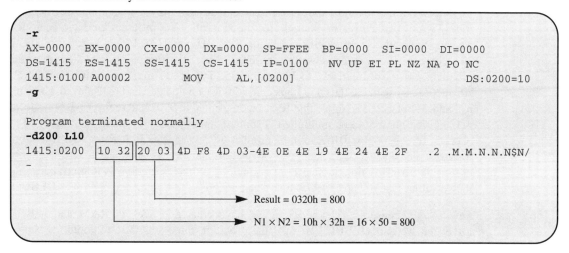

---

[13] This program was not designed to process ASCII data, and thus the ASCII interpretation is gibberish. Also note that DEBUG displays non-ASCII characters as a period.

[14] When DEBUG is first started it sets register IP to 0100 and all of the segments to fully overlapping (i.e., CS = DS = ES = SS).

Table 4.4   Flag Names in DEBUG

	Flag Name	**Reset (0)**	**Set (1)**
Status	Auxiliary carry	NA	AC
	Carry	NC	CY
	Overflow	NV	OV
	Parity	PO	PE
	Sign	PL	NG
	Zero	NZ	ZR
Control	Interrupt	DI	EI
	Direction	UP	DN

The value of each flag bit—in mnemonic form—is also shown. For example, NV indicates no overflow (OF = 0). Table 4.4 lists the mnemonic associated with each flag value.

Finally, recognizing that the current instruction references memory location 200, DEBUG displays the data at this location (DS:0200 = 10—the number 10 we entered previously).[15]

Running the Program.   Continuing with Figure 4.9, we type **G** (for **G**o). The program runs and displays the message *Program terminated normally*. With DEBUG back in control, we type D200 L10—display 10H bytes beginning at address 200H. Studying the last lines of Figure 4.9, notice that locations 202 and 203 now contain the result of the multiplication in *little endian* format. Reversing the order of the bytes (0320) and converting to decimal (800), we see that the program has indeed run correctly.

Single-Stepping the Program.   DEBUG's GO command causes the computer to run at full speed until the end of the program is encountered. For debugging and testing purposes, however, it may be more useful to *single-step* through the program one instruction at a time. Figure 4.10 shows an example for the multiplication program we have been discussing. We begin by entering new data for N1 (4DH) and N2 (29H) in locations 200 and 201. Next, the R command is used to confirm that register IP is pointing at the start of the program. Now we are ready to begin tracing. Typing **T**, the first instruction (MOV AL,[0200]) is executed, the CPU registers and flags are updated and redisplayed, and control returns to DEBUG. Notice that IP has incremented to 0103 and register AL now stores 4D, the first number to be multiplied. Typing **T** again causes the multiply instruction to execute, IP advances to 0107, and the product (0C55) appears in register AX. One more trace and the contents of register AX is written to memory. IP advances to 010A, the site of the INT 20 instruction. It is best not to single-step this instruction, as it jumps back into the operating system and executes many instructions before returning control to DEBUG.

Saving the Program.   The program we have created resides in RAM and will be lost when we quit DEBUG. To save the program, three steps are required, as shown in Figure 4.11(a). First we use the **N** (**N**ame) command to give the program a name—

---

[15]Recall that when accessing general data the data segment is used. Because all of the segments in this program overlap, location 200 in the data segment (DS:200) is the same as location 200 in the code segment (CS:200).

Figure 4.10 Using the T command to trace through the multiplication program one line at a time.

```
-e200
1415:0200  10.4d   32.29   20.0    03.0
-r
AX=0000  BX=0000  CX=0000  DX=0000  SP=FFEE  BP=0000  SI=0000  DI=0000
DS=1415  ES=1415  SS=1415  CS=1415  IP=0100   NV UP EI PL NZ NA PO NC
1415:0100 A00002       MOV    AL,[0200]                         DS:0200=4D
-t

AX=004D  BX=0000  CX=0000  DX=0000  SP=FFEE  BP=0000  SI=0000  DI=0000
DS=1415  ES=1415  SS=1415  CS=1415  IP=0103   NV UP EI PL NZ NA PO NC
1415:0103 F6260102      MUL    BYTE PTR [0201]                  DS:0201=29
-t

AX=0C55  BX=0000  CX=0000  DX=0000  SP=FFEE  BP=0000  SI=0000  DI=0000
DS=1415  ES=1415  SS=1415  CS=1415  IP=0107   OV UP EI PL NZ NA PO CY
1415:0107 A30202        MOV    [0202],AX                        DS:0202=0000
-t

AX=0C55  BX=0000  CX=0000  DX=0000  SP=FFEE  BP=0000  SI=0000  DI=0000
DS=1415  ES=1415  SS=1415  CS=1415  IP=010A   OV UP EI PL NZ NA PO CY
1415:010A CD20          INT    20
-
```

MULTIPLY.COM in this example. Next, register CX must be loaded with the number of bytes in the program. This is done by typing **RCX** to examine the contents of CX. We then enter C, as there are 12 bytes in this program. Finally, typing **W** Writes the program to disk (it will be stored in the default directory). To exit DEBUG and return to the DOS prompt, type **Q** (Quit).

Running the Program from the DOS Prompt. By default, DEBUG writes programs to disk in *COM* format. Such programs are directly executable from the DOS prompt by simply typing their primary name. For example, to run the multiply program:

```
C:\>multiply
```

If you try this, nothing will appear to happen. This is because the multiply program does not write to the video screen or access any other hardware. It does modify the contents of memory—but there is no way to view this (except to run the program under DEBUG). Section 4.3 and Chapters 5 and 6 illustrate DEBUG programs that utilize the BIOS services and MS-DOS functions to write to the system video screen.

Retrieving the Program. To load a program into DEBUG, simply include the program name when DEBUG is first started; that is, type DEBUG MULTIPLY.COM to start DEBUG and load the file MULTIPLY.COM. This is shown in Figure 4.11(b). To confirm that the program has loaded, give the **U** command to unassemble the program instructions (this is also shown in the figure).

Figure 4.11   (a) To save a DEBUG program it must be named (N), register CX loaded with the number of program bytes, and then written to disk (W). (b) To load a program into DEBUG, type **DEBUG** followed by the program name.

```
-n multiply.com          ;Name the program
-rcx                     ;Examine register CX
CX 0000
:c                       ;Load CX with the number of bytes in the program
-w                       ;Write the file to disk
Writing 0000C bytes
-q                       ;Quit DEBUG

C:\DOS>

                              (a)



C:\DOS>debug multiply.com
-u100 Lc
1446:0100 A00002         MOV     AL,[0200]
1446:0103 F6260102       MUL     BYTE PTR [0201]
1446:0107 A30202         MOV     [0202],AX
1446:010A CD20           INT     20

                              (b)
```

DEBUG Command Summary.   Figure 4.12 presents a summary of all of the commands available in DEBUG.

Editing a Program in DEBUG.   DEBUG has limited editing capabilities. Although you can backspace and correct errors on a given line, once that line has been entered you cannot delete it (except by typing a new instruction in its place, and then only if the new instruction has the same number of bytes as the original). In addition, if you have forgotten an instruction, there is no way to insert the new instruction without retyping all of the commands following it.

However, if you have access to Microsoft Windows there is a way to edit a DEBUG program. As shown in Figure 4.13, begin by typing the program instructions into a text file using an editor (in this example, Window's Notepad.) Next, select all of the text and copy it to the clipboard. Now start DEBUG in a *DOS window*. At DEBUG's "-" prompt, type A100 (assuming assembly is to begin at 0100H), but instead of typing the program instructions, select the DOS window's *Edit* menu and *paste* the instructions into DEBUG from the clipboard. In this way, if you have forgotten an instruction, it is an easy task to insert it in the original text file via the editor and then repaste it into DEBUG. Using this technique, you will always have two versions of your programs: a text file (MULTIPLY. TXT) the machine code version created by DEBUG (MULTIPLY.COM).

Figure 4.12 DEBUG command list summary.

	DEBUG Command List Summary	
assemble	A	[address]
compare	C	range address
dump	D	[range]
enter	E	address [list]
fill	F	range list
go	G	[=address] [addresses]
hex	H	value1 value2
input	I	post
load	L	[address] [drive] [firstsector] [number]
move	M	range address
output	O	port byte
proceed	P	[=address] [number]
quit	Q	
register	R	[register]
search	S	range list
trace	T	[=address] [value]
unassemble	U	[range]
write	W	[address] [drive] [firstsector] [number]
allocate expanded memory	XA	[#pages]
deallocate expanded memory	XD	[handle]
map expanded memory pages	XM	[Lpage] [Ppage] [handle]
display expanded memory status	XS	

Figure 4.13 Window's Notepad can be used to create a text file corresponding to the program instructions. These can then be *pasted* into DEBUG via a DOS window.

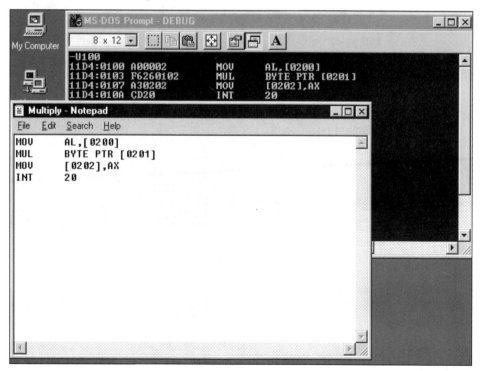

Self-Review 4.2 (Answers on page 172)

4.2.1   In Figure 4.7, if N1 = 6EH, and N2 = DBH, predict the (hexadecimal) values of the product P(LSB) and P(MSB).

4.2.2   In Figure 4.8(b) , the hexadecimal code for the instruction INT 20 is _____.

4.2.3   In Figure 4.8(c), the hexadecimal value of the data stored in memory location 20F is

   _____.

4.2.4   Which of the following DEBUG commands displays ten bytes of memory in machine code format beginning at address 200H?
   (a) D200 LA
   (b) A200 L10
   (c) E200 L10
   (d) U200 LA

4.2.5   In Figure 4.10, after tracing the MOV AL,[200] instruction, register AX = _____.

4.2.6   What three steps must be taken to save a DEBUG program?

4.3   MS-DOS Functions and BIOS Calls

Introduction

Many software programs written for 80x86 computers are designed to run under the MS-DOS operating system.[16] Included as part of this operating system are the DOS functions and BIOS calls. These are subprograms, callable from applications software, that can be used to access the hardware of the PC. The intention is to save the programmer from having to "reinvent the wheel" with each new applications program. In addition, by providing a standard set of input/output routines, these subprograms ensure software compatibility between computers with different hardware configurations.

   In this section we:

• Show the structure of MS-DOS and explain the roles of the BIOS and the MS-DOS kernel.
• Explain the difference between hardware and software interrupts.
• Provide a list of standard interrupt vectors for an 80x86 computer running MS-DOS.
• Use DEBUG to write a program that accesses the BIOS services and MS-DOS functions.

The Structure of MS-DOS

The BIOS (Basic Input/Output System).   As shown in Figure 4.14, the BIOS routines are the most *primitive* in a computer as they "talk" directly to the system hardware. Accordingly, the BIOS is hardware specific; that is, it must know the exact port address and control bit configurations for each I/O device in the computer. Typically, the BIOS is supplied by the computer manufacturer and resides in one or two ROM chips on the system board of the computer. Computer users refer to the BIOS in their computer by

---

[16]IBM computers typically run PC-DOS. Although MS-DOS and PC-DOS are different programs, they are functionally equivalent. Unless otherwise stated, all comments in this section regarding MS-DOS apply equally well to PC-DOS.

Figure 4.14 The BIOS interacts directly with the system hardware. The MS-DOS kernel accepts requests from the applications programs and passes these on to the BIOS and system hardware.

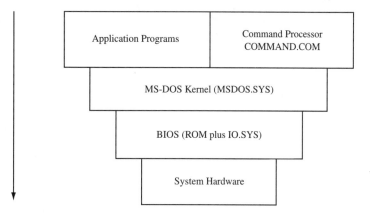

manufacturer name; for example, "*I have the Phoenix BIOS*" or "My system board uses AMI BIOS."

By definition, the code stored in ROM is unchangeable (read-only). However, many manufacturers are beginning to select "flash" memory for the BIOS. This is a type of ROM that can be selectively reprogrammed without removing the chip from the system board. This allows users to upgrade their BIOS from a manufacturer-supplied floppy disk.

With MS-DOS computers, the BIOS is actually made up of two parts. The first is the *resident* portion described above, which resides in ROM; the second is *nonresident* and is loaded into RAM when the computer is booted. This is the file IO.SYS (IBMIO.SYS in PC-DOS). It contains extensions to the resident BIOS and allows data to be passed between the higher levels of DOS and the system hardware. In addition, IO.SYS provides a convenient way of adding new features to the BIOS.

The MS-DOS Kernel.   In between the BIOS and the high-level applications software is the MS-DOS kernel (see Figure 4.14). It is loaded into RAM when the system is booted via the file MSDOS.SYS (IBMDOS.SYS in PC-DOS). Unlike the BIOS, the kernel provides *hardware-independent* functions. For example, function 39 is used to create a disk subdirectory. To use this function the user "points" register DX at the directory name (stored as a string of characters in memory), loads register AH with 39H (the function number), and then executes the software interrupt INT 21. MS-DOS function 39 takes care of all the details: calling various BIOS routines to turn on the disk drive, locating an available disk sector, and writing the data.

You can see that the kernel is designed to provide *higher level* functions than the BIOS. And because it is hardware independent, users can safely code these calls into their software without having to worry about I/O address compatibility. Indeed, it is the kernel that allows the same program to work in computers with different disk drives, different video cards, and different keyboards.

80x86 Interrupts

An interrupt is an event that causes the processor to suspend its present task and transfer control to a new program called the *interrupt service routine (ISR)*. There are three sources of interrupts in an 80x86 computer: (1) processor interrupts, (2) software interrupts, and

(3) hardware interrupts.[17] Each interrupt must supply a *type number* or *vector,* which is used by the processor as a pointer into an *interrupt vector table (IVT)* to determine the address of that interrupt's service routine. As shown in Figure 4.15, 256 different interrupt

Figure 4.15 The interrupt vector table (IVT) stores a pointer to the ISR for each of the 256 possible interrupts.

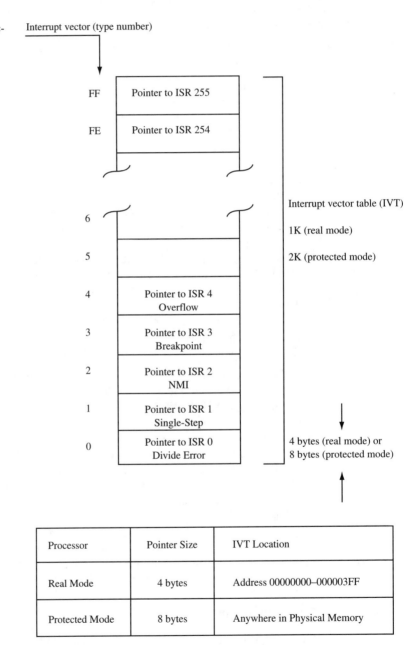

Processor	Pointer Size	IVT Location
Real Mode	4 bytes	Address 00000000–000003FF
Protected Mode	8 bytes	Anywhere in Physical Memory

---

[17]Intel uses the term *interrupt* to refer to hardware-initiated requests and *exception* to refer to those initiated in software or by the processor itself. In this book, the term *interrupt* will be used to include both types.

vectors are allowed (00–FF). Each entry in the IVT points to the location of its corresponding ISR. Of course, when the processor is first started, this table is "empty." Therefore, loading the IVT with the proper subprogram addresses is one of the first operations that must be performed by the processor.

Before transferring control to the ISR, the processor performs one very important task: *It saves the current program address and the flags on the stack*. Control then transfers to the ISR. When the ISR finishes, it uses the instruction IRET—*return from interrupt*—to recover the flags and "old" program address from the stack. In this way, the processor can resume execution of the original program.

Many of the vectors in the IVT are reserved for the processor itself; others have been reserved by MS-DOS for the BIOS and kernel. Still others have become de facto standards for specific hardware features in the PC. Table 4.5 lists the vector numbers (00–FF), their description, and their source. Note that, depending on the processor, some interrupts may or may not be available. For example, interrupt 11, *alignment check,* occurs only with 486-vintage processors or newer. Some of the interrupts have two functions (number five, for example). These require special ISRs to determine the source of the interrupt and the appropriate action to be taken.[18]

Processor Interrupts (Types 0–12).   These interrupts are generated by the processor itself, usually in response to an error condition. For example, a type 0 interrupt occurs when an attempt to divide by zero (or any other divisor that would yield a result too large for the destination register) occurs. Interrupt 0D—*general protection fault*—is another example. This interrupt will be generated whenever a Protected Mode program attempts to access data or code at a higher privilege level.

A type 1 interrupt occurs at the completion of each instruction—but only if the *trap flag* has been set. The purpose of this interrupt is to provide a mechanism for single-stepping the processor. DEBUG's trace mode takes advantage of this concept.

Note that although the processor automatically generates these interrupts, it is up to the user (via the operating system software) to write the corresponding service routines and place the addresses of these routines in the IVT.

Software Interrupts.   Not all of the processor interrupts are due to an error condition. Interrupt types 3 and 4 are *software interrupts*. These are special 80x86 instructions that trigger an interrupt response from the processor. The general form of the software interrupt instruction is:

```
INT type_number
```

For example, the instruction INT 3 (op-code CCH) calls the ISR whose address is stored at entry three in the IVT (see Figure 4.15). Intel designed this interrupt to assist in program debugging (they refer to it as a *breakpoint*). Because its op-code is a single byte, it can easily be inserted into a program, temporarily replacing the instruction at that location. When executed, the program runs at full speed until the INT 3 is encountered; control then

---

[18]In 1978, when the 8086 was first announced, Intel reserved interrupts 0–1F for the processor (and future generations of 80x86 processors). However, when the original IBM PC was designed, only interrupts 0–4 were in use by Intel. The PC designers therfore selected several interrupts in the reserved range. This was not a problem with the 8088-based PC, but has led to conflicts with the more recent processors. For example, with some systems, execution of the BOUND instruction (interrupt type 5) can cause a print screen to occur!

Table 4.5 80x86 Family Interrupts

Interrupt Vector Number	Description	Interrupt Initiated by:			
		CPU	BIOS	MS-DOS	PC
0	Divide error	all			
1	Single-step	all			
2	Non-maskable interrupt (NMI)	all			
3	Breakpoint	all			
4	Interrupt on overflow	all			
5	Bound	$\geq$286			
	Print screen				
6	Invalid op-code	$\geq$286			
7	Coprocessor not available	286, 386			
7	Device not available	$\geq$486			
8	Double fault	$\geq$286			
	Timer				IRQ0
9	Coprocessor segment overrun	286,386			IRQ1
	Reserved	$\geq$486			
	Keyboard				
A	Invalid task state segment	$\geq$386			
	Video				IRQ2
B	Segment not present	$\geq$386			
	Serial port 2				IRQ3
C	Stack fault	$\geq$386			
	Serial port 1				IRQ4
D	General protection fault	$\geq$286			
	Second parallel port				IRQ5
E	Page fault	$\geq$386			
	Floppy disk				IRQ6
F	Reserved	X			
	First parallel port				IRQ7
10	Coprocessor error	$\geq$286			
	Video services		X		
11	Alignment check	$\geq$486			
	Equipment list service		X		
12	Machine check	$\geq$Pentium			
	Memory size service		X		
13	Disk services		X		
14	Communications services		X		
15	System services		X		
16	Standard keyboard services		X		
17	Printer services		X		
18	Activate ROM BASIC		X		
19	Activate bootstrap start-up routine		X		
1A	Time and data service		X		
1B–1F	PC hardware specific				X
20	Program terminate			X	
21	General MS-DOS services			X	

Table 4.5 (continued)

Interrupt Vector Number	Description	Interrupt Initiated by:			
		CPU	BIOS	MS-DOS	PC
22	Terminate address			X	
23	Control-C handler			X	
24	Critical error handler address			X	
25	Absolute disk read			X	
26	Absolute disk write			X	
27	Terminate and stay resident			X	
28	MS-DOS idle interrupt			X	
29–2E	MS-DOS internal use			X	
2F	Multiplex interrupt			X	
30-3F	MS-DOS internal use			X	
40-FF	PC hardware specific				IRQ8-15

transfers to the breakpoint ISR. Typically this routine displays all of the CPU registers so that the programmer can inspect the state of the machine to this point. If all is well, the breakpoint is moved further into the program and debugging continues until it is determined that the program is working correctly.

One of the main advantages of software interrupts is that they provide a way for applications software to access subprograms without having to know the absolute addresses of these programs. For example, the programmer need not know the absolute address of the breakpoint ISR. He or she simply inserts the INT 3 instruction in the program. The processor then looks up the ISR address in the IVT and transfers control to it.

In a similar way, software interrupts provide access to the BIOS and MS-DOS kernel. In Table 4.5, note that interrupts 10–1A are used by the BIOS (with some overlap with the processor) and interrupts 20–3F are used by the MS-DOS kernel. Each interrupt provides access to a particular BIOS service or MS-DOS function. Many of the interrupts have *subservices* or *subfunctions*. Table 4.6 lists the 22 subservices associated with interrupt 10—the BIOS video services.[19] Typically these subservices and functions are accessed by putting the service or function number in register AH before executing the interrupt instruction. For example, to write one character to the video screen using the current video mode, the following code is required:

```
MOV AH,0AH    ;BIOS service 10 to register AH
MOV AL,CHAR   ;ASCII code for character to be displayed in AL
INT 10H       ;Call the BIOS interrupt routine
```

Additional examples using these services and functions are provided later in this chapter and in Chapters 5 and 6.

Hardware Interrupts. Hardware interrupts are interrupt requests initiated by external hardware. The 80x86 processors have two pins reserved for this purpose. The first is called

---

[19]Appendix A provides a detailed description of the BIOS services and MS-DOS functions used in this book. An excellent reference on this subject is *The Peter Norton PC Programmers Bible* (Microsoft Press: Redmond, Wa., 1995).

Table 4.6   The BIOS Video Services

Interrupt	Subservice	Description
10H	0	Set video mode
	1	Set cursor size
	2	Set cursor position
	3	Read cursor position
	4	Read light-pen position
	5	Set active display page
	6	Scroll window up
	7	Scroll window down
	8	Read character and attribute
	9	Write character and attribute
	0A	Write character
	0B	Set 4-color palette
	0C	Write pixel
	0D	Read pixel
	0E	Write character in teletype mode
	0F	Get current video mode
	10	Color palette interface
	11	Character generator interface
	12	Alternate select
	13	Write character string
	14	(PC-convertible only)
	15	(PC-convertible only)
	1A	Read/write display combination page
	1B	Return functionality state information
	1C	Save/restore video state

NMI—nonmaskable interrupt. The rising edge of the signal on this pin causes a type 2 interrupt to be generated, and control is then transferred to the corresponding ISR. This interrupt is *nonmaskable,* meaning it cannot be blocked. In the PC this interrupt is used to shut the system down due to a memory parity error.

The second interrupt pin is INTR. This pin allows external hardware to activate any of the 256 interrupt types in Table 4.4. This is done by placing the type number on the data bus when the processor acknowledges the interrupt request. With this single input pin, it would seem that the processor is limited to one hardware interrupt request. However, using the 8259 programmable interrupt controller (PIC), as many as eight inputs can be accommodated (64 with 8 PICs wired in cascade). The PC uses this technique to support 16 interrupt requests on IRQ0–IRQ15.

A Program Example: The PC Typewriter

Problem Statement.   Write an 80x86 program to input keystrokes from the PC's keyboard and display the characters on the system video monitor. Pressing any of the function keys F1–F10 should cause the program to end.

Outlining the Solution.   Machine language programs can be among the most difficult to write—especially if you start the problem without a "game plan." By game plan we mean

Figure 4.16 Outlining the solution to the PC typewriter program.

```
  I. Get the code for the key pressed
     A. Call Keyboard BIOS Service 0
        1. AH = 0                          I.A    mov   ah.0
        2. INT 16                                 int   16

 II. If this code is ASCII, display the key
 pressed on the monitor and continue
     A. Check for non-ASCII character
        1. AL = 0?                                cmp   al,0
           i. Yes: Goto III.A                     jz    III.A
          ii. No. continue
     B. Display the character                     mov   ah,0e
        1. Call Display BIOS service 0E           int   10
           i. Character to AL
          ii. AH = 0E
         iii. INT 10
     C. Repeat the loop                           jmp   I.A
        1. Goto 1-A

III. Quit when a non-ASCII key is pressed
     A. Return control to MS-DOS       III.A    int   20
        1. INT 20
```

a step-by-step plan of what you want the program to do. Figure 4.16 shows such a plan written in outline format.[20] We first visualize the solution at the highest level. Three steps are identified:

  I. Get the code for the key pressed.
  II. If this code is ASCII, display the key pressed on the monitor and continue.
  III. Quit when a non-ASCII key is pressed.

Note that we write these three steps in "plain English"—not computer instructions. At this level in the outline we want to make it clear *what* we want our program to do—not *how* we plan to accomplish it.

The next step is to refine each of the main points. To do this, we need to study the BIOS services and DOS functions in Appendix A, as these provide our "gateway" to the hardware of the PC. To accomplish step I, we select interrupt 16, BIOS service 0—*Read next keyboard character*. Note that this requires that register AH store a 0 (the service number) when the interrupt is called.

Step II requires three operations:

A. Check for a non-ASCII character.
B. Display the ASCII character.
C. Repeat the loop.

Noting that interrupt 16 returns 0 in AL for non-ASCII characters; step II.A can be accomplished by testing this register and branching accordingly. To display the character (step

---

[20]Traditionally, flowcharts have been used for this purpose. In recent years, however, flowcharts seem to have fallen out of favor (perhaps no one likes drawing boxes and arrows). The method shown here takes advantage of the *outliner* available with most word processors.

IIB), we select interrupt 10, BIOS service 0E—*Write character in teletype mode*. Note that this requires register AH to hold the service number (0E), and AL to hold the character to be displayed. Also note that, as it turns out, that character is already in AL due to the previous BIOS call. Finally, step II.C is accomplished by jumping back to the start of the program to retrieve the next keyboard character.

The last step is to quit the program when a non-ASCII key is pressed. This is accomplished by calling interrupt 20—*Program terminate*.

Coding the Program.   Once the outline is complete, we can begin coding the program. This we have done in the right half of Figure 4.16. With the program logic already worked out, this coding phase becomes quite simple. One problem does occur, however: The two jump instructions require an address to jump to, but until we actually determine the instruction object codes, we can't predict these addresses. For now we enter symbolic addresses, III.A and I.A, the outline locations.

Writing the Program with DEBUG.   The final step is to type the program into DEBUG, test it, and save it. The steps are shown in Figure 4.17. We begin assembly at address 0100, as is customary for all COM programs. Once the codes have been entered, we type U100 L10 to unassemble the 16 bytes of the program and verify that all instructions have been entered correctly. Note that the two jump addresses can now be resolved. I.A becomes 0100, and III.A becomes 010E.[21] The next few lines save the program using the name TYPER.COM.

At this point we are ready to test the program. Before doing so, however, we type R to allow the CPU registers to be examined. In particular, we want to be sure that register IP is pointing at address 0100, the start of the program. Verifying this address, we type G to run the program. DEBUG's prompt disappears and we are free to type any text we want. Pressing a function key causes the program to terminate and DEBUG's prompt to reappear.

Adding a Sign-On Message.   Because TYPER was saved as a COM program, it can be run from the DOS prompt. Assuming the program was saved to the DOS directory, we can type:

```
C:\DOS>typer
```

If you try this, you will find that the DOS prompt disappears and you are left with a blinking cursor. For the user's benefit, it would be better if a *sign-on message* appeared explaining the function of the program. Figure 4.18 shows how TYPER is modified to include such a message.

The new program is nearly identical to the old one except for the first three lines, which call upon interrupt 21, DOS function 9—*String output*. As explained in Table A.2 of Appendix A, this function outputs a string of characters to the standard output device (normally the video system). The $ character is used to indicate the end of the string; registers DS:DX point to the first byte in the string.

---

[21] This is a little bit "trickier" than it appears. Although the starting address is known to be 0100, the end address (needed by the JZ instruction) is not known until all instructions have been entered. A good plan to follow here is take *two* passes. On the first pass (when the end address is not yet known) enter the current address as a "dummy" (JZ 0106). Then, after all instructions have been entered (and the end address is known), reenter the JZ instruction using the proper address (A106 JZ 010E).

Figure 4.17   Writing the code for the PC typewriter program.

```
C:\DOS>debug
-a100
1415:0100 mov      ah,0              ;Keyboard BIOS service 0
1415:0102 int      16               ;Wait for keypress
1415:0104 cmp      al,0             ;Check for a function key
1415:0106 jz       10e              ;If found, then quit
1415:0108 mov      ah,0e            ;Video BIOS service 0E
1415:010A int      10               ;Write character to screen
1415:010C jmp      100              ;Do another loop
1415:010E int      20               ;Return to MS-DOS
1415:0110
-
-u100 L10
1415:0100 B400           MOV     AH,00
1415:0102 CD16           INT     16
1415:0104 3C00           CMP     AL,00
1415:0106 7406           JZ      010E
1415:0108 B40E           MOV     AH,0E
1415:010A CD10           INT     10
1415:010C EBF2           JMP     0100
1415:010E CD20           INT     20
-
-n typer.com
-rcx
CX 0000
:10
-w
Writing 00010 bytes
-
-r
AX=0000  BX=0000  CX=0010  DX=0000  SP=FFEE  BP=0000  SI=0000  DI=0000
DS=1415  ES=1415  SS=1415  CS=1415  IP=0100  NV UP EI PL NZ NA PO NC
1415:0100 B400           MOV     AH,00
-
-g
The program seems to work correctly.
Note that after typing ENTER control-J is required for a line feed.
Program terminated normally
-
```

Studying Figure 4.18, note that the message to be displayed is added to the end of the program beginning at address 0117.[22] The pseudo-op *db* (define byte) tells DEBUG that the codes that follow are to be interpreted as data and not program instructions. If

---

[22]Technically, DOS function 9 expects the message to be loaded in the *data* segment. However, when DEBUG is started, it sets all of the segments to be fully overlapping. Therefore, address 0117 in the code segment is the same as address 0117 in the data segment.

Figure 4.18   The improved version of the PC typewriter includes a sign-on message via MS-DOS function 9, interrupt 21.

```
-a100
1415:0100 MOV    DX,0117           ;Point DX at message
1415:0103 MOV    AH,09             ;MS-DOS function 9
1415:0105 INT    21                ;Output message to screen
1415:0107 MOV    AH,00             ;Keyboard BIOS service 0
1415:0109 INT    16                ;Wait for keypress
1415:010B CMP    AL,00             ;Check for a function key
1415:010D JZ     0115              ;If found,then quit
1415:010F MOV    AH,0E             ;Video BIOS service 0E
1415:0111 INT    10                ;Write character to screen
1415:0113 JMP    0107              ;Do another loop
1415:0115 INT    20                ;Return to MS-DOS
1415:0117 db     'Type any letter, number or punctuation key.'
1415:0142 db     'Any F1 to F10 to end program.'
1415:0161 db     0d,0a,0a,'$'
1415:0165
-
-u100 L17
1415:0100 BA1701      MOV    DX,0117
1415:0103 B409        MOV    AH,09
1415:0105 CD21        INT    21
1415:0107 B400        MOV    AH,00
1415:0109 CD16        INT    16
1415:010B 3C00        CMP    AL,00
1415:010D 7406        JZ     0115
1415:010F B40E        MOV    AH,0E
1415:0111 CD10        INT    10
1415:0113 EBF2        JMP    0107
1415:0115 CD20        INT    20
-
-d100 L65
                                                    Op-Codes
1415:0100  BA 17 01 B4 09 CD 21 B4-00 CD 16 3C 00 74 06 B4    ......!....<.t..
1415:0110  0E CD 10 EB F2 CD 20 54-79 70 65 20 61 6E 79 20    ...... Type any
1415:0120  6C 65 74 74 65 72 2C 20-6E 75 6D 62 65 72 20 6F    letter, number o
1415:0130  72 20 70 75 6E 63 74 75-61 74 69 6F 6E 20 6B 65    r punctuation ke
1415:0140  79 2E 20 20 41 6E 79 20-46 31 20 74 6F 20 46 31    y.  Any F1 to F1
1415:0150  30 20 74 6F 20 65 6E 64-20 70 72 6F 67 72 61 6D    0 to end program
1415:0160  2E 0D 0A 0A 24                                     ....$
                    ASCII Codes
-
-g
Type any letter, number or punctuation key.  Any F1 to F10 to end program.


Again the program seems to work.  Note that this time we get a sign-on
message followed by two blank lines.
Program terminated normally
-
```

this data is enclosed within quote marks, DEBUG treats the data as ASCII and generates the proper hex code values. This is the case for the first two lines. The last line, at address 0161, ends the string (note the *$* character) with a carriage return (0D) and two line feeds (0A).

After the codes have been entered and the new jump addresses resolved, the command U100 L17 is given. This displays all of the program lines in machine code format. Note that we do not want to display the data, as DEBUG would interpret these lines as 80x86 instructions that would make no sense. To verify that the data has been entered correctly, we give the command D100 L65. DEBUG responds by displaying this area of memory in hex and ASCII forms. The first 17H bytes represent the program op-codes; the remaining bytes are the data as can be seen on the far right. Finally, the G command is given to verify program operation.

Self-Review 4.3 (Answers on page 172)

4.3.1   With an MS-DOS computer, the nonresident portion of the BIOS is supplied as the file _____.

4.3.2   The MS-DOS kernel supplies *hardware-* (a) *dependent* (b) *independent* functions for the applications programmer.

4.3.3   List the three sources of interrupts with 80x86 computers.

4.3.4   The program that responds to an interrupt is called the _____ _____ _____.

4.3.5   How does the applications programmer access particular BIOS services and DOS functions?

4.3.6   80x86 processors have two hardware interrupt inputs: _____ and _____.

4.3.7   Which software interrupt below provides access to the BIOS video services?
   (a) INT 10H
   (b) INT 16H
   (c) INT 20H
   (d) INT 21H

Chapter 4 Self-Test

1. Identify the op-code and operand for each instruction below.
   (a) INC AX
   (b) WAIT
   (c) MOV DX,CX
   (d) MOV AL,[BX+6]

2. Which of the following instructions are *invalid*? Explain your answer.
   (a) MOV AX,SI
   (b) MOV AL,1234H
   (c) MOV CX,BL
   (d) MOV [100H],EAX

3. Determine the contents of register DH after the following instructions have executed. Assume the content of memory is as shown in Figure 4.2.

   ```
   MOV BX,0201H
   MOV DH,[BX]
   ```

4. Using the direct addressing mode, give the single instruction that adds 1 to the memory word stored at address 0200H.

5. The following instructions are executed on an 80386 in Real Mode. Which of these instructions, if any, are invalid? Explain.
   - (a) INC   EAX
   - (b) MOV   CX,[AX+32]
   - (c) AND   AL,[10000000H]
   - (d) MOV   EBX,[SI]
   - (e) MOV   DX,[ESI]   ;ESI = 0000A000H

6. Refer to Figure 4.19 and determine the contents of registers AX, BX, and SP after the following instructions have executed:

```
MOV    SP,0700H
POP    AX
POP    BX
```

7. Assume register AL = B7H and the instruction AND AL,3CH is given. Determine the new value of register AL.

8. The program below will (a) *loop* (b) *exit the loop* when the data input is the carriage return character.

```
A1:    IN     AL,36H
       CMP    AL,0DH
       LOOPE  A1
```

9. If register AX = 100H and register BX = 200H, determine the contents of registers AX and DX after the instruction MUL BX is given.

10. What is the DEBUG command to begin assembling instructions at location 560H in the default code segment?

11. To enter hexadecimal codes into memory with DEBUG, use the _____ command. To display these same codes in hexadecimal and ASCII, use the _____ command.

12. Assume a machine code program resides in memory beginning at address 350H. If the program is 20 bytes long, what is the DEBUG command to display the program instructions in *mnemonic* form?

13. Typing G in DEBUG causes the program whose offset address is stored in register _____ to begin executing.

14. The instruction MOV AL,[200] moves the (a) *byte* (b) *word* (c) *doubleword* at offset address 200 in the (a) *code* (b) *data* (c) *stack* (d) *extra* segment to register AL.

Figure 4.19   Figure for Chapter 4 Self-Test, 6.

0704	3A
0703	DC
0702	6E
0701	5F
0700	48
06FF	29
06FE	3C

15. Before writing a DEBUG program to disk, the number of bytes in that program must be stored in register _____.
16. Which file listed below adds high-level functions callable by the applications programmer to the MS-DOS operating system?
    (a) COMMAND.COM
    (b) MSDOS.SYS
    (c) IO.SYS
    (d) IBMDOS.SYS
17. Interrupt requests received via the 80x86's NMI input are examples of:
    (a) processor interrupts
    (b) software interrupts
    (c) hardware interrupts
18. The IVT stores the _____ for up to 256 different ISRs.
    (a) address
    (b) type number
    (c) code
    (d) subprogram service or function number
19. When accessing the BIOS video service (interrupt 10H) and the *write character in TTY mode* subservice (0EH):
    (a) Register AH should hold _____.
    (b) The software interrupt type number should be _____.
20. DEBUG programs in COM format typically begin at offset address _____.

Analysis and Design Questions

Section 4.1

4.1 Calculate the physical address of the memory operand for the instruction MOV AX,[BP+12H]. Assume BP = 0350H, DS = E000H, AND SS = F910H.

4.2 For each of the following, determine the value of the operand after the instruction has executed. Assume register BX = 0600H for each question, and the contents of memory are as shown in Figure 4.3. *Hint:* Recall that the 80x86 processors access memory operands using *little endian* format.
    (a) INC BX
    (b) INC BYTE PTR [BX]
    (c) INC WORD PTR [BX]
    (d) INC DWORD PTR [BX]

4.3 The instruction PUSHA pushes the following registers onto the stack: AX, CX, DX, BX, SP, BP, SI, and DI. Determine the value of register SP after the following instructions have executed.

```
MOV  SP,F000H
PUSHA
```

4.4 Determine the memory offset address of the operand in the instruction MOV AX,[BX+SI*8+5]. Assume BX = 7E00H and SI = 0004H.

4.5 Thinking of the data in Figure 4.20 as an *array* of bytes with a base address of 8800H, write a program that initializes a pointer to the array base and then adds array elements two and six, storing the result as element 12H. Use the base-plus-displacement addressing mode.

4.6 The data in Figure 4.20 could be thought of as an array with four elements per record and a base address of 8800H. Element zero of record one would then be 40H. Keeping this organization in mind, write a program that adds elements three of records one and two. Store the

Figure 4.20 Figure for Analysis and Design Question 4.5.

880B	6A
880A	DD
8809	3B
8808	EA
8807	47
8806	29
8805	8A
8804	40
8803	F2
8802	39
8801	4E
8800	27

result as element two, record three, of a new array with base address A000H. Use the base-plus-index × scaling factor plus displacement addressing mode. *Hint:* Use register SI as a record pointer. The instruction INC SI can then be used to adjust this pointer to consecutive records.

4.7 Determine the contents of the BX and CX registers and all flags after the following program has run. Refer to Figure 4.20 for the contents of memory.

```
MOV    BX,8802H
MOV    CX,3C7AH
AND    CX,[BX]
HALT
```

Section 4.2

4.8 The 80x86 instruction DIV r8/m8 divides register AX by an 8-bit register or memory operand.[23] The quotient is returned in register AL, and the remainder in register AH. Figure 4.21 shows a DEBUG program written to divide the contents of memory location 200 (N1) by the contents of memory location 201 (N2). The result is stored in memory locations 202 and 203. Answer the following questions about this program.

(a) What are the *decimal* values of N1 and N2?

(b) The quotient is stored in memory location _____, and the remainder in memory location _____.

(c) What is the purpose of the first instruction, MOV AH,0? That is, why is this instruction needed?

---

[23] r/8 is any 8-bit CPU register. m/8 is any 8-bit memory location.

Figure 4.21   Figure for Analysis and Design Question 4.8.

```
-a100
1415:0100 mov ah,0
1415:0102 mov al,[200]
1415:0105 div byte ptr [201]
1415:0109 mov [202],ax
1415:010C int 20
1415:010E
-e200
1415:0200   4D.32   E2.4   4D.0   ED.0   4D.
-r
AX=0000  BX=0000  CX=0000  DX=0000  SP=FFEE  BP=0000  SI=0000  DI=0000
DS=1415  ES=1415  SS=1415  CS=1415  IP=0100   NV UP EI PL NZ NA PO NC
1415:0100 B400             MOV     AH,00
-g

Program terminated normally
-d200 L4
1415:0200   32 04 0C 02                                        2...
-
```

(d) How many total bytes are required for this program?

4.9 Assume register AX = 1234H and BX = 5678H. Determine the contents of registers DX and AX after the instruction MUL BX is executed.

4.10 Using DEBUG, enter the following six bytes into memory: 4D 53 2D 44 4F 53. How does DEBUG interpret these bytes as (a) ASCII characters? (b) 8086 instruction mnemonics?

4.11 Modify the 8086 multiply program presented in this section so that it multiplies two 16-bit numbers, N1 and N2, storing the result as a doubleword in memory.
(a) Provide a memory utilization map similar to Figure 4.7.
(b) Provide a printed copy of your unassembled instruction mnemonics similar to Figure 4.8(b).
(c) Provide a printed copy of memory showing N1, N2, and the doubleword result. Let N1 = 1234H and N2 = 5678H.
(d) Trace your program one instruction at a time and provide a printed copy similar to Figure 4.10.

Section 4.3

4.12 The following questions refer to the PC typewriter program in Figure 4.17.
(a) Calculate the *physical address* of the first byte of this program.
(b) What is the *offset address* of the last byte of this program?
(c) How many total bytes does this program require?
(d) What are the hexadecimal object codes corresponding to the instruction JZ 010E?

4.13 The following questions refer to the PC typewriter program in Figure 4.18.
(a) This program uses interrupt _____, MS-DOS function _____, to display the ASCII message whose starting address is stored in the ____:____ register pair.
(b) To include hexadecimal data values in a program, use the pseudo-op _____.
(c) The ASCII portion of the program ends with the code 24. What ASCII character does this hex code represent?
(d) If the jump instruction in 0113 was changed to jump to the start of the program in 0100, how would this change the operation of the program?

4.14   Write an 80x86 program that displays your name on the video screen. Provide a printed copy of the program and save it as a COM file. (*Hint:* Use DOS function 9, interrupt 21, to display the message.)

4.15   Modify the program written in Problem 4.14 so that your name appears centered horizontally and vertically on a blank screen. (*Hint:* Output several line feed characters to clear the screen before writing your name.)

4.16   Write a program called WAIT.COM that displays the message "Press any key to continue" and then waits for a single keystroke: Control is then returned to DOS. Provide a printed copy of your program.

Self-Review Answers

4.1.1   Op-code: CMP, operand:CX,DX

4.1.2   (b)

4.1.3   (c)

4.1.4   word, stack, BP, AX

4.1.5   MOV AL,[BX+6]

4.1.6   0AH (and the carry flag is set)

4.1.7   BL > AL

4.2.1   P(LSB) = 1A, P(MSB) = 5E

4.2.2   CD20

4.2.3   2F

4.2.4   (d)

4.2.5   004D

4.2.6   Name the program with the *N* command, enter the number of bytes in the program into register CX, and write the program to disk with the *W* command.

4.3.1   IO.SYS

4.3.2   independent

4.3.3   Processor, software, hardware

4.3.4   interrupt service routine

4.3.5   Put the service or function number in register AH and issue the appropriate software interrupt.

4.3.6   INTR and NMI

4.3.7   (a)

5 80x86 Programming Techniques

Radio Shack was at first skeptical about offering a personal computer. Its success at the time was based on the sale of audio equipment and citizen's band radios. Would its customers really want to purchase a difficult to set up and operate personal computer? Radio Shack gambled that they would, and in the summer of 1977 announced the TRS-80 Model 1 for just $400. It featured the Zilog Z-80 microprocessor (a compatible but more powerful version of Intel's 8080), 4K of RAM, and a version of BASIC stored in ROM. User programs could be saved to cassette tape and later to $5^1/4''$ floppy disks. The monitor was a conventional television receiver without the tuner. (Photo courtesy of Smithsonian)

Outline

Objectives

After completing this chapter you should be able to:

1. Develop a machine language program using a top-down design approach.
2. Set up a program loop using the compare and conditional jump instructions.
3. Show how to document a machine language program.
4. Construct a logical mask to force selected bits of an operand low.
5. Use the rotate and logical AND instructions to unpack a packed BCD number.
6. Convert a BCD number to its ASCII equivalent.
7. Input and store in a memory buffer a string of characters from the system keyboard.
8. Convert an ASCII number to BCD.
9. Add two packed BCD numbers, ensuring that the sum remains a valid BCD number.
10. Link two programs by calling the second as a subroutine.
11. Show how to control the PC's built-in speaker.
12. Explain how to program the PC timer chip to generate square waves of various frequencies.
13. Use the 80x86's I/O instructions to read data from an input port and transfer data to an output port.
14. Write a COM program that returns an error code to DOS.
15. Use the batch file *if errorlevel* command to test for a specific error code.
16. Modify the AUTOEXEC.BAT file to allow different boot sequences based on the left and right alternate key status.
17. Write a COM program that tests for the presence of a disk in a specified drive.
18. Pass a parameter to a COM program via the command line.
19. Construct a translation table.
20. Write an 80x86 program that uses 32-bit instructions.
21. Convert a two-digit ASCII number to binary.
22. Write an 80x86 program that generates a 1- to 99-second programmable time delay.

Overview

Learning to write a computer program is not unlike learning a foreign language. Typically, you begin by studying the meanings and spellings of a few simple words (the instruction set). Next, you focus on putting these words together to form logical sentences (simple instruction sequences). Finally, you refine these sentences, incorporating the proper grammar for that language to write complete stories (assembly language programs).

In this case the "foreign language" you will be learning is 80x86 machine language. Using DEBUG, we will construct seven different programs in COM format.

Each program contains the following sections:

1. **New Instructions.** A description of the instructions used in the program.
2. **New DOS Features.** A description of the BIOS services and DOS functions used in the program.

3. **Discussion.** The solution to the program presented in outline form. The program listing in DEBUG format is then given.
4. **Self-Review.** Several questions (with answers at the end of the chapter) so that you can test your understanding of the program.

5.1 Program 5.1: Displaying the ASCII Character Set

Introduction

The ASCII character set consists of all of the letters of the alphabet, the numbers 0–9, and various punctuation symbols and control codes. In all, 128 codes are defined (see Table 2.5). In Program 5.1, we create a COM program that displays a symbol for each of these codes on your PC's video monitor. This is accomplished by setting up a program loop that passes the ASCII codes one by one to the BIOS video service (interrupt 10H, service number 0EH). DEBUG is used to write and test the program, which will run on any 80x86 computer.

In this section we:

- Develop a machine language program using a top-down design approach.
- Set up a program loop using the compare and conditional jump instructions.
- Show how to document a machine language program.

New Instructions

MOV destination,source. The move instruction is used to copy data from one CPU register to another, from memory to a CPU register, or from a CPU register to memory. It *cannot* be used to move data from one memory location to another (move the data to a CPU register first, then to the new memory location).

When using this instruction, the size of the destination and source operands must *match*. The following are examples of valid and invalid move instructions:

```
MOV AL,BL    ;Valid-8-bit register to 8-bit register
MOV AL,BX    ;Invalid-Attempting to copy a 16-bit register
               into an 8-bit register
MOV BX,AL    ;Invalid-Although AL fits "inside" BX, the processor
               would not recognize which bits to replace
```

When accessing memory, the size of the register operand defines the size of the data moved.

```
MOV AL,[0800]     ;The byte in memory location 0800 is copied
                    into register AL
MOV EAX,[0800]    ;The four bytes (doubleword) beginning at
                    address 0800 are copied into register EAX
```

INC destination. The increment instruction is used to add 1 to the contents of a CPU register or memory location. The flags are changed to reflect the result. For example, consider the following two instructions:

```
MOV AL,FF   ;AL = FF
INC AL      ;AL = FF + 1 = 00
```

The flags are affected as follows:

```
CF = X    ;Not affected
PF = 1    ;The number of 1s in the result is even
            (0 is considered even)
AF = 1    ;There is a carry from bit 3 to bit 4
ZF = 1    ;The result is 0
SF = 0    ;Bit 7 of the result is 0
OF = 0    ;There was no overflow
```

A similar instruction is **DEC** *destination,* which subtracts one from the destination operand and sets the flags accordingly.

CMP operand1,operand2. The compare instruction is used to compare a CPU register with another CPU register, memory location, or immediate data. This is done by subtracting operand2 from operand1 and setting the flags according to the result. Note that neither operand is affected, only the flags. Typically, a conditional jump instruction follows the compare.

JNZ destination. This instruction transfers control to the instruction at the destination address if the zero flag is *not* set. When used with the compare instruction, it allows a program to determine if two operands are equal and branch accordingly.

```
CMP AL,BL    ;Compare AL with BL
JNZ 0121     ;If AL ≠ BL, transfer control to location 0121
INC CX       ;If AL = BL, the jump is not taken and control
               "falls into" this instruction
```

There are many different conditional jump instructions (see Table 4.2[f]) corresponding to the various tests possible. Some have different but equivalent mnemonics. For example, JE *(jump if equal)* is equivalent to JZ *(jump if zero)*. If the target address is in another segment (a *far* jump), an unconditional jump must be used. For example, the following is *invalid:*

```
    JNZ New_Segment_Address
A1:  If zero, the program continues here
```

To accomplish this far jump, use the following:

```
    JZ A1
    JMP New_Segment_Address
A1:  If zero, the program continues here[1]
```

INT type number. This is the software interrupt instruction. It is used to call interrupt service routines (ISRs) without having to know the address of these routines. This is done by using the type number as an index into a table (the *interrupt vector table,* or *IVT*) that stores the addresses of the various ISRs.

When executed, the INT instruction pushes the flags and current address onto the stack. This allows the IRET instruction (return from interrupt) to pop these values back off the stack, thereby returning control to the calling program.

---

[1]When using the 8086 (and DEBUG), the target address for a conditional jump is limited to +127 or −128 bytes relative to the address of the first byte of the next instruction. The 386 and later processors are limited to +32,767 to −32,768 in a 64K segment or $+2^{31} - 1$ to -2^{31} in a 4 GB segment.

Many of the interrupt type numbers are reserved for use by the processor (see Table 4.5). MS-DOS and PC-DOS make extensive use of software interrupts to provide services and enhanced functions to applications programs (see Appendix A for a description of these interrupts).

New DOS Features

BIOS INT 10H, Service 00 (Set video mode).   Service 00 is used to configure the video interface card to a particular mode. Appendix A.1 lists the basic operating modes. Many video cards support additional modes via their onboard BIOS. Program 5.1 takes advantage of the fact that accessing this function *clears the screen* (even if the same video mode is specified).[2] Analysis and Design Problem 5.2 explores using this service to set the video mode to 80×25 16-color text.

BIOS INT 10H, Service 02 (Set cursor position).   Service 02 is used to move the cursor to a particular column (register DL) and row (register DH) on the video screen. The upper left corner of the screen has the coordinates 0,0. Depending on the video mode, several display pages may be supported. This allows the screen contents to be changed very quickly by selecting a new display page. Register BH holds the page number, which in Program 5.1 is set to 0.

BIOS INT 10H, Service 0EH (Write character in TTY mode)   Service 0EH is used to write one character (passed in register AL) to the screen at the current cursor position in the current screen mode. In the color graphics modes, register BL holds the color attribute (see Appendix A.3).

DOS INT 20H (Program terminate).   INT 20H is used to end a program and return control to DOS. It should only be used with "simple" programs that do not open files or change the value of register CS.

Problem Statement

Write an 80x86 program that prints the ASCII character set codes 0–127 beginning on line 10, column 0 of the PC's video monitor.

Discussion

Program Outline.   Figure 5.1 outlines the program solution. Note the top-down approach. We begin by identifying three tasks the program must accomplish:

1. Clear the screen and position the cursor on line 10, column 0.
2. Print the ASCII characters.
3. Return to DOS.

Next we work our way down, refining each task into ever-smaller pieces. We end up with a word description of all of the steps required. In the right-hand column, we convert these steps to machine code instructions.

---

[2]To override this, add 80H to the video mode code in register AL. In this way, the new video mode will be set, but the screen will *not* be cleared.

Figure 5.1   Outline for
Program 5.1. The program is
designed using a *top-down*
approach.

I. Clear Screen and Position Cursor	
on Line 10 Column 0	
A. (Re) Set Video Mode to 80 × 25	mov ax, 0002
1. BIOS INT 10H, service 00	int 10h
i. AH = 0 ;Service 0	
ii. AL = 2 ;Video mode 2	
B. Move cursor to line 10 column 0	mov ah, 2
1. BIOS INT 10H, service 2	mov dx, 0a00
i. AH = 2	mov bh, 0
ii. DX = 0A00 (row = 10,	int 10h
column = 0)	
iii. BH = 0 (page)	
II. Print the ASCII Characters	
A. Print ASCII code	mov ax, 0e00
1. BIOS INT 10H, service 0EH	II.A Int 10h
i. AH = 0EH	
ii. AL = character code	
(first code is 0)	
B. Increment code and repeat II.A until	inc al
all 128codes have been printed	cmp al, 80h
1. AL = AL + 1	jnz II.A
2. AL = 128	
3. No: goto II.A	
4. Yes: continue	
III. Return to DOS	
A. INT 20H	int 20h

Program Listing.   The next step is to type the program into DEBUG, beginning at address 0100H. This is shown in Figure 5.2. As DEBUG assembles the instructions, the address for the JNZ instruction can now be determined. The last step is to name the pro-

Figure 5.2   DEBUG listing for Program 5.1.

```
-a100
1415:0100 mov    ax,0002      ;BIOS service 0, video mode 2
1415:0103 int    10           ;Set video mode and clear screen
1415:0105 mov    ah,2         ;BIOS service 2
1415:0107 mov    dx,0a00      ;Row 10, column 0
1415:010A mov    bh,0         ;Page 0
1415:010C int    10           ;Position cursor
1415:010E mov    ax,0e00      ;BIOS service 0E, first character 0
1415:0111 int    10           ;Print character
1415:0113 inc    al           ;Next
1415:0115 cmp    al,80        ;Done?
1415:0117 jnz    0111         ;No: loop again
1415:0119 int    20           ;Yes: back to DOS
1415:011B
-
```

Figure 5.3   Sample output for Program 5.1.

```
☺☻♥♦♣
►◄↕‼¶§▬↨↑↓→←↔▲▼ !"#$%&'()*+,-./0123456789:;<=>?@ABCDEFGHIJKLMNOPQRSTUVWXYZ[\]
^_`abcdefghijklmnopqrstuvwxyz{|}~⌂
```

Figure 5.4   Instruction listing for Program 5.1 without comments.

```
mov     ax,0002
int     10
mov     ah,2
mov     dx,0a00
mov     bh,0
int     10
mov     ax,0e00
int     10
inc     al
cmp     al,80
jnz     0111
int     20
```

gram (**n prog1.com**), load register CX with the program length (**rcx 1B**), and write the program to disk (**w**).

To run the program, type **G** (or exit to DOS and type **prog1**). Figure 5.3 shows the result. The first 32 characters are control codes that display as "odd" symbols. However, beginning with 20H (space) and 21H (exclamation mark), each succeeding character appears as expected.

Documenting the Program.   Assembly language programs can be very difficult to understand, especially if the author chooses not to annotate each program line. Figure 5.4 shows Program 5.1 without these comments. Although this is the same program, it would be very difficult to identify its function without a great deal of study.[3]

Self-Review 5.1 (Answers on page 218)

5.1.1   The instruction sequence below will loop (take the jump) _____ times before "falling out of" the loop.

```
        MOV AL,0
A1:     INC AL
        JNZ A1
```

5.1.2   To set the video display to 320×200 four-color graphics, the software interrupt INT 10H should be given with AX = _____.

---

[3] You might argue that it is a waste of time typing comments into a DEBUG program, as they cannot be saved as part of the program file. And this is true. However, by creating a *text* version of the program (PROG1.TXT) and then "pasting" this file into DEBUG, the annotated version of the program can be saved. This method was described at the end of Section 4.2.

5.2   Program 5.2: BCD to ASCII Conversion

Introduction

BCD numbers consist of the binary combinations 0000 through 1001. One byte can therefore store two BCD numbers. This is referred to as a *packed BCD* number. In ASCII, the numbers 0 through 9 have the hexadecimal codes 30H through 39H. Therefore one byte stores one ASCII number. Program 5.2 converts the packed BCD number in register AL to two ASCII numbers, which are then passed to the BIOS video service and displayed on the system monitor. For example, if AX = 12H, the screen displays 12. This is accomplished by separating the two BCD numbers and adding 30H (the *ASCII bias*) to each digit. DEBUG is again used to write and test the program, which will run on any 80x86 DOS computer.

⁕In this section we:

- Construct a logical mask to force selected bits of an operand low.
- Use the rotate and logical AND instructions to unpack a packed BCD number.
- Convert a BCD number to its ASCII equivalent.

New Instructions

AND operand1,operand2.   The AND instruction functions like multiple AND gates, performing a *bit-by-bit* AND of the two operands, which may be a CPU register or memory location and another CPU register or immediate value. Operand1 stores the result. For example, if AL = 6DH and BL = 27H, the instruction AND AL,BL will produce the following result:

$$
\begin{array}{r}
\text{AL} = \text{6DH} = 0110\ 1101 \\
\bullet\ \text{BL} = \ \ 27\text{H} = 0010\ 0111 \\
\hline
\text{AL} = \ \ 25\text{H} = 0010\ 0101
\end{array}
$$

The AND instruction is often used as a "mask" or filter. In this way, only selected bits are allowed to pass through the filter. For example, suppose we want to examine only bits 4–7 of register AL. We accomplish this by ANDing AL with 1111 0000 (F0H). Now if AL = 6DH:

$$
\begin{array}{r}
\text{AL} = \text{6DH} = 0110\ 1101 \\
\bullet\ \text{mask} = \ \text{F0H} = 1111\ 0000 \\
\hline
\text{AL} = \ \ 60\text{H} = 0110\ 0000
\end{array}
$$

Notice how the mask allows bits 4–7 of register AL to pass through the filter unchanged. Bits 0–3, however, are all forced to be zero.

There are three other logical instructions: OR, exclusive-OR, and NOT. These are also performed bit by bit between the two operands. The OR function can be used to set selected bits, the exclusive-OR to invert selected bits, and the NOT to invert all bits.

ROR operand,CL.   The ROR instruction rotates all of the bits of the operand, which may be a CPU register or memory location, right CL times. That is, if CL = 4, four rotate rights are performed. (Figure 4.5 diagrammed this instruction.) Beginning with the 386 processor, an immediate value may be specified. For example, if AL = 64H and the instruction ROR AL,2 is given, the result is:

```
0110 0100 -> first rotate: 0011 0010
0011 0010 -> second rotate: 0001 1001
```

Notice that rotating right is the same as dividing the operand by 2. Thus, 64H (100) when rotated right twice becomes 19H (25).

Other similar instructions are ROL, which rotates the operand left, and RCL and RCR, which rotate the operand through the carry flag (see Figure 4.5). The shift instructions are also similar, but the end bits are allowed to "drop off" and do not recirculate (again, see Figure 4.5).

ADD operand1,operand2.   The add instruction is used to add two operands, which may be a CPU register or memory location and another CPU register or immediate value. Operand1 stores the result. By selecting the appropriate operand size, 8-, 16-, and 32-bit additions can be performed. For example, if register AX = F3D9H and the instruction ADD AX,16A2H is given, the result is:

$$\begin{array}{r} AX = F3D9H \\ +\quad 16A2H \\ \hline 0A7BH \text{ and } CF = 1 \end{array}$$

Because the addition of the last two bits generated a carry (1 + F = 10), the carry flag is set. The ADC instruction is similar but includes the carry flag as part of the addition. For example, consider the 64-bit addition problem EDX:ECX = EDX:ECX + EBX:EAX.

```
ADD ECX,EAX    ;Add the low-order registers
ADC EDX,EBX    ;Add the high-order registers plus carry from
               the low-order addition
```

Problem Statement

Write an 80x86 program that displays the packed BCD number in register AL on the system video monitor.

Discussion

Program Outline.   Figure 5.5 outlines the program solution. The packed BCD number is assumed to be in register AL. The first number to be displayed should be the most significant digit (MSD). It is found by masking the least significant digit (LSD) and then rotating the (MSD) into the LSD position. The result is converted to ASCII by adding 30H. The BIOS video service is then called to display the result.

Extracting and converting the LSD is simpler, as no rotate operation is required. Note the importance of saving the original number: The MSD conversion process "wipes out" the AL register.

Program Listing.   Figure 5.6 shows the annotated machine language program. It follows the outline exactly.

Figure 5.5 Outline for Program 5.2.

I. Get Most Significant Digit (MSD), Convert to ASCII, and Display
A. Save original number	`mov    bl,al`
B. Force bits 0-3 low	`and    al,f0h`
1. AND AL with F0H	
C. Rotate MSD into LSD position	`mov    cl,4`
1. Four rotate rights	`ror    al,cl`
D. Convert to ASCII	`add    al,30h`
1. Add 30H to result	
E. Display result	`mov    ah,0eh`
1. BIOS INT 10, video service 0EH	`int    10h`
i. AH = 0EH	
ii. AL = character to display	

II. Get Least Significant Digit, Convert to ASCII and Display
A. Recover original number	`mov    al,bl`
B. Force bits 4–7 low	`and    al,0fh`
1. AND AL with 0FH	
C. Convert to ASCII	`add    al,30h`
1. Add 30H to result	
D. Display result	`int    10h`
1. BIOS INT 10, video service 0EH	
i. AH = 0EH	
ii. AL = character to display	

III. Return to DOS
A. INT 20	`int    20h`

Testing the Program. To test the program, load register AL with a packed BCD number. For example, to load AL with 12H (and AH with 00), give the DEBUG command RAX and then enter 0012. Now type **G** for GO. The number 12 should appear followed by the usual *Program terminated normally* statement.

In the next section, we will convert Program 5.2 into a subroutine that can be called by any program requiring a packed BCD to ASCII conversion.

Figure 5.6 Listing for Program 5.2.

```
10B9:0100 mov    bl,al     ;Save original number
10B9:0102 and    al,f0     ;Force bits 0-3 low
10B9:0104 mov    cl,4      ;Four rotates
10B9:0106 ror    al,cl     ;Rotate MSD into LSD position
10B9:0108 add    al,30     ;Convert to ASCII
10B9:010A mov    ah,0e     ;BIOS video service 0E
10B9:010C int    10        ;Display character
10B9:010E mov    al,bl     ;Recover original number
10B9:0110 and    al,0f     ;Force bits 4-7 low
10B9:0112 add    al,30     ;Convert to ASCII
10B9:0114 int    10        ;Display character
10B9:0116 int    20        ;Return to DOS
```

Self-Review 5.2 (Answers on page 218)

5.2.1   Determine the contents of register AL after the following instructions have executed:

```
MOV AL,47H
AND AL,0FH
```

5.2.2   Repeat 5.2.1 for the following instructions:

```
MOV AL,18H
MOV CL,3
ROR AL,CL
```

5.2.3   Determine the contents of register AL after the following instructions have executed. Assume CF = 1.

```
MOV AL,37H
ADC AL,19H
```

5.3   Program 5.3: Two-Digit BCD Adder

Introduction

When adding BCD numbers, care must be taken to avoid results that produce invalid BCD numbers. For example, 1001 + 0001 yields 1010—the correct binary result, but an *invalid* BCD number. In Program 5.3 we develop an 80x86 program that inputs two two-digit BCD numbers from the system keyboard, adds the numbers, and displays the results on the system video display. For example, typing *87 + 46 =* will produce the result *123* on the next line. This is accomplished by inputting the ASCII numbers to be added to a memory buffer, converting the numbers to packed BCD, performing the addition, adjusting the result for decimal, and finally sending the sum to Program 5.2, which displays the result.

In this section we:

- Input and store in a memory buffer a string of characters from the system keyboard.
- Convert an ASCII number to BCD
- Add two packed BCD numbers, ensuring that the sum remains a valid BCD number.
- Link two programs by calling the second as a subroutine.

New Instructions

SUB operand1,operand2.   The subtract instruction is used to subtract two operands, which may be a CPU register or memory location and another CPU register or immediate value. Operand1 stores the result. By selecting the appropriate operand size, 8-, 16-, and 32-bit subtractions can be performed. For example, if register EAX = 12345678H and the instruction SUB EAX,246E7A10H is given, the result is:

$$
\begin{array}{r}
EAX = 1234\ \ 5678H \\
-\ \ \ \ \ 246E\ \ 7A10H \\
\hline
EDC5\ \ DC68H\ \text{and CF} = 1
\end{array}
$$

Because the subtraction of the last two bits required a borrow, the carry flag is set. Like the ADC instruction discussed in Section 5.2, SBC is used with multiple subtractions. If the carry flag is set, this instruction subtracts 1 from the result (in effect accounting for the borrow in the previous subtraction). For example (and assuming CF = 1):

```
MOV AL,27   ;AL = 27
SBC AL,5    ;AL = 27-5-1 = 21
```

DAA. This instruction performs a decimal adjust for addition on the quantity in register AL. As such, it is used to ensure that the addition of two BCD numbers contains a valid BCD result. It works by noting if the result of an addition has resulted in a carry out of bit 7 (CF = 1) or bit 3 (AF = 1), or if the high- or low-order nibbles of the result are greater than 9. If either condition is met, the DAA instruction automatically adds 6 to the corresponding nibble. Consider the following example:

```
  47H
+ 24H
  6BH   ;AF and CF = 0, but low-order nibble >9
+ 06H   ;So add 6
  71H   ;Corrected result (47 + 24 = 71)
```

Sometimes both digits will need to be corrected.

```
   47H
 + 59H
   A0H   ;AF = 1 and high-order nibble >9
 + 66H   ;So add 66H
 1 06H   ;Corrected result (47 + 59 = 106)
```

Note that in this last result CF = 1, representing the carry from the addition of A + 6. When subtracting BCD numbers, the DAS instruction can be used with similar effect.

The following two points should be noted when using the DAA and DAS instructions:

1. Both instructions are restricted to adjusting only the number in register AL.
2. Neither instruction will convert a binary number to BCD: They should only be used following an addition (DAA) or subtraction (DAS) operation.

CALL destination. This instruction transfers control to another program or procedure at the destination address. In Real Mode, the address may be within the current code segment (a *near* call) or to a procedure in a different code segment (a *far* call). In Protected Mode, the destination may specify a *call gate* to allow transfers between different privilege levels.

Procedures (or subroutines) simplify the programming task because they allow sections of code to be used over and over within other programs. Indeed, the concept of *modular programming* is one in which a program is broken into small modules, or procedures, which are then called by the main program. This allows several programmers to work on the same project, each with responsibility for one module only. Another advantage is that libraries of procedures can be maintained. Programmers can "pick and choose" from these libraries and avoid reinventing the wheel with each new program they write.

RET. When a CALL instruction is executed, the processor first pushes the address of the instruction immediately following the CALL (the return address) onto the stack (see page 142 for a review of stack operation). This ranges from two bytes for a near call (only the

16-bit instruction pointer need be saved) to four bytes for a Real Mode far call (2 bytes each for IP and CS) to six bytes for a Protected Mode far call (4 bytes for IP and 2 for CS). With the return address safely stored on the stack, control then transfers to the called procedure. To return control to the calling program, an RET (return from subroutine) instruction is given. This *pops* the top of the stack back into IP (and CS, for a far call). It is important, therefore, that each CALL instruction be balanced with a corresponding RET instruction. In addition, if multiple CALLs are performed (nested subroutines), they must be returned in the reverse order in which they were called.

New DOS Features

DOS INT 21H, Function 0AH (Buffered Keyboard Input).   Function 0AH is used to input characters from the keyboard to a memory buffer whose address is specified in DS:DX. The first byte of the buffer should hold the total buffer size. The second byte is updated by DOS and represents the actual number of bytes input to the buffer. The keyboard characters themselves are stored beginning with the third byte of the buffer. DOS closes the buffer when the return character (0DH) is input.

Function 0AH is useful when complete strings of keyboard input are required rather than the single bytes input by BIOS INT 16H service 00. In addition, input characters are automatically echoed to the screen, and the backspace key can be used to edit input before pressing return.

Problem Statement

Write an 80x86 program that adds two packed BCD numbers input from the system keyboard and computes and displays the result on the system video monitor. Data should be input in the form: 64+89=. The answer, 153, should appear on the following line.

Discussion

Program Outline.   Figure 5.7 is an outline for Program 5.3. Four major tasks are identified:

1. Get two two-digit ASCII numbers to be added and convert to BCD.
2. Add the numbers.
3. Display decimal result in ASCII.
4. Return to DOS.

The user is expected to enter the two two-digit numbers in the form:

$$64+89=$$

The result will appear on the line below. Figure 5.8 shows how the input buffer would look for the above numbers. The first part of the program sets up an eight-byte input buffer and then calls function 0AH. Because this buffer will be placed at the end of the program, and this address is not yet known, we use the name *buffer_address* to temporarily mark this location. The cursor is then positioned on the next line by outputting a line feed character via BIOS service 0E.

Figure 5.7   Outline for Program 5.3.

```
I.  Get Two Two-Digit ASCII Numbers to
    be Added and Convert to BCD
    A.  Get input string                         mov    dx,buffer-address
        1.  Set up eight-byte input buffer       mov    ah,0ah
        2.  DOS INT 21H, function 0AH            mov    si,dx
            i.   AH = 0AH                         mov    byte ptr [si],8
            ii.  DS:DX point to buffer            int    21h

    B.  Position cursor for result               mov    ah,0eh
        1.  BIOS INT 10H, service 0E             mov    al,0ah
            i.   AL = 0A (line feed)              int    10

    C.  Convert the numbers to BCD               sub    byte ptr [si+2],30h
        1.  Subtract 30H from each number        sub    byte ptr [si+3],30h
            i.   Numbers are at offset 2,3,5, and sub    byte ptr [si+5],30h
                 6 from start of buffer           sub    byte ptr [si+6],30h
        2.  Form BCD numbers                      mov    cl,4
            i.   For both numbers:                rol    byte ptr [si+3],cl
                 a.  Rotate LSD four places left  rol    byte ptr [si+6],cl
                 b.  Rotate 16 bit MSD/LSD        ror    word ptr [si+2],cl
                     four places right            ror    word ptr [si+5],cl
            ii.  Packed BCD numbers are now
                 at offsets 3 and 6

II.  Add the Numbers
    A.  Add and adjust for decimal               mov    al,[si+3]
        1.  Result is low-order sum              add    al,[si+6]
    B.  Save the result                          daa
        1.  AL will be overwritten               mov    bh,al

III. Display Decimal Result in ASCII
    A.  If sum >99 then display 1                jnc    III.B
        1.  AL = 1, call Program 2               mov    al,1
                                                 call   prog2
    B.  Display sum                     III.B    mov    al,bh
        1.  AL = sum, call Program 2             call   prog2

IV.  Return to DOS
    A.  INT 20H                                   int    20h
```

Figure 5.9 shows how the first two ASCII numbers are converted to packed BCD. In the first step, 30H is subtracted from each number. Next, the LSD is rotated left four bits. Finally, the 16-bit MSD/LSD is rotated four bits right. This packs the two BCD numbers into a single register.

Figure 5.8   Eight-byte input buffer storing the problem "64 + 89 =."

Offset:	0	1	2	3	4	5	6	7
	Working size of buffer in bytes	Number of bytes in the buffer	Digit 1 Number 1 6	Digit 2 Number 1 4	Operator +	Digit 1 Number 2 8	Digit 2 Number 2 9	Operator =
ASCII Value			36H	34H	2BH	38H	39H	3DH

Figure 5.9 Three steps are required to convert a two-digit ASCII number to packed BCD.

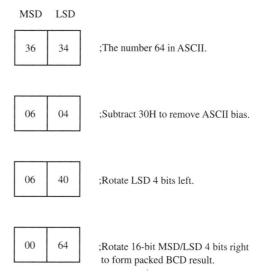

Returning to the outline, note that register SI is pointed at the base of the input buffer (*buffer_address*). The *indexed-plus-displacement* addressing mode is then used to select each digit one by one, subtract the ASCII bias (30H), and perform the rotates. In this way, the absolute address of each byte in the buffer need not be given.

Once the numbers have been packed, they can be added and adjusted for decimal. Remember, however, that this must take place in register AL. Thus, the first number (at SI + 3) is brought into register AL and then added to the second (at SI + 6). If a carry is generated, the result must be greater than 99 and the program first outputs a 1, and then the sum. This test occurs with the JNC instruction. The numbers to be displayed are then loaded into AL and Program 5.2 is called as a subroutine. This program converts the packed BCD number in AL to ASCII and displays it.

Program Listing.   Figure 5.10 provides the complete listing for Program 5.3 with the buffer, conditional jump, and call addresses resolved.[4] The input buffer is placed after the program at address 0160 (the program ends in 015D).[5] Program 5.2 has been added to the bottom of the program, beginning at address 0147. The two call instructions then reference this address. Also note that the last instruction in the Program 5.2 procedure has been changed to an RET so that control returns to Program 5.3 after each call.

Program Trace.   When testing a program such as this, it is a good idea to single-step the program to avoid a program crash (a loss of program control requiring the computer to be rebooted). Figure 5.11 illustrates the process using DEBUG's trace (**t**) command. Comments have been inserted in bold print to make the trace easier to follow. The display command (**d**) is used to view the input buffer at appropriate times.

---

[4]As mentioned in Chapter 4, this is not as simple as it looks. "Dummy" addresses must be inserted when the program is first entered. The DEBUG listing is then studied to determine the actual addresses required, and the program edited accordingly.

[5]Recall that a COM program requires that all of the segment registers have the same value. Therefore, address 0160 in the data segment is the same as address 0160 in the code segment.

Figure 5.10 Listing for Program 5.2. Note that Program 2 is used as a subroutine. The input buffer begins at address 0160.

```
10B9:0100 mov    dx,0160                 ;Point DX at input buffer
10B9:0103 mov    ah,0a                   ;DOS function 0AH
10B9:0105 mov    si,dx                   ;Point Si at input buffer
10B9:0107 mov    byte ptr [si],8         ;8 byte buffer
10B9:010A int    21                      ;Get the two numbers
10B9:010C mov    ah,0e                   ;BIOS video service
10B9:010E mov    al,0a                   ;ASCII line feed
10B9:0110 int    10                      ;
10B9:0112 sub    byte ptr [si+2],30      ;Convert each digit to BCD
10B9:0116 sub    byte ptr [si+3],30
10B9:011A sub    byte ptr [si+5],30
10B9:011E sub    byte ptr [si+6],30
10B9:0122 mov    cl,4                    ;Four rotates
10B9:0124 rol    byte ptr [si+3],cl      ;Form LSD
10B9:0127 rol    byte ptr [si+6],cl
10B9:012A ror    word ptr [si+2],cl      ;Add to MSD
10B9:012D ror    word ptr [si+5],cl
10B9:0130 mov    al,[si+3]               ;Fetch first BCD number
10B9:0133 add    al,[si+6]               ;Add to second
10B9:0136 daa                            ;Keep results decimal
10B9:0137 mov    bh,al                   ;Save results
10B9:0139 jnc    0142                    ;Check for hundredths digit
10B9:013B mov    al,1                    ;Set hundredths digit
10B9:013D call   0147                    ;Display it
10B9:0140 mov    al,bh                   ;Recover low order result
10B9:0142 call   0147                    ;Display low order result
10B9:0145 int    20                      ;Return to DOS


;****************************************************************
;   This is Program 5.2 modified to end with an RET instruction
;****************************************************************
10B9:0147 mov    bl,al                   ;Save original number
10B9:0149 and    al,f0                   ;Force bits 0-3 low
10B9:014B mov    cl,4                    ;Four rotates
10B9:014D ror    al,cl                   ;Rotate MSD into LSD
10B9:014F add    al,30                   ;Convert to ASCII
10b9:0151 mov    ah,0e                   ;BIOS video service 0E
10B9:0153 int    10                      ;Display character
10B9:0155 mov    al,bl                   ;Recover original number
10B9:0157 and    al,0f                   ;Force bits 4-7 low
10B9:0159 add    al,30                   ;Convert to ASCII
10B9:015B int    10                      ;Display character
10B9:015D ret                            ;Return to calling program

10B9:0160                                ;Input buffer begins here
```

Figure 5.11   Using DEBUG's trace command to single-step Program 5.3. Comments are shown in boldface print.

```
C:\PROGRAMS>debug prog3.com
-u100       ;Check the first few lines to verify that the program has loaded.
10DC:0100 BA6001        MOV     DX,0160
10DC:0103 B40A          MOV     AH,0A
10DC:0105 89D6          MOV     SI,DX
10DC:0107 C60408        MOV     BYTE PTR [SI],08
10DC:010A CD21          INT     21
10DC:010C B40E          MOV     AH,0E
10DC:010E B00A          MOV     AL,0A
10DC:0110 CD10          INT     10
10DC:0112 806C0230      SUB     BYTE PTR [SI+02],30
10DC:0116 806C0330      SUB     BYTE PTR [SI+03],30
10DC:011A 806C0530      SUB     BYTE PTR [SI+05],30
10DC:011E 806C0630      SUB     BYTE PTR [SI+06],30
-g 112      ;Run at full speed to address 0112 (breakpoint).
64+89=      ;Enter two test numbers in the expected format.

AX=0E0A  BX=0000  CX=005E  DX=0160  SP=FFFE  BP=0000  SI=0160  DI=0000
DS=10DC  ES=10DC  SS=10DC  CS=10DC  IP=0112    NV UP EI PL NZ NA PO NC
10DC:0112 806C0230      SUB     BYTE PTR [SI+02],30               DS:0162=36
-

-d160 110   ;Display the input buffer and note that the numbers are as expected.
10DC:0160   08 06 36 34 2B 38 39 3D-0D D9 21 D8 43 D9 21 D8   ..64+89=..!.C.!.
-

-t          ;Begin tracing instructions one at a time.

AX=0E0A  BX=0000  CX=005E  DX=0160  SP=FFFE  BP=0000  SI=0160  DI=0000
DS=10DC  ES=10DC  SS=10DC  CS=10DC  IP=0116    NV UP EI PL NZ NA PE NC
10DC:0116 806C0330      SUB     BYTE PTR [SI+03],30               DS:0163=34
-t

AX=0E0A  BX=0000  CX=005E  DX=0160  SP=FFFE  BP=0000  SI=0160  DI=0000
DS=10DC  ES=10DC  SS=10DC  CS=10DC  IP=011A    NV UP EI PL NZ NA PO NC
10DC:011A 806C0530      SUB     BYTE PTR [SI+05],30               DS:0165=38
-t

AX=0E0A  BX=0000  CX=005E  DX=0160  SP=FFFE  BP=0000  SI=0160  DI=0000
DS=10DC  ES=10DC  SS=10DC  CS=10DC  IP=011E    NV UP EI PL NZ NA PO NC
10DC:011E 806C0630      SUB     BYTE PTR [SI+06],30               DS:0166=39
-t

AX=0E0A  BX=0000  CX=005E  DX=0160  SP=FFFE  BP=0000  SI=0160  DI=0000
DS=10DC  ES=10DC  SS=10DC  CS=10DC  IP=0122    NV UP EI PL NZ NA PE NC
10DC:0122 B104          MOV     CL,04
-

-d160 110   ;Display the input buffer again and note the ASCII bias has been removed.
10DC:0160   08 06 06 04 2B 08 09 3D-0D D9 21 D8 43 D9 21 D8   ....+..=..!.C.!.
-

-t          ;Next we trace the two rotate left instructions.
```

(continued on next page)

Figure 5.11   *(continued)*

```
AX=0E0A  BX=0000  CX=0004  DX=0160  SP=FFFE  BP=0000  SI=0160  DI=0000
DS=10DC  ES=10DC  SS=10DC  CS=10DC  IP=0124    NV UP EI PL NZ NA PE NC
10DC:0124 D24403        ROL     BYTE PTR [SI+03],CL          DS:0163=04
-t

AX=0E0A  BX=0000  CX=0004  DX=0160  SP=FFFE  BP=0000  SI=0160  DI=0000
DS=10DC  ES=10DC  SS=10DC  CS=10DC  IP=0127    NV UP EI PL NZ NA PE NC
10DC:0127 D24406        ROL     BYTE PTR [SI+06],CL          DS:0166=09
-t


AX=0E0A  BX=0000  CX=0004  DX=0160  SP=FFFE  BP=0000  SI=0160  DI=0000
DS=10DC  ES=10DC  SS=10DC  CS=10DC  IP=012A    OV UP EI PL NZ NA PE NC
10DC:012A D34C02        ROR     WORD PTR [SI+02],CL          DS:0162=4006
-
-d160 110   ;Check the input buffer again.  Note the LSDs have been rotated left.
10DC:0160   08 06 06 40 2B 08 90 3D-0D D9 21 D8 43 D9 21 D8   ...@+..=..!.C.!.
-
-t          ;Now trace the two rotate rights and move the first number to AL.

AX=0E0A  BX=0000  CX=0004  DX=0160  SP=FFFE  BP=0000  SI=0160  DI=0000
DS=10DC  ES=10DC  SS=10DC  CS=10DC  IP=012D    OV UP EI PL NZ NA PE NC
10DC:012D D34C05        ROR     WORD PTR [SI+05],CL          DS:0165=9008
-t          ;

AX=0E0A  BX=0000  CX=0004  DX=0160  SP=FFFE  BP=0000  SI=0160  DI=0000
DS=10DC  ES=10DC  SS=10DC  CS=10DC  IP=0130    OV UP EI PL NZ NA PE CY
10DC:0130 8A4403        MOV     AL,[SI+03]                   DS:0163=64
-t

AX=0E64  BX=0000  CX=0004  DX=0160  SP=FFFE  BP=0000  SI=0160  DI=0000
DS=10DC  ES=10DC  SS=10DC  CS=10DC  IP=0133    OV UP EI PL NZ NA PE CY
10DC:0133 024406        ADD     AL,[SI+06]                   DS:0166=89
-
-d160 110   ;The two BCD numbers have been formed.  AL holds the first number (64).
10DC:0160   08 06 00 64 2B 00 89 3D-0D D9 21 D8 43 D9 21 D8   ...d+..=..!.C.!.
-
-t

AX=0EED  BX=0000  CX=0004  DX=0160  SP=FFFE  BP=0000  SI=0160  DI=0000
DS=10DC  ES=10DC  SS=10DC  CS=10DC  IP=0136    NV UP EI NG NZ NA PE NC
10DC:0136 27            DAA
-t          ;Add the two numbers.  Note result is not decimal.

AX=0E53  BX=0000  CX=0004  DX=0160  SP=FFFE  BP=0000  SI=0160  DI=0000
DS=10DC  ES=10DC  SS=10DC  CS=10DC  IP=0137    NV UP EI PL NZ AC PE CY
10DC:0137 88C7          MOV     BH,AL
-t          ;But the DAA fixes that problem.  Note carry flag is set.
```

Figure 5.11 *(continued)*

```
AX=0E53  BX=5300  CX=0004  DX=0160  SP=FFFE  BP=0000  SI=0160  DI=0000
DS=10DC  ES=10DC  SS=10DC  CS=10DC  IP=0139    NV UP EI PL NZ AC PE CY
10DC:0139 7307         JNB    0142
-t      ;The result is saved in BH.

AX=0E53  BX=5300  CX=0004  DX=0160  SP=FFFE  BP=0000  SI=0160  DI=0000
DS=10DC  ES=10DC  SS=10DC  CS=10DC  IP=013B    NV UP EI PL NZ AC PE CY
10DC:013B B001         MOV    AL,01
-t      ;The jump is not taken and AL is therefore set to 1.

AX=0E01  BX=5300  CX=0004  DX=0160  SP=FFFE  BP=0000  SI=0160  DI=0000
DS=10DC  ES=10DC  SS=10DC  CS=10DC  IP=013D    NV UP EI PL NZ AC PE CY
10DC:013D E80700        CALL   0147


-g      ;Run the rest of the program at full speed and the correct result appears.
0153
Program terminated normally
-
```

Self-Review 5.3 (Answers on page 218)

5.3.1   For the instruction sequence below, determine the contents of register AL (a) after the add instruction and (b) after the DAA instruction.

```
MOV AL,28H
ADD AL,35
DAA
```

5.3.2   When using DOS INT 21 function 0AH (buffered keyboard input), if DX = 0200H, the user keyboard characters are stored beginning at offset address _____.

5.3.3   One byte can store _____ ASCII character(s) or _____ BCD digit(s).

5.4   Program 5.4: 80x86 Music Machine

Introduction

Today's PC is a multimedia computer capable of displaying full-motion video with stereo sound. This is accomplished via the addition of CD-ROM drives and sound cards with on-board digital signal processors. Program 5.4 shows how to create computer music through a much less sophisticated method: the PC's integrated 8253/54 timer and onboard speaker. The technique involves programming the timer to generate square waves at an audio frequency and then routing these waveforms to the PC's built-in speaker. While not exactly "high fidelity," surprising results can be obtained. In addition, this program provides an opportunity to examine the 80x86's IN and OUT instructions used for accessing I/O ports.

In this section we:

- Show how to control the PC's built-in speaker.
- Explain how to program the PC timer chip to generate square waves of various frequencies.
- Use the 80x86's I/O instructions to read data from an input port and transfer data to an output port.

New Instructions

LODSW (load string word).   This instruction moves the word pointed to by register SI to register AX. Register SI is then incremented (if the direction flag is reset) or decremented (if the direction flag is set) by 2 to point at the next word in the string. Thus, LODSW can be used in place of the two instructions:

```
MOV AX,[SI]    ;Fetch word to AX
ADD SI,2       ;Increment pointer (or decrement) to next word
```

Two other versions of this instruction can be used: LODSB (load string byte) and LODSD (load string double word). The former loads AL with the *byte* pointed to by SI (incrementing or decrementing SI by 1). The latter loads EAX with the *doubleword* pointed to by SI; in this case SI is incremented (or decremented) by 4.

Program 5.4 uses the LODSW instruction to fetch music note-codes from a table. These codes are then output to the timer chip and converted to square waves.

CLD (clear direction flag).   This instruction is used with the LODSB, LODSW, and LODSD instructions as explained above. It causes these instructions to auto-increment by 1, 2, or 4, respectively, when executed. The STD instruction performs the opposite function. It sets the direction flag, thereby enabling the *auto-decrement* mode for the string instructions.

OUT Port,AL.   This instruction outputs the byte in register AL to the 8-bit output port whose address is specified. 16- and 32-bit ports are also supported using the instructions *OUT Port,AX* and *OUT Port,EAX*. In all three cases, the port address must be between 0 and 255. Also note that all output data must pass through the accumulator (registers AL, AX, or EAX). The following instructions are all *invalid:*

```
OUT 625,AL    ;Immediate port address must be less than 256
OUT 32,BL     ;8-bit output port must use AL
OUT CL,AL     ;8-bit port address must be an immediate value
OUT 32,48     ;Immediate output data is not allowed
```

The 80x86 processors use address lines A0–A15 to generate I/O port addresses. This accommodates 65,536 different port addresses from 0000 to FFFFH. Port addresses greater than 255 require that the address be placed in register DX. For example, to output 3C0H to port 625H, the following instructions are required:

```
MOV AX,3C0H    ;Data to output in AX
MOV DX,625     ;I/O port address in DX
OUT DX,AX      ;Output the data
```

IN AL,Port.   This instruction inputs data to register AL from the specified port. The same conditions and restrictions described for the output instructions apply. The following are examples of valid and invalid input instructions:

```
IN    AL,192    ;Valid. 8-bit data from port 192 is input to AL.
IN    EAX,192   ;Valid. 32-bit data from port 192 is input to EAX.
IN    AX,DX     ;Valid. 16-bit data from the port whose address
                 is stored in register DX is input to AX.
IN    AL,314    ;Invalid. Immediate port address cannot exceed 255.
IN    BL,DX     ;Invalid. Destination must be AL, AX, or EAX.
```

New DOS/DEBUG Features

The System Timer.   All members of the PC family include a three-channel programmable timer.[6] The three channels are allocated as follows:

- **Channel 0.** When the PC is booted, the ROM BIOS programs this channel to operate at 18.2 ticks/second. These timer ticks are used by various programs to activate tasks that must occur at regular intervals. DOS, for example, uses this function to keep track of the time of day.
- **Channel 1.** On most PCs this channel is dedicated to generating a memory refresh signal. This signal is used to initiate a "dummy" read cycle—that is, a read cycle that refreshes the memory but does not actually store any data.
- **Channel 2.** This channel is dedicated to the PC's built-in speaker. By programming the timer to operate as a square-wave oscillator, various sounds can be produced.

Controlling the PC's Speaker.   Figure 5.12 shows how the timer's output signal is routed to the PC's speaker. An 8255 PPI (programmable peripheral interface) is used to control the gating between the timer output and the speaker.[7] On all PCs, the time base signal applied to the timer has a frequency of 1.193186 MHz. To produce an audio output, timer port 42H must receive a 16-bit frequency divisor that reduces this to a frequency in the audio range.

Table 5.1 lists the frequencies for eight octaves of musical notes. Note that the frequency of each note doubles with each succeeding octave. Middle C on a piano's keyboard corresponds to tone C, octave 5, and has a frequency of 261.6 Hz. To program the timer for this frequency, we first compute the divisor as:

$$1,193,186 \div 261.6 = 4561 = 11D1H$$

To play this note on the PC's speaker, three steps are required:

1. Program channel 2 of the timer to function as a square-wave oscillator. This is done by sending the data byte B6H to port 43H.

---

[6]On the original PC this was accomplished via the 8253 timer chip. On modern PCs this chip (or its equivalent) has been integrated into a single chip that performs all of the PC's system-board-level I/O functions.

[7]This is another chip that has been integrated and is no longer "visible" on the system board. It contains three programmable I/O ports and a control port (ports 60–63H). The timer interface uses only bits 0 and 1 of port 61. Chapter 8 provides specific details on the 8255's architecture and programming.

Figure 5.12 Equivalent diagram for controlling the PC's speaker. Channel 2 of the timer will drive the speaker when bits 0 and 1 of port 61H are both high.

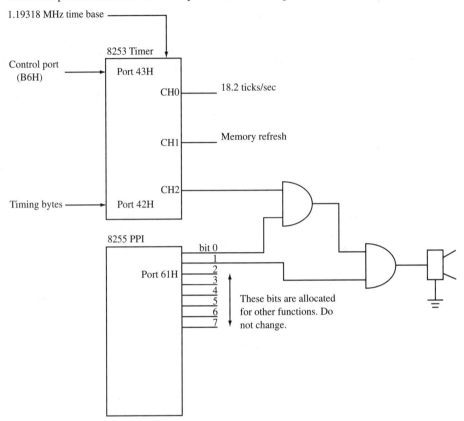

Table 5.1   Eight Octaves of Musical Notes

Tone	Octave 1	Octave 2	Octave 3	Octave 4	Octave 5	Octave 6	Octave 7	Octave 8
C	16.4	32.7	65.4	130.8	261.6	523.2	1046.5	2093.0
C#	17.3	34.6	69.3	138.6	277.2	554.4	1108.7	2217.5
D	18.4	36.7	73.4	146.8	293.7	587.3	1174.6	2349.3
D#	19.4	38.9	77.8	155.6	311.1	622.2	1244.5	2489.0
E	20.6	41.2	82.4	164.8	329.6	659.3	1318.5	2637.0
F	21.8	43.7	87.3	174.6	349.2	698.5	1396.9	2793.8
F#	23.1	46.3	92.5	185.0	370.0	740.0	1480.0	2960.0
G	24.5	49.0	98.0	196.0	392.0	784.0	1568.0	3136.0
G#	26.0	51.9	103.8	207.7	415.3	830.6	1661.2	3322.4
A	27.5	55.0	110.0	220.0	440.0	880.0	1760.0	3520.0
A#	29.1	58.3	116.5	233.1	466.2	932.3	1864.7	3729.3
B	30.9	61.7	123.5	246.9	493.9	987.8	1975.6	3951.1

2. Output the frequency divisor (low byte then high byte) to port 42H: In this example, D1H followed by 11H.

3. Enable the speaker by setting bits 0 and 1 of PPI port 61H. Note: Bits 2–7 of this port are used for other functions and their values should not be changed.

Testing with DEBUG.   Using DEBUG's built-in I/O commands, we can test the above programming sequence. At the DEBUG prompt, type:

```
-o43,b6    ;Output 43 to port B6 (timer control code)
-o42,d1    ;Output low-order divisor byte to port 42
-o42,11    ;Output high-order divisor byte to port 42
-i61       ;Input the data at port 61-get back 20H⁸
20
-o61,23    ;Output this same data but with bits 0 and 1
             set(turn on speaker)
-o61,20    ;Now reset these same bits (turn off speaker)
```

After the o61,23 command, a tone should be heard. The o61,20 command should turn off the speaker and stop the tone. With the hardware now verified, we are ready to write the program.

Problem Statement

Write an 80x86 program that plays the eight notes from middle C to high C on the PC's internal speaker. Each time a key is pressed, the next note in succession should be played.

Discussion

Program Outline.   Figure 5.13 shows the program outline. Three major steps have been identified:

1. *Initialize the data table.* The music note-codes will be stored in a table immediately following the program instructions. Because the string instructions will be used to access these note-codes, register SI must be pointed to the base of this table and the direction flag set to auto-increment.

2. *Each time a key is pressed, play a new note.* This part of the program uses BIOS INT 16H service 0 to detect that a key has been pressed. The LODSW instruction is then used to fetch a note-code. If the code is 0000, the program ends; if not zero, the timer chip is programmed to function as an oscillator by outputting B6H to port 43H. Then the low and high bytes of the note-code are sent to port 42H. Finally, the speaker is enabled by setting bits 0 and 1 of port 61. Note that this requires the contents of this port to first be read with an input instruction. The instruction OR AL,3 then sets bits 0 and 1 (without disturbing bits 2–7), enabling the speaker.

3. *Return to DOS when all notes have been played.* When a note-code of 0000 is detected, the program ends. This requires that the speaker first is turned off and then the DOS INT 20H instruction is executed. Notice that to reset bits 0 and 1 without changing bits 2–7, the data input from port 61 is ANDed with FCH (1111 1100) and then output.

---

[8]Depending on your PC, you may or may not receive the data 20H. No matter. Simply modify this number so that bits 0 and 1 are set to turn on the PC's speaker.

Figure 5.13   Outline for Program 5.4.

I. Initialize Data Table	
A. Point SI at the note table	`mov    si,music_table`
B. Clear direction flag to auto-increment table access	`cld`
C. Load note-codes in memory	
1. Table assumed to immediately follow the program codes	
2. 0000 = code for end of data	
II. Each Time a Key Is Pressed, Play a New Note	
A. Wait for a key to be pressed	`II.A  mov    ah,0`
1. BIOS INT 16H, Service 00	`      int    16`
i. AH = 0	
ii. Keyboard character returned in AL	
(value = "don't care")	
B. Fetch a note from table and save	`lodsw`
1. AX = Word Ptr [SI]	`mov    bx,ax`
2. SI = SI + 2 ;Point to next word	
C. End of Table?	`cmp    AX,0000`
1. AX = 0000?	`jz     III`
i. Yes: Goto III	
ii. No: Play the Note	`mov    al,b6`
a. Program timer	`out    43,al`
1) Port 43 = B6H	
b. Output the divisor	`mov    al,bl`
1) Retrieve saved note-code	`out    42,al`
2) Port 42 = low byte then high byte	`mov    al,bh`
c. Enable speaker	`out    42,al`
1) Set bits 0–1 of Port 61	`in     al,61`
d. Goto II.A	`or     al,3`
	`out    61,al`
	`jmp    II.A`
III. Return to DOS When All Notes Have Been Played	`III   in     al,61`
A. Turn off speaker	`      and    al,1c`
1. Reset bits 0–1 of Port 61	`      out    61,al`
B. DOS INT 20H	`int    20`

Program Listing.   Figure 5.14 shows the program listing. The note-codes are added to the end of the program beginning at address 012C using the *dw (define word)* pseudo-op. In this case, the codes shown correspond to the eight notes in octave five from middle C to high C.

Self-Review 5.4 (Answers on page 218–219)

5.4.1   What 80x86 instruction can be used to fetch a string of words stored in memory, automatically incrementing the memory pointer?

5.4.2   Assume the data 27H must be output to port 9EH. Give the 80x86 instruction sequence required.

Figure 5.14   Listing for Program 5.4. The eight notes from middle C to high C will be played.

```
1446:0100 mov    si,012c        ;Point SI at music table
1446:0103 cld                   ;Direction flag to auto-increment
1446:0104 mov    ah,0           ;BIOS service 0
1446:0106 int    16             ;Wait for keypress
1446:0108 lodsw                 ;Fetch note code
1446:0109 mov    bx,ax          ;Save note code
1446:010B cmp    ax,0000        ;Check for last
1446:010E jz     0124           ;If it is, then quit
1446:0110 mov    al,b6          ;Timer-enable code
1446:0112 out    43,al          ;Output to timer
1446:0114 mov    al,bl          ;Retrieve low order note code
1446:0116 out    42,al          ;Ouptut to timer
1446:0118 mov    al,bh          ;Retrieve high order note code
1446:011A out    42,al          ;Output to timer
1446:011C in     al,61          ;Access speaker control port
1446:011E or     al,3           ;Set speaker control bits
1446:0120 out    61,al          ;Enable speaker
1446:0122 jmp    0104           ;Go and wait for another keypress
1446:0124 in     al,61          ;Access speaker control port
1446:0126 and    al,fc          ;Reset speaker control bits
1446:0128 out    61,al          ;Turn off speaker
1446:012A int    20             ;Return to DOS
1446:012C dw     11d1           ;Note code for middle C
1446:012E dw     0fdf           ;D
1446:0130 dw     0e24           ;E
1446:0132 dw     0d59           ;F
1446:0134 dw     0be4           ;G
1446:0136 dw     0a98           ;A
1446:0138 dw     0970           ;B
1446:013A dw     08e9           ;High C
1446:013C dw     0000           ;End of data
```

5.4.3   Channel _____ of the PC's system timer is used for driving the loudspeaker.

5.4.4   What is the DEBUG command equivalent to the instruction sequence in Question 5.4.2?

5.4.5   Calculate the hexadecimal value of the divisor required to play the note F# in octave five using the PC's timer chip.

5.5   Program 5.5: Testing the Alternate Keys During Boot-Up

Introduction

In Figure 2.6 we listed the sequence of events that occur when an MS-DOS–based computer is booted. The last event in that sequence is the execution of any commands in the AUTOEXEC.BAT file. In Program 5.5, we write a program that tests the left and right alternate keys and returns their status to DOS in the form of an *error code* that can be tested in AUTOEXEC.BAT. Based on this code, different boot sequences can be initiated.

In this section we:

- Write a COM program that returns an error code to DOS.
- Use the batch file *if errorlevel* command to test for a specific error code.
- Modify the AUTOEXEC.BAT file to allow different boot sequences based on the left and right alternate key status.

New DOS Features

BIOS INT 16H, Service 12H (Get Extended Shift Key Status).   Service 12H returns the status (pressed or not pressed) of all of the shift keys on the 101/102-key keyboard in registers AL and AH. Figure 5.15 shows the bit assignments. If a key is pressed, its corresponding bit position is set; for example, if both alternate keys (only) are pressed, register AH = 0000 1010 = 0AH.

DOS INT 21H, Function 4CH (Terminate with Error Code).   Function 4CH is similar to DOS INT 20H, which we have been using to end our programs and return to DOS. Function 4CH, however, closes any open files and allows a user-specified error code to be returned to DOS in register AL. Note that the error code is determined by the user: There is no standard error code message. In Program 5.5 we pass back the shift key status as the error code.

If ErrorLevel* n *Goto Label.   This statement is used in a DOS batch file to test an error code returned by a program. If the error code is equal to or greater than *n*, control in the batch file transfers to the statements immediately following the label. For example, assuming the error code corresponds to the extended shift key status shown in Figure 5.15 for register AH, the following batch file can be used to test the right alternate key.

```
if errorlevel 8 goto right
goto done
:right
Echo Right alternate key is pressed
:done
```

Figure 5.15   BIOS INT 16H, service 12H returns the extended shift key status in registers AL and AH.

Bit:	7	6	5	4	3	2	1	0
	System request	Caps lock	Num lock	Scroll lock	Right alternate	Right control	Left alternate	Left control

Register AH

Bit:	7	6	5	4	3	2	1	0
	Insert	Caps lock	Num lock	Scroll lock	Alternate	Control	Left shift	Right shift

Register AL

If you were to test this batch file, you would find that the message *Right alternate key is pressed* appears if *any* of the Right Alternate, Scroll Lock, Num Lock, Caps Lock, or System Request keys are pressed. Why? The *if errorlevel* statement transfers control if the error code is *equal to or greater than* 8. Because the keys mentioned have values of 8 or higher, they *all* pass the errorlevel test.

We can fix this problem by modifying the test as follows:

```
if errorlevel 8 if not errorlevel 9 goto right
```

This line is interpreted by DOS as "if the errorlevel is greater than or equal to 8 but not greater than or equal to 9, transfer control to the label right." Because only an errorlevel of 8 will pass this test, the statement is equivalent to "if the errorlevel equals 8, transfer control to the label right."

Problem Statement

Write an 80x86 program that scans the keyboard and returns the extended shift key status as an error code to DOS. Modify the system AUTOEXEC.BAT file to test this code as follows:

1. If the left alternate key is pressed, open the AUTOEXEC.BAT file for editing.
2. If the right alternate key is pressed, open CONFIG.SYS for editing.
3. If both the right and left alternate keys are pressed, start Windows.
4. If neither alternate key is pressed, display the DOS version.

Discussion

Program Listing.   Two steps are required to accomplish this project. The first is to write the COM program that gets the shift key status (get_alt.com). This turns out to be quite simple, as shown in Figure 5.16. BIOS service 12H scans the keyboard and returns with the shift key status in registers AL and AH. We then mask off all bits in register AH except for the alternate keys in bits 1 and 3. The resulting code is then transferred to register AL, where it is returned as the error code by DOS function 4CH.

The second step in the project is to test the error code in AUTOEXEC.BAT. Figure 5.17 provides an example. The first seven lines are typical; @echo off hides the execution of the commands to follow, the path is set, the mouse driver and doskey are loaded, the default dir command and prompt are set, and the screen is cleared. Get_alt is then run and the status is returned as an errorlevel code that is tested in the next four lines. Four options are then presented via the labels *:none, :left, :right,* and *:both.* Each ends with a *goto end* statement, which transfers control to the end of the batch file, causing it to terminate.

Figure 5.16   Listing for Program 5.5.

```
1415:0100 mov    ah,12       ;BIOS Service 12
1415:0102 int    16          ;Get extended shift key status
1415:0104 and    ah,0a       ;Test ALT keys only
1415:0107 mov    al,ah       ;Return code
1415:0109 mov    ah,4c       ;DOS Function 4C
1415:010B int    21          ;Return to DOS with error code
```

Figure 5.17   Sample AUTOEXEC.BAT file to test Program 5.5 (get_alt.com). Four different key combinations are tested.

```
@echo off
path c:\dos;c:\windows;c:\util
mouse.com /Y
doskey
set dircmd=/l/o:-g
prompt $p$g
cls

get_alt                  'Get alternate key status

if errorlevel 0 if not errorlevel 1 goto none
if errorlevel 2 if not errorlevel 3 goto left
if errorlevel 8 if not errorlevel 9 goto right
if errorlevel 10 if not errorlevel 11 goto both

:none                    'No keys down
ver
goto end

:left                    'Left alternate key down
edit c:\autoexec.bat
goto end

:right                   'Right alternate key down
edit c:\config.sys
goto end

:both                    'Left and right alternate keys down
win

:end
```

Because get_alt.com does not wait for a key to be pressed, it is important to hold down the desired alternate keys *before* AUTOEXEC.BAT starts. This can be done by holding down the desired keys when the message *Starting MS-DOS* appears during boot-up. In progrom 5.7 we will add a time delay to this routine that negates this requirement.

Self-Review 5.5 (Answers on page 219)

5.5.1   If only the Num Lock key is pressed when BIOS INT 16H, service 12H is called, the hex value returned in AX will be _____.

5.5.2   In Program 5.5, if the left alternate key (only) is pressed, what is the value of the error code returned to DOS?

5.5.3 The batch file command *if errorlevel 5 if not errorlevel 6 goto print* will transfer control to the print label:

(a) Only if the errorlevel is equal to 5

(b) If the errorlevel is greater than or equal to 5

(c) If the errorlevel is less than 5

(d) None of the above

5.6 Program 5.6: Floppy Disk Media Check

Introduction

With regard to their physical outline, floppy disks are commonly described as being 3.5- or 5.25-inch. Both disk types are further divided into high- and low-density versions. Program 5.6 checks the media size of the user-specified drive and reports back its capacity in bytes. This is accomplished by accessing the *media byte* for that drive and using the returned information as a pointer into a translation table. The data in this table is then used as a pointer to the appropriate disk-size message.

In this section we:

- Test for the presence of a disk in a specified drive.
- Pass a parameter to a COM program via the command line.
- Construct a translation table.

New Instructions

Push operand.[9]   This instruction pushes the operand, which may be any 16- or 32-bit register or memory location or a 16- or 32-bit immediate value, onto the stack (*Note:* Immediate data is not allowed with the 8086 or DEBUG). The value of the stack pointer is decremented by 2 for word operands and 4 for 32-bit operands. The next paragraph provides an example.

POP operand.   This instruction is used to recover data from the stack top to the destination operand. For example, the instruction POP EBX pops the 32-bit value currently atop the stack into the EBX register. The stack pointer is then incremented by 4.

The PUSH and POP instructions are almost always used together, as they offer a convenient way of saving a CPU register, particularly when all other registers are in use. For example, suppose the word in register BX must be output to the I/O port whose address is in register DX. Furthermore, assume register CX is being used as a loop counter and registers SI and DI as memory pointers. Moving the data in BX to AX will wipe out important input data in this register. How can the data in BX be output? The following sequence can be used:

```
PUSH AX      ;Save AX on the stack
MOV  AX,BX   ;Transfer the data to be output to AX
OUT  DX,AX   ;Output the data
POP  AX      ;Recover the original contents of AX
```

---

[9]See page 142, *Using the Stack,* for a description of the stack and the stack pointer.

Notice how the POP instruction works in coordination with the PUSH instruction to re-cover the data saved on the stack. To the programmer, the advantage of these two instruc-tions is their *transparency;* that is, the data is simply saved on the stack without the pro-grammer needing to know (or care about) the exact memory address.

LOOP destination.   The LOOP instruction decrements register CX (or ECX) and, if the result is not zero, transfers control to the destination address, which must be in the range from 128 bytes before the next instruction to 127 bytes after the next instruction. No flags are affected. The loop instruction is used to repeat a group of instructions several times. For example, the following instructions output 256 bytes of data stored in memory to out-put port 27H.

```
        MOV    CX,100    ;Set loop counter to 256
A1:     LODSB            ;Fetch a data byte to AL
        OUT    27,AL     ;Output the byte
        LOOP   A1        ;Repeat 256 times (until CX = 0)
```

XLAT.   This instruction uses the contents of register AL as an *offset* into a table whose base address is in DS:BX (or DS:EBX). The byte at this location is then moved into reg-ister AL (overwriting the offset value). Symbolically, the instruction can be written as: AL ← [DS:BX + AL]. In Program 5.6 we compute a unique number (code) in register AL for each disk drive type. XLAT is then used to "look up" the address where the ASCII message describing that drive type is stored. Thus, the instruction offers a way of *trans-lating* a code value into a memory address.

New DOS Features

BIOS INT 13H, Service 2 (Read Disk Sectors).   Service 2 is for reading one or more floppy disk sectors into a memory buffer whose address is in ES:BX. AL holds the num-ber of sectors to be read, CL the sector number, CH the cylinder (or track) number, DH the head number, and DL the drive number (drive A is 0, B is 1, etc.). If more than one sector is to be read, all sectors must be on the same track. Upon return, the carry flag is reset and AH = 0 if the operation was successful; if not, the carry flag is set and AH holds an error code.

Program 5.6 calls this service repeatedly to determine that a disk is ready in the spec-ified drive. If after ten attempts the carry flag continues to be set, the program displays a message indicating that the drive is not ready (no disk present or drive door not closed). Any data read into memory is ignored.

DOS INT 21H, Function 1CH (Get Specified Drive Information).   Function 1CH returns important information about the drive specified in DL (DL is 0 for the current drive, 1 for drive A, 2 for drive B, etc.). (Caution: Note that this assignment is not the same as that used by BIOS INT 13H, service 2 described above).

- If successful, AL contains the number of sectors per cluster; FF if unsuccessful.
- CX contains the size in bytes of the disk sectors (normally 512).
- DX contains the total number of disk clusters.
- DS:BX points to the location of the *media byte* associated with the specified drive.

Table 5.2   Program 5.6 Message Coding

Disk Type/Message	Sectors/Cluster	Media Byte	Code*	Message Address
360K 5.25″	2	FD	FF	0175H
1.2 MB 5.25″	1	F9	FA	0181H
720K 3.5″	2	F9	FB	018D
1.44 MB 3.5″	1	F0	F1	0198H
Drive not ready	—	—	00	0165H
Invalid drive	—	—	01	013DH

*Sectors/cluster + media byte.

Table 5.2 gives the number of sectors per cluster and media byte values for the various disk sizes. Studying this table, you can see that the media bytes for a 720K floppy disk and 1.2 MB floppy disk are the same. In order to distinguish between these two disk types, Program 5.6 adds the number of sectors per cluster to the media byte to obtain a unique code for each disk type. This is shown in the Code column.

The Message Address column indicates the starting address for each message. This will be explained in more detail later in this section.

The Program Segment Prefix (PSP).   When MS-DOS loads a program into memory, it sets aside a 256-byte block of memory immediately ahead of the program instructions. Because it precedes the program itself, it is often called the *Program Segment Prefix* or *PSP*. This should help explain why all of the programs we have written begin at offset 0100H—the PSP occupies memory from 0000 to 00FFH.

The PSP stores information that DOS uses to help run the program. Table 5.3 provides a brief description of the most common PSP fields and their offset addresses. In Program 5.6 we take advantage of the fact that any command line parameters (characters typed after the program name itself) are stored in the PSP beginning at offset 81H. By examining this area, we can determine which drive the user wants to check.

Problem Statement

Write an 80x86 program that determines the size in bytes of the specified drive. For example, with a high-density 3.5-inch disk in drive A, the command CHECK A should return 1.44 MB.

Table 5.3   Common PSP Fields and Their Offset Addresses

Offset	Description
00H	Code for the INT 20 instruction. A call to this address can be used to terminate your program.
0AH	The address of the system routine that will gain control when your program ends.
2CH	Segment address of the memory block that holds the system environment variables (DOS path, prompt, etc.).
80H	The length of the parameters on the command line.
81H	The first character in the command line (usually a space).

Discussion

Program Outline.   In Figure 5.18 we show the program outline. The first task is to check that the user-specified drive is ready. This is accomplished by retrieving the drive letter from the PSP at offset 82H (the byte at 81H should be a space). By forcing bits 4–7 of this byte low and subtracting 1 from the result, we end up with a number that is equal to the drive letter as defined by BIOS INT 13H.[10] The next step is to set up the CPU registers for

Figure 5.18   Outline for Program 5.6.

I. Check for Specified Drive to Be Ready	
A. Get drive letter from user	`mov   al,[82h]`
1. Access byte at offset 82H in the PSP	`and   al,0fh`
2. Convert drive letter to number	`dec   al`
i. Mask bits 4–7	
ii. Subtract 1 (drive A = 0)	
B. Test for a disk in this drive	
1. Attempt to read head 0, sector 1, track 0 of the	`mov   dl,al`
specified drive	`mov   cx,000a`
i. BIOS INT 13, service 2	`mov   ax,0201h`
a. AH = 2	`mov   dh,0`
b. DL = drive number	`mov   bx,0300h`
c. DH = head number (0)	`I.B.1   push  cx`
d. CL = sector number (1)	`mov   cx,0001h`
e. CH = track number (0)	`int   13h`
f. AL = number of sectors to read	
g. ES:BX = address of buffer	
2. Success (CF = 0)?	`pop   cx`
i. No:	`jnc   II.A`
a. Repeat 10 times	`loop  I.B.1`
b. Display error message (II.B.1.ii)	`mov   al,0`
ii. Yes: Goto II.A	`jmp   II.B.1.ii`
II. Determine and Display Drive Size	
A. Access media byte	`II.A   push  ds`
1. DOS INT 21, function 1C	`inc   dl`
i. DS:BX points to media byte (save DS)	`mov   ah,1ch`
ii. DL = drive letter	`int   21h`
a. Add 1 for function 1C compatibility	
B. Display appropriate drive size message	`add   [bx],al`
1. Convert media byte into message pointer	`mov   al,[bx]`
i. Form code: Media byte + sectors/cluster	`pop   ds`
ii. Translate code into low-byte message	`II.B.1.ii mov   bx,xlat_table`
offset address	`xlat`
2. Display message	`mov   dl,al`
a. DOS INT 21, function 9	`mov   dh,01`
1) DS:DX points to message	`mov   ah,9`
	`int   21h`
III. Return to DOS	
A. INT 20H	`int   20`

---

[10]Strictly speaking, this is not correct. We actually end up with the low four bits of the ASCII character typed at the command line. This means any ASCII character whose last digit is a 1 or 2 will be interpreted as drive A or drive B. Analysis and Design Question 5.14 examines a program modification that provides a more thorough test.

the BIOS call. In this case we will make ten attempts to read the sector at head 0, track 0, sector 1. The data read (which is unimportant) will be stored beginning at offset 0300H.

In the program instructions, notice that register CX is used to store the attempt-counter. However, because this same register must also store the sector and track number, we must temporarily save CX on the stack via the PUSH CX instruction. After the BIOS call, CX is recovered via the POP CX instruction. The success or failure of the operation is indicated by the carry flag status: If reset, the drive has been successfully read and control moves on to the next block; if set, the loop instruction decrements the attempt-counter in CX and transfers control back to the BIOS 13H call for another attempt. Ten consecutive failures cause the program to fall out of the loop. In this case a 0 is moved into AL, a code value that will be used to indicate that the drive is not ready (see Table 5.2).

The second program task is to determine the disk size and display the appropriate message. This is accomplished by first calling DOS INT 21H, function 1CH. Upon return, DS:BX points to the *media byte* and AL holds the number of sectors per cluster. Because the BIOS call will change the DS segment register, a PUSH DS instruction is used prior to executing the call to save this register. Also notice that register DL must be incremented by 1 to agree with the drive number definition used by function 1CH.

The next step is to add the contents of AL to the media byte to form the drive code (described in Table 5.2.) After pointing register BX to the base of the translation table, the XLAT instruction is used to retrieve the offset address of the message for the specified drive. Moving this to DL and setting the high-order address to 01 (all messages share this high-order address), DOS INT 21H, function 9 is called to display the message. Finally, INT 20H ends the program.

Program Instructions.   Figure 5.19 shows the annotated program listing derived from the outline. Notice that the drive-size messages are added immediately after the program instructions using the *db* operator and each is terminated with a *$*, as required by function 9.

Memory Usage.   Figure 5.20 shows the three blocks of memory used by the program. The first, from 0000 to 00FFH, is the PSP. In this example, the user has typed *CHECK A*. Examining the command line parameters beginning at offset 0080H, we interpret these bytes as:

[80H] = 02.   The number of bytes in the command line (a space and the letter A).
[81H] = 20.   This is the first byte in the command line (ASCII space).
[82H] = 41H.   This is the second byte in the command line (ASCII A).
[83H] = 0DH.   The end of the command line (ASCII return).

The program itself begins at offset 0100H. The six ASCII messages follow, beginning at 013DH: each is terminated with a 24H *($)*. Notice that the offset addresses of these messages (in agreement with Table 5.2) are:

013DH   Invalid drive specification or bad disk.
0165H   Drive not ready.
0175H   360KB 5.25″.
0181H   1.2MB 5.25″.
018DH   720KB 3.5″.
0198H   1.44MB 3.5″.

The last memory block is the *translation table*. It stores the offset address of the message for each code. For example, a code of F1 was used to signify a 1.44 MB floppy disk

Figure 5.19 Listing for Program 5.6. Note that the ASCII messages are stored at the end of the program beginning at offset 013DH.

```
1415:0100 mov    al,[82]              ;Get drive letter
1415:0103 and    al,0f                ;Convert to number
1415:0105 dec    al                   ;Adjust for BIOS drive offset
1415:0107 mov    dl,al                ;Drive number to DL
1415:0109 mov    cx,000a              ;Prepare for 10 loops
1415:010C mov    ax,0201              ;BIOS service 2, read one sector
1415:010F mov    dh,0                 ;Head 0
1415:0111 mov    bx,0300              ;Buffer address
1415:0114 push   cx                   ;Save loop counter
1415:0115 mov    cx,0001              ;Cylinder 0, sector 1
1415:0118 int    13                   ;Read one sector
1415:011A pop    cx                   ;Recover loop counter
1415:011B jnc    123                  ;If successful, continue
1415:011D loop   114                  ;Else try to read it again
1415:011F mov    al,0                 ;Set error code to 0 (10 failures)
1415:0121 jmp    12f                  ;Go and display the error
1415:0123 push   ds                   ;Save DS (changed by function 1C)
1415:0124 inc    dl                   ;Adjust drive number for DOS
1415:0126 mov    ah,1c                ;DOS function 1CH
1415:0128 int    21                   ;Get media byte
1415:012A add    [bx],al              ;Add sectors/cluster
1415:012C mov    al,[bx]              ;Code to AL for data look-up
1415:012E pop    ds                   ;Recover DS
1415:012F mov    bx,0200              ;BX points to base of message table
1415:0132 xlat                        ;Look up message
1415:0133 mov    dl,al                ;Offset of message in DX
1415:0135 mov    dh,01                ;All messsage are on page 01
1415:0137 mov    ah,9                 ;DOS function 9
1415:0139 int    21                   ;Display message
1415:013B int    20                   ;return to DOS
1415:013D db 'Invalid drive specification or bad disk$'
1415:0165 db 'Drive not ready$'
1415:0175 db '360KB 5.25"$'
1415:0181 db '1.2MB 5.25"$'
1415:018D db '720KB 3.5"$'
1415:0198 db '1.44MB 3.5"$'
```

(see Table 5.2). The XLAT instruction, with AL = F1, retrieves the contents of memory location 0200 + F1 (BX + AL), or 02F1. Studying Figure 5.20, the byte in this location is 98H. Moving this to DL and 01 to DH points the DX register at 0198, the offset address of the 1.44 MB message.

In Program 5.6 we define six different disk-size codes. The translation table, however, has room for 256 entries (by definition). In this example we have programmed the unused code "slots" with address 3D—the invalid drive message.

Figure 5.20   Memory usage for Program 5.6.

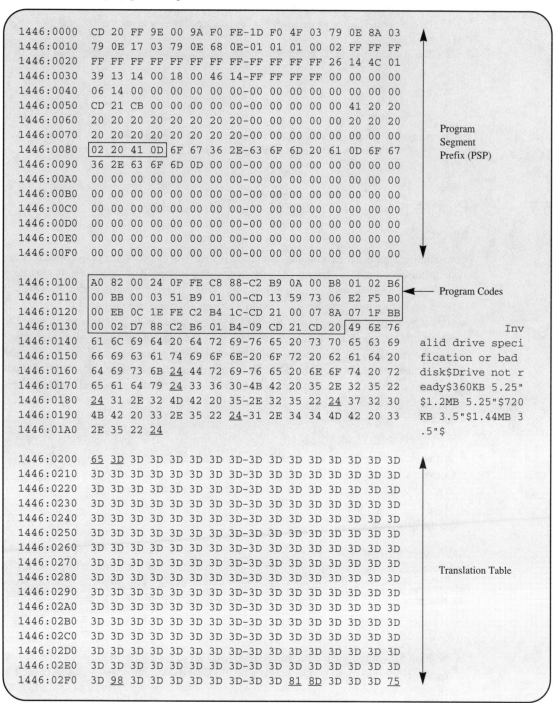

```
1446:0000   CD 20 FF 9E 00 9A F0 FE-1D F0 4F 03 79 0E 8A 03
1446:0010   79 0E 17 03 79 0E 68 0E-01 01 01 00 02 FF FF FF
1446:0020   FF FF FF FF FF FF FF FF-FF FF FF FF 26 14 4C 01
1446:0030   39 13 14 00 18 00 46 14-FF FF FF FF 00 00 00 00
1446:0040   06 14 00 00 00 00 00 00-00 00 00 00 00 00 00 00
1446:0050   CD 21 CB 00 00 00 00 00-00 00 00 00 00 00 41 20 20
1446:0060   20 20 20 20 20 20 20 20-00 00 00 00 00 20 20 20
1446:0070   20 20 20 20 20 20 20 20-00 00 00 00 00 00 00 00
1446:0080   02 20 41 0D 6F 67 36 2E-63 6F 6D 20 61 0D 6F 67
1446:0090   36 2E 63 6F 6D 0D 00 00-00 00 00 00 00 00 00 00
1446:00A0   00 00 00 00 00 00 00 00-00 00 00 00 00 00 00 00
1446:00B0   00 00 00 00 00 00 00 00-00 00 00 00 00 00 00 00
1446:00C0   00 00 00 00 00 00 00 00-00 00 00 00 00 00 00 00
1446:00D0   00 00 00 00 00 00 00 00-00 00 00 00 00 00 00 00
1446:00E0   00 00 00 00 00 00 00 00-00 00 00 00 00 00 00 00
1446:00F0   00 00 00 00 00 00 00 00-00 00 00 00 00 00 00 00

1446:0100   A0 82 00 24 0F FE C8 88-C2 B9 0A 00 B8 01 02 B6
1446:0110   00 BB 00 03 51 B9 01 00-CD 13 59 73 06 E2 F5 B0
1446:0120   00 EB 0C 1E FE C2 B4 1C-CD 21 00 07 8A 07 1F BB
1446:0130   00 02 D7 88 C2 B6 01 B4-09 CD 21 CD 20 49 6E 76
1446:0140   61 6C 69 64 20 64 72 69-76 65 20 73 70 65 63 69
1446:0150   66 69 63 61 74 69 6F 6E-20 6F 72 20 62 61 64 20
1446:0160   64 69 73 6B 24 44 72 69-76 65 20 6E 6F 74 20 72
1446:0170   65 61 64 79 24 33 36 30-4B 42 20 35 2E 32 35 22
1446:0180   24 31 2E 32 4D 42 20 35-2E 32 35 22 24 37 32 30
1446:0190   4B 42 20 33 2E 35 22 24-31 2E 34 34 4D 42 20 33
1446:01A0   2E 35 22 24
```

```
Program
Segment
Prefix (PSP)
```

← Program Codes

```
                Inv
alid drive speci
fication or bad
disk$Drive not r
eady$360KB 5.25"
$1.2MB 5.25"$720
KB 3.5"$1.44MB 3
.5"$
```

```
1446:0200   65 3D 3D 3D 3D 3D 3D 3D-3D 3D 3D 3D 3D 3D 3D 3D
1446:0210   3D 3D 3D 3D 3D 3D 3D 3D-3D 3D 3D 3D 3D 3D 3D 3D
1446:0220   3D 3D 3D 3D 3D 3D 3D 3D-3D 3D 3D 3D 3D 3D 3D 3D
1446:0230   3D 3D 3D 3D 3D 3D 3D 3D-3D 3D 3D 3D 3D 3D 3D 3D
1446:0240   3D 3D 3D 3D 3D 3D 3D 3D-3D 3D 3D 3D 3D 3D 3D 3D
1446:0250   3D 3D 3D 3D 3D 3D 3D 3D-3D 3D 3D 3D 3D 3D 3D 3D
1446:0260   3D 3D 3D 3D 3D 3D 3D 3D-3D 3D 3D 3D 3D 3D 3D 3D
1446:0270   3D 3D 3D 3D 3D 3D 3D 3D-3D 3D 3D 3D 3D 3D 3D 3D
1446:0280   3D 3D 3D 3D 3D 3D 3D 3D-3D 3D 3D 3D 3D 3D 3D 3D
1446:0290   3D 3D 3D 3D 3D 3D 3D 3D-3D 3D 3D 3D 3D 3D 3D 3D
1446:02A0   3D 3D 3D 3D 3D 3D 3D 3D-3D 3D 3D 3D 3D 3D 3D 3D
1446:02B0   3D 3D 3D 3D 3D 3D 3D 3D-3D 3D 3D 3D 3D 3D 3D 3D
1446:02C0   3D 3D 3D 3D 3D 3D 3D 3D-3D 3D 3D 3D 3D 3D 3D 3D
1446:02D0   3D 3D 3D 3D 3D 3D 3D 3D-3D 3D 3D 3D 3D 3D 3D 3D
1446:02E0   3D 3D 3D 3D 3D 3D 3D 3D-3D 3D 3D 3D 3D 3D 3D 3D
1446:02F0   3D 98 3D 3D 3D 3D 3D 3D-3D 3D 81 8D 3D 3D 3D 75
```

```
Translation Table
```

Self-Review 5.6 (Answers on page 219)

5.6.1 To retrieve the data word currently atop the stack and store it in register DX, use the instruction _____.

5.6.2 The instruction sequence below will output _____ bytes to port 27H.

```
        MOV   CX,200H
A1:     LODSB
        OUT   27,AL
        LOOP  A1
```

5.6.3 A media byte value of _____ indicates a 1.44 MB floppy disk.

5.6.4 The PSP for an MS-DOS program begins at offset _____ and ends at offset _____.

5.7   Program 5.7: Programmable Time Delay

Introduction

Computer engineers are continually searching for ways to improve the performance of the systems they design. It is a tribute to their success that the speed of today's PC is measured in millions of instructions executed per second. When interfacing with a user, however, it is often necessary to adjust the machine to a slower (human) time frame. In Program 5.7 we develop a program that creates a 1- to 99-second time delay programmable from the command line. This is accomplished by retrieving the desired time delay from the operator, converting it to microseconds, and then programming the onboard timer chip for the desired time interval. Because the numbers involved become quite large, we will find it advantageous to write the program using several 80x86 32-bit instructions and registers.[11] Finally, we will use Program 5.7 in a DOS batch file to display a menu of choices for several seconds.

In this section we:

- Write an 80x86 program that uses 32-bit instructions.
- Convert a two-digit ASCII number to binary.
- Write an 80x86 program that generates a 1- to 99-second programmable time delay.

New Instructions

ROR operand, immediate value.   The rotate and shift instructions were described in Program 5.2. In that program, register CL was programmed with the number of bits to rotate. Beginning with the 80286, this number can be given as an *immediate* value. Thus, the instruction ROR AL,4 is equivalent to the two instructions:

```
MOV CL,4
ROR AL,CL
```

In Program 5.7 we use the instruction ROR EAX,10H to rotate the 16 most significant bits of register EAX into register AX. In this way, the 32-bit contents of EAX can be copied to

---

[11]Because of this, Program 5.7 will not run on an 8086- or 8088-based PC.

two 16-bit registers. For example, assume we want to copy EAX to the CX:DX register pair. The following instructions can be used.

```
MOV DX,AX      ;Copy low-order 16 bits of EAX to DX
ROR EAX,10H    ;Rotate high-order bits of EAX into AX
MOV CX,AX      ;Copy low-order 16 bits of EAX to CX
```

New DOS Features

BIOS INT 15H, Service 86H (Wait for Time Delay).   Service 86H suspends operation of the program until the time delay specified in the CX:DX register pair has expired. The value in these registers is interpreted as the wait period in *microseconds*. Thus, a time delay of one second requires a delay parameter of 1,000,000, or 000F4240H (CX = 000FH, DX = 4240H).

Problem Statement

Write an 80x86 program that generates a time delay of between 1 and 99 seconds specified by the user on the command line. For example, typing WAIT 05 should suspend program operation for 5 seconds.

Discussion

Program Outline.   Figure 5.21 outlines the program. The first task is to retrieve the delay parameter from the command line. This can be done by noting the memory locations in the PSP where the command line parameters will be stored. For example, suppose the user types **WAIT 05.** The contents of the PSP beginning at offset 0080H will then be as follows:

WAIT   0   5

[0080H] = 03H	The number of characters on the command line.
[0081H] = 20H	ASCII space.
[0082H] = 30H	ASCII 0.
[0083H] = 35H	ASCII 5.
[0084H] = 0DH	ASCII return.

The program begins by checking for a return character in 0084H (thus requiring the user to enter a two-digit delay value). If this is not found, the user is assumed to have typed an in-

Figure 5.21 Outline for Program 5.7.

```
I.  Get Time Delay Parameter and Convert
    to Binary
    A. Verify Valid Input                       mov   al,[0084]
       1. [84] = return?                         cmp   al,0d
          i.  No: Goto III                       jnz   III.A
          ii. Yes: continue
    B. Prepare EAX to hold result                mov   eax,0
    C. Strip ASCII Bias from Time Delay Parameter sub   word ptr[0082],3030
       1. Word Ptr[82] = Word Ptr[82] - 3030H
    D. Convert Ten's Digit                       mov   al,[0082]
       1. AL = [82]        ;Ten's digit          mov   bl,0a
       2. AX = 10 * AL     ;Convert to units in AX mul   bl
    E. Add Units
       1. AX = AX + [83]   ;AX = 1 to 99         add   al,[83]

II. Do Time Delay
    A. Convert Time Delay to Microseconds        mov   ebx,000f4240
       1. Multiply Parameter by 1,000,000 us/sec mul   ebx
          i.   EAX = AX
          ii.  EDX:EAX = EAX * F4240H
               a. If EAX is 99 or less, EDX will be 0
    B. BIOS INT 15H, service 86H                 mov   dx,ax
       1. CX:DX = EAX                            ror   eax,10
          i.   DX = AX    ;Low-order timing word mov   cx,ax
          ii.  Rotate EAX right 16 bits
          iii. CX = AX    ;High-order timing word mov   ah,86
       2. AH = 86                                int   15

III. Return to DOS
    A. INT 20H                          III.A int   20
```

valid delay parameter and the program terminates. Next, 30H is subtracted from both ASCII digits to convert them to binary.[12] The ten's digit in 0082H is multiplied by 10 and the units digit is added to this result. At this point AX holds the desired time delay value in binary. And because EAX was initially set to 0, EAX = AX.

In Part II of the program, register EBX is loaded with one million (000F4240H). The instruction MUL EBX multiplies EAX by EBX, storing the result in the 64-bit register pair EDX:EAX. Note, however, that before the multiplication, EAX is no larger than 99. The EDX:EAX product can therefore be no larger than 99,000,000 (05E69EC0), and register EDX will always be 0. Accordingly, Program 5.7 breaks the product in EAX into two 16-bit numbers that are copied to DX (low-order timing word) and CX (high-order timing

---

[12]Of course, this assumes the user has entered a number and not a letter or punctuation symbol. A more elaborate program could verify that the characters entered have an ASCII code between 30H and 39H.

word) as required by BIOS INT 15H. The time delay is then called, after which control returns to DOS.

DEBUG32.   Because of the 32-bit instructions DEBUG cannot be used to enter and test Program 5.7. Instead we use DEBUG32, a 32-bit debugger written by Gary Larson and included with this book. DEBUG32 provides several enhancements over DEBUG.

1. Any 80x86 instruction through the Pentium processor may be entered.
2. Breakpoints can be set via the BP command. The program runs at full speed until the breakpoint is encountered and then stops and displays the contents of all CPU registers. The BL command lists all currently set breakpoints.
3. The CMOS command allows the contents of CMOS (configuration) memory to be viewed (see Figures 7.50 and 7.51).
4. The CPU command displays the CPU type and operating mode.
5. The display command has been enhanced to display memory in byte, word, or doubleword format.
6. The DR command displays the processor's internal debug registers.
7. The help command (?) can be pointed at a specific command. Example: ? R.
8. The HEX command displays the sum and difference of two hex numbers.
9. The PR command displays the values of the privileged registers as well as the Flags.
10. The PT command traces one or more instructions and highlights any changed register or flag bits. The command also lets you trace through a subroutine call or software interrupt without stepping each instruction in that subroutine or interrupt.
11. The R16/R32 command causes the CPU registers to be displayed in 16- or 32-bit format.

Program Listing.   Figure 5.22 shows the annotated program listing written with DEBUG32. It follows the program outline exactly. Note that several of the 32-bit instructions require 6-byte operation codes.

Typical Application.   Often, when writing a DOS batch file, it is necessary to give the user time to read a message and press a key. Program 5.7 can be used to generate the time delay required in such files. Figure 5.23 shows the AUTOEXEC.BAT file used to test Program 5.5, but now modified to include a *menu*. When this file runs, the Boot Menu appears on the screen for 5 seconds. This gives the user time to read the menu and hold down the appropriate alternate keys before get_alt scans the keyboard. Without the time delay, the user must know and hold down the appropriate keys before AUTOEXEC.BAT has started.

Self-Review 5.7 (Answers on page 219)

5.7.1   What single instruction can be given to rotate the contents of register BL left 5 bits?

5.7.2   Calling BIOS INT 15H, service 86H with CX:DX = 0020 0000 will cause a _____s time delay.

5.7.3   The instruction MUL EBX computes the product of _____ and _____, and stores it in the 64-bit register pair _____.

Figure 5.22 Program 5.7 listing. Note that several 32-bit instructions are required.

```
2988:0100 8A068400      MOV   AL,[0084]                ;Get third key stroke
2988:0104 3C0D          CMP   AL,0Dh                   ;Is it return?
2988:0106 752D          JNZ   Short 0135               ;If not then quit
2988:0108 66B800000000  MOV   EAX,00000000h            ;Prepare EAX to hold time delay
2988:010E 812E82003030  SUB   Word Ptr [0082],3030h    ;Strip ASCII bias from input
2988:0114 8A068200      MOV   AL,[0082]                ;Get tens digit
2988:0118 B30A          MOV   BL,0Ah                   ;Multiplier = 10
2988:011A F6E3          MUL   BL                       ;Convert to units
2988:011C 02068300      ADD   AL,[0083]                ;Add units digit
2988:0120 66BB40420F00  MOV   EBX,000F4240h            ;Multiplier = 1 million
2988:0126 66F7E3        MUL   EBX                      ;Convert units to microseconds
2988:0129 8BD0          MOV   DX,AX                    ;Store low word result in DX
2988:012B 66C1C810      ROR   EAX,10h                  ;Rotate high word result to low word
2988:012F 8BC8          MOV   CX,AX                    ;Store low word result in CX
2988:0131 B486          MOV   AH,86h                   ;BIOS INT 15, service 86
2988:0133 CD15          INT   15h                      ;Wait for time delay
2988:0135 CD20          INT   20h                      ;Return to DOS
```

212

Figure 5.23   Program 5.5's AUTOEXEC.BAT file modified to display a boot menu for
five seconds.

```
@echo off
path c:\dos;c:\windows;c:\util
mouse.com/Y
doskey
set dircmd=/l//o:-g
prompt $p$g
cls


Echo              Boot Menu
Echo.
Echo Press the left alternate key to edit AUTOXEC.BAT
Echo.
Echo Press the right alternate key to edit CONFIG.SYS
Echo.
Echo Press both alternate keys to start Windows
Echo.
Echo No keys pressed displays the DOS version
Echo.
Echo.

wait 05

get_alt          'Get alternate key status

if errorlevel 0 if not errorlevel 1 goto none
if errorlevel 2 if not errorlevel 3 goto left
if errorlevel 8 if not errorlevel 9 goto right
if errorlevel 10 if not errorlevel 11 goto both

;none            'No keys down
ver
goto end

;left            'Left alternate key down
edit c:\autoexec.bat
goto end

;right           'Right alternate key down
edit c:\config.sys
goto end

;both            'Left and right alternate keys down
win
```

Chapter 5 Self-Test

1. When accessing the BIOS services, register _____ holds the service number.

2. Which instruction sequence below transfers control to a memory location named A1 if register AL = 40H?

```
;Sequence 1          ;Sequence 2          ;Sequence 3
CMP AL,40H           MOV BL,40H           CMP AL,40H
JNZ A1               CMP AL,BL            JA  A1
                     JZ  A1
```

3. The ASCII code defines _____ different letters, numbers, punctuation marks, and control codes.

4. Determine the contents of register AL after the following instructions have executed:

```
MOV AL,58H
AND AL,F0H
```

5. Determine the contents of register AL after the following instructions have executed:

```
MOV AL,E2H
MOV CL,5
ROR AL,CL
```

6. Determine the contents of register BL after the following instructions have executed:

```
MOV BL,79H
MOV AL,82H
SUB BL,AL
SBB BL,13H
```

7. For the instruction sequence below, determine the contents of register AL (a) after the add instruction and (b) after the DAA instruction.

```
MOV AL,46H
ADD AL,85H
DAA
```

8. When using DOS INT 21, function 0AH (buffered keyboard input), the first byte of the buffer represents:
   (a) the actual length of the buffer
   (b) the maximum length of the buffer
   (c) the first character typed from the keyboard

9. What single 80x86 instruction is equivalent to the following 80x86 instruction sequence? Assume the direction flag is reset.

```
MOV AL,[SI]
INC SI
```

10. Which of the following I/O instructions are *invalid?*
    (a) OUT 256,AL
    (b) IN BL,AL
    (c) IN AL,DX
    (d) OUT DX,3CE0

11. What is the DEBUG *immediate mode* command to input the byte from port 15H?

12. Write an 80x86 instruction sequence that inputs data from port 57H, sets bits 6 and 7 without changing the other bits, and outputs this data back to the same port.

13. BIOS INT 16H, service 12H returns AX = 0080H. Which key on the system keyboard is pressed?

14. To return an error code to DOS, use DOS INT _____ function 4CH with the error code in register _____.

15. The batch file command *if errorlevel 3 goto input* will transfer control to the input label:
    (a) Only if the errorlevel is equal to 3
    (b) If the errorlevel is greater than or equal to 3
    (c) If the errorlevel is less than 3
    (d) None of the above

16. To save register BX on the stack, use the instruction _____.

17. The instruction sequence below outputs _____ consecutive bytes of memory, beginning at address _____, to I/O port _____.

```
        CLD
        MOV CX,1000H
        MOV DX,200H
        MOV SI,300H
A1:     LODSB
        OUT DX,AL
        LOOP A1
```

18. Because of the PSP, the first instruction of an MS-DOS program begins at offset address _____.

19. To rotate the contents of register EAX right 16 bits, the single instruction _____ can be given.

20. In Program 5.7, if the user types WAIT 12, the 32-bit delay parameter passed to BIOS INT 15H, service 86H in the register pair CX:DX is _____H.

Analysis and Design Questions

Program 5.1

5.1 The extended ASCII character set includes those characters and symbols with ASCII codes between 80H and FFH. Modify Program 5.1 to print only these extended characters. Provide a complete program listing of your solution with comments.

5.2 Study the program listing shown in Figure 5.24. Behind each program line, add a meaningful comment. You may find it useful to enter the program into memory using DEBUG and run it. You should see the ASCII character set printed in bright green on a blue background (*Hint:* Refer to Appendix A.1 and A.3 for descriptions of the BIOS services and color codes used). Now answer the following questions about this program.
    (a) What video mode does the program set?
    (b) Which instruction defines the screen colors?
    (c) What is the purpose of the instruction MOV CX,07D0? Try loading smaller numbers into CX and note the effect.
    (d) What is the effect of changing the MOV AX,0920 instruction to MOV AX,0924?
    (e) What change is required to display the ASCII characters in *red* on a *white* background?

Program 5.2

5.3 Determine the contents of registers AL, AH, BL, and BH after the following instructions have executed.

```
MOV AX,EA7BH
MOV BX,AX
AND AL,3CH
```

Figure 5.24   Figure for Analysis and Design Question 5.2.

1446:0100 B400	MOV	AH,00
1446:0102 B002	MOV	AL,02
1446:0104 CD10	INT	10
1446:0106 B82009	MOV	AX,0920
1446:0109 B31A	MOV	BL,1A
1446:010B B9D007	MOV	CX,07D0
1446:010E CD10	INT	10
1446:0110 B402	MOV	AH,02
1446:0112 BA000A	MOV	DX,0A00
1446:0115 B700	MOV	BH,00
1446:0117 CD10	INT	10
1446:0119 B40E	MOV	AH,0E
1446:011B B000	MOV	AL,00
1446:011D CD10	INT	10
1446:011F FEC0	INC	AL
1446:0121 3C80	CMP	AL,80
1446:0123 75F8	JNZ	011D
1446:0125 CD20	INT	20

```
OR  AH,0FH
XOR BL,F0H
NOT BH
```

5.4   Write a program called BEEP.COM that causes a short "beep" to occur from the system speaker each time it is executed. (*Hint:* "Print" a control-G.) Provide an outline and annotated listing of your program similar to Figure 5.5 and 5.6.

Program 5.3

5.5   Refer to the listing for Program 5.3 in Figure 5.10. Assume the user enters the problem: 28+79=. Determine the contents of the following just *before* the JNC instruction in 0139 executes:

(a) SI
(b) Byte Ptr [SI+1]
(c) Word Ptr [SI+2]
(d) Word Ptr [SI+5]
(e) AX
(f) BH
(g) CL
(h) DX
(i) CF

5.6   Write a program to display the two packed BCD numbers in register AX. Example: AX = 1234H, video display shows 1234. Provide a complete program listing of your solution with comments. (*Hint:* Call Program 5.2 as a subroutine twice; replace the INT 20H at the end of Program 5.2 with RET).

5.7   Write a program to add the 4-digit BCD number in AX to the similar number in BX, maintaining a valid BCD result. Example: if AX = 4682H and BX = 2734H, the sum in AX should be 7416 (the results need not be displayed). Provide an outline and annotated listing of your program. (*Hint:* Don't forget that DAA works only on the quantity in register AL.)

Program 5.4

5.8   Using a spreadsheet, create a table similar to Table 5.1 but with the *hexadecimal* value of
        the required divisor shown for each tone. (*Hint:* Notice that the frequency of each tone dou-
        bles as its octave number increments.)

5.9   Write a program that steps through tone A in octaves 1-8 with each succeeding key press.
        Rather than use a data table as in Program 5.4, note that the frequency of each note halves
        as its octave number increases and have your program *compute* the divisor value for each
        new note. (*Hint:* To divide a number by 2, *shift* that number right 1 bit.) Provide an outline
        and annotated listing of your program.

Program 5.5

5.10   Write a DOS batch file that tests for errorlevels 0–3 takes the following action, and then
        ends.
        (a) Display the DOS version if errorlevel 0
        (b) Give the tree command if errorlevel 1
        (c) Give the chkdsk command if errorlevel 2
        (d) Display the time if errorlevel 3
        (e) Ends if the errorlevel is 4 or greater

5.11   Write a program called YES.COM that waits for a key to be pressed and returns with an
        error code of 1 if the *y* or *Y* key has been pressed, a 0 if not. Provide an annotated listing of
        your program.

5.12   Because DOS's FORMAT command erases all data on a disk, it should be used with
        caution. To guard against erasing data, rename the command to XFORMAT.COM. Now
        write a batch file called FORMAT.BAT that cautions the user that all data on the specified
        drive is about to be lost. The user must then type *y* or *Y* to proceed with the format (via
        XFORMAT.COM). Use the program from Question 5.11 to test for these two key values.
        Provide a listing of your batch file.

Program 5.6

5.13   Write an instruction sequence that tests bit 0 of *byte* input port 2000H and transfers control
        to symbolic location A1 if this bit is high. If, after five consecutive failures, bit 0 is still low,
        transfer control to symbolic location A2.

5.14   Program 5.6 does not do a thorough job of testing for the proper drive letter. Answer the
        following questions about this program.
        (a) What response does the program give if the user types CHECK F (and there is no phys-
            ical drive F)? Explain.
        (b) Repeat (a) for drive Q.
        (c) Show the changes required to Program 5.6 so that only drive letters A and B will be tested.
            All other letters should result in the message *Invalid drive specification or bad disk.*

5.15   Refer to the hardware in Figure 5.25 and write an 80x86 program that inputs the binary
        value set on a 4-switch DIP switch and outputs the 7-segment code corresponding to the
        hexadecimal value set on the switch. For example, if the switches are set to 0000, the
        7-segment output code should be X100 0000 (segments *a–f* are on, segment *g* is off). The
        program should loop indefinitely, displaying each new switch value as it is entered. Provide
        an outline and annotated listing of your program. (*Hint:* Store the sixteen 7-segment codes
        in a translation table and use the binary number input from the switch as an index into this
        table. The XLAT instruction can then be used to retrieve the proper code.)

Program 5.7

5.16   Rewrite Program 5.7 so that the delay value entered by the user is interpreted in tenths of a
        second. For example, if the user types WAIT 75, a 7.5s time delay occurs. Provide an anno-
        tated program listing.

Figure 5.25   Figure for Analysis and Design Question 5.15.

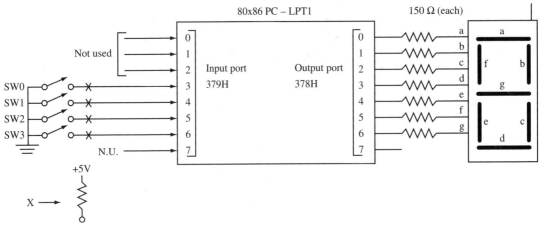

5.17   Rewrite Program 5.7 to allow the user to enter a 3-digit time delay value. For example, typing WAIT 850 causes an 850s time delay. Provide an annotated program listing.

5.18   Add the following feature to the batch file written in Question 5.12: When the user types *format*, a message should appear that warns the user that formatting a disk causes all data on that disk to be lost. After 5 seconds (via Program 5.7), the screen should clear and the batch file should then operate the same as described in Question 5.12. Provide a listing of the new batch file.

5.19   Using DEBUG32 load Program 5.7 into memory. Perform the following steps:
(a) Beginning at address 0080 enter the following numbers: 03, 20, 31, 32, 0D. What time delay does this represent? Run the program at full speed to verify your answer.
(b) Examine memory locations 0082 and 0083. You should see 01 and 02. Explain why.
(c) With a printer connected to your computer, press the Control and Print Screen keys to enable printer echoing.
(d) Reload memory as described in (a). Now use the PT (procedure trace) command to step through the program one line at a time. On the printed copy, provide an explanation of each instruction as it is executed.

Answers to Self-Review Questions

5.1.1   255 (the jump "falls through" on the 256th test)
5.1.2   0004
5.2.1   07H
5.2.2   03H
5.2.3   51H
5.3.1   (a) 5DH   (b) 63H
5.3.2   0202H
5.3.3   1,2
5.4.1   LODSW with the direction flag reset.
5.4.2   MOV AL,27H
         OUT 9E,AL

5.4.3   2

5.4.4   O9E,27

5.4.5   1, 193, 186 ÷ 370 = 3225 = 0C99H

5.5.1   0010 0000 0010 0000 = 2020H

5.5.2   02H

5.5.3   (a)

5.6.1   POP DX

5.6.2   512

5.6.3   F0

5.6.4   0000, 00FFH

5.7.1   ROL BL,5

5.7.2   2.097

5.7.3   EAX and EBX, EDX:EAX

6 80x86 Assembly Language Programming

First announced in 1977, the Apple II personal computer was an instant success. Although far more expensive than the competing Radio Shack TRS-80 ($1200 vs. $400), it offered an open architecture, color graphics, and an elegant floppy disk interface. Beginning a tradition that continues to this day, it did not use an Intel microprocessor chip, but rather the MOS Technology 6502 (later Apple computers used Motorola processors). System clock speed was 1 MHz. The popularity of the Apple II was legendary and Apple became the fastest growing computer company in history. Its two founders—Steven Jobs and Steve Wozniak—became millionaires before their thirtieth birthdays. (Photo courtesy of Smithsonian)

Outline

Objectives

After completing this chapter you should be able to:

1. Explain the four steps for developing an assembly language program: edit, assemble, link, and test and debug.

2. Identify by three-letter extension the file types created in the assembly process.
3. Show how to use MASM's Programmer's Workbench (PWB) to manage all of the tools required for processing an assembly language program.
4. List and identify the function of each CodeView window.
5. Explain the difference between tracing and stepping a program in CodeView.
6. Set conditional and unconditional breakpoints in a CodeView program.
7. Show how to write an 80x86 assembly language program with separate code, data, and stack segments.
8. Explain how the linker combines program segments to create an executable file in EXE format.
9. Show how to set up a CodeView watch window to view the contents of a symbolic memory location.
10. Use the equate operator to assign a label to a constant.
11. Place and reference ASCII messages in a data segment.
12. Create a template for a general assembly language program.

Overview

In Chapter 5 we learned how to use DEBUG to put together 80x86 machine instructions to create useful programs. In this chapter you are introduced to Microsoft's Programmer's Workbench (PWB).[1] This is a program that integrates all of the tools of the assembly language programmer. These include editors, assemblers, linkers, and debuggers. Using PWB you will find it much easier to create and test an 80x86 program than using DEBUG. The chapter concludes by creating an assembly language program *template* that can be used as a model for all future 80x86 programs.

6.1   The Edit, Assemble, Link, and Test and Debug Cycles

Introduction

If you worked through any of the programs in Chapter 5, you should be familiar with the limitations of using DEBUG to create 80x86 programs. Program addresses must be computed manually (usually requiring two passes—one to enter the instructions and a second to resolve the addresses), no inserting or deleting of instructions is possible, symbolic addresses cannot be used, and although comments can be entered, they are not saved as part of the program. All of these limitations can be overcome by using the proper assembly language tools.

In this section we:

- Explain the four steps for developing an assembly language program: edit, assemble, link, and test and debug.

---

[1]PWB integrates all of the programming tools included with the Microsoft Macro Assembler (MASM). Another popular package is Borland's Turbo Assembler and its Programmer's Platform. The examples presented in this chapter are developed using MASM 6.1 and PWB.

- Identify by three-letter extension the file types created in the assembly process
- Show how to use MASM's Programmer's Workbench (PWB) to manage all of the tools required for processing an assembly language program.

The Assembly Process—Using PWB

The development of an assembly language program follows a four-step process:

1. Create or edit the *source code*.
2. Assemble the program to create the *object code*.
3. Link the program to create the *executable code*.
4. Test and debug the program.

This process is flowcharted in Figure 6.1. Each step results in the creation of one or more files with the extensions as shown in the figure. The following paragraphs explain each of these steps in detail.

Creating the Source Code.   The source code contains the 80x86 program mnemonics plus any pseudo-ops and assembler directives. This file is created with a *text editor* (built into PWB—use the File-New menu option) and should be given the extension ASM (PWB will *not* do this automatically). When editing this file, PWB renames the current version with a BAK (backup) extension (for example, PROG51.ASM becomes PROG51.BAK). This allows you to retrieve the older version if you decide to "take back" the current changes.

   In Figure 6.2 we show Program 5.1 (PROG51) written in 80x86 assembly language form (compare this figure with the original listing in Figure 5.2).[2] Refer to this figure as we explain each line of this program.

Line 1: The page directive affects the list file (LST) output by the assembler (it has no effect on the ASM source code). In this example we are setting the length of each page to 58 lines and the width of each page to 132 columns. (The latter number is to ensure that the comments do not wrap around to the next line; of course your printer must be capable of printing columns this wide.)

Line 2: The Title directive indicates the title that will be printed near the top of each page in the list file.

Lines 3–9: Lines that begin with a semicolon are ignored by the assembler. In this case we are creating a *header block* to identify the name and purpose of the program.

Line 10: This line indicates that the instructions that follow are part of a memory segment named *cseg* (for a brief review on memory segments, refer to the *80x86 Memory Segment Refresher* sidebar on page 224). The optional 'code' at the end of the line is used to indicate a *class type*. The linker will arrange program segments so that all segments with the same class name are next to each other in the executable file. Adding the class type also causes the assembler and linker to add information to the executable file that will allow the actual source statements to be viewed in the debugger (see *Debugging with CodeView* later in this section).

---

[2]The line numbers in this listing are mine and are not part of the assembly file. Although they make it easy to refer to specific parts of the program, these numbers should *not* be entered when creating the source code.

80x86 Memory Segment Refresher

Processors in the 80x86 family divide their memory space into segments. In Real Mode these segments are 64K in length. Six segments are defined called the *code, stack, data, extra, F,* and *G segments.* By default, instructions are stored in the code segment, the stack is located in the stack segment and general data is stored in the data segment. The physical location of these segments is determined by the values in the CS, SS, DS, ES, FS, and GS registers. Segments may be separate, partially overlapped or fully overlapped.

    The two types of executable files (COM and EXE) program these segments differently. COM programs are limited to 64K and consist of a single fully overlapped segment. In such programs, all of the segment registers are typically set to the same value. That is, the program instruction codes, stack and data re all stored in the same segment. In assembly language, COM programs should define a single segment with all of the segment registers set to this value via the assume statement. Such programs do not need a stack segment as DOS will set this up automatically.

```
cseg      segment    'Code'
          assume     cs:ceg, ds:cseg, ss:cseg, es:cseg
```

    EXE files have no file size restriction and may contain several program segments. In fact, it is considered good programming practice to separate the program instructions, its data, and the stack into separate segments. In addition, complex programs are ofter written in modular form with several code, data, and stack segments. This is shown below. Notice that multiple segments must be aligned on *paragraph*(16 byte) boundaries. In the example below, DSEG2 begins at the first paragraph address after DSEG1. When multiple segments are defined, the linker will automatically concatenate segments on paragraph boundaries. The "class" directive can be used to ensure that similar segments are grouped together.

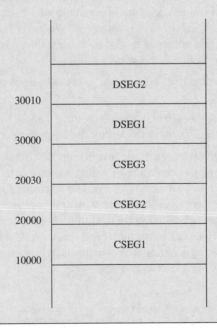

Figure 6.1   The development of an assembly language program requires four steps: edit, assemble, link, and debug. Several different file types are created in the process. The three-letter extension associated with each is shown.

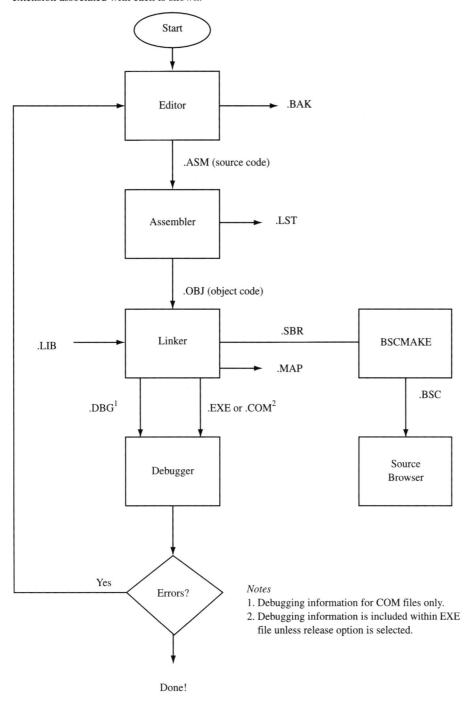

Done!

Figure 6.2   Program 5.1 rewritten in assembly language form.

```
1           Page    58,132
2           Title   Program 5.1

3  ;*********************************************
4  ;          Display ASCII Character Set       *
5  ;*                                           *
6  ;*  This program displays all of the ASCII   *
7  ;*  characters with codes 0-127.             *
8  ;*                                           *
9  ;*********************************************

10 cseg       segment 'code'
11            assume  cs:cseg, ds:cseg, ss:cseg, es:cseg

12            org     100h                  ;Leave room for PSP

13 start:     mov     ax,0002               ;BIOS service 0, video mode 2
14            int     10h                   ;Set video mode and clear screen
15            mov     ah,2                  ;BIOS service 2
16            mov     dx,0a00h              ;Row 10, column 0
17            mov     bh,0                  ;Page 0
18            int     10h                   ;Position cursor
19            mov     ax,0e00h              ;BIOS service 0E, first character is 0
20 IIA:       int     10h                   ;Print character
21            inc     al                    ;Next
22            cmp     al,80h                ;Done?
23            jnz     IIA                   ;No: loop again
24            int     20h                   ;Yes: back to DOS

25 cseg       ends
26            end     start
```

Line 11: Complex programs may contain many different segments. During the assembly process, the assembler needs to know which *particular* segments to assume. For example, a JMP instruction is coded differently if the target address is within the same segment (a near jump) or in an entirely new segment (a far jump). The ASSUME statement tells the assembler which segments to assume as the assembly process begins.[3]

Line 12: The ORG statement is used to specify the starting offset address for the following instructions. In this (COM file) example, we want the assembly to begin at 100H. This is to allow room for the 256-byte PSP (program segment prefix), which begins at offset 0000. *Be sure to include the letter H when specifying a hexadecimal number:* If this is left off, the assembler assumes a decimal number.[4]

---

[3]Note that the ASSUME statement does not actually load the segment registers with the appropriate values. It is up to the programmer to accomplish this task (Section 6.3 provides an example). With COM files like Program 5.1, the operating system automatically loads all of the segment registers with the same value.

[4]This is different from DEBUG. which assumes all numbers are hexadecimal and does not even allow the H suffix.

Line 13: The program instructions begin on this line. The word START: is used as a *label* to mark the memory location of this instruction. Note that a colon is required after the label.

Line 16: In this instruction we move the hexadecimal number 0A00H to register DX. It is important to include the leading zero in this address. If this is not done, the assembler will look for a label named A00H and generate a corresponding error message. In general, *hexadecimal numbers that begin with a letter (A–F) must be preceded with a zero.*

Line 20: IIA: is a label given to the memory location storing the first byte of the INT 10H instruction (the name was chosen to correspond to its position in the outline in Figure 5.1). Note that the JNZ instruction in line 23 uses this name as its target address. During assembly, this label will be converted to the proper offset address.

Line 25: Every segment must have an end statement (ENDS—end segment). In this example, the CSEG segment ends here.

Line 26: Every program must end with an *END* statement. The optional operand (START in this example) tells the assembler the name of the memory location that should be used to start the program. This is only important when multiple segments are defined.

Once the source code has been written, edited, and saved, we will find two files on our disk:

1. PROG51.ASM ;The program source code in ASCII text form.
2. PROG51.BAK ;The backup (previous version of PROG51.ASM).

Building the Program.   The next step is to assemble and link the program. In PWB this is called *building* the program. Before the actual build command is given, several options in PWB should be set.

1. *Project Template.* PWB uses the concept of a "project" to manage the files, commands, and options involved in compiling files and building the resulting target. A project consists of a list of files and the commands to convert those files into the result. A project *template* is a named set of Build switches (rules) that describes how PWB is to compile a file. Because PROG51 is to be compiled as a COM file, we select this project template.
2. *Build Options.* The project can be built using Debug or Release options. The former causes debugging information to be generated (used by the CodeView debugger); the latter does not. In this case, since our program has not yet been tested, we choose the Debug option.
3. *Language Options.* PWB can be used with many different programming languages. In this case, we select MASM to indicate our choice of assembly language. Several additional options are then presented, most of which are self-explanatory. Under Set Debug Options we choose Generate Listing File so that the machine code associated with our program can be viewed.

The Project Build menu option can now be selected. This causes PWB to assemble the program, creating the object code module (OBJ). This file contains the "raw" instruction codes that make up the program. We can examine the object code (in hexadecimal form) together with the original source code by viewing the *list* file (LST), also output by the assembler. This is shown in Figure 6.3(a). Studying this figure, notice that memory (offset)

Figure 6.3 The list file shows (a) the object code associated with each instruction and (b) a summary list of the segments and symbols used in the program.

```
Microsoft (R) Macro Assembler Version 6.11
Program 5.1                                        Page     1 - 1

                                    Page    58,132
                                    Title   Program 5.1

                   ;**************************************
                   ;       Display ASCII Character Set   *
                   ;*                                     *
                   ;*  This program displays all of the ASCII *
                   ;*  characters with codes 0-127.       *
                   ;*                                     *
                   ;**************************************

0000               cseg    segment  'code'
                           assume   cs:cseg, ds:cseg, ss:cseg, es:cseg

                           org      100h              ;Leave room for PSP

0100  B8 0002      start:  mov      ax,0002           ;BIOS service 0, video mode 2
0103  CD 10                int      10h               ;Set video mode and clear screen
0105  B4 02                mov      ah,2              ;BIOS service 2
0107  BA 0A00              mov      dx,0a00h          ;Row 10, column 0
010A  B7 00                mov      bh,0              ;Page 0
010C  CD 10                int      10h               ;Position cursor
010E  B8 0E00              mov      ax,0e00h          ;BIOS service 0E, first character is 0
0111  CD 10        IIA:    int      10h               ;Print character
0113  FE C0                inc      al                ;Next
0115  3C 80                cmp      al,80h            ;Done?
0117  75 F8                jnz      IIA               ;No: loop again
0119  CD 20                int      20h               ;Yes: back to DOS

011B               cseg    ends
                           end      start

(a)
```

Figure 6.3(b) *(continued)*

Segments and Groups:

N a m e	Size	Length	Align	Combine Class
cseg	.16 Bit	011B	Para	Private 'CODE'

Symbols:

N a m e	Type	Value	Attr
IIA	.L Near	0111	cseg
start	. .L Near	0100	cseg

0 Warnings
0 Errors

(b)

addresses are shown along the far left, with the machine code associated with each instruction beside it. This is similar to the Debug listings presented in Chapter 5. This listing is a good one to study when debugging your program, as any syntax errors will be listed immediately beneath the line in error.

Figure 6.3(b) shows the last page of the list file. It lists the segments and symbols used in the program. In this example we see that we have a single 16-bit (64K) segment named CSEG whose length is 011BH bytes. It is aligned on paragraph (16 byte) boundaries, has a combine type of *Private* (the code in this module cannot be accessed by another program module), and class type of *Code*.

If the object code assembles without error, PWB proceeds to *link* the program.

The linker creates relocateable, executable files that the operating system can load into any unused sections of memory. It does this by combining the segments in the object code file with any library files you specify.[5] The operand addresses for all instructions that reference memory locations are then resolved. The result is an executable file in EXE or COM form.

The linker can also be instructed to produce a map (MAP) file. This file lists the program segments by name and class, and shows their starting and ending addresses and the length of each segment in bytes. (This command will be illustrated in the next section.)

At this point, typing DIR PROG51.* reveals that our simple ASCII character set program has grown to nine files![6] This is shown in Figure 6.4. Table 6.1 provides a summary for each file type by extension. Most of these files should now be familiar to you, but three we have not discussed.

Figure 6.4   After the build command is given, Prog51 grows to nine files.

```
C:\8086\CHAP6>dir prog51.*

 Volume in drive C is DRIVE C
 Volume Serial Number is 1D1F-99DC
 Directory of C:\8086\CHAP6

prog51   lst         2,002 08-18-95  10:35a
prog51   sbr             0 08-18-95  10:32a
prog51   bak         1,035 08-17-95   6:40a
prog51   dbg           684 08-18-95  10:38a
prog51   obj           372 08-18-95  10:38a
prog51   map           528 08-18-95  10:38a
prog51   bsc           402 08-18-95  10:32a
prog51   asm         1,020 08-17-95   6:44a
prog51   com            27 08-18-95  10:38a
         9 file(s)          6,070 bytes
                    121,864,192 bytes free
```

---

[5]Rather than rewrite the same routines over and over, PWB allows object code libraries to be maintained. Selected modules (in LIB form) can then be linked to the current project.

[6]You may see fewer. The MAP and SBR files will only be created if you have turned these options on. The BAK file is created after you edit the original ASM file.

Table 6.1   File Extensions Created During the Assembly Process

Extension	Meaning
.ASM	Source code created by the editor
.BAK	Source code backup
.BSC	Project database created by BSCMAKE
.COM	Executable program limited to a single segment
.DBG	Debug file created by the linker for .COM files only
.EXE	Executable program with multiple segments
.LIB	Library file
.LST	List file, created by the assembler, containing object and source code
.OBJ	Object code created by the assembler
.MAP	Map file created by the linker showing program segments
.SBR	Database file created by the assembler for the current module

PROG51.DBG is a file created by the linker that contains debugging information. This file is created only if the executable file is of type COM and you have selected *Use Debug Options* in the Build Options menu. EXE files have this debugging information built in.

By default, PWB maintains a database of information about your program. Using a tool called the Source Browser, you can quickly move around in this database to locate pieces of code or find where certain functions are invoked or where a variable is used. For example, in PWB, selecting the commands Browse-Goto Definition, will cause a window to open that displays all of the symbols in the current project. Clicking any of these symbols reveals the line number(s) of that symbol in the corresponding assembly file; double-clicking the symbol takes you to that line.

To see how the database files are created, refer to the flowchart in Figure 6.1. During the assembly process, PWB creates SBR (Source Browser) files for each module in your program. These files contain information about the code in that module. The SBR files are examined and combined by the database-creation program (BSCMAKE) to create the actual database file for the project. This database file is given the extension BSC. As each SBR file is examined, its length is truncated to zero. Until the code for that module changes, this zero length indicates that this particular SBR file has already been included in the database and need not be reexamined. This allows updating the database to proceed more efficiently.

Testing and Debugging

Running the Program.   After giving the build command and assembling your program, PWB offers the following choices:

<View Results> <**R**un Program> <**D**ebug Program> <Cancel> < Help >

If the build completed without errors, select Run. You will be switched to the output screen, where the results of the program will be displayed. A message to "Strike a key when ready . . ." indicates completion of the program and allows control to return to PWB.

Syntax Errors.   If the build fails or errors were encountered in assembly, you can **View** the results. This screen shows the assembly commands issued by PWB and any corresponding errors. The error messages are a bit cryptic and take some study to understand. For example, in Figure 6.2, changing line 16 from MOV DX,0A00H to MOV DX,A00H causes the following error to be reported:

```
Assembling: ..\8086\CHAP6\PROG51.ASM
..\8086\CHAP6\PROG51.ASM(20): error A2006: undefined symbol : a00h
NMAKE : fatal error U1077: 'ML' : return code '1'
```

Without the leading zero, the assembler "thinks" the hexadecimal number A00 is a symbol or label (and it cannot find any definition for this symbol). If you are not clear about the error, open the LST file. In this example, the assembler highlights the error immediately below the program statement, making it easy to find.

```
0105 B4 02                          mov     ah,2          ;BIOS service 2
                                    mov     dx,a00h       ;Row 10, column 0
PROG51.ASM(20): error A2006: undefined symbol : a00h
0107 B7 00                          mov     bh,0          ;Page 0
```

Another option is to select *Next Error* under the Project menu in PWB (or press shift-F3). The source code window will be opened, the line in error will be highlighted, and the error message will appear at the bottom of the screen.

Logical Errors.   What if the assembly proceeds without errors but the program does not work? This indicates a program *bug*—an error in the program's logic. In Figure 6.2, if we forget the INC AL instruction in line 21, the character displayed will have a code of 0, which displays nothing. The program will never end, and the output screen will be blank. How do we locate this error?

Errors in program logic require a debugger. PWB includes a powerful debugger called CodeView. In the next section we learn how to use CodeView to locate errors in a program's logic.

Self-Review 6.1 (Answers on page 264–265)

6.1.1   The first step in writing an assembly language program is to create the _____ code.

6.1.2   Use the assembly pseudo-op _____ _____ to begin assembly at offset address 0100H.

6.1.3   In PWB, the set of files and commands associated with a particular program are called a

_____.

6.1.4   To see the memory address for each instruction in your program, examine the _____ file.

6.1.5   The assembler converts the source code into _____ code, which is then linked with any library files to produce the _____ code.

6.1.6   After assembly, any errors in program syntax can be found by examining the _____ file.

6.2 Debugging Assembly Language Programs

Introduction

In Chapter 5 we learned how to use Debug and Debug32 to examine 80x86 CPU registers and memory locations. By single-stepping our programs one instruction at a time using Debug's *trace* command, we were able to spot errors in program logic. CodeView provides all of these capabilities and more. With CodeView we can set *watch windows* that will allow us to watch memory locations as our program executes. 80x86 CPU registers can be viewed in 16- or 32-bit mode and can be changed by simply overtyping the current value. The *trace mode* allows procedures (such as DOS functions and BIOS services) to be executed at full speed while the program instructions are single-stepped. An *animate mode* executes one instruction, pauses, and then repeats the cycle. Finally, CodeView is a *symbolic debugger*. This means the actual source code can be viewed while debugging. In addition, the values taken on by program variables can be watched, or evaluated, and changed as needed as the program runs.

In this section we:

- List and identify the function of each CodeView window.
- Explain the difference between tracing and stepping a program in CodeView.
- Set conditional and unconditional breakpoints in a CodeView program.

CodeView Windows

The screen presented by CodeView is organized into several windows. In Figure 6.5 we show an example with four windows. Each window can be sized and placed as desired on the screen. In addition to the windows shown in Figure 6.5, additional windows showing watch variables and the coprocessor registers can be opened. The following paragraphs provide a brief description of each window.

The Source Window. The source window is used to view the program instructions. Options allow the code to be viewed in assembly format (as shown), source code format (like the ASM file), or mixed-assembly format (like the LST file).[7] If desired, a second source window can be opened to allow two views of the program simultaneously. The arrow, page up, and page down keys can be used to scroll through the entire program.

The Memory Window. The memory window is used to examine the contents of memory. By typing over the address field, new memory locations can be accessed quickly. Eleven different display formats are supported (ASCII byte values are shown). These can be cycled through via the shift-F3 keys. Two memory windows can be opened at a time to allow two different areas of memory to be viewed. The contents of memory can be changed by overtyping present values. ASCII characters can be entered simply by typing the characters in the desired locations.

The Register Window. The register window shows the contents of the various CPU registers and the flags. New values can be entered by typing over the old ones. The registers can be viewed in 16- or 32-bit format, depending on an option.

---

[7]Only assembly language programs compiled in EXE form can be debugged symbolically.

Figure 6.5 The CodeView screen for Program 5.1 showing four open windows: *memory1, source1, command,* and *reg.*

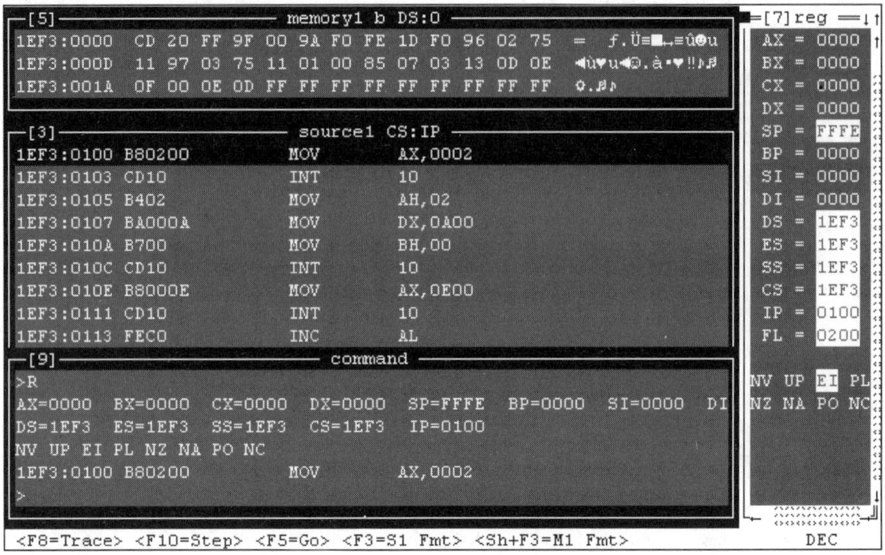

```
┌─[5]──────────────────── memory1 b DS:0 ──────────────────┐═[7]reg ═↓↑
│1EF3:0000  CD 20 FF 9F 00 9A F0 FE 1D F0 96 02 75  =  ƒ.Ü≡■„=ûθu│AX = 0000 ↑
│1EF3:000D  11 97 03 75 11 01 00 85 07 03 13 0D 0E  ◄û▼u◄Θ.à•▼‼♪ß│BX = 0000
│1EF3:001A  0F 00 0E 0D FF FF FF FF FF FF FF FF FF  Θ.♫♪      │CX = 0000
│                                                          │DX = 0000
├─[3]──────────────────── source1 CS:IP ───────────────────┤SP = FFFE
│1EF3:0100 B80200          MOV        AX,0002              │BP = 0000
│1EF3:0103 CD10            INT        10                   │SI = 0000
│1EF3:0105 B402            MOV        AH,02                │DI = 0000
│1EF3:0107 BA000A          MOV        DX,0A00              │DS = 1EF3
│1EF3:010A B700            MOV        BH,00                │ES = 1EF3
│1EF3:010C CD10            INT        10                   │SS = 1EF3
│1EF3:010E B8000E          MOV        AX,0E00              │CS = 1EF3
│1EF3:0111 CD10            INT        10                   │IP = 0100
│1EF3:0113 FEC0            INC        AL                   │FL = 0200
├─[9]──────────────────────── command ─────────────────────┤
│>R                                                        │
│AX=0000  BX=0000  CX=0000  DX=0000  SP=FFFE  BP=0000  SI=0000  DI│NV UP EI PL
│DS=1EF3  ES=1EF3  SS=1EF3  CS=1EF3  IP=0100              │NZ NA PO NC
│NV UP EI PL NZ NA PO NC                                   │
│1EF3:0100 B80200          MOV        AX,0002              │
│>                                                         │
└──────────────────────────────────────────────────────────┘
 <F8=Trace> <F10=Step> <F5=Go> <F3=S1 Fmt> <Sh+F3=M1 Fmt>      DEC
```

The Command Window. CodeView understands most of DOS Debug's commands. For example, Figure 6.5 shows the R command being given to display the 80x86 CPU registers. Other commands supported are the U (unassemble), D (display), and T (trace) commands. Most users will find it more convenient to select these commands via the menu bar at the top of the screen and view the results in the appropriate window.

The Output Window. When your program runs, all output is directed to the *output window.* This is a full-screen window separate from the others. To view the output window, press the F4 function key. Pressing any key then restores the view to the normal CodeView screen.

Other Windows. To open additional windows, select the *Windows* option in the menu bar. Multiple source and memory windows can be opened along with watch (explained in Section 6.3), coprocessor, and help windows.

Debugging Techniques

CodeView offers several features that can be used to help locate program bugs. Many of these are controlled via the F1–F10 function keys. Table 6.2 summarizes this information. Once you become familiar with the debugging capabilities of CodeView, you will be able to develop your own program-debugging strategies.

Starting CodeView. After giving the build command in PWB (and assuming no assembly errors), you can select *Debug Program* to start CodeView and load the executable program file. Alternately, you can select this same command from PWB's Run menu.[8]

---

[8]If you try the techniques illustrated in this section with the ASCII character set program, you will need to set the *Swap Screen in Buffers* option under the *Options—CodeView Options* menu. This will allow the program to reset the video mode without producing a warning message.

Table 6.2   CodeView Function Key Reference

Function Key	Description
F1	Context-sensitive help
F3	Program display format: mnemonics and object code, source code with comments, both
F4	View program output screen
F5	Execute program beginning at current IP value
F6	Select active window
F8	Single-step (including procedures)
F10	Single-step (excluding procedures)
Shift-F1	General help
Shift-F3	Memory display format:ASCII, hex, decimal, integer, floating point
Shift-F9	Set quick watch

Single-Stepping.   One of the most effective ways of troubleshooting a program is to run the program one instruction at a time. CodeView offers two ways of doing this. The first is the *trace* command (type **T** in the command window or press the F8 function key). With each key press, you will see the highlight bar step down through the program instructions while the memory and register windows update accordingly. The animate command (*Run—Animate*) automates the process and allows you to watch your program execute in slow motion.

To avoid having to step through DOS function and BIOS calls, use the program *step* command (**P** or F10). This will step through your program line by line without tracing into these procedures.

Breakpoints.   If you are not sure where the program bug is located, you can use the "*divide and conquer*" technique. Move the cursor to the midpoint of your program and select the *Data—Set Breakpoint—Break at Location* menu option (double-clicking any-where on the desired program line will also set—or reset—a breakpoint). Now, under the *Run* menu select *Restart* to reset all data registers and point IP to the start of your program. Press F5 to run the program at full speed to the breakpoint. If the breakpoint is never "hit," move it closer to the start of your program. Using this technique, you should be able to quickly locate the line(s) in error. Use the *Data—Edit Breakpoints—Remove* command to delete breakpoints.

Sometimes your program runs fine but then fails when certain data is encountered. One way of debugging this type of problem is to set a *conditional* breakpoint. Figure 6.6 shows an example in which we have set a breakpoint (with pass count = 30H) in offset lo-cation 0113. The program breaks in this location (see the Command window), with reg-ister AL = 2F confirming that we have made 30H passes (2F plus one for the first pass when AL= 0). Press F4 to view the output of the program to this point. You should see the first 30 characters of the ASCII character set.

You can also set breakpoints that occur only when an expression is true. For example, if you have a memory variable in your program named COUNT, you can set a breakpoint to occur when COUNT = 5. You can also set breakpoints to occur whenever an expression *changes* or whenever data is written to a block of memory.

Figure 6.6   Setting a conditional breakpoint for 30 program loops.

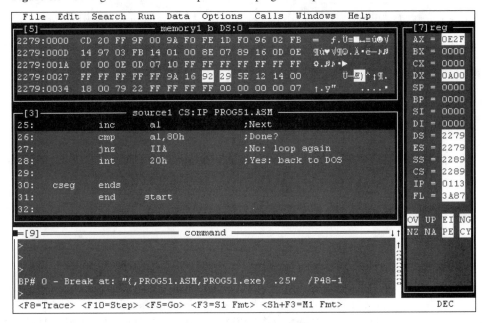

Watch Windows.   Rather than watch the program data in a memory window, you can open a Watch window (Ctrl-W)and enter the name of a memory location. Now, as your program runs you can view this window to see if this variable changes as expected.

If you want to know the value of a memory variable, a Quick Watch window (Shift-F9) can be opened and the name of the desired memory variable entered. In Section 6.3 we will write a program that uses memory variables. Watch windows are also illustrated in that section.

Self-Review 6.2 (Answers on page 264)

6.2.1   In CodeView you view your program instructions in the _____ window.

6.2.2   To trace your program line by line without tracing into procedure calls, use CodeView's _____ command.

6.2.3   To check the value of a memory variable, open a _____ _____ window.

6.2.4   List two different debugging techniques supported by CodeView.

6.3   Working with Separate Code, Data, and Stack Segments

Introduction

The simplest format for an 80x86 program is the COM file. COM files may have only a single (Real Mode) memory segment and are thus limited to 64K bytes in length. And because DOS takes care of the stack, even a stack segment need not be set up. While this format is adequate for simple programs, it does not take full advantage of the power of the 80x86 processors. In particular, it does not allow program data to be stored in its own segment, separate from the program instructions.

In this section we:

- Show how to write an 80x86 assembly language program with separate code, data, and stack segments.
- Explain how the linker combines program segments to create an executable file in EXE format.
- Show how to set up a CodeView watch window to view the contents of a symbolic memory location.

Defining Program Segments in the Assembly File

In this section we will use the 8-bit BCD adder program from Chapter 5 (Program 5.3) as an example. Several changes will be required to convert this program to executable form (EXE). These will be explained in the next few subsections. The list (LST) form of the program is shown in Figure 6.7.

Choosing the Build Options.   In Section 6.1 we described the process of "building" the program. Before issuing the build command, the *project template* should be selected. In this example, because we are creating an EXE file, this template should be chosen. The build options should again be set for *Debug,* and the language option to *MASM.* In the latter case, be sure the Debug options are set to create a listing file.

Program Header.   The first few lines of Figure 6.7(a) specify the page settings and program title. Note that with 43 lines/page, the intention is to print this file in *landscape* format. This should prevent the comments from "wrapping around" to the next line.

The .8086 directive tells the assembler to allow assembly of any instruction in the 8086 processor's instruction set. Typically, you set this directive to the *lowest* (least capable) processor that you want your program to be able to run on. In this way you will not be able to assemble an instruction for a higher level processor. The default is .8086.

A description of the program follows, together with an example of typical input and output.

Stack Segment.   Programs written in EXE format must set up their own stack segment.[9] Figure 6.7(a) shows how this is done. The line:

```
SSEG    SEGMENT    STACK
```

creates a segment called SSEG of combine type STACK. Note that any name can be used for this segment, but the combine type must be STACK. The next line:

```
DB      32    DUP  (?)
```

uses the define byte operator (db) to duplicate (or reserve) 32 consecutive memory locations. The question mark (?) indicates that the value to be put in these locations is of no concern (that is, we just want to reserve 32 consecutive memory locations).[10]

---

[9]Recall that the stack is necessary to allow temporary storage of program variables via the PUSH and POP instructions. It is also required to save subroutine and software interrupt return addresses.

[10]In this example, we have decided that a 32-byte stack is adequate. Depending on the program, however, a larger stack may be required. The PUSHA instruction, for example, pushes all eight CPU data registers onto the stack. This one instruction thus requires a stack of at least 16 bytes (assuming 16-bit registers).

Figure 6.7 Program 5.3 written in EXE form: (a) the stack and data segments; (b) the code segment; (c) The display procedure; and (d) The program summary.

```
                    Page43,132
                    Title    Program 5.3

                    .8086

        ;********************************************
        ;*                                          *
        ;*             8-Bit BCD Adder              *
        ;*                                          *
        ;* This program inputs two packed BCD numbers from *
        ;* the keyboard, computes their sum and outputs the *
        ;* result to the screen.                     *
        ;*                                          *
        ;* Example: The user types:  62+34=        *
        ;* The computer responds:       96          *
        ;********************************************

        ;****************************
        ;*     Stack Segment     *
        ;****************************
        sseg    segment  stack
0000    0000            db        32 dup  (?)                      ;32 bytes for stack
          00
        ]
0020    sseg    ends


        ;****************************
        ;*     Data Segment      *
        ;****************************
        dseg    segment
0000    0000    buff     db       8 dup   (?)                      ;8 byte input buffer
          00
        ]
0008    dseg    ends
```

(a)

Figure 6.7 *(continued)*

```
                        ;********************************
                        ;      Code Segment             *
                        ;********************************
0000                            cseg    segment    'code'
                                assume  cs:cseg, ds:dseg, ss:sseg

0000  B8 ---- R         main:   mov    ax,dseg              ;Get address of data segment
0003  8E D8                     mov    ds,ax                ;and store in DS

0005  8D 16 0000 R              lea    dx,buff              ;Point DX at input buffer
0009  B4 0A                     mov    ah,0ah               ;DOS function 0AH
000B  8B F2                     mov    si,dx                ;Point Si at input buffer
000D  C6 04 08                  mov    byte ptr [si],8      ;8 byte buffer
0010  CD 21                     int    21h                  ;Get the two numbers
0012  B4 0E                     mov    ah,0eh               ;BIOS video service
0014  B0 0A                     mov    al,0ah               ;ASCII line feed
0016  CD 10                     int    10h

0018  80 6C 02 30               sub    byte ptr [si+2],30h  ;Convert each digit to BCD
001C  80 6C 03 30               sub    byte ptr [si+3],30h
0020  80 6C 05 30               sub    byte ptr [si+5],30h
0024  80 6C 06 30               sub    byte ptr [si+6],30h
0028  B1 04                     mov    cl,4                 ;Four rotates
002A  D2 44 03                  rol    byte ptr [si+3],cl   ;Form LSD
002D  D2 44 06                  rol    byte ptr [si+6],cl
0030  D3 4C 02                  ror    word ptr [si+2],cl   ;Add to MSD
0033  D3 4C 05                  ror    word ptr [si+5],cl
0036  8A 44 03                  mov    al,[si+3]            ;Fetch first BCD number
0039  02 44 06                  add    al,[si+6]            ;Add to second
003C  27                        daa                         ;Keep results decimal
003D  8A F8                     mov    bh,al                ;Save results
003F  73 05                     jnc    IIIB                 ;Check for hundredths digit
0041  B0 01                     mov    al,1                 ;Set hundredths digit
0043  E8 0009                   call   dspy                 ;Display it
0046  8A C7             IIIB:    mov    al,bh                ;Recover low order result
0048  E8 0002                   call   dspy                 ;Display low order result
004B  B4 4C                     mov    ah,4ch               ;Terminate
004D  CD 21                     int    21h                  ;Return to DOS
```

(b)

(continued on next page)

Figure 6.7 (continued)

```
                ;*************************
                ;*  Display Procedure  *
                ;*************************
                ;  Function:  Display Two Digit BCD Number
                ;  Inputs:    BCD number in AL
                ;  Outputs:   None
                ;  Calls:     BIOS interrupt 10H
                ;  Destroys:  AX, BL, CL, flags

004F            dspy    proc                ;Display procedure
004F  8A D8             mov     bl,al       ;Save original number
0051  24 F0             and     al,0f0h     ;Force bits 0-3 low
0053  B1 04             mov     cl,4        ;Four rotates
0055  D2 C8             ror     al,cl       ;Rotate MSD into LSD
0057  04 30             add     al,30h      ;Convert to ASCII
0059  B4 0E             mov     ah,0eh      ;BIOS video service 0E
005B  CD 10             int     10h         ;Display character
005D  8A C3             mov     al,bl       ;Recover original number
005F  24 0F             and     al,0fh      ;Force bits 4-7 low
0061  04 30             add     al,30h      ;Convert to ASCII
0063  CD 10             int     10h         ;Display character
0065  C3                ret                 ;Return to calling program
0066            dspy    endp

0064            cseg    ends
                        end     main
```

(c)

Figure 6.7 *(continued)*

Segments and Groups:

N a m e	Size	Length	Align	Combine	Class
cseg	16 Bit	0066	Para	Private	'CODE'
dseg	16 Bit	0008	Para	Private	
sseg	16 Bit	0020	Para	Stack	

Procedures, parameters and locals:

N a m e	Type	Value	Attr
dspy	P Near	004F	cseg Length= 0017 Public

Symbols:

N a m e	Type	Value	Attr
IIIB	.L Near	0046	cseg
buff	.Byte	0000	dseg
main	L Near	0000	cseg

    0 Warnings
    0 Errors

(d)

241

The last line in the stack segment is:

```
SSEG     ENDS
```

This tells the assembler that this is the end of the segment. Every segment must end with a similar line.

Data Segment.   Program 5.3 requires 8 bytes of memory to store the user input (see Figure 5.8). In Figure 6.7(a) we create a data segment called DSEG and label the first memory location in this segment BUFF (for buffer).

Code Segment.   The code segment [Figure 6.7(b)] contains the program instructions. We begin by naming the segment CSEG and specifying the combine type as CODE. Next, the ASSUME statement tells the assembler which segments to assume for the code, data, and stack.

Because the program will be calling a procedure to display the result, we name the first line of the program MAIN. In general, you may place a name (followed by a colon) beside any instruction in the program. However, it only makes sense to do this if that instruction is the target of a jump or the first instruction in the program.

The next two lines, in memory locations 0000 through 0003, load the DS segment register. Although we told the assembler what to *assume* for DS, it is still up to us to load these registers with the proper address. And this requires two steps. First, load the address of the segment into a data register. For example:

```
MOV    AX,DSEG      ;Get address of data segment
```

Now copy the segment address to the segment register:

```
MOV    DS,AX     ;Transfer segment address to DS[11]
```

Note that the CS and SS segment registers will automatically be loaded with the proper values when the EXE file is loaded by DOS. Thus, these registers need not be programmed. DOS also points register SP at the "top" of the stack to allow the stack to grow downward. (See the subsection *Comparing COM and EXE Files* later in this section.)

The next instruction in Figure 6.7(b) uses the LEA (load effective address) instruction to point register DX at the start of the input buffer. Notice the letter *R* in the object code column for this instruction (and the first instruction referencing DSEG). This indicates that the address is *relative*. When the various program segments are linked, these addresses will be resolved.[12]

The remaining lines of the program in Figure 6.7(b) follow the original version of this program (see Figures 5.7 and 5.10). Notice, however, that the name IIIB has been given to the MOV AL,BH instruction in location 0046. Also notice that the CALL instructions in 0043 and 0048 simply reference the display procedure as DSPY. The assembler automatically determines the proper object codes to get to these new addresses.

---

[11]The more straightforward approach would seem to be MOV DS,DSEG. However, this instruction is not allowed. This is to avoid the possibility of an interrupt occurring while the segment register is being loaded, possibly causing an incorrect value to be stored in this register.

[12]This problem of resolving addresses should be familiar to you if you tested any of the programs in Chapter 5 with DEBUG. Analysis and Design Question 6.7 explains how to determine the actual run-time addresses used for these instructions.

Procedures.   Figure 6.7(c) shows the code for the display procedure. It begins with a header block that identifies the procedure name, its function, the expected input and output data, and a list of the registers that it modifies. Including this header block is good programming practice. You may want to use this procedure in another program and will need to know which registers the procedure uses or modifies.[13]

The line

```
DSPY    PROC
```

indicates that the following lines are part of a procedure and that the name of that procedure is DSPY. The end of the procedure is then indicated with the line

```
DSPY    ENDP
```

The last two lines of the program end the CSEG (code) segment and end the entire program listing. By following the pseudo-op END with MAIN, we identify to the linker the starting address of the program.

Program Summary.   Figure 6.7(d) shows the last page of the list file. It gives a description of each segment, identifies the display procedure (type Near means the procedure is located in the same segment as the code), and lists the program symbols. In the latter case, notice that IIIB and MAIN are identified as Near target addresses, while BUFF is described as a byte memory location.

Program Map

The Map File.   The MAP file provides information that is similar to the program summary. To request that this file be produced during the program build, select *Options—Link Options—Additional Debug Options—Map File—Standard*. The output for Program 5.3 is shown in Figure 6.8. The three program segments are listed by name along with their starting and ending addresses and segment length. Notice that the three segments have now been combined, and the starting address of each segment is given relative to 00000. The starting address for the display procedure and program entry point are given relative to the base of the code segment.

The actual addresses used by DOS when loading Prog53.EXE can be determined by loading the program with Debug and giving the R command to view the CPU registers. The result is shown below:[14]

```
C:\8086\CHAP6>debug prog53.exe
-r
AX=0000 BX=0000 CX=0434 DX=0000 SP=0020 BP=0000 SI=0000 DI=0000
DS=1033 ES=1033 SS=1043 CS=1046 IP=0000 NV UP EI PL NZ NA PO NC
1046:0000 B84510      MOV    AX,1045
```

We interpret the values in the segment registers as follows:

1. ES and DS point to the base of the 256-byte PSP (program segment prefix). In this example, DS = ES = 1033H.

---

[13]Analysis and Design Question 6.9 explores "transparent" procedures; that is, writing a procedure so that, to the calling program, none of the CPU registers (or flags) appear to change.

[14]These addresses will vary depending on available memory at the time the program is loaded.

Figure 6.8   PROG53.MAP. This file shows the length of each program segment, the starting address of the display procedure, and the starting address of the first program instructon.

```
Start   Stop   Length Name                        Class
00000H 0001FH 00020H SSEG
00020H 00027H 00008H DSEG
00030H 00093H 00064H CSEG                          CODE


 Address              Publics by Name


 0003:004D            dspy


 Address              Publics by Value


 0003:004D            dspy


Program entry point at 0003:0000
```

2. SS points to the base of the stack, and SP points to the stack top. In this example, SS=1043H and SP=0020H.
3. CS points to the base of the code, and IP points to the first instruction. In this example, CS=1046 and IP=0000.

Recall that the first two instructions in Program 5.3 load register DS with the address of the data segment:

```
MOV AX,DSEG      ;Get address of data segment
MOV DS,AX        ;and store it in DS
```

The Debug listing shows the first program instruction as MOV AX,1045. From this we conclude that DOS has located the program's data segment (where the keyboard strokes will be stored) at 1045H.

The Program Memory Map.   Figure 6.9 summarizes all of this information in the form of a *program memory map*. The stack, data, and code segments are shown along with the PSP. The addresses are shown in segment:offset form on the left, and the offset address from the base of the PSP is shown on the right. It is interesting to see that the 8-byte data segment is actually 16 bytes long. This is because segment addresses must begin on paragraph (16 byte) boundaries. The code segment therefore begins at the next paragraph address following 1045:0000, or 1046:0000.

Comparing COM and EXE Files.   As we mentioned at the beginning of this chapter, COM files are limited to a single 64K memory segment. When DOS loads such a program, it sets the CS, SS, DS, ES, FS, and GS segment registers all to the same value. Thus, these registers need not be loaded by your program. The stack pointer, register SP, is set to FFFEH, one byte less than the top of the segment. This allows the stack to grow downward without conflicting with the program instructions.

As we learned in Chapter 5, all COM files begin with a 256-byte program segment prefix, or PSP. The first line of code in a COM file should therefore include the pseudo-op ORG 0100H to ensure that program assembly begins immediately following this segment.

When an EXE file is loaded, DOS again expects a 256-byte PSP. However, unlike a COM file, DOS sets the DS, ES, FS, and GS segment registers to point to the base of this

Figure 6.9   Memory map for PROG53.EXE. The specific segment addresses are found by loading the program with Debug and then viewing the CPU registers with the R command.

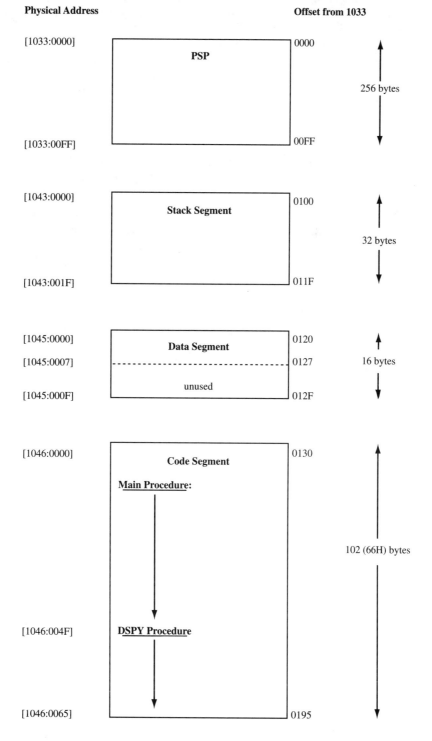

area; in effect placing the PSP in its own data segment. Therefore, the source code need not load these segment registers with the PSP address.[15] Of course, these registers will have to be initialized if data segments other than the PSP are utilized (as was the case with PROG53.EXE, discussed in this section).

EXE files require that a separate stack segment be created. When such a program is loaded, DOS automatically loads register SS with the address of this segment and points register SP at the top of the segment.

The program instructions are placed in the code segment at offset 0000 (i.e., IP = 0000) by DOS. Register CS is automatically pointed to the base of this segment.

Table 6.3 summarizes the differences between COM and EXE files.

Testing and Debugging with CodeView

Viewing the Source with Code.   We can debug PROG53.EXE by following these steps. With the ASM version of the program loaded, select *RUN* from the PWB menu bar, and then select *Debug PROG53.EXE*. CodeView will start and PROG53.EXE will be loaded into memory. Three different source window program display formats can now be selected:

1. Source code
2. Object code
3. Combined object and source code

Use the F3 function key to step through these three views.

Setting Up Memory and Watch Windows.   Before we begin testing the program, we will set up memory and watch windows to help us analyze program operation. Figure 6.10 shows CodeView configured with four windows: *memory1*, *watch*, *source1*, and *registers*. In the watch window we have decided to watch the 4 bytes that hold the 2 numbers input by the user. For example, the line:

$$by \qquad \&buff+2,x$$

has the meaning "display the byte (by) at memory location buff+2 (&buff+2) in hexadecimal (x)."[16] By choosing offsets 2, 3, 5, and 6, the four digits input by the user can be watched.

Stepping the Program.   From CodeView's Run menu, select *Restart*. This will reset all registers and memory locations and move the highlight to the first instruction in the

Table 6.3   Default Values for COM and EXE Segment and Pointer Registers

File Type	Segment Registers			Pointers	
	CS	**SS**	**DS, ES, FS, GS**	**IP**	**SP**
COM	All segment registers set to the same value			0100H*	FFFEH
EXE	Points to code	Points to stack	Points to PSP	0000	—†

*IP should be set to this address via the pseudo-op ORG 0100H.
†Set to top of user defined stack.

---

[15]See Analysis and Design Question 6.10 for an example EXE program that accesses the PSP.
[16]To view the word at this location, replace *by* with *wo*.

Figure 6.10 PROG53.EXE loaded into CodeView. The memory window displays the 8-byte memory buffer. The watch window is set to watch the four digits entered by the user.

```
 File   Edit   Search   Run   Data   Options   Calls   Windows   Help
┌─[5]──────────── memory1 b 0x1F05:0x0000 ────────────┐    ■═[7]reg ═┐
│1F05:0000  08 06 31 32 2B 33 34 3D 0D  □▲12+34=▶     │    AX = 0AOD│
│                                                      │    BX = 0000│
│ ┌─[2]──────────── watch ────────────────┐           │    CX = 0000│
│ │ by &buff+2,x = 0x0031                  │           │    DX = 0000│
│ │ by &buff+3,x = 0x0032                  │           │    SP = 0020│
│ │ by &buff+5,x = 0x0033                  │           │    BP = 0000│
│ │ by &buff+6,x = 0x0034                  │           │    SI = 0000│
│ │                                        │           │    DI = 0000│
│ └─[3]──────────── source1 CS:IP PROG53.ASM ──────────┤    DS = 1F05│
│ 39:                                                  │    ES = 1EF3│
│ 40:   main:   mov   ax,dseg          ;Get address of dat│ SS = 1F03│
│ 41:           mov   ds,ax            ;and store in DS  │  CS = 1F06│
│ 42:                                                  '│  IP = 0012│
│ 43:           lea   dx,buff          ;Point DX at input│ FL = 3202│
│ 44:           mov   ah,0ah           ;DOS function 0AH │            │
│ 45:           mov   si,dx            ;Point Si at input│ NV UP EI PL│
│ 46:           mov   byte ptr [si],8  ;8 byte buffer   │  NZ NA PO NC│
│ 47:           int   21h              ;Get the two number│          │
│ 48:           mov   ah,0eh           ;BIOS video service│          │
│ 49:           mov   al,0ah           ;ASCII line feed  │            │
│ 50:           int   10h                               │            │
└──────────────────────────────────────────────────────┘            │
 <F8=Trace> <F10=Step> <F5=Go> <F3=S1 Fmt> <Sh+F3=M1 Fmt>       DEC
```

program. Examining the register window, we see that CodeView has loaded the PSP (via ES and DS) at 1EF3, the stack at 1F03 (via SS), and the program itself (via CS) at 1F06. Now, using the F10 function key, we step through the first two instructions, which load DS with the address of the data segment (1F05). With this information in mind, we can adjust the memory window to show the 8-byte data buffer.

As we continue to step the program, we see register SI loaded with the offset address of the data buffer. The two numbers to be added are then input. We can see these in the memory window and the watch window. For example, assuming the user has typed "12+34=", we interpret the data in the memory window as:

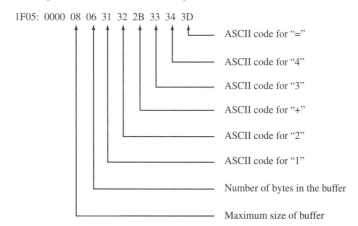

1F05: 0000 08 06 31 32 2B 33 34 3D

ASCII code for "="

ASCII code for "4"

ASCII code for "3"

ASCII code for "+"

ASCII code for "2"

ASCII code for "1"

Number of bytes in the buffer

Maximum size of buffer

Now view the watch window to see the program convert the ASCII numbers to BCD. After the display procedure runs, press F4 to view the output screen. You should see the sum of the two input numbers.

Once the program is debugged, you can run it at full speed by pressing F5. You can also exit CodeView and PWB and run the program from the DOS prompt. Typing DIR PROG53.* reveals the following files:

```
1. prog53 sbr    ;Placemarker file used by PWB database
2. prog53 bsc    ;Project database
3. prog53 asm    ;Source code
4. prog53 obj    ;Object code
5. prog53 map    ;Map file
6. prog53 exe    ;Executable file (with debugging extensions)[17]
7. prog53 bak    ;Source code backup
8. prog53 lst    ;List file
```

Self-Review 6.3 (Answers on page 265)

6.3.1   Assume a data segment of 256 bytes is to be created. Using the name MY_DATA, show the assembly pseudo-ops required. Label the first byte location in the data FIRST_BYTE.

6.3.2   Give the assembly language instructions required to load register DS with the address of the data segment described in 6.3.1. Point register DX at FIRST_WORD.

6.3.3   A near procedure is one that is located in the _____ segment as the calling program.

6.3.4   A 100-byte data segment has been created. If DOS loads this segment at address 1AFA:0000, the starting address for the code segment that immediately follows is _____: 0000.

6.3.5   When DOS loads an EXE file into memory, all of the data segment registers (DS, ES, FS, and GS) will initially be pointing at the _____.

6.3.6   A word memory variable named TEST is to be viewed in hexadecimal form in a CodeView Watch window. Give the Watch command required.

6.4   Programming Strategies—A Game Program Example

Introduction

In this final section we develop a game program called NIM in EXE form .NIM will provide us with the opportunity to apply all of our programming skills. In particular, we will need to place several ASCII messages on the screen, get and process input from the user, perform table look-ups and output the resulting data in ASCII form, generate variable time delays, and set up a structure that causes the program to loop until the quit option is selected.

In this section we:

- Use the equate operator to assign a label to a constant.
- Place and reference ASCII messages in a data segment.
- Create a template for a general assembly language program.

---

[17]Once the program has been debugged, you may want to rebuild it, selecting *Release Options* instead of *Debug* options. This removes the debugging information from the EXE file, making it smaller.

The Game of NIM

Description.   NIM is a game played with 15 "sticks." When it is your turn, you may select one, two, or three sticks. Your opponent (in this case, the computer) then takes his or her turn. The person to pick up the last stick (or sticks) wins. A sample game is shown in Figure 6.11. As you might expect, we can program the computer so that it usually (but not always) wins.[18]

Figure 6.11   The game of NIM.

```
NIM - A Game of Skill


I have 15 sticks.  You may pick 1, 2, or 3 sticks.   Then I will pick.
You win if you pick up the last 1, 2, or 3 sticks.
Type q at any time to quit.


There are now 15 sticks remaining.
Your choice: 2

There are now 13 sticks remaining.
My choice: 1

There are now 12 sticks remaining.
Your choice: 3

There are now 9 sticks remaining.
My choice: 1

There are now 8 sticks remaining.
Your choice: 1

There are now 7 sticks remaining.
My choice: 3

There are now 4 sticks remaining.
Your choice: 1

There are now 3 sticks remaining.
My choice: 3

I WIN!
```

---

[18]I won't ruin the game by giving you the winning combination!

Outline.   Figure 6.12 outlines the game. Notice that four basic steps are required:

1. Initialize.
2. Get user's choice and evaluate.
3. Get computer's choice and evaluate.
4. Return to DOS (when the user selects Quit).

In the program solution we will use a memory location named STICKS to hold the current number of sticks in the "pile." As the computer and its opponent make their choices, the number in this location is reduced. When the number reaches zero, a winner is declared and the game starts over.

The computer will determine its choices using the XLAT instruction and a data table. For example, if 13 sticks remain in the pile, the thirteenth entry in this table will be accessed to determine the computer's choice (1 in this instance). To add realism, we will program the computer to appear to "think" for several seconds before making its move.

Much of the program will be concerned with outputting ASCII messages to the screen. We can use DOS INT 21H, function 09 for this purpose. This function expects register DX to point to the message in the data segment. The end of the message must be

Figure 6.12   Outline for the game of NIM. Four basic tasks are required.

The Game of NIM

  I. Initialize
     A. Clear screen
     B. Show sign-on message
     C. Set stick counter to 15
     D. Display instructions

  II. Get user's choice and evaluate
     A. Quit?
        1. Yes: Goto IV
        2. No: Continue
     B. Subtract choice from stick counter
        1. Counter = 0?
           i. No:
               a. Display current number of sticks in the pile
               b. Goto III
           ii. Yes:
               a. Display "You Win!"
               b. Wait for keypress and then restart game

  III. Get computer's choice and evaluate
     A. Use number of sticks as an index into a choice table
     A. Subtract computer's choice from stick counter
     A. Counter = 0?
        1. No:
           i. Display current number of sticks in the pile
           ii. Goto II
        2. Yes:
           i. Display "I Win!"
           ii. Wait for keypress and then restart game

  IV. Return to DOS

denoted with a *$*. The current stick count can be output using BIOS INT 10H, service 0EH. This service writes the (ASCII) character in AL to the screen at the current cursor position.

The user's keyboard input can be obtained using BIOS INT 16H, service 0. This service waits for a keystroke and then returns with the key value in register AL. Note that pressing the enter key after each input is therefore not required. We can also use this function to restart the game after a winner has been displayed.

BIOS INT 15H, service 86H can be used to generate the "think time." This service uses the 32-bit register pair CX:DX to generate a time delay in microseconds. If we set DX to 0, the number in CX sets the time delay in multiples of 65,536 microseconds (.065 seconds); for example, if CX:DX = 00320000H, the time delay will be 32H × .065s = 50 × .065s = 3.25s.

Program Description

The Program Header and Equates [Figure 6.13(a)].   The program begins with the usual header information. The .286 directive is required to allow assembly of the PUSHA and POPA instructions, which will be used to make the procedures transparent (any CPU registers changed by the procedure will be restored before returning). The next statements use a new assembler pseudo-op called the *equate operator*. These statements allow us to assign a label to program constants. For example, *cr* is equated to *0dh* (the ASCII code for a carriage return). Using this label, whenever we want to place a return in an ASCII message, we simply enter *cr*.

As you can see in Figure 6.13(a), we can also use equates to describe the BIOS and DOS services and functions. For example, suppose an ASCII message begins at address NIM. The following code can be used to display this message:

```
LEA DX,NIM                  ;Point DX at the message
MOV AH,DISPLAY_MESSAGE      ;Load AH with function number 09H
INT 21H                     ;Display the message
```

Besides making your program easier to read, the equate operator allows global changes to be made to your program with a single line. For example, if we desire to change the time delay from 3.3s to 5s, we need only change the DELAY equate. Every line in the program that references this parameter will automatically be updated.

The Data Segment [Figure 6.13(b)].   The first line in this segment reserves a single byte for the stick counter. The "?" indicates that the assembler need not initialize this location to any particular value. All of the ASCII messages required by the game are also placed in this segment. Be sure to notice the following about these messages:

1. Each message ends with the *$* character, as required by DOS function 9.
2. If enclosed within a single quote, the ASCII messages can be entered in text form. During assembly, the actual ASCII codes will be generated.
3. Whenever a carriage return or line feed is required, the equates allow expressing this as *cr* or *lf*.

The last entry in the data segment is the choice table. Fifteen choices are stored, corresponding to 0–14 sticks remaining. For example, when 7 sticks remain, the computer's choice will be 3.

Figure 6.13 (a) The program header, equates, and stack segment; (b) the data segment; (c) and (d) The main program; and (e), (f), and (g) the procedures.

```
        Page    43,132
        Title   NIM

        .286

;*****************************************
;*                                       *
;*   The Game of NIM                      *
;*                                       *
;* The game of NIM is played with 15 "sticks." When  *
;* it is your turn, you may pick 1, 2, or 3 sticks.   *
;* The player to pick up the last stick wins.         *
;*                                       *
;*                                       *
;*****************************************


;The following equate statements assign constants to the labels shown.
;This makes the program more readable and will allow global changes to
;the program to be mde more easily.

display_message   equ   09h       ;DOS INT 21h function 9 (string output)
video_mode        equ   0002h     ;BIOS INT 10h service 0, video mode 2 (80x25)
cr                equ   0dh       ;carriage return
lf                equ   0ah       ;line feed
get_key           equ   0         ;BIOS INT 16h service 0 (read next keyboard character)
quit              equ   'q'       ;Exit by typing q
delay             equ   50        ;50 x 65,536 = 3.3s
BIOS_Wait         equ   86h       ;Bios INT 15h service 86h (wait for time delay)
terminate         equ   4ch       ;DOS INT 21h function 4c (terminate with error code)
write_character   equ   0eh       ;Bios INT 10h service 0e (write character in TTY mode)


;*****************************
;*   Stack Segment   *
;*****************************
sseg    segment stack
        db   100 dup (?)          ;100 bytes for stack
sseg    ends
```

(a)

Figure 6.13 *(continued)*

```
;************************
;*    Data Segment      *
;************************
dseg    segment

sticks  db      ?               ;This location stores the number of sticks in the pile

nim     db      'NIM - A Game of Skill'
        db      cr,lf,lf,'$'

instruc db      'I have 15 sticks.  You may pick'
        db      ', 1, 2, or 3 sticks.  Then I will'
        db      ' pick.'
        db      cr,lf
        db      'You win if you pick up the last'
        db      ', 1, 2 or 3 sticks.'
        db      cr,lf,lf,'$'

uchce   db      'Your choice: $'

lost    db      cr,lf
        db      'YOU WIN!$'

won     db      cr,lf
        db      'I WIN!$'

update  db      cr,lf,lf
        db      'There are now $'

up_end  db      ' sticks remaining.'
        db      cr,lf,'$'

mychce  db      'My choice is: $'

;This is the table of choices for the computer
choices db      0,1,2,3,1
        db      1,2,3,1,1
        db      1,1,1,1,2

dseg    ends
```

(b)

(continued on next page)

253

Figure 6.13 (continued)

```
;*************************
;     Code Segment      *
;*************************
cseg    segment 'code'
assume  cs:cseg, ss:sseg, ds:dseg

start:  mov     ax,dseg                 ;Load DS
        mov     ds,ax

;Clear the screen by setting the video mode
        mov     ax,video_mode           ;BIOS service: set video mode
        int     10h

;Show NIM sign-on message
        lea     dx,nim                  ;Point DX at sign-on message
        call    show                    ;Show the message

;Set number of sticks to 15
        mov     ds:[sticks],15

;Display the program instructions
        lea     dx,instruc              ;Point DX at instructions
        call    show                    ;Show the message

;Display the number of sticks remaining in the pile
Turn:   call    process

;Get the user's choice
        lea     dx,uchce                ;Point to message
        call    show                    ;Show the message

        mov     ah,get_key              ;DOS function: wait for next keypress
        int     16h                     ;Character to AL

        cmp     al,quit                 ;Quit?
        jz      dos                     ;Return to DOS

        call    cout                    ;Else display character
```

(c)

Figure 6.13 *(continued)*

```
;Update the stick counter
        sub     al,30h              ;Remove ASCII bias
        sub     ds:[sticks],al      ;Adjust counter
        jz      uwin                ;If 0, user wins
        call    process             ;Show the new count

;Look up the computer's choice
        lea     dx,mychce           ;Point to message
        call    show                ;Show the message
        call    think_time          ;Time to "think"
        lea     bx,choices          ;Point to base of choice table
        mov     al,ds:[sticks]      ;Get current number of sticks
        xlat                        ;Use this as index into table
        mov     bl,al               ;Save in BL
        add     al,30h              ;Add ASCII bias
        call    cout                ;Display choice

;Update the stick counter and check to see if computer wins
        call    think_time          ;More think time
        sub     ds:[sticks],bl      ;Adjust counter
        jz      iwin                ;If 0, computer wins
        jmp     turn                ;Else next turn

;Come here to process the winner and start over
uwin:   lea     dx,lost             ;Point to message
        call    show                ;Show the message
        jmp     skip

iwin:   lea     dx,won
        call    show

skip:   mov     ah,get_key          ;Any key restarts game
        int     16h
        jmp     start

;Come here to return to DOS
dos:    mov     ah,terminate        ;DOS function: terminate
        int     21h
```

(d)

(continued on next page)

Figure 6.13 *(continued)*

```
;************************************
;*Procedure Think_Time              *
;*                                  *
;* Function: Create time delay      *
;* Inputs:   nothing                *
;* Calls:    BIOS INT 15H service 86H *
;* Modifys:  flags                  *
;************************************

think_time      proc

;Adjust delay equate for desired time interval
                pusha                   ;Save all registers
                mov     dx,0            ;Time delay in CX:DX (microseconds)
                mov     cx,delay
                mov     ah,bios_wait
                int     15h             ;Do time delay
                popa                    ;Restore registers
                ret

think_time      endp

;************************************
;* Procedure Process                *
;*                                  *
;* Function: Display number of sticks *
;*   remaining in the pile.         *
;* Inputs:   Counter in [sticks]    *
;* Calls:    SHOW and COUT          *
;* Modifys:  flags                  *
;************************************

process proc

                pusha                   ;Save all registers

;Print the update message
                lea     dx,update       ;Point DX at message
                call    show            ;Show message
```

(e)

Figure 6.13 *(continued)*

```
;Display the number of sticks remaining
        mov     bl,ds:[sticks]          ;Copy stick counter to BL
        cmp     bl,0ah                  ;Fewer than 10 sticks?
        jb      units                   ;Yes:
        mov     al,31h                  ;No: So first digit is ASCII '1'
        call    cout                    ;Display 1
        sub     bl,10                   ;Get units digit
units:  add     bl,30h                  ;Add ASCII bias
        mov     al,bl                   ;COUT wants character in AL
        call    cout                    ;Display units

        lea     dx,up_end               ;Point DX to end of update message
        call    show                    ;Show message

        popa                            ;Restore registers
        ret

process endp

;************************************************
;*          Procedure Show                      *
;*                                              *
;* Function: Display ASCII message              *
;*           terminated with $                  *
;* Inputs:   DX points to message               *
;* Calls:    DOS INT 21 service 09H             *
;* Modifys:  flags                              *
;*                                              *
;************************************************

show    proc
        pusha                           ;Save all registers
        mov     ah,display_message      ;DOS function: string output
        int     21h
        popa                            ;Restore registers
        ret

show    endp
```

(f)

(continued on next page)

257

Figure 6.13 *(continued)*

```
;*********************************
;*       Procedure COUT           *
;*                                *
;* Function: Write one character at *
;*   current cursor position.     *
;* Inputs: character in AL        *
;* Calls: BIOS INT 10H service 0EH *
;* Modifys: flags                 *
;*********************************

cout    proc

        pusha                        ;Save all registers
        mov     ah,write_character   ;BIOS service: write character in TTY mode
        int     10h
        popa                         ;Restore registers
        ret

cout    endp

cseg    ends
        end     start
```

(g)

The Main Program [Figure 6.13(c) and (d)]. The program is of course stored in the code segment. It is organized as a main program and several procedures. Each section of the program is preceded by a comment line describing the purpose of the instructions to follow. This is good programming practice, as it makes it easier to understand the logic of the program.

After loading the DS segment register, the screen is cleared (this occurs automatically when the video mode is set) and the sign-on message is displayed. Notice that after pointing DX to the message, a procedure named SHOW is called. Because several messages will have to be output as the program runs, calling this procedure simplifies the job of displaying these messages.

The instruction MOV DS:[STICKS],15 initializes the stick counter (in memory location STICKS) to 15. Although we have come to understand that an address enclosed in parentheses indicates the *contents* of that memory location, the assembler does not require this. However, a constant expression (like STICKS) *cannot* be used as an address expression unless it has a *segment override*. That is the purpose of the DS: preceding the address expression (store 15 in the memory location STICKS in the data segment). Also notice that because STICKS has been previously defined as a byte location (via the db pseudo-op), it is not necessary to use the BYTE PTR pseudo-op in the MOV instruction.

After displaying the program instructions, a second procedure called PROCESS is called to display the number of sticks remaining in the pile. Next, the user's input is retrieved and compared with the ASCII letter *q* (via the *quit* equate). If this letter is not found, the number input by the user is echoed back to the screen via a third procedure called COUT.

To evaluate the user's choice, the number must first be converted to binary (by subtracting 30H). The result is then subtracted from the stick counter. If not zero, the PROCESS procedure is called to display the new value of the stick counter. If the result is zero, the user has won and control is transferred to a location named UWIN.

Assuming the user has not won, the screen is updated and the computer's choice is determined. After displaying the MY CHOICE message, a fourth procedure named THINK_TIME is called to generate a time delay. The computer's choice is found via the XLAT instruction. Notice that this requires register BX to point to the base of the choice table, and register AL to hold the current value of the stick counter. The routine ends by converting the computer's choice to ASCII via the ADD AL,30H instruction.

The stick counter is then updated and displayed; if zero, control transfers to location IWIN. If not zero, the program loops back to process another set of turns.

When a winner is found, register DX is pointed at the appropriate message and the CALL SHOW instruction is used to display the winner. The program then waits for a keypress before starting over.

The Procedures [Figure 6.13(e) and (f)]. The four procedures are placed immediately following the main program. Each of these has a header block describing its function, the expected inputs and outputs, and a list of any registers modified by the procedure. In this case, because each procedure begins with the instruction PUSHA (push all registers onto the stack) and ends with the instruction POPA (pop all registers from the stack), only the flags are affected.

The following is a brief description of each procedure.

1. THINK_TIME. This procedure uses BIOS INT 15H, service 86H to generate a time delay whose value is set by the DELAY equate.
2. PROCESS. This procedure displays the current number of sticks in the pile. Notice that if the total is greater than 9, an ASCII 1 is first output, and then the units digit.

3. SHOW. This procedure calls DOS interrupt 21H with AH = 09 to display the ASCII message pointed to by register DX (which should be set before calling this procedure).
4. COUT. This procedure uses BIOS INT 10H, service 0EH to write one character to the screen.

General Assembly Language Program Template

Figure 6.14 shows a template that you can use for developing 80x86 assembly language programs. Note the following about this listing:

1. Use the page directive to format the output to your printer. Set the number of columns high enough to avoid having the comments wrap around to the next line.

Figure 6.14   Template for an 80x86 assembly language program in EXE form.

```
          Page lines,columns
          Title

          .CPU

;*****************************************
;*                 Program Name          *
;*                                       *
;*    Put a description of the program here.*
;*****************************************


; Program equates
var1              equ     xx
var2              equ     xx


;*****************************************
;*               Stack Segment           *
;*                                       *
;*****************************************
sseg             segment         stack
                 db              100 dup (?)               ;100 byte stack
sseg             ends




;*****************************************
;*              Data   Segment           *
;*                                       *
;*****************************************
dseg             segment

first            db              ?                         ;One byte
second           db              100     dup  (?)          ;100 bytes
ASCII            db              'Put ASCII messages inside quotes'

dseg             ends
```

(a)

Figure 6.14 *(continued)*

```
;*********************************
;*             Code Segment      *
;*                               *
;*********************************

cseg            segment         'code'
assume          cs:cseg, ss:sseg, ds:dseg
                mov             ax,dseg         ;Load DS
                mov             ds,ax
start:                                          ;Main program begins here


;Place procedures in the code segment

procedure1      proc
                pusha
                                                ;Body of procedure
                popa
procedure1      endp


procedure2      proc
                pusha
                                                ;Body of procedure
                popa
procedure2      endp


cseg            ends                            ;End of code segment
                end             start           ;End of program
```

(b)

2. The title directive determines the name placed on the top of each page in the listing.
3. All programs should have a name and description. Putting this in a box highlights this information.
4. Use the equate pseudo-op to assign a name to most program constants. Define these equates at the beginning of the program.
5. All EXE programs require a stack. Set the stack size based on expected usage.
6. All program data must go in the data segment. ASCII messages can be entered directly if placed in single quotes.
7. The program instructions must be placed in the code segment. The first few instructions should load the data segment registers (SS and CS are automatically loaded by DOS when the program is started).
8. Procedures must also be placed in a code segment. Typically, these are entered after the main program.
9. The end statement must be the last line in the program. Follow this with the label of the starting address of the program.

Self-Review 6.4 (Answers on page 265)

6.4.1   Use a(n) _____ to name a memory location

6.4.2   Use a(n) _____ to represent a program constant.

6.4.3   To store an ASCII message in memory, use the _____ pseudo-op and enclose the message in single _____.

6.4.4   To place a comment line in a program, precede that comment with a _____.

6.4.5   If your program requires at least an 80386 processor, use the _____ directive at the beginning of the program listing.

6.4.6   Unlike COM files, all EXE programs require a _____ segment.

6.4.7   Procedures called by the main program should be placed in a _____ segment.

Chapter 6 Self-Test

1. An 80x86 assembly language program in source code form has the extension _____.

2. Give the assembler pseudo-op required to create a segment called TEST of class Code.

3. To mark the end of a segment named TEST, use the pseudo-op _____ _____.

4. The _____ file shows the hexadecimal object code and program instructions associated with a particular program.

5. When linking an assembly language program, the input to the linker is the _____ code. The output is the executable file in _____ or _____ format.

6. Errors in program logic (a) *will* (b) *will not* be caught during program assembly.

7. In CodeView, to change the contents of memory, simply overtype the values shown in the _____ window.

8. To view the value of a memory variable while your program is running, open a _____ window.

9. In CodeView, to run your program using the current value in register IP as the starting address, press the _____ function key.

10. CodeView supports two single-step commands called _____ and _____.

11. To force your program to stop on a particular instruction, set a _____ at this location.

12. What are two different methods for entering a new value for register AX using CodeView?

13. Assume a data segment of 500 bytes is to be created with uninitialized data. Using the name D1, show the assembly pseudo-ops required. Label the first location in the segment TEST.

14. Give the assembly language instructions required to load register DS with the address of the data segment described in Question 13. Point register DI at location TEST.

15. If DOS loads the data segment described in Question 13 at address 217C:0000, the starting address for the code segment which immediately follows is _____ : 0000.

16. Assume a procedure named TEST is to be written. Give the first- and last-line pseudo-ops required.

17. Explain how to identify to the Linker the starting instruction of an 80x86 assembly language program.

18. (*True/False*) When an EXE file is loaded by DOS, the stack and code segment registers will automatically be set to their proper values.

19. Use the _____ operator to assign a name to a constant in an 80x86 assembly language program.

20. Show the code required to create a data segment called SAMPLE. In this segment store the ASCII message *First Line of Sample* using the label M1.

Analysis and Design Questions

Section 6.1

6.1   Create, assemble, and link the source code for PROG51 shown in Figure 6.2. Verify that the program operates correctly. Now, for each of the following, modify the source code as indicated, reassemble, and indicate how the change affects program operation and/or assembly. If an error occurs, explain the error message.

(a) In the segment definition, delete the 'Code' classification.

(b) Change the ORG 100H statement to ORG 200H.

(c) Change line 19 to MOV AX,E00H.

(d) Change the interrupt instruction in line 20 to INT 10 (delete the H).

(e) In line 23, change the JNZ IIA to JNZ IIIA.

(f) Delete the statement CSEG ENDS.

(g) Delete the label START from the program end statement.

(h) Change line 25 to 'CSEG ENDS (add the apostrophe).

6.2   Rewrite PROG51.ASM to display the entire ASCII and extended character set (codes 00 through FFH). Assemble, link, and test your program. Correct all errors; print a copy of the new list file.

6.3   Write the program described in Analysis and Design Question 5.2 in assembly language format. Verify proper program operation and print a copy of the list file.

Section 6.2

6.4   Using CodeView, load PROG51.COM and arrange the windows as shown in Figure 6.5 (the COM file is available on the student disk). Use print screen to provide a hard copy of the CodeView screen.

6.5   Complete Analysis and Design Question 6.2 and load the resulting program into CodeView. Place a breakpoint at the JNZ instruction such that the program halts after A0H loops. Use PrintScreen to capture a copy of the CodeView window screens and output screen at this point.

Section 6.3

6.6   Create PROG53.ASM, assemble, and load into CodeView. Arrange the CodeView windows as shown in Figure 6.10 and use PrintScreen to obtain a hard copy.

6.7   Refer to Figure 6.9 and express the physical address for the data and code segments as 1043:*xxxx,* where *xxxx* is the offset from the start of the stack segment. You should find that these offsets agree with the results shown in the map file in Figure 6.8.

6.8   Rewrite the PC typewriter program from Chapter 4 (see Figure 4.18) in EXE assembly language form. Note the following:

(a) Provide a 100 byte stack.

(b) Use the db pseudo-op and place the sign-on message in a data segment.

(c) Load register DS with the address of the data segment.

(d) Point register DX at the first byte in the data segment.

(e) Test your program by stepping through each instruction in CodeView.

(f) Provide a hard copy of the list file.

(g) Provide a hard copy and the CodeView screen (via PrintScreen) showing the ASCII sign-on message in a memory window.

(h) Provide a hard copy of the map file.

(i) Obtaining the physical addresses from CodeView, draw a diagram similar to Figure 6.9, identifying any *unused* areas of memory.

Figure 6.15 Figure for Analysis and Design Question 6.12.

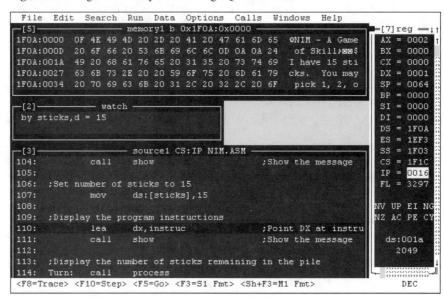

```
 File   Edit   Search   Run   Data   Options   Calls   Windows   Help
┌[5]──────────────── memory1 b 0x1F0A:0x0000 ──────────────   ■[7] reg ═┐↑
│1F0A:0000  0F 4E 49 4D 20 2D 20 41 20 47 61 6D 65  ♦NIM - A Game   AX = 0002 │ ↑
│1F0A:000D  20 6F 66 20 53 6B 69 6C 6C 0D 0A 0A 24   of Skill▮▮$    BX = 0000 │
│1F0A:001A  49 20 68 61 76 65 20 31 35 20 73 74 69   I have 15 sti  CX = 0000 │
│1F0A:0027  63 6B 73 2E 20 20 59 6F 75 20 6D 61 79   cks.  You may  DX = 0001 │
│1F0A:0034  20 70 69 63 6B 20 31 2C 20 32 2C 20 6F   pick 1, 2, o   SP = 0064 │
│                                                                   BP = 0000 │
├[2]───────────── watch ──────────────                            SI = 0000 │
│ by sticks,d = 15                                                  DI = 0000 │
│                                                                   DS = 1F0A │
│                                                                   ES = 1EF3 │
├[3]──────────── source1 CS:IP NIM.ASM ──────────────             SS = 1F03 │
│104:       call     show                   ;Show the message      CS = 1F1C │
│105:                                                              IP = 0016 │
│106: ;Set number of sticks to 15                                  FL = 3297 │
│107:       mov      ds:[sticks],15                                          │
│108:                                                             NV UP EI NG│
│109: ;Display the program instructions                          NZ AC PE CY│
│110:       lea      dx,instruc            ;Point DX at instru              │
│111:       call     show                  ;Show the message      ds:001a   │
│112:                                                               2049     │
│113: ;Display the number of sticks remaining in the pile                   │
│114: Turn:  call    process                                                │
└<F8=Trace> <F10=Step> <F5=Go> <F3=S1 Fmt> <Sh+F3=M1 Fmt>           DEC      ┘
```

6.9 A procedure is said to be *transparent* if, upon return, none of the CPU registers or flags are altered by the procedure. Rewrite the display procedure in Figure 6.7(c) to make it transparent.

6.10 Rewrite Program 5.7 (see Figure 5.21) in EXE form. Note that because DOS automatically loads register DS (and ES) with the address of the PSP, you will *not* need to create a data segment or initialize this register. Provide a hard copy of the LST file. *Hint:* To access the 32-bit registers, use the .386 assembly directive.

Section 6.4

6.11 Assume the game of NIM as written in Figure 6.13 has 14 "sticks" remaining in the pile: How many sticks will the computer choose?

6.12 Load NIM into CodeView (the program is available on the student disk) and arrange the windows as shown in Figure 6.15. Note that memory location STICKS has been placed in a Watch window. Use PrintScreen to obtain a hard copy of the CodeView screen.

6.13 Assume NIM is loaded such that the stack segment begins at address 1AD0:0000. Give the offset address of the following:
    (a) 1AD0: _____ The start of the data segment.
    (b) 1AD0: _____ The start of the code segment.
    (c) 1AD0: _____ The first byte of the SHOW procedure.
    (d) 1AD0: _____ The very last byte of the program.

6.14 Rewrite Program 5.4 (the 80x86 music machine) in EXE form. Use the equate operator to assign labels to the program constants and include a sign-on message. Terminate your program via DOS INT 21H, function 4CH. Provide a hard copy of the debugged LST file.

Answers to Self-Review Questions

6.1.1   source
6.1.2   ORG 0100H

6.1.3   project
6.1.4   list
6.1.5   object, executable (EXE or COM)
6.1.6   list
6.2.1   source
6.2.2   step
6.2.3   quick watch
6.2.4   Single-stepping and breakpoints
6.3.1   MY_DATA   segment
        FIRST_BYTE   db   256   dup (?)
        MY_DATA   ends
6.3.2   MOV AX,MY_DATA
        MOV DS,AX
        LEA   DX,FIRST_BYTE
6.3.3   same
6.3.4   1AFA:0000 + 63H = 1AFA0 + 63H = 1B003H = end of data segment. Next paragraph
        address = 1B010 = 1B01:0000.
6.3.5   PSP
6.3.6   WO &TEST,x
6.4.1   label
6.4.2   equate
6.4.3   db, quotes
6.4.4   semicolon
6.4.5   .386
6.4.6   stack
6.4.7   code

7 Memory Chips and Memory Interfacing

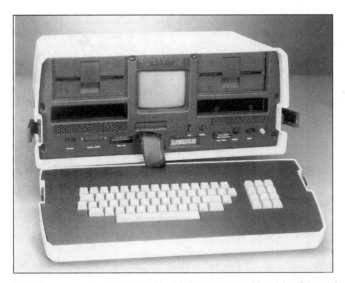

The Osborne computer was announced in 1981 by company president Adam Osborne. It represented the first portable personal computer (if a 28 lb. computer can be considered portable) and was the precursor to today's laptop and notebook computers. Osborne's transportable featured an Z-80 processor, two $5^{1}/4''$ floppy disk drives, and a 5" CRT screen. All necessary software, including a database, word processor, and the CP/M operating system, was included for $1795. Unable to view an entire 80-character line on the small screen, users had to view their text in a scrollable "window." The computer was a huge success—perhaps too successful. Two years later the company was out of business, unable to keep up with its hypergrowth (and the new 16-bit IBM PC and MS-DOS operating system). (Photo courtesy of Smithsonian)

Outline

Objectives

After completing this chapter you should be able to:

1. Compare programmable, one time programmable, UV-light erasable, and electrically erasable read-only memory technologies.
2. Describe the structure of a flash memory part and list common applications.
3. Compare static and dynamic RAM technologies based on bit density, access time, and power consumption.
4. Sketch read/write timing diagrams for the 80x86 processors.
5. Compute the memory access time provided by each of the 80x86 processors running at various clock frequencies.
6. Compare the data transfer rate for the 80x86 processors.
7. Describe the pin functions of the HM62864 64K × 8 SRAM.
8. Show how to interface an array of 64K × 8 SRAMs to each of the 80x86 processors.
9. Explain how the memory decoder positions the memory array at a specific set of memory addresses.
10. Explain how AND, NAND, OR, and NOR gates can be used as address decoders.
11. Show how the 74LS138 can be used as a block decoder.
12. Construct a programmable decoder using PAL technology.
13. Describe common DRAM control signals and access time parameters.
14. Compare conventional DRAMs with page mode, extended data out, and synchronous DRAM technologies.
15. Show the timing for $\overline{\text{RAS}}$-only, $\overline{\text{CAS}}$ before $\overline{\text{RAS}}$, and hidden refresh techniques.

Overview

Computers typically have two types of memory: *main memory* and *secondary memory*. Main memory is used to store the processor's program instructions. However, because most main memory technologies are *volatile*—the information is lost when power is removed—secondary memory is required to provide permanent storage. Secondary memory is typically based on magnetic or optical technologies. Examples of the former are floppy and hard disk drives; CD-ROM drives and optical disks are examples of the latter.

In this chapter we focus on the semiconductor memory chips typically used for main memory and the techniques used to interface these chips to the microprocessor. Technologies covered include programmable read-only memory (PROM), static and dynamic random access memory (SRAM and DRAM), and flash memory, a memory technology that combines the attributes of ROM and RAM.

We will also show the techniques for interfacing these chips to the microprocessor and mapping the parts to specific memory addresses; a process called *address decoding*. Several types of decoders will be examined, including logic gate, block, and programmable array logic (PAL) devices.

7.1   Main Memory Technologies

Introduction

If you could build the ideal memory chip, what characteristics would it have? The *access time*—time to read or write data to the chip—would be very short (0 ns). The data, once written, would never be lost, even if power is interrupted (i.e., the part would be *non-volatile*). The chip itself would be very *dense*, requiring only a small amount of printed circuit board space. Finally, *power consumption* would be minuscule to minimize the current drain on the system power supply or battery.

In this section we examine several different main memory technologies. Each meets some of the criteria listed above, but falls short in others. ROMs, for example, are non-volatile, but cannot be easily written to. Static RAMs (SRAMs) can be read from or written to and have very short access times, but lose their data when power is turned off. Dynamic RAMs (DRAMs) provide very high bit densities, but are relatively slow and also volatile. Flash memory comes the closest to our ideal, as it is nonvolatile, has relatively high bit densities, and has (memory read) access times comparable to those of DRAMs. However, single bytes cannot be written: The entire chip (or a subset) must first be erased, and then the new data block written.

In this section we:

- Compare programmable, one time programmable, UV-light erasable, and electrically erasable read-only memory technologies.
- Describe the structure of a flash memory part and list common applications.
- Compare static and dynamic RAM technologies based on bit density, access time, and power consumption.

Mask-Programmable ROM

It is possible to view a ROM as a device with n inputs and m outputs. For each of the 2^n input combinations, there is one output word of m bits. This is shown in Figure 7.1.

A ROM is made up of an *address decoder,* a *programmable memory array,* and a set of *output buffers.* In Figure 7.1, $n = 4$ and $m = 5$. When a 4-bit address is applied to the ROM, one of the 16 row lines will go low. A diode connected between a row line and a column line will program that output bit low (via the conducting diode); the absence of a diode will program a logic 1 (via the column pull-up resistors).

In essence, a ROM is nothing more than a truth-table generator. It provides one m-bit output word for each possible input combination. Because of this, ROMs can be used to replace combinational logic networks.

A *mask-programmable* ROM is one in which the diode connections are programmed at the factory according to a truth table supplied by the user. In this way, the manufacturer can sell the same ROM chip to many different customers, altering only the mask that defines the diode connections.

The economics of integrated-circuit manufacture are such that it would be impractical to make only one ROM chip. The integrated-circuit dies are grouped together on a wafer containing several hundred potential ROMs. Because there is no guarantee that a particular

Figure 7.1 A diode ROM illustrating the *n*-input address decoder, $2^n \times m$ memory array, and *m* output buffers. (From J. Uffenbeck, *Microcomputers and Microprocessors: The 8080, 8085, and Z-80.* Prentice Hall, Englewood Cliffs, N.J., 1991)

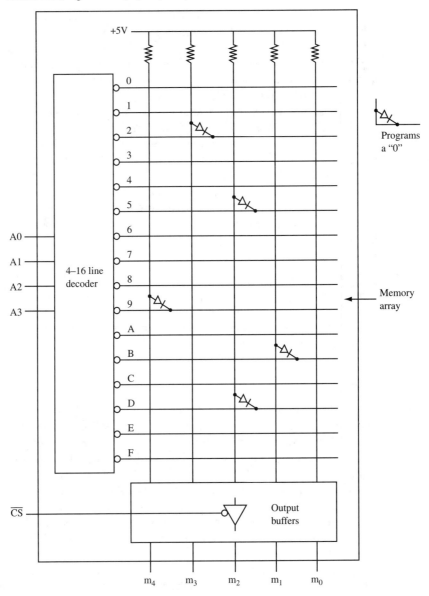

wafer will test as good, several wafers must be manufactured. For this reason, mask-programmable ROMs are limited to production runs of several thousand parts. Needless to say, it is imperative that the truth table supplied to the manufacturer be accurate![1]

---

[1]Until the advent of flash memory, most PCs used mask-programmable ROMs to store the boot-up and BIOS routines.

Figure 7.2 OTP ROMs use titanium tungsten (TiW) fuses that can be selectively "blown" using a special programmer.

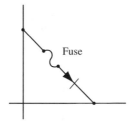

Fuse

Field-Programmable ROMs

There are several types of ROMs that can be programmed by the OEM or end user. These devices are referred to as *PROMs,* or *programmable read-only memories.*

One-Time Programmable PROM (OTP). One type of PROM uses a low-current fusible link in series with each diode in the array (see Figure 7.2). By applying a current pulse to the desired location, the fuse can be melted and a logic 1 permanently programmed. Of course once a fuse has been "blown," it cannot be altered. Fusible-link PROMs are therefore referred to as *one-time programmable,* or *OTPs.*

UV-Light Eraseable PROM (EPROM). A more versatile—but more expensive—type of PROM is the UV-EPROM. This device can be programmed, erased, and reprogrammed by the user many times over. EPROMs use a *floating-gate avalanche-injection* MOS (FAMOS) transistor cell to store charge [Figure 7.3(a)]. Applying a special programming voltage (V_{pp}) to the chip causes a high electric field to be developed in the channel region

Figure 7.3 (a) Basic UV EPROM cell structure. A logic 0 is stored by trapping charge on the floating-gate electrode. (b) The E²PROM has a thin tunnel oxide covering the drain diffusion of the MOS transistor. Electrons are able to "tunnel" through this thin oxide to or from the floating gate. In this way, programming and erasure are both done electrically. (Courtesy of Intel Corporation)

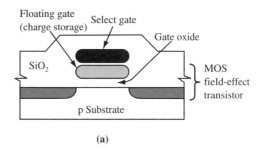

(a)

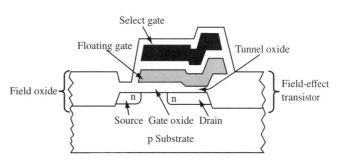

(b)

of the transistor. This, in turn, causes electrons to jump the silicon dioxide barrier between the channel region and the floating gate.

During programming, the select gate is given a positive bias, which helps attract these electrons to the floating-gate electrode. Because the floating gate is surrounded by silicon dioxide (an excellent insulator), the injected charge is effectively trapped. The storage period is projected to exceed 20 years.

Cells with trapped charge cause the transistor to be biased ON, whereas those cells without trapped charge are biased OFF. Blank EPROMs have no trapped charge, and each cell stores a logic 1. The EPROM can be erased by subjecting each gate to ultraviolet (UV) light, which has a wavelength of 2537 angstroms. The electrons on the floating gate absorb photons from the UV-light source and acquire enough energy to reverse the programming process and return to the substrate.

EPROMs are placed in special ceramic packages with quartz windows to allow erasure. Commercial erasers are available that will erase several EPROMs at once in 15 to 20 minutes. In practice, the EPROM window should be covered with an opaque label because normal fluorescent lighting could erase the device (Intel reports that approximately three years of exposure to fluorescent lighting or one week of direct sunlight would be required).

UV EPROMs are programmed by wiring their V_{pp} programming pin to +13V. The data to be written is then applied to the data-out lines, the desired address to the address lines, and the $\overline{PGM}$ pin pulsed low for 100 μs. Typically, this is accomplished using a PC, an interface card, and a programming module (see Figure 7.4). Proprietary software is then used to program the selected EPROM. A typical EPROM can be programmed in 2 to 5s.

Electrically Erasable PROM (E^2PROM).   There are several disadvantages to the UV EPROM:

1. The device must be removed from the circuit board to be erased.
2. Byte erasure is not possible—all cells are erased when exposed to UV light.
3. The quartz-window package is expensive.

Figure 7.4 EPROM programmer consisting of a PC interface card and programming module.

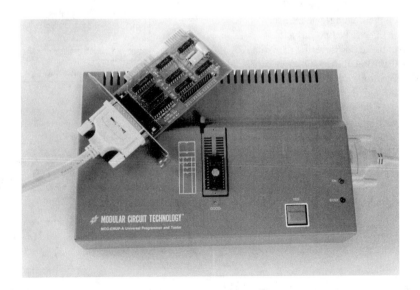

Because of these problems, much research has been devoted to developing an electrically erasable nonvolatile memory device. Two different technologies have emerged. The first is the electrically erasable PROM, or E²PROM. These devices can be programmed and erased without removing the chip from its socket. In addition, both byte and bulk erasure modes are possible.

The most recent development is called *flash memory*. Similar to the E²PROM, these devices can be erased electrically, but unlike the E²PROM, they do not allow individual bytes to be erased. Flash memory is covered in the next section.

Figure 7.3(b) shows the difference between the FAMOS cell and the E²PROM cell. Like the FAMOS cell, a floating gate and a select gate are used. However, a very thin tunnel oxide is provided over the drain diffusion of the MOS transistor in the E²PROM cell. With a positive voltage applied to the select gate, electrons are attracted to the floating gate. Applying a positive voltage to the drain terminal discharges (erases) the cell.

Because the gate oxide over the drain is so thin, the process is controlled by a *tunneling* phenomenon instead of avalanche injection. Tunneling has the advantage that a large amount of charge can be injected during the write cycle, but only a small amount of charge is lost during a read cycle. Data retention is said to be greater than 10 years.

Unfortunately, each read and write cycle causes a small amount of charge to be trapped in the gate oxide. Eventually the E²PROM cannot be reprogrammed. This lifetime is between 10,000 and 1,000,000 read/write cycles.

E²PROM read access times are comparable to present EPROM chips, but write times are slow (25 ms is typical) compared to conventional RAM devices. For this reason, *wait* states (extra clock cycles in which the processor's bus interface unit does nothing but wait for the memory chip to respond) will be required for all write cycles.

Flash Memory

In recent years, E²PROMs, with their complex cell structures, have fallen out of favor and have been replaced by *flash memory*. Like E²PROM, flash memory parts can be electrically erased and reprogrammed without removing the chip from the circuit board. Unlike E²PROM, however, the entire chip (or a subblock) must be erased at one time: Individual byte erasure is not possible.

Despite this limitation, flash memory offers several advantages over E²PROM. The flash memory cell is much simpler, thus lowering costs and improving reliability. In addition, very *dense* memory parts can be manufactured. Intel's 28F020, for example, provides two million bits of storage organized as 256K bytes. Flash memory devices are available in credit-card-size (PCMCIA—Personal Computer Memory Card International Association) units that store 40 MB of nonvolatile read/write memory. These cards effectively function as *silicon hard disks*. Figure 7.5 shows examples of two PCMCIA cards: one a modem, the other an Ethernet adapter.

Bulk Erase. Figure 7.6 provides a description of the 28F020 256K × 8 CMOS flash memory. Note the following about this chip:

1. Typical erase time is 2s.
2. A single byte can be written in 10 μs. Four seconds are required to write to all 256K locations.

Figure 7.5 PCMCIA modem and Ethernet adapter.

3. 100,000 erase/program cycles are allowed.
4. Read access time is 70 ns (comparable to high-speed DRAMs, but slower than static RAM).
5. Two power supplies are required: V_{CC} = 5V and V_{PP} = 12V (the latter is required only for programming).
6. Current consumption is typically 10mA (similar-size DRAMs typically require 65–90mA).
7. Only bulk (entire-chip) erasure is possible.

Flash memory components differ from conventional memory parts in that access is controlled via an onboard *command register*. Typically, V_{PP} is raised to 12V, and one, two, or three commands are written to the chip (Table 7.1 provides the details.) For example, to read from the memory array, a 00 data byte is first written; subsequent reads then occur from the memory array. Similarly, to erase the chip, two write cycles with the data byte 20H are required.

Boot Block.   A recent development in flash memory technology is the introduction of the *boot block* memory device. Figure 7.7 lists key features of the 28F400B. This chip provides four million bits of storage organized as 256K 16-bit words or 512K 8-bit bytes. The memory is further divided into seven memory blocks as follows:

1	Boot block	16K
2	8K parameter blocks	16K
1	Main block	96K
3	128K main blocks	384K
		512K

Figure 7.6   Description of the 28F020 256K × 8 flash memory part. (Courtesy of Intel Corporation)

28F020
2048K (256K x 8) CMOS FLASH MEMORY

- **Flash Electrical Chip-Erase**
  - **— 2 Second Typical Chip-Erase**
- **Quick-Pulse Programming Algorithm**
  - **— 10 μs Typical Byte-Program**
  - **— 4 Second Chip-Program**
- **100,000 Erase/Program Cycles**
- **12.0V ±5% V_{PP}**
- **High-Performance Read**
  - **— 70 ns Maximum Access Time**
- **CMOS Low Power Consumption**
  - **— 10 mA Typical Active Current**
  - **— 50 μA Typical Standby Current**
  - **— 0 Watts Data Retention Power**
- **Integrated Program/Erase Stop Timer**

- **Command Register Architecture for Microprocessor/Microcontroller Compatible Write Interface**
- **Noise Immunity Features**
  - **— ±10% V_{CC} Tolerance**
  - **— Maximum Latch-Up Immunity through EPI Processing**
- **ETOX Nonvolatile Flash Technology**
  - **— EPROM-Compatible Process Base**
  - **— High-Volume Manufacturing Experience**
- **JEDEC-Standard Pinouts**
  - **— 32-Pin Plastic Dip**
  - **— 32-Lead PLCC**
  - **— 32-Lead TSOP**
  - (See Packaging Spec., Order #231369)
- **Extended Temperature Options**

Intel's 28F020 CMOS flash memory offers the most cost-effective and reliable alternative for read/write random access nonvolatile memory. The 28F020 adds electrical chip-erasure and reprogramming to familiar EPROM technology. Memory contents can be rewritten: in a test socket; in a PROM-programmer socket; on-board during subassembly test; in-system during final test; and in-system after-sale. The 28F020 increases memory flexibility, while contributing to time-and cost-savings.

The 28F020 is a 2048-kilobit nonvolatile memory organized as 262,144 bytes of 8 bits. Intel's 28F020 is offered in 32-pin plastic DIP, 32-lead PLCC, and 32-lead TSOP packages. Pin assignments conform to JEDEC standards for byte-wide EPROMs.

Extended erase and program cycling capability is designed into Intel's ETOX (EPROM Tunnel Oxide) process technology. Advanced oxide processing, an optimized tunneling structure, and lower electric field combine to extend reliable cycling beyond that of traditional EEPROMs. With the 12.0V V_{PP} supply, the 28F020 performs 100,000 erase and program cycles well within the time limits of the Quick-Pulse Programming and Quick-Erase algorithms.

Intel's 28F020 employs advanced CMOS circuitry for systems requiring high-performance access speeds, low power consumption, and immunity to noise. Its 70 nanosecond access time provides no-WAIT-state performance for a wide range of microprocessors and microcontrollers. Maximum standby current of 100 μA translates into power savings when the device is deselected. Finally, the highest degree of latch-up protection is achieved through Intel's unique EPI processing. Prevention of latch-up is provided for stresses up to 100 mA on address and data pins, from −1V to V_{CC} + 1V.

With Intel's ETOX process base, the 28F020 levers years of EPROM experience to yield the highest levels of quality, reliability, and cost-effectiveness.

These blocks are located sequentially in memory, but the boot block can be placed at the top or bottom of the memory space. In addition, each block can be individually erased. The boot block can also be *locked* via the $\overline{RP}$ input pin: When low, no program or erase cycles are possible within this block.

Table 7.1 Flash Memory Command Definitions (Courtesy of Texas Instruments)

Command	Bus Cycles Required	First Bus Cycle			Second Bus Cycle		
		Operation	Address[1]	Data[2]	Operation	Address[1]	Data[2]
Read Memory	1	Write	X	00H			
Read Intelligent Identifier Codes[3]	3	Write	X	90H	Read	[3]	[3]
Set Up Erase/Erase	2	Write	X	20H	Write	X	20H
Erase Verify	2	Write	EA	A0H	Read	X	EVD
Set Up Program/Program	2	Write	X	40H	Write	PA	PD
Program Verify	2	Write	X	C0H	Read	X	PVD
Reset[4]	2	Write	X	FFH	Write	X	FFH

[1]IA = Identifier address: 00H for manufacturer code, 01H for device code.
EA = Address of memory location to be read during erase verify.
PA = Address of memory location to be programmed.
Addresses are latched on the falling edge of the write-enable pulse.
[2]ID = Data read from location IA during device identification (Mfr = 89H, Device = BDH).
EVD = Data read from location EA during erase verify.
PD = Data to be programmed at location PA. Data is latched on the rising edge of write-enable.
PVD = Data read from location PA during program verify. PA is latched on the Program command.
[3]Following the Read Intelligent ID command, two read operations access manufacturer and device codes.
[4]The second bus cycle must be followed by the desired command register write.

Applications.   There are numerous applications for flash memory. Each takes advantage of the nonvolatile nature of the part along with the capability to (occasionally) reprogram some or all memory locations.

1. In Chapters 4 and 5 we learned that DOS stores boot-up code and BIOS routines in ROM. Using conventional ROM technology, BIOS updates require the user to locate and replace the ROM BIOS chips—a task most users are unsuited for. Using flash memory, however, BIOS upgrades are accomplished by running a software program that erases the flash ROM and reprograms it with the new code, a relatively routine task. In fact, reprogramming could even be accomplished *remotely* by a technician with a modem connection to the target computer.

2. Networks have become increasingly popular in recent years, and many PCs today are equipped with Ethernet network interface cards. These cards must be configured with I/O addresses and interrupt numbers. Although this can be accomplished with "jumpers," most cards today use flash memory to allow these settings to be specified via software and then stored by the card.

3. Laser printers typically require "font cards" to support various font styles. Using flash memory, users can select the fonts they want and download them to the printer. If a different font set is desired, the old one can be erased and a new font set programmed.

4. In the automotive industry, flash ROMs can be used to store "trouble codes" that provide diagnostic information to the mechanic. The nonvolatile nature of the flash memory part allows these codes to be stored for several weeks or months after the actual fault occurs. These codes can then be studied by the technician at the next service interval.

Figure 7.7 The 28F004B is a boot block flash memory part. Unlike conventional flash memory parts, individual blocks can be erased and reprogrammed. (Courtesy of Intel Corporation)

intel®

28F400BX-T/B, 28F004BX-T/B
4 MBIT (256K x16, 512K x8) BOOT BLOCK FLASH MEMORY FAMILY

- x8/x16 Input/Output Architecture
  - 28F400BX-T, 28F400BX-B
  - For High Performance and High Integration 16-bit and 32-bit CPUs

- x8-only Input/Output Architecture
  - 28F004BX-T, 28F004BX-B
  - For Space Constrained 8-bit Applications

- Optimized High Density Blocked Architecture
  - One 16-KB Protected Boot Block
  - Two 8-KB Parameter Blocks
  - One 96-KB Main Block
  - Three 128-KB Main Blocks
  - Top or Bottom Boot Locations

- Extended Cycling Capability
  - 100,000 Block Erase Cycles

- Automated Word/Byte Write and Block Erase
  - Command User Interface
  - Status Registers
  - Erase Suspend Capability

- SRAM-Compatible Write Interface

- Automatic Power Savings Feature
  - 1 mA Typical I_{CC} Active Current In Static Operation

- Very High-Performance Read
  - 60/80 ns Maximum Access Time
  - 30/40 ns Maximum Output Enable Time

- Low Power Consumption
  - 20 mA Typical x8 Active Read Current
  - 25 mA Typical x16 Active Read Current

- Reset/Deep Power-Down Input
  - 0.2 μA I_{CC} Typical
  - Acts as Reset for Boot Operations

- Extended Temperature Operation
  - −40°C to +85°C

- Write Protection for Boot Block

- Hardware Data Protection Feature
  - Erase/Write Lockout During Power Transitions

- Industry Standard Surface Mount Packaging
  - 28F400BX: JEDEC ROM Compatible
    44-Lead PSOP
    56-Lead TSOP
  - 28F004BX: 40-Lead TSOP

- 12V Word/Byte Write and Block Erase
  - V_{PP} = 12V ±5% Standard
  - V_{PP} = 12V ±10% Option

- ETOX III Flash Technology
  - 5V Read

Static RAM

RAM stands for *random access memory*. In practice, however, a better definition would be *read/write memory*, to differentiate it from ROM, which is read-only. Static RAM, or SRAM, is a type of RAM that uses a flip-flop as the basic storage element.

SRAM Storage Cell. Figure 7.8 shows a typical SRAM memory cell. In this cell, Q1 and Q2 form a cross-coupled flip-flop, with Q3 and Q4 acting as pull-up resistors. Transistors

Figure 7.8 Basic six-transistor static memory cell. (From J. Uffenbeck, *Microcomputers and Microprocessors: The 8080, 8085, and Z-80.* Prentice Hall, Englewood Cliffs, N.J., 1991)

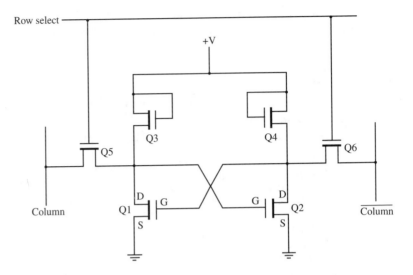

Q5 and Q6 provide access to the cell. To write data into the flip-flop, the row-select line is made active, turning on transistors Q5 and Q6. Now, to store a logic 1, the Column line is driven high and $\overline{\text{Column}}$ low. Via Q5, the high level on the column line is applied to the gate of Q2, turning this transistor ON and forcing its drain lead low.

Similarly, the low level on $\overline{\text{Column}}$ forces Q1 OFF and its drain lead pulls high—reinforcing the high level applied to the gate of Q2. In effect, the cell *latches* itself into the applied state. Row-select transistors Q5 and Q6 can now be turned off and the information is retained. To store a logic 0, the process is repeated, but this time the column input is driven low and $\overline{\text{Column}}$ high.

To read the data stored by the SRAM cell, the row-select line is again made active, but this time the voltage *difference* between the column lines is sensed. A positive voltage indicates a logic 1 is stored; a negative voltage between these same lines indicates a logic 0 is stored.

Because of the SRAM's internal latching mechanism, data is retained without the need for any refresh signals. For this reason, the cell is referred to as *static*. However, if power is removed from the cell, the data is lost. Furthermore, when power is reapplied, the state of each flip-flop will be unpredictable.

Applications. To avoid inserting *wait states*, most high-speed microcomputer systems require a *cache memory* subsystem. These systems are normally designed using SRAMs because they provide the fastest access times of any of the current memory technologies. The 7C1024-15 SRAM, for example, provides 128K of storage and has an access time of just 15 ns. Four of these chips would allow a 32-bit-wide, 512K cache to be constructed. Most microcomputer system boards have sockets designed to accommodate several different sizes of SRAM chips: The user can adjust the size of the cache as needed, based on the amount of installed DRAM and cost.[2]

---

[2]These high-speed SRAM chips are not especially cheap. A single 7C1024-15, for example, currently costs $15.

Dynamic RAM (DRAM)

Storage Cell. If we assume that one of the goals of main-memory technology is to produce a high-bit-density component, a part that requires six transistors per cell may not be the best choice. This drawback of static RAM has led designers to *dynamic RAM (DRAM)* technology.

Figure 7.9 shows the internal structure of a DRAM. The memory cell has been shrunk to a single bit-select transistor and storage capacitor. Each cell in the array is identified by its unique row and column address. A 1 Mb (1 million bits) chip, for example, might be organized as 1024 rows by 1024 columns.

Figure 7.9 Dynamic RAMs use an MOS transistor and capacitor as the basic storage cell. Particular cells are selected via a row and column address.

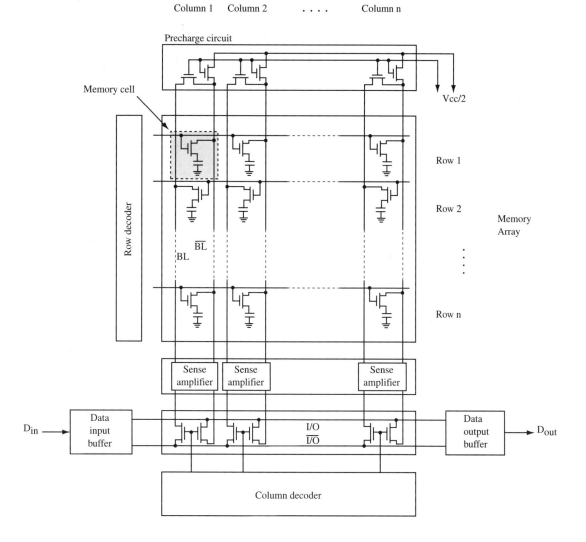

Read Cycle.   Data is read from the DRAM by sensing the voltage on the bit cell capacitor. The row address decoder turns on all of the transistors in a given row. The charge on the selected capacitors is then placed on the bit sense lines (BL and $\overline{BL}$). However, because these capacitors are very tiny, the charge stored is very tiny. The *precharge circuit* is used to precharge the bit sense lines to $V_{CC}/2V$. When the row transistors are turned on, this level is either increased (if the capacitor is charged) or decreased (if the capacitor is empty). The amount of *change* is very small, however, typically only 100 mV. *Differential amplifiers* (sense amplifiers) are thus required to convert this change into valid logic levels (0V or 5V).

The read cycle is completed by supplying a column address, which is used to select one bit in the active row now stored in the sense amplifiers. The output of the selected sense amplifier is then gated to the data output buffer, where it can be read by the processor. In this example, the DRAM stores one bit at each address, but other organizations are possible ($\times 4, \times 8, \times 16$). This is discussed later in this section.

In summary, four steps are required to read data from the DRAM:

1. Precharge the bit sense lines.
2. Apply the row address and turn on all of the transistors in that row.
3. Sense and amplify the potential difference on the bit sense lines.
4. Apply the column address to select the specific bit (or bits) in the selected row to be gated to the output.

Write Cycle.   DRAM write cycles are similar to read cycles. However, after precharging the bit sense lines and applying the row address, the data to be written is gated through one of the sense amplifiers and allowed to change the charge stored on the selected capacitor; that is, if a 1 is to be written, the charge level is increased, and if a 0 is to be written, the charge level is decreased.

Refresh.   You are probably familiar with the DRAM's greatest shortcoming—the storage node is not perfect and will become discharged over a period of time. This necessitates a *refresh* operation—that is, sense the charge, amplify it, and then rewrite the data. Depending on the DRAM, a refresh must be carried out once per memory cell every 1 to 16 ms.

Refresh may not be as difficult to implement as it may at first seem. Referring to Figure 7.9, each time a row in the DRAM is accessed, the precharge circuit restores the charge on that capacitor—and on all of the other capacitors in that row. Thus, simply reading (or writing) the contents of memory also refreshes the memory. In Section 7.5 we discuss several different DRAM-refresh strategies.

Access Time.   When DRAMs were first introduced, access times were typically greater than 150 ns. This was no problem, as microprocessors of this era had just 4 to 5 MHz clock speeds. In recent years the access times for DRAMs have leveled off at 60 to 80 ns, while processor clock speeds have risen to well over 100 MHz. To make up for this failing, most microcomputer systems now include a high-speed SRAM cache memory, as described previously. In Section 7.5 we discuss several new DRAM technologies that may make this external cache obsolete.

SIMMs and DIMMs.   Because of their high bit density, DRAMs form the "core" memory for most microcomputer systems. For example, it is not uncommon for a microcomputer to have 16 MB of (DRAM) main memory, 2 MB of (DRAM) video memory, and another 2 to 4 MB of hard disk (DRAM) cache memory. To minimize the amount of circuit board space required to support all of these DRAMs, the chips are commonly soldered on thin circuit boards called *single in-line memory modules,* or *SIMMs* (see Figure 7.10). Single-byte (30-pin) and 4-byte (72-pin) SIMMs are available. Figure 7.11 shows the pin-outs for an 8M × 32 (32 MB) 72-pin SIMM; its equivalent schematic is shown in Figure 7.12.

To accomodate the 64-bit (8-byte) data bus width of the Pentium processors, manufacturers have recently introduced *DIMMs (dual in-line memory modules).* These are SIMMs with pins on both sides of the board. Eight bytes are provided per DIMM with 168 total module pins.

Figure 7.10 High bit density memory arrays are constructed by soldering DRAM chips to small circuit boards. The resulting component is referred to as a SIMM—*single in-line memory module.* 30- and 72-pin SIMMs are popular.

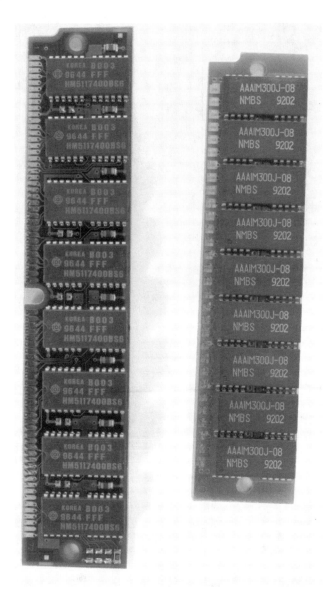

Figure 7.11   Pinouts for an 8M × 32 (32 MB) SIMM. (Courtesy of Texas Instruments)

(Top view)   (Side view)

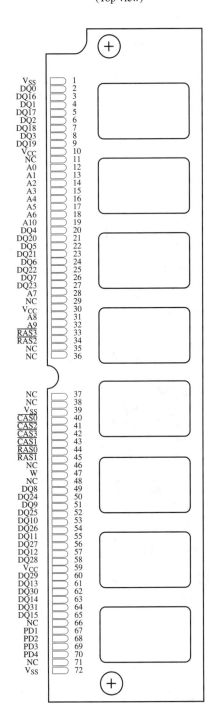
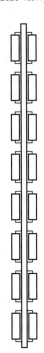

Pin Nomenclature	
A0–A10	Address inputs
$\overline{CAS0}$–$\overline{CAS3}$	Column-address strobe
DQ0–DQ31	Data in/data out
NC	No connection
PD1–PD4	Presence detects
$\overline{RAS0}$–$\overline{RAS3}$	Row-address strobe
V_{CC}	5V supply
V_{SS}	Ground
$\overline{W}$	Write enable

Presence Detect					
Signal (PIN)		PD1 (67)	PD2 (68)	PD3 (69)	PD4 (70)
TM893CBK32	80 ns	NC	V_{SS}	NC	V_{SS}
	70 ns	NC	V_{SS}	V_{SS}	NC
	60 ns	NC	V_{SS}	NC	NC

Figure 7.12 Equivalent circuit for the 32 MB SIMM shown in Figure 7.11. (Courtesy of Texas Instruments)

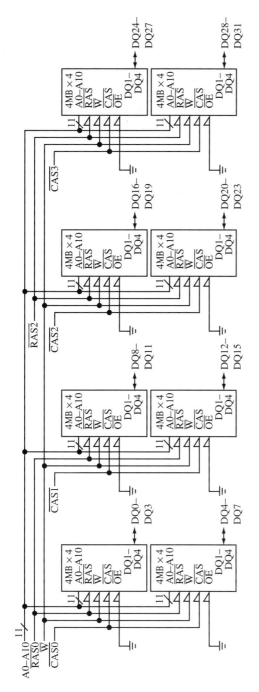

Functional block diagram (side 1)

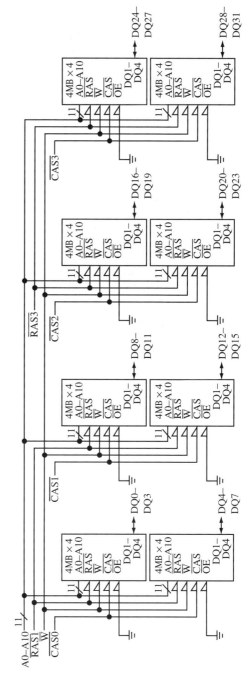

Functional block diagram (side 2)

Memory Organization

The *organization* of a memory chip refers to the way in which the storage cells are arranged to provide external data access. For example, a particular chip may have a total of 16 Mb of storage. Externally, however, these 16 Mb may be accessed in several different ways:

1. $16M \times 1$ (i.e., 16M bits)
2. $4M \times 4$ (i.e., 4M nibbles)
3. $2M \times 8$ (i.e., 2M bytes)
4. $1M \times 16$ (i.e. 16M words)

SRAMs and ROMs are typically arranged $\times 8$: This is referred to as *byte-wide*. The organization of a memory chip is important because it determines how many chips will be required in a memory interface.

Example 7.1

Using $64K \times 8$ SRAMs, determine the *minimum* number of chips required to construct a memory interface to each of the following processors. For each interface, calculate the total memory capacity provided.

(a) 8088   (b) 8086   (c) 80486   (d) Pentium

Solution
The bus width of the processor dictates the number of memory chips that will be required. Thus, the 8088 with its 8-bit bus requires only a single chip. The Pentium, however, with a 64-bit data bus, will require eight memory chips. Table 7.2 summarizes the results for all four processors.

Memory Part Numbers

Interpreting the part number of a memory chip is tricky, because no particular standard has been established. Nevertheless, you can usually identify four components of the part number:

WWW XX YYYY-ZZ

where WWW is the *manufacturer code,* XX identifies the *type* of memory (EPROM, SRAM, DRAM, etc.), YYYY represents the total *bit storage* of the chip, and ZZ represents the *access time* in nanoseconds. Let's try an example. A certain memory chip has the number MC27256-10. We interpret this as:

- WWW = MC, the code for Motorola Semiconductor
- XX = 27, the code used to identify EPROMs[3]
- YYYY = 256, the total storage capacity of the chip (256K bits)
- ZZ = 10, the access time is 100 ns

Notice that the part number does not give a hint as to how these 256K bits are organized. However, EPROMs are almost always byte-wide, and thus we surmise that this particular chip provides 32K ($32K \times 8 = 256K$).

---

[3]The XX code for DRAMs is typically 41 or 51, flash memories use 28, SRAMs are often indicated by 62 or 7C. Use caution, however, as there are many inconsistencies.

Table 7.2 Minimum Memory Capacity for Various 80x86 Processors*

Processor	Data Bus Width (bits)	Minimum Number of Chips Required	Total Memory Capacity Supplied
8088	8	1	64K
8086	16	2	128K
80386/486	32	4	256K
Pentium/Pro	64	8	512K

*Assumes 64K × 8 memory chips

You might have expected the *-10* in the part number to indicate a 10 ns access time. Unfortunately, most manufacturers use only two digits to represent access time. Users therefore have to make an *educated guess* at the actual access time. Because EPROMs are relatively slow—access times are generally 100 ns or more—we conclude that for this part the correct interpretation is 100 ns. Table 7.3 provides examples for several common memory chips.

Table 7.3 Specifications for Common Memory Chips

Part Number	Manufacturer	Technology	Total Bits	Organization	Access Time
TMS4164-100	Texas Instruments	DRAM	64K	64K × 1	100 ns
TMS4464-80	Texas Instruments	DRAM	256K	64K × 4	80 ns
UPD411000-60	NEC	DRAM	1M	1M × 1	60 ns
HY514256P-60	Siemens	DRAM	1M	256K × 4	60 ns
TMS44100-70	Texas Instruments	DRAM	4M	4M × 1	70 ns
TMS417400-60	Texas Instruments	DRAM	16M	4M × 4	60 ns
TMS464800-60	Texas Instruments	DRAM	64M	8M × 8	60 ns
TMM2016-150	Toshiba	SRAM	16K	2K × 8	150 ns
HM6264LP-10	Hitachi	SRAM	64K	8K × 8	100 ns
HM62256LP-12	Hitachi	SRAM	256K	32K × 8	120 ns
HM62832-12	Hitachi	SRAM	256K	32K × 8	12 ns
ATT7C1024-15	AT&T	SRAM	1M	128K × 8	15 ns
TMS27C128-15	Texas Instruments	EPROM	128K	16K × 8	150 ns
TMS27C256-12	Texas Instruments	EPROM	256K	32K × 8	120 ns
TMS27C512-80	Texas Insruments	EPROM	512K	64K × 8	80 ns
27C101-70	Microchip Technology	EPROM	1M	128K × 8	70 ns
TMS27C210A-120	Texas Instruments	EPROM	1M	64K × 16	120 ns
27C201-100	Microchip Technology	EPROM	2M	256K × 8	100 ns
27C401-80	Microchip Technology	EPROM	4M	512K × 8	80 ns
TMS27C240-80	Texas Instruments	EPROM	4M	256K × 16	80 ns
28F256-120	Intel	Flash	256K	32K × 8	120 ns
TMS29F256-170	Texas Instruments	Flash	256K	32K × 8	170 ns
28F010-65	Intel	Flash	1M	128K × 8	65 ns
28F020-70	Intel	Flash	2M	256K × 8	70 ns
29LV040-25PC	Atmel	Flash	4M	512K × 8	250 ns

Self Review 7.1 (Answers on page 340–341)

7.1.1 The diode ROM in Figure 7.1 can store _____ words, where each word is _____ bits wide.

7.1.2 Fusible-link PROMs are said to be _____ _____ _____.

7.1.3 Which of the following PROMs can be erased without requiring that the chip be removed from its socket?
(a) UV-EPROM
(b) E²PROM
(c) OTP ROM
(d) Mask-programmable ROM

7.1.4 _____ memory offers bit densities comparable to that of DRAMs but is limited to _____ erase/program cycles.

7.1.5 _____ provides the fastest memory access times.

7.1.6 The storage cell for a DRAM is actually a _____.

7.1.7 72-pin SIMMs are _____ bytes wide.

7.1.8 A certain SRAM stores 1 Mb. If this chip is organized ×8, it stores _____ bytes.

7.1.9 A memory chip with part number 4164-10 probably uses _____ technology, stores _____ bits, and has an access time of _____ ns.

7.2   80x86 Processor Read/Write Bus Cycles

Introduction

From a hardware standpoint, one can view a microprocessor as a complex timing unit. Turn the machine on and a carefully orchestrated set of signals can be observed on the data, address, and control buses. The timing of these signals defines the "window of opportunity" that the memory chips must match in order for data to be reliably read or written.

In this section we:

- Sketch read/write timing diagrams for the 80x86 processors.
- Compute the memory access time provided by each of the 80x86 processors running at various clock frequencies.
- Compare the data transfer rate for the 80x86 processors.

Read/Write Timing

8086/8088 Processors.   Figure 7.13 illustrates read and write bus cycle timing for the 8086 and 8088 processors. As shown, each bus cycle is divided into four clock cycles, or T states. These are labeled T1–T4 in Figure 7.13. Each cycle begins with the T1 state, in which the 20-bit memory (or 16-bit I/O) address is output. During T2 the processor identifies the cycle type—*read or write*—by activating the memory (or I/O) read or write lines. For a read cycle the processor takes no further action: It is up to the memory or I/O device to supply the data to be read. The T3 state is provided for this purpose. During T4 the data is latched by the processor and the read control signal is removed.

If a write cycle is to occur, the data to be written is output during T2 and held throughout the remainder of the bus cycle. It is up to the external hardware (the I/O port or memory interface) to latch this data. Typically, the write control signal is used for this purpose.

Figure 7.13   Read and write bus cycle timing for the 8086 and 8088 microprocessors. Each bus cycle requires four T states.

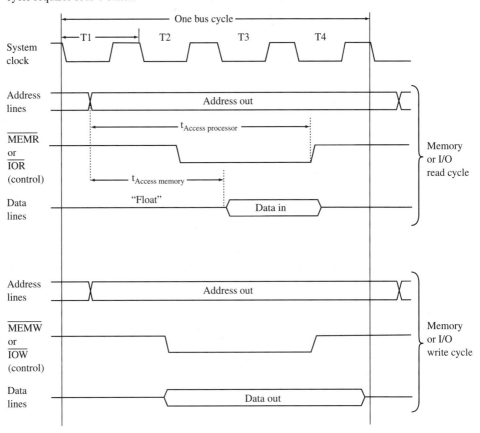

Access Time.   As we learned in Section 7.1, memory chips are rated by their access times. This is the time measured from receipt of the memory address until valid data is output by the chip. In Figure 7.13 this is called $t_{Access\ memory}$. Also shown in this figure is the access time provided by the processor $t_{Access\ processor}$. If the memory interface is to work properly:

$$T_{Access\ processor} > T_{Access\ memory}$$

In fact, because the memory address and data must pass through buffers, it is desirable that the access time provided by the processor exceed that of the memory chip by several nanoseconds.

The 8086 and 8088 processors provide an access time of about 2.3 T states. A 4.77 MHz 8088 used in a typical PC or XT computer thus provides $2.3 \times 1/4.77$ MHz = 2.3×209 ns = 481 ns for the memory chips to respond. Memory parts of this era typically had 200–300 ns access times and thus met this specification without a problem, even accounting for buffer delays.

Wait States.   What if the memory chip cannot supply data within the processor's pre-
scribed window of opportunity? When the processor attempts to access the memory chip,
invalid data will be read and the system will most likely "crash"—refuse to boot or mys-
teriously "hang up." The latter symptom may be caused by a memory chip with an access
time that is *close* to meeting the processor's access time requirements.

There are three solutions to this problem:

1. *Decrease the system clock frequency.* Some computers have a TURBO switch that may
   be pressed to slow the processor down. Of course, this penalizes the entire system when
   only the memory is at fault.
2. *Purchase faster memory parts.* This is a simple enough solution, but may be costly if
   several banks of memory must be replaced.
3. *Program the memory unit to request wait states with each memory access.* The 80x86
   processors, for example, provide a READY input which is sampled at the start of each
   T3 state. If this pin is found low—indicating memory is *not ready*—additional T3 states
   are added until READY goes high.

In the previous example, one wait state adds 209 ns (one processor T state) to the
memory access time. Memory chips as slow as 481 ns + 209 ns = 690 ns could thus be accommodated. Note that the memory subsystem must be designed to allow that wait states
be requested (via the READY input). On many computers, this is accomplished via the
CMOS setup software.

80386/486 and Pentium Processors.   Figure 7.14 illustrates read/write timing for 386,
486, and Pentium processors. Note that each bus cycle requires only two T states (T1 and
T2). Like the 8086, each cycle begins with the output of the memory (or I/O) address. The
type of cycle—read or write—is indicated by the logic level on the W/$\overline{R}$ pin. The $\overline{READY}$
input then pulls high, indicating that valid data is not yet present on the data bus.

If a read cycle is occurring, a period of time—the memory access time—is then provided while the processor waits for the input data. At the end of T2, the processor checks
its READY input and, if low, latches the data. If the access time provided by the processor
is not sufficient, the memory system must hold the READY line high to request one or
more wait states. According to Intel's data sheets, 1.5 T states of memory access time are
provided.

Write cycles are similar. The data to be written is output by the processor during T1
and held on the bus for the remainder of the cycle. The W/$\overline{R}$ signal can then be used by the
memory chip or output port to latch this data.

Table 7.4 compares clock rates and memory access times for the various 80x86
processors. Note that beginning with the 386, processor access times are all less than 50
ns; with a 66 MHz bus, only 22.5 ns is provided. As DRAM chips typically have 60–80 ns
access times, you can see why fast SRAM caches are necessary in most microcomputer
systems today.

Burst Cycles.   As we have seen, the 386, 486, and Pentium processors require two clock
cycles to read or write one quantity of data. However, beginning with the 486, a new *burst
bus* mode has been implemented. A burst cycle begins with a two-T-state bus cycle as
before. However, subsequent cycles transfer *one quantity* of data (four bytes for a 486,

Figure 7.14 Basic read and write bus cycle timing for the 386, 486, and Pentium processors. Each bus cycle requires two T states.

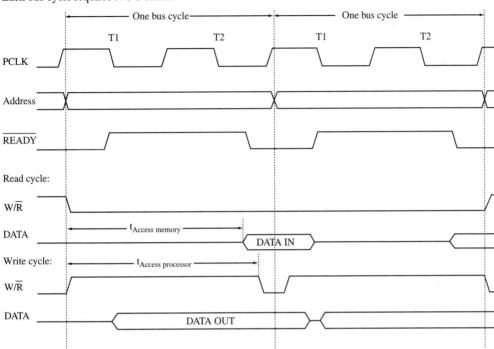

eight bytes for a Pentium) per clock pulse. The data transfer rate thus doubles compared to nonburst cycles.

The primary purpose of this new bus mode is to allow the internal processor cache to be filled as quickly as possible. However, burst cycles can be implemented for any memory access. Some limitations do apply, as described below.

1. With a 486 processor, the cycle is restricted such that only 16 bytes (the line size of the internal cache) may be transferred per burst cycle. In addition, all of the data items must

Table 7.4 80x86 Processor Memory Access Times

	External Clock		Processor Access Time	
Processor	Frequency	Period	T States	Seconds
8088	4.77 MHz	209 ns	2.3	480.0 ns
8086	10 MHz	100 ns	2.3	230.0 ns
80386	33 MHz	33 ns	1.5	49.5 ns
80486	50 MHz	20 ns	1.5	30.0 ns
Pentium	66 MHz	15 ns	1.5	22.5 ns
Pentium Pro	66 MHz	15 ns	1.5	22.5 ns

fall within a 16-byte aligned area beginning at address XXXXXXX0 and ending with XXXXXXXF. Within this area, four different *burst orders* are possible:

(1) 0-4-8-C   (2) 4-0-C-8   (3) 8-C-0-4   (4) C-8-4-0[4]

2. With the Pentium processors the burst cycle transfers 32 bytes (again the line size of the internal cache). In this case all of the data items must lie within a 32-byte aligned area beginning at address XXXXXXX0 and ending with XXXXXXX1F. Again four different burst orders are possible:

(1) 0-8-10-18   (2) 8-0-18-10   (3) 10-18-0-8   (4) 18-10-8-0

3. The 486 cannot burst write cycles; the Pentium processors can burst both read and write cycles.

When data is transferred in burst mode, four bus cycles are required. These are often described as 2-1-1-1. This means the first bus cycle requires two clock pulses, while the remaining three cycles require only a single clock pulse. Using *address pipelining,* in which the memory address is output before the start of the data transfer bus cycle, the Pentium can run 1-1-1-1 burst cycles.

Types of Memory Access

Byte, Word, Doubleword, and Quadword Transfers.   Depending on the processor, the quantity of data transferred per memory cycle varies from a single byte (the 8088) to eight bytes (the Pentium and Pentium Pro processors). To indicate which bits of the data bus will be involved in the data transfer, the 80x86 processors provide *byte enable* output pins (Figure 7.15).

The 386 and 486 [Figure 7.15(a)], each with a 4-byte (32-bit) data bus, provide four byte enable signals ($\overline{BE3}$–$\overline{BE0}$). The Pentium processors [Figure 7.15(b)], with 8-byte (64-bit) data buses, require eight byte enable signals ($\overline{BE7}$–$\overline{BE0}$).[5] Via these byte enable signals, the 80x86 processors can indicate that:

1. A single byte is to be transferred (only one byte enable signal active).
2. A word is to be transferred (two byte enable signals active).
3. A doubleword is to be transferred (four byte enable signals active).
4. A quadword is to be transferred (all eight byte enable signals active).

Of course, when a memory transfer occurs, consecutive memory locations must be accessed, as illustrated in the following example.

---

[4]For example, to burst the 16 bytes beginning at address 00000100, four bus cycles will be required. One possible sequence is:

    Cycle 1—bytes 100–103
    Cycle 2—bytes 104–107
    Cycle 3—bytes 108–10B
    Cycle 4—bytes 10C–10F

[5] The 8086 has a 16-bit data bus and two byte-enable signals. The first is called $\overline{BHE}$ (bus high enable) and is used to indicate that D7–D15 will be active in the data transfer. The A0 address line acts as the second byte enable. It will be active when D0–D7 are involved in the data transfer. This is explained in more detail later in the next section.

Example 7.2

Assume a Pentium processor executes the following instructions. Indicate the logic state of the $\overline{BE7}$–$\overline{BE0}$ byte enables for each associated memory access.

(a) MOV AL,[0000]   (b) MOV AX,[0000]   (c) MOV EAX,[0000]

Solution

The answers are as follows:

Instruction	$\overline{BE7}$	$\overline{BE6}$	$\overline{BE5}$	$\overline{BE4}$	$\overline{BE3}$	$\overline{BE2}$	$\overline{BE1}$	$\overline{BE0}$
(a) MOV AL,[0000]	1	1	1	1	1	1	1	0
(b) MOV AX,[0000]	1	1	1	1	1	1	0	0
(c) MOV EAX,[0000]	1	1	1	1	0	0	0	0

Figure 7.15 The byte enable signals identify the data lines that will be involved in the data transfer. (a) Processors with a 32-bit data bus require four byte enables. (b) Processors with a 64-bit data bus require eight byte enables.

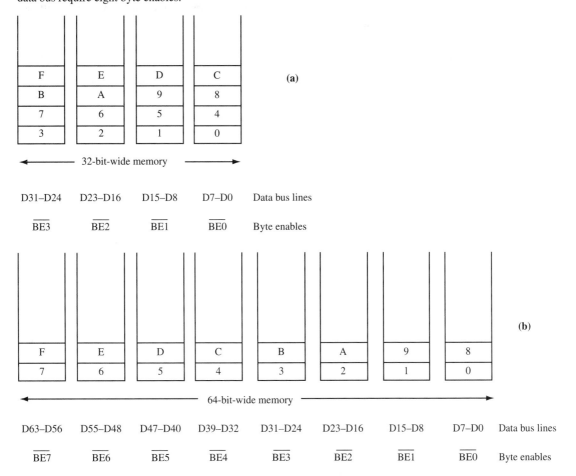

Alignment.   Table 7.5 illustrates how the 386 and 486's four byte enable pins ($\overline{BE3}$–$\overline{BE0}$) are used to indicate byte, word, and doubleword transfers. In this table, data is said to be *aligned* if all of the bytes to be accessed are located within the *same* 4-byte boundary. Four such address boundaries are possible:

1. XXXXXXX0 through XXXXXXX3

2. XXXXXXX4 through XXXXXXX7

3. XXXXXXX8 through XXXXXXXB

4. XXXXXXXC through XXXXXXXF

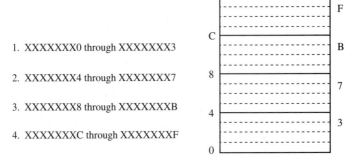

Data items that span *across* two of these boundaries are said to be *misaligned* and will require that two bus cycles be performed. Table 7.5 shows the combinations for addresses in the first (and spanning into the second) address range.[6]

Example 7.3

Assume a 486 processor executes the instruction MOV EAX, [0005]. Which byte enable signals will be active? How many bus cycles will be required?

Solution
The doubleword (four bytes) at address 0005–0008 is to be accessed. This corresponds to note (a) in Table 7.5. Two bus cycles will be required. The first will be run with only $\overline{BE3}$ active. This will transfer the byte at address 0008. The second bus cycle will be run with $\overline{BE0}$–$\overline{BE2}$ active and transfer the three remaining bytes at address 0005–0007.

Data Transfer Rate.   The quantity of data (measured in bytes) that a processor can transfer in one second is called the *data transfer rate*. It can be computed as:

$$\text{Data Transfer Rate} = \frac{\text{Number of bytes transferred per bus cycle}}{\text{time for one bus cycle}} \qquad \textbf{(7-1)}$$

The time for one bus cycle can be written as

$$n \times T_{\text{clock}} = n/f$$

where n represents the number of system clock pulses per bus cycle, T_{clock} is the period of the external bus clock, and f is the frequency of the bus clock. Substituting into Equation 7-1, we obtain:

$$\text{Data Transfer Rate} = \frac{\text{Number of bytes transferred per bus cycle} \times f}{n} \qquad \textbf{(7-2)}$$

---

[6]A similar table could be constructed for the Pentium processors. In this case, memory accesses must be confined to 8-byte boundaries to avoid the extra memory cycle.

Table 7.5 80386 and 80486 Byte, Word, and Doubleword Transfers

Memory Access Type	Number of Bus Cycles	BE3	BE2	BE1	BE0	7 B F 3	6 A E 2	5 9 D 1	4 8 C 0	3 7 B F	2 6 A E	1 5 9 D	0 4 8 C	
														8-Byte Address Range
Byte	1	1	1	1	0								X	Single-byte transfers can occur at any address and require only a single bus cycle.
	1	1	1	0	1							X		
	1	1	0	1	1						X			
	1	0	1	1	1					X				
Word	1	1	1	0	0							X	X	Two consecutive bytes within a four-byte boundary transfer in a single bus cycle.
	1	1	0	0	1						X	X		
	1	0	0	1	1					X	X			
	2	0	1	1	1				X	X				Two single-byte transfers are required for bytes that span two four-byte boundaries.
Doubleword	1	0	0	0	0					X	X	X	X	Four consecutive bytes within a four-byte boundary transfer in one bus cycle.
	2*	0	0	0	1				X	X	X	X		When bytes span the four-byte boundary, two bus cycles are required.
	2†	0	0	1	1			X	X	X	X			
	2**	0	1	1	1		X	X	X	X				

*High-order byte followed by 3 low-order bytes
†High-order word followed by low-order word
**High-order 3 bytes followed by low-order byte

Table 7.6   80x86 Processor Data Transfer Rates

Microprocessor	Data Bus Width (bytes)	Bytes Transferred per Memory Cycle	Number of Clocks per Memory Cycle	External Bus Operating Frequency	Data Transfer Rate[1]
8088	1	1	4	8 MHz	2 MB/s
8086	2	2	4	10 MHz	5 MB/s
80386	4	4	2	33 MHz	66 MB/s
80486	4	4	2	50 MHz	100 MB/s
		16	5		160 MB/s[2]
Pentium	8	8	2	66 MHz	264 MB/s
		32	5		422 MB/s[3]
		32	4		528 MB/s[4]
Pentium Pro	8	8	2	66 MHz	264 MB/s
		32	5		422 MB/s[3]
		32	4		528 MB/s[4]

[1](Operating frequency × number of bytes transferred per memory cycle)/number of clock pulses per memory cycle.
[2]2-1-1-1 burst mode, data must be aligned on 16-byte boundaries, read cycles only, 16 bytes per cycle.
[3]2-1-1-1 burst mode, read or write cycles, 32 bytes per cycle.
[4]1-1-1-1 burst mode with address pipelining.

Example 7.4

Calculate the data transfer rate for an 8088 processor running at 4.77 MHz. Compare this result to a Pentium processor with a 66 MHz bus frequency.

Solution

The 8088 has an 8-bit data bus width and requires four clock pulses per bus cycle. Its data transfer rate is therefore:

$$\frac{1 \text{ byte} \times 4.77 \text{ MHz}}{4 \text{ clock pulses/transfer}} = 1.19 \text{ MB/s}$$

The Pentium transfers eight bytes per data transfer and requires two clock pulses per bus cycle. Its data transfer rate is:

$$\frac{8 \text{ bytes} \times 66 \text{ MHz}}{2 \text{ clock pulses/transfer}} = 264 \text{ MB/s}$$

The 66 MHz Pentium therefore transfers data more than 221 times faster than a 4.77 MHz 8088!

Table 7.6 compares the data transfer rates for all of the 80x86 processors. Notice that in burst mode, the 486 can transfer 16 bytes in five clock cycles using a 2-1-1-1 burst cycle. The Pentium processors transfer 32 bytes using this same mode. The highest transfer rate occurs when the Pentium processors use *address pipelining* to transfer 32 bytes in four clock cycles using a 1-1-1-1 burst cycle.

Self-Review 7.2 (Answers on page 341)

7.2.1   For a memory interface to work properly, the access time provided by the processor must be _____ _____ the access time of the memory chip.

7.2.2   Compute the access time provided by a 33 MHz 80386 processor with one wait state.

7.2.3   Using burst mode, a 486 processor can read _____ bytes of information in _____ clock cycles.

7.2.4   What is the penalty incurred with the 80x86 processors for accessing *misaligned* data items?

7.2.5   Calculate the maximum data transfer rate for a 25 MHz 386 processor.

7.3   80x86 SRAM Interface Examples

Introduction

To *interface* means to connect in a compatible manner. When interfacing memory, all three system buses—the address, control, and data buses—are involved. Via the address bus, the processor specifies the *memory locations* to be accessed. Via the control bus, the *direction* of the data transfer—into or out of the processor—is specified. And finally, it is via the data bus that the actual data transfer takes place. In this section we:

- Describe the pin functions of the HM62864 64K × 8 SRAM
- Show how to interface an array of 64K × 8 SRAMs to each of the 80x86 processors.
- Explain how the memory decoder positions the memory array at a specific set of memory addresses.

Interfacing the HM62864

Control Signals.   Figure 7.16 is a portion of the data sheet for the HM62864 64K × 8 SRAM. This byte-wide RAM has three active-low control inputs labeled $\overline{CS1}$, $\overline{OE}$, and $\overline{WE}$ and one active-high pin called CS2. These pins control the operation of the chip as follows:

1. The two chip select inputs ($\overline{CS1}$ and CS2) "turn the chip on." Unless $\overline{CS1}$ is low and CS2 high, all of the other pins are disabled and the chip operates in a low-power standby mode.
2. The $\overline{OE}$ (output enable) input enables the tristate output buffers. This pin is used during memory read cycles to gate the selected data onto the data pins.
3. The $\overline{WE}$ (write enable) input enables the tristate input buffers. This pin is used during memory write cycles to gate the memory write data into the chip (the rising edge of $\overline{WE}$ causes the data to be latched).

In addition to the control inputs, 16 address pins (A0–A15) are provided. They permit access to all 64K locations (2^{16} = 64K). Three versions of the chip are available: the HM62864-5 with a 55 ns access time; the HM62864-7 with a 70 ns access time; and the HM62864-8 with an 85 ns access time. Operating current is 55 mA, but only 0.4 mA in standby mode.

Interfacing the 8088 Processor

One Bank Will Do.   Figure 7.17 shows an interface between the 8088 processor and the HM62864. Because of the 8088's 8-bit data bus, only a single HM62864 is required.[7]

---

[7]Of course, additional chips can be added, but a working memory is constructed with this single memory chip.

Figure 7.16 Specifications for the MH62864 64K × 8 SRAM. (Reprinted with permission (and without edits and revisions) of Hitachi America, Ltd.)

Pin Arrangement

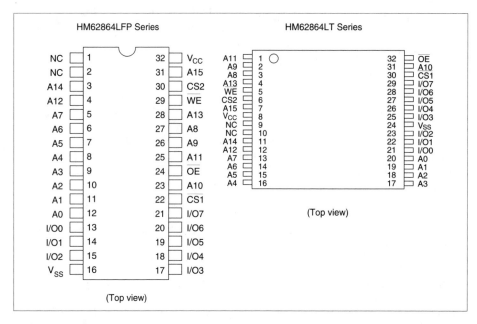

(Top view)

Pin Description

Pin Name	Function
A0 to A15	Address
I/O0 to I/O7	Input/output
CS1	Chip select 1
CS2	Chip select 2
WE	Write enable
OE	Output enable
NC	No connection
V_{cc}	Power supply
V_{ss}	Ground

Function Table

CS1	CS2	OE	WE	Mode	V_{cc} Current	I/O Pin	Ref. Cycle
H	X	X	X	Not selected	I_{SB}, I_{SB1}	High-Z	—
X	L	X	X	Not selected	I_{SB}, I_{SB1}	High-Z	—
L	H	H	H	Output disable	I_{cc}	High-Z	—
L	H	L	H	Read	I_{cc}	Dout	Read cycle (1) to (3)
L	H	H	L	Write	I_{cc}	Din	Write cycle (1)
L	H	L	L	Write	I_{cc}	Din	Write cycle (2)

Note: X: High or Low

Figure 7.16 *(continued)*

AC Characteristics (Ta = 0 to +70°C, V_{CC} = 5 V ± 10%, unless otherwise noted.)

Read Cycle

Parameter		Symbol	Min	Max	Min	Max	Min	Max	Unit	Notes
Read cycle time		t_{RC}	55	—	70	—	85	—	ns	
Address access time		t_{AA}	—	55	—	70	—	85	ns	
Chip select access time	$\overline{CS1}$	t_{CO1}	—	55	—	70	—	85	ns	
	CS2	t_{CO2}	—	55	—	70	—	85	ns	
Output enable to output valid		t_{OE}	—	30	—	40	—	45	ns	
Chip selection to output in low-Z	$\overline{CS1}$	t_{LZ1}	5	—	10	—	10	—	ns	2
	CS2	t_{LZ2}	5	—	10	—	10	—	ns	2
Output enable to output in low-Z		t_{OLZ}	5	—	5	—	5	—	ns	2
Chip deselection in output in high-Z	$\overline{CS1}$	t_{HZ1}	0	20	0	25	0	30	ns	1, 2
	CS2	t_{HZ2}	0	20	0	25	0	30	ns	1, 2
Output disable to output in high-Z		t_{OHZ}	0	20	0	25	0	30	ns	1, 2
Output hold from address change		t_{OH}	5	—	10	—	10	—	ns	

Notes: 1. t_{HZ} and t_{OHZ} are defined as the time at which the outputs achieve the open circuit conditions and are not referred to output voltage levels.

2. This parameter is sampled and not 100% tested.

Read Timing Waveform (1) (WE = V_{IH})

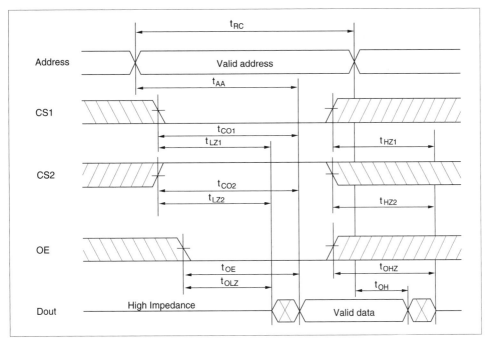

(continued on next page)

Figure 7.16 *(continued)*

Write Timing Waveform (1) (OE Clock)

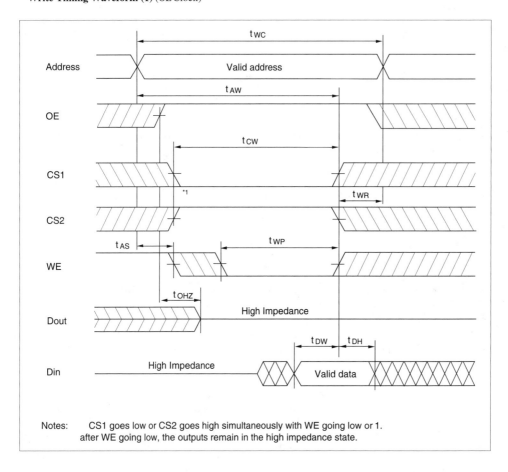

Notes: CS1 goes low or CS2 goes high simultaneously with WE going low or 1.
          after WE going low, the outputs remain in the high impedance state.

Most of the connections are straightforward—the data lines connect to the 8088's data bus, and the memory read and write lines to the $\overline{OE}$ and $\overline{WE}$ control pins, respectively. The address lines, however, may need some explaining.

The 8088 has a 20-bit address bus; the HM82864, however, has only 16 address pins. If we connect address lines A0–A15 to the memory, what is to be done with the four remaining address lines—A16–A19? In Figure 7.17 we show these lines connected to a box labeled *decoder*. Figure 7.18 shows an example of what might be in the box—a simple NAND gate and inverter. Notice, however, that the output of this NAND gate drives the $\overline{CS1}$ input of the RAM chip. Because the RAM is enabled only when this input is low and CS2 high, we can conclude that the memory will be enabled only when A16 is low and A17–A19 are high.

Example 7.5

Draw an *address map* for the memory interface in Figure 7.17, assuming the decoder is as shown in Figure 7.18. From this map, determine the *range* of addresses occupied by the memory interface.

Solution

The address map shows the range of addresses, in binary, that enable the memory interface. This is shown below.

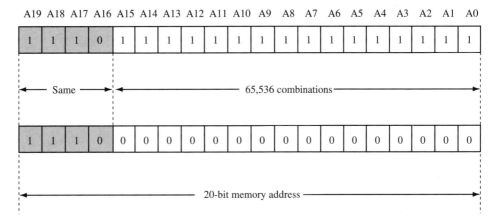

A19 A18 A17 A16 A15 A14 A13 A12 A11 A10 A9 A8 A7 A6 A5 A4 A3 A2 A1 A0

Because A19–A16 must always equal 1110 (to chip-select the memory), the 64K RAM is effectively mapped to the address range E0000H—EFFFFH. This is shown in the 8088 memory map in Figure 7.19.

Figure 7.17 64K x 8 8088 SRAM interface. Only a single memory chip is required.

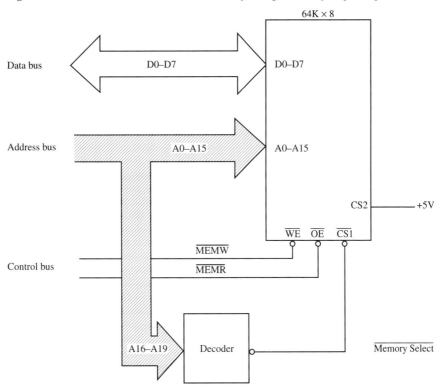

Figure 7.18 Example of an address decoder for the 8088 memory interface in Figure 7.17. The memory will be enabled only when A19–A16 = 1110.

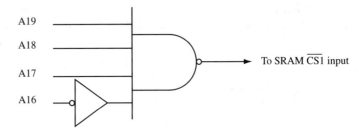

To SRAM $\overline{CS1}$ input

Figure 7.19 Memory map for the 8088 interface in Figure 7.17 and decoder in Figure 7.18. The 64K SRAM is mapped to the address range E0000H to EFFFFH.

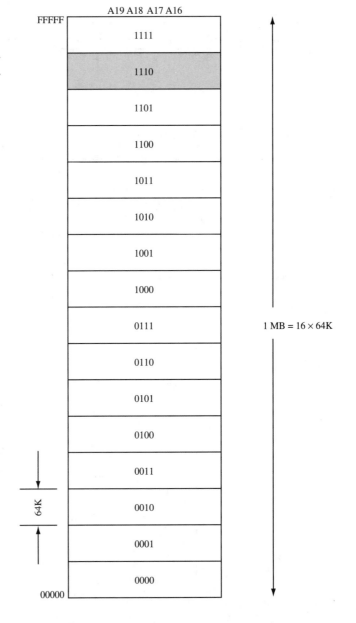

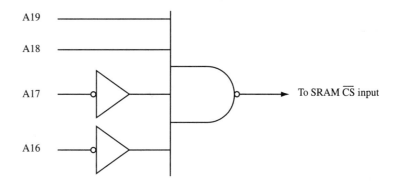

Figure 7.20 Decoder to map the SRAM in Figure 7.17 to the range C0000–CFFFFH.

As you can see by studying Figure 7.19, there are 16 different 64K blocks in the 8088's memory address space. By modifying the decoder, we can map the interface to any one of these 16 ranges.

Example 7.6

Show the decoder required to map the 64K memory interface in Figure 7.17 to the address range C0000H to CFFFFH.

Solution
The circuit is shown in Figure 7.20. Only when address lines A19–A16 = 1100 will the memory interface be enabled.

Interfacing the 8086 Processor

Even and Odd Memory Banks. Figure 7.21 shows an interface between the 8086 processor and the HM82864. Because of the 8086's 16-bit data bus, two SRAMs are required—one stores the *even bytes* and connects to D0–D7, the other stores the *odd bytes* and connects to D8–D15. The interface thus provides a total of 128K of memory.

Studying this circuit further, we see that address lines A1–A16 are wired in parallel to the A0–A15 address inputs of the two SRAM chips. This may seem odd: Why not begin with A0, as in the 8088 interface? Table 7.7 should help explain. To allow the processor to access individual bytes as well as 16-bit words, a new processor control signal called $\overline{\text{BHE}}$ (bus high enable) is provided. As shown in Table 7.7, when this line is low, the processor

Table 7.7 8086 Memory Access Encoding

$\overline{\text{BHE}}$	A0	Action
0	0	Access 16-bit word
0	1	Access odd byte to D8–D15
1	0	Access even byte to D0–D7
1	1	No action

Source: J. Uffenbeck, *Microcomputers and Microprocessors: The 8080, 8085, and Z 80.* Prentice Hall, Englewood Cliffs, N.J., 1991.

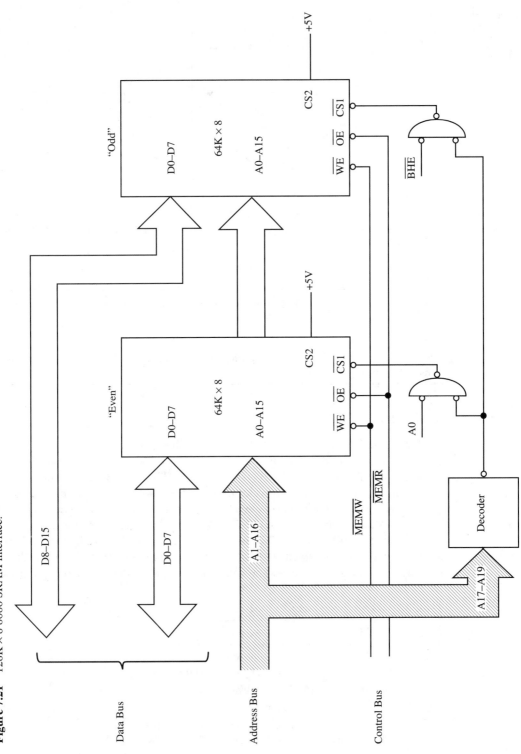

Figure 7.21 128K × 8 8086 SRAM interface.

is accessing a word or an *odd* memory byte. In both cases, the high-order part of the data bus (D8–D15) is involved. On the other hand, when A0 is low, the processor is either accessing a word or an *even* memory byte. In this case the low-order part of the data bus (D0–D7) is involved.

The logic behind the interface in Figure 7.21 should now be clear. The decoder verifies that the high-order address lines match the address assigned to this circuit. A0 and $\overline{BHE}$ are then used to enable the even (A0 = 0) or odd ($\overline{BHE}$ = 0) SRAM chip.[8] Both chips are enabled for a word access. Note that this implies *that words must begin at an even memory address* (that is, an address with A0 = 0). Words that begin at an odd address will require two memory cycles: one to access the odd byte, the second to access the even byte.

In summary, we can view the 20 address lines (and $\overline{BHE}$ control signal) output by the processor as follows:

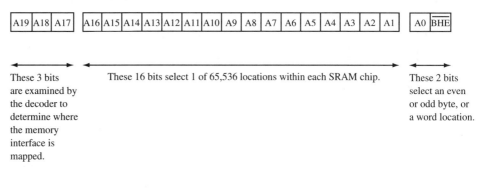

These 3 bits	These 16 bits select 1 of 65,536 locations within each SRAM chip.	These 2 bits
are examined by		select an even
the decoder to		or odd byte, or
determine where		a word location.
the memory		
interface is		
mapped.		

Example 7.7

Assume the decoder in Figure 7.21 is a three-input NAND gate and determine the range of addresses occupied by this interface.

Solution

The starting and ending addresses are:

Start:	**1110**	0000	0000	0000	0000	;E0000H
End:	**1111**	1111	1111	1111	1111	;FFFFFH

128K total bytes of memory are provided. The chip marked "even" stores the even bytes over this range; the chip marked "odd" stores the odd bytes over this range.

Interfacing the 80386 and 80486 Processors

Four Memory Banks Required.   Interfacing the 386 and 486 processors to the HM82864 is similar to the 8086 circuit. However, because the 386 and 486 each have a 32-bit data bus, *four* memory chips (banks) will be required. The total capacity of the interface will therefore be 256K (4 × 64K). (Figure 7.22 provides the details.)

---

[8]The two "AND gates" shown are actually OR gates drawn with their alternate (active-low input and output) symbol. This can be justified via DeMorgan's Theorem: $\overline{AB} = \overline{A} + \overline{B}$.

Figure 7.22 256K × 8 80386/486 SRAM interface.

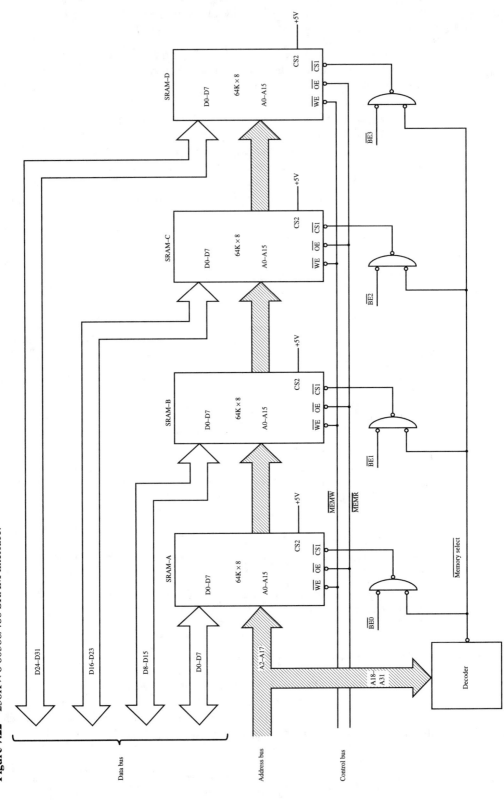

As described in Section 7.2, the 386 and 486 are restricted to accessing memory on 4-byte memory boundaries (see Table 7.5). For this reason, the A0 and A1 address lines, which would define addresses within a 4-byte boundary, are not present with these processors. Instead, the four byte enable signals—$\overline{BE0}$–$\overline{BE3}$—are used to define the memory bank to be selected. For example, if a doubleword whose hexadecimal memory address ends in 0, 4, 8, or C is to be accessed, all four byte enable signals will be low and all four memory banks will be selected (assuming the decoder's output is active). On the other hand, if a 16-bit word within the 4-byte boundary is to be transferred, two consecutive byte enables will be made active. Finally, if a single byte is to be accessed, then only that single byte enable will be active. Table 7.5 summarizes the combinations possible.[9]

Example 7.8

Describe the decoder required to map the interface in Figure 7.22 to the "bottom" of physical memory (that is, address 00000000H). What is the ending address of the last byte in this interface? Which chip stores this byte?

Solution

Because the 386 and 486 each have a 32-bit memory address, and because only lines A2–A17 are wired to the memory chips, the decoder must examine the remaining 14 address lines: A18–A31. To map this circuit to the bottom of memory, a 14-input NAND gate with 14 inverters will be required. Rather than construct such a ("messy") circuit, Figure 7.23 shows an alternative. It uses the 74ALS677 *address comparator*. This 24-pin chip is essentially a 16-input programmable NAND gate. When enabled ($\overline{G}$ 0V), the four *P* inputs define the number of NAND gate inputs that will be inverted. In this example, *P* = 14 (1110), causing inputs A1–A14 to become active-low. Inputs A15–A16 remain active-high.

The *ending* memory address can be computed in binary as:

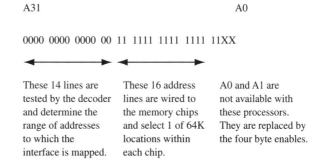

A31		A0
	0000 0000 0000 00 11 1111 1111 1111 11XX	
These 14 lines are tested by the decoder and determine the range of addresses to which the interface is mapped.	These 16 address lines are wired to the memory chips and select 1 of 64K locations within each chip.	A0 and A1 are not available with these processors. They are replaced by the four byte enables.

Choosing 1s for A0 and A1, the topmost memory address corresponds to address 0003FFFFH. Because this is the last byte in the 4-byte boundary beginning at address 3FFFCH, SRAM-D stores this byte.

Interfacing the Pentium and Pentium Pro Processors

Eight Banks Required.   With the preceding sections as background, you should have a pretty good idea of what is required to interface the HM82864 to the Pentium and Pentium

---

[9]When the data is *misaligned*, two bus cycles will be performed by the processor. Various combinations of the byte enables will then be required, as described in Table 7.5.

Figure 7.23 To map the interface in Figure 7.22 to the bottom of memory, the decoder must "look for" an address combination with A18–A31 all low. Using the 74LAS677 this is accomplished by programming the first 14 inputs to be active-low.

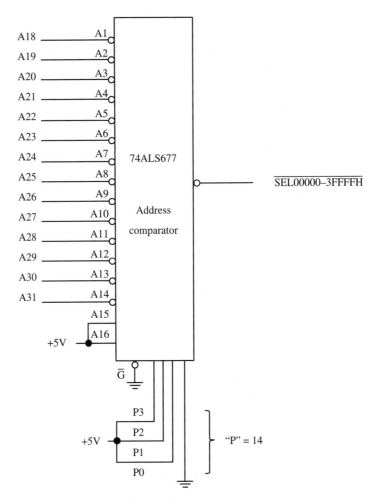

Pro processors. The circuit is shown in Figure 7.24. Because the Pentium processors have 64-bit data buses, *eight* memory chips (banks) will be required in the interface, providing a total memory capacity of 512K. Like the 386 and 486, byte enable signals are provided to select the appropriate chips.

The 16 low-order address lines A3–A18 are wired in parallel to each memory chip. The decoder is then required to examine the remaining 13 address lines: A19–A31. When these address lines match the requirements set by the decoder, its output goes low, enabling the eight active-low input NAND gates. Now, depending on the memory cycle, the byte enable signals will allow selection of individual bytes, words, doublewords, or quadwords. Other combinations are possible for *misaligned* data.

Example 7.9

The address decoder determines the memory *range* to which the circuit in Figure 7.24 is mapped. How many different memory ranges are possible?

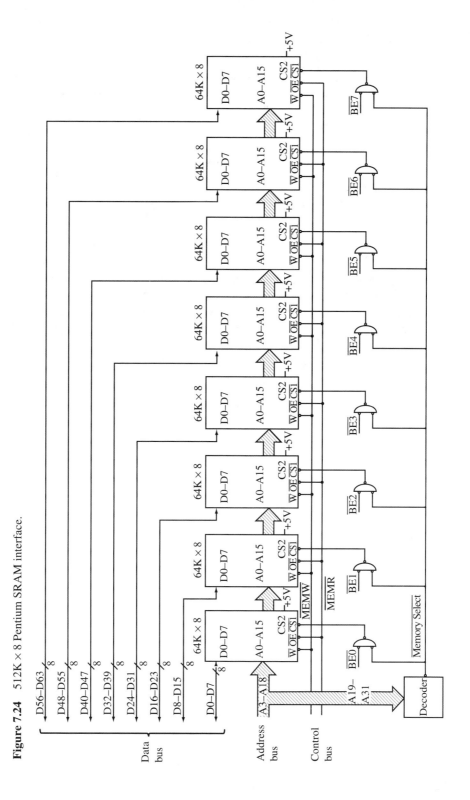

Figure 7.24 512K × 8 Pentium SRAM interface.

Solution

There are two ways to determine this answer.

1. Noting that the decoder inputs 13 address lines (A19–A31), we can calculate that there must be 2^{13} different decoder combinations. This corresponds to 8192 different address ranges.
2. Recalling that the Pentium (and 386 and 486) processors have a 4 GB physical memory capacity (2^{32}), we can compute the number of possible address ranges as 4 GB/512K = 4096 MB/.5 MB = 8192 different address ranges. (This means it would take 8192 copies of the circuit in Figure 7.24 to fully populate the 4 GB address space!)

Synchronous SRAM.   Conventional SRAMs are asynchronous. After the memory address is applied to the chip, the data appears on the output pins some time later (that time being the access time). Because the access time is not synchronized to the system clock, designers must use care to celect sufficiently fast memory parts. Slow parts will require additional clock cycles (wait states) while the system waits for the memory to deliver the data.

Synchronous SRAMs are changing this. With these devices, control signals are strobed into the memory on a rising clock edge. The data then becomes available on the *next* rising clock edge (that is, two cycles per memory access). Notice that in this scheme the memory is *synchronized* to the system clock. In effect, the SRAM access time adjusts itself to the speed of the clock.

Two additional features make synchronous SRAMs even more attractive:

1. *Burst capability.* Synchronous burst SRAMs incorporate a small amount of logic that allows the memory to self-cycle through sequential locations without the need for external addresses. In this way data can be accessed once every clock cycle (after the initial address has been applied).
2. *Pipelining.* This is a technique in which the memory address for the next cycle can be applied before the data from the previous cycle has been read. This is accomplished by incorporating on-board data registers. The end result is a chip that can be accessed at a higher rate.

With Pentium and Pentium Pro processors now operating with clock speeds over 150 MHz, synchronous SRAMs have become the dominant technology for fast (zero wait state) cache memory. Micron Technology, for example, offers parts with clock cycle times as short as 7 ns (143 MHz) and with storage capacities up to 256K (organized as 64K locations of four bytes each).

Self-Review 7.3 (Answers on page 341–342)

7.3.1   Describe the logic level (high, low, or X—don't care) required on the $\overline{OE}$, $\overline{CS1}$, CS2 and $\overline{WE}$ pins of the HM82864 for memory read and write cycles.

	$\overline{CS1}$	CS2	$\overline{OE}$	$\overline{WE}$
Memory Read				
Memory Write				

7.3.2   A certain SRAM is organized as 32K × 8. How many address pins do you predict for this chip?

7.3.3 Describe the decoder required to map the HM82864 to the address range 00000–0FFFFH in Figure 7.17.

7.3.4 When the 8086's A0 and $\overline{BHE}$ pins are both low, we know the processor is accessing a(n) _____ location.

    (a) even byte

    (b) odd byte

    (c) word

7.3.5 The 80486 byte enables $\overline{BE3}$–$\overline{BE0}$= 0111. This indicates that a _____ is being accessed.

    (a) byte

    (b) word

    (c) doubleword

    (d) quadword

7.3.6 With the 80x86 processors, two bus cycles will be required to access data that is _____.

7.3.7 The minimum total memory capacity when interfacing 32K × 8 SRAMs to the Pentium processors is

    (a) 32K

    (b) 128K

    (c) 256K

    (d) 512K

7.4   Address Decoding Techniques

Introduction

Beginning with the 80386 microprocessor, the 80x86 processors provide a 32-bit memory address that allows up to 4 GB of main memory. No memory interfaces, however, fill this entire range.[10] This means that for a given memory design, several of the address lines are going to be "unused." However, these unused lines are very important, because they determine the *range* of addresses the memory interface will occupy.

An *address decoder* is a circuit that examines these extra address lines and enables the memory for a specified range of addresses. This is an important part of any memory design, as one block of memory must not be allowed to overlap another. In this section we:

- Explain how AND, NAND, OR, and NOR gates can be used as address decoders.
- Show how the 74LS138 can be used as a block decoder.
- Construct a programmable decoder using PAL technology.

Logic Gate Decoders

ANDs, ORs, NANDs, and NORs.   A digital decoder is a circuit that recognizes a particular binary pattern on its input lines and produces an active output indication. This implies a logic AND condition, as the output of the decoder should be active only when this one input combination occurs. For example, a two-input NAND gate recognizes the input pat-

---

[10]At least not with today's memory prices!

Figure 7.25 (a) NAND, (b) AND, (c) OR, and (d) NOR gates can be used as address decoders, depending on the logic levels to be detected and the output level required.

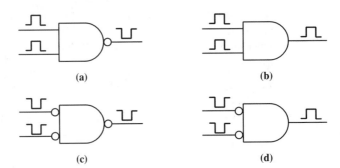

tern *11* and produces an *active-low* output only when this input combination is applied. A two-input AND provides a similar function but produces an *active-high* output indication.

OR and NOR gates can also be used as decoders when their alternate (active-low input) logic symbols are used. The four possible logic gate decoder combinations are shown in Figure 7.25.

Example 7.10

Design a decoder for the 8086 SRAM memory interface in Figure 7.21 such that the memory is mapped to the address range 00000–1FFFFH.

Solution

If we examine the 8086 memory addresses over this range:

```
A19                        A0
  0000 0000 0000 0000 0000     00000H
  0001 1111 1111 1111 1111     1FFFFH
```

we notice that the "unused" address lines A19–A17 must always be low. Figure 7.26 shows two ways of building the decoder. Notice that the second, which uses an OR gate drawn as an active-low input and on active-low output AND gate, requires only the single gate.

Block Decoders

Building a 128 MB Memory Array.   In a practical microcomputer, the "core" memory often consists of an array of SIMMs or DIMMs. Typical system boards have 4–8 such sockets that can be populated with various-size DRAM modules. This type of interface will require a separate decoder for each SIMM or DIMM socket, unless a special *block decoder* is built.

A 32-bit memory interface capable of supporting 128 MB of memory is shown in Figure 7.27. It consists of eight 16 MB SIMMs (SIMM0–7) and a *74LS138 3-to-8 line decoder*. Each SIMM has four 4 MB memory modules (typically, two 4 M × 4 DRAM chips). To access all 4 M memory locations within each DRAM, 22 two-address lines (A2–A23) will be required.[11] Byte enable control signals $\overline{BE0}$–$\overline{BE3}$ are then used to selec

---

[11]Recall that the 32-bit 80386/486 processors do not have A0 and A1 address pins.

Figure 7.26   Two equivalent 8086 address decoder circuits. (a) NAND gate implementation. (b) OR gate implementation.

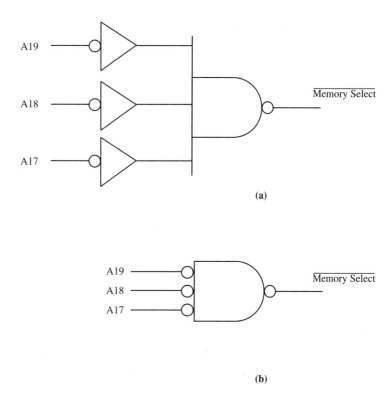

the appropriate DRAM, depending on the memory access type (byte, word, or double-word). The *direction* of data flow—into or out of the processor—is controlled by the $\overline{\text{MEMR}}$ and $\overline{\text{MEMW}}$ control signals, which are also wired to each SIMM.

It is the job of the decoder to examine the *unused address lines* A24–A31 and select the appropriate SIMM. Notice, however, that the decoder itself will only be enabled if A27 and A28 are low and the output of U2 is high. This requires that A29–A31 be low.

When the decoder is enabled, address lines A24–A26 select one of the eight SIMMs. For example, if these three lines are low, SIMM 0 is enabled. If these same lines are high, SIMM 7 is selected. Figure 7.28 summarizes the function of the address and byte enable lines in the interface in Figure 7.27. The corresponding memory map is shown in Figure 7.29. In this map you can see that because the interface requires A27–A31 to be low, the circuit is mapped to the bottom of the 4 GB address space. Thirty-two such circuits (256 SIMMs) would be required to fill the entire memory space.

PAL Decoders

Limitations of Block Decoders.   Each output of the decoder in Figure 7.27 defines a 16 MB address range. This is characteristic of all block decoders—the block size must be the same for each output. In a practical microcomputer, however, the block sizes are often different. Consider, for example, the 8-bit 8088 memory map shown in Figure 7.30. In this map, three 256K blocks and two 64K blocks are defined. If we were to construct a block

Figure 7.27 128 MB memory array consisting of eight 16 MB SIMMs. A 74LS138 is used as a block decoder.

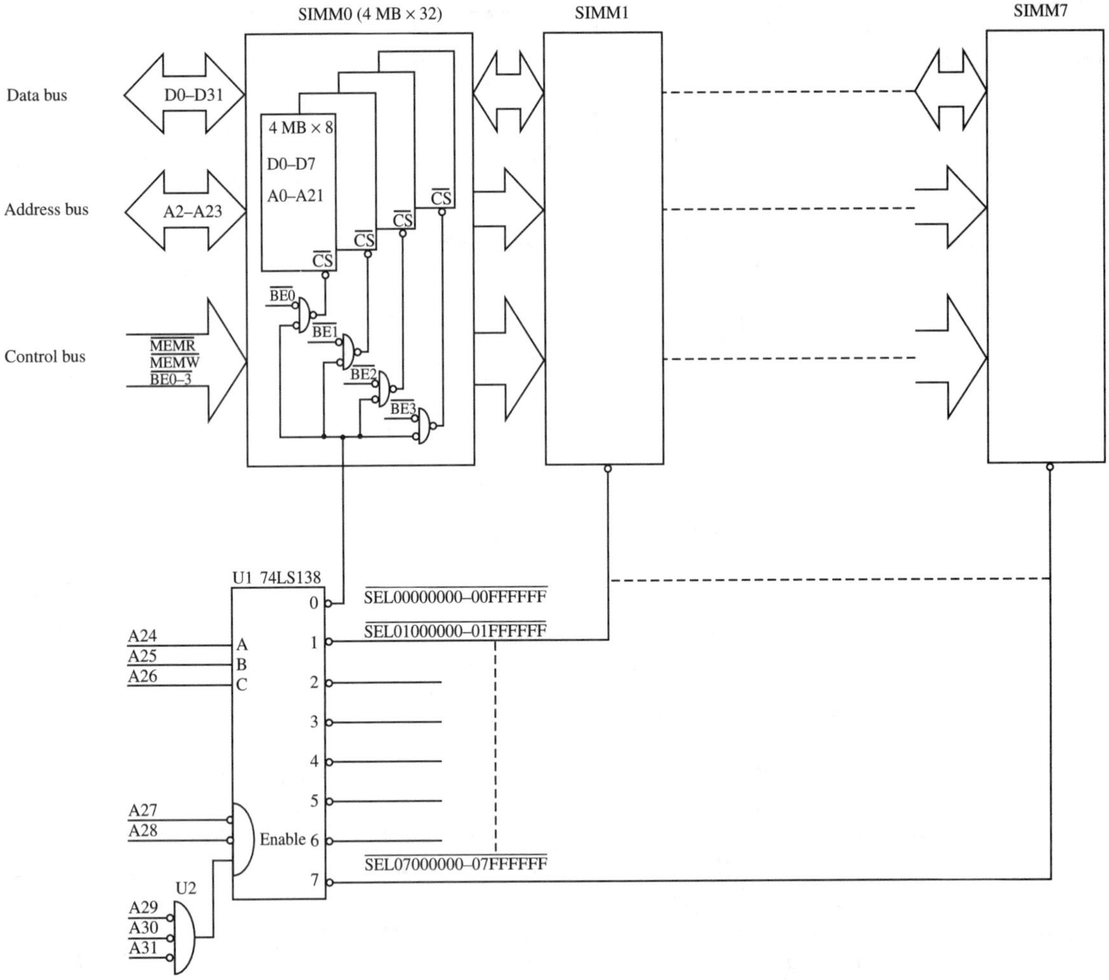
SIMM0 (4 MB × 32)
SIMM1
SIMM7
Data bus
D0–D31
Address bus
A2–A23
Control bus
MEMR
MEMW
BE0–3
4 MB × 8
D0–D7
A0–A21
CS
BE0
BE1
BE2
BE3
U1 74LS138
A24
A25
A26
A
B
C
A27
A28
Enable
U2
A29
A30
A31
SEL00000000–00FFFFFF
SEL01000000–01FFFFFF
SEL07000000–07FFFFFF

decoder for this circuit, it would have to have a "resolution" of 64K (the smallest block size) and would therefore require 16 outputs to cover the full 1 MB address space (1MB/64K). And, because the RAM blocks are 256K long, additional gating would be required to combine four consecutive memory selects for each of these chips. The resulting circuit is beginning to sound pretty "messy."

Figure 7.28 Address and byte enable line usage for the 128 MB memory interface in Figure 7.27.

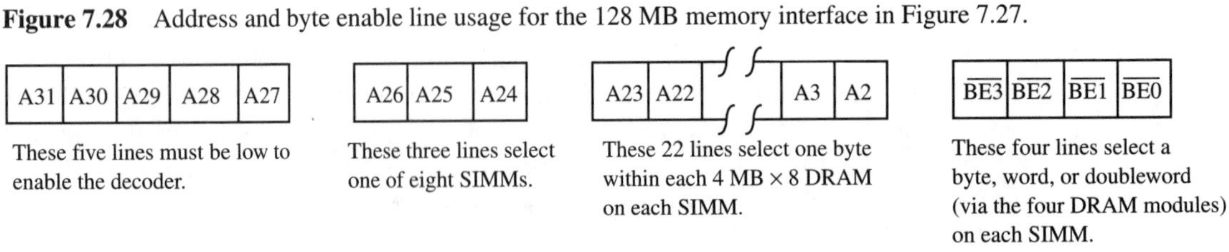
A31 A30 A29 A28 A27
These five lines must be low to enable the decoder.
A26 A25 A24
These three lines select one of eight SIMMs.
A23 A22 A3 A2
These 22 lines select one byte within each 4 MB × 8 DRAM on each SIMM.
BE3 BE2 BE1 BE0
These four lines select a byte, word, or doubleword (via the four DRAM modules) on each SIMM.

Figure 7.29   Memory map for the 128 MB memory interface in Figure 7.27. The circuit is mapped to the bottom 128 MB.

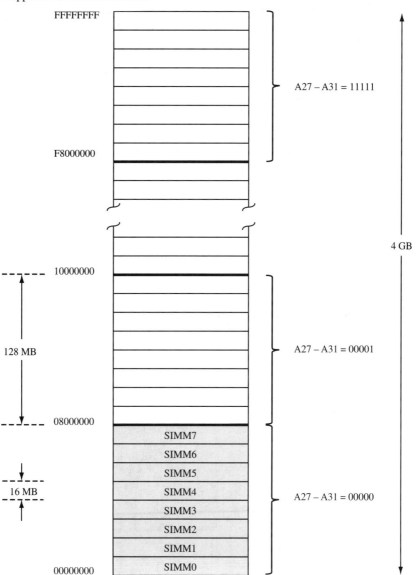

A better solution would be to design a circuit like the one shown in Figure 7.31. This uses a single *programmable array logic (PAL)* device to examine the unused address lines and select the appropriate memory chip. Certainly an *elegant* solution, but what is a PAL16L8 and how is this part programmed?

What Is a PAL?   In its simplest form, a PAL is nothing more than an array of AND and OR gates. As shown in Figure 7.32, these gates are arranged in *sum-of-products* form (that

Figure 7.30 Memory map for an 8088 microcomputer. Because the memory block sizes are different, a conventional block address decoder will be inefficient.

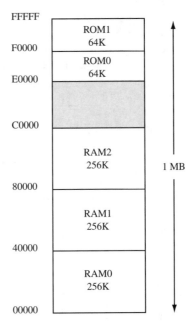

Figure 7.31 Memory interface corresponding to the map in Figure 7.30. A PAL16L8 is used as the address decoder.

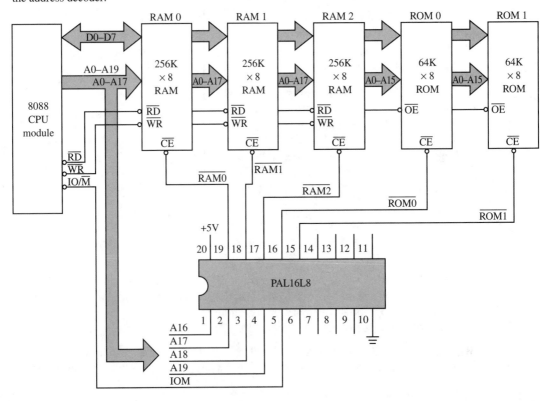

Figure 7.32   Partial diagram of a PAL. The AND gate connections are fuse programmable, but the inputs to the OR gate are fixed. (From J. Uffenbeck, *Digital Electronics, A Modern Approach,* Prentice-Hall, Englewood Cliffs, N.J., 1994)

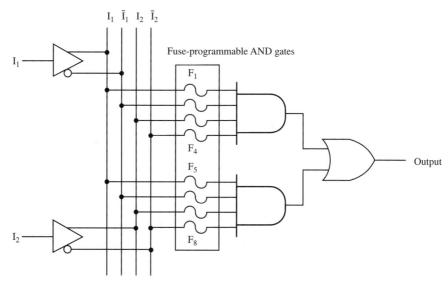

is, each output is obtained via an OR gate, which is used to sum the AND gate product terms). In this example, only two inputs (I_1 and I_2) and one output are shown, but practical PALs have as many as 20 input lines and 10 outputs.

In Figure 7.32, notice that each input and its complement are connected (via fuses) to each AND gate. Thus, each AND gate can be *programmed* to form any one combination of the (2^n possible) input variable combinations.

Example 7.11

Determine the logic function for the PAL in Figure 7.32 if fuses 1, 3, 6, and 8 are blown.

Solution
We assume a blown fuse results in a logic 1 at that AND gate input. The resulting logic equation is thus:

$$\text{OUTPUT} = \overline{I}_1\,\overline{I}_2 + I_1\,I_2$$

PAL Limitations.   The PAL in Figure 7.32 allows complete flexibility in programming the product terms; that is, each AND gate can be programmed to form any one of the 2^n possible product terms (for n inputs). The OR gate connections, however, are *fixed*. In this example, only two product terms can be summed. Some PALs allow as many as eight product terms (that is, the output OR gates have eight inputs). When selecting a PAL chip, it is therefore important to choose a part that provides an adequate number of OR gate inputs.

PAL Logic Notation.   The fuse symbology shown in Figure 7.32 becomes impractical as the number of gate inputs increases. In its place, PAL designers have adopted the

Figure 7.33 Equivalent symbology for a three-input AND gate: (a) standard notation; (b) PAL notation.

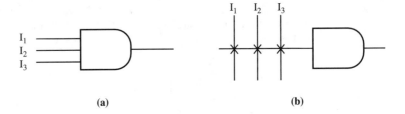

(a)   (b)

notation shown in Figure 7.33. The Xs in this figure indicate fuses that are left intact (*not blown*).

Figure 7.34 compares standard logic symbology and PAL notation for the logic equation $OUT = \overline{I_1 I_2} + I_1 I_2$. Inputs I_1 and I_2 are first passed through buffers with complementary outputs and then into the fuse array. In this example fuses 1, 3, 6, and 8 are blown and are therefore not shown. Note the "tiny" AND gate symbology. This is necessary because some PALs have OR gates with as many as eight AND gate inputs.

The PAL16L8 (16 inputs and 8 active-low outputs). Figure 7.35 shows how the PAL16L8, the part we have chosen for our address decoder, is internally organized. This part has 10 conventional inputs (pins 1–9 and 11), 6 bidirectional input/outputs (pins 13–18), and 2 standard outputs (pins 12 and 19). Each output is passed through an inverting tristate buffer, with the buffer enable controlled by one of the AND gates from the fuse array.

Each OR gate in this PAL has seven inputs, allowing it to sum seven different product terms. The product terms themselves can be made up of any combination of the 16 input pins (that is, each AND gate has 32 inputs).

PAL Programming.   Before a PAL can be programmed, a *fuse map* must be created, listing the locations of the blown fuses. Typically, this is accomplished using a *PAL compiler*. This is a computer program that inputs logic equations and outputs a PAL fuse map (in JEDEC format) ready for downloading to a PAL programmer. Several such programs are available, including proLOGIC, PLDesigner, ABEL, and CUPL. In the next section, we will use CUPL to program our address decoder.[12]

Figure 7.34 Two equivalent logic diagrams for the function $OUT = \overline{I_1} \, \overline{I_2} + I_1 \, I_2$; (a) standard symbology; (b) PAL notation.

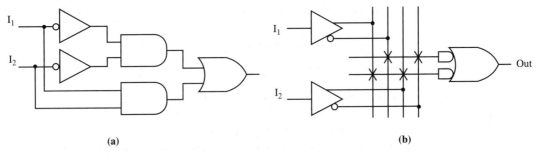

(a)   (b)

---

[12]CUPL (Universal Compiler for Programmable Logic) is available from Logical Devices, Inc., 692 South Military Trail, Deerfield Beach, FL, 33442, (800) 331–7766.

Figure 7.35 Logic diagram for the 16-input 8-output PAL16L8. (Copyright Advanced Microdevices, Inc. Reprinted with permission of the copyright owner. All rights reserved.)

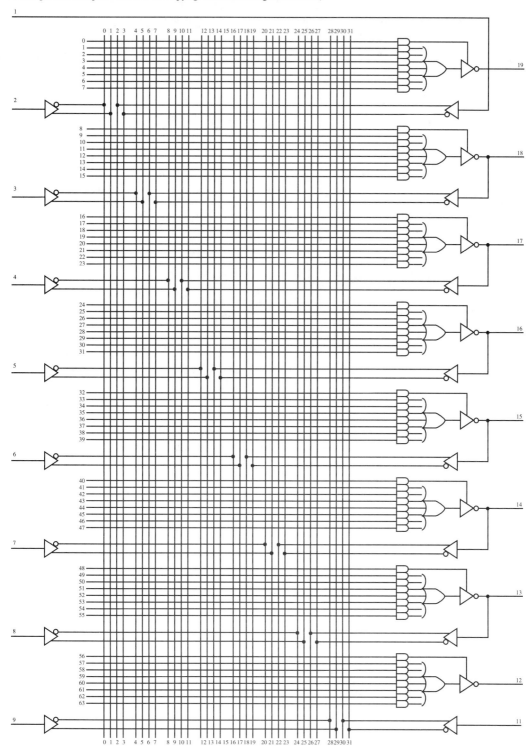

Figure 7.36   Address map corresponding to the memory map in Figure 7.30.

ROM1	FFFFF	1 1 1 1	1 1 1 1	1 1 1 1	1 1 1 1	1 1 1 1
	F0000	1 1 1 1	0 0 0 0	0 0 0 0	0 0 0 0	0 0 0 0
ROM0	FFFFF	1 1 1 0	1 1 1 1	1 1 1 1	1 1 1 1	1 1 1 1
	E0000	1 1 1 0	0 0 0 0	0 0 0 0	0 0 0 0	0 0 0 0
RAM2	BFFFF	1 0 1 1	1 1 1 1	1 1 1 1	1 1 1 1	1 1 1 1
	80000	1 0 0 0	0 0 0 0	0 0 0 0	0 0 0 0	0 0 0 0
RAM1	7FFFF	0 1 1 1	1 1 1 1	1 1 1 1	1 1 1 1	1 1 1 1
	40000	0 1 0 0	0 0 0 0	0 0 0 0	0 0 0 0	0 0 0 0
RAM0	3FFFF	0 0 1 1	1 1 1 1	1 1 1 1	1 1 1 1	1 1 1 1
	00000	0 0 0 0	0 0 0 0	0 0 0 0	0 0 0 0	0 0 0 0

Address Decoder Design Example.   In Figure 7.36 we show the *address map* corresponding to the memory map in Figure 7.30. The range of addresses occupied by each block of memory can readily be seen. For example, ROM1 should be enabled whenever A16–A19 are all high. On the other hand, RAM0 should be enabled only when A18 and A19 are both low.

The PAL used in this design must have at least five outputs—one for each of the five memory blocks. And, based on the address map in Figure 7.36, it must have at least four inputs for address lines A16–A19. One other input is also required. This is the 8088's IO/$\overline{\text{M}}$ signal, which will tell us (when low) that the address on the bus is indeed a mem address and not an I/O port address.

The next step is to create the *source code* for the PAL using a text editor. Figure 7.37 shows an example written in CUPL format. It begins with a header block that contains the name of the file (DECODER.PLD), the part number, and other related information. Next, the input and output pins are defined. Note how CUPL allows several pins to be named at once by inserting the beginning and ending pin numbers in brackets separated by periods. The "!" symbol is used to define the output pins as active-low.

The declarations section follows, and the variable name memadr is given to represent address lines A19–A16. The intermediate variable memreq is then defined as being active when IO/$\overline{\text{M}}$ is low. Intermediate variables are signals that are convenient to define, but are not brought out to the package pins.

Figure 7.37   Source code for the PAL address decoder.

```
NameDecoder
Partno    P000001;
Date      0/7/27/92;
Revision  0;
Designer  Uffenbeck;
Company   WITC;
Assembly  PC Memory;
Location  U106;

/**********************************************************/
/* This device generates chip select signals for two     */
/* 64Kx8 ROMs and three 256Kx8 RAMS.                      */
/**********************************************************/
/** Allowable Target Device Types : PAL16L8             **/
/**********************************************************/
/**   Inputs   **/

PIN [1..4]   = [a16..19] ;   /* CPU Address Bus         */
PIN [5]      = IOM ;         /* IO/M control signal     */

/**   Outputs   **/

PIN [19..17] = ![ram0..2] ;    /* Ram Chip Selects      */
PIN [15..14] = ![rom0..1] ;    /* ROM Chip Selects      */

/** Declarations and Intermediate Variable Definitions **/

Field memadr = [a19..16] ; /* Give The Address Bus       */
                           /* the Name "memadr"          */

memreq = !IOM ;         /* Create the intermediate       */
                        /* Variable "memreq"             */

/**   Logic Equations   **/

rom0 = memreq & memadr:[E0000..EFFFF] ;

rom1 = memreq & memadr:[F0000..FFFFF] ;

ram0 = memreq & memadr:[00000..3FFFF] ;

ram1 = memreq & memadr:[40000..7FFFF] ;

ram2 = memreq & memadr:[80000..BFFFF] ;
```

Finally, the logic equations themselves are written. Notice how easy this is. Simply define the desired address range and AND this term with the memreq signal (the latter term is necessary to ensure that the select signal is enabled only for memory cycles).

After the source code has been written, it is compiled by giving the command:[13]

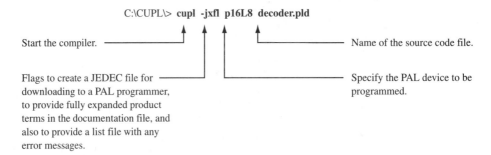

Figure 7.38 shows the fist page of the documentation file (DECODER.DOC) produced by CUPL. It repeats the header block and then lists the detailed logic equations for each variable. Notice, for example, that ROM1 will be active when A16, A17, A18, and A19 are high and IO/$\overline{\text{M}}$ is low.[14] Checking, this is indeed in agreement with the address map in Figure 7.36. The four signals on the bottom of Figure 7.38 are the output enables for the tristate buffers. Note that CUPL has permanently enabled these by connecting them to a logic 1.

A nice feature of the DOC file is the inclusion of a *chip diagram* for the target PAL. This diagram, shown in Figure 7.39, is in agreement with the pin definitions we chose in Figure 7.31.

Finally, the last page of the DOC file is the fuse map itself in JEDEC-compatible format (decoder.jed). This is shown in Figure 7.40. We are now ready to download this file to the PAL programmer. Most PAL programmers are designed to be controlled by a host PC and come with the appropriate control software. Figure 7.41 shows the screen presented by one such device. In the upper right corner the manufacturer and type of PAL are specified. Next the name and location of the JEDEC file to be loaded is given. The first 16 lines of the fuse map are shown directly beneath this: 1s in this map indicate a blown fuse and 0s represent an intact fuse. Note that the XY coordinates of each fuse in this map can be traced back to the similar numbers in the PAL16L8 schematic in Figure 7.35.

GALs (Generic Array Logic).   The previous example has illustrated the versatility of using a PAL as an address decoder. Unfortunately, if a new address map is required, the (fuse-programmable) PAL must be discarded and the new logic programmed. For this reason, most designers today prefer to use GALs instead of PALs. GALs can be (bulk) erased electrically, allowing the same part to be used several times. In addition, particular GALs are designed to emulate several different PAL chips. Thus, by stocking just a few GALs, any of the various PAL devices can be built. For this reason, GALs are thought of as *generic* logic devices.

---

[13]Recent versions of CUPL are menu driven and allow the compile options to be set via a menu selection.

[14]CUPL uses the "&" symbol for the AND function and the "#" symbol to represent the OR function. Inversion is shown with the "!" symbol.

Figure 7.38 The equations implemented by CUPL can be seen in the decoder.doc file.

```
**********************************************************************
                              Decoder
**********************************************************************

CUPL            2.11c Serial# 2-99999-001
Device          p1618  Library DLIB-f-23-8
Created         Wed Jul 29 14:07:10 1992
Name            Decoder
Partno          P000001
Revision        01
Date            07/27/92
Designer        Uffenbeck
Company         WITC
Assembly        PC Memory
Location        U106


====================================================================
                      Expanded Product Terms
====================================================================

memadr =>
    a19 , a18 , a17 , a16

memreq =>
    !IOM

ram0 =>
    !a18 & !a19 & !IOM

ram1 =>
    a18 & !a19 & !IOM

ram2 =>
    !a18 & a19 & !IOM

rom0 =>
    !a16 & a17 & a18 & a19 & !IOM

rom1 =>
    a16 & a17 & a18 & a19 & !IOM

ram0.oe  =>
    1

ram1.oe  =>
    1

ram2.oe  =>
    1

rom0.oe  =>
    1

rom1.oe  =>
    1
```

Self-Review 7.4 (Answers on page 342)

7.4.1   When used as an address decoder, an OR gate functions as an AND gate with active-_____ inputs and an active-_____ output.

7.4.2   If a 128K memory array is interfaced to an 8086 (1 MB address space) microcomputer system, how many address lines must be examined by the address decoder?

Figure 7.39 Package outline for the PAL16L8 address decoder.

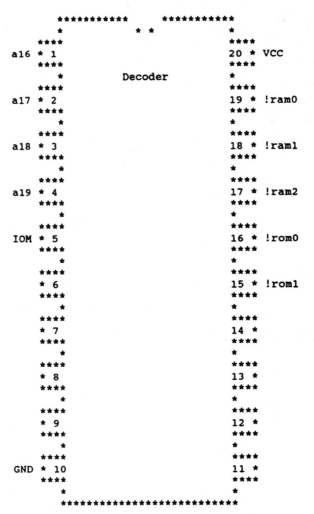

```
======================================================================
                            Chip Diagram
======================================================================

                ***********     ***********
                    *          *   *           *
                   ****                       ****
            a16 *  1                   20 *  VCC
                   ****                       ****
                    *          Decoder        *
                   ****                       ****
            a17 *  2                   19 *  !ram0
                   ****                       ****
                    *                         *
                   ****                       ****
            a18 *  3                   18 *  !ram1
                   ****                       ****
                    *                         *
                   ****                       ****
            a19 *  4                   17 *  !ram2
                   ****                       ****
                    *                         *
                   ****                       ****
            IOM *  5                   16 *  !rom0
                   ****                       ****
                    *                         *
                   ****                       ****
                *  6                   15 *  !rom1
                   ****                       ****
                    *                         *
                   ****                       ****
                *  7                   14 *
                   ****                       ****
                    *                         *
                   ****                       ****
                *  8                   13 *
                   ****                       ****
                    *                         *
                   ****                       ****
                *  9                   12 *
                   ****                       ****
                    *                         *
                   ****                       ****
            GND *  10                  11 *
                   ****                       ****
                    *                         *
                ***************************
```

7.4.3 When used as an address decoder, the 74LS138 provides _____ separate block decode outputs.

7.4.4 Which output _____ (0–7) of the decoder in Figure 7.27 is active when the data at memory address 053C2E00 is being accessed?

7.4.5 In a PAL, the input signals are applied to _____ gates. The outputs of these gates are then applied to an output _____ gate.

7.4.6 Each output in the PAL16L8 is limited to summing _____ product terms.

7.4.7 The source code file in CUPL has the extension _____.

7.4.8 If the ROM1 block in Figure 7.31 is moved to start at address C0000, what changes to the PAL source code in Figure 7.38 are required?

Figure 7.40 PAL programmer-compatible (JEDEC format) download file for the 8088 address decoder. A "1" indicates a blown fuse.

```
CUPL              2.11c  Serial# 2-99999-001
Device            p1618  Library DLIB-f-23-8
Created           Wed Jul 29 14:07:10 1992
Name              Decoder
Partno            P000001
Revision          01
Date              07/27/93
Designer          Uffenbeck
Company           WITC
Assembly          PC Memory
Location          U106
*QP20
*QF2048
*G0
*F0
*L0000 11111111111111111111111111111111
*L0032 11111011101110111111111111111111
*L0256 11111111111111111111111111111111
*L0288 11110111101110111111111111111111
*L0512 11111111111111111111111111111111
*L0544 11111011101110111111111111111111
*L0768 11111111111111111111111111111111
*L0800 01100111011101111111111111111111
*L1024 11111111111111111111111111111111
*L1056 01010111011101111111111111111111
*C26B3
*9E50
```

Figure 7.41 Screen copy of the PAL programmer control program. The first 15 lines of the 64-line fuse map can be seen.

```
MCT      PAL PROGRAMMER     V1.1      * MFG.: TI
MODEL : MCT-MUP  (C)  SEP 1988        * TYPE: 16L8
By Modular Circuit Technology         * FUSE MAP: c:\cup1\decoder.jed

        MAIN MENU:                    00000000001111111111222222222233333333333
====================================  01234567890123456789012345678901234567890
  1. DIR                              +=========================================+
  2. LOAD FUSE MAP FROM DISK      0  |11111111111111111111111111111111
  3. SAVE FUSE MAP TO DISK        1  |11111011101110111111111111111111
  4. EDIT FUSE MAP                2  |00000000000000000000000000000000
  M. MANUFACTURER                 3  |00000000000000000000000000000000
  T. TYPE                         4  |00000000000000000000000000000000
  B. BLANK CHECK                  5  |00000000000000000000000000000000
  P. PROGRAM      A. AUTO         6  |00000000000000000000000000000000
  R. READ         V. VERIFY       7  |00000000000000000000000000000000
  S. SECURITY FUSE BLOW           8  |11111111111111111111111111111111
  Q. QUIT                         9  |11110111101110111111111111111111
EDIT FUSE MAP BUFFER :           10  |00000000000000000000000000000000
  <ESC> back to main menu.       11  |00000000000000000000000000000000
     F. feed blank form          12  |00000000000000000000000000000000
  Screen editing key :           13  |00000000000000000000000000000000
    <PGUP>,<PGDN>,<HOME>,<END>    14  |00000000000000000000000000000000
    <UP>,<DN>,<LF>,<RT>          15  |00000000000000000000000000000000
```

7.5   DRAM Specifications and Timing

Introduction

Because of their dynamic nature, DRAMs are more complex to interface than SRAMs. The memory address must be supplied in row-and-column format and, because of the capacitive nature of the storage cell, the entire chip must be refreshed on a periodic basis. The timing to accomplish these operations is critical or data will be lost. In this section we:

- Describe common DRAM control signals and access time parameters.
- Compare conventional DRAMs with page mode, extended data out, and synchronous DRAM technologies.
- Show the timing for $\overline{RAS}$-only, $\overline{CAS}$ before $\overline{RAS}$, and hidden refresh techniques.

DRAM Control Signals

Address Multiplexing.   Figure 7.42 shows the package pin-outs for a popular DRAM—the 4M × 4 TMS417400. A block diagram of the chip is also shown. The following is a brief description of the pin functions.

- **Power and Ground.** +5V is applied to the V_{CC} pin and ground to V_{SS}.[15]
- **Data In/Out.** The four data bits to be read or written are accessed at DQ1–DQ4.
- **Read/Write.** To write data to the chip, the $\overline{W}$ input must be taken low. When this pin is high, the chip operates in the read mode.
- **Output Enable.** The $\overline{OE}$ pin enables the output buffers for memory read cycles. Only when this pin is low will the selected data be placed on the data pins.
- **Address Control.** The memory address must be applied to the chip in the form of a *row* address followed by a *column* address. When $\overline{RAS}$ (row address strobe) is low, the address applied to the address pins is interpreted as the row address. When $\overline{CAS}$ (column address strobe) is low, the address on these pins is interpreted as the column address.
- **Memory Address.** These pins receive the row and column addresses of the memory location desired.

Because of the need to supply separate row and column addresses to the address pins, DRAMs are said to employ *address multiplexing*. The TMS417400, for example, has 11 address pins (A0–A10). However, when multiplexed, these 11 pins allow a *22-bit* memory address to be supplied (an 11-bit row address followed by an 11-bit column address). The full address is therefore 22 bits wide, which allows access to the 4M memory locations (2^{22} = 4M). In effect, we can view this chip as having 2K rows and 2K columns.

The row and column addresses are not always the same size. Another version of this same chip—the TMS416400—is internally organized as 4K rows and 1K columns. It requires a 12-bit (A0–A11) row address but only a 10-bit (A0–A9) column address.

$\overline{RAS}$ and $\overline{CAS}$ Timing.   Figure 7.43 illustrates basic timing for DRAM memory read and write cycles. A read or write cycle begins with the falling edge of the $\overline{RAS}$ clock signal. This will latch the address currently applied to the chip, which should correspond to the high-order, or row address. The address lines must then change and become the low-order

---

[15]Two versions of this chip are available: one with V_{cc} = 5V, the other with V_{cc} = 3.3V.

Figure 7.42   (a) Chip pinout for the TMS417400 4 M × 4 DRAM;. (b) Block diagram.

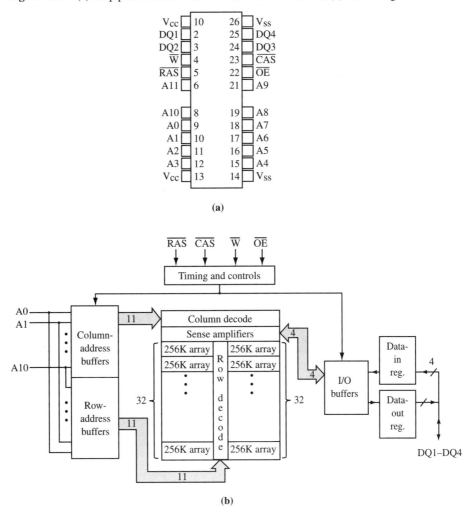

(a)

(b)

or column address. The falling edge of $\overline{\text{CAS}}$ latches this address and also gates the data onto the data-out pin of the DRAM (assuming $\overline{\text{OE}}$ is low).

There are three access times:

1. The row acess time (t_{RAC}) measured from the falling edge of $\overline{\text{RAS}}$ to valid data out.
2. The column access time (t_{CAC}) measured from the falling edge of $\overline{\text{CAS}}$ to valid data out.
3. The address accesst time (t_{AA}) measured from the time the column address is applied until valid data is output.

Normally, DRAMs are characterized by their row access time. Thus a 60 ns 417400 is interpreted as having t_{RAC} = 60 ns.

The memory read cycle must include the cycle *precharge* time t_{RP}. This is the time required to charge the bit sense line (see Figure 7.9) in preparation for the next memory cycle. The memory read *cycle time* (t_{RC}) determines how rapidly the DRAM can be

Figure 7.43 Dynamic RAM timing. Two clock signals ($\overline{RAS}$ and $\overline{CAS}$) are required to latch the multiplexed row and column addresses. Valid data appears t_{CAC} ns after the clock goes low and remains until $\overline{CAS}$ returns high.

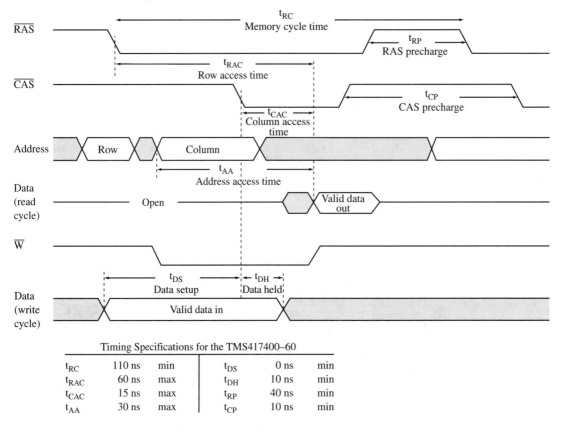

Timing Specifications for the TMS417400–60						
t_{RC}	110 ns	min		t_{DS}	0 ns	min
t_{RAC}	60 ns	max		t_{DH}	10 ns	min
t_{CAC}	15 ns	max		t_{RP}	40 ns	min
t_{AA}	30 ns	max		t_{CP}	10 ns	min

accessed. In particular, it defines the *valid data-out window*. This is the time that valid data remains on the system data bus lines.

Example 7.12

Using the specifications given in Figure 7.43, calculate the width of the valid data-out window for the TMS417400-60.

Solution

The data-out window can be calculated as:

$$t_{RC} - t_{RAC} - t_{RP} = 110 \text{ ns} - 60 \text{ ns} - 40 \text{ ns} = 10 \text{ ns}$$

The data-out window can be extended by keeping the $\overline{CAS}$ clock low as necessary. When this clock goes high, the data pin of the DRAM returns to a high impedance state. In effect, $\overline{CAS}$ "turns the data off" when it goes high. The frequency of the $\overline{CAS}$ clock thus determines the cycle time of the DRAM.

With many of today's PCs operating with a 66 MHz bus clock frequency (15 ns period), the cycle time of the memory must be kept as short as possible. The DRAM memory interface in these systems includes a latch to "catch" the data during the brief data-out window.

DRAM Write Cycles. A DRAM memory write cycle occurs when the $\overline{W}$ input is active. In this case data will be latched by the falling edge of $\overline{CAS}$ or $\overline{W}$, whichever occurs last. Because the DRAM's data lines are bidirectional, care must be taken to *deactivate* these lines for write cycles. If this is not done, the write data may conflict with the read data still on the data lines from a previous cycle. Typically, this is accomplished by keeping the $\overline{OE}$ pin *inactive* throughout the write cycle.

Many DRAM controllers perform an *early-write* cycle; that is, $\overline{W}$ occurs *before* the falling edge of $\overline{CAS}$. The advantage of this technique is that the data lines will be forced a high-impedance state independent of $\overline{OE}$. (Recall that when $\overline{OE}$ is high, the data pin of the DRAM is off.) No conflicts can occur and more flexibility is achieved in the memory subsystem design (i.e., $\overline{OE}$ is a "don't care").

Wait States. It is important to note that DRAMs are *asynchronous*. Once the row and column addresses have been strobed into the chip, the data appears on the output pins t_{CAC} ns later. The data is then held on these pins—but for just a few nanoseconds (as long as $\overline{RAS}$, $\overline{CAS}$, and $\overline{OE}$ remain active and $\overline{W}$ inactive). It is up to the memory interface to *latch* the data before it disappears. This is quite different from an SRAM interface, in which the data out remains valid through the end of the memory cycle.

To further complicate matters, the DRAM does not provide a synchronizing signal that can be monitored by the processor to determine when valid data is available. The memory controller must therefore detect the falling edge of $\overline{CAS}$, wait t_{CAC} ns, and then latch the data. If the processor attempts to access the data too soon, invalid data will be read and the system will crash.

When the access time provided by the processor is shorter than the memory access time, *wait states* —T states provided by the processor to give the memory more time to respond (read cycle) or latch the current data (write cycle)—must be inserted.

Example 7.13

Calculate the number of wait states required to interface the TMS417400-60 to a 50 MHz 80486 processor running nonburst cycles.

Solution
Two calculations must be performed—one to check the access time and one to check the DRAM cycle time.

Access time: In Table 7.4 it was shown that the 486 provides 1.5 T states for a memory access. At 50 MHz, this corresponds to 30 ns. To meet the 60 ns row access time of the 417400, 60 ns – 30 ns = 30 ns of additional time is required. This time is provided in the form of *wait states,* where one wait state equals one processor T state. In this example, with a 50 MHz clock frequency, one wait state provides an additional 20 ns of memory access time. Two wait states will therefore be required (the number of wait states must be an integer multiple of clock cycles).

DRAM cycle time: The 417400 has a read or write cycle time of 110 ns. In nonburst mode, the 486 requires two clock cycles per memory cycle (see Table 7.6). At 50 MHz, this corresponds to 40 ns. The difference, 110 ns – 40 ns = 70 ns will require *four* wait states. Thus we see that the DRAM cycle time is the limiting factor in this interface, not the row access time.

As mentioned in Section 7.2, wait states are *not* inserted automatically by the processor. Most system boards are designed to allow a variable number of wait states to be set via the CMOS setup software. It is up to the operator, however, to judge the number of wait states required, based on the access time of the DRAM chips.[16]

Faster DRAMs

Page Mode.   Because DRAM access times are so slow (relative to the bus clock frequency), most PCs are designed with high speed *cache* memories. In these systems DRAM accesses occur infrequently—only when a cache miss occurs. When the DRAMs are accessed, one cache line's worth of data will be read or written. Notice that this implies read or write cycles to consecutive memory locations.

Most DRAMs support a fast page mode that can be taken advantage of in this situation. After the $\overline{RAS}$ clock falls low, all of the memory cells in the selected row pass their data on to the sense amplifiers. In the case of the 417400, the column address is 11 bits wide, and each row therefore stores 2K nibbles (one page).

With one page of data stored in the sense amplifiers, the $\overline{CAS}$ clock can now be used to select random (or consecutive) memory locations on this page. The advantage, of course, is that the column access time is much faster than the row access time. For the 417400-60, t_{RAC} is 60 ns while t_{CAC} is only 15 ns.

Figure 7.44 illustrates page-mode timing. After the row address has been output, multiple column addresses are applied in sequence via the $\overline{CAS}$ clock. The data being accessed appears t_{CAC} ns after the falling edge of each $\overline{CAS}$ pulse.

The cycle time of the memory is now determined by t_{CAC} (the column access time), the valid data out window, and t_{CP} (the precharge time). The 417400-60 lists a 40 ns page-mode cycle time (compared to 110 ns for a conventional access).

Extended Data Out (EDO).   Conventional DRAMs have the drawback that during the $\overline{CAS}$ precharge time the output data is turned off. In order to maintain a reasonable (10 ns) data out window, the width of the $\overline{CAS}$ low pulse must be extended. The effect is to increase the cycle time of the memory (and decrease overall system performance).

EDO DRAMs offer one new feature. During the $\overline{CAS}$ precharge time (that is, when $\overline{CAS}$ is high), valid data remains on the output pins. That is, $\overline{CAS}$ no longer turns the output data off. This is shown in the bottom waveform in Figure 7.44.

This simple change has far-reaching effects. Because the time when valid data is available has been extended to the end of the memory cycle, the cycle time can be reduced while still maintaining a reasonable data out window.

In Table 7.8 we list the important timing specifications for the non-EDO 417400-60 and the EDO 416169-60. Notice that both parts have identical row and column access times, and nonpage-mode cycle times. However, when operated in page mode, the EDO part can be accessed every 25 ns, compared to every 40 ns for the non-EDO part. The 416169 could thus keep up with a 40 MHz memory cycle rate processor, while the non-EDO 417400 would be restricted to 25 MHz.

---

[16]This must be done on an experimental basis—set the CMOS for one wait state and see if the computer runs. If not, try two wait states, etc. Also note that using one set of slow DRAMs will penalize the entire system, as wait states cannot usually be set for individual DRAM banks.

Figure 7.44 Comparing conventional page-mode DRAMs with EDO DRAMs. The EDO parts can be cycled faster because the output data is available throughout the clock cycle.

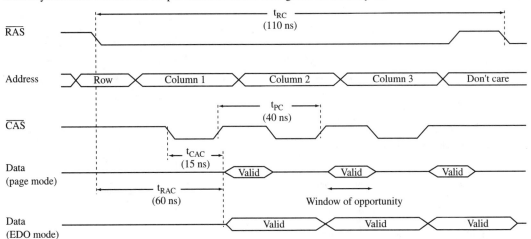

Synchronous DRAM (SDRAM).   The drawback to conventional DRAM (and SRAM) technology has always been the asynchronous nature of the part. DRAMs in particular require a complex sequencing of row and column address clocks before data can be accessed. As processor clock speeds move well past 100 MHz, it becomes increasingly difficult to work with parts who deliver their data only after some (unsynchronized) time delay occurs.

With synchronous DRAMs, the control signals ($\overline{RAS}$ and $\overline{CAS}$) are latched on the rising edge of the system clock. The data output is then available on a subsequent clock rising edge.

Figure 7.45 describes the Texas Instruments TMS626802 1 M × 8 bits × 2 banks synchronous DRAM (SDRAM). This chip has a maximum clock frequency of 100 MHz, allowing data to be read or written once every 10 ns. It is organized as two separate 1 MB banks. (Figure 7.46). Each bank is, in turn, organized as 2K rows with 512 bytes per row. Like conventional DRAMs, the $\overline{RAS}$ clock is used to strobe in the (11-bit) row address and the $\overline{CAS}$ clock strobes in the (9-bit) column address. Address line A11 is used to select the two banks—low to select bank B (the *bottom* bank), high to select bank T (the *top* bank).

Table 7.8 Common DRAM Memory Specifications

Parameter	Description	417400-60 4 MB × 4 non-EDO	416169-60 1 MB × 16 EDO
t_{RAC}	Access time from $\overline{RAS}$ low	60 ns	60 ns
t_{CAC}	Access time from $\overline{CAS}$ low	15 ns	15 ns
t_{RC}	Cycle time (nonpage mode)	110 ns	110 ns
t_{PC}	Cycie time (page mode)	40 ns	25 ns

Figure 7.45   Catalog description for the TMS626802 synchronous DRAM. (Courtesy of Texas Instruments)

TMS626802
1048576-WORD BY 8-BIT BY 2-BANK
SYNCHRONOUS DYNAMIC RANDOM-ACCESS MEMORY

SMOS182A – FEBRUARY 1994 – REVISED JUNE 1995

- Organization . . . 1M × 8 × 2 Banks
- 3.3-V Power Supply (±10% Tolerance)
- Two Banks for On-Chip Interleaving (Gapless Accesses)
- High Bandwidth – Up to 100-MHz Data Rates
- Burst Length Programmable to 1, 2, 4, or 8
- Programmable Output Sequence – Serial or Interleave
- Chip Select and Clock Enable for Enhanced-System Interfacing
- Cycle-by-Cycle DQ-Bus Mask Capability
- Programmable Read Latency From Column Address
- Self-Refresh Capability
- High-Speed, Low-Noise LVTTL Interface
- Power-Down Mode
- Compatible With JEDEC Standards
- 4K Refresh (Total for Both Banks)
- 2-Bit Prefetch Architecture for High Speed Performance
- Performance Ranges:

	ACTV	
SYNCHRONOUS CLOCK CYCLE TIME	COMMAND TO READ OR WRITE COMMAND	REFRESH TIME INTERVAL
t_{CK} (MIN)	t_{RCD} (MIN)	t_{REF} (MAX)
'626802-10 10 ns	30 ns	64 ms
'626802-12 12.5 ns	35 ns	64 ms
'626802-15 15 ns	40 ns	64 ms

DGE PACKAGE
(TOP VIEW)

V_{CC}	1	44	V_{SS}
DQ0	2	43	DQ7
V_{SSQ}	3	42	V_{SSQ}
DQ1	4	41	DQ6
V_{CCQ}	5	40	V_{CCQ}
DQ2	6	39	DQ5
V_{SSQ}	7	38	V_{SSQ}
DQ3	8	37	DQ4
V_{CCQ}	9	36	V_{CCQ}
NC	10	35	NC
NC	11	34	NC
$\overline{W}$	12	33	DQM
$\overline{CAS}$	13	32	CLK
$\overline{RAS}$	14	31	CKE
$\overline{CS}$	15	30	NC
A11	16	29	A9
A10	17	28	A8
A0	18	27	A7
A1	19	26	A6
A2	20	25	A5
A3	21	24	A4
V_{CC}	22	23	V_{SS}

PIN NOMENCLATURE

A0–A10	Address Inputs
	A0–A10 Row Addresses
	A0–A8 Column Addresses
	A10 Automatic-Precharge Select
A11	Bank Select
$\overline{CAS}$	Column-Address Strobe
CKE	Clock Enable
CLK	System Clock
$\overline{CS}$	Chip Select
DQ0–DQ7	SDRAM Data Input/Data Output
DQM	Data/Output Mask Enable
NC	No External Connect
$\overline{RAS}$	Row-Address Strobe
V_{CC}	Power Supply (3.3 V Typ)
V_{CCQ}	Power Supply for Output Drivers (3.3 V Typ)
V_{SS}	Ground
V_{SSQ}	Ground for Output Drivers
$\overline{W}$	Write Enable

description

The TMS626802 series are high-speed 16777216-bit synchronous dynamic random-access memories (DRAMs) organized as two banks of 1048576 words with eight bits per word.

All inputs and outputs of the TMS626802 series are compatible with the low-voltage TTL (LVTTL) interface.

The synchronous DRAM employs state-of-the-art enhanced performance implanted CMOS (EPIC™) technology for high performance, reliability, and low power. All inputs and outputs are synchronized with the CLK input to simplify system design and enhance use with high-speed microprocessors and caches.

The TMS626802 synchronous DRAM is available in a 400-mil, 44-pin surface-mount TSOP (II) package (DGE suffix).

EPIC is a trademark of Texas Instruments Incorporated.

Figure 7.46 The TMS626802 is organized as two separate 1M × 8 memory banks. (Courtesy of Texas Instruments)

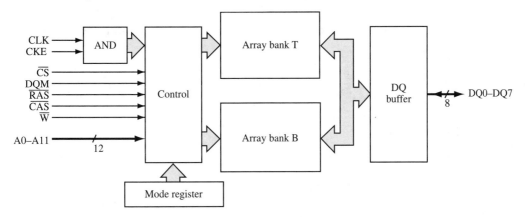

Unlike a conventional DRAM, the 626802 is accessed by giving various *commands*. The seven basic functions are:

1. Mode register set
2. Bank activate/row address entry
3. Column-address entry/write operation
4. Column-address entry/read operation
5. Bank deactivate
6. $\overline{CAS}$ before $\overline{RAS}$ refresh
7. Self-refresh

A unique feature of the 626802 is that data is read or written in one-, two-, four-, or eight-byte bursts. The bursts can be *serial* or *interleaved* with the chip automatically generating the required column addresses. In serial mode, sequential addresses are used. In interleave mode, the address sequence can be programmed. For example, an eight-byte burst may be accessed as bytes 1, 0, 3, 2, 5, 4, 7, 6.

A basic read operation requires four steps:

1. Program the mode register with the burst type and length, and the access latency (see below).
2. Issue the bank-activate command with the row address on A0–A10 and the bank select on A11.
3. Issue the read command with the column address on A0–A8. The data then appears on the output pins one, two, or three clock pulses later, depending on the latency.[17]
4. Issue the deactivate-bank command.

With two separate banks, the 626802 has the unique ability to access random columns in two separate rows (one in bank B, the other in bank T). Figure 7.47 shows an example. First the two banks are activated (ACTV B and ACTV T) by placing the row addresses (R0 and

---

[17]In effect, the programmable latency allows the designer to adjust the 626802 to operate in accordance with the system's capability to latch the output data.

Figure 7.47   Using column interleaving, the 626802 can access column addresses from two different row addresses. The access time is set by the clock period, which can be as short as 10 ns with the 100 MHz part. (Courtesy of Texas Instruments)

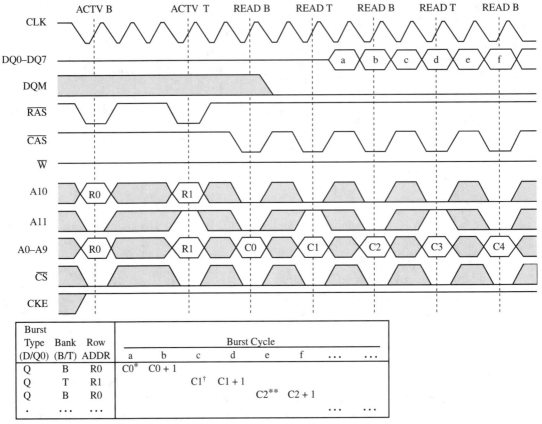

*Column-address sequence depends on programmed burst type and C0.

†Column-address sequence depends on programmed burst type and C1.

**Column-address sequence depends on programmed burst type and C2.

R1) on A0–A10. The random column addresses are then output, with A11 used to select bank B or T. In this example, the burst length is set to two—meaning two bytes are read at each column address (a and b, c and d, etc.). Notice that the first byte read (a) is accessed three clocks after its column address is output, corresponding to a read latency of three.

Refresh

As mentioned in Section 7.1, the storage cell for a dynamic RAM is a capacitor. And because this capacitor will eventually lose its charge, the charge in each cell must be rewritten on a periodic basis. Typically, this is accomplished by accessing successive rows once every 15.625 μs. The refresh period (maximum time one row can go without a refresh cycle) for a DRAM with an n-bit row address can thus be calculated as:

$$\text{Refresh period} = 2^n \times 15.625 \ \mu s$$

Example 7.14

Calculate refresh period for the TMS417400 4M × 4 DRAM.

Solution
The row address for this chip is 11 bits wide. The refresh period is thus $2^{11} \times 15.625\mu s = 32$ ms.

There are three different methods of refreshing a DRAM.

$\overline{RAS}$-*Only Refresh [Figure 7.48(a)].*   In this technique, only a row address is sent to the DRAM, the $\overline{CAS}$ clock remains high, and no data is therefore actually read and output to the data pins. All of the bits in the selected row are refreshed. For an *n*-bit row address, all 2^n rows must be cycled within the refresh period. Although simple to describe, the technique is not so simple to implement, because external hardware is required to generate and keep track of the refresh address.

$\overline{CAS}$ *Before* $\overline{RAS}$ *(CBR) Refresh [Figure 7.48(b)].*   Modern DRAMs have the capability of generating the refresh address internally without the aid of external hardware. In the CBR technique, the $\overline{CAS}$ clock is made active *before* the $\overline{RAS}$ clock goes low. This causes the DRAM to generate a row address and refresh all of the cells in that row. Multiple $\overline{RAS}$ clocks with $\overline{CAS}$ low will cause sequential row addresses to be generated internally and refreshed.

Self-Refresh.   Self-refresh is the same as CBR refresh, but with $\overline{RAS}$ and $\overline{CAS}$ held low for at least 100μs. An onboard oscillator then generates the refresh addresses automatically. Upon exiting this mode, a burst refresh (see below) must be performed to ensure that the DRAM is fully refreshed.

Distributing the Refresh Cycles.   There are three methods of distributing the necessary refresh cycles over the DRAM refresh period.

1. *Burst refresh.* In this technique, the processor is forced into a wait state and all rows are refreshed in one burst. Normal processing is then resumed until the next refresh period is required. During this time the memory cannot be accessed.[18]
2. *Distributed refresh.* Rather than refresh the entire memory at once, the refresh cycles can be distributed over the entire refresh period. This will require a refresh cycle every 15.625 μs. Most DRAM controllers use this technique.[19]
3. *Hidden refresh.* This method is shown in Figure 7.48(c). After completing a normal memory read or write cycle, the $\overline{CAS}$ clock is left low. This will maintain data on the output pins. Now any number of $\overline{RAS}$ clocks can be applied, as the row address is incremented internally by the DRAM. Hidden refresh is essentially a $\overline{RAS}$-only refresh with the $\overline{CAS}$ clock held low. The technique can be used to "hide" refresh cycles amon processor cycles that require that data be held on the bus but do not require a new memory or I/O access.

---

[18]Analysis and Design Question 7.16 shows that the time to refresh a DRAM is actually an insignificant portion of the refresh period.

[19]Analysis and Design Question 7.17 shows that a large number of instructions can be executed between refresh cycles.

Figure 7.48 DRAM refresh methods.

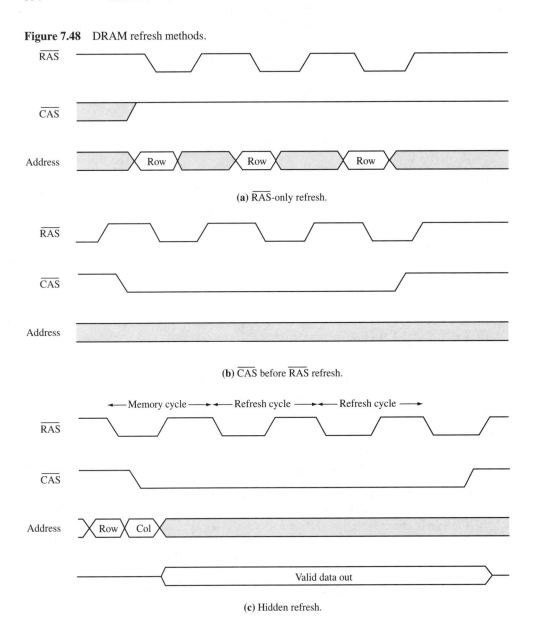

(a) $\overline{\text{RAS}}$-only refresh.

(b) $\overline{\text{CAS}}$ before $\overline{\text{RAS}}$ refresh.

(c) Hidden refresh.

DRAM Controllers

The PC/XT. The IBM PC and XT computers use discrete logic to interface the DRAMs to the 8088 processor. A distributed $\overline{\text{RAS}}$-only refresh technique is used, initiated by the system timer every 15 µs. A "dummy" read cycle *(access the memory data but do not store it)* is then performed by the DMA controller. During the DMA refresh cycle, the memory cannot be accessed. On the PC/XT, this amounts to about 5 percent of the processor's time.

Figure 7.49 Typical system board showing the processor and support chips. The combination is referred to as the *system board chipset*.

Modern Computers. While it is easy to spot the DMA controller, the system timer, or the address decoding logic on a PC/XT computer, it is not so easy on a modern microcomputer. Typically, these machines contain a processor chip and 4–5 custom support chips. The combination is referred to as a *chipset*. Figure 7.49 is a photograph of a typical system board. The chip set is programmable via the BIOS setup program (often called *the CMOS*), which can be activated during boot-up.[20] The CMOS settings are critical, as they affect many different features of the computer: Incorrect values may prevent the computer from booting at all.

Figure 7.50 shows the Advanced CMOS Setup screen presented by the popular AMI BIOS. Notice how, via this program, the internal and external SRAM cache memory can be enabled or disabled. In addition, the video, system, and adapter ROMs can be *shadowed*. This is a technique in which the contents of ROM are copied to RAM. The ROM is then disabled and the RAM mapped to its address space (*shadowing* the ROM). Because the access time of RAM is much faster than that of the ROM chips, overall system performance is improved.

Figure 7.51 shows the Advanced Chipset Setup screen. It is here that the operation of the SRAM cache and core-memory DRAMs can be fine-tuned. Included are options to set the clock cycles in burst mode, the number of read and write wait states, and the cache type—write back or write through. Several options are available for controlling the DRAMs, including fast or slow page mode, read and write wait state selection, $\overline{\text{RAS}}$ precharge time, and hidden refresh selection.

Typically, users start with the default settings built into the BIOS. Then, depending on the speed and size of installed memory, each parameter is adjusted, the computer is rebooted, and system performance is tested. Eventually, the optimum settings are found.

---

[20]One popular scheme is to hold the DEL key pressed while the computer is booting.

Figure 7.50   The Advanced CMOS Setup screen presented by the AMI BIOS.

```
          AMIBIOS SETUP PROGRAM - ADVANCED CMOS SETUP
          (C)1993 American Megatrends Inc., All Rights Reserved

Typematic Rate Programming : Enabled    Video   ROM Shadow C000,32K: Enabled
Typematic Rate Delay (msec): 500        Adaptor ROM Shadow C800,32K: Disabled
Typematic Rate (Chars/Sec) : 30         System  ROM Shadow F000,64K: Enabled
Mouse Support Option       : Enabled    BootSector Virus Protection: Disabled
Above 1 MB Memory Test     : Disabled   IDE Block Mode Transfer    : Disabled
Hit <DEL> Message Display  : Enabled
Hard Disk Type 47 RAM Area : 0:300
Wait For <F1> If Any Error : Enabled
System Boot Up Num Lock     : On
Numeric Processor Test      : Enabled
Floppy Drive Seek At Boot   : Enabled
System Boot Up Sequence     : A:, C:
System Boot Up CPU Speed    : High
1MB Cache Installed         : Disabled
External Cache Memory       : Enabled
Internal Cache Memory       : Enabled
Turbo Switch Function       : Enabled
Password Checking Option    : Setup

======= ESC:Exit  ↓→↑Sel  (Ctrl)Pu/Pd:Modify  F1:Help  F2/F3:Color =======
======= F5:Old Values  F6:BIOS Setup Defaults   F7:Power-On Defaults =======
```

Figure 7.51   The Advanced Chipset Setup screen. Several options for controlling the cache and DRAM memory are provided.

```
          AMIBIOS SETUP PROGRAM - ADVANCED CHIPSET SETUP
          (C)1993 American Megatrends Inc., All Rights Reserved

Auto Configuration Function: Disabled
CPU Frequency Select       : 40Mhz
SRAM Read Burst Control    : 3-2-2-2
SRAM Write Wait States     : 1 W/S
Cache Type Control         : WB
DRAM Paged Mode Type       : Slow
DRAM Write Wait State      : 1 W/S
DRAM Read Wait State       : 2 W/S
RAS Precharge Time         : 3 Sysclk
System BIOS is Cacheable   : Disabled
Video BIOS is Cacheable    : Disabled
Reset Wait For Halt        : Enabled
Hidden Refresh Control     : Disabled
Cacheable Range            : 128 MB
Address 16 Mbyte Access    : Normal
Block-0 Function Select    : Disabled
Block-0 Size Select        : 64 KB
Block-0 Base Address Select: 0 KB

======= ESC:Exit  ↓→↑Sel  (Ctrl)Pu/Pd:Modify  F1:Help  F2/F3:Color =======
======= F5:Old Values  F6:BIOS Setup Defaults   F7:Power-On Defaults =======
```

Self-Review 7.5 (Answers on page 342)

7.5.1   A certain DRAM has a 10-bit memory address and is organized ×4. If the number of rows and columns is equal, this chips stores _____ bits.

7.5.2   In a DRAM, the row address is latched by applying the _____ clock; the column address is latched by applying the _____ clock.

7.5.3   Explain what is commonly meant by a 70 ns access time as applied to a DRAM.

7.5.4   Why is the access time in page mode faster than nonpage mode for a DRAM? Why not operate the DRAM in page mode all the time?

7.5.5   What determines the access time for a synchronous DRAM?

7.5.6 Calculate the refresh period for the DRAM described in 7.5.1.

7.5.7 Of the following refresh techniques, which require external hardware or software to generate the refresh address?
(a) $\overline{\text{RAS}}$-only refresh
(b) $\overline{\text{CAS}}$ before $\overline{\text{RAS}}$ refresh
(c) Self-refresh

7.5.8 In a modern computer, how does the operator control the number of wait states for the DRAM memory array?

Chapter 7 Self-Test

1. Which of the following memory types are nonvolatile?
(a) EPROM (b) SRAM (c) DRAM (d) Flash

2. Which of the following memory types allow individual bytes to be erased and rewritten?
(a) EPROM (b) E^{2}PROM (c) Flash (d) OTP ROM

3. Which of the following memory types requires that one to three command bytes be sent to the chip in order to access it?
(a) DRAM (b) Flash (c) SRAM (d) E^{2}PROM

4. A certain byte-wide SRAM has the part number HM6116LP-1. We interpret this to mean that the chip stores _____ bytes and has an access time of _____ ns.

5. Calculate the access time provided by a 486 processor with a 40 MHz bus frequency.

6. Repeat Question 5, assuming two wait states are added.

7. Why is a burst cycle faster than a conventional memory bus cycle?

8. Of the memory addresses listed below, which are misaligned with a 486 processor? Assume a doubleword access.
(a) 00000000 (b) 00FE03CA (c) 0003489B (d) FFFFEEEC

9. A certain SRAM has $\overline{\text{CS}} = 0$, $\overline{\text{WE}} = 0$, and $\overline{\text{OE}} = 1$. This chip is operating in its _____ mode.
(a) read (b) write (c) standby

10. An 8086 memory interface is to be built using 32K × 8 SRAMs. The minimum interface will require _____ SRAMs with a _____ input NAND gate decoder.

11. A 486 processor is accessing a memory word at address 00000036H. Determine the logic levels required on the processor's A31–A2 address pins and the four byte enables $\overline{\text{BE3}}$–$\overline{\text{BE0}}$.

12. When the $\overline{\text{BE7}}$–$\overline{\text{BE0}}$ outputs of the Pentium processors = 11110000, we know that a _____ is being accessed.
(a) byte (b) word (c) doubleword (d) quadword

13. When used as an address decoder, a four-input NOR gate provides four active- _____ inputs and an active-_____ output.

14. When interfaced to an 80486 processor, a 16 MB memory array will require an address decoder that examines _____ address lines.

15. When enabled and with its CBA inputs = 110, only output _____ of the 74LS138 will be _____.

16. Convert the CUPL equation OUT = !A & (B # !C) to standard logic notation.

17. A certain DRAM has address pins numbered A0–A8 and is organized ×16. What is the total storage capacity of this chip in bits? Assume equal row and column address bits.

18. Number the following DRAM timing parameters in order (1 = shortest, 3 = longest)
(a) _____ row access time
(b) _____ memory cycle time (nonpage mode)
(c) _____ column access time

19. Which type of DRAM has as access time that follows the system clock?
    (a) page-mode DRAM   (b) EDO DRAM   (c) synchronous DRAM
20. A certain DRAM has a 12-bit row address and a 10-bit column address. Calculate the refresh period.

Analysis and Design Questions

Section 7.1

7.1   In Figure 7.1, determine the values (high, low, or open circuit) on outputs m_0–m_4 for each of the following input combinations:

Inputs					Outputs				
$\overline{CS}$	A3	A2	A1	A0	m_4	m_3	m_2	m_1	m_0
0	0	0	1	0					
0	0	1	1	0					
0	1	1	0	1					
1	1	1	1	1					

7.2   Match each of the phrases listed below with one of the following memory technologies: mask-programmable ROM, OTP ROM, UV-EPROM, E²PROM, flash memory, cache SRAM, DRAM. Some phrases may have more than one answer.
      (a) Volatile
      (b) Capacitor storage cell
      (c) Fastest access times
      (d) Nonvolatile and byte erasable
      (e) Nonvolatile with access times comparable to that of DRAMs
      (f) Fusible links
      (g) Core memory SIMMs and DIMMs
      (h) Quartz-glass window

7.3   For each of the following memory part numbers, identify the manufacturer, memory type, total bit capacity, and access time.
      (a) TMS4116-12
      (b) MC2764A-250
      (c) TMS29F512-100
      (d) HMM628128LP-10
      (e) TMS44400-10

Section 7.2

7.4   A certain DRAM has a 60 ns access time. Determine the maximum allowable clock frequency (without wait states) if this chip is to be used in a 486 computer. Ignore buffer delays.

7.5   Explain how an 80x86 memory subsystem requests wait states of its processor.

7.6   Which has the highest data transfer rate, a 50 MHz 486 processor operating in *burst mode* or a 33 MHz Pentium processor operating in *pipelined burst mode?* Show the calculations to support your answer.

Section 7.3

7.7　Draw a diagram similar to Figure 7.21 using 128K × 8 SRAMs instead of the 64K × 8 parts shown. Show the decoder required to map your circuit to the address range C0000–FFFFFH.

7.8　Describe the changes required to the 386/486 memory interface in Figure 7.22 if 128K × 8 SRAMs are used in place of the 64K × 8 parts shown. What is the total memory capacity of this new interface? If the decoder requires that all of its address inputs be low, what address range will this circuit be mapped to?

7.9　The Pentium processors access data on 8-byte boundaries via the $\overline{BE7}$–$\overline{BE0}$ byte enable signals. For each memory access listed in the table below, determine the logic level required on the byte enable signals for the memory access described.

Address	Type of Access	$\overline{BE7}$	$\overline{BE6}$	$\overline{BE5}$	$\overline{BE4}$	$\overline{BE3}$	$\overline{BE2}$	$\overline{BE1}$	$\overline{BE0}$
00000000	Quadword								
00000003	Doubleword								
00000006	Word								
00000001	Byte								

Section 7.4

7.10　Draw a schematic diagram similar to Figure 7.21 showing two 32K × 8 SRAMs interfaced to an 8086 processor and mapped to cover the address range A0000–AFFFFH.

7.11　Refer to the address decoder in Figure 7.52. (a) What range of addresses correspond to the output labeled $\overline{SIMM3}$? (b) Calculate the number of memory locations in the $\overline{SIMM3}$ range. (c) Calculate the total number of bytes in all ranges decoded by this circuit.

7.12　For each memory address specified below, determine the SIMM in Figure 7.27 being accessed and the *type* of access (byte, word, doubleword).
(a) $^{A31}00000\ 001\ 000000000000000000000^{A2}\ ^{\overline{BE3}}0000^{\overline{BE0}}$
(b) $^{A31}00000\ 110\ 000000000000000000000^{A2}\ ^{\overline{BE3}}0110^{\overline{BE0}}$

7.13　Refer to the 8088 memory map shown in Figure 7.53. (a) Draw the schematic of the required memory interface similar to Figure 7.31. (b) Write the required source code file in CUPL format.

Section 7.5

7.14　The following questions refer to the TMS417400 whose block diagram is shown in Figure 7.42.
(a) The chip is organized as ＿＿＿＿＿＿ × ＿＿＿＿＿＿.
(b) The row and column addresses are both ＿＿＿＿＿＿ bits wide.
(c) The total storage capacity of the chip is ＿＿＿＿＿＿ bits.
(d) The memory array is made up of ＿＿＿＿＿＿ 256K bit arrays.
(e) When operated in page mode, ＿＿＿＿＿＿ nibbles are accessible per page.

7.15　A certain DRAM has the following specifications: t_{RAC} = 70 ns, t_{CAC} = 25 ns, and t_{RC} = 125 ns. Calculate the number of wait states required (if any) if this chip is interfaced to (a) a 10 MHz 8086 processor, (b) a 33 MHz 386 processor, and (c) a 66 MHz 486 processor (running nonburst cycles).

7.16　Answer the following questions about the TMS417400-60 DRAM shown in Figure 7.42 with specifications in Table 7.8:
(a) Calculate the refresh period.
(b) Assuming a $\overline{RAS}$-only refresh cycle requires t_{RC} ns, calculate the time required to refresh the entire chip in one burst.

Figure 7.52   Figure for Analysis and Design Question 7.11.

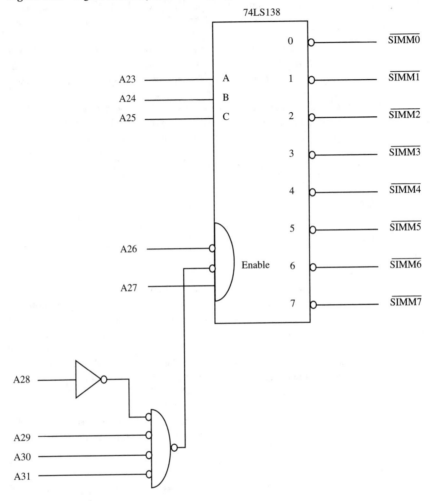

(c) Keeping in mind that the DRAM cannot be accessed while the burst refresh is occurring, for what percentage of the refresh period is the DRAM accessible by the processor?

7.17   If a distributed refresh is used, successive DRAM rows must be refreshed every 15.625 μs. Calculate the number of instructions a 66 MHz processor can execute between refresh cycles. Assume one instruction per clock cycle.

Self-Review Answers

7.1.1   16, 5
7.1.2   one-time programmable
7.1.3   (b)

Figure 7.53 Figure for Design and Analysis Question 7.13.

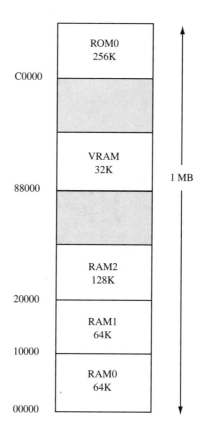

7.1.4   Flash, 100,000

7.1.5   SRAM

7.1.6   capacitor

7.1.7   four

7.1.8   128K

7.1.9   DRAM, 64K, 100

7.2.1   greater than

7.2.2   2.5 clock pulses × 1/33 MHz = 76 ns

7.2.3   16, 5

7.2.4   One extra bus cycle must be run.

7.2.5   (4 × 25 MHz)/2 = 50 MB/s

7.3.1

	$\overline{CS1}$	CS2	$\overline{OE}$	$\overline{WE}$
Memory Read	0	1	0	1
Memory Write	0	1	1	0

7.3.2   15 (2^{15} = 32K)

7.3.3   A four-input NAND gate with inverters on each input connected to A16–A19. A four input OR gate would also work.

7.3.4   (c)

7.3.5   (a)

7.3.6   misaligned

7.3.7   (c) $8 \times 32K = 256K$

7.4.1   low, low

7.4.2   3 (A17–A19)

7.4.3   8

7.4.4   5

7.4.5   AND, OR

7.4.6   7

7.4.7   PLD

7.4.8   ROM1 = memreq & memadr:[C0000..CFFFF]

7.5.1 $2^{20} \times 4$ bits = 4M bits

7.5.2 $\overline{RAS}$, $\overline{CAS}$

7.5.3   Valid data is available 70 ns after the falling edge of $\overline{RAS}$.

7.5.4   Page mode is faster because all of the data for the selected page is stored in the column buffers. Only the $\overline{CAS}$ clock need be cycled to access this data. Page mode limits you to selecting data on the specified page only. A new page (row) address must be input (via $\overline{RAS}$) to select data on another page.

7.5.5   The clock frequency applied to the chip.

7.5.6 $2^{10} \times 15.625\mu s = 16$ ms

7.5.7   (a)

7.5.8   Via the CMOS setup software.

8 Input/Output Techniques: Programmed I/O

To many people, the IBM PC legitimized the personal computer industry. Until the PC arrived in 1982, personal computers were by and large viewed as "toys" or "game machines." The IBM PC was an unusual machine for IBM. It featured an open architecture and utilized many components from other vendors. Its operating system was written by and licensed from Microsoft Corporation—a decision which helped that company become the world's largest supplier of computer software. Similarly, the choice of Intel's new 16-bit 8088 processor secured Intel's future as a major supplier of microprocessor chips. (Photo courtesy of Smithsonian)

Outline

8.1 Parallel I/O
8.2 Programmed I/O
8.3 The 8255A Programmable Peripheral Interface

Objectives

After completing this chapter you should be able to:

1. Compare the direct and indirect 80x86 I/O instructions.
2. Show how to decode the processor's address and control buses to generate a device-select pulse, and use this signal to enable parallel input and output ports.
3. Compare memory-mapped I/O with I/O-mapped I/O.

4. Explain the "handshaking" signals exchanged between a parallel printer and microcomputer.
5. Write a printer driver using programmed I/O.
6. Explain why polling is an inefficient method of controlling an I/O device.
7. Show how to determine the control byte for the 8255A when operated in mode 0.
8. Show how to interface the 8255A to the 80x86 processors.
9. Write an 80x86 program to control a matrix keyboard interfaced using an 8255A.

Overview

This chapter is the first of three dealing with microprocessor I/O. Its intention is to present the basic *concepts* of parallel I/O ports and the techniques used to control the flow of data through these ports. We will begin by showing how to construct 8- and 16-bit input and output ports. The focus here will be on the specific hardware (chips) required with each of the 80x86 processors.

With the ports designed, we will then turn our attention to *programmed I/O*—the simplest, but least efficient, method for controlling or synchronizing the data flow through an I/O port. In Chapter 9 we will introduce two more-efficient I/O-control methods based on interrupts and DMA.

We conclude this chapter with an introduction to the 8255A *Programmable Peripheral Interface* (PPI). This single chip contains all of the hardware required to construct three programmable I/O ports. Although not included on the system boards of today's PCs, its *functionality* is included in many chipsets today.

8.1   Parallel I/O

Introduction

The I/O devices can be likened to the "arms" and "legs" of a computer system. It is through these devices that information is input, processed, and then output to perform useful work. The I/O devices connect to the microprocessor through *ports*. An I/O port is similar to a memory location in that each port must have its own address. With the 80x86 processors, the port address is 16 bits long, allowing addresses in the range 0000 through FFFFH. The ports themselves may be 8, 16, or 32 bits wide. The resulting interface is therefore said to be using parallel I/O.[1] In this section we:

- Compare the direct and indirect 80x86 I/O instructions.
- Show how to decode the processor's address and control buses to generate a device-select pulse, and use this signal to enable parallel input and output ports.
- Compare memory-mapped I/O with I/O-mapped I/O.

80x86 I/O Instructions

I/O Space vs. Memory Space.   The 80x86 processors use the $M/\overline{IO}$ signal to separate I/O space from memory space (Figure 8.1). When this signal is high, addresses output by the

---

[1]In Chapter 10 we consider serial I/O, in which the data is transmitted and received one bit at a time.

Figure 8.1 The M/$\overline{\text{IO}}$ signal is used to identify the current address as a memory location or an I/O location.

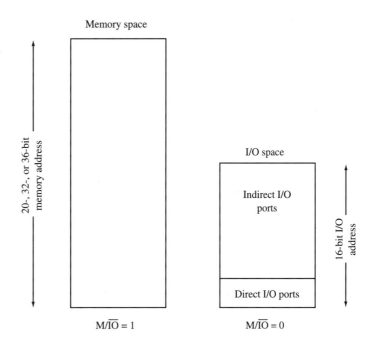

processor will be interpreted as memory locations. However, when this line is low, those same addresses will be interpreted as I/O locations. Because I/O addresses are restricted to 16 bits, valid I/O addresses range from 0000 to FFFFH.

Types of I/O Instructions. Oddly enough, the 80x86 processors have just two basic I/O instruction mnemonics—IN and OUT. However, there are several variations of each, depending on the size of the data to be input or output (byte, word, or doubleword), the method of specifying the port (direct or indirect), and the method of specifying the source and destination of the data. These are summarized in Table 8.1.

Direct I/O. The direct I/O instructions supply the port address (which must be a number between 0 and FFH) as part of the instruction. For example:

```
IN    AL, 27H       ;Input the byte at port 27H to register AL
```

Note that all data must flow through the accumulator. Thus, to output the 16-bit quantity in register BX to port 27H, two instructions are required:

```
MOV   AX,BX         ;Data to accumulator
OUT   26H, AX       ;Output the 16-bit accumulator to port 26H
```

In this last instruction, AL is output to port 26H and AH to port 27H.

Indirect I/O. To access the full range of I/O ports from 0 to FFFFH, the *indirect* I/O instructions must be used. For these instructions, register DX must be preloaded with the port address. For example, to input the 32-bit quantity at port 1000H, use the instructions:

```
MOV   DX,1000H      ;Port address to DX
IN    EAX,DX        ;Input the doubleword whose port address
                    is in DX to register EAX
```

Table 8.1   80x86 I/O Instructions

Type	Instruction	Description
Direct	IN AL, *port* IN AX, *port* IN EAX, *port*	Input the byte, word, or doubleword to the accumulator register. The port address must be in the range 0–FFH.
	OUT *port*, AL OUT *port*, AX OUT *port*, EAX	Output the byte, word, or doubleword from the accumulator register. The port address must be in the range 0–FFH.
Indirect	IN AL, DX IN AX, DX IN EAX, DX	Input the byte, word, or doubleword to the accumulator register. Register DX holds the port address, which must be in the range 0–FFFFH.
	OUT DX, AL OUT DX, AX OUT DX, EAX	Ouptut the byte, word, or doubleword from the accumulator register. Register DX holds the port address, which must be in the range 0–FFFFH.
String	INSB INSW INSD	Input the byte, word, or doubleword to the memory location ES:DI or ES:EDI. Register DX holds the port address, which must be in the range 0–FFFFH.
	OUTSB OUTSW OUTSD	Output the byte, word, or doubleword from the memory location DS:SI or DS:ESI. Register DX holds the port address, which must be in the range 0–FFFFH.

Because four bytes of data are being input, ports 1000, 1001, 1002, and 1003 will all be accessed for this last instruction.

String I/O.   The direct and indirect I/O instructions require that all data pass through the accumulator. The string I/O instructions allow data to pass directly to or from a memory location. For example, assume 4K of data (in a segment named D_DATA with the first byte at an offset called TOP) is to be output to a disk drive at port 47H. The following instructions can be used.

```
MOV    AX,D_DATA      ;Get segment address
MOV    DS,AX          ;and copy to DS
LEA    SI,TOP         ;Offset address of the data to SI
CLD                   ;Clear direction flag (set to auto-increment)
MOV    DX,47H         ;DX points to the I/O port
MOV    CX,1000H       ;CX is the byte counter (4K)
REP    OUTSB          ;Output the contents of the data table to the
                       I/O port
```

Coupled with the REP prefix, the string I/O instructions are very powerful. In this example, the REP OUTSB instruction outputs a byte from memory pointed to by DS:SI, increments SI to point to the next memory location, and decrements the byte counter in CX. The instruction is repeated until CX equals zero.

"Where Are the A0 and A1 Address Lines?"

The 386 and 486 processors have a 32-bit data bus and can thus access four bytes of memory (or four consecutive I/O ports) in one bus cycle. The A0 and A1 address lines, which would identify bytes within this four-byte boundary, are not present. Instead four active-low byte enable signals called $\overline{BE3}$ through $\overline{BE0}$ are provided. The table below shows which set of data bus lines will be active for each byte enable.

$\overline{BE3}$	$\overline{BE2}$	$\overline{BE1}$	$\overline{BE0}$	Data Bus
1	1	1	0	D0–D7
1	1	0	1	D8–D15
1	0	1	1	D16–D23
0	1	1	1	D24–D31

When the 386 or 486 executes the instruction IN AL,0, it places the 14-bit I/O address 0000 0000 0000 00_ _ on bus lines A15 through A2. It also activates the $\overline{BE0}$ byte enable. Similarly, the instruction IN AL,1 outputs the same 14-bit memory address, but this time $\overline{BE1}$ is made active. A 16-bit word access causes two byte enables to be active simultaneously. For example, when the instruction IN AX,0 is executed, the same 14-bit I/O address is output, but this time $\overline{BE0}$ and $\overline{BE1}$ are made active. $\overline{BE2}$ and $\overline{BE3}$ would be active for the instruction IN AX,2. All four ports can be accessed at once with the instruction IN EAX,0. In this case, all of the byte enables are made active.

$\overline{BE3}$	$\overline{BE2}$	$\overline{BE1}$	$\overline{BE0}$	Instruction	Ports Accessed
1	1	1	0	IN AL,0	0
1	1	0	1	IN AL,1	1
1	0	1	1	IN AL,2	2
0	1	1	1	IN AL,3	3
1	1	0	0	IN AX,0	0 and 1
0	0	1	1	IN AX,2	2 and 3
0	0	0	0	IN EAX,0	0, 1, 2, and 3

The Pentium processors are similar to the 386 and 486 processors but access eight bytes at a time. For these chips, the A0–A2 address lines are not needed. Eight byte enable signals are provided.

Finally, the 8086 processor has a 16-bit data bus. It uses the A0 address line and the $\overline{BHE}$ (bus high enable) signal to identify which data lines will be involved in the data transfer. When A0 only is low, data is transferred on D0–D7. When $\overline{BHE}$ only is low, data is transferred on D8–D15. When A0 and $\overline{BHE}$ are both low, data is transferred on all 16 data lines.

I/O Port Design

Designing a Parallel Input Port.   Figure 8.2 shows the design for a 16-bit 80386/486 input port.[2] Sixteen switches are used to simulate the input data. IC1 decodes the port address on A2–A15. In this example, any address in the range 0–3 (0–1 for an 8086 processor) will be accepted. The output of IC1 is the *port select signal* $\overline{SEL0\text{–}3}$. IC2c examines

---

[2]The signals shown in parentheses are the 8086 signal names.

Figure 8.2 Sixteen-bit 80x86 input port. Tristate buffers are used to place the input data on the data bus lines.

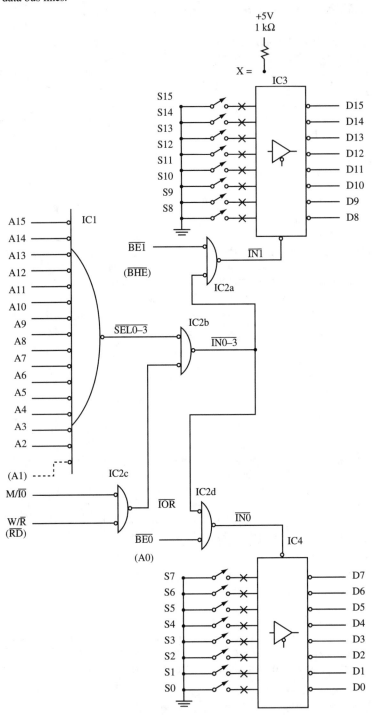

the control signals M/$\overline{\text{IO}}$ and W/$\overline{\text{R}}$. Its output, $\overline{\text{IOR}}$, will be active for I/O read cycles only. IC2b combines this signal with $\overline{\text{IOR}}$ to generate the *device-select pulse* (DSP) signal $\overline{\text{IN0–3}}$. This signal is so called because it will be active only for input instructions that select the devices wired to ports 0–3H.

Similar to a 16-bit memory interface, a 16-bit I/O port must be divided into two 8-bit ports. Data from port 0 is transferred via D0–D7, while D8–D15 are used to transfer data from port 1. As shown in Figure 8.2, $\overline{\text{BE0}}$ and $\overline{\text{BE1}}$ are combined with $\overline{\text{IN0–3}}$ to generate separate port 0 and port 1 device-select pulses ($\overline{\text{IN0}}$ and $\overline{\text{IN1}}$). These signals are then used to enable the tristate buffers and allow the data set up on the switches to be placed onto the data bus lines.

Example 8.1

Describe the changes required to the I/O port interface in Figure 8.2 if the circuit is to be used with the Pentium processors.

Solution

Only one change is required: The A2 address line, which is not present in the Pentium, should be removed. Notice that this change causes IC1 to decode eight consecutive ports from 0 through 7 (instead of four). Each of these ports can then be selected via the eight byte-select signals $\overline{\text{BE0–BE7}}$.

Example 8.2

Write a procedure (subroutine) for the input port in Figure 8.2 to check if switches 13, 11, 3, or 2 are open. If the condition is met, return with CF = 1; if the condition is not met, return with CF = 0.

Solution

An open switch will present a logic 1 level on its input line. Thus, the problem becomes one of determining if any of bits 13, 11, 3, or 2 are logic 1s. This can be done with the instruction TEST AX,280CH. A nonzero result means that at least one of the bits is set. Figure 8.3 provides a listing for the program. The statement PUBLIC FIG8_3 will allow this routine to be linked by another calling program. This will be done in Example 8.4.

The input port in Figure 8.2 will work with any of the instructions:

```
IN AL,0H      ;SW0-SW7 -> AL via D0-D7
IN AL,1H      ;SW8-SW15 -> AL via D8-D15
IN AX,0H      ;SW0-SW15 -> AX via D0-D15
IN AL,DX      ;If DX = 0000H then SW0-SW7 -> AL
              ;If DX = 0001H then SW8-SW15 -> AL
IN AX,DX      ;If DX = 0000H then SW0-SW15 -> AX
```

Note that for byte input the destination is always register AL. This is true even though the data may be transferred via the D0–D7 (even ports) or D8–D15 (odd ports) data bus lines. The processor automatically selects the proper set of data lines.

Figure 8.3   Control program for Example 8.1.

```
                        ;Function:  Test if bits 13, 11, 3 or 2 of
                        ;           the 16-bit data port are high.
                        ;Inputs:    Status information from IPORT.
                        ;Outputs:   CF=1 if condition TRUE, else CF=0.
                        ;Destroys:  AX, flags.

                                 PUBLIC FIG8_3
= 0000                           IPORT   EQU     0H               ;Data input port

0000                    CODE     SEGMENT BYTE PUBLIC 'CODE'
                                 ASSUME CS:CODE

0000                    FIG8_3   PROC    NEAR
0000    F8                       CLC                              ;Be sure CF=0
0001    E5 00                    IN      AX,IPORT                 ;Sample data
0003    A9 280C                  TEST    AX,0010100000001100B     ;Test input data
0006    74 01                    JZ      DONE                     ;No bits high
0008    F9                       STC                              ;At least 1 bit high
0009    C3              DONE:    RET
000A                    FIG8_3   ENDP
000A                    CODE     ENDS
                                 END
```

Example 8.3

Explain how to troubleshoot the circuit in Figure 8.2 using DEBUG.

Solution

First set up a simple test program that will "exercise" the port.

```
-a100
1BFA:0100 IN AX,0
1BFA:0102 JMP 100
```

Run the program in DEBUG using *trace* mode. A logic probe can be used to locate the input read bus cycle. This can be identified by the $\overline{IN0}$ and $\overline{IN1}$ DSP signals both pulsing low. $\overline{IOR}$, $\overline{BE0}$, $\overline{BE1}$, and $\overline{SEL0-3}$ should also pulse low. IC3 and IC4 should be enabled and, as each data switch is changed, the data displayed by DEBUG for register AX should also change.

Designing a Parallel Output Port.   The hardware required for an output port is similar to that of an input port except that the DSP signal is used to strobe a *latch* instead of the tristate buffers. The latch is required due to the short time that data is placed on the bus by the processor.

Figure 8.4 shows the design for an 8-bit output port mapped to address 0. IC2a is used to decode I/O write bus cycles ($M/\overline{IO} = 0$ and $W/\overline{R} = 1$). IC2b combines this signal with the address decode signal $\overline{SEL0-3}$ from Figure 8.2. This creates the DSP $\overline{OUT0-3}$. This signal will be active for any I/O write cycle to ports in the range 0–3. So that only the data for port 0 is latched, IC2c is used to combine the DSP with $\overline{BE0}$.

Figure 8.4   Eight-bit 80x86 output port. Eight latches are rquired to store the output data.

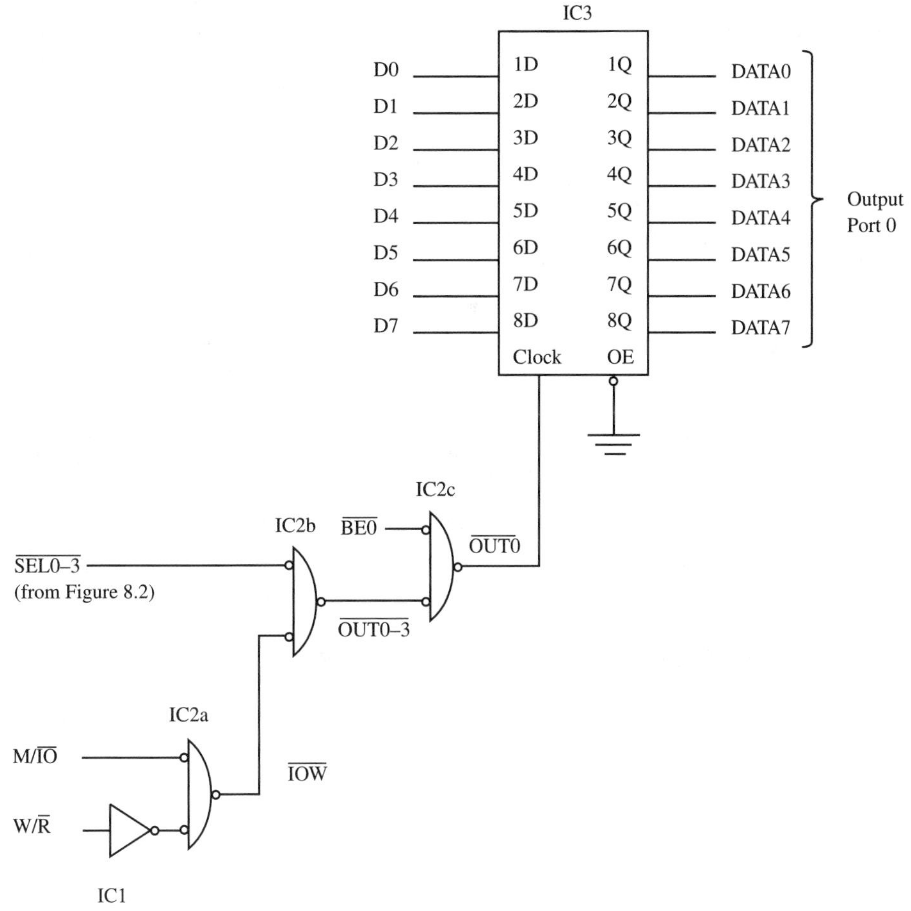

There are two ways of using this port. In the direct mode, simply issue the instruction:

```
OUT   0,AL    ;Output register AL to port 0
```

The second method is to use the indirect mode:

```
MOV   DX,0    ;Port 0 address to DX
OUT   DX,AL   ;Output register AL to the port whose address is in DX
```

Although not logical, several other instructions will also work. For example, the instruction OUT 0,AX sends the contents of register AL to port 0, and register AH to port 1. As there is no latch to "catch" the port 1 data, this information will be lost. A similar result occurs with the instruction OUT 0,EAX.

Example 8.4

Write a program that tests if any of the switches 13, 11, 3, or 2 in the input port of Figure 8.2 are open. If the condition is met, output FFH to port 0 in Figure 8.4; if the condition is not met, output 00 to this port. The program should cycle indefinitely.

Solution

We can take advantage of the procedure written in Example 8.2 to test the input port. Depending on the condition of CF (the carry flag), FFH or 00 can then be output to port 0. Figure 8.5 is a listing of the program. FIG8_3 is declared as an external symbol so that this routine can be linked to the program in Figure 8.5 without having to rewrite that procedure's code.

Applications for the Device-Select Pulse

ON/OFF Control of a Relay.   Normally, the DSP signal is used to enable a latch or set of tristate gates. However, in some cases, the pulse alone is sufficient. Figure 8.6 provides an example. Using the $\overline{IN0}$ and $\overline{OUT0}$ DSP signals from the decoders in Figures 8.2 and 8.4, this circuit controls a mechanical relay. An IN AL,0 instruction *resets* the flip-flop and turns on the transistor. This, in turn, allows current to flow through the relay coil. The normally open (N.O.) contact closes, allowing the external device to be turned on. An OUT 0,AL instruction turns the relay off.

The 74LS05 is an open-collector buffer. This allows its output to be pulled to +5V and the transistor base drive to be supplied through the pull-up resistor. Transistor Q1 is required because the relay's ON current exceeds the sink capability of the 74LS05.

A similar application for the DSP is to trigger a one-shot to generate pulse widths of a particular length. Note that only the DSP is used: No data is transferred. For this reason, the contents of register AL is a "don't care" when an output instruction is executed, and indeterminate when an input instruction is executed.

Figure 8.5   Control program for Example 8.4.

```
                          ;This program calls the routine in Fig. 8.3.
                          ;If switches 13, 11, 3 or 2 are open, FFH is
                          ;output to OPORT, else 00 is output.

                              EXTRN    FIG8_3:NEAR
= 0000                        OPORT    EQU      0     ;Output port

0000                  CODE    SEGMENT  'CODE'
                              ASSUME   CS:CODE

0000   B3 FF          START:  MOV      BL,0FFH        ;Open switches code is FF
0002   E8 0000 E              CALL     FIG8_3         ;Test switches
0005   72 02                  JC       SET            ;Condition met
0007   B3 00                  MOV      BL,0           ;Condition not met code is 00
0009   8A C3          SET:    MOV      AL,BL          ;Code to AL
000B   E6 00                  OUT      OPORT,AL       ;Program the port
000D   EB F1                  JMP      START          ;Monitor continuously
000F                  CODE    ENDS
                              END      START
```

Figure 8.6   Using device-select pulses to control a relay. An IN AL,0 instruction will turn the relay on; an OUT 0,AL instruction will turn it off.

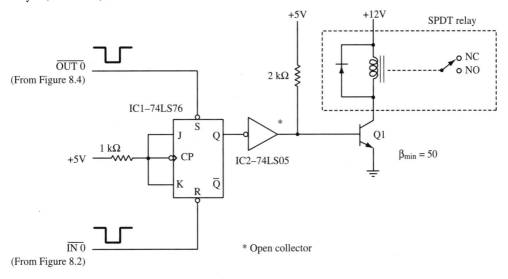

Memory-Mapped I/O

The address space of the 80x86 processors is divided into 4 GB of memory space and 64K of I/O space.[3] To ensure that these two regions do not overlap, the control bus signal $M/\overline{IO}$ is provided. Memory instructions cause the control signal to be high; I/O instructions cause this signal to be low.

But consider designing a one-byte (or word or doubleword) read/write memory. We would use latches to store the data written during a memory write cycle, and tristate gates to drive the bus during a memory read cycle—exactly the same hardware we would use for an output or input port.

This is the essence of *memory-mapped I/O*. In hardware, it appears to be a conventional I/O port. But because it is mapped to a *memory* address, it is accessible in software using any of the memory read or write instructions. For example, the instruction MOV BH,[1000] becomes an input instruction (input the data at "port" 1000 to register BH). Indirect I/O is also possible. The instruction sequence

```
MOV   SI,1000H     ;Point SI at the port
MOV   [SI],CX      ;Output CX to the port
```

allows CX to be output to the 16-bit port at address DS:1000H.

As you can see, the advantage of memory-mapped I/O is the large number of instructions and addressing modes available for referencing memory. All of these now become potential I/O instructions. With I/O-mapped ports we are restricted to the simple IN and OUT instructions. Even using string I/O, the port address must be specified in register DX. Memory-mapped ports allow this address to be computed using any of the 80x86's addressing modes.

---

[3]The 8086/88 has 1 MB of memory space; the 286 has 16 MB.

Self-Review 8.1 (Answers on page 381–382)

8.1.1   When the instruction IN AL,01H is executed, the 80486 inputs the data byte over the
_____ data bus lines.
(a) D0–D7
(b) D8–D15
(c) D16–D32
(d) D24–D31

8.1.2   For direct I/O, the 80x86 processors are restricted to _____ I/O ports with addresses
in the range _____ to _____.

8.1.3   Indicate the logic levels required (1 or 0) on W/$\overline{\text{R}}$ and M/$\overline{\text{IO}}$ for (a) an I/O read cycle and (b)
an I/O write cycle.

8.1.4   When an I/O port select signal is combined with the $\overline{\text{IOR}}$ or $\overline{\text{IOW}}$ control signals, the resulting signal is referred to as a _____ _____ _____.

8.1.5   Describe the change required to the output port in Figure 8.4 if it is to be mapped to port 3.

8.1.6   Which of the following instructions could *not* be used for memory-mapped input?
(a) INC AX
(b) CMP DX,[1000]
(c) MOV BX,[1000]
(d) MOV BP,[BX]

8.2   Programmed I/O

Introduction

The I/O ports of a computer typically operate at different data rates. A hard disk drive, for
example, might require the computer to input data at 10 MB/s. CD-ROM drives operate at
300–600K/s. However, when inputting keystrokes from the operator, the data rate may fall
to only one or two characters per second. If the processor is to operate efficiently, we will
need to develop a strategy to control or *synchronize* the flow of data between the processor
and the widely varying data rates of its I/O devices.

In this section we will :

- Explain the "handshaking" signals exchanged between a parallel printer and microcom-
puter.
- Write a printer driver using programmed I/O.
- Explain why polling is an inefficient method of controlling an I/O device.

Parallel Printer Interface Example[4]

Printers typically have buffers that can be filled by the computer at high speed. Once full,
the computer must wait while the data in the buffer is printed. The buffer is then refilled
and the process repeated. To facilitate the control process, most printer manufacturers have
settled on a standard set of control and data signals that is now referred to as the *Centronics
Parallel Printer Interface*. In this section we will study this interface as an example of
programmed I/O.

---

[4]In Appendix B we provide a schematic diagram of the parallel printer port used in the PC. The discussion in this
section is based on an analysis of this hardware.

Table 8.2 Parallel Printer Port Bit Definitions

Port A—DATA		8-Bit Output Port					
PA7	PA6	PA5	PA4	PA3	PA2	PA1	PA0
Data 8	Data 7	Data 6	Data 5	Data 4	Data 3	Data 2	Data 1

Port B—Status		5-Bit Input Port					
$\overline{\text{PB7}}$	PB6	PB5	PB4	PB3	PB2	PB1	PB0
BUSY	$\overline{\text{ACKNLG}}$	PE	SLCT	$\overline{\text{ERROR}}$	Not Used	Not Used	Not Used

Port C—Control		5-Bit Output Port					
PC7	PC6	PC5*	PC4	$\overline{\text{PC3}}$	PC2	$\overline{\text{PC1}}$	$\overline{\text{PC0}}$
Not Used	Not Used	DIR	IRQEN	$\overline{\text{SLCT IN}}$	$\overline{\text{INIT}}$	$\overline{\text{AUTO}}$	$\overline{\text{STROBE}}$

*In modern computers port A is bidirectional. When bit 5 of port C is set, the bidirectional mode is enabled. Software can then control the direction of the port by writing to an additional register.

Signal Definitions.   In the PC, the parallel printer port is usually referred to as LPT1 or LPT2. Each of these "ports" is actually made up of three ports:

- Port A—the printer data port
- Port B—the printer control signal status port
- Port C—the printer control port

Table 8.2 gives the (parallel printer) signal names associated with the bits in each port. When interfaced as LPT1, the three ports are mapped to I/O addresses 378–37AH; when interfaced as LPT2, the addresses are 278–27AH.[5]

In the Centronics standard the computer and printer are connected via a cable with 25 pins at the computer end and 36 pins at the printer end. Table 8.3 provides the details on the specific pin assignments: Figure 8.7 shows the hardware interface.

The 8-bit data byte to be output to the printer is sent to port A. Data output to this port will be latched when the $\overline{\text{STROBE}}$ input (bit $\overline{\text{PC0}}$) is pulsed low for 0.5 μs or longer.[6] Figure 8.8 illustrates the timing. The data requires a 0.5 μs setup time before the leading edge of $\overline{\text{STROBE}}$ occurs. A 0.5 μs hold time is also required after the $\overline{\text{STROBE}}$ signal returns high.

Two other control signals are provided by the printer, labeled BUSY and $\overline{\text{ACKNLG}}$. Returning to Table 8.3, BUSY is an active-high signal that indicates that the printer is "busy" printing a character, has some error condition, or is in an OFFLINE state. Taken literally, it means *I am busy now and can't accept data from you.*

---

[5]A parallel printer port may also be found at address 3BCH (this is used on early monochrome video adapters). In addition, a fourth parallel port may be mapped to base address 2BCH. During the boot-up process, the BIOS scans ports 3BCH, 378H, 278H, and then 2BCH. The first active port it finds is assigned the name LPT1, the second LPT2, etc. Four different ports are thus possible. Some BIOS versions support only LPT1 and LPT2—even though the hardware for LPT3 and LPT4 may be present.

[6]The $\overline{\text{PB7}}$, $\overline{\text{PC3}}$, $\overline{\text{PC1}}$, and $\overline{\text{PC0}}$ signals in Table 8.2 are input or output through inverters in the PC's parallel port hardware (see Appendix B). Thus, writing a logic 1 to bit 0 of port C will actually result in a logic 0 being output by the parallel interface card. Similarly, a logic 1 input from bit 7 of port B will be input as a logic 0.

Table 8.3   Parallel Printer Signal Descriptions

Port	Printer 36-pin	Computer 25-pin	Signal	Direction	Description
$\overline{\text{PC0}}$	1	1	$\overline{\text{STROBE}}$	In	STROBE pulse to read data in. Pulse width must be more than 0.5 µs at receiving terminal. The signal level is normally "HIGH"; read-in of data is performed at the "LOW" level of this signal.
PA0	2	2	DATA 1	In	
PA1	3	3	DATA 2	In	
PA2	4	4	DATA 3	In	These signals represent information of the first to eighth bits of parallel data, respectively. Each signal is at "HIGH" level when data is logical 1 and "LOW" when logical 0.
PA3	5	5	DATA 4	In	
PA4	6	6	DATA 5	In	
PA5	7	7	DATA 7	In	
PA6	8	8	DATA 8	In	
PA7	9	9	DATA 9	In	
PB6	10	10	$\overline{\text{ACKNLG}}$	Out	Approx. 5-µs pulse. "LOW" indicates that data has been received and that the printer is ready to accept other data.
$\overline{\text{PB7}}$	11	11	BUSY	Out	A "HIGH" signal indicates that the printer cannot receive data. The signal becomes "HIGH" in the following cases: 1. During data entry 2. During printing operation 3. In OFFLINE state 4. During printer error status
PB5	12	12	PE	Out	A "HIGH" signal indicates that the printer is out of paper.
PB4	13	13	SLCT	Out	This signal indicates that the printer is in the selected state.
$\overline{\text{PC1}}$	14	14	$\overline{\text{AUTO}}$ $\overline{\text{FEED XT}}$	In	With this signal being at "LOW" level, the paper is automatically fed one line after printing.
—	15	—	NC		Not used.
—	16	—	0V		Logic GND level.
—	17	—	CHASSIS-GND	—	Printer chassis GND. In the printer, the chassis GND and the logic GND are isolated from each other.

Table 8.3   *(continued)*

Port	Printer 36-pin	Computer 25-pin	Signal	Direction	Description
—	18	—	NC	—	Not used.
—	19 to 30	18–25	GND	—	TWISTED-PAIR RETURN signal GND level.
PC2	31	16	$\overline{\text{INIT}}$	In	When the level of this signal becomes "LOW," the printer controller is reset to its initial state and the print buffer is cleared. This signal is normally at "HIGH" level, and its pulse width must be more than 50 μs at the receiving terminal.
PB3	32	15	$\overline{\text{ERROR}}$	Out	The level of this signal becomes "LOW" when the printer is in: 1. PAPER END state 2. OFFLINE state 3. Error state
—	33	18–25	GND	—	Same as with printer pins 19 to 30.
—	34	—	NC	—	Not used.
—	35	—			Pulled up to +5V through 4.7-kΩ resistance.
$\overline{\text{PC3}}$	36	17	$\overline{\text{SLCT IN}}$	In	Data entry to the printer is possible only when the level of this signal is "LOW."

Notes

1. "Direction" refers to the direction of signal flow as viewed from the printer.

2. "Return" denotes "TWISTED-PAIR RETURN" and is to be connected at signal ground level. As to the wiring for the interface, be sure to use a twisted-pair cable for each signal and never fail to complete connection on the Return side. To prevent noise effectively, these cables should be shielded and connected to the chassis of the host computer and the printer, respectively.

3. All interface conditions are based on TTL level. Both the rise and fall times of each signal must be less than 0.2 μs.

4. Data transfer must not be carried out by ignoring the $\overline{\text{ACKNLG}}$ or BUSY signal. (Data transfer to this printer can be carried out only after confirming the $\overline{\text{ACKNLG}}$ signal or when the level of the BUSY signal is "LOW.")

Source: Seiko Epson Corporation.

The $\overline{\text{ACKNLG}}$ signal is an active-low *pulse* provided by the printer after a character has been accepted and printed. Note the difference between these two signals. BUSY is best suited for a *level-triggered* input; $\overline{\text{ACKNLG}}$ is most appropriate with an edge-triggered input.[7]

---

[7]As shown in Figure 8.7, setting bit PC4 allows the $\overline{\text{ACKNLG}}$ signal to drive the IRQ7 interrupt input of the PC. Interrupts are covered in detail in Chapter 9. In addition, an interrupt-driven parallel printer interface is also discussed in that chapter.

Figure 8.7 PC to parallel printer interface. Three ports—A, B, and C—are required. In this example the port assignments correspond to LPT1.

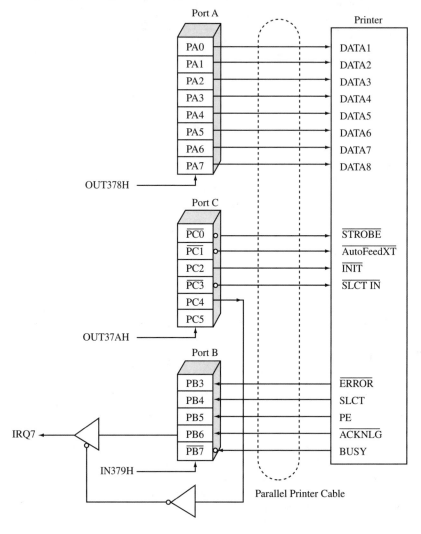

Figure 8.8 Parallel printer timing showing the relationship between the handshaking signals. (Courtesy of Seiko Epson Corporation)

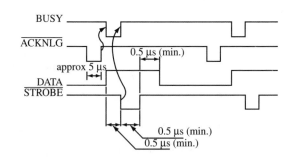

The $\overline{\text{STROBE}}$, BUSY, and $\overline{\text{ACKNLG}}$ signals form a set of "handshaking" signals exchanged between the computer and printer. The computer extends its "hand" with the $\overline{\text{STROBE}}$ pulse, saying, *Here is the data.* The printer acknowledges via the $\overline{\text{ACKNLG}}$ pulse saying, *I've got it. You can send me some more.* BUSY is the same as $\overline{\text{ACKNLG}}$ bu provides a *level* to be monitored instead of a pulse.

Controling the Printer.   Before data can be writing to the printer, the printer must be *initialized.* This is accomplished by writin to the control port (Port C).

Example 8.5

Determine the code to be written to the LPT1 control port in Figure 8.7 such that the printer port operates unidirectionally, IRQ7 is disabled, the printer is selected, the printer controller is reset, line feeds are automatically added after each line, and the STROBE input is inactive.

Solution

Referring to Table 8.2 for the Port C bit definitions, the following bit pattern is required:

(a) PC7 and PC6 are "don't cares"
(b) PC5 = 0 (The printer port is unidirectional)
(c) PC4 = 0 (Disable IRQ7)
(d) PC3 = 0 (Put the printer in the selected state)
(e) PC2 = 0 (Reset the printer controller)
(f) PC1 = 0 (Enable automatic line feeds)
(g) PC0 = 1 ($\overline{\text{STROBE}}$ = high)

The code to output would appear to be XX00 0001. However, as shown in Figure 8.7, bits PC3, PC1, and PC0 are inverted by the printer adapter before being output to the printer. Taking this into account, the proper initialization code is XX00 1010 = 0AH (choosing the Xs to be 0).

Once the printer is initialized, it is ready to receive data. This is accomplished by outputting the data to port A, and then taking the $\overline{\text{STROBE}}$ input momentarily low. The next character is then output, and the process repeated. The $\overline{\text{STROBE}}$ signal can be generated in software by outputting a 1, a 0, and then a 1 again. The result will be a brief active-low pulse.

Example 8.6

Determine the codes to write to the LPT1 control port in Figure 8.7 such that (a) $\overline{\text{STROBE}}$ is high; and (b) $\overline{\text{STROBE}}$ is low. Assume the printer operates as described in Example 8.5.

Solution

The printer's $\overline{\text{INIT}}$ input must first be made inactive so that the printer controller is not continuously being reset. This requires PC2 = 1. Now to make the $\overline{\text{STROBE}}$ signal high, PC0 = 0 (recall that this bit is inverted). The code is thus: XX00 1110 = 0EH. To make the $\overline{\text{STROBE}}$ signal low, PC0 = 1. The codes is XX00 1111 = 0FH.

Polling.   Figure 8.9 flowcharts the printer driver software required to transfer data between the computer and printer. In this example, we assume the data to be printed is stored in consecutive memory locations thought of as a *print buffer.* A pointer is used to identify the head of this buffer; a counter is used to store the total number of bytes to be printed.

Figure 8.9 Flowchart for the printer control program.

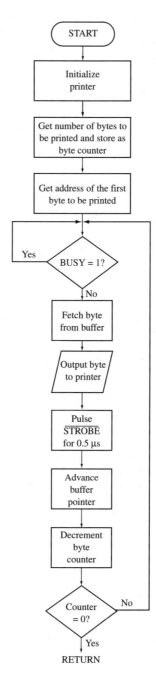

The decision block, *BUSY = 1?*, forms a *polling* loop in which the computer continually tests the printer's BUSY flag. When this line goes low, the processor fetches a byte from the buffer, outputs it to the printer, pulses the $\overline{\text{STROBE}}$ input, advances the table pointer, and decrements the byte counter. If more data remains to be printed, control returns to the polling loop.

Control Program.   Figure 8.10 lists the 80x86 code required to control the parallel printer interface in Figure 8.7. We begin by setting up a PRINT_DATA segment, where the
number of bytes to be printed and the starting address of this data (in segment:offset format) are stored. [Figure 8.10 (a)]. The program is written as a *procedure,* so it is up to the
calling program to initialize this PRINT_DATA segment before calling the main program.

Several *equates* are used to make the program more readable. Note that the I/O addresses are assumed to be 378–37AH corresponding to LPT1 on the PC. S_HIGH and
S_LOW are defined such that, when written to the printer control port, the $\overline{\text{STROBE}}$ signal
will go high or low accordingly.

The program code begins in Figure 8.10(b). Register CX is used as the byte counter
and DS:SI as the data pointer. Following printer initialization, the program drops into the
polling loop waiting for the printer to be ready. When it is, the LODSB instruction fetches
the data byte to AL, where it is then output to the data port. The $\overline{\text{STROBE}}$ signal is then
pulsed low and back high (via software). The sequence is then repeated until all bytes have
been written (CX = 0).

The most important point to note about this program is the use of the $\overline{\text{STROBE}}$ and
BUSY signals to *synchronize* the microprocessor and peripheral. Because the transfer of data
to the printer is done under program control, the technique is referred to as *programmed I/O.*

Figure 8.10   Control program for the parallel printer interface in Figure 8.7.

```
                        ;Function:  Polled printer driver for LPT1.
                        ;           Written as a far procedure.

                        ;Inputs:    PRINT_DATA segment holds number of bytes
                        ;           to be printed and the address of the buffer.
                        ;Outputs:   Characters in the buffer are output to LPT1.
                        ;Calls:     None
                        ;Destroys:  AX, CX, SI, DS, flags


0000                    PRINT_DATA      SEGMENT WORD
0000 0000                       NUMB    DW   ?          ;Number of bytes to print
0002 00000000                   ADR     DD   ?          ;Address of first byte

0006                    PRINT_DATA ENDS

= 0378                  LPT1    EQU     378H            ;Printer data port
= 0379                  STATUS  EQU     379H            ;Printer status port
= 037A                  Control EQU     37AH            ;Printer control port
= 000A                  INIT    EQU     0AH             ;Unidirectional, no IRQ,
                                                        ;select printer, init, auto
                                                        ;STROBE=1
= 000E                  S_HIGH  EQU     0EH             ;STROBE=1 and no init
= 000F                  S_LOW   EQU     0FH             ;STROBE=0 and no init
```

(a)

(continued on next page)

Figure 8.10 (*continued*)

```
0000                    CODE      SEGMENT  'CODE'
0000           FIG8_10  PROC      FAR
                        ASSUME    CS:CODE, DS:PRINT_DATA

               ;Initialize pointers:
               ;    DS:SI to start of data
               ;    CX with number of bytes to be printed

0000  B8 ---- R         MOV       AX,PRINT_DATA    ;Load DS with
0003  8E D8             MOV       DS,AX            ;address of PRINT_DATA.
0005  8B 0E 0000 R      MOV       CX,NUMB          ;Get number of bytes
0009  C5 36 0002 R      LDS       SI,ADR           ;Get address of data
                                                   ;to DS:SI
000D  FC                CLD                        ;Auto increment

               ;Initialize and select printer, auto line feed, STROBE=1

000E  B0 0A             MOV       AL,INIT          ;Initialization code
0010  BA 037A           MOV       DX,CONTROL       ;Control port access
0013  EE                OUT       DX,AL            ;Write the code

               ;Poll the printer waiting for BUSY to be low

0014  B0 0E      NEXT:  MOV       AL,S_HIGH        ;Be sure STROBE is high
0016  EE                OUT       DX,AL            ;Write to control port
0017  BA 0379    POLL:  MOV       DX,STATUS        ;Status port access
001A  EC                IN        AL,DX            ;Get BUSY status
001B  A8 80             TEST      AL,10000000B     ;Test BUSY bit
001D  74 F8             JZ        POLL             ;Wait until READY
```

(b)

Figure 8.10 (*continued*)

```
                              ;Printer is ready, fetch and output a byte
001F   AC              LODSB             ;Get byte
                                         ;and advance pointer.
0020   BA 0378         MOV    DX,LPT1    ;Data port access
0023   EE              OUT    DX,AL      ;Output to printer

                              ;Strobe the printer
0024   B0 0F           MOV    AL,S_LOW   ;STROBE=0
0026   BA 037A         MOV    DX,CONTROL ;Control port access
0029   EE              OUT    DX,AL      ;Write to LPT1 control port

                              ;Repeat the polling loop until all data has been printed
002A   E2 E8           LOOP   NEXT       ;Do CX times

002C   CB              RET               ;Then return
002D           FIG8_10  ENDP
002D           CODE     ENDS
                        END
```

(b)

The Polling Loop.   In Figure 8.10, the four instructions

```
POLL:    MOV    DX,STATUS
         IN     AL,DX
         TEST   AL,10000000B
         JZ     POLL
```

form the polling loop. In effect, they ask the printer, "Are you ready for more data?" Initially, when the printer's buffer is empty, the answer will be *Yes.* However, because the data rate of the computer is so fast (even a 5 MHz 8086 can output more than 60,000 characters/s), the buffer will quickly fill up. Several seconds may then elapse before the printer is ready for more data. During this time, the computer will be repeatedly asking the printer if it is ready. Several thousand such requests may occur before the answer is finally *Yes.*

This may suggest that polling is a rather inefficient way of controlling the printer. Most of the time the processor is simply waiting for the printer to be READY. And even when it is, only a few milliseconds are required to refill the print buffer. Then it's back to waiting for the data to be printed.

But maybe you are thinking, "What does it matter? What else does the processor have to do anyway?" Depending on the system, perhaps nothing. But if the printer is being used to print a 100-page report, you may have a long wait before the system can be used for some other job. It also seems intuitively *wrong* to have a microprocessor as powerful as the Pentium (or 386, or 486, etc.) simply "spinning its wheels" waiting for the slow printer to be done.

So now you ought to be thinking about a way to improve the efficiency of this process. Ideally, it would let the processor "periodically check in on the printer" while most of its time is devoted to other (more useful) tasks. In Chapter 9 we will see exactly how to do this.

Self-Review 8.2 (Answers on page 382)

8.2.1   Polling a peripheral's BUSY/READY flag is one way of _____ the microprocessor to a slow-speed peripheral.

8.2.2   List the handshaking signals supplied by the printer in Figure 8.7.

8.2.3   Why is polling an *inefficient* way of controlling a peripheral?

8.2.4   Determine the contents of the PRINT_DATA segment in Figure 8.10 if 25 bytes beginning at IFOC:0040 are to be printed.

8.2.5   In Figure 8.7, the printer's BUSY/READY status can be read as bit _____ of input port _____.

8.3   The 8255A Programmable Peripheral Interface

Introduction

Intel has developed several peripheral controller chips designed to support the 80x86 processor family. The intent is to provide a complete I/O interface in one chip. The 8255A Programmable Peripheral Interface (PPI) provides three 8-bit I/O ports in one 40-pin package. The chip interfaces directly to the data bus of the processor, allowing its function to be *programmed;* that is, in one application a port may appear as an output, but in another, by reprogramming it, as an input. Other peripheral controller chips include the 8259 Programmable Interrupt Controller (PIC), the 8253/54 Programmable Interval Timer (PIT), and the 8237 Programmable DMA Controller.

In PC/XT computers, these chips are built into the system board and can be seen by inspection. In modern computers, the *functionality* of these chips has been built into the system board chipsets. In, this section we will:

- Show how to determine the control byte for the 8255A when operated in mode 0.
- Show how to interface the 8255A to the 80x86 processors.
- Write an 80x86 program to control a matrix keyboard interfaced using an 8255A.

Description

The 8255A is a general-purpose parallel I/O interfacing device. It provides 24 I/O lines organized as three 8-bit I/O ports labeled A, B, and C. Pin definitions and a block diagram are provided in Figure 8.11.

Programming of the ports is restricted to bytes or nibbles (4 bits). Each of the ports, A or B, can be programmed as an 8-bit input or output port. Port C can be divided in half, with the topmost or bottommost four bits programmed as inputs or outputs. Individual bits of a particular port cannot be programmed.

Figure 8.11   8255 programmable peripheral interface (PPI). Twenty-four I/O pins are provided grouped as three 8-bit I/O ports. There is one 8-bit control port. (Courtesy of Intel Corporation)

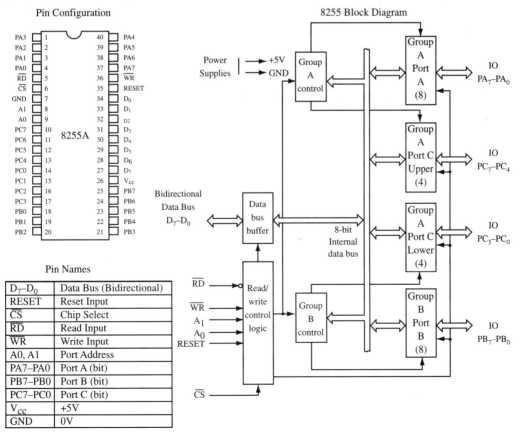

The 8255A is a very versatile device. It can be programmed to look like three simple I/O ports (called *mode 0*), two handshaking I/O ports (called *mode 1*), or a bidirectional I/O port with five handshaking signals (called *mode 2*). The modes can also be intermixed. For example, port A can be programmed to operate in mode 2, while port B operates in mode 0. There is also a *bit set/reset mode* that allows individual bits of port C to be set or reset for control purposes.

Accessing the Chip.   Table 8.4 shows how the four internal registers (or ports) are accessed by the processor for read and write operations. Two address input lines labeled A0 and A1 determine which register is to be selected. For example, port A is accessed when A1 A0=00.

The $\overline{RD}$ and $\overline{WR}$ input pins determine the direction of data flow over the chip's 8-bit bidirectional data bus. Note that each of the *data* ports can be read from or written to. The *control* port, however, can only be written to. As you will see, the byte written to this port determines the mode of operation of the three data ports.

Similar to the memory devices discussed in Chapter 7, the 8255A can only be accessed when its $\overline{CS}$ (chip select) input is low. Thus, this input is normally driven by an address decoder, to assign the device to a specific range of I/O addresses.

If you are wondering about compatibility with the 16-, 32-, and 64-bit buses of the 80x86 processors, remember the ability of these chips to access its I/O (or memory) in bytes as well as words. The next section illustrates a typical interface.

Interfacing to the 80x86 Processors

Figure 8.12 shows how the 8255A can be interfaced to the 32-bit bus of the 80386 or 80486 processors. In this example we have (arbitrarily) chosen to connect the PPI chip to the low eight bits (D0–D7) of the data bus. IC1 functions as the address decoder and, in this example, provides an active output when the address on A4–A15 is in the range 0–FH.

Table 8.4   Truth Table for the 8255A PPI (Courtesy of Intel Corporation)

A_1	A_0	$\overline{RD}$	$\overline{WR}$	$\overline{CS}$	
					Input operation (READ)
0	0	0	1	0	Port A → data bus
0	1	0	1	0	Port B → data bus
1	0	0	1	0	Port C → data bus
					Output operation (WRITE)
0	0	1	0	0	Data bus → port A
0	1	1	0	0	Data bus → port B
1	0	1	0	0	Data bus → port C
1	1	1	0	0	Data bus → control
					Disable function
X	X	X	X	1	Data bus tristate
1	1	0	1	0	Illegal condition
X	X	1	1	0	Data bus tristate

Figure 8.12   Interfacing the 8255 to the 386/486 processors. The four PPI ports are mapped to addresses 0, 4, 8, and C.

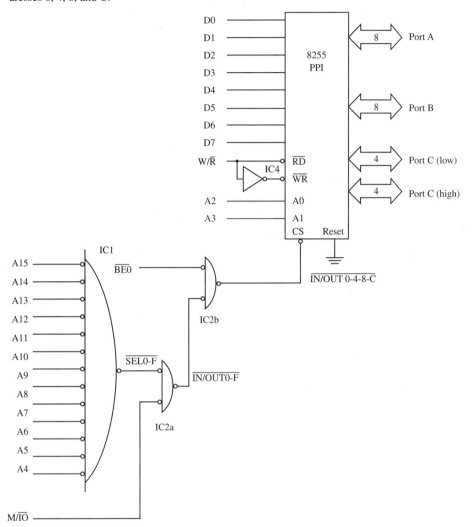

IC2a combines this signal with M/$\overline{\text{IO}}$ to produce the signal $\overline{\text{IN/OUT0–F}}$, which will be active for any I/O read or write cycle to any port in the range 0–FH.

Because the interface is connected to the low-order data bus lines, $\overline{\text{BE0}}$ is used to qualify the $\overline{\text{IN/OUT0–F}}$ signal. The result is the device-select signal $\overline{\text{IN/OUT0-4-8-C}}$. No that this signal is active only for the four ports at addresses 0, 4, 8, and CH. If we connected the PPI to the D8–D15 data bus lines, we would qualify the $\overline{\text{IN/OUT0–F}}$ signal with $\overline{\text{BE1}}$. IC2b's output would then be active for ports 1, 5, 9, and DH.

If you are wondering why we are allowing four different addresses to enable the 8255A, remember that internally it is organized as four separate I/O ports. Its A0 and A1 address inputs (connected to A2 and A3 in our design) define the specific port selected.

Example 8.7

Determine the addresses of ports A, B, C, and the control port in the interface in Figure 8.12.

Solution

IC2b selects the chip if the I/O address is 0, 4, 8, or CH. Note that over this range the processor's A0 and A1 address lines (if present) would have to be 00. Combining this information with the port definitions given in Table 8.4, we can draw the following table:

	Processor Address Lines			
PPI Port	A15–A4*	A3 A2†	A1 A0**	Hex Address
A	0000 0000 0000	0 0	0 0	0
B	0000 0000 0000	0 1	0 0	4
C	0000 0000 0000	1 0	0 0	8
Control	0000 0000 0000	1 1	0 0	C

*The address decoder requires all of these lines to be low.
†These lines are connected to the A1 and A0 PPI inputs and select one of four internal ports.
**These lines are not actually output by the processor. However, because $\overline{BE0}$ is low, they are effectively 00. If $\overline{BE1}$ was substituted for $\overline{BE0}$, these lines would equate to 01.

Programming

Specifying the Control Byte.   Applying an active high pulse to the 8255A's RESET input will leave the three data ports programmed as inputs. Thus, the first few instructions of the applications software will normally program the PPI for the desired operating mode and I/O configuration. This will require one to three bytes to be output to the control port.

Figure 8.13 shows how the control byte is formed. Bit 7 determines if a *bit set/reset* or *mode-definition* byte is to be written. The bit set/reset function is not really a control byte (it does not alter the previously specified operating mode); instead, it allows individual bits of port C to be set or reset. This is discussed further in the next section.

When bit 7 of the control byte is a 1, one of three operating modes can be specified. As Figure 8.13 illustrates, the three data ports are separated into two groups, labeled Group A and Group B. The ports in Group A can be programmed for any of modes 0, 1, or 2. The ports in Group B can only be programmed for modes 0 or 1.

Example 8.8

Write the 80x86 initialization routine required to program the 8255A in Figure 8.12 for mode 0, with port A an output and ports B and C inputs.

Solution

Referring to Figure 8.13, the control word is formed as:

$$1\ 00\ 0\ 1\ 0\ 1\ 1 = 8BH$$

The program is very simple:

```
MOV   AL,8BH     ;Control byte to AL
OUT   0CH,AL     ;Write to control port
```

Figure 8.13   Two types of 8255A control bytes. (a) When bit 7 = 0, a bit set/reset operation is indicated; (b) When bit 7 = 1, any of the modes 0, 1, or 2 can be programmed. (From J. Uffenbeck, *Microcomputers and Microprocessors: The 8080, 8085 and Z 80,* Prentice Hall, Englewood Cliffs, N.J., 1991)

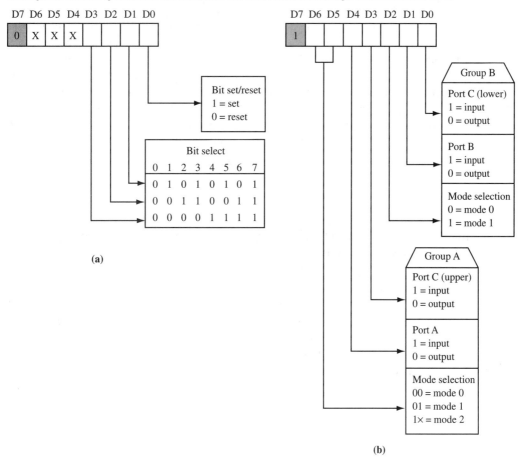

(a)

(b)

   One of the most powerful features of the 8255A is that only one control byte is required to program the mode selection—this is true no matter how complex the configuration may be. The following example will illustrate the ease of programming and versatility of the 8255A.

Example 8.9

Write an 80x86 program to input a byte from port B of the PPI chip in Figure 8.12 and output this byte to port A of the same chip. Assume both chips have been programmed as in Example 8.8

Solution
The program requires two instructions.

```
IN    AL,04      ;Get data from port B
OUT   0,AL       ;Output the data to port A
```

Mode 0 Design Example

Interfacing a Matrix Keyboard.   When programmed for mode 0 operation, as in Example 8.8, the PPI offers three simple (nonhandshaking) I/O ports. This mode is appropriate for I/O devices that do not need special synchronizing signals to exchange data with the processor. A common example is a keyboard used for data entry: This could range from a full-size ASCII keyboard to a calculator-like keypad used to control an industrial process.

Figure 8.14 shows an example of the latter case, in which a 16-key switch matrix is to be interfaced to a microcomputer using the 8255A. In this example, port A is programmed as a mode 0 input port, while the high-order nibble of port C is programmed as an output port. Before discussing the details of this interface, three problems associated with interfacing a keyboard to a microcomputer should be mentioned.

1. *Detect* that at least one key in the matrix is closed.
2. *Debounce* the switch closure and release.
3. *Encode* the key with a particular value.

There are many approaches that can be taken to solve these problems. They range from an all-hardware solution, in which the keyboard is simply "plugged into" an available input port, to an all-software solution in which only the bare keyswitches themselves are connected to the computer. As you can see in Figure 8.14, this example will follow the latter approach.

Detecting a Keypress.   Our first problem is to be able to detect that one of the switches in the matrix is closed. This can be done by inputting the byte from PPI port A. With all switches open, the result will be FFH. Now consider outputting a 0 to PC6 and PC7, the two column lines. If one of the switches, say switch 6, is closed, the code 10111111 or BFH will be read. The following instruction sequence can be used to detect this non-FFH code:

```
MOV   AL,00XXXXXX      ;Make PC6 and PC7 low
OUT   PORT_C,AL        ;Both column lines now low
IN    AL,PORT_A        ;Scan the keyboard for a closed switch
CMP   AL,0FFH          ;Compare with all-keys-up code
JNE   KEY_DOWN         ;A nonzero result means a key is down
```

Debouncing.   Once it is known that a key has been pressed, it must be debounced, because the contacts of all mechanical switches will bounce open and closed for several milliseconds after first being depressed or released. If you are not careful, the computer will process the first contact closure and return in time to pick up several of the bounces. In most cases this will result in erroneous operation of the control function.

Debouncing can be handled in software by inserting *time delays* of sufficient length to ensure that the switch contacts are stable. This will have to be done when the switch is first detected closed, and also when the switch returns open.

Encoding.   The final problem of encoding the key with a particular value is solved by setting up a *data table* of desired keyboard values. The "raw" code read from the keyboard is then used as an *index* into this table to extract that key's value. This is a particularly elegant solution because it allows the key values (or functions) to be changed to suit the application.

Figure 8.14 Interfacing a 16-key switch matrix to the 8255A (assumed interfaced to the 386/486 circuit shown in Figure 8.12). Port A is programmed as a mode 0 input port and port C (upper) as a mode 0 output port.

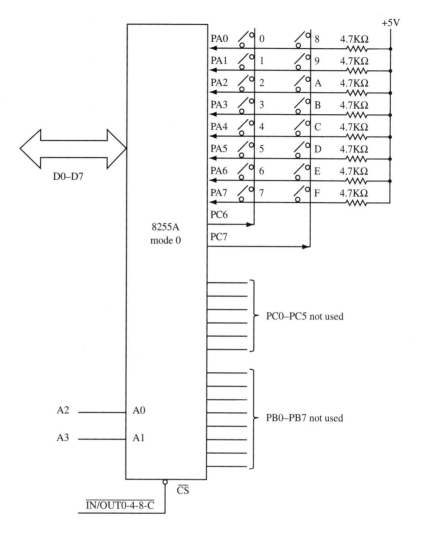

PPI Initialization. Studying Figure 8.14, we see that the PPI's port A must be programmed as an input, and the upper bits of port C as an output. The remaining ports are "don't cares". Referring to Figure 8.13, the control byte is formed as:

$$1\ 00\ 1\ 00\ X\ X$$

Choosing the Xs to be 0, the code is 90H. The PPI is then programmed with the sequence:[8]

```
MOV   AL, 90H     ;Control byte to AL
OUT   0CH,AL      ;Write to control port
```

Program Flowchart. Figure 8.15 flowcharts the entire process of detecting, debouncing, and encoding. Notice that we begin by ensuring the keyboard is clear (all keys up). This

---

[8]In the keyboard controller program to follow we assume this initialization has been performed.

Figure 8.15   Flowchart of the process required to detect a key closure, debounce the key, and encode with a value between 0 and F.

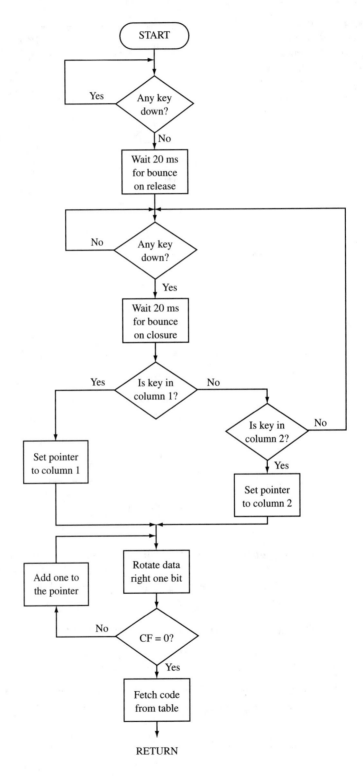

is done to prevent the computer from processing the same key over and over due to the operator holding the key down longer than it takes the program to process that key.

To encode the key with a value, its particular column must be found. This is done by first testing column 1 (PC6 = 0, PC7 = 1). An input of FFH means the key must be in column 2.

After setting a pointer into the key-value data table, the contents of AL can be rotated right, the table pointer incremented, and CF tested. When CF = 0, the pointer will have located the key's value in the table. This code can then be fetched to register AL.

Program Listing.   Figure 8.16 is the 80x86 assembly language listing for the keyboard problem (written as a procedure). It begins with a title block that explains the program function and then identifies the expected inputs and outputs, procedures called, and registers modified.

A KEY_CODE data segment is used to store the hexadecimal values to be assigned to the keys. The labels COL1 and COL2 identify the beginning of the column one and column two code values, respectively.

Equates are used to make the program more readable. In addition, if the I/O port assignments change, it will be a simple matter to change the I/O address equates.

The time delay for the debounce routine is created in software via the DELAY procedure. The LOOP SELF instruction will loop back to itself CX times. The time delay thus generated will depend on the processor and the bus clock frequency: For example, with a 486 processor, seven T states are required to execute the LOOP instruction. At 25 MHz, this is 280 ns (7 × 1/25 MHz). To achieve a 10 ms time delay, 10 ms/280 ns = 35,714 (8B82H) loops will be required.[9]

The main program is written as a procedure so that other programs need only call this routine to read the keyboard. The calling program can then process the key value as desired.

Bit Set/Reset

When bit 7 of the 8255A control byte is a 0, a *bit set/reset* operation will be performed. In this mode any one bit of port C can be set to a logic 1 or reset to a logic 0. Note that only one bit can be set or reset at a time.

One of the advantages of this mode is that individual bits of port C can be changed without changing any of the others. This is important when port C is used to control the ON/OFF status of several external devices. The device connected to PC4, for example, can be turned ON without affecting the status of the devices connected to the other seven outputs.

The bit set/reset mode also lends itself to easy generation of *strobe* pulses. Consider the following instruction sequence:

```
MOV   AL,000001001   ;Bit set control byte (PC4=1)
OUT   CTRL_PORT,AL    ;Write to control port
DEC   AL             ;Change control byte to bit reset mode (PC4=0)
OUT   CTRL_PORT,AL    ;Write to control port
```

---

[9]Calculating exact instruction execution times is difficult. Some experimentation with the time delay parameter in this routine may be required.

Figure 8.16 Program listing for the keyboard interface in Figure 8.13 corresponding to the flowchart in Figure 8.14.

```
                    ;Function:   Scan the keyboard shown in Fig. 8.14
                    ;            and return with the encoded key
                    ;            value in register AL.
                    ;Inputs:     none
                    ;Outputs:    hex key value in AL.
                    ;Calls:      10 ms delay procedure for debouncing
                    ;Destroys:   AX and flags

                    ;********
                    ; Set up segment to store key values
                    ;********

0000                KEY_CODE    SEGMENT BYTE
0000 00 01 02 03 04 COL1        DB      0,1,2,3,4
0005 05 06 07                   DB      5,6,7
0008 08 09 0A 0B 0C COL2        DB      8,9,0AH,0BH,0CH
000D 0D 0E 0F                   DB      0DH,0EH,0FH
0010                KEY_CODE    ENDS

0000                CODE        SEGMENT BYTE
                                ASSUME  CS:CODE,DS:KEY_CODE

                    ;********
                    ;Program equates
                    ;********

= 00F0              PORT_A       EQU    00H         ;PPI port A address (see Fig. 8.12)
= 00F2              PORT_C       EQU    08H         ;PPI port C address
= 00BF              COL_1_LOW    EQU    10111111B   ;PC6 low
= 007F              COL_2_LOW    EQU    01111111B   ;PC7 low
= 003F              BOTH_COL_LOW EQU    00111111B   ;PC6 and PC7 low
= 00FF              KEY_UP       EQU    0FFH        ;Input 0FFH when no keys are down
= 16FA              T1           EQU    8B82H       ;~ 10 ms time delay assuming 25 MHz 80486
```

Figure 8.16 (continued)

```
                                ;********
                                ;   10 ms time delay for debouncing
                                ;********

0000                            DELAY       PROC    NEAR
0000    B9 8B82                             MOV     CX,T1
0003    E2 FE                   COUNT:      LOOP    COUNT
0005    C3                                  RET
0006                            DELAY       ENDP


                                ;********
                                ;  Main program begins here
                                ;********

0006                            KEYBOARD    PROC    NEAR
0006    1E                                  PUSH    DS              ;Save registers about to be used
0007    51                                  PUSH    CX
0008    56                                  PUSH    SI
0009    B8 ---- R                           MOV     AX,KEY_CODE     ;Point DS to the key codes
000C    8E D8                               MOV     DS,AX

                                ;Wait for previous key to be released

000E    B0 3F                               MOV     AL,BOTH_COL_LOW ;Scan both columns
0010    E6 08                               OUT     PORT_C,AL       ;Column lines on PC6 and PC7
0012    E4 00                   POLL1:      IN      AL,PORT_A       ;Read keyboard
0014    3C FF                               CMP     AL,KEY_UP       ;All keys up?
0016    75 FA                               JNE     POLL1           ;No - so wait
0018    E8 0000 R                           CALL    DELAY           ;Yes - wait for bounce on release

                                ;Wait for a new key to be pressed

001B    E4 00                   POLL2:      IN      AL,PORT_A       ;Read keyboard
001D    3C FF                               CMP     AL,KEY_UP       ;Any keys down?
001F    74 FA                               JE      POLL2           ;No - so wait
0021    E8 0000 R                           CALL    DELAY           ;Yes - wait for bounce
```

(Continued on next page)

Figure 8.16 *(continued)*

```
                    ;See if the key is in column 1

0024  B0 BF                     MOV    AL,COL_1_LOW     ;Test for column 1
0026  E6 08                     OUT    PORT_C,AL        ;PC6 low
0028  E4 00                     IN     AL,PORT_A        ;Read column 1 keys
002A  3C FF                     CMP    AL,KEY_UP        ;Any key down?
002C  74 07                     JE     CHECK_COL_2      ;No - check for column 2
002E  8D 36 0000 R              LEA    SI,COL1          ;Yes - point SI at the key values 0-7
0032  EB 0F 90                  JMP    LOOKUP           ;Now lookup code

                    ; If not column 1 then column 2

0035  B0 7F         CHECK_COL_2:  MOV  AL,COL_2_LOW     ;Test for column 2
0037  E6 08                     OUT    PORT_C,AL        ;PC7 low
0039  E4 00                     IN     AL,PORT_A        ;Read column 2 keys
003B  3C FF                     CMP    AL,KEY_UP        ;Any key down?
003D  74 DC                     JE     POLL2            ;No - false input so repeat
003F  8D 36 0008 R              LEA    SI,COL2          ;Yes - point SI at key values 8-F

                    ;Now lookup the key's value and store in AL

0043  D0 D8         LOOKUP:     RCR    AL,1             ;Rotate keyboard input code right
0045  73 03                     JNC    MATCH            ;If 0 key is found - so retrieve it
0047  46                        INC    SI               ;No - advance pointer to next value
0048  EB F9                     JMP    LOOKUP           ;Repeat the loop

004A  8A 04         MATCH:      MOV    AL,[SI]          ;Get the key code
004C  5E                        POP    SI               ;Restore all registers
004D  59                        POP    CX               ; (except AX and flags)
004E  1F                        POP    DS
004F  C3                        RET
0050          KEYBOARD   ENDP
0050          CODE       ENDS
                         END
```

Port Assignments in the PC/XT

In the PC/XT computer, the 8255A was used to read the system configuration settings, input the keyboard scan code, and provide various control functions. Table 8.5 summarizes the port assignments. Note that the four ports of the 8255A are mapped to I/O addresses 60–63H.

Depending on the state of bit 7 of port B, port A can be used to read the system configuration (set on a DIP switch) or the keyboard scan code. For example, to test if the coprocessor chip is installed, the following instructions are required:

```
IN     AL,61H    ;Get status of port B control bits
AND    AL,7FH    ;Reset bit 7 without changing the other bits
OUT    AL,61     ;Port A now set to read system board switch
IN     AL,60H    ;Get configuration information
TEST   AL,02H    ;Test coprocessor bit
JZ     NO        ;If zero then not installed
JMP    YES       ;Else it is installed
```

Port B is the only output port and is used to control the keyboard, to enable parity checking of memory, and to enable the timer and speaker. The original PC came with a cassette recorder interface, and bit 3 of port B was used to turn the motor on and off.

Port C is another input port. It returns parity error information, the timer output signal, and the cassette data signal. Depending on the state of PB2, the port was also used to read the size of memory in 32K blocks.

Most of these port assignments have become obsolete in newer computers. Configuration information, for example, is now stored in CMOS RAM; the addresses assigned to the 8255A are now given to the keyboard controller. Some assignments remain: Port A, for example, can still be read to obtain the keyboard scan codes, and bits 0 and 1 of port B are still used to control the timer and speaker.

Electrical Characteristics of the Ports

Two versions of the 8255A are available: the 8255A-5 and the 82C55. The former part has an access time of 200 ns, and the latter 125 ns. Both parts are thus woefully slow compared to today's processors and will require several wait states. Keep in mind, however, that the *functionality* of the 8255A can be designed into the system board chipset with a corresponding increase in operating frequency.

The I/O ports of the 8255A–5 have an I_{OL} specification of 1.7 mA and an I_{OH} specification of 200μA. This means they can drive one standard TTL load or four LSTTL loads. The 82C55 is somewhat better, with high- and low-level currents rated at 2.5 mA. Note that the outputs *cannot* sink the typical 10–20 mA current required to light an LED—a buffer will be required for such loads.

Self-Review 8.3 (Answers on page 382)

8.3.1   The 8255A provides a total of _____ pins that can be programmed as inputs or outputs.

8.3.2   In Figure 8.12, if IC2b is enabled with $\overline{BE2}$ instead of $\overline{BE0}$, what I/O address will the 8255A control port be mapped to?

8.3.3   Assuming the interface in Figure 8.12, write an 80x86 program that programs the 8255A for mode 0 with port A an input, port B an output, PC4–7 as inputs, and PC0–3 as outputs.

Table 8.5 8255 Port Assignments in the PC/XT

Bit	7	6	5	4	3	2	1	0
60H	F1	F0	V1	V0	M1	M0	CO	T
	Port A (if PB7 = 0) — Input							

- *F1 F0:* Number of installed floppy drives
  00 = 1, 01 = 2, 10 = 3, 11 = 4
- *V1 V0:* Primary video adapter
  00 = EGA, VGA 01 = CGA 40 characters/line
  10 = CGA 80 characters/line 11 = monochrome
- *M1 M0:* System board memory (640K board)
  00 = 256K, 01 = 512K, 10 = 576K, 11 = 640K
- *CO:* Coprocessor 0 = not installed, 1 = installed
- *T:* Self test

Bit	7	6	5	4	3	2	1	0
60H	KP			— Scan Code —				
	Port A (if PB7 = 1) — Input							

- *KP:* 0 = key not pressed, 1 = key pressed

Bit	7	6	5	4	3	2	1	0
61H	PA	KBC	NME	NMI	PE/MTR	MTR	SB2	TM1	TM2
	Port B — Output							

- *PA:* Port A control 0 = configuration, 1 = keyboard
- *KBC:* Keyboard clock enable/disable (1/0)
- *NME:* NMI error enable on adapter card enable/disable (1/0)
- *NMI:* Main memory parity check enabled/disabled (1/0)
- *MTR:* Cassette motor on/off (0/1)
- *SB2:* Port C control
- *TM1:* Timer drives cassette/speaker (0/1)
- *TM2:* Timer enable/disable (1/0)

Bit	7	6	5	4	3	2	1	0
62H	PE1	PE2	TMR	CAS	MM5	MM4	MM3	MM2
	Port C (if PB2 = 0) — Input							

- *PE1:* Main memory parity error/no error (1/0)
- *PE2:* Adapter card parity error/no error (1/0)
- *TMR:* Output signal from timer
- *CAS:* Output signal from cassette
- *MM5-2:* See below

Bit	7	6	5	4	3	2	1	0
62H	— As above —				— reserved —			MM6
	Port C (if PB2 = 1) — Input							

- *MM6-2:* Size of main memory above 64K in 32K blocks
  00000 = 0K
  00001 = 32K
  00010 = 64K

8.3.4   In the 8255A keyboard interface shown in Figure 8.14, if PC6 is low and the data read from port A is EFH, which key is being pressed?

8.3.5   Using the 8255A's bit set/reset mode, what is the command byte to set bit 5 of port C without changing any of the other bits?

Chapter 8 Self-Test

1. Using *indirect* I/O, the 80x86 processors can access up to _____ different I/O ports.
2. When M/$\overline{\text{IO}}$ is low and W/$\overline{\text{R}}$ is high, what type of bus cycle is occurring?
   (a) memory read   (b) I/O read   (c) memory write   (d) I/O write
3. Give two different input instructions that can be used to input the byte (only) at input port 0 in Figure 8.2.
4. When used for memory-mapped I/O, the instruction MOV CL,[SI] (a) *inputs* (b) *outputs* the (a) *byte* (b) *word* (c) *doubleword* from the port whose address is stored in (a) *SI* (b) *the contents of memory pointed to by SI.*
5. In the polling routine shown below, the BUSY/READY status bit is _____ when the printer is busy, and is input as bit _____ of port _____.

```
POLL:   IN      AL,5
        TEST    AL,01000000B
        JZ      POLL
```

6. In the Centronics standard parallel printer interface, when the $\overline{\text{STROBE}}$ signal becomes active, the BUSY signal goes _____.
7. The instruction sequence shown below produces an active-_____ strobe pulse on bit _____ of port _____. Assume the routine is called repeatedly.

```
MOV     DX,800H
MOV     AL,80H
OUT     DX,AL
MOV     AL,0
OUT     DX,AL
```

8. *(True/False)* In the printer control program of Figure 8.10, the data to be printed is stored in the PRINT_DATA segment.
9. Determine the 8255A mode 0 control byte required to program port A as an output, port B as an output, PC4–7 as outputs, and PC0–3 as inputs.
10. A single 8255A PPI chip occupies _____ I/O port addresses. When interfaced to a 486 processor's D0–D7 data bus lines with base I/O address of 10H, the addresses of the remaining ports are _____, _____, and _____.
11. When the 8255A is operated in bit set/reset mode, the command byte 01H (a) *sets* (b) *resets* bit _____ of port C.
12. List the three tasks that must be accomplished when interfacing a keyboard to a computer.

Analysis and Design Questions

Section 8.1

8.1   Complete the following table, indicating the logic level (1 or 0) on each signal for the I/O instructions listed (a–d).

	A19–A2	$M/\overline{IO}$	$W/\overline{R}$	$\overline{BE3}$	$\overline{BE2}$	$\overline{BE1}$	$\overline{BE0}$	Instruction
(a)								IN AX,0
(b)								IN AL,3
(c)								OUT 0,EAX
(d)								OUT 2,AL

8.2 Design an 80486 8-bit input and output port both mapped to port FFFCH. Write a program to read data from the input port and output this data to the output port.

8.3 Modify the output port in Figure 8.4 to become a 32-bit port spanning the ports 0–3.

8.4 The following questions refer to the I/O port shown in Figure 8.17.
  (a) Is this port I/O or memory mapped?
  (b) What is the size of the port (8, 16, or 32 bits)?
  (c) Is this an input or output port?
  (d) What range of addresses will the port respond to? How many ports are in this range?
  (e) Give an example of an instruction that can be used to access this port.

Section 8.2

8.5 Refer to the printer control program in Figure 8.10. Assume bytes 0–5 of the Print_Data segment store 00 30 00 02 10 E0, and answer the following questions about this program:
  (a) How many bytes will the program output to the printer?
  (b) Which instruction is used to fetch these bytes from memory?
  (c) Which instruction outputs these bytes to the printer?
  (d) What is the *segment* address of the memory location where these bytes are stored?
  (e) What is the *offset* address of the memory location where these bytes are stored?

8.6 The bit assignments for an industrial control system are shown in the table below. Write a polling routine that tests each assigned bit and, if active, transfers control to a routine with the same bit name. For example, if $\overline{AH0}$ is low, transfer control to a routine name AH0. Write your routine so that the highest numbered bits are given priority (that is, tested first).

Figure 8.17 Figure for Analysis and Design Question 8.4.

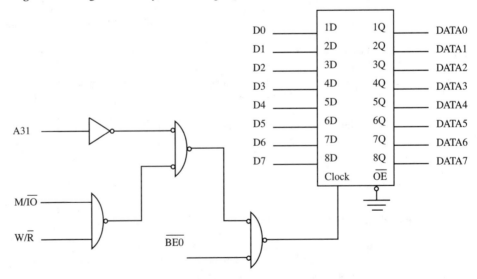

Figure 8.18 Figure for Analysis and Design Question 8.9.

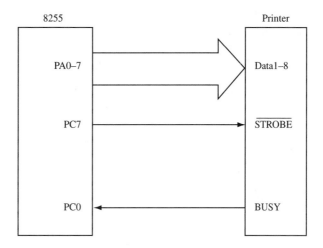

x indicates that that bit is unassigned. Assume the port address is E000H. Be sure to add meaningful comments to each program line.

	Status Port Bit Assignments							
Bit number	7	6	5	4	3	2	1	0
Bit function	x	$\overline{\text{SPL}}$	x	NPL	x	AH2	$\overline{\text{AH1}}$	$\overline{\text{AH0}}$

8.7 Using the bit and port assignments in Problem 8.6, write a polling program that transfers control to location READY if NPL is inactive *and* AH2 *or* $\overline{\text{AH0}}$ is active. If the condition is not met, continue to poll. Be sure to add meaningful comments to each program line.

Section 8.3

8.8 Describe the changes required to the 8255A circuit in Figure 8.12 if the chip is to be interfaced to a Pentium processor. If the base I/O address of the interface remains 0, determine the addresses of the remaining three ports.

8.9 Figure 8.18 shows a parallel printer interface using an 8255A PPI chip. Write a printer driver procedure for this circuit that accepts a single character to be printed in register AL and then prints that character using polling. Use the *bit set/reset* mode of the 8255A to create the STROBE pulse.

8.10 Refer to the scanning keyboard software in Figure 8.16. Assuming key 6 (only) is held down, determine the contents of registers AL, SI, CX, and the carry flag as the program is about to execute the RCR AL,1 instruction in location 0043.

Self-Review Answers

8.1.1 (b) D8–D15

8.1.2 256, 0–FFH

8.1.3

W/$\overline{\text{R}}$	M/$\overline{\text{IO}}$	Cycle
0	0	$\overline{\text{IOR}}$
1	0	$\overline{\text{IOW}}$

8.1.4   device-select pulse

8.1.5   On IC2, change $\overline{\text{BE0}}$ to $\overline{\text{BE3}}$. Connect the data inputs of IC3 to D24–D31.

8.1.6   (a)

8.2.1   Synchronizing

8.2.2 $\overline{\text{STROBE}}$, BUSY, $\overline{\text{ACKNLG}}$

8.2.3   The processor spends most of its time waiting for the peripheral to be ready.

8.2.4   19 00 40 00 0C IF

8.2.5   7, 379H

8.3.1   24

8.3.2   0EH

8.3.3   ```
MOV   AL,98H
OUT   0CH,AL
```

8.3.4   4

8.3.5   0BH
```

9 Input/Output Techniques: Interrupts and DMA

The Macintosh was offered by Apple Computer Company as an alternative to the IBM PC and its clones. Utilizing icons to represent files and programs, a pointing device called a "mouse," and overlapping "windows" to hold the user's work, the Mac (as it became known) was touted for its ease of use—simply take it out of the box, plug it in, and begin using it. The Macintosh used Motorola's 68000 32-bit microprocessor and was one of the first PC's to use $3^1/2''$ floppy disks. The Mac was initially put down as a "toy" by many business users. However, one need look no further than Windows 3.1 and Windows 95 to see the ultimate vindication of the Apple Macintosh and its graphical user interface. (Photo courtesy of Smithsonian)

Outline

Objectives

After completing this chapter you should be able to:

1. Describe the sequence of events that occurs in response to an 80x86 hardware or software interrupt.
2. Identify the function of the 80x86's INTR and NMI interrupt inputs.

3. Explain how the type number of an interrupt is input by the processor during interrupt acknowledge cycles.
4. Identify the operating modes of the 8259A PIC, including fully nested, special fully nested, nonspecific rotating, specific rotating, special mask, and polling.
5. Explain how to program the initialization and operation control registers of the 8259A PIC.
6. Develop the interrupt-driven control software for a parallel printer.
7. Describe the DMA protocol used by the 80x86 processors.
8. Compare the byte, burst, and block DMA transfer modes.
9. List the advantages and disadvantages of programmed I/O, interrupt-driven I/O, and DMA.

Overview

In Chapter 8 we learned how to construct microcomputer input and output ports. We also learned how to control the transfer of data between those ports and the processor using *programmed I/O* or *polling*. In this chapter, two new I/O-control techniques are introduced. The first is *interrupts*. Interrupts are more efficient than polling because they allow the processor to perform other tasks while waiting for the I/O device to request service. The 80x86 processors support several different types of interrupts, including processor interrupts, software interrupts, and hardware interrupts. These are described in Section 9.1. Hardware interrupts are most often controlled using the 8259A *Programmable Interrupt Controller (PIC);* this chip is described in detail in Section 9.2.

Another I/O-control technique is called *Direct Memory Access* or *DMA*. In this method, the processor is temporarily disabled while the I/O device and memory transfer data directly. DMA offers very high data transfer rates but requires a special DMA controller separate from the processor. DMA is described in Section 9.3.

The chapter concludes with a brief comparison of the three I/O techniques covered in this chapter and Chapter 8.

9.1   Interrupt-Driven I/O

Introduction

In Chapter 4 we learned that the 80x86 processors receive interrupts from three different sources: (1) the processor itself, due to an internal fault (an attempt to divide by zero, for example), (2) the software interrupt instruction INT *n* (commonly used in the PC to access the BIOS and DOS functions), and (3) external hardware. I/O devices that interface to the processor using a hardware interrupt are said to be *interrupt driven*. In this section we:

- Describe the sequence of events that occurs in response to an 80x86 hardware or software interrupt.
- Identify the function of the 80x86's INTR and NMI interrupt inputs.
- Explain how the type number of an interrupt is input by the processor during interrupt acknowledge cycles.

Hardware Interrupts

A More Efficient Approach.   When interfacing a peripheral to a microprocessor, the real problem for the microprocessor is not knowing when the peripheral is ready; that is, the peripheral operates *asynchronously* with respect to the microprocessor. As we learned in Chapter 8, one way of synchronizing the computer and peripheral is to program the processor to repeatedly poll the peripheral's BUSY/READY flag. However, this has a built-in disadvantage, in that all of the resources of the processor are devoted to waiting for this flag: No other tasks can be performed. If the peripheral is ready only once every 10 ms (10,000 µs), as might be true with a parallel printer, the processor will spend most of its time waiting.

A more logical approach would be to have the peripheral *tell the processor* when it is ready. This is the purpose of the microprocessor's *interrupt* input. Using this technique, the processor can spend most of its time with other tasks, only servicing the I/O device briefly when interrupted.

Responding to Hardware Interrupts.   At the end of each instruction, the processor samples its interrupt input. If active, control is transferred to a special *interrupt service routine (ISR)*. Figure 9.1 diagrams this process. During time 1, the processor is assumed to be executing its main task. At time 2, the peripheral's READY flag causes an interrupt to occur. After finishing the current instruction at time 3, the CS, IP (or EIP), and flag registers are pushed onto the stack at time 4. Control then transfers to the ISR at time 5. During time 6, the ISR is executed, terminating with the instruction IRET (interrupt return). The CS, IP, and flag registers are recovered from the stack during time 7, and the original task is resumed at time 8.

If we assume that 100 µs are required to respond to the interrupt and supply the peripheral with data (filling its internal buffer), then in the case of the 10,000 µs per READY pulse peripheral, 9,900 µs will be available to the processor for its main task. In effect, the processor can perform two jobs at the same time.

Figure 9.1   When an interrupt occurs, normal processing is suspended while a special interrupt service routine (ISR) is executed. Normal processing resumes when this routine is completed.

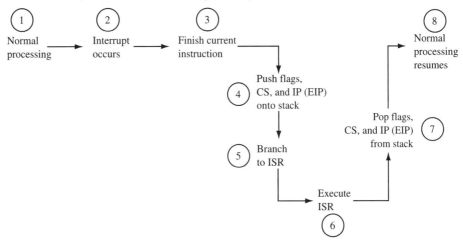

INTR and NMI.   The 80x86 processors have just two hardware interrupt pins. These are labeled INTR and NMI. NMI is a *nonmaskable interrupt,* which means it cannot be blocked—the processor must respond to it. For this reason the NMI input is usually reserved for critical system functions, for example, saving the processor state when a power failure is eminent. INTR, on the other hand, is maskable via the IF flag. Using the instruction STI—set interrupt flag—interrupts are enabled on INTR. Similarly, the instruction CLI—clear interrupt flag—disables interrupts on this input.

Figure 9.2 flowcharts the 80x86 processors' response to internal (divide by zero, for example) and external interrupts. Notice that internal interrupts have the highest *priority* (they are serviced first when multiple interrupts are received). Also notice that the processor automatically clears IF when an interrupt (internal or external) is received. This means an INTR interrupt cannot interrupt a previous service routine that has not yet completed (unless that routine specifically sets IF to allow this). When the IRET instruction is given, the flags are restored, and if IF was previously set, INTR interrupts will again be enabled.

TF is the trap flag. When set, the processor will execute a type 1 interrupt after each program instruction. Typically, this is used in debugging, as it allows the processor to be *single-stepped* one instruction at a time. As shown in Figure 9.2, this interrupt has lowest priority (it is serviced last when multiple interrupts occur).

Other Hardware Interrupts.   In addition to INTR and NMI, the 80x86 processors support several other hardware interrupt inputs. None are intended for general-purpose I/O, however, as each has a dedicated function.

1. **RESET.** This interrupt forces the processor to begin execution at a known state. Program execution resumes at address FFFF0H.
2. **INIT.** This interrupt is only available with the Pentium processors. It is similar to RESET except that the internal caches, write buffers, and floating-point registers retain their data. Program execution begins at address FFFFFFF0H.
3. **BUSCHK.** This Pentium-only signal allows the system to signal an unsuccessful bus cycle. Control then transfers to the machine check-exception address previously established.
4. **R/S.** This Pentium-only signal is designed to be used with a debugging port. When active, the processor leaves the run mode and enters an idle state in which debugging information can be gathered.
5. **FLUSH.** This signal causes the internal cache of the 486 and Pentium processors to be emptied (invalidated). Any changed lines in the data cache are first written back.

Computing the ISR Address.   In Real Mode the address of the interrupt service routine is stored in four consecutive memory locations (a doubleword) in an interrupt vector table beginning at address 00000H.[1] (This table was introduced previously as Figure 4.15.) When an interrupt occurs, an 8-bit type number is supplied to the processor, which identifies the appropriate entry in this table. The method for determining the type number depends on the interrupt source. Software interrupts supply the type number as part of the instruction (INT *n,* where *n* is the type number). Internal interrupts have

---

[1]In Protected Mode the interrupt vectors use 32-bit addressing, and 8 bytes are thus required to store the segment and offset address. The 8-byte vectors are stored in a special interrupt descriptor table.

Figure 9.2 80x86 interrupt processing sequence. Internal interrupts are processed first, followed by NMI and INTR (if IF is set). If TF (the trap flag) is set, the processor operates in a single-step mode, branching to the single-step service routine between each instruction. (Courtesy of Intel Corporation)

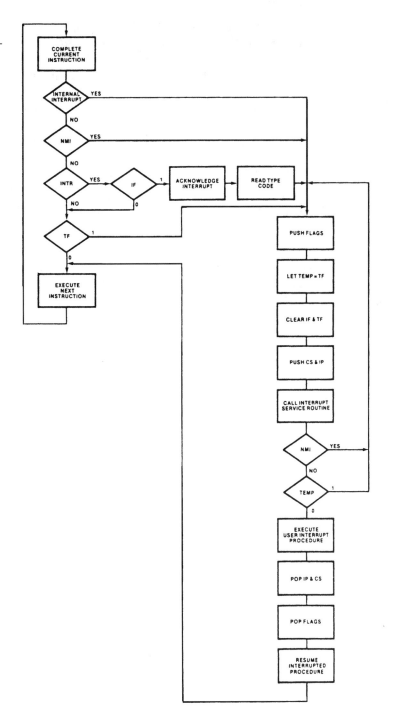

predefined type numbers: For example, a divide-by-zero error causes a type 0 interrupt, a general-protection fault initiates a type 0D interrupt. (Refer to Table 4.5 on page 160 for a complete list.)

As shown in Table 4.5, the NMI hardware interrupt is predefined as type 2 and extracts its vector from locations 00008–0000BH. INTR, however, must gate its type number onto data bus lines D0–D7 during a special interrupt acknowledge cycle. The timing for this cycle and the hardware required to read the type number are explained in the next section.

The address where the vector is to be stored is computed by the processor by multiplying the type number by four (or by eight in Protected Mode). The resulting number is then used as a pointer to one of the 256 possible interrupt vectors.

Example 9.1

A particular Real Mode interrupt has a type number $n = 41H$. If the corresponding ISR begins at address 09E3:0010H, determine the locations in the vector table to store this address.

Solution
The vector address is calculated by multiplying 41H by four. This is done most easily by rotating 41H left twice. 41H = 0100 0001; rotate left twice –> 01 0000 0100 = 104H. The offset address of the ISR is stored in the low-word location and the segment address in the high-word location. This is shown below.

00107	09
00106	E3
00105	00
00104	10

Hardware Interrupt Timing

INTR and NMI. The 80x86 processors sample the INTR and NMI inputs at the end of each currently executing instruction. The NMI input is *rising-edge-triggered* and internally synchronized. The INTR input is *level-triggered* and must be held high until acknowledged by the processor. The 8086 and 8088 provide the $\overline{INTA}$ signal for this purpose; the 386 and later processors provide a unique bus cycle that can be decoded for this purpose. The NMI input (and all internal interrupts) are not acknowledged.

Interrupt Acknowledge Cycles. Regardless of the processor, when the INTR interrupt is accepted, two interrupt acknowledge cycles are executed (two $\overline{INTA}$ pulses), separated by four idle clock pulses (to allow for 8259A programmable interrupt controller recovery time). The first cycle acknowledges the interrupt request and alerts the external hardware to prepare to gate the type number onto the data bus lines. During the second cycle, the processor inputs the contents of its D0–D7 data lines, which it interprets as one of the 256 possible type numbers.

Figure 9.3 (a) Latching an interrupt request (for example, the ACKNOWLEDGE pulse from a printer). (b) Gating the type number onto the low-order data bus lines with the second pulse.

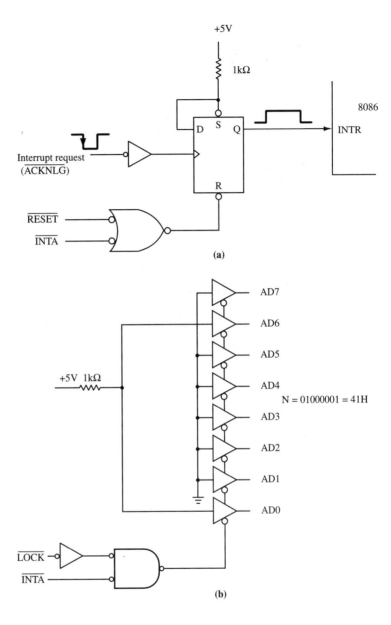

Figure 9.3(a) shows a circuit that can be used to drive the INTR input of the 8086.[2] In this case the peripheral is assumed to supply a falling edge to indicate that it is ready for more data. This signal clocks the flip-flop, driving INTR high. The first $\overline{\text{INTA}}$ pulse resets Q, removing INTR before it can be interpreted as a second interrupt request. The $\overline{\text{RESET}}$ input ensures that INTR will be low after the system is reset.

[2]A similar circuit can be designed for the 386 and above processors by decoding the address and bus enable signals. No $\overline{\text{INTA}}$ signal is provided by these processors.

Figure 9.3(b) illustrates a technique for gating the type number onto the low data bus lines. The $\overline{LOCK}$ signal is combined with $\overline{INTA}$ to enable the tristate gates during the second $\overline{INTA}$ pulse, when the processor expects the type number.[3] In this example, the gates are wired to input $n = 41H$.

The 8259A.   The circuits in Figure 9.3 limit the 80x86 processors to one (maskable) hardware interrupt. This will be inadequate in all but the simplest of systems. For this reason, Intel has developed the 8259A Programmable Interrupt Controller (PIC).

The PIC is a very flexible peripheral controller chip programmed via software commands from the 80x86. It accepts eight interrupt inputs (expandable to 64), each of which can be masked. Various priority schemes can also be programmed. When an interrupt occurs, the PIC determines the highest priority request, activates the 80x86 via its INTR input, and gates the type number onto the data bus during the $\overline{INTA}$ bus cycle. The PIC is discussed in detail in the next section.

Self-Review 9.1 (Answers on page 427)

9.1.1   Why is interrupt-driven I/O more efficient than polling?

9.1.2   An 80x86 processor stores the bytes 3A 49 2F 1C beginning at address 0008CH. What interrupt type number does this address correspond to? What is the address of the ISR?

9.1.3   The 80x86 processors have two general-purpose hardware interrupt inputs, labeled _____ and _____.

9.1.4   Which registers are saved by an 80x86 processor when an interrupt occurs?

9.1.5   What is the purpose of the interrupt acknowledge bus cycle? Which interrupt types will cause this cycle to occur?

9.2   The 8259A PIC

Introduction

In the preceding section we learned that controlling the peripheral devices of a computer using interrupts is more efficient than using programmed I/O (polling). However, because all general-purpose 80x86 interrupt requests must be channeled through the processor's single INTR input, some means of managing the interrupt requests is desirable. This is the purpose of the 8259A Programmable Interrupt Controller (PIC). It is designed specifically to support the 80x86 processors. Originally included as a separate IC on the system board, today's computers include the functionality of the PIC in their chipsets.[4] In fact, most chipsets incorporate the equivalent of *two* 8259A chips. In this section we will:

- Identify the operating modes of the 8259A PIC, including fully nested, special fully nested, nonspecific rotating, specific rotating, special mask, and polling.
- Explain how to program the initialization and operation control registers of the 8259A PIC.
- Develop the interrupt-driven control software for a parallel printer.

---

[3]The $\overline{LOCK}$ signal ordinarily goes active to tell system bus masters that access to the bus is denied at this time. During 8086 $\overline{INTA}$ cycles, $\overline{LOCK}$ is low during the first $\overline{INTA}$ cycle and high during the last (when the type number is expected by the processor).

[4]The Pentium Pro processor includes the functionality of the 8259A onboard via the Advanced Programmable Interrupt Controller (APIC).

Figure 9.4 Block diagam and pin definitions for the 8259A Programmable Interrupt Controller (PIC). (Courtesy of Intel Corporation.)

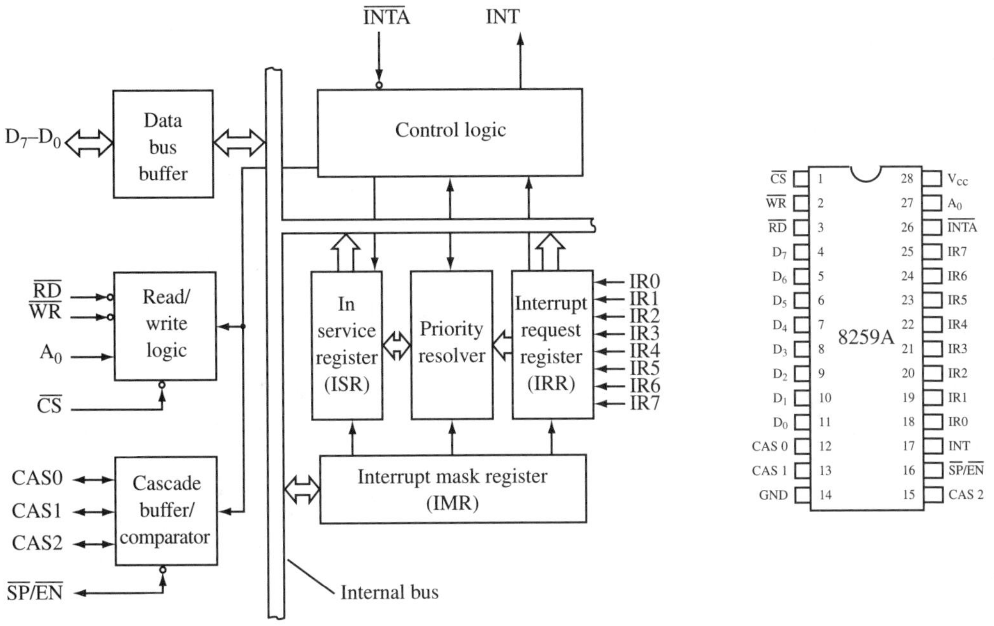

Overview

Hardware Interface. Figure 9.4 provides a block diagram of the 8259A and includes the pin number descriptions (for the discrete version of the part). Like the 8255A, the PIC is programmed via an 8-bit bidirectional data bus. To the 80x86 processors, the PIC appears to be two memory- or I/O-mapped 8-bit ports selected by the (PIC's) A0 input. The direction of data flow, to or from the PIC, is controlled by the $\overline{RD}$ and $\overline{WR}$ inputs. The output of an address decoder should be used to enable the PIC via its $\overline{CS}$ (chip select) input.

The CAS0–2 input/outputs are used when several PICs are wired together in cascade mode. This will be explained later. The $\overline{SP/EN}$ signal is a dual-function pin. When operated in Buffered Mode, it functions as an output intended to enable the system data bus buffers when the type number is being input from the PIC. When used as an input, it is used to designate a slave ($\overline{SP/EN}$ = 0) or master ($\overline{SP/EN}$ = 1) PIC.

Interrupt requests are output on INT (normally connected to the processor's $\overline{INTR}$ input). The interrupt acknowledge signal from the processor is received via the INTA input. Finally, the IR0–IR7 inputs allow eight separate interrupt requests to be input and controlled by the PIC.

Example 9.2

Determine the I/O port addresses occupied by the PIC-386/486 interface shown in Figure 9.5.

Solution

The output of address decoder IC1 will be active for inputs in the range A15–A3 = 0000 0000 0000 0XXX = 0000–0007H. By qualifying this signal with $\overline{BE0}$ via IC2a, the $\overline{CS}$ signal $\overline{SEL0,4}$ is

Figure 9.5   Interfacing the PIC to the 386 and 486 processors. Two I/O ports are required.

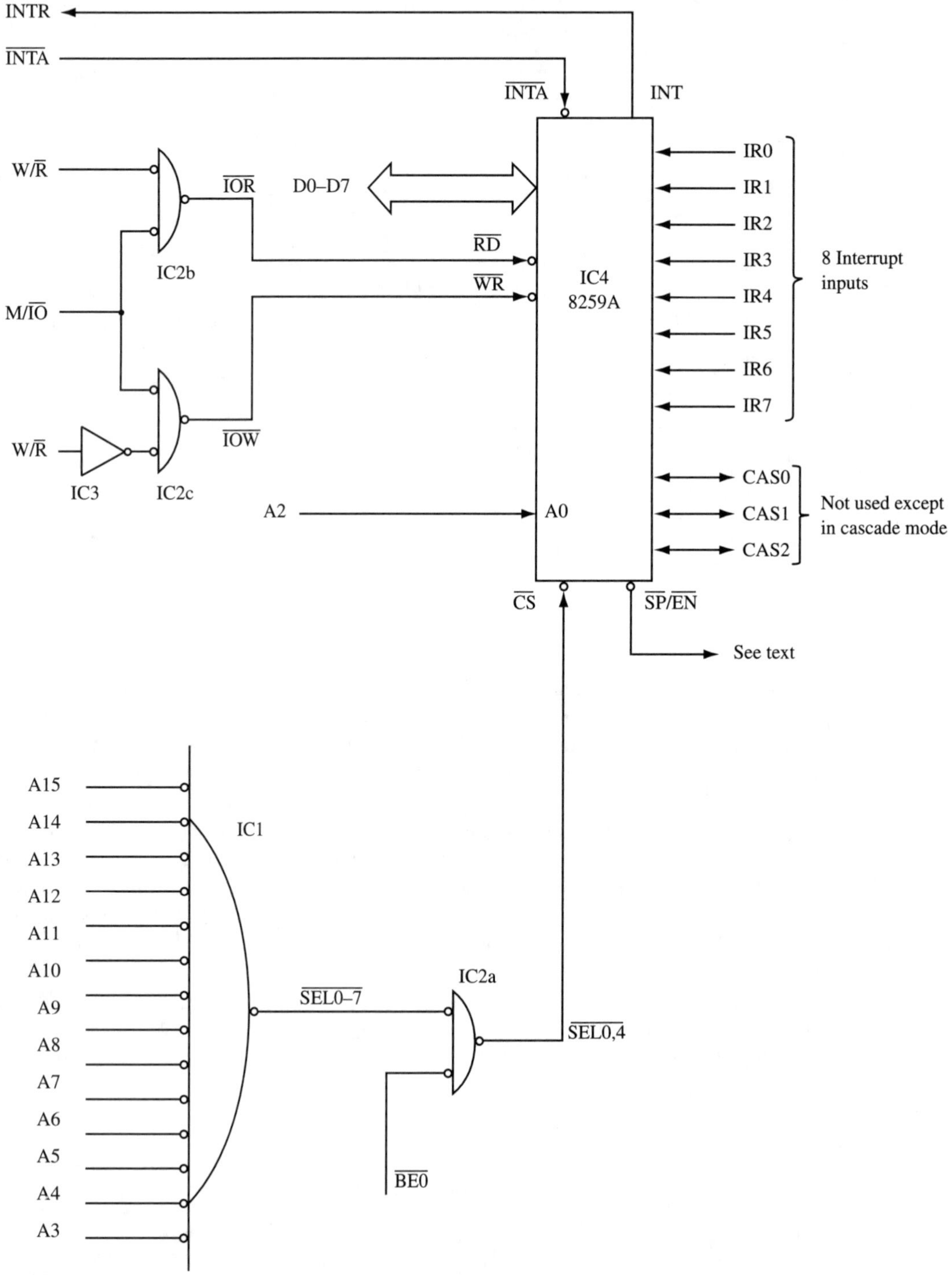

produced. This signal will be active when the I/O address is 0 or 4, and these are the two port addresses occupied by this interface. When A2 is low, port 0 will be accessed; when this line is high, port 4 will be accessed.

PC Port Assignments.   In the PC, the PIC is mapped to I/O ports 20H and 21H. As explained later in this section, AT-class computers add a second PIC (called the *slave*) and this chip is mapped to ports A0H and A1H.[5]

Basic Operation.   Before the PIC can be used, the interrupt *type* numbers must be programmed. In addition, the operating mode and priority scheme must be selected. These software codes are written via the 8-bit bidirectional data bus lines.

Once initialized, the PIC responds to interrupt requests on IR0 through IR7. For example, if an interrupt request occurs that is of a higher priority than that currently being serviced (if any), the PIC drives its INT output high. Assuming IF (the processor's interrupts enabled flag) is set, the processor finishes the current instruction and responds by outputting the first of two $\overline{INTA}$ pulses. This pulse freezes (stores) all interrupt requests within the PIC in a special *interrupt request register (IRR)*. The interrupt signal can now be removed.

When the second $\overline{INTA}$ pulse is received by the PIC, one bit of the *in-service (IS)* register is set (see Figure 9.4). For example, if a request on IR3 is acknowledged by the processor, the PIC will set IS3 to indicate that this input is now active. Furthermore, inputs of equal or lower priority will be inhibited.

The PIC then outputs a *type number* corresponding to the active IR input. This number is multiplied by four within the processor and then used as a pointer into the interrupt vector table located at address 00000 through 003FFH. Thus, if the PIC outputs a type number of A0H (1010 0000), the processor will retrieve the vector stored in 00280H–00283H (10 1000 00XX).[6]

Before transferring control to the vector address, the processor pushes CS, IP, and the flag register onto the stack. The interrupt service routine (ISR) then executes. Upon completion, the ISR must issue a special *end-of-interrupt (EOI)* command to the PIC. This resets the IS register bit corresponding to the active IR input. If this bit is not reset, all interrupts of equal or lower priority will remain inhibited by the PIC.

The interrupt cycle ends when the IRET instruction is executed. This retrieves CS, IP, and the flags, and transfers control back to the interrupted program.

Cascading.   PC and XT computers use a single PIC, allowing eight different interrupt requests (IRQ0–7). When the AT was designed, a second PIC was added, increasing the number of interrupt inputs to 15. Figure 9.6 shows the circuit. One PIC is designated the

---

[5]Because the PC is based on the 8-bit 8088 microprocessor, port addresses are naturally consecutive in this computer. As we have learned, when interfacing 8-bit ports to 16-, 32-, and 64-bit processors, the port assignments are *staggered*. Using a technique called *dynamic bus sizing,* the 386 and later processors can temporarily change their data bus width to 8 bits. When this is done, I/O port addresses can be accessed consecutively (albeit, 8 bits at a time). Another approach is to interface the I/O device using a *data bus multiplexer*. Analysis and Design Problem 9.6 shows an example of this technique.

[6]In Protected Mode, the interrupt type number is multiplied by eight and the ISR address is retrieved from an interrupt descriptor table.

Figure 9.6 PCs use two PICs wired in cascade. Fifteen different interrupts are supported.

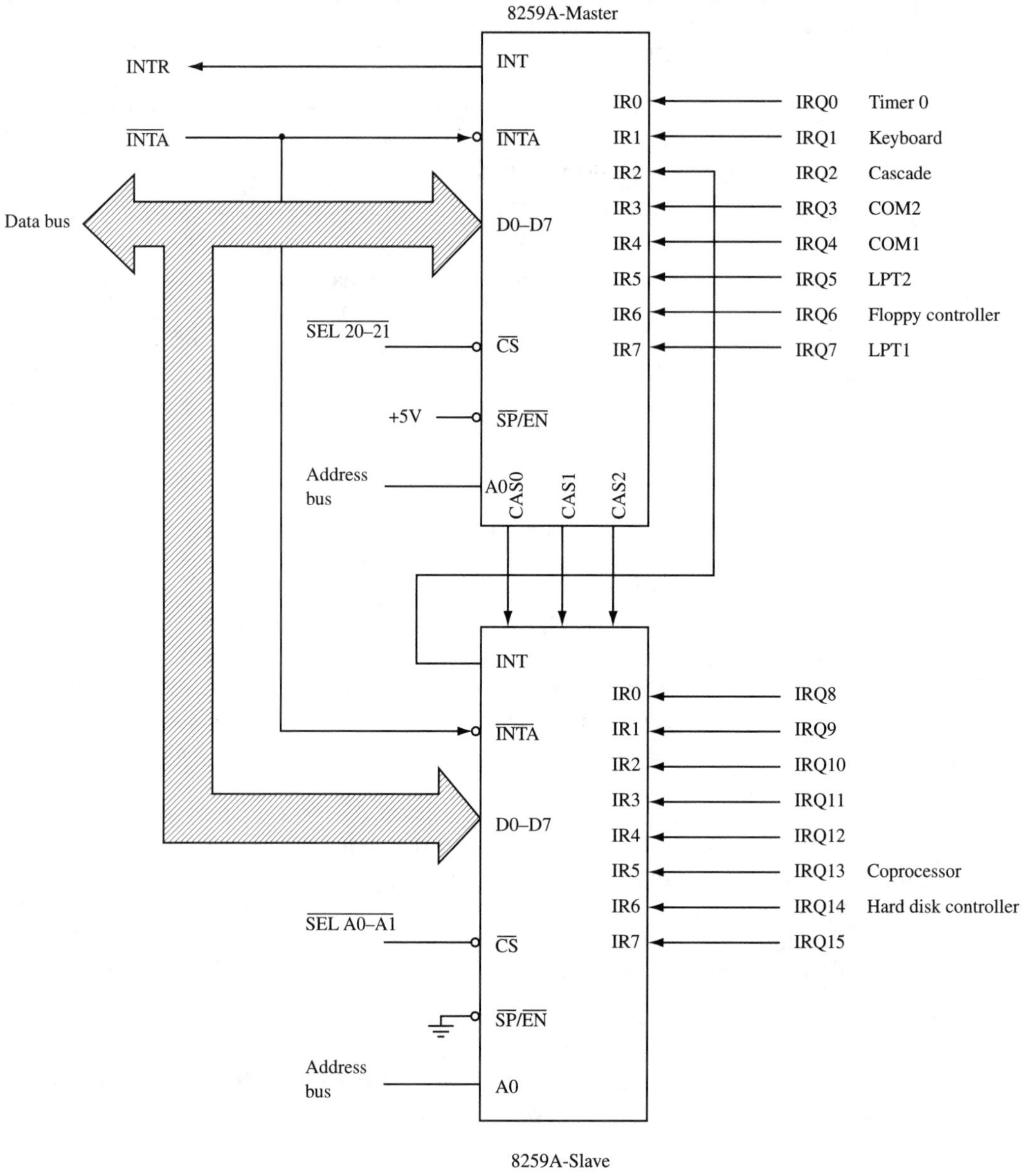
8259A-Master
INTR
INT
INTA
INTA
IR0 IRQ0 Timer 0
IR1 IRQ1 Keyboard
IR2 IRQ2 Cascade
IR3 IRQ3 COM2
IR4 IRQ4 COM1
IR5 IRQ5 LPT2
IR6 IRQ6 Floppy controller
IR7 IRQ7 LPT1
Data bus
D0–D7
SEL 20–21
CS
+5V
SP/EN
Address bus
A0
CAS0
CAS1
CAS2
INT
INTA
IR0 IRQ8
IR1 IRQ9
IR2 IRQ10
IR3 IRQ11
IR4 IRQ12
IR5 IRQ13 Coprocessor
IR6 IRQ14 Hard disk controller
IR7 IRQ15
D0–D7
SEL A0–A1
CS
SP/EN
Address bus
A0
8259A-Slave

master ($\overline{SP}/\overline{EN}$) = +5V) and the second becomes the *slave* ($\overline{SP}/\overline{EN}$ = 0V). Notice that all of the slave interrupts are input via IRQ2 of the master.[7] Although not implemented in the AT, eight different slaves can be accommodated by the master PIC, allowing as many as 64 different interrupt requests.

[7]On the PC, the interrupt inputs are named IRQ*n;* on the PIC, these inputs are called IR*n.*

Priority.   On the PC, the PIC is operated in the *fully nested* mode. This means that the *lowest numbered* IRQ input has highest priority. Interrupts of a lower priority will not be acknowledged by the PIC (and therefore not forwarded to the processor) until the higher priority interrupts have been serviced.

The PC assigns the timer interrupt on IRQ0 highest priority. Notice that because the slave PIC's INT output is connected to the IRQ2 input of the master, IRQ8–15 all have higher priority than IRQ3–7.

When an interrupt request occurs on one of the slave's IR inputs, its priority is resolved among the other inputs within the slave. If this input is enabled, the request is passed on to the master. Again, the priority is resolved—this time between IR0, IR1, and the cascaded IR2. If the former are inactive, the master requests an interrupt by forcing its INT output high.

Now, assuming processor interrupts to be enabled, the processor outputs the first $\overline{\text{INTA}}$ pulse. Upon receipt of this pulse, the master PIC outputs a *cascade address* on CAS0–CAS2—in this example 010, corresponding to IR input 2. This enables the slave PIC, causing it to output its type number onto the data bus lines during the second $\overline{\text{INTA}}$ pulse.

Notice that this interconnection scheme allows the slave to be programmed separately from the master. Indeed, each PIC can be programmed to operate in a different mode.

When the service routine completes, it issues an EOI command to the slave PIC, resetting the appropriate IS bit (corresponding to IRQ8–15). Next, the IS register of the slave should be read to ensure that another interrupt from the slave in not in progress. If this read returns zero, an EOI command can also be sent to the master. If the slave's IS register is not zero, the master IS bit should be left high until the lower priority routine completes.

The Interrupt Control Registers

The Interrupt Request Register (IRR).   All interrupt requests must pass through three registers within the PIC, as shown in Figure 9.7. The first register is IRR, the *interrupt request register.* This is a transparent latch clocked by the $\overline{\text{FREEZE}}$ signal. Bits in this register are not latched until the first $\overline{\text{INTA}}$ pulse occurs.

The Interrupt Mask Register (IMR).   Because the IRR is transparent, all requests are passed on to the *interrupt mask register (IMR).* If the corresponding mask bit is a zero, the request is routed to the *priority resolver*—a circuit designed to select the highest priority input when simultaneous requests occur, or when the request has higher priority than the routine currently executing.

The In-Service Register (IS).   If the request meets either of these two criteria, the INT output is driven high. When the processor acknowledges this request, the $\overline{\text{FREEZE}}$ signal is generated, latching the IR input. When the $\overline{\text{INTA}}$ cycle completes, the appropriate IS bit is set, indicating that the interrupt is now *in-service.* Simultaneously, all bits of IRR are cleared.

Notice that the PIC does not "remember" interrupt requests that are not acknowledged. It is up to the interrupting device to hold the request until the $\overline{\text{FREEZE}}$ signal latches it. If an interrupt is requested but no IR bit is found high during $\overline{\text{INTA}}$—that is, IR is removed before being acknowledged—the PIC will default to an IR7. For this reason, this input can be reserved for "spurious" interrupts and a single IRET instruction can be used for the IR7 service routine. If the IR7 input is used for a legitimate device, the service routine should read the IS register and test to be sure that bit 7 is high.

Figure 9.7 All interrupt requests must pass through the PIC's interrupt request register (IRR) and interrupt mask register (IMR). If put in sevice, the appropriate bit of the in-service (IS) register is set.

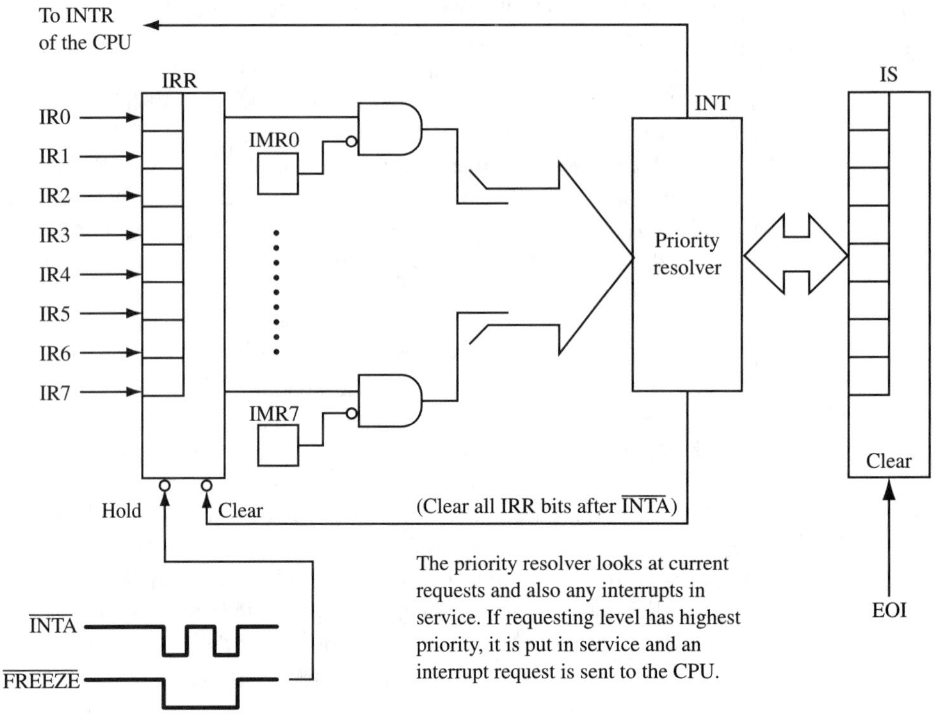

It is important to remember that the processor has ultimate control over its interrupt input via the STI (set interrupt flag) and CLI (clear interrupt flag) instructions. In fact, when servicing an interrupt, the processor automatically clears IF. Thus, it is quite possible that the PIC could receive an interrupt request of higher priority than that currently executing, but not receive an acknowledge from the processor. For this reason, an STI instruction must be explicitly placed in the ISR if the priority capabilities of the PIC are to be extended to interrupts in progress.

Operating Modes

The PIC can be programmed to operate in one of six modes. The following is a brief description of each.

1. Fully Nested. This is the default mode of the PIC and the one used by the PC. It prioritizes the IR inputs such that IR0 has highest priority and IR7 the lowest priority. This priority structure extends to interrupts currently in service, as well as simultaneous interrupt requests.

For example, if an interrupt on IR3 is being serviced (IS3 = 1) and a request occurs on IR2, the PIC will issue an interrupt request because the IR2 input has higher priority. But if an IR4 is received, the PIC will not issue the request. Note, however, that the IR2 request will not be acknowledged unless the processor has set IF within the IR3 service routine.

In all operating modes, the IS bit corresponding to the active routine must be reset to allow other lower priority interrupts to be acknowledged. This can be done by outputting a special *nonspecific EOI* instruction to the PIC. Normally, this is done just before the IRET instruction within the service routine; alternately, the PIC can be programmed to perform this nonspecific EOI automatically when the second $\overline{INTA}$ pulse occurs. Note, however, that, in the latter case, lower priority interrupts will be enabled throughout the higher priority service routine.

2. Special Fully Nested.   This mode is selected for the master PIC in a cascaded system. It is identical to the fully nested mode but extends the priority structure to the cascaded PICs. For example, if the service routine for IRQ12 in Figure 9.6 is in progress, a request from IRQ8 will be honored because it has higher priority (even though both requests use the same master IRQ2 input). In effect, the special fully nested mode allows the master PIC to accept requests on a (master) IR input that is already in service.

3. Nonspecific Rotating.   This mode is intended for systems with several interrupt sources, all of equal priority. When the EOI command is issued, the IS bit is reset and then assigned lowest priority. The priority of the other inputs rotates accordingly. Figure 9.8 illustrates the technique. Simultaneous interrupts are shown to arrive on IR4 and IR6. The IR4 routine is put in service (IS4 = 1), as it has highest priority [Figure 9.8(a)].

When the rotate on nonspecific EOI command is given by the IR4 service routine, IS4 is reset and becomes the lowest priority [Figure 9.8(b)]. Notice that this moves IR6 up to second-highest priority. A second rotate on nonspecific EOI command, given on completion of the IR6 service routine, resets IS6, leaving the IR7 input with highest priority [Figure 9.8(c)]. The rotate on nonspecific EOI mode ensures that no input will ever have to wait for more than seven devices to be serviced before being serviced itself. The rotate on nonspecific EOI command can be output within the service routine or programmed to occur automatically after the second $\overline{INTA}$ pulse occurs.

There is one caution to be observed with this mode: The EOI command always resets the *lowest numbered* IS bit. In the fully nested mode this will always correspond to the routine in service. However, in the rotating priority mode this may not always be the current in-service bit. Figure 9.9 shows an example in which an IR4 is in progress, but is interrupted by an IR6 (the IR6 is assumed to have higher priority). Issuing a nonspecific EOI command within the IR6 service routine will cause IS4 to be reset—the wrong bit.

There are two solutions to this problem. One is to select the automatic nonspecific rotating mode. This will automatically clear the IS bit as soon as the processor acknowledges the request. Two IS bits will never be set simultaneously, and thus the "wrong" bit can never be cleared. However, this also means that all other IR inputs will be enabled throughout the service routine, which may be undesirable.

The second solution is to select the *specific rotating* mode.

4. Specific Rotating.   This mode again allows the priorities to be rotated, but the EOI command can indicate the specific IS bit to reset and assign lowest priority. Figure 9.9 illustrates how this command can be used to solve the "wrong bit" problem mentioned above.

A variation of this command allows the priorities to be specified without resetting the IS bit. This allows the programmer to control the priority structure within the service routine. For example, while executing the IR4 service routine, it may be important to assign the IR7 input highest priority. The specific rotating command allows you to do this.

Figure 9.8 (a) Simultaneous interrupt requests arrive on IR4 and IR6. IR4 has highest priority and its IS bit is set as the IR4 service routine is put in service. (b) The IR4 service routine issues a rotate-on-nonspecific-EOI command, resetting IS4 and assigning it lowest priority. IR6 is now placed in service. (c) The IR6 service routine issues a rotate-on-nonspecific-EOI command, resetting IS6 and assigning it lowest priority.

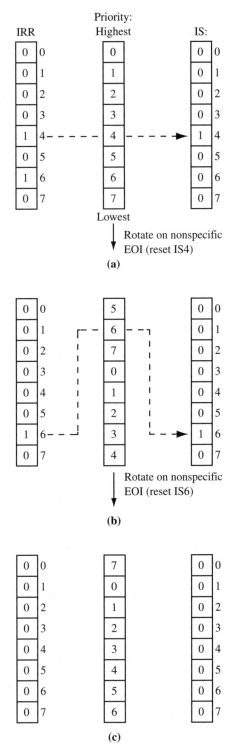

Figure 9.9   Example illustrating the difference between the rotate-on-nonspecific-EOI command and the rotate-on-specific-EOI command.

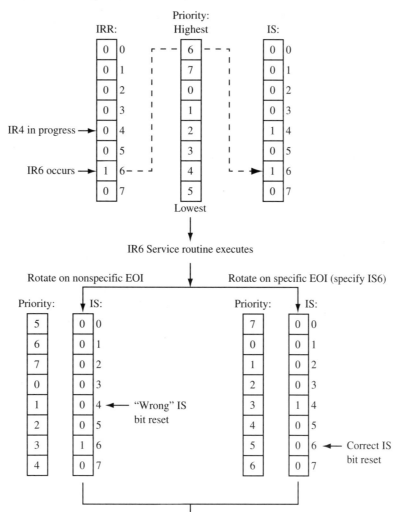

5. Special Mask.   As we have seen, the PIC normally inhibits interrupt requests of equal or lower priority than that currently in service. In the special mask mode, this is altered to allow interrupts on all inputs except the input currently in service.

6. Polling.   In this mode, the INT output of the PIC is inhibited and the device is used as a *prioritized poller*. Performing an I/O read instruction from the PIC (either port address) returns the status word shown in Figure 9.10. Typically, a polling routine is written to test bit 7 of the PIC status word. If this bit is high, bits 0 through 2 encode the highest priority device requesting service.

Figure 9.10 In the polled mode the 8259A acts as a prioritized status port.

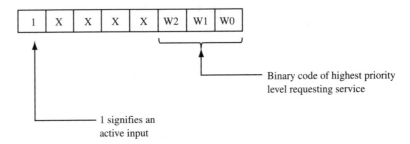

Programming the Initialization Control Registers

As you can imagine, the key to using the PIC is to perform the proper initialization sequence required for the desired operating mode. Figure 9.11 defines the format for the four initialization control words (ICWs).

ICW1. Whenever a command is issued with PIC inputs A0 = 0 and D4 =1, the result is interpreted as *Initialization Control Word 1 (ICW1)*. This byte starts the initialization sequence. As shown in Figure 9.11, bits D7–D5 and D2 are only required when used with the 8-bit 8085 microprocessor. Bit D3 specifies the IR trigger—either level- or rising-edge. Remember, however, that the input must be held until acknowledged by the processor. In addition, if you program for the level-trigger mode, you must be sure to remove the input after the acknowledge pulses occur to avoid multiple interrupt requests. Bit D1 is used to specify that the PIC is to be used in the cascade mode (requiring a subsequent ICW3). Bit D0 must be a 1 for an 80x86 processor.

As an example, the following instructions program the master 8259A in Figure 9.6 for 80x86 mode, rising-edge trigger, and a single PIC.

```
MOV    AL,00010011B      ;Edge trigger, single PIC, 80x86 mode
OUT    20H,AL            ;ICW1 (A0 = 0 and D4 = 1)
```

ICW2. ICW2 is written with A0 = 1 and specifies the five high-order bits (base number) of the interrupt type number to be output by the PIC during the bus cycle. The PIC assigns the three low-order bits 000 through 111 to correspond to the active IR input, IR0 through IR7: Thus, the base type number of the PIC must end with 000B.

Example 9.3

Determine the programming required for the master PIC in Figure 9.6 so that inputs IRQ0–7 correspond to type numbers 08–0FH. From which memory locations will the processor fetch the interrupt vectors? Assume Real Mode.

Solution

ICW2 stores the base address and thus should be programmed for 08H. Table 9.1 summarizes the type numbers output for each IRQ input and the corresponding interrupt vector locations in memory. The latter are obtained by multiplying the type number by four.[8]

---

[8]You may want to compare this table with Table 4.5, which summarizes all of the 80x86 processor interrupts.

Figure 9.11 8259A initilization control word format. (Courtesy of Intel Corporation)

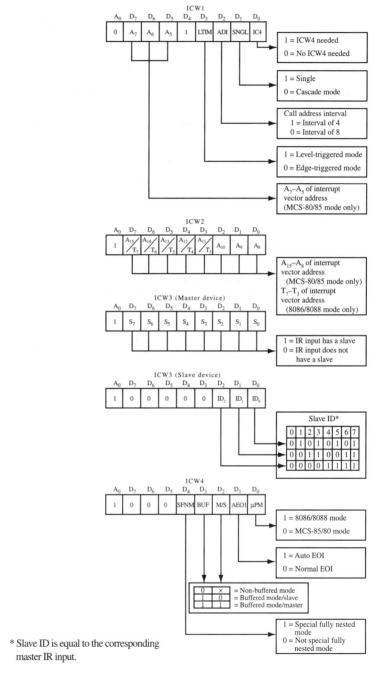

* Slave ID is equal to the corresponding master IR input.

ICW3. If ICW1 bit D1 = 0, the cascade mode is indicated. In this case, a second write to the PIC with A0 = 1 will be interpreted as ICW3.

For the master 8259A, ICW3 specifies the IR input to which a slave is connected. Thus, setting ICW3 to 00000011 indicates that slave PICs are connected to the master's IR1 and IR0 inputs.

Table 9.1   PIC Interrupt Vectors for Example 9.3

Input	Type Number Output by PIC	Interrupt VectorLocation
IRQ0	08H	0000:0020–23H
IRQ1	09H	0000:0024–27H
IRQ2	0AH	0000:0028–2BH
IRQ3	0BH	0000:002C–2FH
IRQ4	0CH	0000:0030–33H
IRQ5	0DH	0000:0034–37H
IRQ6	0EH	0000:0038–3BH
IRQ7	0FH	0000:003C–3FH

For a slave PIC, ICW3 indicates the *cascade address* (master IR input) to which that slave is connected. For example, if the slave is connected to IR6 of the master, ICW3 = 00000 110. During the $\overline{\text{INTA}}$ bus cycle the master will output this address on CAS0–CAS2. If the address matches, the slave will output the type number corresponding to its highest priority active IR input.

ICW4.   If ICW1 bit D0 = 1, 80x86 mode is indicated and ICW4 is required. In this case, the third write with A0 = 1 will be interpreted as ICW4.

Bit D1 of ICW4 activates the automatic EOI instruction used in the fully nested and automatic rotating priority modes. Bits D2 and D3 specify if the PIC is the master or slave in a buffered CPU environment, and thus control the $\overline{\text{SP/EN}}$ the output discussed previously. Bit D4 selects the fully nested or special fully nested operating mode.

The Programming Sequence.   As just explained, ICW2–ICW4 are all written to the same port address. This works because the 8259A expects these bytes to be written *in sequence,* as shown in the flowchart in Figure 9.12. ICW3 and ICW4 are *optional,* depending on the presence of slave PICs in the system and if an 80x86 processor is to be used.

Programming the Operation Control Registers

I am sure you are getting the idea that the 8259A is a complex device to program—and we are still not quite done! After the three (or four) initialization control words have been written, the PIC is ready to receive interrupts on IR0 through IR7 and will operate in the fully nested or special fully nested mode. Subsequent writes to the 8259A will be interpreted as *Operation Control Words.* These bytes specify the rotating priority modes, the special mask mode, the polled mode, the interrupt mask, and the EOI commands. Figure 9.13 provides the details.

OCW1.   This register can be written to or read from using the high (A0 = 1) port address. Bits set to a 1 mask the corresponding IR input, inhibiting it from requesting an interrupt.

Figure 9.12 8259A initialization sequence. (Courtesy of Intel Corporation)

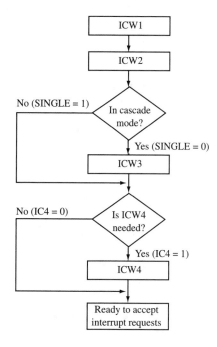

Example 9.4

Using DEBUG, write the following two programs to disable and enable the timer interrupt on the PC.

(a) TIMEROFF.COM   ;Mask interrupts on IRQ0 of the PC
(b) TIMERON.COM   ;Enable interrupts on IRQ0–7of the PC

Devise a means of verifying correct operation.

Solution
The programs are as follows:

TIMEROFF.COM:

```
1BFA:0100 B001    MOV    AL,01    ;Mask IRQ0
1BFA:0102 E621    OUT    21,AL    ;Output to OCW1
1BFA:0104 CD20    INT    20       ;Return to DOS
```

TIMERON.COM:

```
1BFA:0100 B000    MOV    AL,00    ;Enable IRQ0-7
1BFA:0102 E621    OUT    21,AL    ;Output to OCW1
1BFA:0104 CD20    INT    20       ;Return to DOS
```

TEST.BAT

```
@echo off
:start
time <cr.dat
cls
goto start
```

The batch file (TEST.BAT) and data file (CR.DAT) can be used to test the two programs. CR.DAT is a text file that contains only the return character. The line

```
time <cr.dat
```

gets its input from this file and allows the TIME command to be given over and over without having to press the enter key each time the *Enter new time:* prompt appears.

To test the programs, type TIMEROFF and then TEST. You should see the time of day displayed, with the seconds unchanging. This is because DOS is not receiving timer "ticks" used to update the clock (they have been masked). Now enter TIMERON and then TEST. The seconds should now increment, showing that the timer interrupts are again being received.

Figure 9.13   8259A operation control word format. (Courtesy of Intel Corporation)

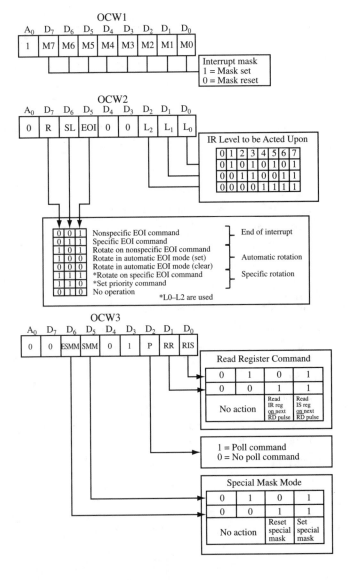

Table 9.2　OCW2 Command Summary

R	SL	EOI	Command	Description
0	0	1	Nonspecific EOI	Use in fully nested mode to reset IS bit; if ICW4 bit 1 is set, this command is performed automatically during INTA bus cycles.
0	1	1	Specific EOI	Use to reset a specific IS bit; bits D0–D2 specify IS bit to reset
1	0	1	Rotate on non-specific EOI	Use to operate in nonspecific rotating mode; resets lowest numbered IS bit and assigns that input lowest priority.
1	0	0	Set rotate in auto EOI mode	If ICW4 bit 1 is set, this command will automatically cause the PIC to perform a rotate on nonspecific EOI command during INTA bus cycles.
0	0	0	Clear rotate in auto EOI mode	Use to disable the auto rotate mode.
1	1	1	Rotate on specific EOI command	Use to operate in specific rotating mode; bits D0–D2 specify the IS bit to reset and assign lowest priority.
1	1	0	Set priority command	Use to assign a specific IR input lowest priority, thus fixing all other priorities.

OCW2.　OCW2 is written to the low port (A0 = 0) and is used to specify the EOI command to the PIC. Note that bit D4 is a 0, so the PIC will not confuse this byte with ICW1 (in which bit D4 = 1). Table 9.2 summarizes the commands that can be written to this register.

Example 9.5

Describe the form of the interrupt service routine when the PIC has been programmed for the fully nested mode. Assume the master PIC port assignments in Figure 9.6.

Solution
```
ISR    PROC     FAR
           .                      ISR begins
           .                      ISR ends
       MOV      AL,00100000B      ;Nonspecific EOI
       OUT      20H,AL            ;OCW2
       IRET
ISR    ENDP
```

There is no need to worry about resetting the wrong IS bit when operating in the fully nested mode, because the nonspecific EOI instruction always resets the lowest numbered IS bit. In the fully nested mode, this will always correspond to the currently executing routine. Thus, the *IR level to be acted upon* in Example 9.5 is a "don't care."

OCW3.   This is a write register accessible using the low (A0 = 0) port address. It is distinguished from ICW1 and OCW2 by bits D3 and D4, which must be 1 and 0, respectively. Bits D5 and D6 allow the special mask mode to be programmed, allowing lower priority interrupts to be accepted. For example, consider the following instructions given within the service routine for the PC's COM1 port using IRQ4:

```
MOV    AL,00010000B       ;Mask IRQ4
OUT    21H,AL             ;OCW1 (IMR)
MOV    AL,01101000B       ;Special mask mode
OUT    20H,AL             ;OCW3
```

By masking itself and selecting the special mask mode, interrupts on IRQ5 through IRQ7 will now be accepted by the PIC (as well as those of higher priority on IRQ0 through IRQ3).

Bit D2 of OCW3 is used to select the poll mode; D0 and D1 allow IRR or IS to be read.

Example 9.6

Write a service routine to verify that the interrupt on the PC's IRQ7 input is "legitimate."

Solution

Recall that the PIC defaults to an IR7 if the interrupt request is not held until acknowledged by the processor. In this case, IS7 will *not* be set. The program is as follows:

```
ISR7    PROC   FAR
        MOV    AL,00001011        ;Read IS on next IO read
        OUT    20H,AL             ;OCW3
        IN     AL,20H             ;Get IS status
        TEST   AL,80H             ;IS7 set?
        JZ     FALSE              ;no-spurious input
                                  ;yes-process good interrupt
         .
         .
         .
FALSE:  IRET
ISR7    ENDP
```

8259A Design Example: Controlling a Parallel Printer

In Figure 8.7 we developed an interface between an 80x86 processor and a Centronics-compatible parallel printer. The control software was written using programmed I/O (polling). In this section we will modify that interface to use interrupts (via the 8259A). The (interrupt-driven) software will also be presented.

Hardware Interface.   The printer interface remains the same as shown in Figure 8.7; however, the printer's $\overline{\text{ACKNLG}}$ signal should be connected to one of the IR0–7 PIC interrupt inputs. To model the PC environment, we have chosen IRQ7 in the PIC interface in Figure 9.6. In this circuit, the master PIC is assumed to be interfaced to ports 20–21H.

Planning the Software.   When the printer is ready to accept new data, the $\overline{\text{ACKNLG}}$ pulse will request an interrupt. The 80x86 will suspend its current task and transfer control to the printer service routine. This program will output new data to the printer and then return control to the suspended program by executing an IRET instruction.

The software required to control an interrupt-driven peripheral like this parallel printer is called a *device driver*. This program is actually made up of two parts: a *command processor* and the *interrupt service routine*. Figure 9.14 shows how the command processor is activated from within the mainline program. The main program begins by per-

Figure 9.14 The printer command processor is called from within the mainline program whenever the user requires a print operation.

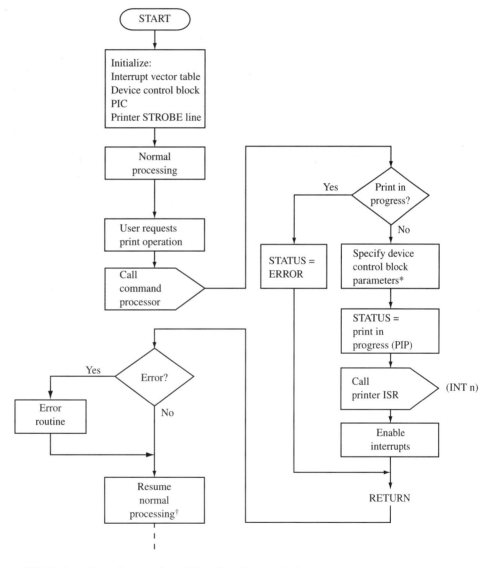

* This block could transfer control to a disk read routine, transferring
 one sector of data to the print buffer.
† Printer periodically interrupts as necessary for additional data.

Table 9.3 Printer Device Control Block Definitions

Name	Description
STATUS	A one-byte field used to identify if the previous print has completed (GOOD), is in progress (PIP), or if an error has occurred (ERROR).
BUF_ADDR	A four-byte field storing the base address of the data table containing the characters to be printed.
CHAR_COUNT	A two-byte field storing the number of bytes to be printed.
CHAR_XFER	A two-byte field storing the current number of bytes transferred.

forming a system initialization. This is a sequence of instructions that program the I/O devices to a known state ($\overline{\text{STROBE}}$ = high, for example), initialize the PIC, and load initial data into any memory tables. The program then begins normal processing, depending on its function.

Flowcharting the Command Processor.   At some point in the main program, the user requests that a print operation occur. The program responds by transferring control to the printer command processor. This procedure checks to make sure that a previous print is not in progress, and then specifies the parameters of the printer device control block (DCB). This is a section of memory used to transfer data between the main program and the interrupt service routine. Table 9.3 defines the DCB parameters used for this example.

The command processor may transfer control to another routine that retrieves the data to be printed and fills in the DCB parameters. Alternately, these parameters might be passed from the main program when the print is first requested. In either case, the STATUS byte is loaded with PIP (print in progress), and a software interrupt is used to transfer control to the printer's interrupt service routine. This is done to start the print process for the first time.

Upon returning from the ISR, the command processor enables interrupts. This allows the printer's $\overline{\text{ACKNLG}}$ signal to initiate all further print requests. The command processor is not executed again until the user requests another print operation.

Flowcharting the ISR.   Figure 9.15 flowcharts the printer ISR. Because most printers have an internal *buffer*, polling is used to write bytes to this buffer until the BUSY flag is set. In this way, several hundred (thousand) bytes may be output to the printer with each $\overline{\text{ACKNLG}}$ pulse. When the number of characters transferred equals the character count, the print job is finished and the ISR sets the STATUS to GOOD. The assembly language listing for the entire program is given in Figure 9.16. There are several important points to note about this program; these are described in the following paragraphs.

Setting Up the Interrupt Vector Table.   The statements in Figure 9.16(a) set up an interrupt vector table segment and DCB. Note the use of the SEGMENT AT statement. Although this cannot be used to force code to be loaded at a particular address, it does allow a label to be defined at specific locations in memory.

In this example, the ORG 0FH*4 statement causes the location counter to associate the label PRINT_INT with address 0000:003C. This corresponds to the vector location for a type 7 interrupt, assumed to have been generated by the PIC.

Figure 9.15   Flowchart for the printer interrupt service routine.

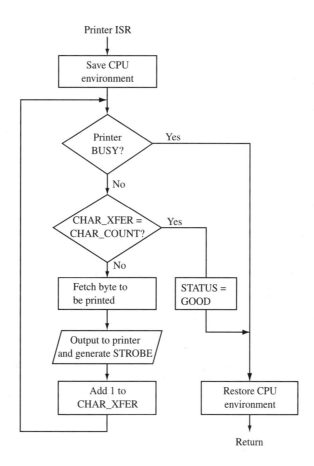

Setting Up the Device Control Block.   The DCB is defined as a segment with the DB, DW, and DD operators used to reserve space for the appropriate parameters (to be specified later by the command processor). The print buffer is arbitrarily selected to begin at 2000:0000H.

Printer and PIC Equates.   The port addresses for the LPT1 data, status, and control ports are specified using equates. The initialization code, and strobe high and low codes are also defined. The initialization codes for the PIC are also defined using the EQUATE operator. In this way, the codes are easily recognized and changed if necessary. The following conditions are established:

1. ICW1 programs a rising-edge trigger, a single PIC, and 80x86 mode (ICW4 to follow).
2. ICW2 holds the vector base address (08H), with $\overline{\text{ACKNLG}}$ wired to IRQ7. The PIC will then generate a type number of 0FH as desired.
3. ICW4 programs the *not special fully nested mode* (lowest numbered IR input has highest priority), nonbuffered, and a normal EOI (the interrupt input will not be automatically reset by the PIC).
4. 20H will be written to OCW2 and, in this example, specifies a nonspecific EOI command. This will cause the current IS bit to be reset, re-enabling interrupts on this input.

Figure 9.16 (a) Program to set up the interrupt vector segment and device control block. Equates are used to identify the printer and PIC program codes. (b) Interrupt vector and PIC initialization. (c) Mainline program showing how control is transferred to the command processor. (d) Command processor routine. (e) Printer interrupt service routine.

```
                          .386
                          ;*******
                          ; Parallel Printer Device Driver -
                          ;    Interrupt vector table, device control
                          ;    block, program equates
                          ;*******

                          ; Set up segment at absolute address 0000
                          ; Printer generates type 0F (IRQ7) interrupt
                          ;    See Table 4.5

00000000        INT_VEC_TABLE   SEGMENT AT 0
                          ORG    0FH*4
0000003C        PRINT_INT       LABEL   DWORD
003C            INT_VEC_TABLE   ENDS

                ;Set up and initialize the device control block

00000000        DEV_CTRL_BLK    SEGMENT BYTE

                ;The following equates define the status byte

= 00000000        GOOD      EQU   00H         ;Good transfer
= 00000001        ERROR     EQU   01H         ;Previous print in progress
= 00000002        PIP       EQU   02H         ;Print in progress flag

00000000 00       STATUS      DB   GOOD        ;Current print status
00000001 20000000 BUF_ADDR    DD   20000000H   ;Print buffer starting address
00000005 0000     CHAR_COUNT  DW   ?           ;Number of bytes to be printed
00000007 0000     CHAR_XFER   DW   ?           ;Current number of bytes
                                               ;transferred

0009            DEV_CTRL_BLK    ENDS
```

(a)

Figure 9.16 (continued)

```
                    ;Printer equates (see Fig. 8.7 for hardware interface)

= 0378              PR_PORT         EQU     378H        ;LPT1 port A
= 0379              PR_STATUS       EQU     379H        ;LPT1 status
= 037A              PR_CTRL         EQU     37AH        ;LPT1 control
= 001A              INIT            EQU     1AH         ;Unidirectional, IRQ7 enable,
                                                        ;sel printer, init, auto
= 001F              STROBE_LOW      EQU     1FH         ;STROBE low
= 001E              STROBE_HIGH     EQU     1EH         ;STROBE high
= 0080              BUSY            EQU     80H         ;Mask for BUSY/READY - bit D7

                    ;8259A PIC equates (see Fig. 9.6 for hardware interface)

= 0013              ICW1            EQU     00010011B   ;Edge triggered,single,ICW4 to follow
= 0008              ICW2            EQU     00001000B   ;PIC base vector = 08H (IRQ7 = type 0FH)
= 0001              ICW4            EQU     00000001B   ;NSFNM,non buffered,normal EOI,8086
= 0020              PIC_A           EQU     20H         ;PIC base port address
= 0021              PIC_B           EQU     21H         ;Second port
= 0020              EOI             EQU     20H         ;OCW2 - nonspecific EOI
```

(a)

(continued on next page)

Figure 9.16 (continued)

```
                ;*******
                ;  Parallel Printer Device Driver -
                ;      Initialization routines
                ;*******

00000000        CODE    SEGMENT 'CODE'
                ASSUME  CS:CODE, DS:INT_VEC_TABLE

                ;Load printer interrupt vector

00000000  FA            START:  CLI                             ;No interrupts until initialized
00000001  66| B8 0000           MOV     AX,0                    ;Base of INT_VEC_TABLE
00000005  66| 8E D8             MOV     DS,AX                   ;Point DS at INT_VEC_TABLE
00000008  C7 05 0000003C R      MOV     PRINT_INT,OFFSET PR_ISR ;Store offset of printer ISR
          0000007D R
00000012  C7 05 0000003E R      MOV     PRINT_INT+2,SEG PR_ISR  ;Store segment of printer ISR
          00000000 R

                ;Ouptut PIC program codes

0000001C  B0 13         MOV     AL,ICW1                         ;Program PIC
0000001E  E6 20         OUT     PIC_A,AL
00000020  B0 08         MOV     AL,ICW2
00000022  E6 21         OUT     PIC_B,AL
00000024  B0 01         MOV     AL,ICW4
00000026  E6 21         OUT     PIC_B,AL

                ;Initialize printer, set STROBE line high

00000028  B0 1A         MOV     AL,INIT                         ;Initialization code
0000002A  66| BA 037A   MOV     DX,PR_CTRL
0000002E  EE            OUT     DX,AL
0000002F  B0 1E         MOV     AL,STROBE_HIGH
00000031  EE            OUT     DX,AL
```

(b)

Figure 9.16 (*continued*)

```
                                    ;********
                                    ;  Parallel Printer Device Driver -
                                    ;      Main program
                                    ;********


                                    ;Normal processing occurs

                                    ;User requests a file to be printed

                             ASSUME CS:CODE, DS:DEV_CTRL_BLK    ;Following labels are in DEV_CTRL_BLK
00000032  1E                 PUSH   DS                          ;Save main program's DS
00000033  66| B8 ---- R      MOV    AX,DEV_CTRL_BLK             ;Point DS at DEV_CTRL_BLK
00000037  66| 8E D8          MOV    DS,AX
0000003A  E8 0000000F        CALL   COM_PROC                    ;Transfer control to command processor

                                    ;Command processor returns control to main
                                    ;program after starting the I/O.  STATUS
                                    ;holds error condition (if any).

0000003F  80 3D 00000000 R   CMP    STATUS,ERROR
       01
00000046  1F                 POP    DS                          ;Was a print already in progress?
00000047  74 03              JE     ERROR_ROUTINE               ;Recover main program's DS
                                                                ;Notify user of error

                                    ;Normal processing now resumes (simulated by
                                    ;the closed loop that follows)

00000049  90          SIMU:   NOP
0000004A  EB FD              JMP    SIMU

0000004C                     ERROR_ROUTINE:
                                    ;This routine might notify the user that a
                                    ;previous print job is already in progress.
                                    ;Control then returns to the main program.

0000004C  EB FB              JMP    SIMU                        ;Just a dummy in this case
```

(c)

(continued on next page)

Figure 9.16 (continued)

```
        ;********
        ;   Parallel Printer Device Driver -
        ;   Command processor procedure
        ;********

        ;Function:   Process print command and specify
        ;            DEV_CTRL_BLK parameters.
        ;
        ;Inputs:     DS assumed to point at DEV_CTRL_BLK
        ;Outputs:    STATUS=ERROR if previous print in
        ;            progress, else STATUS=PIP.
        ;Calls:      Printer ISR to start I/O.
        ;Destroys:   flags


00000004E                       COM_PROC   PROC   NEAR
00000004E  80 3D 00000000 R               CMP    STATUS,GOOD      ;Make sure previous print complete
           00
000000055  74 09                          JE     SKIP             ;Else
000000057  C6 05 00000000 R               MOV    STATUS,ERROR     ;Let STATUS = ERROR
           01
00000005E  EB 1C                          JMP    SHORT QUIT       ;And quit
000000060  66| C7 05          SKIP:       MOV    CHAR_XFER,0      ;Reset characters transferred to 0
           00000007 R
           0000
000000069  66| C7 05                      MOV    CHAR_COUNT,512   ;This example prints 512 byte buffers
           00000005 R
           0200
000000072  C6 05 00000000 R               MOV    STATUS,PIP       ;Update STATUS to print-in-progress
           02
000000079  CD 0F                          INT    0FH              ;Start the first byte "manually" (IRQ7)
00000007B  FB                             STI                     ;Remaining bytes will print automatically
00000007C  C3                QUIT:        RET                     ;So return to main program
00000007D                    COM_PROC     ENDP
```

(d)

Figure 9.16 (continued)

```
                        ;********
                        ;  Parallel Printer Device Driver -
                        ;    Printer interrupt service routine
                        ;********

                        ;Function:    Output bytes from buffer to
                        ;             printer port until printer is
                        ;             BUSY.
                        ;Inputs:      Data to be printed stored
                        ;             beginning at BUF_ADDR
                        ;Outputs:     Data to be printed at PR_PORT.
                        ;             Returns with STATUS=GOOD when
                        ;             all bytes printed.
                        ;Calls:       Nothing
                        ;Destroys     Nothing


0000007D                PR_ISR  PROC    NEAR
0000007D  66|  56               PUSH    SI              ;Save any registers about to be changed

0000007F       1E               PUSH    DS

00000080  66|  50               PUSH    AX

00000082  66|  BA 0379  POLL:   MOV     DX,PR_STATUS    ;Get printer status
00000086       EC               IN      AL,DX
00000087       A8 80            TEST    AL,BUSY         ;If printer BUSY (or off-line)
00000089       75 44            JNZ     EXIT            ;Then exit this procedure

0000008B  66|  B8 ---- R        MOV     AX,DEV_CTRL_BLK ;Make sure DS points to DEV_CTRL_BLK

0000008F  66|  8E D8            MOV     DS,AX

00000092  66|  A1               MOV     AX,CHAR_XFER    ;Check to see if all bytes
```

(e)

(continued on next page)

Figure 9.16 *(continued)*

```
00000098  66| 3B 05   00000007 R   CMP   AX,CHAR_COUNT        ;have been printed.

0000009F  74 27        00000005 R   JE    JOB_DONE             ;Then the job is done

000000A1  1E                        PUSH  DS                   ;Save DEV_CTRL_BLK segment
000000A2  66| C5 35                 LDS   SI,BUF_ADDR          ;Point DS at base of the print buffer

000000A9  66| 03 F0    00000001 R   ADD   SI,AX                ;Point SI at character to be printed
000000AC  67& 8A 04                 MOV   AL,[SI]              ;Fetch the byte

000000AF  66| BA 0378               MOV   DX,PR_PORT           ;LPT1 port A
000000B3  EE                        OUT   DX,AL                ;Output byte to printer
000000B4  B0 1F                     MOV   AL,STROBE_LOW        ;Strobe the printer
000000B6  66| BA 037A               MOV   DX,PR_CTRL
000000BA  EE                        OUT   DX,AL
000000BB  B0 1E                     MOV   AL,STROBE_HIGH
000000BD  EE                        OUT   DX,AL
000000BE  1F                        POP   DS                   ;Recover DEV_CTRL_BLK segment

000000BF  66| FF 05                 INC   CHAR_XFER            ;Update characters transferred
          00000007 R

000000C6  EB BA                     JMP   POLL                 ;See if printer will accept another

                                  JOB_DONE:
000000C8  C6 05 00000000 R          MOV   STATUS,GOOD          ;When all bytes printed STATUS=GOOD
000000C8  00
```

(e)

Figure 9.16 (continued)

```
000000CF  B0 20      EXIT:    MOV   AL,EOI       ;Reset interrupt within PIC

000000D1  E6 20               OUT   PIC_A,AL

000000D3  66| 58              POP   AX           ;Restore used registers

000000D5  1F                  POP   DS

000000D6  66| 5E              POP   SI

000000D8  66| CF              IRET

000000DA            PR_ISR    ENDP
00DA                CODE      ENDS
                              END   START
```

(e)

Finally, the PIC_A and PIC_B equates identify the hardware ports associated with the low (A0 = 0) and high (A0 = 1) ports of the PIC. In this example, we assume the PC assignments of 20H and 21H.

Setting Up the Initial Conditions.   Figure 9.16(b) shows how the offset and segment addresses of the printer ISR are loaded into the interrupt vector. This was the point of defining the label PRINT_INT in Figure 9.16(a). Note the use of the OFFSET and SEG operators to obtain the appropriate addresses for the printer service routine PR_ISR. [see Figure 9.15(e)]. The remaining lines in this figure write ICW1–4 to the PIC. The last instructions initialize the printer and ensure that the $\overline{\text{STROBE}}$ input of the printer is high.

Calling the Command Processor.   Figure 9.16(c) shows how the main program transfers control to the command processor. The error routine is executed if the command processor returns with STATUS = ERROR.

The Command Processor.   Figure 9.16(d) is the command processor procedure. It begins by checking to ensure that any previous print jobs have completed. If so (STATUS = GOOD), it initializes the device control block as follows:

```
Characters transferred = 0
Character count = 512        ;This is the number of bytes that
                             will be printed with one call to the
                             command processor. Alternately, the
                             main program could supply this number.
STATUS = PIP                 ;Print in progress
```

The last instruction—INT 0FH—starts the print procedure (PR_ISR). Subsequent calls to this routine will be initiated by the printer's $\overline{\text{ACKNLG}}$ pulse.

The ISR.   Figure 9.16(e) is the printer interrupt service routine. Because the segment registers will have unknown values when this routine is called, it is necessary to load DS with the DEV_CTRL_BLK address. The CHAR_XFER is used as an index into the buffer so that the instruction ADD SI,AX forms a pointer into this buffer. Data is then output to the printer until its BUSY flag becomes active.

Before the POP instructions restore the processor registers, an EOI byte is written to OCW2. This is required to reset the interrupt request (latched by the PIC). If this is not done, further interrupts will not be honored (by the PIC).

Conclusion.   As you can see, the software required to interface an interrupt-driven peripheral is more complex than that associated with a status-driven or polled peripheral. This is because the interrupt procedure must be written such that other tasks (the mainline program) can be executed while the I/O is in progress.

Of course this is precisely the advantage of interrupt-driven I/O. The processor need only service the peripheral when the peripheral is READY, thus allowing time for other tasks (or peripherals) to be serviced.

The main disadvantage is the software overhead required. Each time the ISR is entered, the buffer address must be retrieved, the character fetched and printed, and the number of characters transferred incremented. In addition, any registers used within the

ISR must be pushed onto the stack. The polled routine must fetch the same variables, but only once, when the program is first started.

Self-Review 9.2 (Answers on page 427)

9.2.1   Using one 8259A, the single INTR input of the 80x86 processors can be expanded to accommodate up to _____ prioritized interrupt inputs.

9.2.2   Interrupt requests received by the PIC must be held until the first _____ _____ cycle occurs.

9.2.3   A certain PIC has ICW2 programmed for 80H. What is the type number output by an interrupt request on IR4?

9.2.4   When operated in the slave mode, the PIC outputs its type number only if the cascade address received on CAS0–CAS2 matches the address programmed in _____ bits D0–D2.

9.2.5   When operated in _____ _____ mode, the EOI command causes the current IS bit to be reset and assigned lowest priority.

9.2.6   To allow interrupts of lower priority than that currently executing, the _____ _____ mode of the PIC should be selected.

9.2.7   In Figure 9.16, the main program initiates a print job by calling the _____ _____.

9.2.8   The program in Figure 9.16 operates the PIC in the:
(a) Fully nested mode
(b) Special fully nested mode
(c) Special mask mode
(d) Specific rotating mode

9.3   Direct Memory Access

Introduction

We have now seen two different methods for controlling the flow of data through a microcomputer I/O port. A third technique, called *direct memory access* or *DMA,* is considered next. Using DMA, the peripheral is synchronized to *main memory,* not the microprocessor. In this section we:

- Describe the DMA protocol used by the 80x86 processors.
- Compare the byte, burst, and block DMA transfer modes.
- List the advantages and disadvantages of programmed I/O, interrupt-driven I/O, and DMA.

The DMA Protocol

The Processor Is the Problem.   To appreciate the DMA concept, you must understand that the real bottleneck in the data transfer process is the microprocessor itself. When a text file is output to a disk drive, we are concerned with transferring data from memory to that drive. Yet with the programmed or interrupt-driven I/O approaches, that data must first be read from memory into the processor—and then transferred to the disk drive. The microprocessor is an unnecessary "middleman" in this process, with the result that the transfer rate is decreased.

The DMAC.   The DMA approach is to "turn off" the processor and let the disk drive access the data file in memory itself: a sort of *direct memory access.* If the memory can supply a new byte of data every 100 ns, data can potentially be transferred at a rate of 10 million bytes per second!

DMA requires that another processor—the *DMA controller* or *DMAC*—take over the buses generating the memory and I/O addresses. While the DMA transfer occurs, the main processor operates in an idle mode.

HOLD and HLDA.   We use the term *protocol* in this section to describe the handshaking mechanism used by the processor to release control of its buses to another processor. The DMA protocol followed by the 80x86 processors involves two control signals, called *HOLD* and *HLDA.* Figure 9.17 shows how these signals are used by the DMAC.

The cycle begins with the peripheral requesting service via the DMARQn (DMA request) input of the DMAC. The DMAC, in turn, drives the 80x86's HOLD input high, requesting that the processor enter a HOLD state. The processor responds by finishing the current bus cycle (if any) and then open-circuits (tristates) its address, data, and (most) control signals. HLDA is then output high by the 80x86, acknowledging the hold request. In a system with address, data, and control bus buffers, HLDA is used to disable these buffers so that the processor is completely disconnected from the memory and I/O.

Upon receiving HLDA, the DMAC applies DMACK (DMA acknowledge) to the peripheral requesting service—normally via the *chip-select* input of the peripheral. The DMAC is now in control of the system, outputting all of the control and address bus signals just as if it were the system processor (which, in fact, it is).

The DMAC is normally programmed by the 80x86 processor prior to the DMA operation for a particular type of transfer. For example, it might be programmed to transfer 100 bytes from memory beginning at address 1000:0000H to I/O port A3H. When the DMAC takes over the buses, it chip-selects the output port at A3H, drives the $\overline{\text{IOW}}$ and $\overline{\text{MEMR}}$ control signals low, and then sequentially outputs the address for each of the 100 bytes to be transferred. Note that the data moves directly from memory to the I/O port—not through the DMAC. This allows a very high transfer rate.

Priority.   The HOLD input has a higher priority than INTR or NMI. Thus, simultaneous HOLD and interrupt requests will result in the HOLD acknowledge cycle being performed first. However, if the HOLD request occurs at the beginning of an interrupt acknowledge cycle, that cycle will be allowed to complete before HLDA is output. The LOCK prefix, however, can be used to delay generation of the HLDA signal until the LOCKED instruction has been executed.

The 8237A DMAC.   To implement DMA cycles, Intel provides the 8237A DMA controller. This chip provides three separate, prioritized DMA channels similar to that shown in Figure 9.17. In the original IBM PC, the 8237A was used to speed up disk-drive read and write operations with the relatively slow 8088 processor. With today's high-speed processors, this is no longer necessary. Instead, the chip is often used to generate row addresses for refreshing dynamic memory. In addition, many sound cards use DMA for transferring data from memory to the onboard digital-to-analog converter.

Like the 8255A and 8259A discussed previously, the 8237A is no longer "visible" on the system board of a modern PC. However, its functionality remains as part of the computer's chipset. In fact, AT computers provide eight DMA channels (0–7).

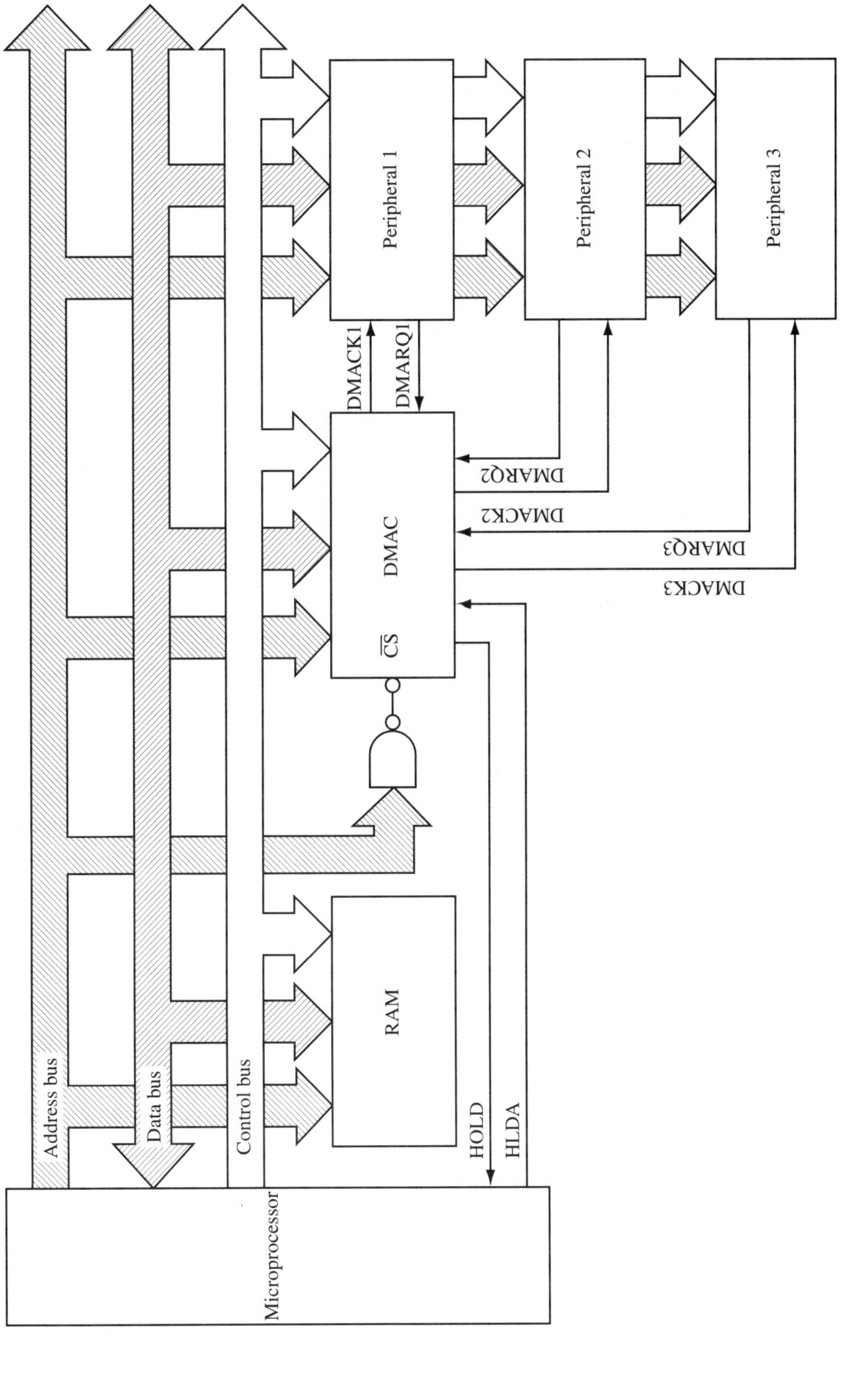

Figure 9.17 A DMA controller allows the peripheral to interface directly with memory without processor intervention. This allows the data transfer rate to approach the access time of memory.

Types of DMA

Sequential DMA.   In *sequential DMA,* the DMAC first performs a read operation, fetching the data byte into the DMAC. Next, a write operation is performed, transferring the data byte to the I/O port. The opposite sequence is also possible—read a byte from the I/O port, and then write the byte to memory. Generally, 2 to 4 clock periods are required for each read or write operation (4 to 8 for the total transfer).

Simultaneous DMA.   With this technique, the read and write operations are performed at the same time (as discussed at the beginning of this section). This requires $\overline{\text{MEMR}}$ and $\overline{\text{IOW}}$ (or $\overline{\text{IOR}}$ and $\overline{\text{MEMW}}$) to both be active simultaneously. In this way, data does not flow through the DMAC at all, but directly from memory to the I/O port (or vice versa). The result is a factor-of-two speed improvement compared to the sequential approach.

In either case, the data transfer is done completely in hardware, involving only the DMAC, the peripheral, and main memory. Because the processor is not involved, there is no software overhead.

Transfer Combinations.   Several DMA transfer combinations are possible. These are:

1. Memory to peripheral
2. Peripheral to memory
3. Memory to memory
4. Peripheral to peripheral

Before the data transfer can occur, the processor must program the DMAC for the type of transfer that is to take place, the destination and source addresses, and the number of bytes to be transferred.

DMA Modes.   For a given DMA type, there are three ways of mixing the DMA cycles among normal processor bus cycles. These are shown in Figure 9.18. In *byte* or *single* mode, the DMAC, after gaining control of the system buses, transfers a single data byte. Control of the buses is then relinquished until the peripheral's READY flag is again active.

The *burst* or *demand* mode is intended for peripherals that have high-speed data buffers. After gaining control of the buses, data is transferred until the peripheral's READY flag is no longer active. Control of the buses is then relinquished to the processor. When READY again becomes active, another burst of DMA occurs. The advantage of this technique is that the peripheral's buffer can be filled very rapidly by the DMAC and then emptied at the peripheral's leisure.

A third type of DMA is called *continuous* or *block* mode DMA. This is similar to burst mode except that control of the buses is not relinquished until the entire data block has been transferred. This technique is very effective with a high-speed peripheral that can keep up with the DMAC; slow peripherals will cause long periods of inactivity on the buses as the DMAC waits for the READY flag.

I/O Summary

In Chapters 8 and 9 we have discussed the design of a parallel I/O port and seen how the 8255A can be used to implement three such ports with a single chip. We have also covered three techniques for *synchronizing* the microprocessor to the data rate of the peripheral.

Figure 9.18 Three methods of DMA operation: (a) byte; (b) burst; (c) block.

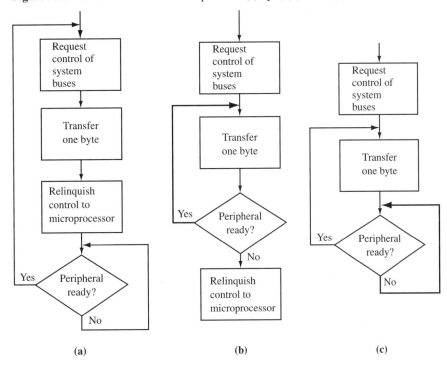

(a)   (b)   (c)

The simplest is *polling,* which provides a fast response time and relatively high transfer rate, provided only one peripheral is to be controlled at a time. Its main disadvantage is that all of the resources of the processor are dedicated to this one peripheral.

The *interrupt* approach is more efficient, as the processor only services the peripheral when data is required. This allows the processor to perform some other task, occasionally stopping to service the peripheral when data is required. The main disadvantage is the software overhead required to save the processor registers and processing environment. This means the response time may be quite lengthy and the transfer rate less than that for polling.

The ultimate in transfer rate and response time is achieved with *DMA*. DMA data transfer rates approach the access time of the memory chips themselves. The disadvantage is that a special DMA controller is required, increasing the overall complexity (and cost) of the system.

All three techniques are supported by special *peripheral controller chips*. These devices can be programmed by the processor so that their configurations can be changed to meet the particular needs of the peripheral interfaced.

Self-Review 9.3 (Answers on page 427)

9.3.1   To request a DMA cycle, the _____ input of the processor must be made active.

9.3.2   (a) *Sequential*   (b) *Simultaneous* DMA provides the fastest data transfer rate.

9.3.3   The _____ mode of DMA is appropriate for peripherals with a data buffer.

9.3.4   When compared with interrupt-driven I/O, the data transfer rate using DMA is faster. Explain.

Chapter 9 Self-Test

1. The 80x86 processors can receive interrupts from three different sources. List these.
2. The 80x86 processors have two general-purpose hardware interrupts, called _____ and _____. Of these, interrupts on _____ can be blocked by giving the _____ instruction.
3. Simultaneous interrupts occur on INTR and NMI. Which one will the 80x86 processors respond to first?
4. Assume a peripheral has an interrupt service routine stored at 0783:0010H. Determine the contents and location of the interrupt vector if type number 200D is used.
5. What type of interrupt causes an interrupt acknowledge cycle to be run? What is the purpose of this cycle?
6. Under what conditions can an interrupt on INTR interrupt an ISR currently running?
7. How does the 8259A PIC indicate interrupts that are currently in service?
8. In the fully nested mode, if an interrupt on IR5 is being serviced, will the 8259A PIC issue an interrupt request from IR0?
9. Under what conditions will a lower priority service routine be allowed to interrupt a higher priority routine using the 8259A PIC?
10. To program PIC input IR5 to produce a type number of 75H, the base address _____ should be written to _____.
11. In the fully nested mode, why is it important to issue an EOI instruction before ending the corresponding interrupt service routine?
12. During DMA cycles, the processor _____ _____ its data, address, and control buses.
13. Assume data is being transferred from a disk drive directly to memory using simultaneous DMA. Indicate the logic level required on the following system control bus signals.
    (a) $\overline{IOR}$
    (b) $\overline{IOW}$
    (c) $\overline{MEMR}$
    (d) $\overline{MEMW}$
14. If the processor receives simultaneous HOLD and NMI requests, which input will be serviced first?
15. Three types of DMA cycles can be run by the DMAC. List these. Which type retains control of the system buses until all of its data has been transferred?

Analysis and Design Questions

Section 9.1

9.1   A divide-by-zero error causes an INT 0 to occur. While servicing this interrupt, a hardware interrupt on NMI occurs. (a) Will the processor suspend the INT 0 interrupt service routine and respond to the NMI? Explain. (b) Instead of NMI, an interrupt on INTR occurs. Will the processor suspend the INT 0 interrupt service routine and respond to this INTR? Explain.

Figure 9.19 Figure for Analysis and Design Question 9.4.

```
ISR    PROC    NEAR
       PUSH    SI              ;Save CPU environment
       PUSH    AX
       PUSH    DS
       PUSH    CX

       POP     SI              ;Recover old data pointer
       POP     DS
       POP     CX

       MOV     AL,[SI]         ;Fetch byte to be printed
       OUT     PR_PORT,AL      ;Output byte to printer
       INC     SI              ;Advance data pointer
       DEC     CX              ;Decrement byte counter

       PUSH    CX              ;Save counter and pointer
       PUSH    DS
       PUSH    SI

       POP     CX              ;Restore CPU registers
       POP     DS
       POP     AX
       POP     SI

       IRET
ISR    ENDP
```

9.2   Assume the interrupt service routine for the NMI input is stored at address C9A0:0100. Draw a diagram similar to the one in Example 9.1, showing the location and contents of the required interrupt vector.

9.3   Describe the changes required to the circuit in Figure 9.3 to support a hardware interrupt with type number 20H.

9.4   The ISR shown in Figure 9.19 is written to service a printer. Each time the printer is ready for a new character, it generates an interrupt that vectors to this routine. Identify any errors you can find in this program.

9.5   Design the hardware such that a pushbutton switch can be used to generate a type 40H interrupt request. Write a test program that increments the count displayed in a seven-segment display wired to output port 56H each time the switch is pushed.

Section 9.2

9.6   Assume the PIC interface shown in Figure 9.5 is to be redesigned to operate with an 8086 processor. If the circuit is to be mapped to I/O ports 0 and 2, show the new interface.

9.7   The following questions refer to the 8259A–80486 interface shown in Figure 9.20.
   (a) For what *range* of addresses will the $\overline{SEL}$ signal output by IC6 be active?
   (b) IC1 and IC2 will place data on the processor's data lines only for _____ cycles.
   (c) What logic levels are required on $\overline{SEL}$, $\overline{BE1}$, and $\overline{BE0}$ to enable IC1?
   (d) What single I/O address is required to enable IC1?
   (e) What single I/O address is required to enable IC2?

Figure 9.20 Figure for Analysis and Design Question 9.7.

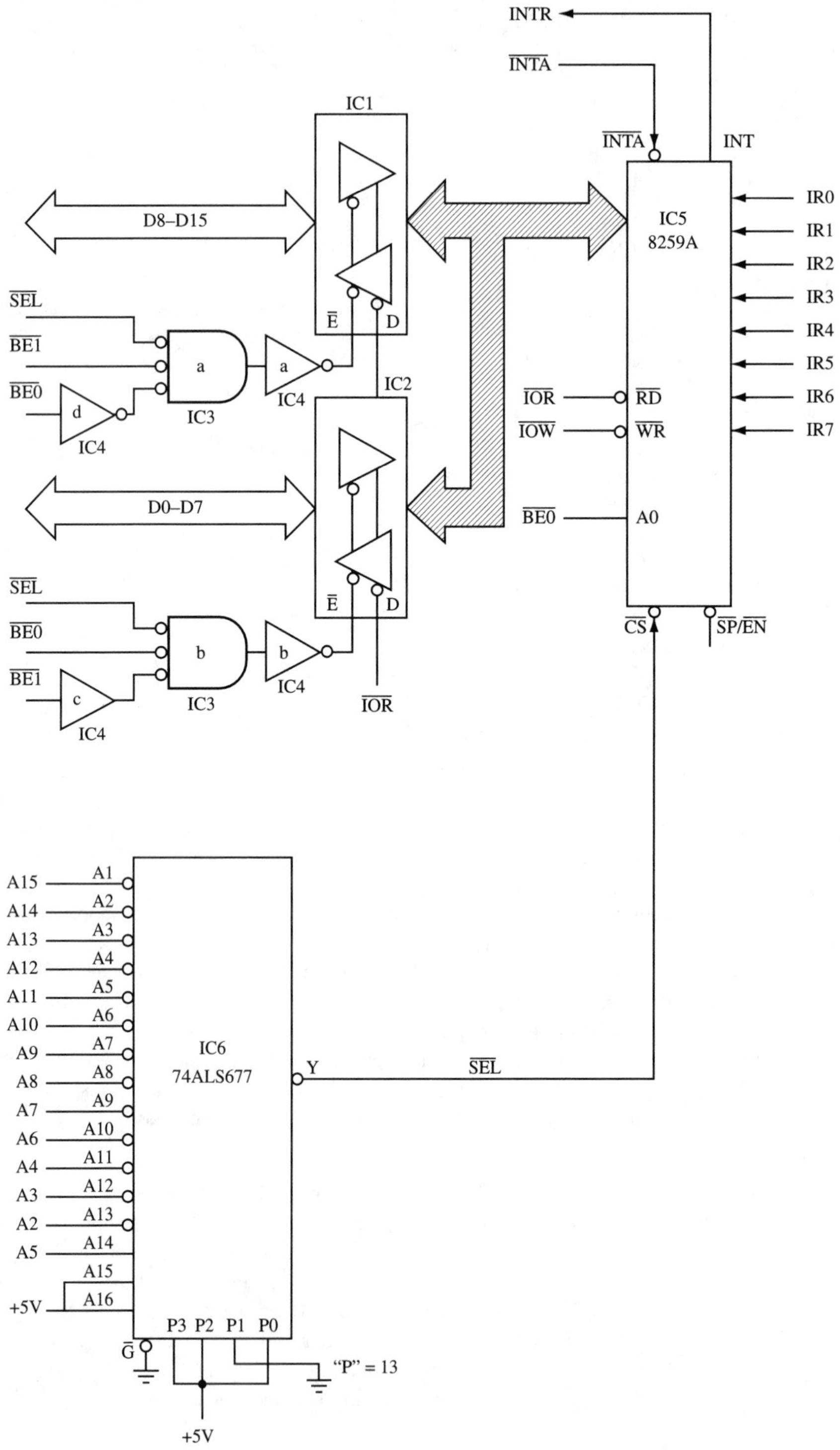

(f) When the PIC's A0 input is low, data is transferred over the _____ data lines. When this input is high, data is transferred over the _____ data lines.

9.8   Write the 8259A initialization instructions required for the following: (a) single PIC, (b) level triggered, (c) IR0 type number E0H, (d) automatic EOI, (e) nonbuffered processor interface, (f) fully nested. Assume the PIC port addresses are F0H and F4H.

9.9   Assume a PIC is operating in the fully nested mode with ICW4 bit 1 low. A request on IR3 occurs and the service routine begins. A second request occurs on IR2, which is serviced and terminated with a nonspecific EOI command. Will this command reset the correct IS bit? Explain.

9.10   Assuming the 386/486 PIC port assignments given in Example 9.2, sketch the resulting priority structure if the IR2 service routine in Problem 9.9 terminates with the instructions:

```
MOV    AL,11100010B
OUT    20H,AL
```

Section 9.3
9.11   Why do the flags, CS, and IP registers not have to be saved during a DMA cycle?

9.12   Which two I/O instructions allow the 80x86 processors to perform the equivalent of sequential DMA? (*Hint:* One outputs data the other inputs data.)

9.13   Which of the following I/O techniques would be most efficient when interfacing a keyboard to a microcomputer? Explain your answer.
(a) Programmed I/O
(b) Interrupts
(c) DMA

Self-Review Answers

9.1.1 The processor need only respond to the peripheral when the peripheral is ready for service.
9.1.2 n = 23H ISR = 1C2F:493A
9.1.3 NMI, INTR
9.1.4 flags, CS, and IP (EIP)
9.1.5 Input the interrupt type number, INTR only
9.2.1 8
9.2.2 interrupt acknowledge
9.2.3 84H
9.2.4 ICW3
9.2.5 nonspecific rotating
9.2.6 special mask
9.2.7 command processor
9.2.8 (a)
9.3.1 HOLD
9.3.2 (b) Simultaneous
9.3.3 Burst (or block)
9.3.4 There is no software overhead with DMA. In addition, data flows directly between the peripheral and memory. There is no processor "middleman."

10 Data Communications

By the mid-1980s the IBM PC had undergone two renovations resulting in the IBM XT and AT computers. To take advantage of the new 32-bit processors becoming available (the 80386), IBM decided to design an entirely new machine family called the Personal System 2 or PS/2 family. In addition to a new, sleeker case, the initial PS/2 computers abandoned the 8- and 16-bit expansion slots of the XT and AT in favor of a new design called Microchannel Architecture (MCA). While technically superior to the old design, it also made the older adapter cards obsolete. This angered many users and led several manufacturers to gang together to produce a PC/XT-compatible alternative bus slot called EISA (Extended Industry Standard Architecture).

Outline

Objectives

After completing this chapter you should be able to:

1. Draw the waveshape for an asynchronous serial data character showing the start, stop, data, and parity bits.
2. Calculate the bits per second and character rates for asynchronous serial data.
3. Identify the function of a UART in a serial interface.
4. Describe the bisync and SDLC synchronous serial data communications protocols.
5. Describe the electrical characteristics of RS-232 and show how to construct a TTL-compatible interface.
6. Identify and describe the function of the signals that make up the RS-232 standard.
7. List the six RS-232 modem control signals and show how they are used to provide hardware flow control between a modem and computer.
8. Describe the internal register set of the PC16550D UART.
9. Explain how the PC16550D's onboard FIFOs allow the processor to operate more efficiently.
10. Describe the PC16550D initialization and interrupt handling software.
11. Compare modem modulation schemes, including FSK, PSK, QAM, and TCM.
12. Identify common national and international modem standards.
13. Show how the AT command set is used to control the functions of a modem.
14. Contrast the two common error control schemes: ARQ and FEQ.
15. Compare common error detection schemes, including parity, checksum, and CRC.
16. Show how the Hamming code is applied to detect and correct data errors on individual data bytes.

Overview

Data communications refers to the ability of one computer to exchange data with another computer or peripheral. Physically, the data communications path may be a short, 5 to 10 ft ribbon cable connecting a microcomputer and parallel printer; it might be a 2- or 3-conductor serial interface cable to a *modem*.

The ability to communicate with other computers and computer peripherals is essential to nearly every computer system—from the mainframe to the micro. And because of this need, it is to everyone's advantage to establish a *standard* data communications port. Equipped with this port, interfacing a computer and peripheral becomes a simple matter of plugging a cable into each device's standard data port.

In practice, there are several different standards. For example, the Centronic's parallel printer interface described in Chapter 8 has become a de facto parallel interface standard simply because everyone uses it. Other standards are more formal: The Electronic Industries Association (EIA), for example, has proposed a series of standards prefaced with the letters *RS*. The best known is RS-232, describing a serial communications standard.

In this chapter we focus on serial communications. We begin by contrasting asynchronous and synchronous serial transmission techniques. The RS-232 standard is then introduced so that you can see how a typical serial port is implemented in a PC. Next, the

PC16550D UART (Universal Asynchronous Receiver/Transmitter) is described. This chip is the key component for converting parallel data to serial form and vice versa. Once converted to serial form, data can be transmitted thousands of miles via a *modem*. Several different modem standards will be discussed, as well as the AT command set—the de facto modem programming language. The chapter concludes with a discussion of common error detection and correction schemes. These are important because they ensure that the received data matches the data that was transmitted.

10.1   Serial I/O

Introduction

Microprocessors are by nature *parallel* machines; that is, data moves from point to point within the machine in parallel data groups (8, 16, 32, or 64 bits at a time). The alternative is to move the data *serially*—one bit at a time. Obviously this will be slower (32 clock pulses will be required to receive or transmit a 32-bit data group), but only a single wire (two, counting a common ground) between receiver and transmitter will be required. If amplifiers are used, the distance between the two stations can be quite large (several thousand feet). If the serial data is converted to audio tones (via a modem), the data can be transmitted thousands of miles over the telephone network. Indeed, serial data is used to communicate with deep-space probes millions of miles from Earth.

In this section we will:

- Draw the waveshape for an asynchronous serial data character showing the start, stop, data, and parity bits.
- Calculate the bits per second and character rates for asynchronous serial data.
- Identify the function of a UART in a serial interface.
- Describe the bisync and SDLC synchronous serial data communications protocols.

Asynchronous Serial Data Communications

One of the most common applications for a serial I/O port is to interface the keyboard on a video display terminal (VDT). In this circuit, each keystroke generates a 7-bit ASCII code that is converted to bit-by-bit serial and then transmitted to a computer over a 2- or 3-conductor cable. Because even the fastest typist cannot exceed data rates of 120 words per minute, this interface is a good match for the relatively slow transmission rate of the serial port.

Note an important characteristic of this interface: At some times the serial port will be required to transfer data at 10 to 20 characters/s, but at other times the data rate may be only 1 or 2 characters/s. Indeed, most of the time the keyboard is not in use at all, and the data rate is 0. Because of this erratic data flow, an *asynchronous communications protocol* (set of universally accepted rules) must be established.

Start Bits, Stop Bits, and the Data Rate.   The accepted technique for asynchronous serial communications is to hold the serial output line at a logic-1 level (a *mark*) until data is to be transmitted. Each character is required to begin with a logic 0 (a *space*) for one bit time. This first bit is called the *start bit* and is used to synchronize the transmitter and receiver. Figure 10.1 illustrates how the data byte 7BH would look when transmitted in the

Figure 10.1 Standard asynchronous serial data format. The data byte is framed between the start bit and one or more stop bits. In this example the data byte is 7BH.

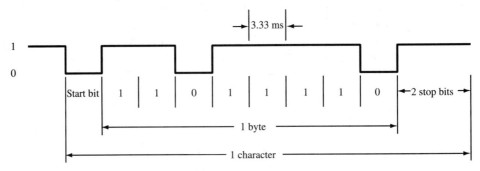

asynchronous serial format. The data is sent least significant bit first and framed between a start bit (always a 0) and one or two stop bits (always a 1).

The start and stop bits carry no information, but are required because of the asynchronous nature of the data. The data rate can be expressed as bits/s (bps) or characters/s.[1]

Example 10.1

Calculate the data rate in bits/s and the character rate for the serial data shown in Figure 10.1.

Solution
Because one bit persists for 3.33 ms, the bits/s rate is 1/3.33 ms = 300 bits/s. Because there are 11 bits per character, it will require 11 × 3.33 ms = 36.63 ms to transmit the entire byte. The character rate is therefore 1/36.63 ms = 27.3 characters/s.

Example 10.2

Modems commonly transmit data over the telephone network at 9600, 14,400 or 28,800 bps. If a 1 MB file is to be transmitted to a another computer via modem calculate the transmission time using one start bit, one stop bit, and eight data bits at (a) 9600 bps and (b) 28,800 bps.

Solution
Ten bits are required to transmit each byte. The two character rates are therefore 960 character/s and 2880 character/s. The transmission times can thus be calculated as:

(a) 1,048,576 characters × 1s/960 characters = 1092s = 18 minutes and 12 seconds
(b) 1,048,576 characters × 1s/2880 characters = 364s = 6 minutes and 4 seconds

Building a Serial I/O Port.   The hardware required for a serial I/O port need not be complex. As shown in Figure 10.2, a serial port is simply a one-bit parallel I/O port. In this example the port is mapped to input and output port 0 (see Figures 8.2 and 8.4 for details on generating $\overline{\text{IN0}}$ the $\overline{\text{OUT0}}$ DSP signals).

---

[1]It is common practice to use the term *baud rate* for the data rate in bits/s. For example, 9600 baud instead of 9600 bps. However, as we will learn in Section 10.4, the baud rate is actually equal to the number of *signal events per second,* which may not be the same as the data rate.

Figure 10.2 One-bit input and output port. With appropriate software this circuit can function as a serial I/O channel.

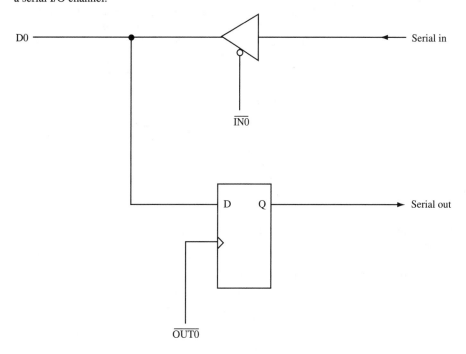

To send one bit of data to this port, the instruction OUT 0,AL can be given. The data in bit 0 of register AL will be output. Similarly, the instruction IN AL,0 will input the serial data to bit 0 of AL.

Generating and Recovering the Serial Data. Of course, to actually transfer serial data through the port in Figure 10.2, the outgoing data will have to be serialized (in software) and start and stop bits added. Similarly, software will be required to detect the incoming start and stop bits and convert the data back to parallel form.

Figure 10.3 is an example of an 80x86 serial transmitter program that could be used with the one-bit I/O port in Figure 10.2. Each bit to be transmitted is rotated to the bit 0 position of the accumulator and then output. The DELAY procedure determines the data rate. Start and stop bits are inserted by first resetting, and then setting, the carry bit and rotating this flag into register AL, where it is output.

Recovering the serial data requires a more complex program but, again, no special hardware is required. Figure 10.4 flowcharts the process. The program begins by waiting for the 1 to 0 transition of the start bit. Once found, the middle of the bit is located by waiting for one half of the DELAY time. If the input bit is still 0, a valid start bit is assumed and the program waits for one additional bit time (thus sampling in the middle of all following bits).

As each bit is read it is rotated right—through the carry—and after eight reads the entire byte has been recovered. The ninth read should return the first stop bit. If this bit is low, a *framing* error is indicated; that is, the program is out of sync with the data. If the bit is high, the data byte can be saved and the program begins searching for the next start bit.

Figure 10.3   80x86 serial transmitter program. Bit 0 of the DPORT is used for the serial output line.

```
                        ;Function:   Serial data transmitter.  DELAY
                        ;            procedure determines data rate.
                        ;Inputs:     Character to be transmitted assumed
                        ;            passed in AL.
                        ;Ouputs:     Serial data on bit 0 of DPORT.

                        ;Destroys:   AL,CX,flags.

                            EXTRN       DELAY:NEAR
= 00F0                      DPORT       EQU    00H

0000                CODE    SEGMENT
                            ASSUME      CS:CODE

0000                FIG10_3 PROC        NEAR
0000  B9 000A               MOV         CX,10       ;10 bits/char
0003  F8                    CLC                     ;Start bit
0004  D0 D0                 RCL         AL,1        ;Move to position 0
0006  E6 F0       TRANS:    OUT         DPORT,AL    ;Transmit bit
0008  E8 0000 E             CALL        DELAY       ;Wait
000B  D0 D8                 RCR         AL,1        ;Next bit
000D  F9                    STC                     ;Stop bit
000E  E2 F6                 LOOP        TRANS       ;Do 10 times
0010  C3                    RET
0011                FIG10_3 ENDP
0011                        CODE        ENDS
                            END
```

Matching the Receiver and Transmitter Clocks.   It has been implied in our discussion thus far that the receiver and transmitter data rates are exactly matched. But is this necessary? Can we tolerate slight differences? For example, using software timing loops, it is unlikely that the DELAY procedure used in the program in Figure 10.3 will produce a time delay that exactly matches the time delay in the receiving computer.

Figure 10.5 illustrates the results of trying to recover data that is too fast or too slow for the receiver. In both cases, note how the error *accumulates*. If sampling is done in the middle of the bit time, the maximum allowable error will cause the ninth bit to be shifted 1/2 bit time to the right or left. If all bits are shifted equally (because of a data rate mismatch), the amount of error in one bit will be 1/2 bit time/9 = 1/18 bit time. This means the received and transmitted data rates must match within 5.6 percent.

This is an interesting result. You might have guessed that the data rates had to match exactly, which would be true if there were no start or stop bits. But because of these bits, synchronization need only be held from the beginning of one start bit to the beginning of the first stop bit. The asynchronous technique *self-synchronizes* after each character. Of course the price we pay for this is that each data byte must be increased in length by two bits, or 25 percent. If these bits were not required, the character rate for a 28.8 modem

Figure 10.4 Flowchart of the process required to recovover asynchronous serial data.

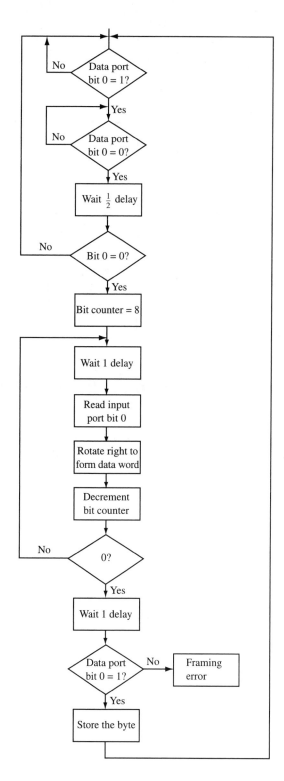

Figure 10.5   (a) Serial data transmitted at the proper rate. (b) The data rate is too fast. (c) The data rate is too slow.

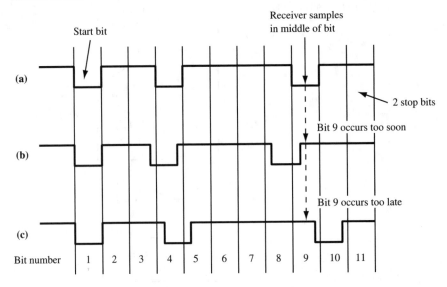

would rise from 2800 characters/s to 3600 characters/s. The time to transmit the 1 MB data file in Example 8.2 would then decrease from 6 minutes and 4 seconds to 4 minutes and 51 seconds.

In some cases, a logic 1 might be delayed more than a logic 0 (or vice versa) when passing through the transmission medium. This can lead to individual bit errors rather than framing errors. Because of this, the rule of thumb is to try to match receiving and transmitting data rates to 1 percent or less.

Standard Data Rates.   As mentioned previously, protocols define certain rules that should be followed to help standardize the communications technique. An example is the adoption of a logic 0 for a start bit and a logic 1 for a stop bit for asynchronous serial data. Certain data rates have also become standard; these are listed in Table 10.1.

Setting the Serial Port Parameters.   When setting up a serial port, several parameters must be specified. The most common are:

1. The number of data bits/character, usually five to eight
2. The number of stop bits, usually one
3. The parity bit, used to detect single bit errors, may be specified as odd, even, stick, or no parity.[2]
4. Baud rate (see Table 10.1 for standard frequencies)

Typically, these parameters are set via the DOS mode command or in the application using the serial I/O port. Figure 10.6 shows an example of the latter using Windows 95.

---

[2]Error detection and correction techniques are discussed in Section 10.5.

Table 10.1 Common Data Rates for Serial Data Communications

75	
110	These first three rates are now obsolete. They were used with early teletype equipment.
150	
300	Early modems operated at 300 baud.
600	
1200	
2400	
4800	
9600	
14,400	This is a popular modem data rate. Referred to as "14.4."
19,200	
28,800	For several years this was the top-of-the-line speed for modems.
33,600	Some 28.8 modems can be upgraded to operate at this speed.
38,400	
57,600	The current maximum data rate for modems.
115,200	28.8 modems can exchange data with the PC at this rate.

Figure 10.6 Setting the data rate for COM2 in Windows 95.

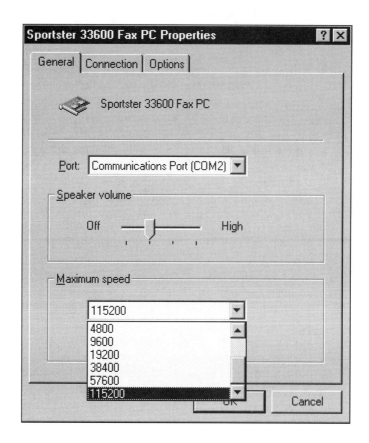

Example 10.3

Explain how to transmit the data file TEST.DAT to the serial printer connected to the PC's COM1 serial port. Set the serial port parameters to 19,200 bps, odd parity, one stop bit, and eight data bits.

Solution

The command is

```
C:\>MODE COM1: BAUD=19200, PARITY=odd, DATA=8, STOP=1.
```

This can be shortened to *MODE COM1: 19,o,8,1.* The file can then be transmitted using the copy command

```
C:\>copy test.dat com1:
```

Troubleshooting Serial I/O Ports.   One of the most common problems with serial ports is not matching the receiver and transmitter communications parameters. The receiver may be set for one data rate and the transmitter to another. The result is "garbage" characters on the screen or paper. Clearly, checking that these settings match should be one of the first steps in troubleshooting a serial I/O port.

Another common problem is the serial cable wiring; this is covered in Section 10.2.

The UART

Writing a program compatible with all of the different asynchronous communications protocols can be quite a task. It is also an *inefficient* use of the microprocessor, since much of its time will be spent in timing loops waiting to transmit or receive another character.

Because of this, the semiconductor companies have developed the *Universal Asynchronous Receiver/Transmitter* chip, or *UART*. Typically this chip features a separate serial transmitter and serial receiver in the same package. Internal registers allow the serial data parameters to be programmed and changed as necessary. Status registers allow the BUSY/READY state of the receiver and transmitter to be monitored. Other status indicators show when a framing error (invalid start bit), parity error, or overrun condition (character received before the previous character has been read) has occurred.

The UART requires an accurate clock signal, which then determines the data for the port. Most UARTs use a signal with a frequency that is 16 times the intended data rate—this effectively breaks each bit time into 16 "slices" and allows the center of the bit to be more accurately located. For example, to operate at 1200 bps, a 19.2 KHz clock signal should be connected to the UART's transmitter and receiver clock inputs.

It is interesting to note that a serial port (the UART) appears to the microprocessor to be a conventional *parallel* port. When the transmitter buffer is empty, all of the bits in the word to be transmitted are output to the port at once (in parallel). Similarly, all bits of the received word are input at once when the received data is ready.

The job of converting the data from serial to parallel, or from parallel to serial, has been transferred to the UART. This is interesting because we usually think of using the microprocessor to replace hardware with software. However, the UART is an example of a case in which it is more efficient to replace software with hardware.

In Section 10.3 we discuss the National Semiconductor PC16550D UART chip popular in most PCs today.

Synchronous Serial Communications

The start and stop bits of asynchronous serial data represent wasted overhead bytes that reduce the overall character rate—no matter what the data rate. Even adding a parity bit can reduce the transfer rate by 10 percent.

But giving up the start and stop bits will require some means of *synchronizing* the data. How will we know when the data starts and when to sample it? In the following paragraphs we will examine two common synchronous serial protocols that answer these questions.

Bisync Protocol.   Because there is no start bit, a special *sync character* is required in all synchronous serial formats. This character tells the receiver that data is about to follow. Accordingly, the UART must have a special "hunt" or "search" mode so that the sync character can be found.

Because there is no stop bit, a clock signal usually accompanies the synchronous data to maintain synchronization. When synchronous serial data is to be transmitted over the telephone network, it is not possible to provide a separate clock channel. In this case, a special *synchronous modem* that encodes the data and clock into a single signal is used. The receiving modem separates the data and clock signals.

Another difference between synchronous and asynchronous serial data is that the clock rate for synchronous data is the same as the data rate (that is, a 1× clock is used).

In the *bisync* protocol, several special ASCII characters are used to control the data transfer, as shown in Table 10.2. Figure 10.7 illustrates one "frame" of a synchronous message. Just as asynchronous data is framed between start and stop bits, synchronous data is framed between special control codes. In Figure 10.7, two sync characters are output followed by *STX*—start of text. The data follows. This block may consist of 100 or more data bytes, or may simply be other control codes. *ETX* signifies end of text. *BCC* is a block check character used for error detection. *PAD* is the character output when no data is being transmitted and corresponds to the "mark" output in asynchronous serial data.

Table 10.2   Special Characters Used in the BISYNC Synchronous Serial Protocol

Character	ASCII Code	Description
SYN	16	Sync character
PAD	FF	End of frame pad
DLE	10	Data link escape
ENQ	05	Enquiry
SOH	01	Start of header
STX	02	Start of text
ITB	0F	End of intermediate transmission block
ETB	17	End of transmission block
ETX	03	End of text

Figure 10.7 One frame of a synchronous message using the bisync protocol.

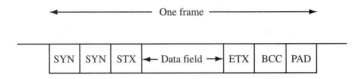

Be sure to note that the bisync protocol is simply a set of rules that everyone has agreed to follow. It is not necessarily any better or worse than some other set of rules.

Example 10.4

Calculate the percentage of "wasted" bits using the bisync protocol compared to eight data bit/one stop bit/one parity bit asynchronous serial. Assume the data block size is 100 bytes.

Solution
The overhead required for the asynchronous character is 38 percent (three extra bits for each byte). The bisync protocol requires six extra bytes (see Figure 10.7 and assume a 16-bit BCC) for the 100 byte block. The overhead is six percent.

The consequences of the reduced overhead should be clear. For a given data rate, synchronous data will have a considerably higher character rate.

Serial Data Link Control (SDLC). This format was developed by IBM for use with its *Systems Network Architecture (SNA)* communications package. Figure 10.8 illustrates one frame of data using this protocol. It is similar to bisync but is not byte oriented.

The SDLC receiver searches for the beginning flag (01111110) as its sync character. An 8-bit address field follows, allowing each frame to be addressed to a particular station among a network of stations. Control characters are identified by a sequence of six or more logic 1s.

The information field can be of any format (that is, it does not have to consist of an integral number of bytes). The transmitter will automatically insert 0s in this field if five or more logic 1s appear in sequence: This will avoid inadvertent control characters appearing in the information field. The receiver automatically deletes these 0s.

The 16-bit frame check is used for error detection, similar to the BCC character in bisync. The frame ends with the ending flag.

SDLC is actually a subset of HDLC (high-level data link control), which is an international synchronous communications protocol. As with bisync, SDLC is simply a set of rules that have been agreed upon for the transfer of serial data.

Figure 10.8 One frame of a synchronous message using the SDLC protocol.

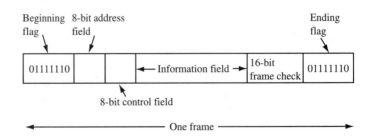

Self-Review 10.1 (Answers on page 495–496)

10.1.1   How long will it take to transmit the ASCII letter *B*, assuming 1200 bps, 7 data bits, 1 start bit, no parity, and 2 stop bits?

10.1.2   Sketch the transmitted waveform for the conditions described in 10.1.1.

10.1.3   A _____ error occurs when the receiver detects a missing stop bit.

10.1.4   The _____ is a microprocessor-compatible peripheral interface chip used to convert parallel data into serial and serial data into parallel.

10.1.5   What *clock rate* is required by a UART transmitting the data described in 10.1.1?

10.1.6   The *character rate* for the conditions in 10.1.1 is _____ characters/s.

10.1.7   Which serial communications technique—synchronous or asynchronous—normally achieves the highest character rate? Why?

10.1.8   _____ is a byte-oriented synchronous serial data technique, while _____ is a bit-oriented synchronous technique.

10.2   The EIA RS-232 Serial Interface Standard

Introduction

RS-232 is by far the most popular serial interface standard. First published in 1969, it was intended to describe the interface between a computer terminal and a modem. In RS-232 jargon, the terminal is referred to as a *DTE (data terminal equipment)* and the modem as a *DCE (data communications equipment)*.[3]

The specifications limit the data rate to 19,200 bps with a 50 foot cable. In practice, much longer cables can be accommodated, but at lower data rates. RS-232 is a voltage standard with typical logic levels of –12V for a logic 1 and +12V for a logic 0.

In addition to the electrical characteristics, two standard connectors (9 pin and 25 pin) are in common use. In this section we will:

- Describe the electrical characteristics of RS-232 and show how to construct a TTL-compatible interface.
- Identify and describe the function of the signals that make up the RS-232 standard.
- List the six modem control signals and show how they are used to provide hardware flow control between a modem and a computer.

Electrical Characteristics of RS-232

Noise Immunity.   Figure 10.9 compares the logic level specifications of RS-232 with those of standard TTL. As you know, standard TTL uses positive logic and provides 0.4V of noise immunity. RS-232 is quite different. It uses *negative logic,* with typical output levels of ±12V. The higher voltages are necessary to ensure reliable operation with long cables. The 2V noise immunity specification allows the cables to be routed through noisy environments that would be a problem for TTL.

Interfacing with TTL.   In order to interface RS-232 with TTL, special line drivers and receivers are required. These are shown in Figure 10.10(a). The MC1488 accepts TTL-level

---

[3]The RS-232 "standard" has gone though several revisions. The current level is RS-232E.

Figure 10.9 Comparing the logic-level specifications of (a) standard TTL, and (b) RS-232. The RS-232 standard uses negative logic (true=low).

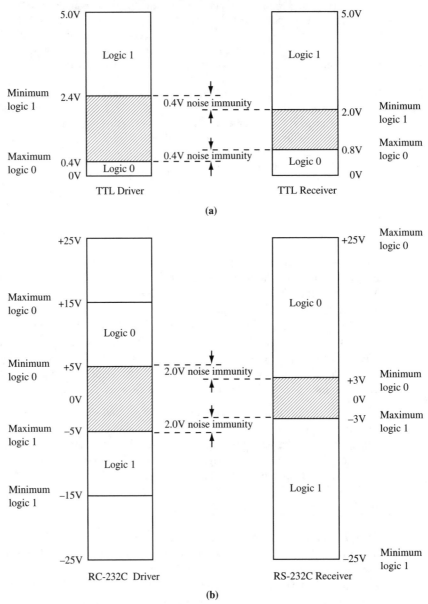

inputs and provides RS-232 output levels. The MC1489 does the opposite, converting the RS-232 levels on the transmission line to TTL levels for the receiving UART. Because of these drivers and receivers, the negative logic aspect of RS-232 is "transparent" to the user.

Figure 10.10 LIne drivers are available to convert TTL levels to any of the three standards: (a) RS-232; (b) RS-423A; (c) RS-422A.

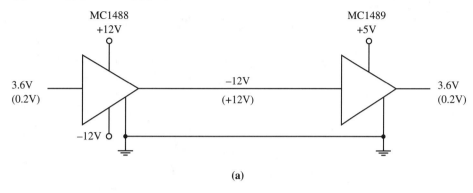

(a)

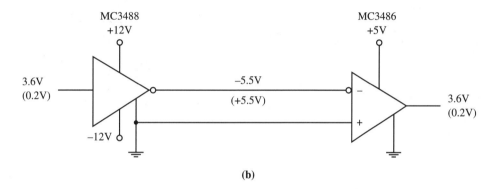

(b)

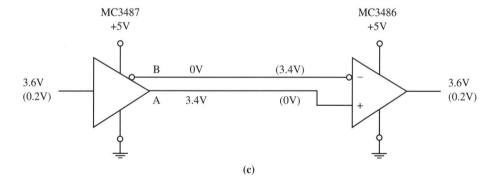

(c)

Figure 10.11 shows an RS-232 *transceiver* manufactured by Maxim Integrated Products. It offers two RS-232 drivers and receivers in one package (thus the term transceiver). In addition, it features an onboard "charge pump" that can generate the ±12V directly from the +5V supply. This single chip thus replaces the two chips shown in Figure 10.10(a) and negates the need to construct separate ±12V power supplies.

Figure 10.11   The MAX232
RS-232 transceiver. (Courtesy of
Maxim Integrated Products, Inc.)

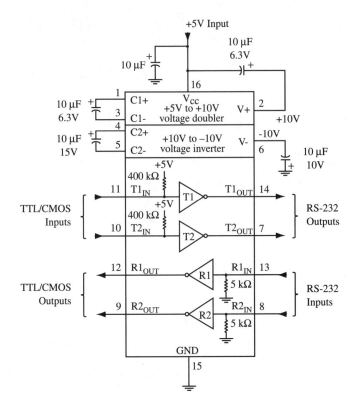

Maximum Cable Length.   One of the requirements of the RS-232 standard is that the transition time from one logic level to the other must not exceed 4 percent of one bit time. Thus, at 19,200 baud the transition time must be less than $.04 \times 1/19,200 = 2.1\mu s$. This, in turn, imposes a limit on the length of cable that can be driven. The longer the cable, the greater the capacitive load on the driver and the slower the transition time. At 19,200 baud, the maximum cable length is restricted to 50 feet.

RS-422A and RS-423A

Differential vs. Single-Ended.   One of the reasons that RS-232 is restricted to relatively short cable lengths is that the drivers and receivers are *unbalanced,* or *single-ended.* This means the input and output signals are referenced to a common ground [see Figure 10.10(a)]. Because it is likely that the ground potentials at the receiving and transmitting nodes will be at different potentials, a current will flow in the common groundwire connection. The resulting *IR* drop in this conductor reduces the 2.0V of noise immunity. The unbalanced nature of the driver and receiver thus becomes another limiting factor in the length of cable that can be used.

Figure 10.10(b) and (c) illustrates two new electrical interface standards: RS–423A and RS-422A. RS-422A uses a *differential* transmitter and receiver: This eliminates the common groundwire. The receiver detects the *difference* between its two inputs as positive or negative. RS–423A is similar but uses a single-ended driver with a differential receiver.

Figure 10.12 Comparing the logic-level specifications of (a) RS-422A, and (b) RS-423A.

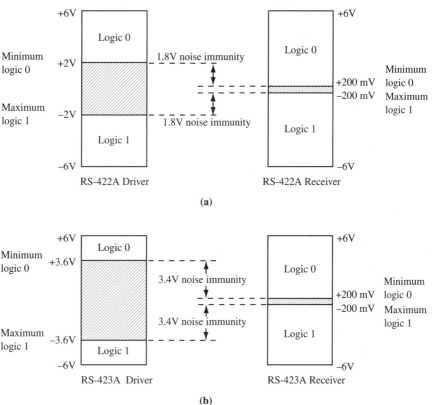

(a)

(b)

Again, no common ground path exists. Figure 10.12(a) and (b) compares the logic-level specifications for these two standards.

Because of its differential design, RS–422A can tolerate a much smaller transition region than RS-232: This in turn allows a much higher data rate. For example, using RS-422A, 100,000 bps is possible with a 4000 ft cable.

The EIA would like to see the electronics industry move to the newer RS-422A standard. However, as you can see by comparing RS-232 in Figure 10.9(b) with RS-422A in Figure 10.12(a), the two are not compatible. This is one of the reasons that RS-423A was developed. An RS-423A driver produces voltages within the RS-232 specifications. In addition, its receiver will correctly convert RS-232 levels to TTL. Thus, RS-423A establishes a sort of interim standard between RS-422A and RS-232.

Table 10.3 compares important electrical characteristics of the three standards discussed. You should be aware that RS-422A and RS-423A actually represent just the *electrical standards* for yet another EIA standard, called RS-449. This is a new serial interface standard comparable with RS-232. However, unlike RS-232, it specifies two data connectors, a 37-pin connector for the main interface signals, and a 9-pin connector for an (optional) secondary channel. For data rates below 20,000 bps, either RS-422A or RS-423A can be used. For data rates above 20,000 bps, RS-422A must be used.

Table 10.3 Electrical Characteristics for RS-232, RS-422A, and RS-423A

Parameter	RS-232	RS-422A	RS-423A
Line length (max.)	50 ft	4000 ft	4000 ft
Frequency (max.)	20 Kbaud/50 ft	10 Mbaud/40 ft	100 Kbaud/30 ft
		1 Mbaud/400 ft	10 Kbaud/300 ft
		100 Kbaud/4000 ft	1 Kbaud/4000 ft
Mode of operation	Single-ended input and output	Differential input and output	Single-ended output, differential input
Driver logic levels			
"0"	> +5 to +15V	> +2 to +5V	> +3.6 to +6V
"1"	< −5 to −15V	< −2 to −5V	< −3.6 to −6V
Noise immunity	2.0V	1.8V	3.4V
Number of receivers allowed on one line	1	10	10
Input impedance	3–7 kΩ and 2500 pF	> 4 KΩ	> 4 kΩ
Output impedance	—	< 100 Ω balanced	< 50 Ω
Short circuit current	500 mA	150 mA	150 mA
Output slew rate	30V/μs maximum	—	Controls provided
Receiver input voltage range	±15V	±7 V	±12V
Maximum voltage applied to driver output	±25V	−0.25 to +6V	±6V

Will RS-449 replace RS-232? At present, the industry is solidly entrenched with RS-232. However, the performance benefits of RS-449 are slowly attracting converts. The best bet is to expect this conversion process to continue for many years.

RS-232 Signal Descriptions and Mechanical Interface

Signal Names.   Table 10.4 lists the signal names, source, and destination for the 25 pins of the RS-232 interface standard. The data pins are grouped into a *primary* and *secondary* channel. The latter is seldom used, but does allow a path for confirmation or interruption of the data flow.

The six control pins $\overline{\text{DTR}}$, $\overline{\text{DSR}}$, $\overline{\text{CTS}}$, $\overline{\text{RTS}}$, $\overline{\text{DCD}}$, and $\overline{\text{RI}}$ establish a *protocol* between the modem (DCE) and the terminal (DTE). They are explained in detail in the next section. The remaining signals are less frequently used and support a secondary data channel, synchronous modems (requiring separate transmit and receive clock signals), and a data-rate select pin for dual-rate modems. Note that the signal names are defined from the DTE's point of view. *This is very important.* Why? If we simply consider pin 2 to be transmitted data, then we could easily end up with two transmitters connected to the same pin. Fortunately, the standard allows any two pins to be shorted without damage—but the interface will certainly not work.

Table 10.4 Signal Designations for the RS-232C Serial Interface Standard

Pin	Signal name	Data – From DTE to DCE	Data – To DTE from DCE	Control – From DTE to DCE	Control – To DTE from DCE
1	Protective ground				
2	Transmitted data	X			
3	Received data		X		
4	Request to send ($\overline{\text{RTS}}$)			X	
5	Clear to send ($\overline{\text{CTS}}$)				X
6	Data set ready ($\overline{\text{DSR}}$)				X
7	Signal ground				
8	Data carrier detect ($\overline{\text{DCD}}$)				X
9/10	Reserved for data set testing				
11	Unassigned				
12	Secondary data carrier detect				X
13	Secondary clear to send				X
14	Secondary transmitted data	X			
15	Transmit signal element timing				X
16	Secondary received data		X		
17	Receive signal element timing				X
18	Unassigned				
19	Secondary request to send			X	
20	Data terminal ready ($\overline{\text{DTR}}$)			X	
21	Signal-quality detector (indicates probability of error)				X
22	Ring indicator				X
23	Data signal rate select (allows selection of two different baud rates)				X
24	Transmit signal element timing			X	
25	Unassigned				

Example 10.5

Show the minimum connections required to interface a microcomputer serial port wired as a DTE to a serial printer wired as a DCE.

Solution

As shown in Figure 10.13, a *straight-through* cable can be used. Three signals are required: transmitted data, received data, and signal ground. Technically, protective ground, pin 1, should also be used to help eliminate the ground loop problem mentioned earlier. However, the connections shown in Figure 10.13 are very common.[4]

---

[4]The connections described in this example do not include any *handshaking* logic. This may cause the printer's buffer to overflow at higher data rates. Later in this section we show an example that uses handshaking to avoid this problem.

Figure 10.13 Interfacing a serial printer wired as a DCE to to a PC wired as a DTE.

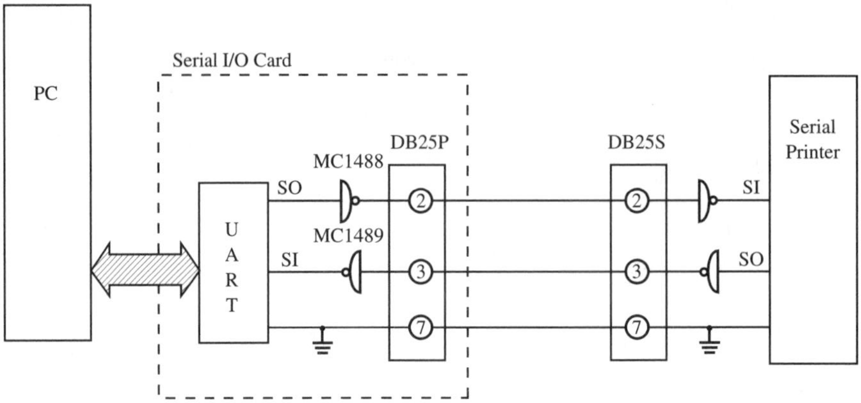

Serial I/O Card

PC

UART

SO   MC1488

DB25P

②

MC1489

SI   ③

⑦

DB25S

②   SI

③   SO

⑦

Serial
Printer

Connectors.   Two different connectors are commonly used with RS-232: These are shown in Figure 10.14. The 25-pin male and female connectors are referred to as DB-25P (for plug) and DB-25S (for socket). Because these connectors are relatively large and many of the 25 pins are not used, manufacturers frequently provide a *subset* of the standard via 9-pin male and female connectors. Table 10.5 compares the pinouts for the two connectors. Adapters are available to convert 9-pin connectors to 25-pin and vice versa.

Caution is required when spotting 9- or 25-pin connectors on the rear of a computer, however. The parallel port on a PC also uses a DB-25 connector, and CGA/EGA video cards (now nearly obsolete) use 9-pin connectors. No confusion should arise, however, as

Figure 10.14 Both DB25 and DB9 connectors are in common use with RS-232 ports.

Table 10.5 DB-9 and DB-25 RS-232 Pin Designations

Signal Name	DB-9	DB-25
DCD	1	8
RxD	2	3
TxD	3	2
DTR	4	20
GND	5	7
DSR	6	6
RTS	7	4
CTS	8	5
RI	9	22

the 9- and 25-pin connectors used by the PC's serial ports are male connectors; the printer and video cards use female connectors.

RS-232 Data Exchange Protocol

The Six Modem Control Signals.   When RS-232 was developed, six active-low (+12V in RS-232) signals were defined to control the transfer of data between a terminal (DTE) and modem (DCE). The word interpretation for each of these signals is as follows:

1. *Data carrier detect ($\overline{DCD}$)*: This signal is output by the DCE and indicates that the modem has detected a valid carrier from a remote site.
2. *Data terminal ready ($\overline{DTR}$)*: This signal is output by the DTE to indicate that it is present and ready for communications. It can be used to switch on a modem.
3. *Data set ready ($\overline{DSR}$)*: This signal is output by the DCE in response to $\overline{DTR}$ and indicates that the DCE is on and connected to the communications channel.
4. *Request to send ($\overline{RTS}$)*: This signal is output by the DTE to indicate that it is ready to transmit data.
5. *Clear to send ($\overline{CTS}$)*: This signal is output by the DCE and acknowledges $\overline{RTS}$. It indicates that the DCE is ready for transmission.
6. *Ring ($\overline{RI}$)*: This signal is output by the DCE (modem) and is active in synchronization with the telephone ring signal.

Figure 10.15 shows the typical cabling required between a PC and a modem. Note that either the standard 25-pin or newer 9-pin connectors can be used. Pin numbers shown are for the 25-pin connector.

Consider now the *handshaking* that goes on between a PC wired as a DTE and a modem wired as a DCE. Two cases will be considered: (a) Placing a call to a remote site and (b) receiving a call from a remote site.

Placing a Call.   Figure 10.16 flowcharts the sequence. Typically, a communications program (PROCOM, TERMINAL, etc.) is used to place the call. When this program starts, it causes $\overline{DTR}$ to become active. If the modem is present and turned on, it responds with $\overline{DSR}$. This establishes the PC-to-modem connection.

Figure 10.15 Interfacing a PC and a modem using RS-232. A nine-conductor cable is required.

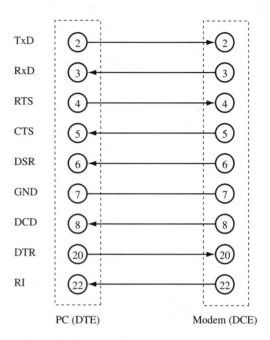

TxD
RxD
RTS
CTS
DSR
GND
DCD
DTR
RI

PC (DTE)   Modem (DCE)

The communications program now sends commands to the modem to take the phone off hook and dial the remote computer.[5] When this computer "answers the phone" it places a high-pitched tone (the *carrier*) on the line. This causes the $\overline{\text{DCD}}$ signal to become active. The PC and remote computer are now connected.

To begin the actual transfer of data, the PC makes $\overline{\text{RTS}}$ active and then waits for the modem to respond with $\overline{\text{CTS}}$. Data is then output to the modem (and transmitted to the remote) as long as $\overline{\text{CTS}}$ remains active. Note that the carrier must be maintained during this transfer or the connection will be lost.

In effect, $\overline{\text{DTR}}$ and $\overline{\text{DSR}}$ handshake the *connection* between PC and modem: $\overline{\text{RTS}}$ and $\overline{\text{CTS}}$ handshake the *transfer of data* between PC and modem.

Receiving a Call.   Figure 10.17 flowcharts the sequence for an incoming call. The only difference, when compared to Figure 10.16, is that the PC does not begin the $\overline{\text{DTR}}/\overline{\text{DSR}}$ handshaking until the phone is detected to be ringing (via $\overline{\text{RI}}$). Thus, the remote computer initiates the connection. The remainder of the sequence follows the protocol shown in Figure 10.16.

Terminating a Call.   When the transfer of data is complete and the connection is to be broken, each computer (local and remote) sends the *on-hook* (ATH0 in the Hayes command set) command to the modem. In effect this "hangs up" the phone and causes the carrier signal to be terminated. The connection then ends.

---

[5]Usually this is done using a standard set of commands developed by Hayes Corporation. The commands are known as the *AT command set* because each command is prefaced with the letters AT (for attention). The command to take the phone off hook, for example, is ATH1. Section 10.4 describes modems and the Hayes AT commands in more detail.

Figure 10.16 The handshaking sequence between a PC and a modem for an outgoing call.

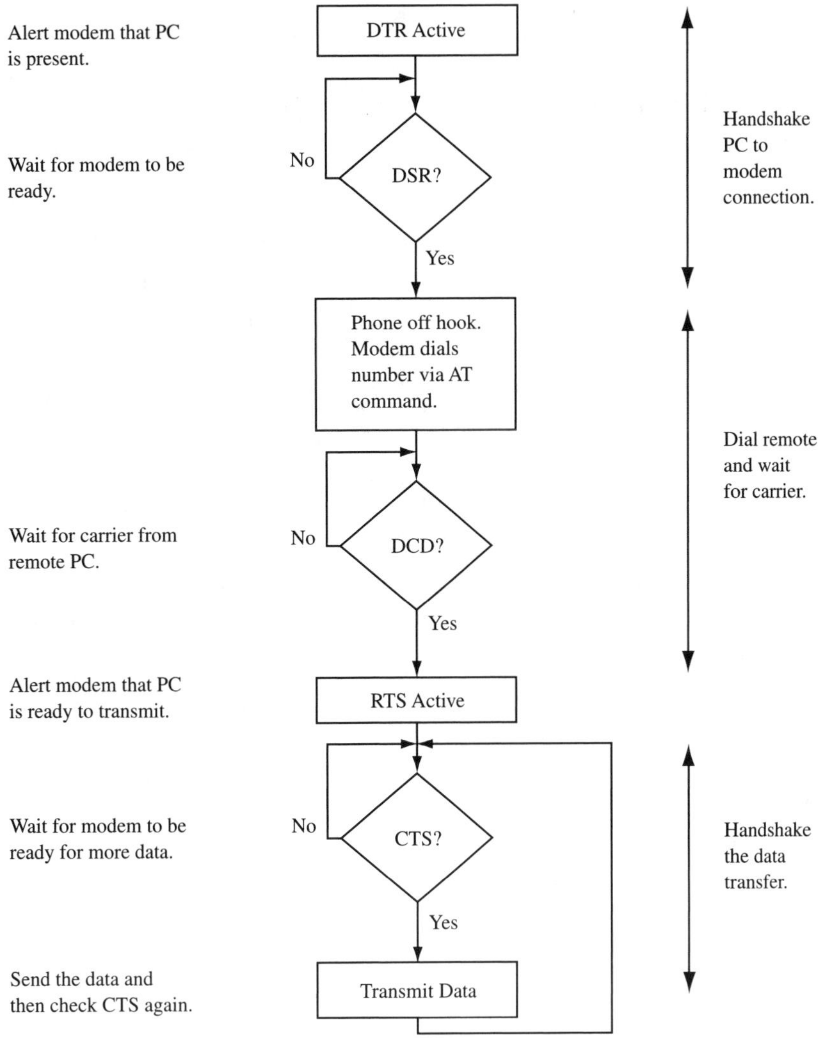

Alert modem that PC is present.

DTR Active

Handshake PC to modem connection.

Wait for modem to be ready.

No

DSR?

Yes

Phone off hook. Modem dials number via AT command.

Dial remote and wait for carrier.

Wait for carrier from remote PC.

No

DCD?

Yes

Alert modem that PC is ready to transmit.

RTS Active

Wait for modem to be ready for more data.

No

CTS?

Handshake the data transfer.

Yes

Send the data and then check CTS again.

Transmit Data

Interfacing Non-Modem Peripherals

Although originally intended to describe the interface between a modem and a terminal, RS-232 is commonly used to interface printers, plotters, and other serial devices to PCs. Indeed, it is common practice to transfer files between a desktop and laptop computer using each computer's COM port. When constructing these interfaces, two problems must be overcome:

1. *Determine the proper cable wiring.* If the serial ports of both devices are wired as DTEs (as is the case when interfacing a desktop PC to a laptop computer), each will attempt to transmit data on pin 2 and receive data on pin 3. Clearly, this will not work.
2. *Establish a handshaking protocol for the data transfer.* Two methods are common: One involves software, the other hardware.

Figure 10.17 The handshaking sequence between a PC and a modem for an in-coming call.

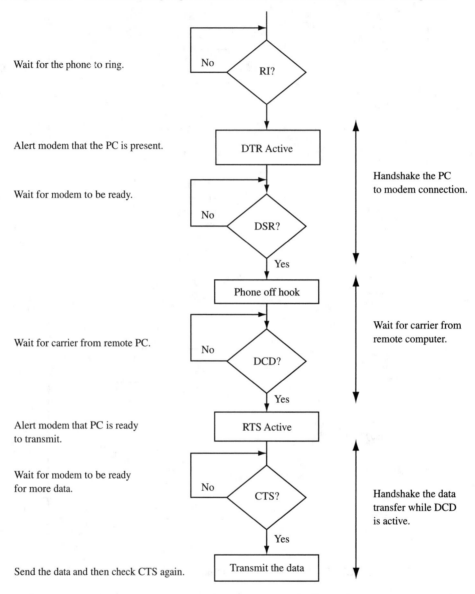

Wait for the phone to ring.

RI?   No

DTR Active — Alert modem that the PC is present.

Wait for modem to be ready.

DSR?   No

Yes

Phone off hook

Wait for carrier from remote PC.

DCD?   No

Yes

RTS Active — Alert modem that PC is ready to transmit.

Wait for modem to be ready for more data.

CTS?   No

Yes

Transmit the data — Send the data and then check CTS again.

Handshake the PC to modem connection.

Wait for carrier from remote computer.

Handshake the data transfer while DCD is active.

Determining the Proper Cable Wiring.   Printers and plotters are often wired as DTEs and therefore require a special cable when interfaced to a PC (which is also a DTE). As an example, consider the interface between a Hewlett Packard plotter and a PC running OrCAD Schematic Design Tools software shown in Figure 10.18. Because the computer and plotter are both DTEs, pins 2 and 3 must be "crossed." In addition, pin 20 of the plotter ($\overline{\text{DTR}}$) is connected to pins 5 and 6 ($\overline{\text{CTS}}$ and $\overline{\text{DSR}}$) of the PC. These latter connections provide hardware handshaking and are explained further in the next section.

Figure 10.18 A null modem cable is required when connecting a DTE and DCE.

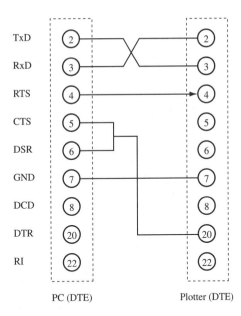

PC (DTE)   Plotter (DTE)

An RS-232 cable with pins 2 and 3 crossed, as shown in Figure 10.18, is often referred to as a *null modem*. That is, the cabling must be adapted to the fact that there is no DCE (modem) in this connection. Many other null modem wiring schemes are in common use. It is important, therefore, to locate the proper wiring diagram for the device you are trying to interface.[6]

Hardware Handshaking.   The need for handshaking signals with a serial data port may not be immediately obvious. Normally, the microcomputer is synchronized to the character rate of the UART by testing the latter's transmitter-ready flag. The flaw in this technique is that the *readiness* of the data receiver is not being tested.

For example, when interfacing a plotter, a command may be given that requires a new pen to be selected. While the new pen is being mounted, data will be lost unless the plotter notifies the PC that it is busy. But without handshaking, the transmitter has no way of knowing that the plotter is "busy" and so continues to output data.

The interface example shown in Figure 10.18 supports *hardware handshaking*. The plotter uses pin 20 (normally $\overline{\text{DTR}}$ in a modem interface) to supply its BUSY/READY status. The OrCAD software then tests this signal via pins 5 and 6 (normally reserved for $\overline{\text{CTS}}$ and $\overline{\text{DSR}}$ in a modem interface) and transmits data only when these pins are low (indicating that the plotter is ready for more data).

Here is where things can get "sticky." Another CAD program might expect the BUSY/READY status to be supplied on pin 8 ($\overline{\text{DCD}}$) instead of pins 5 and 6. In this case, you could have a situation where the plotter works in one program, but not in another. This would lead you to suspect a software problem—but the cable would actually be at fault!

---

[6]When all else fails, *breakout boxes* are available that allow pins on one side of the RS-232 interface to be jumpered to the other side. In this way, the proper cabling can be determined experimentally. This can be a frustrating process, however, as each manufacturer seems to have come up with its own standard.

You may end up having to maintain a stock of cables to support different programs. Of course this is to be expected: RS-232 was designed to support a terminal-to-modem connection—everything else violates the standard.

Software Handshaking.   If the serial device being interfaced can transmit as well as receive data, software handshaking may be possible. In this scheme, the I/O device can request that data transmission be halted by sending the ASCII character 13H (X-OFF or control-S) to the PC. Transmission resumes when the character 11H (X-ON or control-Q) is received. The advantage of this technique is that it eliminates the need for the handshaking wires. The disadvantage is that the UART may have one or two characters stored in its buffer when X-OFF is received. These characters will still be transmitted and thus may be lost.

Another technique is to use the ETX/ACK characters, which provide a block-oriented protocol. After a block of data has been sent, it is terminated with 03H (ETX or end of transmission). Further transmissions are inhibited until 06H (ACK or acknowledge) is received from the I/O device. This technique is suitable for peripherals with data buffers that can be filled as fast as the UART can output data.

Be sure to note, however, that in order to use either of these techniques, the peripheral must be designed to support the protocol, and the PC driver must be designed to recognize it.

Self-Review 10.2 (Answers on page 496)

10.2.1   Standard TTL provides a noise immunity of _____ volts. RS-232 provides _____ volts of noise immunity.

10.2.2   Because it uses a _____ transmitter and receiver, RS–422A offers much higher data rates than RS-232.

10.2.3   Give an example of a device that is considered
(a) a DTE
(b) a DCE

10.2.4   PCs typically use _____ or _____ pin (a) *male* (b) *female* serial connectors.

10.2.5   Which local modem control signal indicates that the remote computer has placed its carrier on the line?

10.2.6   When waiting for a call from a remote computer, how does the PC know when to take the phone off-hook?

10.2.7   When is a null modem cable required?

10.2.8   The X-OFF/X-ON protocol is an example of _____ handshaking.

10.3   The PC16550D Universal Asynchronous Receiver /Transmitter

Introduction

The PC16550D is a UART chip that interfaces directly with the system buses of a microprocessor. It accepts parallel data from the processor via its 8-bit data bus lines, converts that data to serial form, adds start, stop, and optional parity bits, and clocks the data out at the specified data rate (0–256K bps). In a like manner, incoming serial data is converted to parallel and stored for access by the processor. All three I/O control schemes we have studied—polling, interrupts, and DMA—are supported.

The PC16550D is the latest in a succession of UART chips used in the PC. It improves on its predecessors—the NS8250 and NS16450—by offering higher data rates and buffered data input and output FIFO (*first-in/first-out*) registers. Because most PCs provide two separate serial ports—COM1 and COM2—National also offers the NPC16552D, which is a dual version of the PC16550D. That is, it contains two 16550s in one package.

In this section we will:

- Describe the internal register set of the PC16550D UART.
- Explain how the PC16550D's onboard FIFOs allow the processor to operate more efficiently.
- Describe the PC16550D initialization and interrupt handling software.

Block Diagram and Pin Descriptions

The PC16550D is available in three different package types—PLCC, TQFP, and DIP. Its block diagram is shown in Figure 10.19. The pin numbers shown are for the DIP package. The following is a brief description of the pin functions:

D0–D7. Bidirectional data connections between the UART and processor.

A0–A2. These three pins allow selection of eight different control and status registers within the UART. In the PC architecture, the UART is mapped to I/O ports 3F8–3FF (COM1) and 2F8–2FF (COM2).

CSO, CS1, $\overline{CS2}$, and $\overline{ADS}$. The rising edge of $\overline{ADS}$ (address strobe) latches the three chip-select inputs (CS0–2). If these signals are active, the chip is selected.

MR (Master reset). When active, all registers except the receiver and transmitter data registers and the data-rate divisor registers are cleared.

RD, $\overline{RD}$, WR, and $\overline{WR}$. Active-high and and low read and write control inputs. If the chip is selected and either read input is active, a read operation occurs. If the chip is selected and either write input is active, a write operation occurs.

DDIS (Driver disable.) This pin goes low whenever the processor is reading data from the UART. It can be used to enable/disable a data bus driver.

$\overline{TxRdy}$ *and* $\overline{RxRDY}$. Transmitter and receiver DMA request lines. $\overline{TxRDY}$ becomes active when the transmitter FIFO is empty (single-transfer mode) or when there is at least one empty position in the FIFO (multitransfer mode). $\overline{RxRDY}$ becomes active whenever the receiver FIFO contains at least one character (single-transfer mode) or when a predefined trigger level or timeout has occurred (multitransfer mode). The receiver and transmitter FIFOs are discussed further in following sections.

XIN and XOUT. External crystal input and output. Typically, a crystal is connected between these two pins. Two internal divisor registers then allow the data rate of the UART to be programmed.

SIN and SOUT. Serial input from the communications link and serial output to the communications link. SOUT is high following a master reset.

RCLK. Receiver clock input. The data rate of the receiver is determined by the frequency of the clock signal applied to this input, which should be 16 times the intended data rate. Typically, RCLK is wired to $\overline{BAUDOUT}$.

Figure 10.19 The PC16550D UART. (Courtesy of National Semiconductor Corp.)

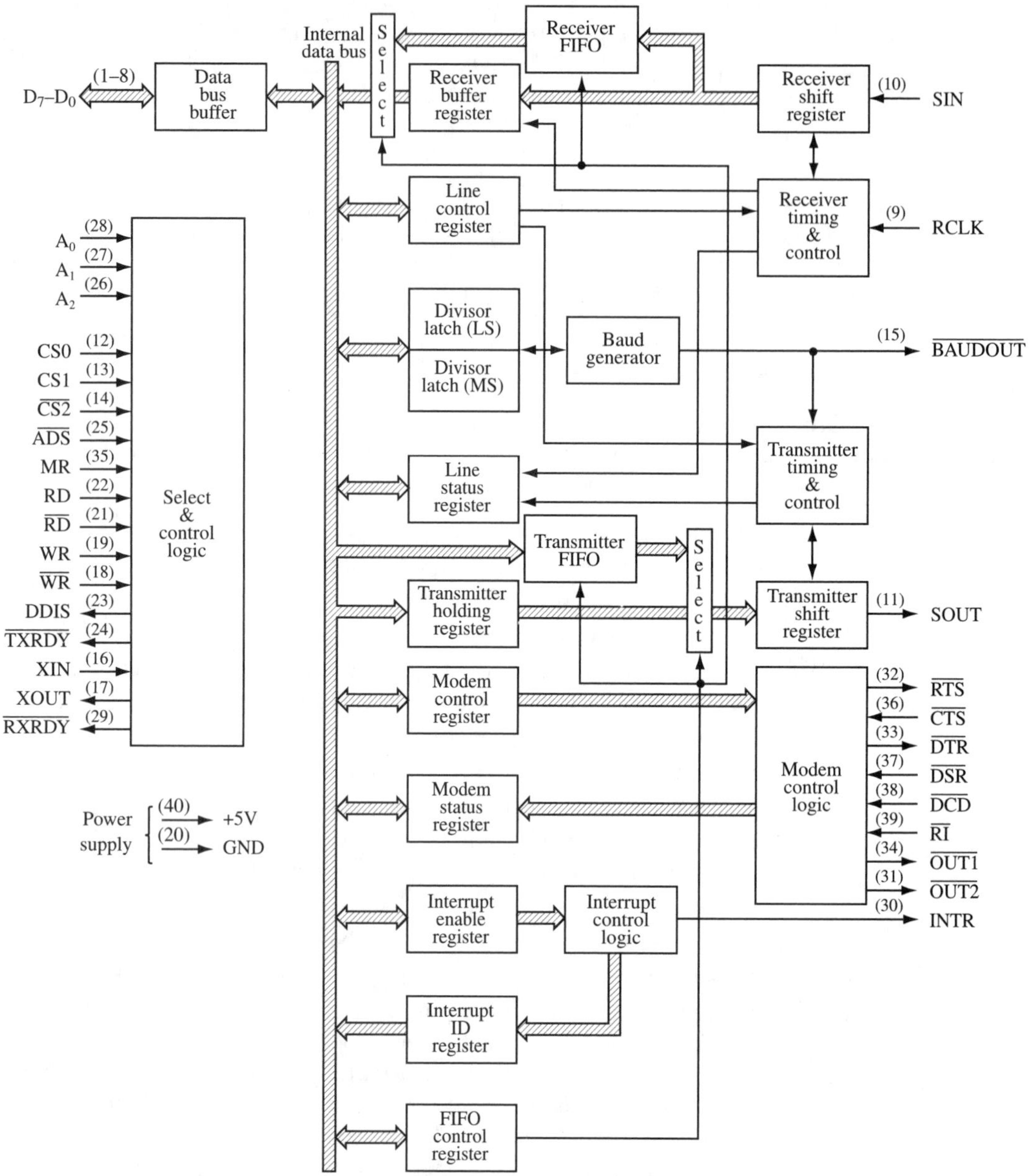

Note: Applicable pinout numbers are included within parentheses.

$\overline{BAUDOUT}$. This is the 16× clock signal equal to the main reference signal (typically the crystal frequency on XIN) divided by the frequency divisor. For example, if the crystal frequency is 1.8432 MHz and the divisor is 6, $\overline{BAUDOUT}$ has a frequency of 307.2 KHz (1.8432 MHz/6). The data rate of the UART is then 19.2K bps (307.2 KHz/16).

$\overline{RTS}$, $\overline{CTS}$, $\overline{DTR}$, $\overline{DSR}$, $\overline{DCD}$, and $\overline{RI}$. These are the modem control signals described in Section 10.2. They can be set or read via the modem control and status registers of the UART, respectively.

$\overline{OUT1}$ and $\overline{OUT2}$. These are general-purpose output pins that can be programmed high or low via the modem control register. A master reset leaves these pins in the high state.

INTR (Interrupt). This pin is connected to IRQ4 (COM1) or IRQ3 (COM2) of the 8259A PIC in a PC system. If enabled via the interrupt enable register, it becomes active whenever one of the following events occur:

1. The receiver detects an error condition, such as a framing error. The specific error can be determined by reading the line status register.
2. The receiver FIFO has "filled up." The *trigger level* can be set to 1, 4, 8, or 14 bytes. An interrupt is also generated if there is at least one character in the FIFO and neither the processor or receiver shift register has accessed the FIFO within four character times of the last byte.[7]
3. The transmitter holding register is empty.
4. Any of the six modem control signals changes state.

Systems Interface

Figure 10.20 is a simplified diagram showing how the PC16550D is interfaced in a typical PC. The data bus connection provides a path for control information and data to be written and read. The address bus connections are necessary to map the chip to the desired I/O ports.

The EIA transmitters and receivers are required to convert the serial output data to RS-232 levels and the incoming serial data to TTL levels.

Control Schemes. One method of controlling the PC16550D is to use *polling*. The status registers can be monitored and new data output when the transmitter FIFO is empty. Similarly, by polling the receiver ready bit, new data can be input from the receiver FIFO.

A more efficient scheme is to use *interrupts*. As shown in Figure 10.20, the INTR output of the UART connects to an IRQ input of the 8259A PIC. When an interrupt is received, the interrupt identification register must be read to determine which interrupt service routine to call based on the nature of the interrupt.

A third control scheme is to use *DMA*. Two channels, activated by $\overline{TxRDY}$ and $\overline{RxRDY}$ will be required. The UART can be programmed to input or output single bytes (mode 0) or multiple bytes (mode 1) each time these signals become active. In the latter case, a trigger level must be programmed to identify the "fullness" of the receiver buffer. When this trigger level is reached, $\overline{RxRDY}$ will become active, initiating the DMA cycle.

Receiver and Transmitter FIFOs

Previous-Generation UARTs. The NS8250 and 16450 had only single-byte data holding registers. This meant the processor had to be interrupted after each character was input or output by the UART. In recent years, serial transmission rates have increased sharply

---

[7]This is to prevent the last few characters of a data block from getting "stuck" in the FIFO unable to meet the interrupt trigger level.

Figure 10.20   Typical PC system including UART and PIC (master and slave). (Courtesy of National Semiconductor Corp.)

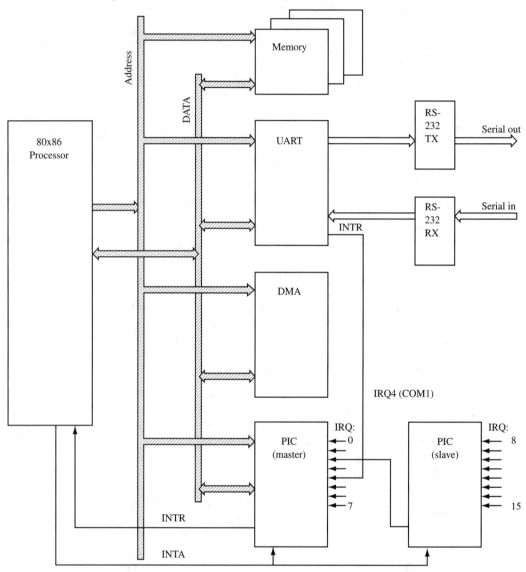

(a 28.8 modem with data compression can accept data at a 115.2K bps rate). This has had the effect of reducing the time available to the processor for other tasks while the serial transfer is occurring.

It is true that the time required to supply data to the UART is quite short when compared to the time required by the UART to transmit or receive one serial character. Nevertheless, the incessant interrupts are a "bother" to the processor (each interrupt requires a certain amount of overhead processing—fetch and update the byte counter, increment

Figure 10.21   A FIFO is a first-in first-out shift register.

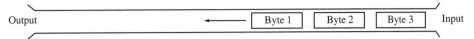

memory pointers, etc.). If the UART could accept more data each time it was accessed, the frequency of interrupts could be reduced and the overhead processing distributed over several bytes of data. The effect would be more processing time made available for other tasks.

The PC16550D accomplishes this by including separate 16-byte *first-in/first-out* (FIFO) receiver and transmitter buffers.

A One-Way Tunnel.   A FIFO can be likened to a one-way tunnel. As shown in Figure 10.21, data enters the FIFO at the "tunnel" entrance, moves through the "tunnel" in single file, and emerges at the "tunnel" output in the same order that it entered. That is, the first byte to enter is the first byte to exit.

In the PC16550D, the "tunnel" is made up of two byte-wide shift registers, each 16 bytes "deep." One buffers data intended for the transmitter, the other buffers data output from the receiver. In this way the processor can be ensured that as many as 16 characters will be transferred with each transmitter interrupt. Similarly, each receiver interrupt can deliver as many as 16 bytes of data to the processor.

Setting the Trigger Level.   The "fullness" of the receiver FIFO can be programmed by writing to the FIFO control register bits 6 and 7. Four levels are allowed:

Bit 7	Bit 6	Trigger Level (Bytes)
0	0	1
0	1	4
1	0	8
1	1	14

This programming allows the software to modify the interrupt trigger levels depending on the current task. It also ensures that the processor will not continually waste time switching context for only a few characters.

The transmitter FIFO operates differently. Interrupts are generated only when the FIFO is empty. Sixteen bytes can then be written, completely filling the buffer. If fewer bytes are written, only those bytes will be transmitted.

The PC16550D Register Set

Overview.   With three address inputs, A0–A2, the PC16550D occupies eight I/O-or memory-mapped port locations. In the PC these are mapped to ports 3F8–3FF for COM1 and 2F8–2FF for COM2. Table 10.6 summarizes the register bit definitions for each of these ports. In this table, note that the port address is given as 0–7 across the top of the table. Thus, port 2 corresponds to the interrupt identification register (and is mapped to

Table 10.6 PC 16550D Registers

	Register Address											
	0 DLAB=0	0 DLAB=0	1 DLAB=0	2	2	3	4	5	6	7	0 DLAB=1	1 DLAB=1
Bit No.	Receiver Buffer Register (Read Only)	Transmitter Holding Register (Write Only)	Interrupt Enable Register	Interrupt Ident. Register (Read Only)	FIFO Control Register (Write Only)	Line Control Register	MODEM Control Register	Line Status Register	MODEM Status Register	Scratch Register	Divisor Latch (LS)	Divisor Latch (MS)
	RBR	THR	IER	IIR	FCR	LCR	MCR	LSR	MSR	SCR	DLL	DLM
0	Data Bit 0 (Note 1)	Data Bit 0	Enable Received Data Available Interrupt (ERBFI)	"0" if Interrupt Pending	FIFO Enable	Word Length Select Bit 0 (WLSO)	Data Terminal Ready (DTR)	Data Ready (DR)	Delta Clear to Send (DCTS)	Bit 0	Bit 0	Bit 8
1	Data Bit 1	Data Bit 1	Enable Transmitter Holding Register Empty Interrupt (ETBEI)	Interrupt ID Bit (0)	RCVR FIFO Reset	Word Length Select Bit 1 (WLS1)	Request to Send (RTS)	Overrun Error (OE)	Delta Data Set Ready (DDSR)	Bit 1	Bit 1	Bit 9
2	Data Bit 2	Data Bit 2	Enable Receiver Line Status Interrupt (ELSI)	Interrupt ID Bit (1)	XMIT FIFO Reset	Number of Stop Bits (STB)	Out 1	Parity Error (PE)	Trailing Edge Ring Indicator (TERI)	Bit 2	Bit 2	Bit 10
3	Data Bit 3	Data Bit 3	Enable MODEM Status Interrupt (EDSSI)	Interrupt ID Bit (2) (Note 2)	DMA Mode Select	Parity Enable (PEN)	Out 2	Framing Error (FE)	Delta Data Carrier Detect (DDCD)	Bit 3	Bit 3	Bit 11

Table 10.6 *(continued)*

Register Address

Bit No.	0 DLAB=0 Receiver Buffer Register (Read Only) RBR	0 DLAB=0 Transmitter Holding Register (Write Only) THR	1 DLAB=0 Interrupt Enable Register IER	2 Interrupt Ident. Register (Read Only) IIR	2 FIFO Control Register (Write Only) FCR	3 Line Control Register LCR	4 MODEM Control Register MCR	5 Line Status Register LSR	6 MODEM Status Register MSR	7 Scratch Register SCR	0 DLAB=1 Divisor Latch (LS) DLL	1 DLAB=1 Divisor Latch (MS) DLM
4	Data Bit 4	Data Bit 4	0	0	Reserved	Even Parity Select (EPS)	Loop	Break Interrupt (BI)	Clear to Send (CTS)	Bit 4	Bit 4	Bit 12
5	Data Bit 5	Data Bit 5	0	0	Reserved	Stick Parity	0	Transmitter Holding Register (THRE)	Data Set Ready (DSR)	Bit 5	Bit 5	Bit 13
6	Data Bit 6	Data Bit 6	0	FIFOs Enabled (Note 2)	RCVR Trigger (LSB)	Set Break	0	Transmitter Empty (TEMT)	Ring Indicator (RI)	Bit 6	Bit 6	Bit 14
7	Data Bit 7	Data Bit 7	0	FIFOs Enabled (Note 2)	RCVR Trigger (MSB)	Divisor Latch Access Bit (DLAB)	0	Error in RCVR FIFO (Note 2)	Data Carrier Detect (DCD)	Bit 7	Bit 7	Bit 15

Notes
1. Bit 0 is the least significant bit. It is the first bit serially transmitted or received.
2. These bits are always 0 in the 16450 mode.
Source: National Semiconductor

461

port 3FA or 2FA in the PC). Similarly, port 0 corresponds to the receiver buffer register (read mode) and the transmitter holding register (write mode).

Ports 0 and 1 also store the low-order and higher *data-rate divisors,* respectively. Bit 7 of the line control register—the data latch access bit, or DLAB—controls this access. When DLAB is low, ports 0 and 1 correspond to the receiver and transmitter holding registers and the interrupt enable register. When DLAB is high, these ports correspond to the data-rate divisor. Following a master reset, DLAB is low.

The following is a brief description of each register:

Receiver and Transmitter Holding Registers (Port 0 with DLAB = 0). These registers are accessed to input data from the receiver FIFO and output data to the transmitter FIFO.

Interrupt Enable Register (Port 1 with DLAB = 0). This register allows each of the four interrupt sources to be enabled or disabled.

Interrupt Identification Register (Port 2). When an interrupt from the UART occurs, the processor cannot tell which event triggered that interrupt. Bits 0–3 of the interrupt identification register encode this information, as shown in Table 10.7.

FIFO Control Register (Port 2). This is a write-only register. Setting bit 0 enables the FIFOs. If this bit is low, the chip operates in 16450 mode with no FIFOs. Setting bits 1 and 2 clears all bytes in the receiver and transmitter FIFOs, respectively. Bit 3 determines the DMA mode (single or multi—0/1) of the $\overline{\text{TxRDY}}$ and $\overline{\text{RxRDY}}$ pins described previously. Bits six and seven program the receiver FIFO "fullness" level, also described previously.

Line Control Register (Port 3). This register programs the format of the asynchronous data communications exchange. The bit definitions are as follows:

1. Bits 0 and 1 specify the number of bits per character.

Bit 1	Bit 0	Character Length
0	0	5 bits
0	1	6 bits
1	0	7 bits
1	1	8 bits

2. Bit 2 specifies the number of stop bits. If low, one stop bit is selected; if high, two stop bits are selected.
3. Bit 3 enables parity detection and generation when high.
4. Bit 4 selects even parity (bit 4 = 1) or odd parity (bit 4 = 0) when parity is enabled.
5. Bit 5, when high, enables stick parity. If bit 4 is high, the parity bit is always low; if bit 4 is low, the parity bit is always high.
6. Bit 6 causes a break condition (SOUT = 0) to be continually transmitted.
7. Bit 7 is the divisor latch access bit (DLAB) described previously.

*Modem Control Register (Port 4).*This register allows the two DTE modem control signals $\overline{\text{DTR}}$ and $\overline{\text{RTS}}$ to be set or reset. The general-purpose output pins $\overline{\text{OUT1}}$ and $\overline{\text{OUT2}}$ are also controlled via this register. Bit 4 provides a local loopback feature for diagnostic testing of the UART. When this bit is set, the transmitter output is internally

Table 10.7 Interrupt Control Functions

FIFO Mode Only	Interrupt Identification Register			Priority	Interrupt Type	Interrupt Set and Reset Functions	
Bit 3	Bit 2	Bit 1	Bit 0			Interrupt Source	Interrupt Reset Control*
0	0	0	1	—	None	None	—
0	1	1	0	Highest	Receiver Line Status	Overrun Error or Parity Error or Framing Error or Break Interrupt	Reading the Line Status Register
0	1	0	0	Second	Received Data Available	Receiver Data Available or Trigger Level Reached	Reading the Receiver Buffer Register or the FIFO Drops Below the Trigger Level
1	1	0	0	Second	Character Timeout Indication	No Characters Have Been Removed From or Input To the RCVR FIFO During the Last 4 Char. Times and There Is at Least 1 Char. In It During This Time	Reading the Receiver Buffer Register
0	0	1	0	Third	Transmitter Holding Register Empty	Transmitter Holding Register Empty	Reading the IIR Register (if source of interrupt) or Writing into the Transmitter Holding Register
0	0	0	0	Fourth	MODEM Status	Clear to Send or Data Set Ready or Ring Indicator or Data Carrier Detect	Reading the MODEM Status Register

*Reading the specified register resets the interrupt (bit 0 of IIR = 1).
Source: National Semiconductor Corp.

connected to the receiver input. Data output is thus immediately received. Note that the SOUT pin is set to the high state and the SIN pin is disabled for this mode.

Line Status Register (Port 5). This register provides status information on the data transfer. The meaning of each bit is as follows:

Bit 0—*Data Ready.* This bit is set whenever a complete character has been received. It is reset when all of the data in the receiver buffer or FIFO has been read.

Bit 1—*Overrun Error.* Set when data in the received buffer is not read and new data has overwritten it.

Bit 2—*Parity Error.* Set when the parity of the received character does not match the parity specified in the line control register. This error is revealed to the processor when the associated character is the current character to be read from the FIFO.

Bit 3—*Framing Error.* Set when the received character does not have a valid (logic 1) stop bit. This error is revealed to the processor when the associated character is the current character to be read from the FIFO.

Bit 4—*Break Interrupt.* Set when a break condition—a solid logic 0 for one full character time—is detected. This error is revealed to the processor when the associated character is the current character to be read from the FIFO.

Bit 5—*Transmitter Holding Register Empty.* This bit is set when the transmitter FIFO is empty or when the holding register is ready for a new character (non-FIFO mode). In addition, an interrupt is generated if the corresponding bit (bit 1) of the interrupt enable register is set.

Bit 6—*Transmitter Empty.* This bit is set whenever the transmitter FIFO (or holding register in non-FIFO mode*)* *and* the transmitter shift register are empty.

Bit 7—*Receiver Error.* This bit is set whenever there is at least one parity error, framing error, or break indication in the FIFO. In non-FIFO mode, this bit is a 0.

Modem Status Register (Port 6). This register monitors the current state of the modem control signals $\overline{\text{CTS}}$, $\overline{\text{DSR}}$, $\overline{\text{RI}}$, and $\overline{\text{DCD}}$ on bits 4–7. In addition, bits 0–3 indicate if any of these indicators have changed since the last modem status register access.

Scratch Register (Port 7). This is a read/write register provided to hold temporary data. It has no effect on UART operation.

Divisor Latch (Ports 0 and 1 with DLAB = 1). These two ports store the low-order (port 0) and high-order (port 1) bytes of the 16-bit data-rate frequency divisor. Table 10.8 provides examples of the required divisors for the most common serial data rates using three different base (crystal) frequencies. For example, if an 18.432 MHz crystal is used to obtain a data rate of 2400 bps, the required divisor is 480, or 01E0H. E0H should thus be written to port 0 and 01H to port 1.

PC16550D Programming

Programming the PC16550D requires two steps. First the UART must be *initialized* to operate at a particular data rate, with the appropriate communications parameters (bits per character, number of stop bits, type of parity, and initial modem control signal states). Once this has been done, individual procedures for the actual transfer of data can be written. Figure 10.22 flowcharts the process.

Table 10.8 Data Rates, Divisors, and Crystals

Baud Rate	1.8432 MHz Crystal		3.072 MHz Crystal		18.432 MHz Crystal	
	Decimal Divisor for 16 × Clock	Percent Error	Decimal Divisor for 16 × Clock	Percent Error	Decimal Divisor for 16 × Clock	Percent Error
50	2304	—	3840	—	23040	—
75	1536	—	2560	—	15360	—
110	1047	0.026	1745	0.026	10473	—
134.5	857	0.058	1428	0.034	8565	—
150	768	—	1280	—	7680	—
300	384	—	640	—	3840	—
600	192	—	320	—	1920	—
1200	96	—	160	—	920	—
1800	64	—	107	0.312	640	—
2000	58	0.69	96	—	576	—
2400	48	—	80	—	480	—
3600	32	—	53	0.628	320	—
4800	24	—	40	—	240	—
7200	16	—	27	1.23	160	—
9600	12	—	20	—	120	—
19,200	6	—	10	—	60	—
38,400	3	—	5	—	30	—
56,000	2	2.86	—	—	21	2.04
128,000	—	—	—	—	9	—

Note: For baud rates of 250K, 300K, 375K, 500K, 750K and 1.5 MB, using a 24 MHz crystal causes minimal error.

Source: National Semiconductor Corp.

Figure 10.22 Programming the PC16550D UART. After the initialization steps have been performed, the UART is ready to respond to interrupts from its COM port. (Courtesy of National Semiconductor Corp.)

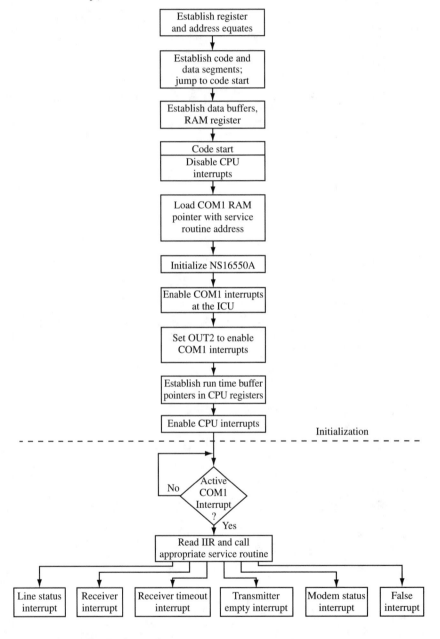

Initialization. Figure 10.23 provides an example of the 80x86 code required to initialize the PC16550D for COM1 operation in a typical PC. The first two blocks consist of a series of equates. The first block assigns a name and address to each UART register. For example, the receiver data register is named *rxd* and assigned the address 3F8H (the base

Figure 10.23 80x86 initialization code for a PC16550D UART interfaced to the PC as COM1. (Courtesy of National Semiconductor Corp.)

```
              TITLE    550APP.AM - NS16550A INITIALIZATION
;
;ESTABLISH NS16550A REGISTER ADDRESS/DATA EQUATES
;
;*********** UART REGISTERS **********************
;
rxd       EQU 3F8H             ;RECEIVE DATA REG
txd       EQU 3F8H             ;TRANSMITT DATA REG
ier       EQU 3F9H             ;INTERRUPT ENABLE REG
dll       EQU 3F8H             ;DIVISOR LATCH LOW
dlh       EQU 3F9H             ;DIVISOR LATCH HIGH
iir       EQU 3FAH             ;INTERRUPT IDENTIFICATION REG
fcr       EQU 3FAH             ;FIFO CONTROL REG
lcr       EQU 3FBH             ;LINE CONTROL REG
mcr       EQU 3FCH             ;MODEM CONTROL REG
lsr       EQU 3FDH             ;LINE STATUS REG
msr       EQU 3FEH             ;MODEM STATUS REG
scr       EQU 3FFH             ;SCRATCH PAD REG
;
;*************** DATA EQUATES ****************
;
BUFSIZE EQU 7CFH               :TX AND RX BUFFER SIZE
dosrout EQU 25H                ;DOS ROUTINE SPECIFICATION
intnum  EQU OCH                ;INTERRUPT NUMBER (OCH = COM1)
icumask EQU OEFH               ;ICU INTERRUPT ENABLE MASK
divacc  EQU 80H                ;DIVISOR LATCH ACCESS CODE
lowdiv  EQU O6H                ;LOWER DIVISOR
uppdiv  EQU OOH                :UPPER DIVISOR
dataspc EQU 1AH                ;DLAB = 0, 7 BITS, 1 STOP, EVEN
fifospc EQU OC1H               ;FIFOS ENABLED, TRIG = 14, DMA MODE = 0
setout2 EQU O8H                ;SETTING OUT2 ENABLES INTRs TO THE ICU
intmask EQU OFH                ;UART INTERRUPT ENABLE MASK
;
;*********** ESTABLISH CODE AND DATA SEGMENTS ****************
;
cseg    SEGMENT PARA PUBLIC "code"
        ORG     100H
        ASSUME  CS:cseg,DS:cseg
INIT:
        PUSH    CS
        POP     DS
        JMP     START
;
;********* ESTABLISH DATA BUFFERS AND RAM REGISTERS ********
;

msflag  DB      0
txflag  DB      0
sbuf    DB      bufsize DUP (*S*)     ; STRING BUFFER
rbuf    DB      bufsixe DUP (*R*)     ; RECEIVE BUFFER
sbufe   EQU     sbuf + bufsize        ; END OF STRING BUFFER
rbufe   EQU     rbuf + bufsize        ; END OF RECEIVE BUFFER
;
START:
        CLI                           ;>>> DISABLE CPU INTERRUPTS <<<
```

(continued on next page)

Figure 10.23   *(continued)*

```
;
;****** LOAD NEW INTERRUPT SERVICE ROUTINE PONTER FOR COM1   ***
;
        PUSH    DS                  ;SAVE EXISTING DATA SEG
        MOV     AH,dosrout          ;DESIGNATE FUNCTION NUMBER
        MOV     AL,intum            ;DESIGNATE INTERRUPT
        PUSH    CS                  ;ALIGN CODE SEG
        POP     DS                  ;WITH DATA SEG
        MOV     DX,OFFSET INTH      ;SPECIFY SERVICE ROUTINE OFFSET
        INT     21H                 ;REPLACE EXISTING INTR VECTOR
        POP     DS                  ;RESTORE CURRENT DATA SEG
;
;****************  INITIALIZE NS16550A  ********************
;
;This enables both FIFOs for data transfers at 19.2 kbaud using
;7 bit data, 1 stop bit and evan parity. The Rx FIFO interrupt
;trigger level is set at 14 bytes.
        MOV     AL,divacc           ;SET-UP ACCESS TO DIVISOR LATCH
        MOV     DX,lcr
        OUT     DX,AL
        MOV     AL,lowdiv           ;LOWER DIVISOR LATCH, 19.2 kbaud
        MOV     DX,dll
        OUT     DX,AL
        MOV     AL,uppdiv           ;UPPER DIVISOR LATCH
        MOV     DX,dlh
        OUT     DX,AL
        MOV     AL,dataspc          ;DLAB = 0, 7 BITS, 1 STOP, EVEN
        MOV     DX,lcr
        OUT     DX,AL
        MOV     AL,fifospc          ;FIFOS ENABLED, TRIGGEER = 14.
        MOV     DX,fcr              ;DMA MODE = 0
        OUT     DX,AL
        MOV     AL,intmask          ;ENABLE ALL UART INTERRUPTS
        MOV     DX,ier
        OUT     DX,AL
        MOV     DX,lsr              ;READ THE LSR TO CLEAR ANY FALSE
        IN      AL,DX               ;STATUS INTERRUPTS
        MOV     DX,msr              ;READ THE MSR TO CLEAR ANY FALSE
        IN      AL,DX               ;MODEM INTERRUPTS
;
;*************** ENABLE COM1 INTERRUPTS ********************
;
        IN      AL,21H              ;CHECK IMR
        AND     AL,icumask          ;ENABLE ALL EXISTING AND COM1
        OUT     21H,AL
        MOV     AL,setout2          ;SET OUT2 TO ENABLE INTR
        MOV     DX,MCR
        OUT     DX,AL

;
;********* ESTABLISH RUN TIME BUFFER POINTERS IN REGISTERS ***
;
        MOV     SI,OFFSET sbuf
        MOV     DI,OFFSET rbuf
        MOV     BX,OFFSET sbuf
        MOV     BP,OFFSET rbuf
        STI     ;>>> ENABLE CPU INTERRUPTS <<<
```

address for COM1 in a PC). The second block assigns names to values that will be written to the UART registers. For example, *dataspc* (data specification) equates to 1AH, and when written to the line control register programs 7 data bits, one stop bit, and even parity.

The next block—Establish Code and Data Segments—sets the data segment to overlap with the code segment. Control then transfers to location START, which temporarily disables interrupts while the UART is being initialized. Also note that two data buffers—sbuf and rbuf—are created, each 2000 (7CFH) bytes in length.

The first block on the second page of the program calls DOS interrupt 21H, service 25H—*set interrupt vector*. This code loads the offset of the interrupt handler routine into the interrupt vector table for a type 0CH (COM1) interrupt.[8] Six different interrupt service routines may then be called by this handler, as shown in Figure 10.22.

The next block of the program outputs the initialization codes to the UART. First the upper and lower divisor bytes are programmed. Next the *dataspc* byte is written to the line control register, as described previously. The *fifospc* byte is then written to the FIFO control register. This enables the FIFOs, sets the trigger level to 14, and programs the $\overline{\text{TXRDY}}$ and $\overline{\text{RXRDY}}$ pins for single-byte DMA transfers (mode 0). The last output instruction enables interrupts for all four interrupt sources. This section of code ends by reading the line and modem status registers to clear any false interrupts.

The next block—Enable COM1 Interrupts—begins by inputting the interrupt mask register byte from the master PIC (port 21H). The *icumask* byte equates to EFH, or 1110 1111. This clears, and therefore enables, bit 4 (IRQ4) of the PIC's interrupt mask register. The last instructions in this block set general-purpose output $\overline{\text{OUT2}}$. This can be used to enable a buffer on the UART's INTR output.

The initialization code ends by pointing SI, DI, BX, and BP at the data buffers established previously and enabling interrupts.

Calling the Appropriate Interrupt Handler. When an interrupt on IRQ4 is received, bits 0 through 3 of the PC16550D's interrupt identification register must be read to determine the source of that interrupt (see Table 10.7). Figure 10.24 shows the 80x86 code required. In this program, equate statements are used to define the bit pattern associated with each interrupt source. Compare and jump instructions are then used to transfer control to the appropriate service routine.

In some cases, further processing will be required. For example, if a line status interrupt occurs, the *ls_int* service routine will have to access the line status register and test bits 1–4 to determine the exact nature of the interrupt—overrun error, parity error, framing error, or break. A modem status interrupt will require similar processing.

Transferring the Data. The actual transfer of data is handled by the *rda_int* and *thre_int* routines listed in Figure 10.24. *rda_int* is called when the receiver FIFO has reached the preset level of "fullness." In the example in Figure 10.23, this was set to 14 bytes via the *fifospc* equate. Bit 0 of the line status register—Data Ready—is then polled and, if high, one byte of data is read from the receiver buffer register (RBR). The process is repeated until all bytes in the RBR have been read.

When the UART's transmitter holding register becomes empty, an interrupt is again generated. In this case, control transfers to the *thre_int* routine. This program writes 16 new bytes of data to the transmitter holding register.

---

[8]COM1 uses IRQ4, which is mapped to interrupt 0CH by the 8259A PIC. This was shown in Table 4.5.

Figure 10.24   When the PC16550D receives an interrupt, the interrupt identification register must be polled to determine the source of that interrupt.

```
;**************** Interrupt Identification ********************************
;
ls        EQU      06H                ;Line status interrupt
rda       EQU      04H                ;Received data available interrupt
cto       EQU      0CH                ;Character timeout interrupt
thre      EQU      02H                ;Transmitter holding register empty interrupt
ms        EQU      0H                 ;Modem status interrupt
;
**************** Process Interrupt ****************************************
;
          pusha                       ;Save registers
          mov      dx,iir             ;Interrupt identification register access
          in       al,dx              ;Read iir

          cmp      al,ls              ;Line status interrupt?
          jmp      ls_int

          cmp      al,rda             ;Received data available interrupt?
          jmp      rda_int

          cmp      al,cto             ;Character timeout interrupt?
          jmp      cto_int

          cmp      al,thre            ;Transmitter holding register empty interrupt?
          jmp      thre_int

          cmp      al,ms              ;Modem status interrupt?
          jmp      ms_int

          popa                        ;Invalid interrupt so return
          iret
```

Note that both routines—*rda_int* and *thre_int*—will be required to maintain separate byte counters and data buffer pointers in memory, and will have to be accessed and updated each time the data transfer routines are called. This is the "price to pay" for interrupt-driven I/O, as explained in Chapter 9. Of course, the PC16550D was designed specifically with this in mind. Because of the internal FIFOs, the overhead software need only be run when the receiver FIFO becomes full or the transmitter FIFO empty. This means as many as 16 bytes can be transferred per overhead cycle.

Self-Review 10.3 (Answers on page 496)

10.3.1   The PC16550D interfaces to the processor using a (a) *parallel* (b) *serial* interface.
10.3.2   To a PC, the PC16550D appears as _____ I/O ports.
10.3.3   List the five events that cause the PC16550D to generate an interrupt.

10.3.4   Because of the PC16550D's onboard FIFOs, each time the transmitter holding register interrupt occurs, _____ bytes of data can be written to the UART.

10.3.5   What PC16550D register must be programmed to specify the "fullness" of the receiver FIFO? What code should be written to enable but not reset both FIFOs, and to select a trigger level of 14 and DMA mode 0?

10.3.6   In the PC's COM1, the PC16550D modem status register corresponds to port _____.

10.3.7   When DLAB = 1, port 0 of the PC16550D stores 06 and port 1 stores 00. What is the UART's data rate if a 1.8432 MHz crystal is used?

10.3.8   The PC16550D IIR stores 04H when an interrupt occurs. To which routine will the program in Figure 10.24 branch?

10.4   Modems

Introduction

The switched telephone network was originally designed to handle analog (voice) communications with a maximum frequency of 3 KHz. However, computer users today routinely transfer data over this network with effective throughputs greater than 50,000 bps. The key component to facilitate this process is the *modem*. In this section we will:

- Compare modem modulation schemes including FSK, PSK, QAM, and TCM.
- Identify common national and international modem standards.
- Show how the AT command set is used to control the functions of a modem.

Telecomputing

Global Communications.   At one time, computer users were satisfied with having their own computer (recall the IBM advertisement promoting the *personal computer* in Chapter 1). Soon, however, users found the need to share information and resources. This spawned the *local area network (LAN)*. Via a LAN, users can access hundreds of megabytes of information on a local file server and direct their print jobs to a shared printer.

Many corporations have branch offices located in different cities around the country or even around the world. To connect these offices, the *wide area network (WAN)* has been developed. Depending on the speed requirements, a WAN may accomplish this connection using dedicated lines, satellite links, or (the least costly approach) a modem connection via the commercial telephone network.

The latter approach also provides a means for individual users to access the worldwide network of computers known as the *Internet*. This, in turn, allows users to communicate directly with major hardware and software vendors. For example, if a company has a new software product, it can be placed on the *World Wide Web* for immediate distribution and testing. Using *e-mail,* information can be transmitted between users anywhere in the world. Compare this with the two-, three-, and four-day delays associated with conventional ("snail") mail.

Modems.   The key component in establishing a connection to the Internet (or any remote computer using the telephone network) is a modem. The reason for using a modem, however, may not be obvious.

Figure 10.25 The switched telephone network has an upper bandwidth limit of just 3300 Hz.

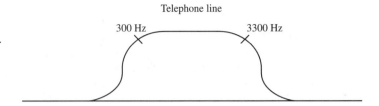

The DC voltage logic levels used by a computer—typically 0V and 5V—require a metallic path (wire) between the two telephones. At best, such a connection occurs only in the local area covered by the Central Office. If loading coils (transformers) are used in the local loop, the DC levels cannot even be transmitted that far.

In addition, because the telephone network has been optimized for *voice transmissions,* a narrow 300 to 3300 Hz bandwidth exists (see Figure 10.25). A digital signal with submicrosecond rise and fall times exhibits frequency components well into the tens of megahertz. The result of attempting to pass such signals through this low-pass filter (the telephone network) would be a signal unrecognizable as a logic 1 or 0.

For this reason, the *modem*—short for *modulator/demodulator*—was invented. When transmitting data, the modem emits a *carrier frequency* that is modulated in some way in synchronization with the input serial data. Several different modulation schemes have been developed, including *amplitude modulation (AM), frequency modulation (FM),* and *phase modulation (PM).* These are discussed in more detail in the next section. The receiving modem demodulates the information riding on the carrier signal and converts it back to standard logic levels. The "trick" is to find a modulation scheme that packs as much information as possible into the carrier wave. Using current technology, data throughput rates greater than 100K bps are possible—quite an accomplishment considering the 3300 Hz bandwidth of the telephone network!

Making a Direct Connection. Early modems connected to the telephone network using an *acoustic coupler.* This was required because the phone company did not allow users to connect wires directly to their system. Since 1976, however, direct connections have been allowed if a *registered protective circuit* is included in the modem. Nearly all modems today come with standard RJ-11 phone jacks. As shown in Figure 10.26, a short cable can then be used to connect the modem to the standard wall interface.

Figure 10.27 shows a typical direct-connect interface circuit. The modulated data is applied and received via the RCVA and TXA signals, respectively. Op-amp A1 is used to amplify the transmitted signal, which is then coupled to the phone line via an isolation transformer. This same transformer tap is used to retrieve the incoming signal, which is amplified by op-amp A2.[9]

The SN75472 relay driver allows the modem to apply an *off-hook* signal which in turn allows automatic dialing.[10] More about this when the Hayes AT command set is covered

---

[9]Careful study shows that op-amp A2 amplifies the received signal by 2 but the transmitted signal by 0, thus preventing the receiver from receiving its own transmitted data. See Analysis and Design Question 10.11.

[10]Pulse dialing is used in this example. Most modems also support tone dialing via a DTMF (dual tone multiple frequency) circuit.

Figure 10.26 Most modems include an RJ-11 connector to allow the device to be directly connected to the telephone lines.

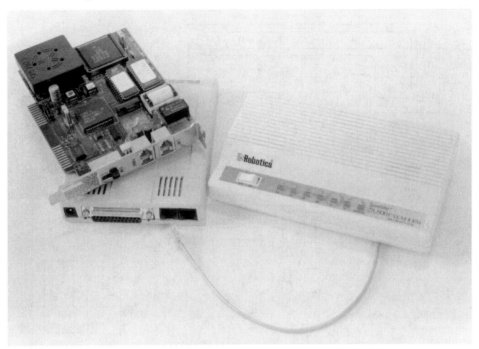

later in this chapter. The ring detection circuit uses an opto-isolator and LM393 comparator to convert the high-voltage (typically 135V RMS) ring signal into an active-low TTL signal.

Types of Modulation

Several modulation methods have been used for impressing the serial data output by a UART onto the carrier wave produced by a modem. The following is a brief description of the most common techniques.

Amplitude Modulation (AM).   This technique is illustrated in Figure 10.28(a). The amplitude of the carrier signal follows the binary data—present for a logic 1 and absent for a logic 0. Some modems transmit several different amplitude levels.

Frequency Modulation (FM).   This technique is shown in Figure 10.28(b). The frequency of the carrier signal is shifted high for a logic 1 and low for a logic 0. In addition to its use in modems, FM is also used to transmit digital data via radio. In the latter case, the transmitter is said to be "keyed" each time it is turned on. The term *frequency shift keying (FSK)* is thus applied. Modems using this modulation scheme are often described as FSK modems.

Phase Modulation (PM).   A third technique for modulating the carrier wave is shown in Figure 10.28(c). In this scheme, each time the logic state changes, the phase angle of the carrier changes. In the example shown, the phase change is 180°. Like FSK modems,

Figure 10.27 Example of a direct connect interface circuit for a modem. The telephone connection is made via the RJ-11 connector. The analog input and output of the modem is attached via the RCVA and TXA connections.

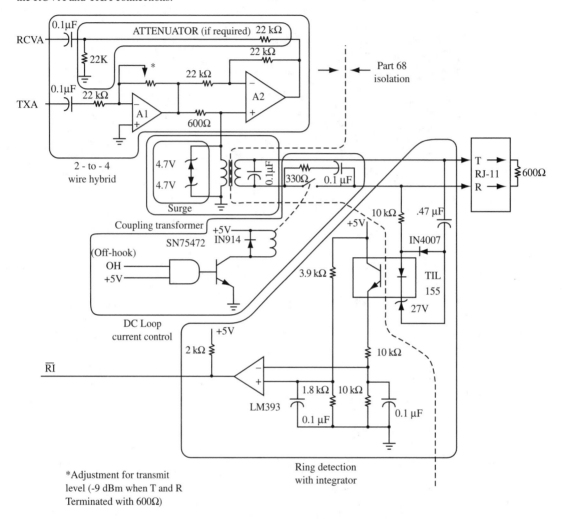

*Adjustment for transmit level (-9 dBm when T and R Terminated with 600Ω)

devices that use this modulation technique are described as *phase shift keying (PSK)* modems. PSK modems need not be limited to 180° phase changes. In fact, current modems encode the data using as many as eight different phase angles.

Baud Rate vs. Data Rate. Much confusion surrounds these two terms. The *baud rate* of a modem describes the number of *signal events* per second. A signal event is a change in amplitude, frequency, or phase of the modem's carrier signal. The *data rate* of a modem describes the number of bits transmitted per second.

In Figure 10.28, a new data bit is transmitted each time a signal event occurs. Thus the baud rate and data rate are the same. But consider a modem that transmits *four different*

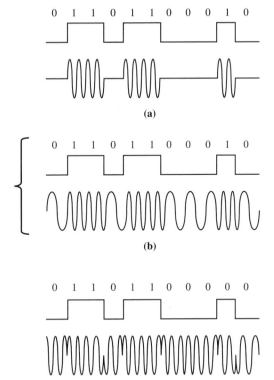

Figure 10.28 The output carrier produced by a modem can be modulated using (a) amplitude modulation; (b) frequency modulation; or (c) phase modulation.

amplitude levels (or four different phase changes). In this case we could associate *two* bits with each unique amplitude level (or phase angle). This is shown below.

Amplitude Level	Bit Pattern
0	0 0
1	0 1
2	1 0
3	1 1

If we could transmit these amplitude level changes at a rate of 600 baud (i.e., 600 amplitude changes per second), the actual data rate (in bits per second) would be 600 baud × 2 bits/baud = 1200 bps.

In Figure 10.29, we show a *constellation pattern* for a modem that transmits two different amplitude levels and eight different phase angles: 16 different amplitude-phase angle combinations are possible (note the 16 different arrowheads). And since 4 bits exactly define 16 combinations, a baud rate of 600 would allow a data rate of 2400 bps.

Modern modems typically transmit several different phase angle and amplitude levels. With these modems, the data rate and baud rate are *not* equal.

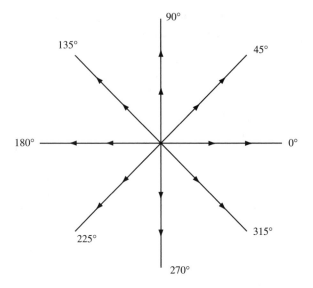

Figure 10.29 Constellation pattern showing two different amplitude levels and eight different phase angles.

Communications Standards

Standards are important for compatibility reasons. The ASCII code developed by the American National Standards Institute, for example, ensures that computer text files can be transferred between different types and makes of computer equipment. The EIA RS-232 standard discussed in Section 10.2 provides a standard serial port for the attachment of modems and other data communications equipment.

National and International Standards.   Until its breakup in 1984, the telephone industry in the United States was controlled by the Bell System. As a result, the Bell System originally supplied all modems that could be attached to the telephone network. By the time other vendors were allowed to sell communications products, a large base of telephone-company devices existed. To be compatible, these vendors followed the protocols established by the Bell System products.

Most modern modems follow a set of international standards developed by the International Telecommunications Union (ITU), a specialized agency of the United Nations. The ITU has in turn formed a committee that deals with technical issues and the development of data communications standards. The group is referred to as the Consultive Committee for International Telephone and Telegraph (CCITT). The standards developed by the CCITT are written as V.xx (pronounced "V dot xx").

The following paragraphs provide a brief description of the most common modem types.

Bell 103 (300 bps FSK). This is a full-duplex (simultaneous reception and transmission) modem. It uses FSK with two different sets of frequencies—one for the originating modem (the one that places the call) and another for the answer modem (the one receiving the call). The frequency assignments are shown in Figure 10.30.

Full-duplex operation is possible because the originating modem transmits using the low set of frequencies and receives using the high set of frequencies. The answer modem uses the opposite frequency set. Because one signal event—the transmission

Figure 10.30   Specifications for the Bell 103 300-bps full-duplex modem standard. (Courtesy of Racal Vadic)

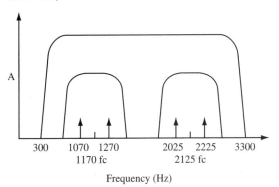

Frequency (Hz)

Specifications and channel assignments for the full-duplex 300 bps asynchronous Bell 103/113 modem are shown in this illustration. The Bell 103 modem can transmit and receive the low or high band. The ability to switch modes has been termed "originate and answer." The Bell 113A/D operates only in the originate mode; the Bell 113B/C operates only in the answer mode.

Specifications

Data:
    Serial, binary, asynchronous, full duplex
Data transfer rate:
    0 to 300 bps
Modulation:
    Frequency shift-keyed (FSK) FM
Frequency assignment:

		Originating end	Answering end
Transmit		1070 Hz space	2025 Hz space
		1270 Hz mark	2225 Hz mark
Receive		2025 Hz space	1070 Hz space
		2225 Hz mark	1270 Hz mark

Transmit level:
    0 to −12 dBm
Receive level:
    0 to −50 dBm simultaneous with adjacent channel transmitter at as much as 0 dBm

of a high or low frequency—corresponds to one data bit, the data and baud rates are the same.

V.21 (200 bps FSK). This is the international standard similar to the Bell 103. However, because it uses a different set of frequencies, it is incompatible with that standard. Notice also that it is limited to a lower data rate.

V.23 (1200 bps FSK). Modems that follow this standard are designed to operate at 1200 bps using half-duplex (only one modem may transmit at a time). It uses FSK, with 1300 Hz representing a mark and 2100 Hz a space. Like Bell 103 modems, the data rate and baud rate are the same. A low-speed (75 bps) reverse channel is also provided, using 390 Hz for a mark and 450 Hz for a space.

Bell 212A (1200 bps DPSK). This modem uses PSK with four different phase angles. In this way, two data bits *(dibits)* can be transmitted with each phase change. The resulting modulation scheme is called *DPSK*. Bell 212A modems operate at 600 baud but, with two bits per baud, the actual data rate is 1200 bps.

V.22 (1200 bps DPSK). This modem standard is similar to the Bell 212A but uses a different phase angle assignment for each dibit. In addition, while Bell 212A modems are compatible with the Bell 103 standard (300 bps), V.22 modems use two-phase PSK to operate at 600 bps for its lower data rate.

V.22bis[11] (2400 bps QAM). Modems that follow this standard operate in full duplex at 600 baud but encode four bits into each signal event. This is done by transmitting 16

---

[11]The term *bis* means *second* in Latin. In data communications standards, it is applied to indicate a second version of an existing standard.

different phase-amplitude combinations. The result is called *quadrature amplitude modulation (QAM)*. At 600 baud, the data rate becomes 2400 bps.

Bell 208 and V.27 (4800 bps PSK). These modems operate in half-duplex at 1600 baud. Eight different phase-angle combinations allow three data bits *(tribits)* to be encoded in each baud. The resulting data rate is therefore 4800 bps. Because the phase-angle assignments for the two modems are different, they are incompatible with each other.

V.32 (9600 bps TCM). This standard defines a full-duplex modem that operates at 2400 baud. Because the transmit and receive frequencies are the same, a sophisticated echo-canceling circuit is required. The modulation scheme uses a differential technique called *trellis coded modulation (TCM)* that looks at the previous output to determine the new output. Like QAM, TCM encodes 16 different phase-amplitude combinations into four bits: The data rate is thus 9600 bps.

The technique also permits the modem to identify misplaced signal points in the signal constellation and to correct most errors. This results in an error rate an order of magnitude less than that of modems without TCM.

V.32bis (14400 bps TCM). Modems that follow this standard also use TCM, but encode six data bits per baud. With a baud rate of 2400, the data rate of the modem becomes 14,400 bps. Like V.32 modems, V.32bis provides full-duplex operation via an echo-cancellation circuit.

V.34 (28800 bps TCM). This is the most complex standard to date. It uses the full bandwidth of the telephone network to operate at 3200 baud. TCM is again employed, and in this standard encodes nine data bits per baud. The resulting data rate is 28,800 bps.

When V.34 modems first connect, they *negotiate* for a compatible data rate. If the phone line conditions permit, both modems will operate at 28,800 bps. If not, the modems will *fall back* to a lower data rate (26,400, 24,000, or 21,600 bps).

The V.34 standard also provides an optional specification for asymmetric transmit and receive speeds. For example, a connection might support a transmit speed of 28,800 bps but a receive speed of 26,400 bps. Without split speed, the connection would be restricted to the slower 26,400 bps rate.

Finally, an improved version of the V.34 standard that will add support for even higher data rates—31,200 and 33,600 bps—is currently being finalized.[12]

Data-Compression Modems

Data compression involves finding a more efficient way of coding and transmitting a block of data. Two methods are in common use: MNP Class 5 and Class 7 and V.42bis.

MNP Class 5 and Class 7.   Microcom Corporation developed a series of networking protocols that are referred to as *MNP (Microcom Networking Protocol)*. Two of the protocols

---

[12]Two even faster modem standards are being proposed by US Robotics (USR) and Rockwell International. Both schemes take advantage of the all-digital nature of the modern telephone network to achieve a 56K bps data rate. This rate, however, is only achievable in the download direction. Uploads will continue to operate at the V.34 rate. Unfortunately the two techniques—called x2 by USR and K56 Flex by Rockwell—are incompatible.

deal specifically with data compression. MNP Class 5 uses a real-time adaptive algorithm for compressing individual characters.[13] Typical compression ratios vary between 1.3:1 and 2:1. MNP Class 7 provides an enhanced data-compression algorithm and can achieve data-compression ratios up to 3:1.

V.42bis.   V.42bis is becoming the preferred standard for data compression. Unlike the MNP protocols, it operates on a *string* of characters using the hardware-based Ziv-Lempel algorithms. Compression ratios as high as 4:1 can be achieved.

Data Compression and DTE Speed.   When interfacing modems that employ data compression, the DTE must supply uncompressed data to the modem at a higher rate than the modem can send the compressed data over the phone lines. For example, a V.34 modem employing V.42bis data compression could achieve a data throughput of 115,200 bps (28,800 bps × 4). In this example, the *line speed* of the modem (the DCE speed) is 28,800 bps, but the *DTE speed* (PC-to-modem data rate) is 115,200 bps. It is therefore important to check the DTE speed setting in the communications software.[14]

Error Detecting and Correcting Modems

Checksum.   When data and program files are transmitted via modem, it is imperative that data be received without error. Imagine misplacing a decimal point when transferring money from your savings account to your checking account! Or consider downloading an EXE file. One incorrect bit could cause the processor to incorrectly interpret an instruction or a jump address. The result? Your system crashes.

Although error detection can be done by the processor in software, increasingly this task is being performed by the modem in real time. Typically, the originating modem groups the data to be transmitted into blocks of characters. A mathematical calculation is then performed on this block, creating a *checksum* byte that is then appended to the block. The receiving modem computes the checksum on the received data. If these characters match, the data block is assumed to be error free. If not, an error signal is sent to the transmitting modem and the block is retransmitted.

Two error detection schemes are in popular use with modems: MNP Class 2–4 and V.42. Although similar, MNP Class 2–4 is designed for modems that support MNP. V.42 was designed specifically to support V.42bis modems.

Synchronous Transmission.   In Section 10.1 we learned that asynchronous serial data is transmitted framed between a start bit and a stop bit. That means 10 bits are required to transmit a single 8-bit byte. MNP Class 3 and V.42 modems strip the start and stop bits received from the serial port and communicate synchronously. The result is a data throughput increase of about 10 percent. For example, a V.34 (28,800 bps) modem will achieve a throughput of 32,000 to 33,000 bps.

---

[13]Using ASCII, a unique seven-bit code is assigned to all characters, independent of their frequency of use. Character-oriented data-compression schemes assign *shorter codes* to frequently occurring characters (vowels, for example) and longer codes to characters that are infrequently used. Adaptive codes continuously adjust themselves to provide maximum data throughput.

[14]As discussed in Section 10.2, the PC16550D UART was designed specifically to support the higher data rates of modern modems.

The AT Command Set

Smart Modems.   Most modems today are considered to be "smart modems" if they respond to commands from the Hayes *AT command set*. These commands were first offered by Hayes Microcomputer Products when it began manufacturing its Hayes Smartmodems. Each command is preceded by the letters *AT* for *attention.* Typically, the commands are issued via a communications program setup to access the COM port the modem is connected to.

Figure 10.31 shows an example using HyperTerminal, the communications program in Windows. The sequence begins with the *at* command. The modem responds *OK*. This verifies the connection between the PC and modem.

Next the command *atdt7984620* is given. This instructs the modem to dial the number 798-4620 using tone dialing. After a short delay, the modem establishes a connection and then leaves the command mode. Note that in this example the message *CONNECT 31200* is indicating the PC-DTE speed. The user is now connected to the remote computer (an Internet provider in this example) for access verification (username and password). After entering point-to-point protocol (ppp) mode, the Internet connection is established (indicated by the odd sequence of characters seen scrolling across the screen). The user now types +++ to force the modem to return to command mode. The modem again responds *OK*. The user hangs up the phone with the command *ath0*. The carrier from the remote computer is lost and the modem returns offline.

Figure 10.31   Typical AT command sequence when connecting a PC to a remote computer (in this example an Internet provider).

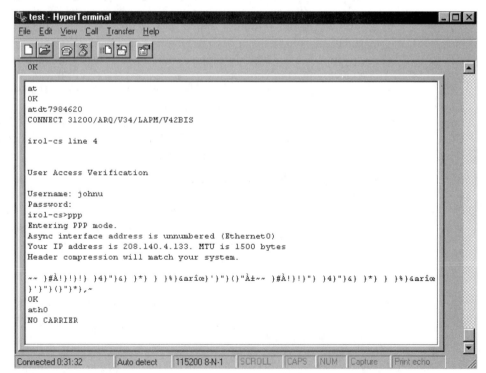

Table 10.9 Some Common AT Commands

Command	Function
ATDTn	Dial the number n using tone dialing
ATDPn	Dial the number n using pulse dialing
ATDSn	Dials the phone number stored in memory at position n ($n = 0$–3)*
ATE0	Local echo on
ATE1	Local echo off
ATF0	Half duplex
ATF1	Full duplex
ATH0	Hang up phone
ATH1	Go off hook (pick up phone)
ATI0	Display modem product code
ATI3	Display call duration
ATI4	Display current modem settings
ATI6	Display link diagnostics (connect speed)
ATK0	Return call duration at I3
ATK1	Return actual time at I3†
ATM0	Speaker always off
ATM1	Speaker on until carrier established
ATM2	Speaker always on
ATO	Return on line after command execution (see +++)
ATSr=n	Set S register r to the value n
ATSr?	Display the contents of S register r
ATS$	Display the contents of all S registers
ATV0	Return result codes in numbers
ATV1	Return result codes in words
ATXn	Set the result code displayed
ATZ	Reset modem
A/	Reexecute last issued command
A>	Reexecute last issued command continuously
+++	Go to command mode

*Phone numbers are stored with the command AT&Zn = s ($n = 0$–3 and s is the phone number)
†Set clock using ATI3 = HH:MM:SS K1

Table 10.9 provides information on several commands in the AT command set. Consult your modem manual for a complete list of commands your modem will execute.

S Registers.   Modems store configuration and status information in a series of registers referred to as the *S registers*. On a US Robotics modem, these can be displayed with the command *ATS$*. Individual registers can be examined with the command *ATS*n*?,* where *n* is the register number. For example, the command *ATS0=5* tells the modem to answer the phone after five rings. Table 10.10 lists the functions of the first twelve S registers for a US Robotics modem (in all, 38 registers are defined for this particular modem).

Table 10.10   S Registers 0 through 12 and Their Defaults*

Register	Range/Value	Default	Function
S0	0–255 rings	1	Number of rings to auto-answer
S1	0–255 rings	0	Counts incoming rings
S2	0–255 ASCII	43	Escape character
S3	0–127 ASCII	13	Carriage return character
S4	0–127 ASCII	10	Line feed character
S5	0–255 ASCII	8	Backspace character
S6	2–255	2	Dial tone wait time before blind dialing
S7	1–255	60	Remote carrier wait time
S8	0–255	2	Comma pause time in dialing
S9	1–$255 \times .1s$	6	Carrier detect response time
S10	1–$255 \times .1s$	7	Delay between carrier loss and hang up
S11	50–255 ms	70	Tone duration and spacing for DTMF dialing
S12	$0\ 255 \times 20$ ms	50	Escape code guard time

*Default values shown are for a US Robotics Sportster.

X Commands.   These commands tell the modem how "smart" it should be; that is, they define the result codes the modem will respond with when an event occurs (for example, detecting a busy signal). At the lowest level *(ATX0)* the modem will report the OK status, the Connect message, a Ring indication, No Carrier, and Error. At the highest level *(ATX6)* the modem can indicate No Dial Tone, Busy, No Answer, Connect *n* (where *n* is the connect speed in bps), Ringing, and Voice. You can measure your modem's IQ by repeatedly giving the *ATXn* command with *n* an ever-larger number. When you get the response ERROR, you have found your modem's "smartness" level.

Initialization String.   Some communications programs require that an *initialization string* be sent to the modem to set initial conditions. For example, one such string might be:

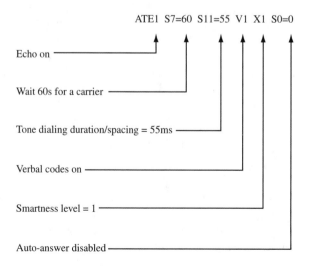

ATE1 S7=60 S11=55 V1 X1 S0=0

Echo on

Wait 60s for a carrier

Tone dialing duration/spacing = 55ms

Verbal codes on

Smartness level = 1

Auto-answer disabled

Many modems today can be initialized with the string AT&F1, which loads the factory configuration and enables hardware flow control. The command AT&F2 does the same but enables software flow control.

A De Facto Standard.   The AT command set has become a de facto standard; that is, it is in such common use that it has become a standard. Having said this, a caution is in order. As new modems are developed, new commands are added to the command set. This has resulted in commands and S-register definitions that are unique to a particular modem.

Fortunately, the AT command set is transparent to most users—it is built into their communications software. It is important therefore to "tell" the communications program about the specific modem you are using. Typically this is accomplished during the modem installation process.

Self-Review 10.4 (Answers on page 496)

10.4.1   The commercial telephone network has an upper bandwidth limit of _____ Hz.

10.4.2   _____ is a modem modulation method in which a logic 1 is transmitted as a high frequency and a logic 0 as a low frequency.

10.4.3   The baud rate of a modem is measured in signal events. What is a signal event?

10.4.4   A 600 baud modem using PSK with eight different phase combinations has a data rate of _____ bps.

10.4.5   What is the *baud* rate for a V.32 modem? What is the *data* rate?

10.4.6   The DTE speed of a 28.8 modem using V.32bis data compression should be set to _____ bps.

10.4.7   How do you "hang up the phone" using an AT command?

10.4.8   What is the AT command to tell the modem to answer the phone on the tenth ring?

10.5   Error Detection and Correction

Introduction

Data errors refer to those errors electrically induced by cross-talk between adjacent conductors, signal distortion, or impulse noise due to lightning, high current, or voltage switching. The long lines of the switched telephone network are particularly susceptible to these noise sources, but data errors can occur on any medium used for data transmissions. This includes the traces on a printed circuit board used to transport data between a microprocessor and its memory chips. In this section we will:

- Contrast the two common error control schemes: ARQ and FEQ.
- Compare common error detection schemes, including parity, checksum, and CRC.
- Show how the Hamming code is applied to detect and correct data errors on individual data bytes.

Error Control Methods

Automatic Request for Repeat (ARQ).   All methods of error control involve *redundancy*—that is, sending extra information that is not a part of the data message. The redundant information is sent in the form of *check bits,* which are used by the receiver to detect errors in the incoming data. ARQ has the receiver request that the last character or block of data be retransmitted if an error has been detected. This has the built-in disadvantage of reducing the data rate of the communications channel in direct proportion to the error rate.

Forward Error Correction (FEC).   This method requires the receiver to have more intricate logic circuitry that not only detects data errors, but also identifies and corrects those bits in error. FEC is based on a data-encoding technique called the *Hamming code* and requires several check bits for each character transmitted. The obvious advantage is the elimination of the need for data retransmission; the disadvantage is the reduction in data throughput due to the presence of the extra check bits.

Error Detection

Parity.   A parity bit is a redundant checking bit added to a data word or stream of bits in such a way that *the total number of logic 1s in the data stream*—including the parity bit—is *even* or *odd* (the receiving and transmitting stations must decide beforehand on even or odd parity). As shown in Figure 10.32, parity can be applied vertically (VRC) or longitudinally (LRC).

Vertical Redundancy Check (VRC).   VRC is a very common form of error control used with asynchronous serial data. One reason for this is that the transmitting and receiving UART can easily append and check the extra parity bit with minimal additional hardware. Used with ASCII-encoded data, the parity bit becomes an eighth data bit chosen to make the number of logic 1s in the resulting byte even or odd.

Example 10.6

The following data bytes are ASCII characters encoded with an even parity bit in the MSB position: D1H,36H,E5H. Which of these bytes, if any, are in error?

Solution
Converting each byte to binary:

$$D1H = 11010001$$
$$36H = 00110110$$
$$E5H = 11100101$$

Inspecting each byte, only E5 has an odd number of ones and must therefore be in error. The actual bit in error, however, is unknown.

The PC16550D UART can be programmed to automatically append a parity bit to each transmitted data character. This is done by setting bit 3 of the line control register (parity enable; see Table 10.6). Once enabled, setting bit 4 of this register selects even parity; resetting this bit selects odd parity. If the parity of the received character does not match the parity setting, a modem status interrupt will be generated by the PC16550D. The line status register can then be tested to determine the source of the interrupt. If bit 2 is set, a parity error is indicated.

Longitudinal Redundancy Check (LRC).   Adding a VRC bit to a data character can only detect *odd* numbers of error bits. For example, if the data byte D1H is received as D2H,

Figure 10.32 Vertical redundancy check (VRC) and longitudinal redundancy check (LRC). One VRC bit is appended to each data character. One LRC character is appended to each block of data.

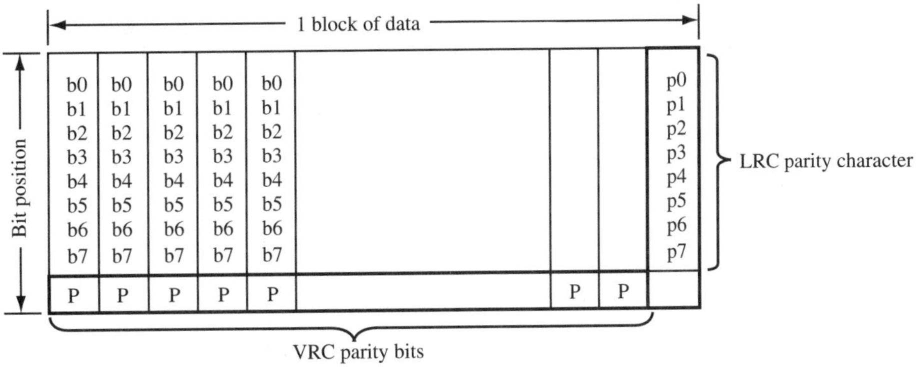

its parity does not change—even though two bits are now in error. VRC is best suited for environments where multiple bit errors are unlikely. A typical situation would be data transmissions between two computers connected via twisted-pair conductors or shielded cable.

Analysis of data errors transmitted over long distances, particularly via a modem and the switched telephone network, reveals that data errors occur in "bursts." A lightning strike may induce noise into the transmission path that may persist for several milliseconds. At 28,800 bps baud, 50–60 bits will be transmitted in 2 ms. Thus, several characters may be affected by the burst noise source.

For this reason, a redundant *block-checking character* or *checksum* is often used to detect multiple bit errors. The block-check character (BCC) may be computed as a LRC parity character, as shown in Figure 10.32, or calculated in software as the *two's complement* of all of the preceding bytes in the data block. Figure 10.33 shows an 80x86 program that calculates and appends a BCC to a block of 255 data bytes. The (256-byte) data block can then be transmitted using serial or parallel techniques as desired.

Example 10.7

Calculate the checksum byte for the four hex data bytes 10, 23, 45, 04.

Solution

The sum is calculated first:

$$
\begin{array}{r}
10 \\
23 \\
45 \\
04 \\
\hline
7C
\end{array}
$$

Inverting 7C and adding 1 (forming the two's complement):

$$\overline{01111100} + 1 = 10000011 + 1 = 10000100 = 84H$$

Figure 10.33   80x86 program to generate the BCC for a 255-byte block of data.

```
                          ;Function:      Append BCC byte to a data block
                          ;Inputs:        Block address passed in DS:SI
                          ;Outputs:       BCC added to the block as last byte
                          ;Calls:         nothing
                          ;Destroys:      flags,CX,SI,AL,BL


                          ;Program Equates

= 00FF                    BLOCK_SIZE      EQU   255


                          ;Procedure Begins

0000                      CODE      SEGMENT   BYTE
                          ASSUME    CS:CODE

0000                      BCC       PROC      NEAR
0000   FC                           CLD                      ;Auto increment
0001   B9 00FF                      MOV       CX,BLOCK_SIZE  ;CX is counter
0004   B3 00                        MOV       BL,0           ;Sum to BL
0006   AC                 SUM:      LODSB                    ;Get one byte
0007   02 D8                        ADD       BL,AL          ;Accumulate sum
0009   E2 FB                        LOOP      SUM            ;Do until CX=0
000B   F6 DB                        NEG       BL             ;Form 2s compl
000D   88 1C                        MOV       [SI],BL        ;Append BCC
000F   C3                           RET                      ;Done
0010                      BCC       ENDP
0010                      CODE      ENDS
                                    END
```

Example 10.8

Assume the following data bytes are received, and the last byte is the checksum character: 10, 23, 45, 04, 84. Has the data been received correctly?

Solution

The receiver need only add the five data bytes:

$$
\begin{array}{r}
10 \\
23 \\
45 \\
04 \\
\underline{84} \\
\hline
1\ 00
\end{array}
$$

Discarding the carry, the result is 00. No error has been detected. The reason for forming the two's complement should now be clear. Correctly received data will always produce a sum of 00 (ignoring the carry).

Besides its ability to detect multiple bit errors, there is another advantage to using BCC error control. For a 255-byte data block, only one extra byte, or 0.4 percent, of redundancy is required. Using a VRC technique, one extra bit is required per byte. This amounts to an overhead of 12.5 percent. Thus BCC is an effective way to detect multiple bit errors without significantly decreasing the data rate of the channel.

BCC is not perfect, however. When an error is detected, the entire data block must be retransmitted. Compare this to VRC, in which only the errant character need be repeated. In addition, some error combinations will go undetected by the BCC. In Examples 10.7 and 10.8, if the data byte 45H changes to 44H, and the data byte 04H becomes 05H, the BCC remains the same. In general, to go undetected, even numbers of bits must change in the same bit position.

Cyclic Redundancy Check (CRC).   CRC is another form of longitudinal redundancy calculated on a block of data. It is commonly used when reading and writing data to a floppy and to hard disks, and to ensure data integrity in programmable ROMs. It is universally used for detecting errors in synchronous data communications.

Unlike the checksum, the CRC method is not byte oriented. Instead, the data block is thought of as a "stream" of serial data bits. The bits in this n-bit block are considered the coefficients of a *characteristic polynomial* [usually referred to as M(X)—pronounced *M of X*]. M(X) has the form

$$M(X) = b_n + b_{n-1}X + b_{n-2}X^2 + \ldots\ldots b_1X^{n-1} + b_0X^n$$

where b_0 is the least significant bit (LSB) and b_n is the most significant bit (MSB).

Example 10.9

Calculate the data polynomial M(X) for the 16-bit data stream 26F0H.

Solution

First visualize this data in binary form:

$$0\ 0\ 1\ 0 \quad 0\ 1\ 1\ 0 \quad 1\ 1\ 1\ 1 \quad 0\ 0\ 0\ 0$$

Now, writing this as M(X):

$$M(X) = 0 + 0X^1 + 1X^2 + 0X^3 + 0X^4 + 1X^5 + 1X^6 + 0X^7 + 1X^8 + 1X^9 + 1X^{10} + 1X^{11} + 0X^{12}$$
$$+ 0X^{13} + 0X^{14} + 0X^{15}$$

and eliminating the 0 terms:

$$M(X) = X^2 + X^5 + X^6 + X^8 + X^9 + X^{10} + X^{11} \tag{10-1}$$

Equation 10–1 is a unique polynomial representing the data in the 16-bit block. If one or more of the data bits changes, the polynomial would also change. The CRC is found by applying the following equation

$$CRC = \frac{M(X) \times X^n}{G(X)} = Q(X) + R(X) \tag{10-2}$$

In this equation, G(X) is called the *generator polynomial*. For the bisync protocol, G(X) is

$$G(X) = X^{16} + X^{15} + X^2 + 1 \tag{10-3}$$

The SDLC protocol uses

$$G(X) = X^{16} + X^{13} + X^5 + 1 \qquad \textbf{(10–4)}$$

When the division is performed, the result will be a *quotient* Q(X) and a *remainder* R(X). The CRC technique consists of calculating R(X) for the data stream and appending the result to the data block. When R(X) is again calculated by the receiver, the result should be R(X) = 0. Also note that because G(X) is of power 16, the remainder, R(X), cannot be of order higher than 15, and is thus represented by two bytes (no matter what the block length itself).

Example 10.9

Calculate the CRC bytes for the data block 26F0H using the bisync generator polynomial.

Solution

Figure 10.34 shows the arithmetic. The remainder is

$$R(X) = X^{15} + X^{13} + X^9 + X^8 + X^6 + X^4 + X^3 + X + 1$$

When expressed in binary, this becomes (recalling that the coefficient of the highest power becomes the LSB):

$$1101\ 1010\ 1100\ 0101 = \text{DAC5H}$$

If the two bytes DAC5 are appended to the 26F0 data stream, the received CRC calculation should result in R(X) = 0, indicating that no errors have been detected. If an error is indicated, a request for retransmission must be made, as with BCC. The effectiveness of CRC for detecting errors can be summarized as follows, assuming a CRC length of *n* bits:

1. All data blocks with an even (or odd) number of errors are detected if *n* is even (or odd).
2. All data blocks with burst errors less than *n* bits long are detected.

Figure 10.34 Generating the CRC bytes from the bisync data stream 26F0H.

$$\frac{M(X)\,X^{16}}{G(X)} = \frac{X^{27} + X^{26} + X^{25} + X^{24} + X^{22} + X^{21} + X^{18}}{X^{16} + X^{15} + X^2 + 1} =$$

$$\begin{array}{rl}
 & X^{11} + X^9 + X^6 + X^2 + X + 1 \\
X^{16} + X^{15} + X^2 + 1 \;\big) & X^{27} + X^{26} + X^{25} + X^{24} + X^{22} + X^{21} + X^{18} \\
 & X^{27} + X^{26} + X^{13} + X^{11} \\ \hline
 & X^{25} + X^{24} + X^{22} + X^{21} + X^{18} + X^{13} + X^{11} \\
 & X^{25} + X^{24} + X^{11} + X^9 \\ \hline
 & X^{22} + X^{21} + X^{18} + X^{13} + X^9 \\
 & X^{22} + X^{21} + X^8 + X^6 \\ \hline
 & X^{18} + X^{13} + X^9 + X^8 + X^6 \\
 & X^{18} + X^{17} + X^4 + X^2 \\ \hline
 & X^{17} + X^{13} + X^9 + X^8 + X^6 + X^4 + X^2 \\
 & X^{17} + X^{16} + X^3 + X \\ \hline
 & X^{16} + X^{13} + X^9 + X^8 + X^6 + X^4 + X^3 + X^2 + X \\
 & X^{16} + X^{15} + X^2 + 1 \\ \hline
R(X) = & X^{15} + X^{13} + X^9 + X^8 + X^6 + X^4 + X^3 + X + 1
\end{array}$$

3. All data blocks with a total number of error bits less then approximately $n/4$ are detected.
4. Of all remaining error patterns, one in 2^n are undetected.

As an example, if a 25-bit CRC is appended to a 1000-bit data stream, only three error bits in 100 million will go undetected!

In practice, the CRC character can be computed in hardware or software. However, it has become common for the data communications peripheral controller chips to implement the function onboard. Intel's 8273 programmable HDLC/SDLC protocol controller automatically checks for CRC errors during reception, and automatically appends R(X) to the end of the data stream during transmission. Thus, the CRC becomes "transparent" to the user.

Error Correction

The preceding error detection techniques—VRC, LRC, BCC, and CRC—all rely on the receiver to request retransmission of the data blocks or characters in which an error was detected. This is called the ARQ (automatic request for repeat) method of data error control.

As mentioned previously, the alternative to ARQ is *forward error correction,* or *FEC.* This is a technique based on work done by mathematician Richard Hamming at Bell Laboratories in the early 1950s. It can be used to *detect and correct* single-bit data errors. Figure 10.35 illustrates how the Hamming code is applied to an 8-bit data byte. Four parity bits are required, each calculated on a different subset of bits in the data byte. In Figure 10.35, the data byte D6H is transmitted as the 12-bit data stream 4D6H. When the data is received, a four-bit *error code* is generated by again calculating the parity on the four subsets of bits (including the four checkbits). This is shown in Figure 10.36. The resulting error code can then be used to identify the particular bit (if any) in error. This is shown in Table 10.11.

Figure 10.36 illustrates the case where the data byte D6H (Hamming-encoded as 4D6H) is received as 456H. The error code generated is 1110, which (correctly) indicates that data bit 7 is in error.

The overhead of four extra parity bits for each data byte makes this technique undesirable for many applications. The data rate of the communications channel is also adversely affected by these four extra bits. However, as the word length increases, the overhead

Figure 10.35 Four parity bits are required to encode one byte in the Hamming code.

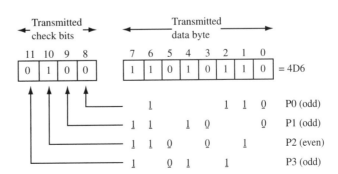

Table 10.11   Error Codes for the 8-Bit
Modified Hamming Code Technique in
Figure 10.27

Error Code	Bit in Error
0000	No error detected
0001	Check bit 0
0010	Check bit 1
0011	Data bit 0
0100	Check bit 2*
0101	Data bit 1
0110	Data bit 3
0111	Data bit 6
1000	Check bit 3
1001	Data bit 2
1010	Data bit 4
1011	All data and parity set to 0
1100	Data bit 5
1101	Multibit error
1110	Data bit 7
1111	Multibit error

*All data and parity bits are set to a 1.

Source: J. Uffenbeck, *Microcomputers and Microprocessors: The 8080, 8085, and Z-80.* Prentice Hall,
Englewood Cliffs, N.J., 1985.

Figure 10.36   The receiver
computes an error code based on
the four check bits and the data
byte. An error code of 0000
indicates that no error has been
detected.

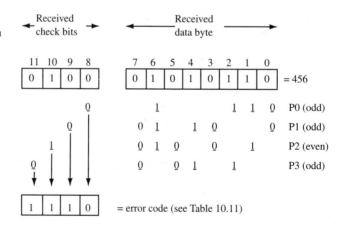

decreases. A 16-bit word requires only five check bits, resulting in a 31 percent overhead.
Such a system has been developed by Data General Corporation: It will correct all single-bit
errors and reportedly detect an average of 97 percent of all multiple-bit errors.[15]

---

[15]George J. Walker, "Error Checking and Correcting for Your Computer," *BYTE,* Vol. 5, No. 5 (1980), p. 260.

Self Review 10.4 (Answers on page 496)

10.5.1   Two general methods for controlling errors in data transmissions are _____ and _____.

10.5.2   List three error detection schemes used with ARQ error control.

10.5.3   When the ASCII character *T* is sent using even parity, the hex code transmitted is _____.

10.5.4   Using the CRC code, the receiving terminal computes a remainder polynomial, which should be _____ if no errors are detected.

10.5.5   What is the advantage of using a block-checking error detection scheme like CRC vs. a character-oriented scheme like parity?

10.5.6   Using the Hamming error detection and correction code, the data byte 3CH would be transmitted as _____.

Chapter 10 Self-Test

1. Calculate the character rate for a serial port programmed for 9600 bps, 8 data bits, 1 start bit, and 1 stop bit.
2. Assume COM2 is to be programmed as described in Question 1. Give the DOS mode command required.
3. Asynchronous serial data is said to be *self-synchronizing*. Explain.
4. When using the bisync synchronous serial protocol, the _____ character replaces the start bit associated with asynchronous serial data.
5. When transmitting a logic 1, an RS-232 transmitter typically outputs _____ volts.
6. RS–422A receivers and transmitters use differential inputs and outputs, respectively. List two performance improvements this provides over RS-232.
7. When interfacing a DTE with a _____, a *straight-through* cable can be used.
8. Which two modem control signals are used to handshake the PC to modem connection (not the data transfer)?
9. What two factors determine the data rate in bps of the PC16550D?
10. To determine if a framing error has occurred, the _____ register of the PC16550D should be read.
    (a) interrupt identification   (b) FIFO control   (c) line status   (d) modem status
11. Without FIFOs, a data ready interrupt is generated by the UART after each character is received. With FIFOs, the PC16550D may store as many as _____ bytes before an interrupt is generated.
12. When the PC16550D's transmitter holding register becomes empty, an interrupt is generated. The source of this interrupt can be verified by reading the _____ _____ register and comparing the contents with _____H. Assume FIFOs enabled..
13. QAM is a modem modulation method that varies the _____ and _____ of the carrier signal.
14. Calculate the baud rate required to achieve a 9600 bps data rate with 4 bits per baud.
15. With V.42bis, the throughput of a modem can be as much as _____ times its specified data rate.
16. Give an example of an AT command that verifies that your communications software is online with your modem. What response from the modem do you predict?
17. Which of the following error-detection schemes are *not* associated with the ARQ method of error control?
    (a) VRC   (b) Hamming codes   (c) BCC   (d) CRC

18. The following bytes are received using odd parity. Which, if any, are in error?
   (a) D6 (b) FF (c) E0H (d) C5H
19. Calculate the checksum byte for the four hex bytes 12, D5, CC, 79.
20. Using a generator polynomial $X^8 + X^5 + X^4 + X^3 + 1$ will result in a _____-bit CRC character.

Analysis and Design Questions

Section 10.1
10.1   Refer to Figure 10.37 to answer the following questions.
   (a) What is the data rate in bits per second for this waveform?
   (b) What is the character rate, assuming 7 data bits, 1 start bit, 1 stop bit, and no parity?
   (c) What ASCII character is being sent?
10.2   The following questions refer to the serial receiver program shown in Figure 10.38 and flowcharted in Figure 10.4; the hardware is as shown in Figure 10.2.
   (a) Give an example of the code that could be used for the BIT_0 procedure.
   (b) What is the purpose of the code in lines 5–7?
   (c) Register _____ holds the number of data bits to be transmitted.
   (d) As each data bit is input, it is moved from register AL bit _____ into _____.
   (e) What is the purpose of the code in lines 13–15?
   (f) Which instruction actually saves the data in memory?
   (g) The procedure returns control to the calling program after _____ byte(s) has (have) been input.
10.3   Assume a 1K (1024 byte) file is to be transmitted serially at 9600 bps. Calculate the total time required and the effective character rate using:
   (a) Asynchronous serial with 8 data bits, 1 start bit, and 1 stop bit.
   (b) Bisync synchronous serial with the data framed as shown in Figure 10.7. Assume the BCC is 16 bits.
   (c) SDLC as shown in Figure 10.8.

Section 10.2
10.4   You are attempting to interface a serial plotter and a PC. The plotter has a 25-pin male DB–25 connector. What test could you perform to determine if the plotter is wired as a DTE or a DCE? (*Hint:* When not actually transmitting data, the output of a serial transmitter should be "marking.")
10.5   Most serial port diagnostic programs require that a *loopback* plug be connected to the computer's serial port. This is a plug that loops the serial output data back to the serial input. It also loops back the modem control signals $\overline{DTR}$, $\overline{DSR}$, $\overline{RTS}$, $\overline{DCD}$, and $\overline{CTS}$. Make a diagram of the required plug. *Hint:* Refer to the flowchart in Figure 10.16.

Figure 10.37 Figure for Analysis and Design Question 10.1.

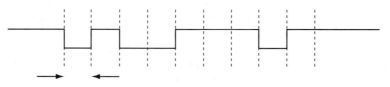

17.36μs

Figure 10.38 Figure for Analysis and Design Question 10.2.

```
        SERIAL_RCVR    PROC     NEAR

1       wait_high      call     bit_0
2                      jz       wait_high

3       wait_low       call     bit_0
4                      jnz      wait_low

5                      call     half_delay
6                      call     bit_0
7                      jnz      wait_high

8                      mov      cx,8

9       form_byte      call     full_delay
10                     in       al,0
11                     ror      al,1
12                     loop     form_byte

13                     call     full_delay
14                     call     bit_0
15                     jz       error
16                     stosb

        SERIAL_RCVR    ENDP
```

10.6   When using a serial plotter, it may be necessary to make separate cables for each program used with that plotter. Explain.

Section 10.3

10.7   Answer the following questions about the PC16550D UART.

  (a) If polling is used to determine if the receiver has new data, which UART register should be accessed and which specific bit tested?

  (b) If a framing error (only) occurs, the interrupt identification register will store the byte _____. In addition, bit _____ of the line status register will be _____. Assume both FIFOs are enabled.

  (c) In (b), an interrupt will be generated only if bit _____ of the _____ _____ register has been set.

  (d) If the UART is to be controlled using multitransfer DMA, bit _____ of the _____ _____ register must be set.

  (e) In (d), which two UART pins are used to initiate DMA requests?

10.8   Write an 80x86 program that sets the data rate for the PC16550D to 56K bps using an 18.432 MHz crystal. Assume the UART is interfaced as COM1 in a PC. (*Hint:* The DLAB must be set without changing the values of the other bits in the LCR.)

10.9   Write a program called *16550.COM* that tests for the presence of a 16550 UART and responds "16550 found" or "16550 not found," depending on the result. The syntax for your program should be *16550 n,* where $n = 1$ to test for a 16550 on COM1 and $n = 2$ to test for a 16550 on COM2. (*Hint:* Attempt to enable the FIFOs and then test to see if they have indeed become enabled.)

10.10   Study the following DEBUG commands given to a PC's COM1 port with a PC16550D UART. Beside each command, provide a comment explaining that line. What is the purpose of the "program'?

```
-o3fc,10
-o3f8,91
-i3f8
91
-o3fc,0
-o3f8,90
-i3f8
90
```

Section 10.4

10.11   Answer the following questions about the modem direct-connect circuit shown in Figure 10.27.

(a) Redraw the A2 op-amp circuit showing that the transmitted data "sees" an inverting and a non-inverting amplifier with a combined gain of 0. (*Hint:* Assume the resistance "looking back into the transformer" is 600 ohms.)

(b) Redraw the A2 op-amp circuit showing that the received data "sees" a non-inverting amplifier with a gain of 2.

(c) Calculate the voltage on the inputs and outputs of the LM393 open-collector comparator when the phone is *not* ringing.

(d) Repeat (c) for when the phone is ringing.

(e) To take the phone off-hook, the OH signal must be _____.

10.12   Figure 10.39 shows the constellation pattern for a particular modem.

(a) What modulation method does this modem use?

(b) How many different amplitude-phase combinations are used?

(c) How many bits are transmitted per baud?

(d) If the baud rate is 2400, calculate the data rate.

Figure 10.39   Figure for Analysis and Design Question 10.12.

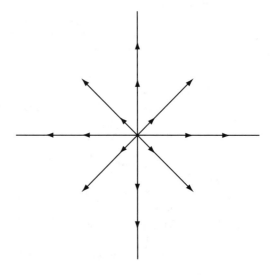

10.13   Complete the table below, giving the AT command required and the expected modem response.

	Action	AT Command	Modem Response
(a)	Verify that PC and modem are connected		
(b)	Display the current modem settings		
(c)	Store the phone number 6824899		
(d)	Set the modem to full duplex		
(e)	Turn the speaker permanently on		
(f)	Set the modem for tone dialing		
(g)	Dial the number previously stored (c)		
(h)	Once connected, escape to command mode		
(i)	Turn the speaker off		
(j)	Return online		
(k)	Hang up the phone		

10.14   Using the AT commands, determine the sequence required to continuously display the current modem settings.

Section 10.5

10.15   Write an 80x86 procedure to check a 256-byte block of BCC-encoded characters (see Figure 10.33 for an example of a program that creates the BCC) for data errors. Return with the carry flag set if an error is detected; reset if there is no error. Assume that the segment address of the data block to be tested is passed in register BX and the offset address in register CX.

10.16   Calculate M(X), Q(X), and R(X) for the 16-bit data stream 8030H. Assume the bisync generator polynomial.

10.17   Write an 80x86 procedure that adds an even parity bit (in bit position 7) to a 7-bit ASCII character passed in register CL. Return with the encoded character in register CL.

Self-Review Answers

10.1.1   10/1200 = 8.3 ms

10.1.2   "B" = 42H = 100 0010

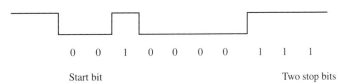

Start bit   0   0   1   0   0   0   0   1   1   1   Two stop bits

10.1.3   Framing

10.1.4   UART

10.1.5   19.2 KHz (assuming a 16X clock)

10.1.6   1200 bps/10 bits/character = 120 characters/s

10.1.7   Synchronous achieves the highest data rate. There is less overhead.

10.1.8   bisync, SDLC

10.2.1   0.4V, 2.0V

10.2.2   differential

10.2.3   (a) PC (b) modem

10.2.4   9- or 25-pin (a) male

10.2.5 $\overline{DCD}$

10.2.6 $\overline{RI}$ becomes active

10.2.7   When two DTEs are to be interfaced

10.2.8   software

10.3.1   Parallel

10.3.2   8

10.3.3   Error condition, receiver FIFO fills up, transmitter buffer is empty, a modem control signal changes state, character timeout

10.3.4   16

10.3.5   FIFO control register, C1H

10.3.6   3FEH

10.3.7   19,200 bps

10.3.8   rda_int

10.4.1   3300

10.4.2   FSK

10.4.3   A signal event is one amplitude, frequency, or phase change.

10.4.4   1800

10.4.5   2400 baud, 9600 bps

10.4.6   115.2K

10.4.7   ATH0

10.4.8   ATS0 = 10

10.5.1   ARQ and FEC

10.5.2   Parity, BCC, CRC

10.5.3   D4H

10.5.4   0

10.5.5   Less overhead and therefore a greater character rate

10.5.6   23CH

11 Personal Computer Architecture and Bus Systems

The IBM Thinkpad is a notebook computer based on Intel's Pentium processor. The machine shown has a 100 MHz processor, 24 MB of RAM, a 1 GB hard drive, a color 600×800 LCD screen, built-in 28.8 Kbps modem, 8X CD-ROM dive, external $3^{1}/_{2}''$ floppy drive and 10 Mbps Ethernet adapter. A comparison with ENIAC is staggering: ENIAC weighed 30 tons, the Thinkpad weighs 7 pounds! ENIAC required 130 kW of power, the Thinkpad is battery powered! ENIAC could perform 5000 additions per second. The Thinkpad (and internal Pentium processor) can perform 150 million floating-point operations per second! Finally, ENIAC cost almost $500,000; the Thinkpad sells for under $3000!

Outline

Objectives

After completing this chapter you should be able to:

1. Describe the architecture of the 8-bit PC and XT computers.
2. Describe the architecture of the 16-bit AT computer and the ISA bus slots.
3. Describe the advantages of Plug and Play and list its hardware and software requirements.
4. Describe the architecture of the MCA bus.
5. Describe the architecture of the EISA bus.
6. Compare the data transfer rates of ISA, MCA, and EISA bus computers.
7. Describe the architecture of the VESA local bus.
8. Describe the architecture of the PCI bus.
9. Compare the data transfer rates for VESA and PCI local bus adapters.
10. List the important features of the SCSI bus, including device IDs, bus termination, and bus operation.
11. Compare the various versions of SCSI, including SCSI-1, SCSI-2, Fast SCSI, Wide SCSI, and SCSI-3.
12. List the important features of USB, including bus topology and protocol, cabling, electrical characteristics, and device types.
13. Compare control, bulk, interrupt, and isochronous USB data transfers for data rate, bandwidth, and bus access.

Overview

In this book we have studied the 80x86 family of microprocessor chips. In the process we have often referred to (IBM-compatible) computer systems using these chips as *PCs*. Over the years, many different PC designs have been developed. Modeled after the hugely successful Apple II, most have featured an *open architecture* with an expansion bus that allows third-party vendors to develop compatible system add-ons (video adapters, disk controllers, modems, serial and parallel ports, etc.).

In this final chapter, we study the architecture and bus systems made popular by the 80x86 processors. We begin with the original 8-bit expansion bus offered in the IBM PC. Now known as the ISA (Industry Standard Architecture) bus, this design is still popular today (in 16-bit form).

With the advent of the 386 processor, two new bus standards became popular. The first is the 32-bit MCA (Microchannel Architecture) bus developed by IBM and first offered in its PS/2 family of computers. Because the MCA bus is proprietary to IBM (and not compatible with ISA), the industry developed an alternative called EISA (extended ISA). This is a 32-bit ISA-compatible bus, but limited to an 8.33 MHz clock frequency.

The newest developments have been *local buses*. This is a design that connects adapters directly to the processor and operates at the (bus) frequency of the processor. The two most popular designs are the VL (Video Local) bus and PCI (Peripheral Component Interconnect). Both support a 64-bit data bus and clock speeds as high as 66 MHz (PCI).

The chapter concludes with a look at two *peripheral buses*—SCSI (Small Computer Systems Interface) and USB (Universal Serial Bus). Both are designed to work in conjunction with system buses. SCSI is a parallel bus best suited for high-speed peripherals such as hard disk drives and digital tape players. USB is a serial bus designed to provide a simple Plug-and-Play interface for video monitors, keyboards, mice, modems, and printers.

11.1   The PC/XT and AT

Introduction

When IBM introduced the 8088-based personal computer in 1982, little did it realize that its design would define the microcomputer architecture to be used for the next four generations of microprocessor chips. Indeed, the struggle to break free of this *dinosaur* (as it is often referred to) continues to this day.

In this section we will:

- Describe the architecture of the 8-bit PC and XT computers.
- Describe the architecture of the 16-bit AT computer and the ISA bus slots.
- Describe the advantages of Plug and Play and list its hardware and software requirements.

The PC/XT

4.77 MHz and 640K.   The IBM PC was introduced in 1982 and featured an 8-bit 8088 microprocessor operating at 4.77 MHz. The system board included 16K of DRAM, 8K of ROM with an abbreviated version of BASIC, a keyboard interface, and a cassette port for mass storage. Five bus slots were provided to allow for system expansion.[1] Typically these were used to add a video adapter and a floppy drive controller. Figure 11.1 outlines the basic architecture of this machine.

Using the 8088 processor, the total memory space was limited to 1 MB. As discussed previously, IBM chose to divide this space into 640K of RAM and 384K of reserved memory. In the first PC, the 640K could only be achieved via expansion memory cards. Later, in the XT version of the computer, all 640K could be had on the system board (two banks of 256K chips and two banks of 64K chips were required).

System Support—The "Glue" Logic.   As can be seen in Figure 11.1, the PC requires several support chips besides the processor. The 8284 clock generator is used to derive the 4.77 MHz system clock signal from the 14.31818 MHz crystal oscillator. The 8087 is a math coprocessor. Typically, this was provided as an empty socket (which few users opted to fill due to the relatively high cost of the chip).

The 8259A provides eight interrupt inputs. Of these, IRQ0 and IRQ1 are used by the 8253 timer chip (to update the system clock) and the 8255A PPI chip (to access the keyboard), respectively. The 8288 bus controller is used to generate most of the system control bus signals. These include the memory and I/O read and write signals.

The 8237 is the DMA controller. Four channels are provided, with channel 0 dedicated to memory refresh. The other three channels are used to transfer data between memory and the I/O (SDLC adapter, floppy disk controller, and hard disk controller). System configuration is read via a DIP switch wired to one 8-bit port in the 8255A PPI. The other PPI ports are used to access the keyboard, cassette recorder, and speaker.

---

[1]In 1983, the XT version of the computer was introduced. It had eight slots and featured a 10 MB hard drive.

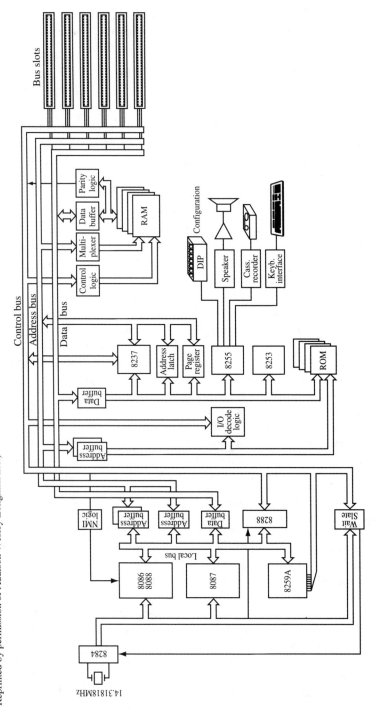

Figure 11.1 The PC/XT architecture is based on the 8088 microprocessor. (From Hans-Peter Messmer, *The Indispensable PC Hardware Book*, second edition, Addison-Wesley Publishing Company, 1995. Reprinted by permission of Addison Wesley Longman Ltd.)

Figure 11.2 The 8-bit bus slot used in the PC/XT.

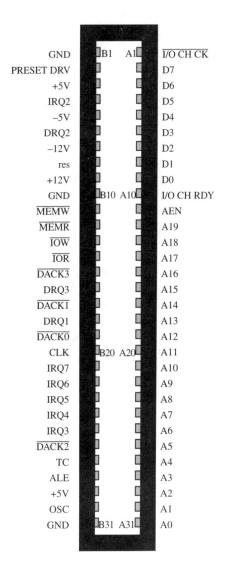

Finally, the three channels of the 8253 timer chip are used to generate internal system clock ticks (~18.2 ticks/s), refresh the DRAMs, and generate tones on the speaker.

System Expansion—The Bus Slots. Each of the five 62-pin bus slots are identical, so an adapter can be plugged into any convenient connector. Figure 11.2 shows the connector configuration; Table 11.1 provides details on the specific signals. Because the data bus width of the slots is limited to 8 bits, cards that plug into these slots are often referred to as *8-bit cards*.[2]

---

[2]Internally, the 8088 is a 16-bit processor; that is, the internal data bus width is 16 bits, as are the data registers. When accessing a 16-bit peripheral or memory card via the slot connectors, two bus cycles are required, one for the low 8 bits and another for the high 8 bits.

Table 11.1   8-Bit PC/XT Bus Signal Descriptions

Signal	Name	Type*	Description
A0–A19	Address Lines	Output	20-bit address bus
AEN	Address Enable	Output	High when DMA controller is controlling the buses.
ALE	Address Latch Enable	Output	High when valid address signals are on the bus.
CLK	System Clock	Output	In the original PC this was 4.77 MHz
D0–D7	Data Lines	Input/Output	8-bit data bus
$\overline{\text{DACK0}}$–$\overline{\text{DACK3}}$	DMA Acknowledge	Output	When low these signals acknowledge a peripheral's DMA request.
DRQ1–DRQ3	DMA Request	Input	High to request a DMA transfer. DRQ0 is dedicated to memory refresh and is therefore not available on the bus.
$\overline{\text{I/O CH CK}}$	I/O Channel Check	Input	Low to indicate an error condition and generate an NMI.
I/O CH RDY	I/O Channel Ready	Input	High when the peripheral is ready. If low, a wait state is inserted into the current bus cycle.
$\overline{\text{IOR}}$	I/O Read	Output	Low when inputting data from an I/O device.
$\overline{\text{IOW}}$	I/O Write	Output	Low when writing data to an I/O device.
IRQ2–IRQ7	Interrupt Requests	Input	High to request an interrupt from the processor.
$\overline{\text{MEMR}}$	Memory Read	Output	Low when reading data from memory.
$\overline{\text{MEMW}}$	Memory Write	Output	Low when writing data to memory.
OSC	Oscillator	Output	Oscillator clock frequency. Normally 14.318180 MHz
RESET DRV	Reset	Output	High during the power-on cycle.
T/C	Terminal Count	Output	High to indicate the end of the DMA cycle.

*Input to or output from the processor/bus controller.

The 8088 processor requires four T states per I/O bus cycle. However, when the PC was designed, it was deemed necessary to add one wait state to each of these cycles to accommodate slow I/O devices. The PC bus thus requires five T states per I/O cycle.

Example 11.1

Calculate the time for one PC bus cycle, assuming a 4.77 MHz clock frequency. What is the data transfer rate for this bus?

Solution

The time for one I/O bus cycle can be computed as

$$5 \text{ T states} \times \frac{1}{4.77 \text{ MHz}} = 1.05 \text{ }\mu\text{s}$$

The data transfer rate is therefore

$$\frac{1 \text{ byte per bus cycle}}{1.05 \text{ μs per bus cycle}} = 0.95 \text{ MB/s}$$

Limited Number of I/O Ports.   As we learned in Chapter 8, the 80x86 processors issue a 16-bit I/O address. This accommodates as many as 65,536 different I/O ports. However, when the PC was designed, IBM decided to decode *only the 10 low-order address bits—* A0–A9. The high-order bits—A10–A15—are ignored by the address decoders. This means the PC is limited to 1024 different I/O port locations (0000–03FFH).[3] The I/O ports are further restricted such that when A9 is low, the ports are located on the system board; when A9 is high, the I/O ports are assigned to the bus slots. This means the bus ports must be in the range 200H–3FFH.

Example 11.2

Show how the 8255A PPI chip can be interfaced to the I/O bus of the PC/XT so that the chip is mapped to ports 3FC–3FFH. What are the commands to program the chip for mode 0 operation with ports A and B operating as input ports and port C as an output port?

Solution
The circuit is shown in Figure 11.3. The data lines of the 8255A connect directly to the data lines of the ISA bus. Similarly, the $\overline{RD}$ and $\overline{WR}$ inputs connect to the $\overline{IOR}$ and $\overline{IOW}$ control signals on the bus. In this way, the PPI can only be accessed for I/O read and write cycles.

The range of I/O addresses to which the chip will respond is determined by the 74ALS677 address comparator. In this example, the top *14* address lines (A2–A15) must correspond to

$$^{A15}0000 \ 0011 \ 1111 \ 11^{A2}$$

The four combinations of the A0 and A1 address lines (connected to the A0 and A1 inputs of the PPI) then define four I/O ports within the PPI chip:

0000 0011 1111 11**00** = 03FCH	'Port A in the PPI
0000 0011 1111 11**01** = 03FDH	'Port B in the PPI
0000 0011 1111 11**10** = 03FEH	'Port C in the PPI
0000 0011 1111 11**11** = 03FFH	'PPI control port

Referring to Figure 8.13, three instructions are required to program the chip:

```
MOV    DX,03FFH      ;Control port access
MOV    AL,92H        ;Mode 0, A and B = inputs, C = output
OUT    DX,AL         ;Program the chip
```

The AT Bus

Advanced Technology.   In 1984, IBM introduced its successor to the PC/XT called the AT—*Advanced Technology*. It featured a 6 MHz 80286 processor with 256K of RAM, a

---

[3]It is possible to exceed this number by decoding (on the adapter card) the six high-order address bits (A10–A15) for which the low-order bits are *unused*. For example, if port 3F0H is unused, 64 ports could be decoded. (See Analysis and Design Question 11.3.)

Figure 11.3   Interfacing the 8255A PPI chip to the PC/XT.

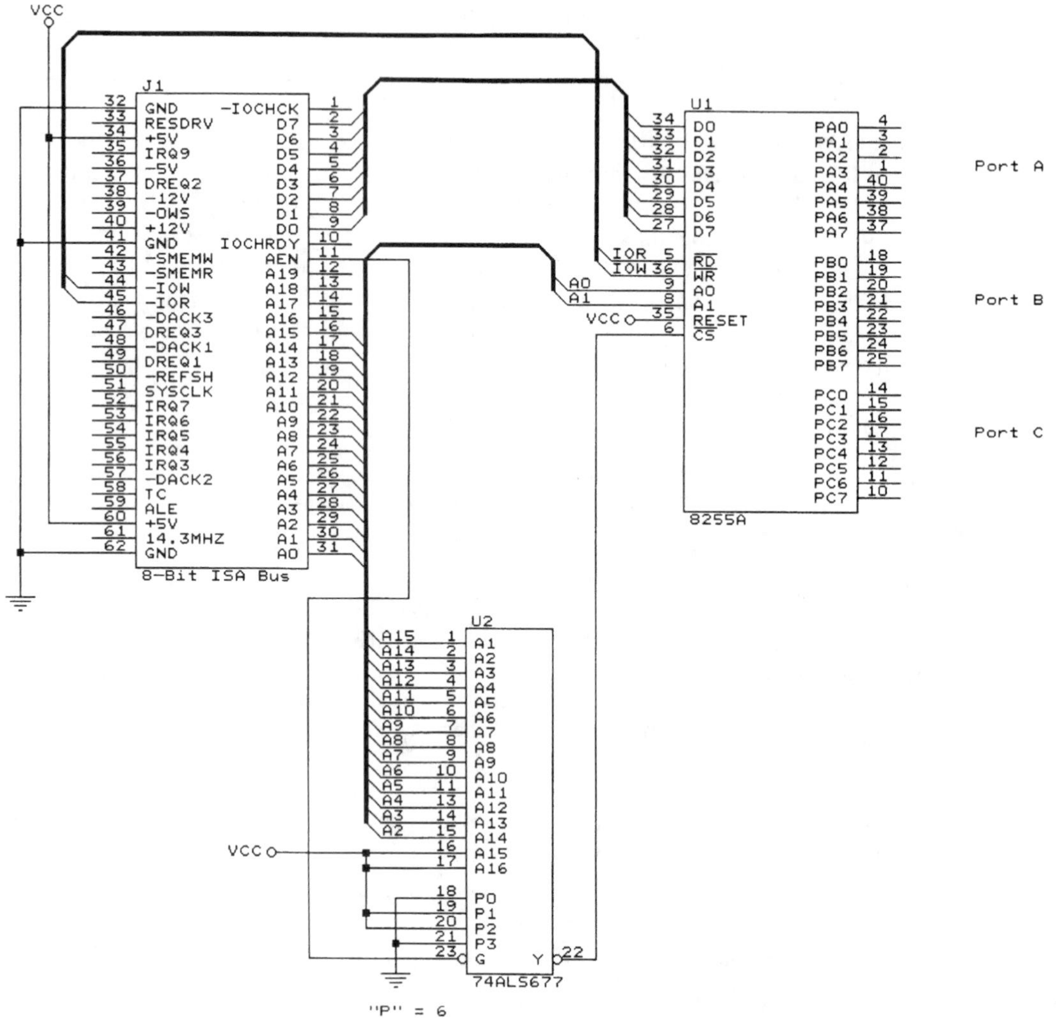

high-density (5¹/4″) floppy disk drive, and a 20 MB hard drive.[4] Although the processor supported a 24-bit memory address (and therefore a 16 MB memory space), memory capacity was limited to 640K for DOS compatibility. Figure 11.4 highlights the features of a typical system.

Fifteen Interrupts and Seven DMA Channels.   Many of the support components used in the AT are updated versions from the PC/XT (the 82284 clock generator vs. the 8284, the 82288 bus controller vs. the 8288, and the 80287 coprocessor vs. the 8087). Two 8259A PICs are provided, expanding the number of interrupt inputs from 8 to 15. Two

---

[4]Versions operating at 8 and 10 MHz soon became available. Using cloned versions of the 286 manufactured by Harris and AMD, clock speeds as high as 25 MHz were achieved.

Figure 11.4 The PC AT architecture is based on the 80286 microprocessor. (From Hans-Peter Messmer, *The Indispensable PC Hardware Book*, second edition, Addison-Wesley Publishing Company, 1995. Reprinted by permission of Addison Wesley Longman Ltd.)

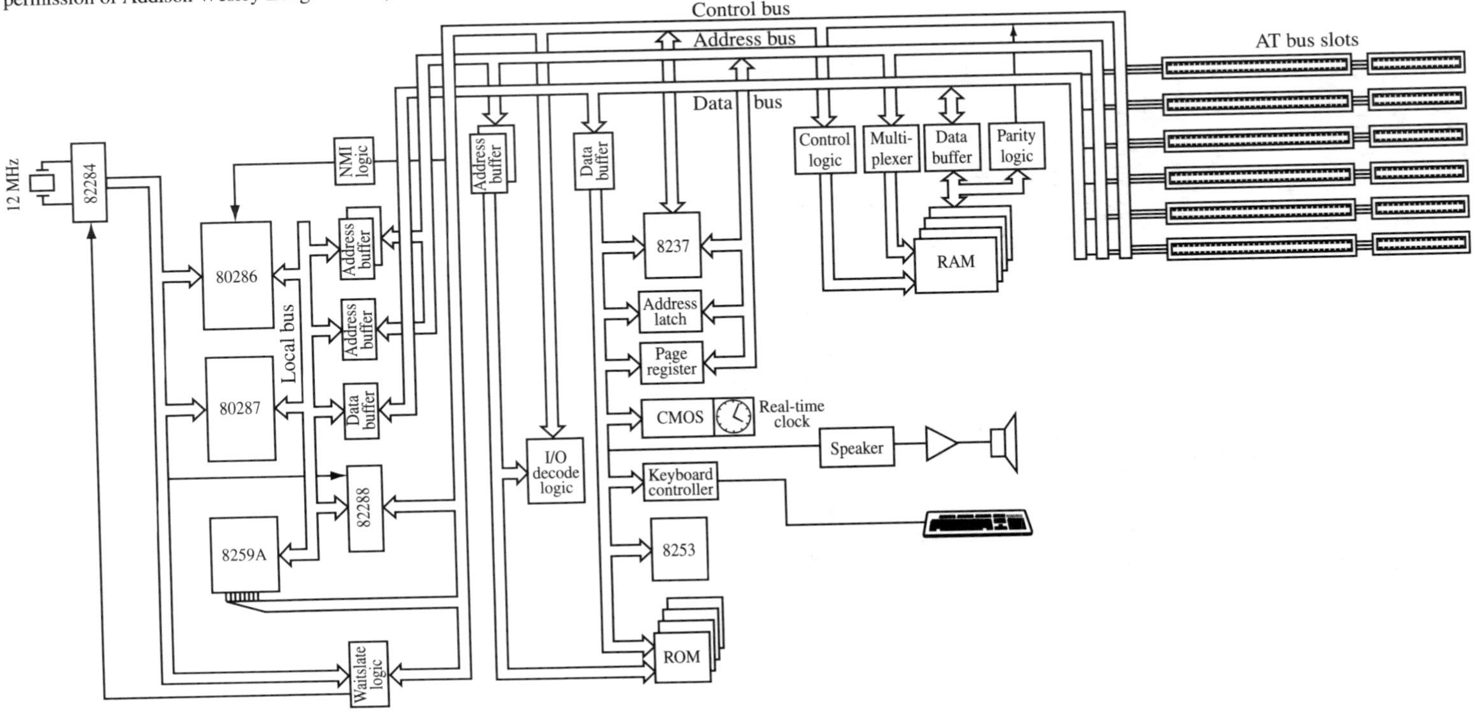

8237 DMA controllers allow seven DMA channels, three of which—channels 5–7–support 16-bit data transfers.

The 8255 PPI has been replaced with a dedicated programmable keyboard controller. In addition, gone are the system board configuration DIP switches. In their place, battery-backed CMOS memory is used to store system configuration information, as well as the time of day and date.

The AT Extension Slot.   In order to accommodate the increased data and address bus widths, plus the additional interrupt and DMA request lines, a new 36-pin bus *extension slot* was added immediately behind the existing 8-bit connector. This is shown in Figure 11.5. Two input signals—$\overline{\text{MEM CS16}}$ and $\overline{\text{I/O CS16}}$—provide a means for a 16-bit adapter to announce its presence and allow 16-bit memory and I/O data transfers. In this way, the AT bus can accommodate both 8- and 16-bit adapter cards. Table 11.2 provides a description of the extension slot signals (and two new 8-bit slot signals—$\overline{\text{OWS}}$ and $\overline{\text{REF}}$).

Data Transfer Rate.   By mutual agreement, most AT manufacturers have standardized on a bus clock frequency of 8.33 MHz (120 ns period). Using a 286 (or 386 or 486) processor, two clock cycles are required per bus cycle. Thus, a zero wait state bus cycle can transfer

$$\frac{2 \text{ Bytes}}{2 \text{ Clock Cycles} \times 120 \text{ ns/cycle}} = 8.33 \text{ MB/s}$$

This compares with 0.95 MB/s in the PC/XT.

Although much faster than the PC/XT, the 8.33 MB/s data rate is much slower than the 386 and 486 processors. In Table 7.6, it was shown that a 50 MHz 486 can transfer data as fast as 160 MB/s. Even a 33 MHz 386 has a 66 MB/s data transfer rate. The AT bus thus represents a "bottleneck" to these processors—especially when accessing *video memory*, which is typically interfaced through a video adapter card and a bus slot. To solve this problem, video local bus (VLB) cards have been developed that interface directly with the processor's local bus and operate at the clock rate of the processor. Most AT system boards similarly provide proprietary main memory slots or SIMM sockets connected directly to the processor.

Standardization—The ISA Bus.   The AT bus has become very popular. In fact, even 386 and 486 (and some Pentium) systems that support this bus structure can be found (albeit offering compromised performance due to the narrow data and address bus widths compared to the 32- or 64-bit buses of these processors).[5] To avoid incompatibilities, the computer industry has agreed to a standard definition for the AT bus—now called the *ISA (Industry Standard Architecture)* bus. The main features of the ISA bus are

1. 16-bit data bus
2. 24-bit address bus
3. 11 interrupt requests (IRQ2–IRQ7, IRQ10–IRQ12, and IRQ14–IRQ15).[6]
4. 7 DMA channels
5. 8.33 MHz maximum bus clock frequency
6. Support for zero wait state bus cycles
7. Support for alternate bus masters (via DMA on an adapter card)

---

[5]It is common for 486 and Pentium system boards to provide 3 to 4 PCI slots and an additional 3 to 4 ISA slots for system expansion. The PCI bus is covered in Section 11.3.

[6]The missing IRQs have dedicated functions on the system board.

Figure 11.5 The 16-bit AT bus incorporates a 36-pin extension to the 8-bit slot used in the PC/XT.

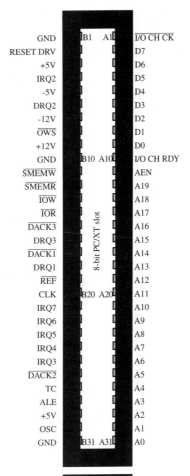

Table 11.2   16-Bit AT ISA Bus Signal Descriptions

Signal	Name	Type*	Description
		8-Bit Slot (see also Table 11.1)	
$\overline{\text{0WS}}$	Zero Wait States	Input	When low from a peripheral, the current bus cycle runs without wait states.
$\overline{\text{REF}}$	Refresh	Output	When low a memory refresh cycle is being performed on the system board.
		16-Bit Slot	
$\overline{\text{DACK0}}$, $\overline{\text{DACK5–DACK7}}$	DMA Acknowledge	Output	When low these signals acknowledge a peripheral's DMA request.
DRQ0, DRQ0–DRQ5	DMA Request	Input	High from a peripheral to request a DMA transfer.
$\overline{\text{I/O CS16}}$	I/O Chip Select 16	Input	Low to indicate that the adapter can support a 16-bit I/O data transfer.
IRQ10–IRQ12, IRQ14–IRQ15	Interrupt Requests	Input	High to request an interrupt from the processor. IRQ8, IRQ9, and IRQ13 are used on the system board and are thus not available at the bus slots.
LA17–LA23	Large Address Lines	Output	High-order address bits. LA17–LA19 overlap with A17–A19. However, the former are output earlier in the bus cycle and may be decoded in advance of A0–A19.
$\overline{\text{MASTER}}$	Master	Input	When low this signal (together with DRQ5–DRQ7) indicates that an adapter card bus master will be driving the buses.
$\overline{\text{MEM CS16}}$	Memory Chip Select 16	Input	Low from a peripheral to indicate that the adapter can support a 16-bit memory data transfer.
$\overline{\text{MEMR}}$	Memory Read	Output	Low to indicate a memory read cycle with an address between 0 and 16M. The similar PC/XT signal (now renamed SMEMR) applies to addresses between 0 and 1M.
$\overline{\text{MEMW}}$	Memory Write	Output	Low to indicate a memory write cycle with an address between 0 and 16M. The similar PC/XT signal (now renamed SMEMW) applies to addresses between 0 and 1M.
$\overline{\text{SBHE}}$	System Bus High Enable	Output	Low to indicate that the high-order eight bits of the data bus (SD8–SD15) will be involved in the data transfer.
SD8–SD15	System Data Bus	Input/Output	High-order system data bus lines

*Input to or output from the processor/bus controller or current bus master.

THE PC/XT AND AT

Plug and Play

IRQs, DMA Channels, and I/O Addresses. The PC as designed by IBM incorporates an "open" architecture via the ISA bus slots. Because of this, users can select expansion cards from a wide variety of third-party vendors. This is both good and bad. It is good because competition keeps the price of these adapters at the lowest levels. However, because the ISA bus does not offer automatic configuration, users are forced to *manually* select the IRQ settings, DMA channels, and I/O port addresses via DIP switches and jumpers.

A typical scenario has the user installing a new sound card only to find that the card does not work due to a *conflict* with another board using the same IRQ setting, DMA channel, or I/O port address. At this point, the user must pull the other adapter cards and check their jumper settings (assuming the documentation is still available).[7] Once a compatible configuration has been found, the drivers and application software will have to be updated with the new values—not exactly a job for the average computer user. *Plug and Play* promises to change this.

Plug-and-Play ISA. Two companies with more than a casual interest in the development of easy-to-use PCs—Intel and Microsoft—announced in May of 1993 a mechanism called *Plug and Play (PnP)* that allows ISA computers to be configured automatically. The goals of PnP are threefold:

1. To make PCs easier to set up and configure.
2. To simplify the task of installing new hardware and software.
3. To allow the configuration of the computer to be changed "on the fly," with the system hardware and software automatically adapting.

To achieve all of these goals, users need to replace existing ISA cards (sometimes called *legacy* devices) with PnP-aware adapters. These cards feature special registers that allow the operating system to determine its function. In addition, commands can be sent to the card telling it to deselect itself, effectively disconnecting from the ISA bus.

In addition to these new adapters, a PnP-aware BIOS, a PnP-aware operating system (Windows 95, OS/2), and PnP-aware applications software are also required. When these conditions are met, users are able to install and remove hardware from their systems without concern for IRQ, DMA, and I/O channel conflicts. "*Just plug it in, and it works.*"

Older PCs that do not have a PnP BIOS or PnP adapters can still benefit from a PnP operating system. Windows 95, for example, can often detect new hardware, suggest configuration settings, and load the proper drivers—all with non-PnP hardware. In addition, PnP is not restricted to the ISA bus. Indeed, the PCI bus (described in Section 11.3) is becoming increasingly popular and has the hardware features of PnP built in by default (some refer to this as *true* Plug and Play).

How Plug and Play Works. The boot-up process for a computer that supports PnP is more complex than that of a non-PnP–compliant machine, because it must bring up the system piece by piece in a compatible manner while managing possible resource conflicts.

---

[7]Diagnostic software is available that can often query the system and provide a description of the current system settings. One example is MSD (Microsoft Diagnostics), provided with DOS and Windows. However, even MSD fails to find some specialized adapters.

Figure 11.6 The Device Manager in Windows 95 can be used to view current resource settings and help resolve adapter conflicts. In this example the interrupt setting for COM2 is conflicting with the interrupt setting for COM1.

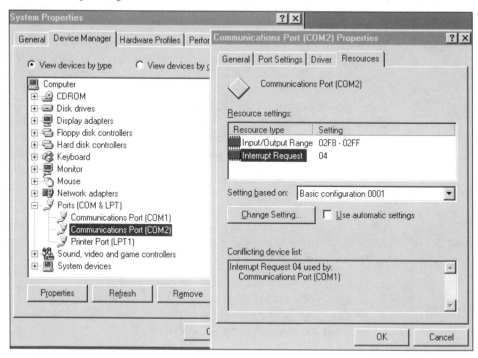

This is especially true when non-PnP adapters are present, as these cards often have inflexible resource settings (via jumpers and switches).

The PnP BIOS and operating system software must work together during system boot-up. Typically, the BIOS isolates all of the PnP adapters not required for the boot process, assigns each a unique *Card Select Number,* and then disables that adapter. Next, the legacy and boot PnP devices are examined, and the resources required by these cards are allocated.

Control now transfers to the (PnP-aware) operating system. At this point, any resource conflicts are presented to the user. In Windows 95, the user may be prompted to start the *Device Manager,* which can then be used to help resolve conflicts with legacy cards (see Figure 11.6). The previously disabled PnP devices are then activated one by one, based on the resources required. If a needed resource is not available, that card remains disabled, but the system continues to run and no conflicts occur.

Self-Review 11.1 (Answers on page 546)

11.1.1   How is a PC/XT system configured? How is this same information specified in an AT computer?

11.1.2   When accessing an I/O device via the bus slots, a PC/XT requires _____ T states or _____ µs with a 4.77 MHz clock.

11.1.3   In the PC/XT design, what range of I/O ports is assigned to the bus slots?

11.1.4   The AT architecture was based on the _____ microprocessor.

11.1.5   Compared to the PC/XT, the AT provides _____ interrupts vs. _____, and _____ DMA channels vs. _____.

11.1.6   The standard clock rate for the ISA bus is _____ MHz.

11.1.7   *(True/False)* To take advantage of Plug and Play, PnP adapter cards must be used.

11.2   Microchannel and Extended ISA

Introduction

The 8.33 MB/s data transfer rate of the ISA bus is woefully inadequate for today's high-end processors with clock rates greater than 100 MHz. In the late 1980s, two new bus standards were proposed. The first is called *Microchannel Architecture (MCA)* and totally abandons the ISA bus. It operates with a 10 MHz bus clock and offers a 160 MB/s data transfer rate (in 64-bit burst mode). The second bus standard is called *EISA,* for *Extended ISA.* Unlike MCA, EISA retains ISA compatibility (via a special two-level connector) while offering a totally new bus to true EISA cards. The bus clock remains at 8.33 MHz. However, using 64-bit burst transfers, the data transfer rate becomes 133 MB/s.

In this section we will:

- Describe the architecture of the MCA bus.
- Describe the architecture of the EISA bus.
- Compare the data transfer rates of ISA, MCA, and EISA bus computers.

The MCA Bus

The PS/2 Family.   In 1987, IBM launched its successor to the PC/XT and AT computers, the PS/2. Not a single computer but rather a family of computers, four different models were announced initially. The Model 30 was based on the 8086 processor, the Models 50 and 60 were based on the 80286 processor, and the Model 80 was based on the 80386 processor. All machines except the Model 30 supported an entirely new system architecture called *MCA—Microchannel Architecture.*[8] This is shown in Figure 11.7.

The PS/2 family of computers marks a radical departure from the PC/XT and AT.[9] Among its most important features are:

1. Integration on the system board of the video display adapter, floppy and hard disk controller, mouse interface (now known as the "PS/2-style" mouse), and the parallel and serial I/O ports.
2. 8-, 16- and 32-bit address and data bus slots (incompatible with the previous-generation ISA slots).
3. Automatic configuration of adapters without setting configuration jumpers or switches.

---

[8]The Model 30 was actually an XT repackaged in a PS/2-style case with a high-density 3.5″ floppy disk drive.

[9]In fact, the changes were so radical that many of the popular computer manufacturers of that time refused to go along. Forming a consortium known as the "Gang of Nine," they created a new (but PC/XT- and AT-compatible) system architecture known as *EISA—Extended Industry Standard Architecture.* EISA is discussed later in this section.

Figure 11.7 The MCA architecture. (From Hans-Peter Messmer, *The Indispensable PC Hardware Book,* second edition, Addison-Wesley Publishing Company, 1995. Reprinted by permission of Addison Wesley Longman Ltd.)

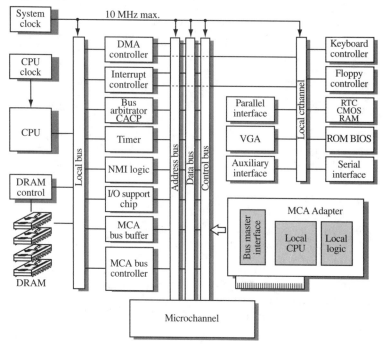

4. A separate video extension slot for higher resolution graphics adapters.
5. Accommodation, via the bus slots, for as many as 16 different bus masters.
6. Support for as many as 255 different (shareable) interrupt inputs.
7. Eight 32-bit DMA channels.
8. 10 MHz bus frequency with 160 MB/s maximum data transfer rate.

10 MHz I/O Bus. The bus slots in the PS/2 operate at 10 MHz and are independent of the processor clock. The standard bus cycle requires two clock cycles (200 ns) and can transfer 32 bits (4 bytes). The data transfer rate is therefore:

$$\frac{4 \text{ Bytes}}{200 \text{ ns}} = 20 \text{ MB/s}$$

This compares to 8.33 MB/s with the AT bus. Even faster data transfer rates are possible using 32- and 64-bit burst modes called *streaming data procedures (SDP).*[10] For these modes, only a single clock pulse is required (100 ns). The data transfer rates become 40 and 80 MB/s, respectively. Finally, a transfer rate of 160 MB/s is possible using *extended 64-bit SDP*. The clock cycle time is 50 ns.

Advanced Features. The MCA bus will allow as many as 16 different processors to control the system buses. The CACP (Central Arbitration Control Point) chip decides which

---

[10]To achieve a 64-bit data transfer, the 32 address lines are temporarily used as additional data lines.

processor to transfer control to when multiple requests are pending. In addition, a watch-dog timer prevents any one processor from keeping control too long, starving the other processors.

DMA channels have been expanded from 16 bits (in the AT) to 32 bits. Eight such channels are provided. Memory refresh is now controlled by dedicated logic, so all eight DMA channels are available for data transfers. Interrupts have also been improved, with support for as many as 255 different requests. By using a *level trigger* (instead of the edge trigger used in the PC/XT and AT designs) each of these interrupts can be *shared* without conflict.[11]

MCA Adapters. Each adapter card in an MCA bus computer is assigned a unique identification number by IBM. This number is stored in two of the eight *programmable option select (POS)* registers required on every MCA card. Table 11.3 lists the register number, I/O address, and register definition. Option bytes one to four are provided for the adapter manufacturer to configure the board—replacing the DIP switches in earlier generation cards.

When a "new" board is placed in an MCA computer, the system BIOS recognizes it and requests that a configuration disk containing an *adapter definition file (ADF)* be inserted. Via software, the user can then configure that card as desired.

MCA Bus Slots. The MCA bus will support 8-, 16-, and 32-bit adapter cards. In addition, an expansion video connector is provided. The structure is shown in Figure 11.8. The 8-bit section contains the key interface signals, with the 16- and 32-bit portions only provided in those computers with similar bus sizes. The connectors themselves have closely spaced pins that are physically incompatible with the earlier PC/XT and AT cards. To minimize noise problems, every fourth contact of a row is a connection to ground.

If the built-in standard VGA video adapter is not sufficient, the video expansion slot can be used. A unique feature is that the new adapter can use the existing video connector. Table 11.4 lists the signals associated with each of the bus slots.

Table 11.3 MCA Programmable Option Select Registers

Number	I/O Address	Meaning
0	0100H	Adapter identification ID (low byte)
1	0101H	Adapter identification ID (high byte)
2	0102H	Option byte 1
3	0103H	Option byte 2
4	0104H	Option byte 3
5	0105H	Option byte 4
6	0106H	Subaddress extension (low byte)
7	0107H	Subaddress extension (high byte)

[11]With a level trigger, as long as the interrupt input remains active the processor "knows" that an additional interrupt on that line is still pending. With an edge trigger, the processor has no way of remembering that a second interrupt request has occurred on that same line.

Figure 11.8 MCA bus slots. Two different connectors are specified.

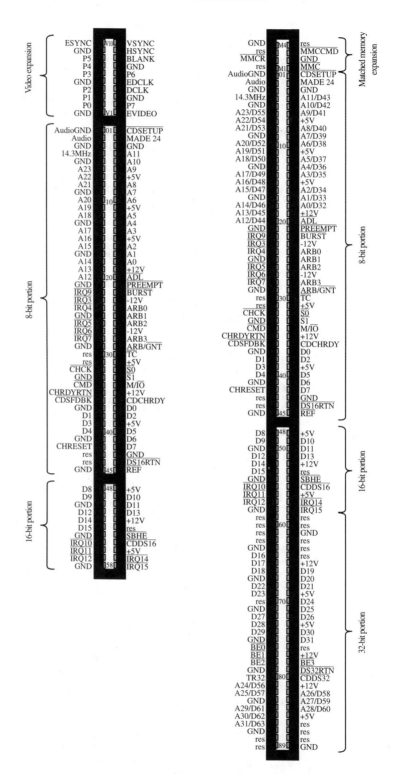

Table 11.4   MCA Bus Signal Descriptions

Signal	Name	Type*	Description
		Video Extension	
Blank	Blank	Output from an adapter and input to system board video controller.	High level blanks the screen.
DCLK	Data Clock		Pixel clock from the video adapter for the DAC.
EDCLK	Enable DCLK		Low level disables system board DCLK and enables DCLK from adapter.
ESYNC	Enable Synchronization		Low level disables system board synchronization signals VSYNC, HSYNC, and BLANK.
EVIDEO	Enable Video		Low level disables system board video.
HSYNC	Horizontal Sync		Active-high horizontal sync signal.
P0-P7	Palette Data Bits		Binary video data signal for the video DAC.
VSYNC	Vertical Sync	↓	Active-high vertical sync signal.
		Matched Memory Extension	
$\overline{\text{MMC}}$	Matched-Memory Cycle	Output	Low from bus controller to indicate a matched-memory cycle.†
$\overline{\text{MMCMD}}$	Matched-Memory Cycle Command.	Output	Low from bus controller to indicate valid address and data on the bus during a matched-memory cycle.
$\overline{\text{MMCR}}$	Matched-Memory Cycle Return	Input	Low from adapter to indicate that it supports matched-memory cycles.
		8-, 16-, and 32-Bit Portions	
14.3 MHZ	14.3 MHz	Output	14.31780 MHz clock signal.
A0–A31	Address Lines	Output	32-bit address bus.
$\overline{\text{ADL}}$	Address Latch	Output	Low to indicate that a valid address is present on the bus.
ARB0–ARB3	Arbitration	Output from bus controller to bus masters.	4-bit binary code indicating which of 16 possible bus masters gets control of the system buses.
ARB/$\overline{\text{GNT}}$	Arbitration/Grant	Output	High to indicate an arbitration cycle is in progress. When low, ARB0–ARB3 are valid and indicate the new bus master.
Audio	Audio	Input	Audio input to system board speaker logic.
AudioGND	Audio Ground	Input	Audio ground connection.

(continued on next page)

Table 11.4   *(continued)*

Signal	Name	Type*	Description
		8-, 16-, and 32-Bit Portions	
BE0–BE3	Byte Enables	Output	Low to indicate which byte(s) of the 32-bit data bus will be involved in the data transfer.
BURST	Burst	Output	Low to indicate a burst bus cycle.
CDDS16	Card Data Size 16	Input	Low by adapter to indicate that it has a 16-bit data bus width.
CDDS32	Card Data Size 32	Input	Low by adapter to indicate that it has a 32-bit data bus width.
CDSETUP	Card Data Setup	Output	Low to instruct the addressed adapter to carry out a setup.
CDSFDBK	Card Data Select Feedback	Input	Low by adapter to indicate that it is ready.
CHCK	Channel Check	Input	Low by adapter to indicate that an error condition on the card has occurred.
CHRDY	Channel Ready	Input	High by an adapter to indicate that the data access is complete and no wait states are required.
CHRDYRTN	Channel Ready Return	Input	High by an adapter to to indicate that the I/O channel is ready.
CHRESET	Channel Reset	Output	High level resets all adapters.
CMD	CMD	Output	Low to indicate that the data on the bus is valid.
D0–D31	Data Lines	Input/Output	32-bit data bus.
DS16RTN	Data Size 16 Return	Input	Low by an adapter to indicate that the device is running with a 16-bit data bus.
DS32RTN	Data Size 32 Return	Input	Low by an adapter to indicate that the device is running with a 32-bit data bus.
IRQ3–IRQ7, IRQ9–IRQ12, IRQ14, IRQ15	Interrupt request connections	Input	Low-level triggered-interrupt requests from adapters.
MADE 24	Memory Address	Ouptut	Address line A24.
M/IO	Memory/IO	Output	Low to indicate an I/O access. High to indicate a memory access.
PREEMPT	Preempt	Input	Low by a bus master to cause an arbitration cycle for passing the bus to another master.
REF	Refresh	Ouptut	Low to indicate that a refresh cycle is being run on the system board. This allows **DRAM** on adapters to be refreshed synchronous to main memory.

Table 11.4 *(continued)*

Signal	Name	Type*	Description
		8-, 16-, and 32-Bit Portions	
$\overline{S0}$, $\overline{S1}$	Status Bits	Output	Microchannel status bits.
SBHE	System Byte High Enable	Output	High to indicate that D8–D15 of the 16-bit data bus hold valid data.
$\overline{TC}$	Terminal Count	Output	High to indicate that the active DMA channel has reached its terminal value.
TR32	Translate 32	Input	Low by bus master to indicate that it is a 32-bit device.

*Input to or output from the processor/bus controller or current bus master.

†A special bus cycle that shortens the bus clock from 100 ns to 93.75 ns (no longer inplemented).

EISA

Frustration with IBM. Personal computer manufacturers were dismayed with IBM's new MCA bus for two reasons. First, the bus structure was incompatible with all of the existing ISA bus cards. Users upgrading to an MCA bus computer would have to scrap these adapters. Second, in order to manufacture an MCA bus computer, a license agreement (and fee) had to be signed with IBM.[12]

EISA (Extended Industry Standard Architecture) grew out of this frustration. First announced in 1988 (and shown schematically in Figure 11.9), EISA offers the following features:

1. A unique bus slot configuration compatible with existing 8- and 16-bit ISA adapter cards, yet providing 90 new contacts.
2. 32-bit address and data bus widths.
3. Automatic configuration of adapters without setting configuration jumpers or switches.
4. Support for multiple processors via bus arbitration.
5. 15 interrupt request lines, each shareable.
6. Seven 32-bit DMA channels (the ISA bus has four 8-bit channels and three 16-bit channels, but is limited to a 24-bit address space and 128K block sizes).
7. 8.33 MHz bus frequency, with 133 MB/s maximum data transfer rate.

The Bus Clock. The bus clock in an EISA computer operates at 8.33 MHz. Typically, two clock pulses are required to transfer one data item (8, 16, or 32 bits). A unique feature is the ability of the EISA bus controller to stretch the bus clock one-half cycle to service slower peripherals without adding a full wait state.

Standard bus cycles transfer data at 16.6 MB/s. Using burst mode (one clock pulse per transfer), this increases to 33 MB/s. Additionally, by triggering a transfer on both edges of the bus clock a 66 MB/s data rate is possible. The fastest transfer rate is achieved by tem-

---

[12]Of course, the proprietary nature of the MCA bus was by design. The open architecture of the PC/XT and AT cost IBM millions of dollars in lost revenue as clones of its machines began to appear.

Figure 11.9 The EISA architecture. (From Hans-Peter Messmer, *The Indispensable PC Hardware Book,* second edition, Addison-Wesley Publishing Company, 1995. Reprinted by permission of Addison Wesley Longman Ltd.)

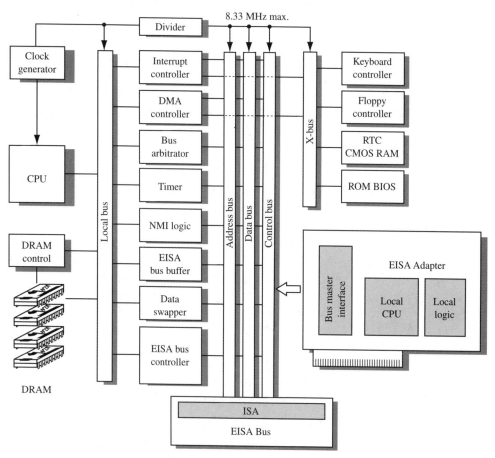

porarily using the 32 address lines as additional data lines—64-bit transfers are then possible. The data transfer rate becomes 133 MB/s.

Advanced Features. Like the MCA bus, EISA supports multiple bus masters. This means an external microprocessor on an adapter card can completely take over the system buses. Thus EISA (and MCA) are designed to function as multiprocessor machines. The AT, by contrast, does not readily permit a second processor to take over the buses (except via a DMA channel, and this is limited to a 16-bit data path and 24-bit memory address).

DMA transfers can take place in ISA (8237A) mode or EISA mode. In the latter case, the full 32-bit data and address bus widths are used. To maintain ISA bus compatibility, 7 data transfer channels are provided. Also like the AT, 15 hardware interrupts are provided. However, unlike the AT, each interrupt may be *programmed* for a trigger level or an edge trigger. Note that when using ISA adapters, an edge trigger must be programmed. EISA adapters can operate with a level trigger and thus support interrupt sharing.

EISA Adapters.   Like MCA cards, every EISA adapter is shipped with a floppy disk containing a configuration (CFG) file. This file is read by the system setup utility and is used to configure the adapter and system to avoid conflicts. Thus, no DIP switches or jumper wires will be found on EISA system boards or adapter cards. Once read, the configuration information is stored in battery-backed CMOS RAM, and the computer can be booted without these disks.

Some EISA adapters require additional setup information. This is provided in the form of overlay files (OVL), which are integrated into the corresponding CFG file via an INCLUDE statement.

EISA Bus Slots.   EISA adapters employ a rather ingenious design with two parallel rows of contacts. Conventional ISA cards, with a single level of contacts, are unable to penetrate the bottommost contact layer and thus "see" only the conventional ISA bus. EISA adapters, on the other hand, reach both sets of contacts. Two signals, $\overline{EX16}$ and $\overline{EX32}$, provide a means for the EISA card to announce its presence and define the width of its data bus. Figure 11.10 shows the bus structure; Table 11.5 provides a description of the new EISA signals.

Self-Review 11.2 (Answers on page 546)

11.2.1   Which of the following adapters are typically found on the system board of a MCA computer? Circle all that apply.
  (a) Video display controller.
  (b) Floppy disk controller.
  (c) Hard disk controller.
  (d) Serial and parallel I/O ports.

11.2.2   A standard MCA bus cycle requires _____ clock pulses or _____ μs.

11.2.3   What is an MCA *adapter definition file*?

11.2.4   Show, via a calculation, that a standard EISA bus cycle transfers data at 16.6 MB/s.

11.2.5   Programming an EISA interrupt as _____ triggered allows that interrupt to be shared by several devices.

11.3   Local Bus: VESA and PCI

Introduction

Although the MCA and EISA buses expanded the data and address bus widths to match those of the 386, 486, and Pentium processors, both remain *I/O buses* operating at relatively low clock speeds (10 MHz and 8.33 MHz, respectively). This is particularly a problem with modern video cards that must move megabytes of data to update a graphics screen. What is needed is a data pathway that connects directly to the processor, operating at or near the clock speed of the processor. This is the idea behind the *local bus*.

Two local bus standards have emerged: VESA (Video Electronics Standards Association) and PCI (Peripheral Component Interconnect). VESA, originally designed to support high-speed video cards, works in combination with the ISA slots. PCI is an entirely new bus standard designed to function on its own (although several ISA slots are also typically provided for low-speed peripherals).

Figure 11.10 EISA bus slots. The connector is designed to accept ISA adapters or EISA adapters.

EISA	ISA		ISA	EISA
GND				
+5V	GND	B1 A1 / F1 E1	I/O CH CK	$\overline{\text{CMD}}$
+5V	RESET DRV		D7	$\overline{\text{START}}$
Manufacturer	+5V		D6	EXRDY
Manufacturer	IRQ2		D5	$\overline{\text{EX32}}$
Code	-5V		D4	GND
Manufacturer	DRQ2		D3	Code
Manufacturer	-12V		D2	$\overline{\text{EX16}}$
+12V	$\overline{\text{OWS}}$		D1	$\overline{\text{SLBURST}}$
M/$\overline{\text{IO}}$	+12V		D0	$\overline{\text{MSBURST}}$
$\overline{\text{LOCK}}$	GND	B10 A10 / F10 E10	I/O CH RDY	W/$\overline{\text{R}}$
res	$\overline{\text{SMEMW}}$		AEN	GND
GND	$\overline{\text{SMEMR}}$		A19	res
res	$\overline{\text{IOW}}$		A18	res
$\overline{\text{BE3}}$	$\overline{\text{IOR}}$		A17	res
Code	$\overline{\text{DACK3}}$		A16	GND
$\overline{\text{BE2}}$	DRQ3		A15	Code
$\overline{\text{BE0}}$/D32	$\overline{\text{DACK1}}$		A14	$\overline{\text{BE1}}$/D33
GND	DRQ1		A13	LA31/D63
+5V	$\overline{\text{REF}}$		A12	GND
LA29/D61	CLK	B20 A20 / F20 E20	A11	LA30/D62
GND	IRQ7		A10	LA28/D60
LA26/D58	IRQ6		A9	LA27/D59
LA24/D56	IRQ5		A8	LA25/D57
Code	IRQ4		A7	GND
LA16/D48	IRQ3		A6	Code
LA14/D46	$\overline{\text{DACK2}}$		A5	LA15/D47
+5V	TC		A4	LA13/D45
+5V	ALE		A3	LA12/D44
GND	+5V		A2	LA11/D43
LA10/D42	OSC		A1	GND
	GND	B31 A31 / F31 E31	A0	LA9/D41

EISA	ISA		ISA	EISA
LA8/D40		D1 C1 / H1 G1		LA7/D39
LA6/D38	MEM CS16		SBHE	GND
LA5/D37	I/O CS16		LA23/D55	LA4/D36
+5V	IRQ10		LA22/D54	LA3/D35
LA2/D34	IRQ11		LA21/D53	GND
Code	IRQ12		LA20/D52	Code
D16	IRQ15		LA19/D51	D17
D18	IRQ14		LA18/D50	D19
GND	$\overline{\text{DACK0}}$		LA17/D49	D20
D21	DRQ0	D10 C10 / H10 G10	$\overline{\text{MEMR}}$	D22
D23	$\overline{\text{DACK5}}$		$\overline{\text{MEMW}}$	GND
D24	DRQ5		SD08	D25
GND	$\overline{\text{DACK6}}$		SD09	D26
D27	DRQ6		SD10	D28
Code	$\overline{\text{DACK7}}$		SD11	Code
D29	DRQ7		SD12	GND
+5V	+5V		SD13	D30
+5V	$\overline{\text{MASTER}}$		SD14	D31
$\overline{\text{MACK}}$	GND	D18 C18 / H18 G18	SD15	$\overline{\text{MREQ}}$

Table 11.5   EISA Bus Signal Descriptions

Signal	Name	Type*	Description
BALE	Address Latch Enable	Output (ISA)	High when valid address signals are present on the I/O channel.
BCLK	Bus Clock	Output (ISA)	Typically 8.33 MHz.
$\overline{BE0}$–$\overline{BE3}$	Byte Enable Signals	Output	Low to indicate which byte(s) of the 32-bit data bus will be involved in the data transfer.
CMD	Command	Output	Low by the EISA bus controller to resynchronize BCLK after a stretched bus cycle.
Code	Coding bridge		Used to prevent an ISA adapter from penetrating too deep into an EISA slot.
D16–D31	Data Lines	Input/Output	High-order 16 bits of the 32-bit data bus. The low 16 bits are transferred via the ISA bus section.
$\overline{EX16}$	Execute 16	Input	Low by an adapter to indicate that it operates with a 16-bit data bus.
$\overline{EX32}$	Execute 32	Input	Low by an adapter to indicate that it operates with a 32-bit data bus.
EXRDY	Ready	Input	High by an adapter to indicate that it is ready and no wait states are required. If low, wait states are inserted.
LA2–LA16, LA24–LA31	Large Address	Output	Nonlatched address signals A2–A16 and A24–A31. Used for fast EISA bus cycles.
$\overline{LOCK}$	Lock	Output	Low by a bus master to indicate that it has exclusive access to memory.
M/$\overline{IO}$	Memory/IO	Output	High to indicate a memory access. Low to indicate an I/O access.
MANUFACTURER	Manufacturer	Input/Output	These four pins are used by EISA OEMs for their own purposes.
$\overline{MACK}$	Master Acknowledge	Input/Output	Low by the system arbitrator to indicate to the current bus master that control has been passed to that master.
$\overline{MREQ}$	Master Request	Input/Output	Low by a bus master to request control of the system buses.
$\overline{MSBURST}$	Master Burst	Input/Output	Low by the bus master to indicate that it can carry out the next bus cycle as a burst cycle.
$\overline{SLBURST}$	Slave Burst	Input	Low by an EISA slave to indicate that the slave can carry out the next bus cycle as a burst cycle.
$\overline{START}$	START	Output	Low to indicate the beginning of a cycle on the EISA bus.
W/$\overline{R}$	Write/Read	Output	High to indicate that the current bus cycle will perform a write operation; low to indicate a read operation.
D32–D63	D32-D63	Input/Output	For 64-bit data transfers, these pins carry the 32 high-order data bits.

*Input to or output from the processor/ bus controller or current bus master.

In this section we will:

- Describe the architecture of the VESA local bus.
- Describe the architecture of the PCI bus.
- Compare the data transfer rates for VESA and PCI local bus adapters.

VESA Local Bus (VLB)

High-Speed Graphics Adapters.   Prior to the widespread acceptance of Microsoft Windows, most PC applications were *character mapped*. A full screen of information consisted of 25 rows with 80 characters per row (2000 characters in all). The time to update such a screen—even with a 4.77 MHz PC/XT—is nearly instantaneous.

Windows changed all this. High-resolution graphics has become the norm. A standard VGA screen with 256 colors requires 300K of memory. Step up to (24-bit) True Color with 1024×768 resolution, and over 2 MB of memory is required. Transferring this much information to the video RAM via the ISA bus can take several seconds. Clearly this is unsatisfactory if multimedia applications supporting full-motion video are to be supported.

The initial solution to this problem was to embed the video adapter into the system board and interface it directly to the processor via its local bus. The drawback to this approach, however, was a lack of *upgradeability*: To add an enhanced video adapter, you either purchased a new system board or plugged that adapter into the slow ISA bus.

Several manufacturers then began developing proprietary local bus designs. Seeing the splintering effect of this approach, the Video Electronics Standard Association (VESA) in 1992 announced a new local bus standard called *VLB* or the *VL bus*. Using data bus widths to 64 bits (Version 2.0), and a 32-bit address bus, data transfer rates as high as 267 MB/s can be achieved (under the best of conditions).

Unlike the other bus standards we have discussed, VLB is designed to *support* an existing bus structure (EISA, ISA, or MCA). In fact, VLB adapters count on the presence of the signals in the standard slots, as this gives them access to the system hardware interrupts and DMA channels. Figure 11.11 shows the most common arrangement, in which three VESA slots have been added directly behind the standard (E)ISA bus connectors. The specifications permit three slots with a system bus frequency of 40 MHz or less, and two slots at 50 MHz.

Bus Frequency and Data Transfer Rate.   The VL bus operates at the bus frequency of the processor, with a theoretical maximum of 66 MHz. However, this can only be achieved if the controller is built into the system board logic. Via the bus slots, 50 MHz is more reasonable. The basic bus cycle requires two clock cycles. However, read operations require one wait state.

The fastest data transfers occur using (486-like) burst cycles. Using a 2-1-1-1 (2 clocks for the first transfer and one for each succeeding transfer) burst cycle, 16 bytes can be written with five clock cycles. The data transfer rate (at 50 MHz) is:

$$\frac{16 \text{ bytes}}{5 \text{ Clock Pulses} \times 20 \text{ ns/pulse}} = 160 \text{ MB/s}$$

Read burst cycles require an additional wait state, and thus run 3-1-1-1 cycles; the transfer rate decreases to 133 MB/s.

Figure 11.11 Typical VESA bus system board. Three VLB connectors are located directly behind the ISA connectors.

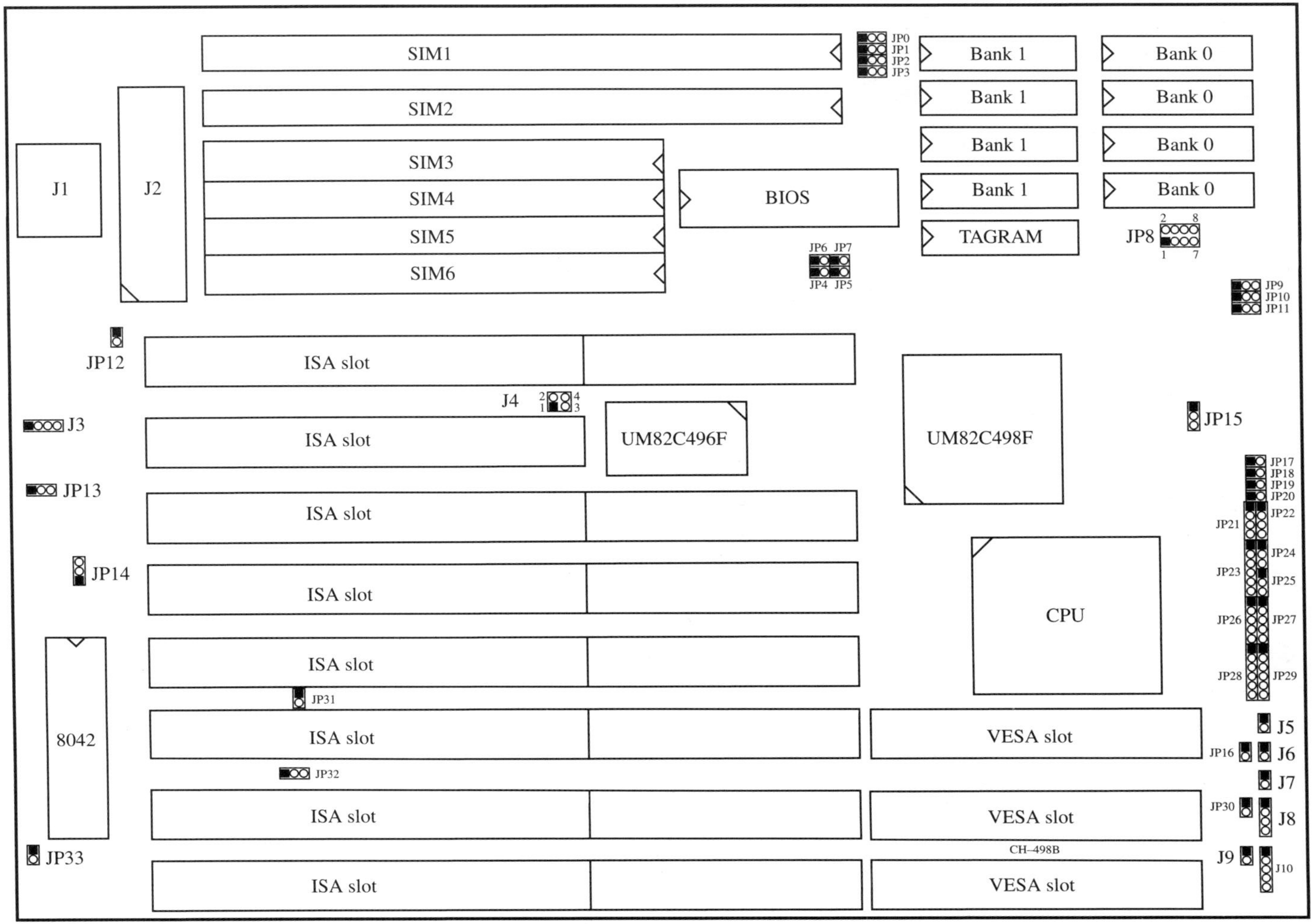

Note: "■" signifies Pin 1.

The 2.0 specification of the standard expands the data bus to 64 bits (to support the Pentium processors). No new pins are added to the connector, however, and multiplexing is therefore used to achieve this greater bus width. As additional time is required to demultiplex these pins, the write and read 64-bit data transfer rates are somewhat less than twice the 32-bit rates: 267 MB/s and 222 MB/s, respectively.

DMA and Interrupts.   The VL bus supports three local bus masters to support high-speed data transfers and has no support for the slower DMA transfers (which it leaves to the standard slots and the standard bus). Only one interrupt input is provided—IRQ9— again leaving this task to the standard slots.

VLB Adapters.   As mentioned, the VL bus was originally designed for high-speed video adapters. Presently, several manufacturers offer VLB hard disk controllers that also can benefit from the high data transfer rate of the VL bus. As the speed of local area networks (LANs) approaches 100 MB/s, these cards will also be good candidates for the VL bus.

VLB adapters require no special system BIOS, but are processor dependent; that is, they will function only in 80x86-based computer systems. In addition, automatic configuration is not part of the specification, so it is not unusual to see DIP switches and jumper plugs on these cards.

VESA Bus Slots.   Figure 11.12 shows the layout of a VL bus slot. To achieve a 64-bit data bus width, some of the pins are required to do "double-duty," as shown. Table 11.6 provides a summary of the pin functions.

PCI

The Next Industry Standard?   Today's multitasking operating systems and multimedia applications require ever-faster throughput from the system peripherals. Unfortunately, the I/O architecture of the popular 16-bit ISA bus is so slow that any improvements in processor technology are made unnoticeable to the system user. The addition of local bus slots (VLB) can only be viewed as a temporary fix, because the local bus components are tied intimately to the CPU and require a complete redesign with each new generation of processors.

The PCI (Peripheral Component Interconnect) local bus was designed with the best features of MCA and EISA in mind, but implemented in such a way that ISA adapters can still be utilized. In a typical system, three PCI slots are provided, together with several ISA slots. Because the component side of a PCI card is opposite that of an ISA card, the two can share the same physical space, with separate bus connectors; that is, the user can insert an ISA card or a PCI card (but not both) in the same slot location.

Figure 11.13 illustrates the architecture of a PCI-based computer. Notice that the processor and the memory subsystem are separate (decoupled) from the PCI and expansion buses. Also notice that all of the PCI units (agents) are connected to the PCI bus, which in turn connects to the processor via the *PCI bridge.* It is this bridge that separates PCI from all of the other buses discussed. More than just a set of buffers between the PCI and processor buses, the PCI bridge is *intelligent,* capable of grouping single data requests into bursts and then exchanging those bursts with memory and the I/O devices. This can be done even though the processor itself may not support a given burst mode (the 486, for example, cannot perform write burst cycles).

Figure 11.12 VL bus slots. To achive a 64-bit data bus width, some of the pins are multiplexed.

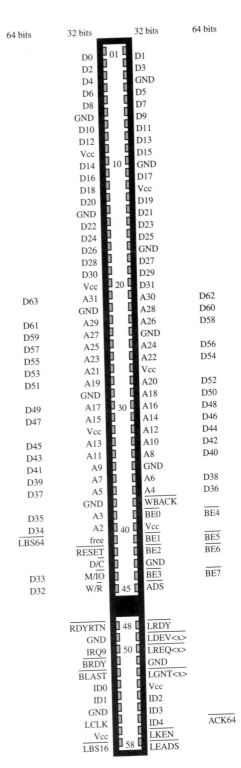

Table 11.6 VESA Local Bus Signal Descriptions

Signal	Name	Type*	Description
		32-bit Section	
A2–A31	Address Lines	Output	VLB address bus.
$\overline{\text{ADS}}$	Address Strobe	Output	Low to indicate the beginning of a bus cycle. Can be used to latch the multiplexed address pins.
$\overline{\text{BE3}}$–$\overline{\text{BE0}}$	Byte Enables	Output	Low to indicate which byte(s) of the 32-bit data bus will be involved in the data transfer.
$\overline{\text{BLAST}}$	Burst Last	Output	Low to indicate that the current transfer is the last of a VLB burst.
$\overline{\text{BRDY}}$	Burst Ready	Input	Low to indicate the end of the current burst transfer.
D0–D31	Data Lines	Input/Output	32-bit VLB data bus.
ID0–ID4	Identification Signals	Output	These pins are intended for VLB adapters and coded to indicate burst capabilities (read, write or none), bus width, write wait states, and processor clock speed.
IRQ9	Interrupt Request	Input	High-level triggered interrupt connected to IRQ9 of the ISA bus.
$\overline{\text{LEADS}}$	Local External Address Strobe	Output	After accessing memory, this signal is set to a low level by a VL bus master to cause the processor to perform a cache write-back operation.
$\overline{\text{LBS16}}$	Local Bus Size 16	Input	Low to indicate to the bus controller that the specified VLB device operates with a 16-bit data bus.
LCLK	Local Clock	Output	VLB clock (66 MHz maximum for an on-board unit and 50 MHz maximum for a VLB slot).
$\overline{\text{LDEV}}$<x>	Local Device	Input	Low by the specified VLB device to indicate that it recognizes that it is the target of the current address.
$\overline{\text{LRDY}}$	Local Ready	Input	Used for single transfers only, this signal is output low by the active VLB device to indicate that it has completed the current request.
$\overline{\text{LREQ}}$<x>	Local Request	Input	Low by the VL bus master in slot x to request control of the VL bus.
$\overline{\text{LGNT}}$<x>	Local Grant	Output	Low by the bus controller granting access to the VL bus to the bus master in slot x.
M/$\overline{\text{IO}}$, D/$\overline{\text{C}}$, W/$\overline{\text{R}}$	Memory/IO, Data/Command, Write/Read	Output	These three signals encode the type of bus cycle: INTA sequence, halt/special, I/O read or write, instruction fetch, halt, memory read or write.
$\overline{\text{RDYRTN}}$	Ready Return	Output	Low by the bus controller to indicate to all bus masters that a VLB cycle has completed.
$\overline{\text{RESET}}$	Reset	Output	Low to reset all VLB units.

Table 11.6   *(continued)*

Signal	Name	Type*	Description
		32-bit Section	
$\overline{\text{WBACK}}$	Write Back	Output	Low to cause the VL bus master to interrupt the current bus cycle and initiate a write-back cycle.
		64-bit Expansion	
$\overline{\text{ACK64}}$	Active Acknowledge	Input	Low to indicate to the controller that the specified VLB device can perform the requested 64-bit data transfer.
$\overline{\text{BE7}}-\overline{\text{BE4}}$	Byte Enables	Output	Low to indicate which byte(s) of the upper 32 bits of the 64-bit data bus will be involved in the data transfer.
D32–D63	Data Lines	Input/Output	The upper 32 bits of the VLB 64-bit data bus.
$\overline{\text{LBS64}}$	Local Bus Size 64	Output	Low to indicate to the target that a 64-bit data transfer should be performed.

*Input to or output from the processor/ bus controller or bus master.

Figure 11.13   The PCI bus connects to the processor through the *PCI bridge*.

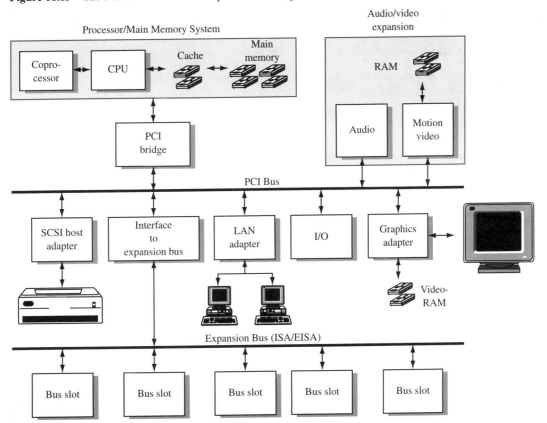

PCI Bus Operation.   The PCI bus clock is rated 0 to 33 MHz (the former is useful in battery-powered systems to reduce power consumption in standby mode). The data bus lines themselves use a multiplexing scheme in which the connector pins are alternately used as address and data lines. A PCI transaction takes place between a *master* (a device that takes control of the system buses) and a *target* (a device that only responds to access requests).

A normal bus access consists of an address phase followed by a data phase. A read cycle, for example, requires three clock pulses: one to output the address, one to switch the address lines around for data access, and one to transfer the data. Using the standard 32-bit bus width, the data transfer rate is 44 MB/s. Write cycles do not require the address lines to be turned around and can complete in just two clocks. The data transfer rate is 50 percent faster—66 MB/s.

As mentioned, PCI also includes a very powerful *burst mode* in which the address phase is followed by an *unlimited* number of data transfers. In this mode, sender and receiver update the address independently. With only one clock pulse per transfer, the data rate approaches 132 MB/s with a 32-bit data bus, and 264 MB/s with a 64-bit data bus.

Two features make the PCI burst mode especially powerful. The first is the ability of the PCI bridge to combine single processor accesses (which may occur at much higher speeds than the 33 MHz of the PCI bus) into a single burst, thus avoiding a potential bottleneck. A second advantage is the ability to transfer an *unlimited* number of bytes in a single burst—even though the processor itself may be limited to a much smaller number (the Pentium, for example, is limited to 32 bytes per burst—the size of one cache line). To avoid having one PCI device "hog" the PCI bus, each device has a latency timer that defines the longest period of time that that device is allowed to control the bus.

Bus Commands.   The PCI bridge is considerably more intelligent than the bus controllers in an (E)ISA or MCA machine. It guides processor accesses through to the proper PCI unit, even filtering those requests to achieve optimum performance. To indicate to the peripherals the type of bus cycle that is about to occur, the PCI bridge can issue 16 different bus commands. This information is multiplexed on the C/$\overline{\text{BE3}}$–C/$\overline{\text{BE0}}$ (command/byte enable) lines and output during the address phase of each bus cycle. Table 11.7 lists the PCI bridge bus commands and provides a brief description of each.

DMA and Interrupts.   You will notice in Table 11.7 that there are no commands referring to DMA cycles. The bus master concept in PCI (and EISA and MCA, for that matter) makes this mode superfluous. This is because the DMA controller must connect through the existing logic on the system board to control the buses. A bus master, on the other hand, shuts down the system board buses and communicates with the adapters via the bus slots. In this way, PCI supports true multiprocessor operating systems.

PCI provides four level-sensitive shareable interrupts ($\overline{\text{INTA}}$–$\overline{\text{INTD}}$). Via the system BIOS, these can be programmed to function as a standard AT IRQ. For example, when installing a hard drive controller in a PCI slot, $\overline{\text{INTA}}$ would be set to IRQ14.

PCI Adapters.   Recognizing the industry's shift toward 3.3V digital signals, PCI defines three different kinds of boards (3.3V, 5V, and universal) and two different slots (3.3V and 5V). The boards are keyed so that a 3.3V board cannot be plugged into a 5V slot and vice versa. Universal boards are designed to work in either slot type and thus are not keyed.

Table 11.7   PCI Bus Commands

C/$\overline{BE3}$–C/$\overline{BE0}$	Name	Bus Transfer Type
0000	INTA sequence	Interrupt vector.
0001	Special cycle	Special information code output to PCI agents.*
0010	I/O read access	Data is input from an I/O device.
0011	I/O write access	Data is output to an I/O device.
0100	Reserved	
0101	Reserved	
0110	Memory read access	Data is input from the memory address area.
0111	Memory write access	Data is output to the memory address area.
1000	Reserved	
1001	Reserved	
1010	Configuration read access	Data is input from the configuration address area.
1011	Configuration write access	Data is output to the configuration address area.
1100	Memory multiple read access	An extended data read cycle greater than a cache line.
1101	Dual addressing cycle	Two consecutive address cycles. Used to transfer a 64-bit address as two 32-bit pieces.
1110	Line memory read access	A memory read access greater than 32 bits (typically to the end of the cache line).
1111	Memory write access with invalidation	A memory write cycle of at least one cache line (thus indicating that that line is now invalid and bypassing a write-back).

*Processor shutdown, processor halt, x86 specific code.

Each PCI card contains a 256-byte *configuration memory*. A standard header of 64 bytes begins the block and contains information about the type of card, manufacturer, revision level, current status of the card, cache line size in 32-byte units, and bus latency (how long a PCI bus operation can take). The remaining 192 bytes depend on the specific card. For example, many cards set up base address registers that allow the onboard RAM, ROM, and I/O ports to be *remapped* to specific address ranges within the 80x86 processor's memory and I/O space.

PCI adapters provide true *plug-and-play support*. At power up, the system scans the configuration memory of all units on the PCI bus and then assigns each device a unique base address and interrupt level. The user simply plugs in a board and it works (at least in theory!).[13]

PCI Bus Signals.   Every signal on the PCI bus is adjacent to a power supply or ground signal. This helps minimize noise pick-up and signal radiation. Figure 11.14 shows the slot configuration for 3.3V and 5V connectors. Table 11.8 provides a brief description of each signal.

---

[13]When adding a new card to a PCI bus computer, software drivers will often have to be added. After recognizing the card, the PCI BIOS will configure the hardware settings. As the computer continues to boot, the operating system should prompt the user to insert the appropriate driver disks.

Figure 11.14 PCI bus slots. Two different connectors are specified.

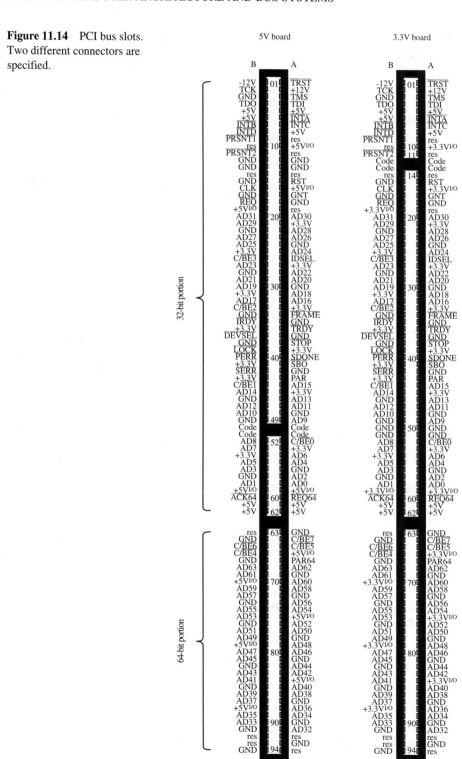

Table 11.8   PCI Bus Signal Descriptions

Signal	Name	Type*	Description
		32-bit Section	
AD0–AD31	Address/Data lines	Input/Output	Multiplexed 32-bit PCI address and data bus.
C/$\overline{BE3}$–C/$\overline{BE0}$	Command/Byte Enables	Input/Output	During the data phase of a bus cycle these lines indicate the type of bus cycle (see Table 11.7). During the address phase these lines are low to indicate which bytes of the 32-bit data bus will be involved in the data transfer.
CLK	Clock	Output	The PCI clock signal (0 to 33 MHz).
$\overline{DEVSEL}$	Device Select	Input	Low by the active PCI device if it has identified itself as the target of a PCI transfer.
$\overline{FRAME}$	Frame	Input/Output	Low by the active PCI bus master at the beginning of every data transfer cycle. It is removed when all data has been transferred or the transfer is interrupted.
$\overline{GNT}$	Grant	Output	Low to indicate to the requesting PCI unit that it can now use the PCI bus as the master. Each PCI master has a separate GNT input.
IDSEL	Initialization Device Select	Output	Low to chip select the configuration memory.
$\overline{INTA}$, $\overline{INTB}$, $\overline{INTC}$, $\overline{INTD}$	Interrupt	Input	Low-level interrupt input. INTA is assigned to a single-function PCI device. Multifunction devices may use INTB-INTD.
$\overline{IRDY}$	Initiator Ready	Input/Output	Low to indicate that the initiating bus master has placed valid data on the bus or is ready to read data off the bus.
$\overline{LOCK}$	Lock	Input/Output	Low to indicate that access to the specified PCI device is blocked. Access to other PCI devices can still be performed.
PAR	Parity	Input/Output	Even parity bit for AD0–AD31 and C/BE3–C/BE0.
$\overline{PERR}$	Parity Error	Input/Output	Low to indicate that a parity error has occurred.
$\overline{PRSNT1}$, $\overline{PRSNT2}$	Present	Input	These two pins are wired to +5V or ground by the PCI adapter to indicate its presence and its power consumption.
$\overline{REQ}$	Request	Input	Low to request control of the PCI bus as a master.
$\overline{REQ64}$	Request 64 Bit Transfer	Input/Output	Low by the current bus master to indicate that a 64-bit data transfer is desired.

(continued on next page)

Table 11.8   *(continued)*

Signal	Name	Type*	Description
		32-bit Section	
$\overline{\text{RST}}$	Reset	Output	Low to reset all connected PCI devices.
$\overline{\text{SBO}}$	Snoop Backoff	Input/Output	Low by a bus master to indicate an inquiry hit to a modified cache line. Used to support a write-through or write-back cache.
SDONE	Snoop Done	Input/Output	High by a bus master to indicate that the current inquiry cycle has completed.
$\overline{\text{SERR}}$	System Error	Input/Output	Low by a bus master to indicate an address parity or other serious system error.
$\overline{\text{STOP}}$	Stop	Target to Master	Low to instruct the master to stop the current operation.
TCK	Test Clock		These five pins are used for system testing.
TDI	Test Data Input		
TDO	Test Data Output		
TMS	Test Mode Select		
$\overline{\text{TRST}}$	Test Reset		
$\overline{\text{TRDY}}$	Target Ready	Target to Master	Low to indicate that the PCI target can accept the write data or that it now has read data ready.
		64-bit Expansion	
AD32-AD63	Multiplexed Address and Data Lines	Input/Output	High-order section of the 64-bit data and address bus.
C/$\overline{\text{BE7}}$-C/$\overline{\text{BE4}}$	Multiplexed Command and Byte Enables	Input/Output	During the data phase of a bus cycle these lines indicate the type of bus cycle. During the address phase these lines are low to indicate which bytes of the high-order 64-bit data bus will be involved in the data transfer.
PAR64	Parity 64	Input/Output	High or low to achieve even parity on the AD32–AD63 address lines and C/BE7–C/BE4.

*Input to or output from the processor/ bus controller or bus master.

Self-Review 11.3 (Answers on page 546)

11.3.1   The VL bus was originally designed to support high-speed _____ adapters.

11.3.2   Using 3-1-1-1 burst cycles, show (via a calculation) that the VL bus operates at 133 MB/s for 32-bit read cycles. Assume a 50 MHz clock frequency.

11.3.3   What types of adapter cards are appropriate for the VL bus?

11.3.4   The PCI bus connects to the processor via the _____ _____.

11.3.5   The PCI bus multiplexes the address and data lines. What does this mean?

11.3.6   In burst mode, the PCI bus can transfer an _____ number of data bytes.

11.3.7   PCI identifies two different slot connectors. What is the difference between these two?

11.4   I/O Buses: SCSI and USB

Introduction

Unlike the *system buses* described in the previous sections, SCSI and USB are designed to function as *peripheral buses*. SCSI, a parallel bus, offers the highest performance and is commonly used to interface hard drives, tape drives, and CD-ROM players. USB is a serial bus intended for low- to medium-speed peripherals such as mice, keyboards, and modems.

In this section we will:

- List the important features of the SCSI bus, including device IDs, bus termination, and bus operation.
- Compare the various versions of SCSI, including SCSI-1, SCSI-2, Fast SCSI, Wide SCSI, and SCSI-3.
- List the important features of USB, including bus topology and protocol, cabling, electrical characteristics, and device types.
- Compare control, bulk, interrupt, and isochronous USB data transfers for data rate, bandwidth, and bus access.

SCSI—The Small Computer Systems Interface

A Peripheral Bus.   As mentioned in the introduction, SCSI (often pronounced *Scuzzy*) is designed as an I/O bus for small computer (microcomputer) peripherals. It was derived from SASI—Shugart Associates Systems Interface—an 8-bit parallel interface between a host computer and a hard disk drive. In addition to hard drives, SCSI is used to control tape backup units, CD-ROM players, video scanners, printers, and other devices. A typical SCSI system is shown in Figure 11.15

SCSI is not a systems bus like (E)ISA, MCA, or PCI. Indeed, typical SCSI adapters run at just 1 to 10 MB/s, nowhere near the 267 MB/s transfer rate of PCI, for example. But that is not the intention. Magnetic drives, optical drives, and CD-ROM readers require data rates of just a few megabytes per second. What SCSI offers is an *intelligent bus* that can accept high-level commands from the processor and then transfer data without further CPU intervention. Indeed, it is even possible for two SCSI devices to transfer information without the host participating (aside from issuing the initial commands). A SCSI hard drive, for example, may be backed up to a SCSI tape drive while the system processor is performing other tasks—true *parallel processing*.

SCSI Signals.   The standard (8-bit) SCSI bus defines 18 different signals. These are made up of:

1. Eight data bit signals
2. One parity bit signal
3. Nine control signals

Each signal wire is surrounded by a ground wire, so that a total of 50 pins are defined. Three different connector configurations are in use. (These are shown in Figure 11.16.) Table 11.9 shows the pin assignments for each connector type.[14]

---

[14]Several different versions of SCSI are in use: SCSI-1, SCSI-2, Fast SCSI, Wide SCSI, and SCSI-3. Wide SCSI and SCSI-3 support a 32-bit data bus width and use a 68-conductor cable. The different versions of SCSI are discussed later in this section.

Figure 11.15   SCSI devices are interfaced via a host adapter that connects to the system bus of the computer.

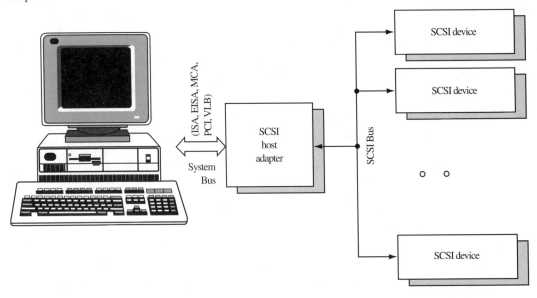

Figure 11.16   SCSI devices are interfaced using a 50-conductor cable. Three connector configurations are in common use.

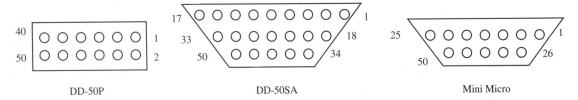

Placing Adapters on the SCSI Bus.   The SCSI bus requires a *host adapter* that interfaces with the processor over the conventional system bus [(E)ISA, MCA, or PCI]. Devices on the SCSI bus communicate with this host via cables wired in a "daisy chain" fashion. (This is shown in Figure 11.17.) Note that each SCSI device therefore requires *two* parallel connectors, and that the host adapter can be placed anywhere on the chain. The SCSI devices themselves may be located internal or external to the computer.

The SCSI ID.   The SCSI bus can accommodate eight devices, one of which must be the host adapter.[15] Accordingly, each device on the bus must be assigned a unique *ID number* in the range 0–7. The higher the ID number, the higher the priority of that device. For that reason, an ID number of 7 is normally assigned to the host adapter.

In general, any SCSI device can be assigned any available ID number: However, the software must be set accordingly. In some cases, the driver software may demand that you

---

[15]With SCSI-3, 16 devices are allowed.

Table 11.9 SCSCI Signal Names and Connector Pinouts

SCSI Signal	Meaning	DD-50P	Mini Micro	DD-50SA
GND	Ground	1	1	1
$\overline{DB(0)}$	Data bit 0	2	26	34
GND	Ground	3	2	18
$\overline{DB(1)}$	Data bit 1	4	27	2
GND	Ground	5	3	35
$\overline{DB(2)}$	Data bit 2	6	28	19
GND	Ground	7	4	3
$\overline{DB(3)}$	Data bit 3	8	29	36
GND	Ground	9	5	20
$\overline{DB(4)}$	Data bit 4	10	30	4
GND	Ground	11	6	37
$\overline{DB(5)}$	Data bit 5	12	31	21
GND	Ground	13	7	5
$\overline{DB(6)}$	Data bit 6	14	32	38
GND	Ground	15	8	22
$\overline{DB(7)}$	Data bit 7	16	33	6
GND	Ground	17	9	39
$\overline{DB(P)}$	Parity bit	18	34	23
GND	Ground	19	10	7
GND	Ground	20	35	40
GND	Ground	21	11	24
GND	Ground	22	36	8
RSR		23	12	41
RSR		24	37	25
Open		25	13	9
TERMPWR	Termination	26	38	42
RSR		27	14	26
RSR		28	39	10
GND	Ground	29	15	43
GND	Ground	30	40	27
GND	Ground	31	16	11
$\overline{ATN}$	Attention	32	41	44
GND	Ground	33	17	28
GND	Ground	34	42	12
GND	Ground	35	18	45
BSY	Busy	36	43	29
GND	Ground	37	19	13
$\overline{ACK}$	Acknowledge	38	44	46
GND	Ground	39	20	30

(continued on next page)

Table 11.9 *(continued)*

SCSI Signal	Meaning	DD-50P	Mini Micro	DD-50SA
$\overline{\text{RST}}$	Reset	40	45	14
GND	Ground	41	21	47
$\overline{\text{MSG}}$	Message	42	46	31
GND	Ground	43	22	15
$\overline{\text{SEL}}$	Select	44	47	48
GND	Ground	45	23	32
$\overline{\text{C/D}}$	Command/Data	46	48	16
GND	Ground	47	24	49
$\overline{\text{REQ}}$	Request	48	49	33
GND	Ground	49	25	17
$\overline{\text{I/O}}$	Input/Output	50	50	50

choose a particular ID. For example, many systems require that the system boot device (typically a hard drive) be given ID number 0.

Single-Ended vs. Differential SCSI.   SCSI allows two types of buses: *single-ended* and *differential*. The single-ended bus uses a signaling system in which the output voltage of a driver is referenced to a common ground. With a differential bus, there is no common ground; instead, the signal is sensed as the difference in potential between two output pins (typically labeled **+** and **−**).

Figure 11.17   SCSI devices are wired in a *daisy chain* configuration with terminating plugs connected to each end of the cable.

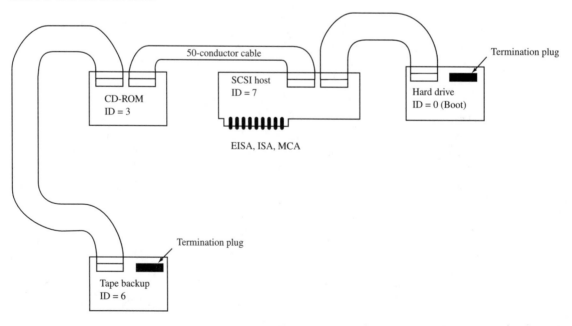

When wired as a single-ended bus, SCSI is limited to a total cable length of six meters. The differential bus, which is less susceptible to noise, can tolerate a total cable length of 25 meters. Unfortunately, the differential bus requires nearly twice as many conductors as the single-ended bus, and thus is used less frequently.

Termination. When a high-frequency voltage pulse is output onto a signal line, it tends to be reflected from the end of that line. The reflected pulse then adds and subtracts energy from the incident pulse, causing distortion. To minimize these reflections, the SCSI bus requires *terminating resistors* at each end of the bus (only). (This is shown in Figure 11.17.)

Two types of termination are in common use: *passive* and *active*. With passive termination, each SCSI signal line is pulled to +5V (via the TERMPWR pin) through a 220Ω resistor and to ground through a 330Ω resistor. The equivalent resistance (132Ω) seen by each SCSI driver approximately matches that of the SCSI transmission line and causes all of the incident energy output by the driver to be absorbed. No reflections should occur.

With active termination, each SCSI signal line is connected to a 2.85V voltage regulator via a 110Ω resistor. This method provides superior noise reduction because the clamping voltage does not vary with the TERMPWR pin, as it does with passive termination. Some SCSI adapters go one step further and clamp the SCSI signal line via diodes to high and low voltage levels. This is called *Forced Perfect Termination (FPT)*.

Passive termination is usually accomplished by inserting a dummy termination plug into the unused SCSI connector at each end of the chain. Active terminators are usually built into the device and can be turned on or off via switches.

Bus Operation. Devices on the SCSI bus function similar to bus masters on the PCI or MCA bus. An arbitration scheme is used to determine which devices can transfer data at a given time. The SCSI device that initiates the transaction is called the *Initiator*; the responding device is called the *Target*. The SCSI bus supports eight different bus phases that ensure an orderly transfer of data between the Initiator and the Target.

1. *Bus Free Phase.* The Initiator begins a transaction by testing the $\overline{\text{BSY}}$ and $\overline{\text{SEL}}$ signals. When these signals are both inactive, the bus is free.
2. *Arbitration Phase.* The unit that wants to control the bus activates the $\overline{\text{BSY}}$ line and then the data bit corresponding to its SCSI ID. A short arbitration delay then occurs, during which the bus is tested to see if another (higher priority) unit is trying to control the bus.
3. *Selection Phase.* Once the Initiator has succeeded in taking over the bus, the $\overline{\text{SEL}}$ line is made active and the SCSI address bits corresponding to the Initiator and Target are placed on the data lines. The Target must then recognize that it has been selected and activate $\overline{\text{BSY}}$ within a certain period of time.
4. *Reselection Phase.* Once the Target receives a command, it carries that command out without further intervention from the Initiator. Depending on the command, several milliseconds may elapse (a long time to a computer). The SCSI bus is thus relinquished during this time. Once the task has finished, the Target, remembering the Initiator's ID, reestablishes connection using the arbitration and selection phases described previously.
5. *Command Phase.* During this phase, device-specific commands are sent to the Target from the Initiator. In effect, these commands represent the *instruction set* for the SCSI bus. As shown in Table 11.10, the $\overline{\text{MSG}}$, $\overline{\text{C/D}}$, and $\overline{\text{I/O}}$ signals are used to identify the type of information on the SCSI data bus lines (command, data, message, or status).

Table 11.10   SCSI Bus Phases

MSG	C/D	I/O	Phase	Transfer Direction
0	0	0	Data out	Initiator → target
0	0	1	Data in	Target → initiator
0	1	0	Command	Initiator → target
0	1	1	Status	Target → initiator
1	0	0	Invalid	
1	0	1	Invalid	
1	1	0	Message out	Initiator → target
1	1	1	Message in	Target → initiator

6. *Data Phase.* Data transfers may occur asynchronously or synchronously. In the former case, the $\overline{REQ}$ and $\overline{ACK}$ signals are used to "handshake" the transfer. With synchronous transfers, the Initiator *assumes* the Target is receiving the data and does not wait for the $\overline{ACK}$ pulse.

7. *Message Phase.* Various messages can be exchanged between the Initiator and the Target. Examples are:

> *Command complete*—The last command has completed successfully.
> *Request Wide Mode*—The SCSI unit wants to perform a 16- or 32-bit data transfer.
> *Request synchronous mode*—The indicated SCSI device wants to use synchronous mode.
> *Terminate I/O*—The target is to terminate (but not abort) the current I/O process.

8. *Status Phase.*   Once a command has completed, the Target transmits a status byte with bits 1–4 used to indicate that the SCSI unit completed the command successfully or that an error has occurred.

SCSI Standards.   The original version of SCSI (SCSI-1) was formally approved in 1986. It featured an 8-bit data bus and permitted asynchronous data transfers of up to 1.5 MB/s. Using synchronous transfers, data rates as high as 5 MB/s could be achieved.

One of the drawbacks to SCSI-1 was the lack of a formal command set, which resulted in compatibility problems between SCSI devices and host adapters manufactured by different companies. SCSI-2 improved this by implementing a Common Command Set (CCS). Not only did the CCS standardize the SCSI instruction set, it defined ten classes of equipment. This allows devices as different as CD-ROM readers, optical disk drives, scanners, streaming tape drives, and printers to all be controlled on the same bus.

By shaving some of the timing margins in SCSI-1, SCSI-2 increased the data transfer rates to 3 MB/s asynchronously and 10 MB/s synchronously (Fast SCSI).[16] In addition, SCSI-2 permits 16- and 32-bit data bus widths (Wide SCSI). Note, however, that these are options and are not required by the standard. With these wider bus widths, data rates as high as 40 MB/s can be achieved (synchronously with differential drivers).

---

[16]The term *Fast SCSI* is generally applied to a SCSI device that can transfer data synchronously at 5 MB/s or faster.

Technically, Wide SCSI–2 requires two cables (called the *A* and *B* cables in the standard). However, most manufacturers have implemented a single 68-pin cable called the *P* cable instead. It is expected that the SCSI-3 version of the standard will formalize the use of this cable (for a 16-bit data bus). Wider buses (32 bits) will require a secondary cable.

Additional enhancements expected with SCSI-3 are support for multi-host systems with as many as 16 SCSI devices, serial SCSI, and fiber optic transmission media. The latter may boost the potential data transfer rate to well over 100 MB/s.

USB—The Universal Serial Bus

Another I/O Bus?　　SCSI is an example of a *parallel* I/O bus. It offers medium-to-high-speed operation but requires a multiconductor (50- or 68-pin) cable of limited length. As such, SCSI tends to be restricted to peripherals "in the computer box."

The alternative to a parallel I/O bus is the *serial* bus. The advantage is simpler cabling with greater distance between devices; the drawback, of course, is slower speed.

Several serial I/O buses have been developed:

- **GeoPort.** This is a serial interface designed by Apple Computer, Inc., to enable Macintosh telephony applications. It uses a 9-conductor cable (limited to 4 feet in length) with RS-422 signaling. The data rate is 2 Mb/s.
- **IEEE P1394** (also called *FireWire*). This is a high-performance serial bus designed primarily for hard disk and video peripherals. It is rated at 100 Mb/s, 200 Mb/s, and 400 Mb/s and uses a 6-conductor cable. FireWire is expected to provide a link between PCs and consumer audio/video electronics.
- **USB** (Universal Serial Bus). This is a low- to medium-speed serial interface that promises to integrate most of the common PC peripherals—keyboard, mouse, printer, and modem—onto a single bus. With USB, users will be able to connect and disconnect peripherals "on the fly," with the system adapting automatically. High-speed (12 Mb/s) and low-speed (1.5 Mb/s) data rates are supported.

USB is particularly attractive because it can simplify the task of connecting basic peripherals to a PC. For example, most 80x86-based PCs require users to struggle with the concept of LPT ports, COM ports, IRQs, I/O addresses, 9-pin serial ports, 25-pin serial ports, 25-pin parallel ports, etc. Select a "wrong" I/O address or IRQ setting and you are in for a long evening of troubleshooting. USB promises to change all of this.

History.　　USB was developed by several companies with a personal interest in the development of easy-to-use PCs: Compaq, Digital Equipment Corporation, IBM, Intel, Microsoft, NEC, and Northern Telecom. Although just emerging as this book was written, USB seems poised to become the next I/O bus standard for the PC. Intel is already announcing PCI chipsets that support the bus, and IBM and Compaq have promised USB systems (and peripherals) by the end of 1996.

USB Devices: Hubs and Functions.　　In a computer that supports USB, *devices* such as keyboards, mice, printers, and modems all connect to the system *host* via *nodes* on USB expansion *hubs*. (This is shown in Figure 11.18.) A typical system may have several hubs accommodating several different devices.

Figure 11.18   USB devices are connected to nodes on hubs. Hubs are then wired in daisy chain fashion to the root hub located in the USB host. (From *USB Specification, Revision 1.0,* January, 1996. Courtesy of Universal Serial Bus Specification.)

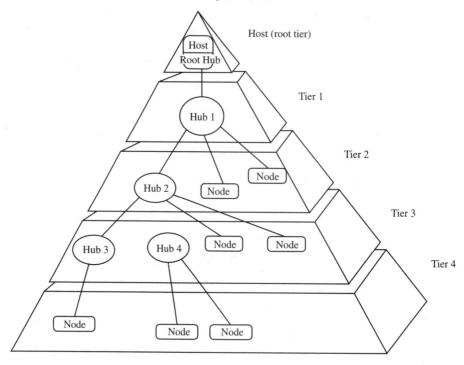

In most cases, the hub will be built into a USB device. In Figure 11.19, for example, the keyboard provides a specific USB *function* (namely the keyboard input device), as well as three nodes for system expansion; that is, it is also a three-port hub.

USB systems require a single host adapter, usually integrated into the chipset of the system board. In addition to interfacing with the system processor, the host provides for system expansion via a *root hub*. In Figure 11.19, the host/root hub provides three expansion ports.

Each device in a USB system is assigned a unique address when first attached. This process is called *bus enumeration*.[17] As many as 127 different devices can be accommodated.

Pipes.   When a USB device is first attached to a hub, the host assigns it an address and establishes a connection between itself and the device. The characteristics of this connection—speed, direction, required bandwidth, error-handling requirements, transfer type, maximum packet size—together are referred to as a *pipe*. The portion of the USB device that communicates with the host is called the *endpoint*. In general, each USB device has several independently operating endpoints. Endpoint 0, however, is reserved for device initialization and configuration.

---

[17]This feature supports the plug-and-play nature of USB. No switches or jumpers need be set by the user: The system automatically addresses devices as they are attached.

Figure 11.19 USB devices typically include a hub for system expansion. (From *USB Specification, Revision 1.0,* January, 1996. Courtesy of Universal Serial Bus Specification.)

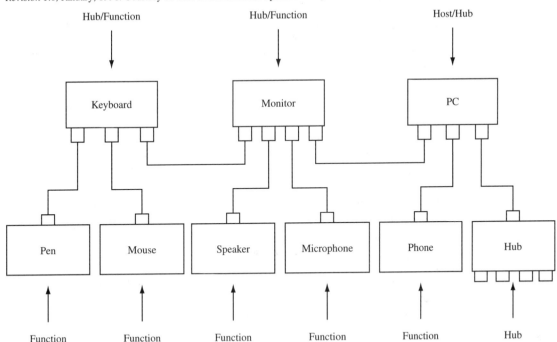

Bus Protocol. USB data is transmitted and received using a *synchronous* serial format (that is, there are no start or stop bits). Synchronization is maintained by encoding the clock signal into the data pattern.

Communication between the USB host and its devices is accomplished via variable-length data *packets*. Each packet begins with a synchronization (SYNC) field to allow the local clock to synchronize itself with the data. The SYNC field is followed by a Packet Identifier Field (PID), used to indicate the type and format of the packet, as well as the type of error detection applied to the packet. The PID is followed by the information portion of the packet and then several CRC bits used to provide error detection. Figure 11.20 summarizes the format for USB packets.

All packets are transmitted over the USB bus distributed over a 1 ms timing frame. Five different packet types may be transmitted:

1. *Start of Frame (SOF).* Each frame must begin with an SOF packet, which can be issued only by the host.
2. *Token.* This packet identifies the direction of the data packets to follow (into or out of the host). A token may also indicate that the following data is *setup* information sent from the host to a device.

Figure 11.20 USB data packets. The information field varies in length depending on the data transfer type.

SYNC	PID	Information	CRC

3. *Data.* These packets carry the data between host and selected USB device.
4. *Handshake.* These packets are used to report the status of a transaction.
5. *Special.* This packet is issued by the host and enables the flow of downstream bus traffic to low-speed USB devices.

Types of Data Transfers. The information transferred by a USB data packet falls into one of four categories:

1. *Control Transfers.* Used by low- and high-speed devices, these transfers are used to configure a device when first attached to a USB hub. A portion of each frame is always reserved for control transfers.
2. *Bulk Transfers.* Limited to high-speed devices, these transfers are intended to communicate large amounts of data, but only when bandwidth—access to the bus—is available. Because all other transfer types have priority, bulk transfers occur at highly variable times. Text data intended for a printer is an example of a bulk transfer.
3. *Interrupt Transfers.* These transfers are always input to the host and may be used by both high- and low-speed devices. They are designed to provide small, spontaneous transfers of data (for example, a mouse click or a keyboard character). Interrupt transfers may occupy as much as 90 percent of a given frame.
4. *Isochronous Transfers.* These transfers are used by high-speed USB devices to communicate *real-time* data (voice or music, for example). Isochronous transfers are guaranteed access to the full bandwidth of the USB channel (that is, they have highest priority), and as long as data is supplied to the pipe, a constant data rate will occur. USB considers the timeliness of isochronous transfers to be more important than correctness, and thus does not support handshaking or data retransmission in this mode.

Plug and Play. Like the PCI bus, USB has Plug and Play built in. The USB host automatically detects new devices, assigns them (nonconflicting) addresses, and alerts the (USB-aware) operating system to issue the proper initialization commands.[18] This can all be done "on-the-fly," allowing the user to add or remove devices from the system at will.

The Universal Serial Bus Driver (USBD). USB devices are accessed via software calls to the Universal Serial Bus Driver (USBD). This driver must be implemented as part of the computer's operating system. The USBD provides both command and pipe mechanisms to its USB clients (USB device-specific software). Command mechanisms allow clients to configure and control a particular USB device; pipe mechanisms allow the client to transfer data with the USB device.

The USB Electrical Interface. USB uses a *differential* output driver to drive the data onto the USB cable. Two pins, called D+ and D– are used to indicate the logic levels as follows:

- Logic 1: D+–D– > 200 mV
- Logic 0: D+–D– < –200 mV

Termination is accomplished via built-in pull-down resistors on D+ and D– at the host and hubs, and a pull up resistor on D+ (full speed) or D– (low speed) at the device ends.

---

[18]Microsoft has announced that Windows 97 (or 98?) will provide USB support.

Figure 11.21 USB devices are connected using a four-conductor cable. (From *USB Specification, Revision 1.0,* January, 1996. Courtesy of Universal Serial Bus Specification.)

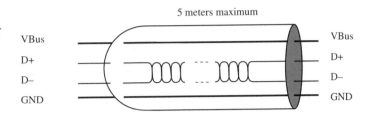

5 meters maximum

VBus   VBus
D+   D+
D−   D−
GND   GND

A full-speed USB connection is made through a shielded twisted-pair cable with a characteristic impedance of 90Ω. (This is shown in Figure 11.21.) The maximum cable length (device to hub) is five meters. Low-speed devices can use an unshielded, untwisted wire cable a maximum of three meters in length.

As shown in Figure 11.21, USB provides power distribution over the cable via the VBus and GND pins. Bus-powered devices rely on the host or a hub for their power source and may draw as much as 500 mA from a suitably powered source. The system keyboard and mouse are typical examples of bus-powered devices. Devices requiring more than 500 mA must be self-powered. A modem would be an example of a self-powered USB device.

Self-Review 11.4 (Answers on page 546)

11.4.1 List the ways in which the SCSI bus differs from a system bus such as (E)ISA, MCA, or PCI.

11.4.2 The host adapter on the SCSI bus is typically assigned ID number _____.

11.4.3 With differential drivers, the SCSI bus may be as long as _____ meters.

11.4.4 Data on the SCSI bus can be transferred _____ or _____.

11.4.5 Most manufacturers implement Wide SCSI using a _____ conductor cable.

11.4.6 Where is the *host* located in a USB system?

11.4.7 How many different devices does USB support?

11.4.8 Data on the USB bus is transmitted in _____ distributed over a 1 ms timing _____.

11.4.9 Real-time audio can be transmitted over a USB bus using _____ transfers.

11.4.10 *(True/False)* USB devices can be added or removed without turning the computer system off.

Chapter 11 Self-Test

11.1 The clock rate in the PC/XT is _____ MHz.

11.2 The bus slots in the PC/XT accommodate a(n) _____-bit data bus width.

11.3 The address bus width for an ISA slot is _____ bits.

11.4 The standard bus clock frequency for an ISA slot is _____ MHz.

11.5 List four system requirements to achieve all of the goals of Plug and Play.

11.6 MCA bus slots first appeared in IBM's _____ family of microcomputers.

11.7 List the adapters typically found on the system board of an MCA computer.

11.8 The MCA bus operates at _____ MHz, and in its highest speed burst mode can transfer as many as _____ bytes in one bus cycle.

11.9 The MCA and EISA buses both provide a _____-bit address bus width.

11.10   How is a "new" adapter card installed and configured in an MCA or EISA bus computer?

11.11   The theoretical maximum bus frequency for the VL bus is _____.

11.12   Using 486-like burst cycles the VL bus can transfer _____ bytes in one burst.

11.13   List two advantages of the PCI bus's burst mode compared to VLB burst mode.

11.14   To minimize the number of pins on the PCI bus, the address and data lines are

_____.

11.15   In what way do PCI cards support Plug and Play?

11.16   SCSI-1 and SCSI-2 support _____ different SCSI devices. SCSI-3 supports
_____ devices.

11.17   With SCSI, the fastest data transfers occur when the bus operates _____.

11.18   How many terminators are required on a SCSI bus? Where should they be placed?

11.19   List the four types of USB data transfers. Which type is used to transfer "mouse clicks"?

11.20   How is Plug and Play accomplished with USB?

Analysis and Design Questions

Section 11.1

11.1   Match each description below with one of the following PC/XT support chips: 8087,
8237, 8255A, 8259A, 8284, 8288.

Support Chip	Description
(a) _____	Math coprocessor
(b) _____	Memory refresh, disk drive data transfers
(c) _____	System configuration, keyboard access, speaker control
(d) _____	Interrupt controller
(e) _____	Clock generator
(f) _____	Bus controller

11.2   Answer the following questions about the 8255A PPI interface shown in Figure 11.3.

(a) How many I/O ports does this interface occupy?

(b) When writing data to port B, we expect A0 = _____; A1 = _____; $\overline{IOR}$ =
_____; $\overline{IOW}$ = _____; and $\overline{CS}$ = _____.

(c) What is the purpose of connecting AEN to the $\overline{G}$ input of the address comparator?

(d) Describe the changes required to map the PPI chip to I/O ports E00–E03H.

11.3   In the PC/XT design there are no I/O ports mapped to the range 360–363H. There are
therefore 64 sets of addresses available with this low-order address (corresponding to the
64 combinations of A10–A15, which are not examined by the onboard decoders). Design
an address decoder circuit that could be used to enable *eight* PPI chips mapped to the following ranges:

(a) 360–363H

(b) 760–763H

(c) B60–B63H

(d) F60–F63H

(e) 1360–1363H

(f) 1760–1763H

(g) 1B60–1B63H

(h) 1F60–1F63H

Hint: Use the circuit in Figure 11.3 but add a 74LS138 three-to-eight line decoder to test A10–A15. When the low-order and high-order addresses match, enable the appropriate PPI chip.

11.4 Calculate the data transfer rate using the ISA bus at 8.33 MHz with one wait state.

Section 11.2

11.5 Show, via a calculation, that the MCA bus has a maximum data transfer rate of 160 MB/s and the EISA bus a maximum rate of 133 MB/s.

11.6 What signal on the MCA bus indicates that that adapter is running with a 16-bit data bus width? What is the name of the similar signal on the EISA bus?

Section 11.3

11.7 Refer to the VLB and PCI signal descriptions in Tables 11.6 and 11.8 and provide the name of the signal that corresponds to the description below.

	Description	VLB Signal Name	PCI Signal Name
(a)	Bus clock		
(b)	Bus master requests control of the buses		
(c)	Request to perform a 64-bit data transfer		
(d)	Byte enables		

11.8 Study the specifications for the various bus standards presented in this chapter and then complete the table below.

	Bus Standard					
Specification	PC/XT	ISA	MCA	EISA	VLB	PCI
Memory address bus width						
Data bus width						
Maximum bus clock frequency						
Maximum data transfer rate						
Support for shared interrupts						
Automatic adapter configuration						
3.3V specific slots						

Section 11.4

11.9 What data transfer rate do you predict for a Wide (16-bit) SCSI-2 device operating synchronously? Explain your answer.

11.10 When testing a passive SCSI terminator with an ohmmeter, 137Ω should be measured between any one signal line and the TERMPWR pin. Show that this is true by:

(a) Drawing a schematic showing the 18 SCSI signal lines with pull-up and pull-down resistors connected as described in the chapter.

(b) Redrawing the circuit in (a) showing the equivalent seen between any one signal pin and TERMPWR. This should be 330Ω in parallel with the resistance of the other 17 lines.

(c) Computing the final equivalent resistance.

Self–Review Answers

11.1.1 The PC/XT is configured by the settings of a DIP switch. The AT is configured via setup software with the configuration data stored in battery-backed CMOS RAM.

11.1.2 5, 1.05

11.1.3 200–3FFH

11.1.4 80286

11.1.5 15, 8, 7, 4

11.1.6 8.33 MHz

11.1.7 False (Even legacy cards can benefit from PnP—provided a PnP-aware operating system is used.)

11.2.1 all

11.2.2 2, 200 ns

11.2.3 ADF files are used to store configuration information about an MCA adapter. When a new adapter card is installed, the BIOS reads this file and configures the card accordingly.

11.2.4 Standard EISA bus cycle:

$$\frac{4 \text{ bytes}}{2 \text{ Clock Pulses} \times 120 \text{ ns/pulse}} = 16.6 \text{ MB/s}$$

11.2.5 Level

11.3.1 Video

11.3.2

$$\frac{16 \text{ bytes}}{6 \text{ Clock Pulses} \times 20 \text{ ns/pulse}} = 133 \text{ MB/s}$$

11.3.3 Video adapters, hard drive controllers, high-speed network interface cards

11.3.4 PCI bridge

11.3.5 The same pins are used for the address and data. During the address phase the lines hold the memory or I/O address. During the data phase the lines switch and input or output the data.

11.3.6 Unlimited

11.3.7 One is designed for 3.3V cards; the other supports 5V cards.

11.4.1 SCSI devices are connected to a host adapter, which in turn connects to the processor via the system bus. As a result, the data transfer rate for SCSI is much slower than that of the system bus. SCSI is an intelligent bus that can operate without processor intervention, thus allowing true parallel processing.

11.4.2 7

11.4.3 25

11.4.4 asynchronously, synchronously

11.4.5 68

11.4.6 All USB systems require a single host located in the system PC (either built into the system board or added as an adapter card).

11.4.7 127

11.4.8 Packets, frame

11.4.9 Isochronous

11.4.10 True

Appendix A

MS-DOS BIOS Services and Functions

Table A.1 Common MS-DOS BIOS Services

Interrupt	Service (AH)	Name	Comments	Registers
10H	00H	Set video mode (and clear screen).	Register AL defines mode (see Registers column).	00H: 40 × 25 16-color text (gray-scaled on composite monitors). 01H: 40 × 25 16-color text. 02H: 80 × 25 16-color text (gray-scaled on composite monitors). 03H: 80 × 25 16-color text. 04H: 320 × 200 4-color graphics. 05H: 320 × 200 4-color graphics (gray-scaled on composite monitors). 06H: 640 × 200 2-color graphics. 07H: 80 × 25 monochrome text (MDA, EGA, VGA). 0DH: 320 × 200 16-color graphics (EGA, VGA). 0EH: 640 × 200 16-color graphics (EGA, VGA). 0FH: 640 × 350 monochrome graphics (EGA, VGA). 10H: 640 × 350 16-color graphics (EGA, VGA). 11H: 640 × 480 2-color graphics (MCGA, VGA). 12H: 640 × 480 16-color graphics (VGA). 13H: 320 × 200 256-color graphics (MCGA, VGA).
10H	02H	Set cursor position.	Cursor is moved to row and column specified in DX.	DH = row number. DL = column number. BH = page number (if applicable).

Table A.1 *(continued)*

Interrupt	Service (AH)	Name	Comments	Registers
10H	09H	Write character and attribute	The character is written CX times at the current cursor position with the specified attributes. The cursor is not advanced.	AL = ASCII character. BL = attribute value (see Table A.3) or foreground color (graphics modes). BH = background color (video mode 13 only) or display page. CX = number of times to write character
10H	0CH	Write pixel.	Writes a pixel to the screen at the column address given in CX and row address in DX with color specified in AL.	AL = pixel color. BH = page number. CX = column number of pixel. DX = row number of pixel.
10H	0DH	Read pixel.	Reads the color value of the pixel whose column address is in CX and row address is in DX. The pixel value is returned in AL.	AL = pixel value. BH = page number. CX = column number of pixel. DX = row number of pixel.
10H	0EH	Write character in teletype mode.	Writes at current cursor position with the current attributes.	AL = ASCII character. BL = foreground color (graphics modes only).
13H	02H	Read disk sectors.	Reads one or more disk sectors into memory.	DL = drive number (A = 0, B = 1, etc.). DH = head number. CH = cylinder number.* CL = sector number. AL = number of sectors to be read. ES:BX = address of buffer. If CF = 0: No error and AH = 0. If CF = 1: Error and AH = error code.

(continued on next page)

*For a hard disk: CH = low-order 8 bits of cylinder number, CL = high-order 2 bits of cylinder number plus 6-bit sector number.

549

Table A.1 *(continued)*

Interrupt	Service (AH)	Name	Comments	Registers
13H	16H	Change of floppy disk status.	Tests the floppy disk specified in DL and returns a code in AH indicating if the disk has changed or the drive is not ready.	AH = floppy disk status. 00H = no floppy disk change. 01H = service called with invalid parameter. 06H = floppy disk changed. 80H = drive not ready.
15H	86H	Wait for time delay.	Suspends program operation until the time delay has expired.	CX:DX = time delay in microseconds. CF = 0 if successful. CF = 1 if not successful. AH = 0 if successful. AH = 80 if invalid command. AH = 83 if a delay is already in progress. AH = 86 if function is not supported.
16H	00H	Read next keyboard character.	Waits for a key to be pressed and then returns with its ASCII code or 0 in AL.	AL: ASCII code or 0 for non-ASCII key. AH: Scan code or character ID.
16H	12H	Get extended shift status.	Shift key status bits returned in AX.	See Figure 5.15 for bit definitions.
19H	—	Reboot computer.	The computer is rebooted. Similar to a cold boot but without the memory check.	

Table A. 2 Common MS-DOS Functions

Interrupt	Function (AH)	Name	Comments	Registers
20H	—	Program terminate.	Returns control to MS-DOS. Does not close open files.	None
21H	09H	String output.	Sends a string of characters terminated with "$" to the standard output device.	DS:DX points to the start of the string.
21H	0AH	Buffered keyboard input.	Inputs a string of characters terminated with the Enter key to a memory buffer pointed to by DS:DX.	DS:DX points to byte (0) of buffer. Buffer byte (0): Desired buffer length. Buffer byte (1): Actual buffer length. Buffer bytes (2 through end): The string
21H	1CH	Get specified drive parameters	Returns specific information about the disk whose drive number is given in DL.	DL = drive number (A = 1, B = 2, etc.). AL = number of sectors per cluster (FF if unsuccessful). CX = size in bytes of disk sectors (512). DX = total number of clusters on disk. DS:BX = pointer to media byte.
21H	2AH	Get date.	Returns with the year, month, day, and day of week.	CX = year (1980–2099). DH = month (1–12). DL = day (1–31). AL = day of week (0–6; Sunday–Monday).
21H	2BH	Set date.	Allows the year, month, and day, to be written.	CX = year (1980–2099). DH = month (1–12). DL = day (1–31). AL = FFH (error) or 00 (no error).

(*continued on next page*)

Table A. 2 *(continued)*

Interrupt	Function (AH)	Name	Comments	Registers
21H	2CH	Get time.	Returns with the time in hours, minutes, seconds, and hundredths of seconds.	CH = hours (0–23). CL = minutes (0–59). DH = seconds (0–59). DL = hundredths of seconds (0–99).
21H	2DH	Set time.	Allows the time in hours, minutes, seconds, and hundredths of seconds to be written.	CH = hours (0–23). CL = minutes (0–59). DH = seconds (0–59). DL = hundredths of seconds (0–99). AL = FFH (error) or 00 (no error).
21H	25H	Set interrupt vector.	Loads the interrupt vector address stored in DS:DX into the interrupt vector table at the type number specified in AL.	DS:DX = address of interrupt service routine. AL = interrupt type number.
21H	4CH	Terminate with error code	Returns control to DOS, closing all open files, and passes back the error code you specify in AL. This code can be tested in a DOS batch file using an "IF ERRORLEVEL" statement.	AL = user-specified error code.

Table A.3   Colors Available in 16-Color Text and Graphics Modes*

Intensity[†]	Red	Green	Blue	Hex	Description
0	0	0	0	00	Black
0	0	0	1	01	Blue
0	0	1	0	02	Green
0	0	1	1	03	Cyan
0	1	0	0	04	Red
0	1	0	1	05	Magenta
0	1	1	0	06	Brown
0	1	1	1	07	White (or gray)
1	0	0	0	08	Black (or dark gray)
1	0	0	1	09	Bright blue
1	0	1	0	0A	Bright green
1	0	1	1	0B	Bright cyan
1	1	0	0	0C	Bright red
1	1	0	1	0D	Bright magenta
1	1	1	0	0E	Yellow
1	1	1	1	0F	Bright white

*The high-order four bits of the attribute byte set the background color; the low-order four bits set the foreground color.
†When setting the background color, if the intensity bit is set, blinking is enabled.

Appendix B

PC/XT/AT Parallel Port

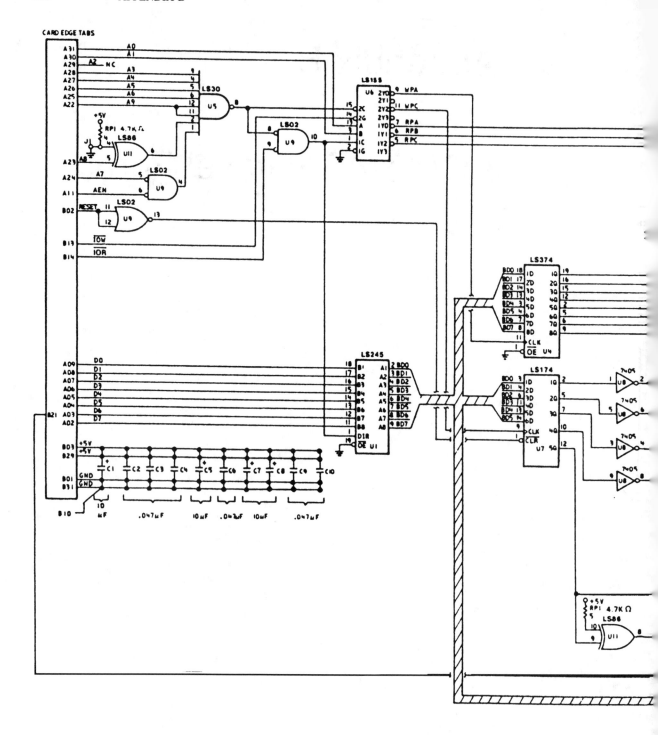

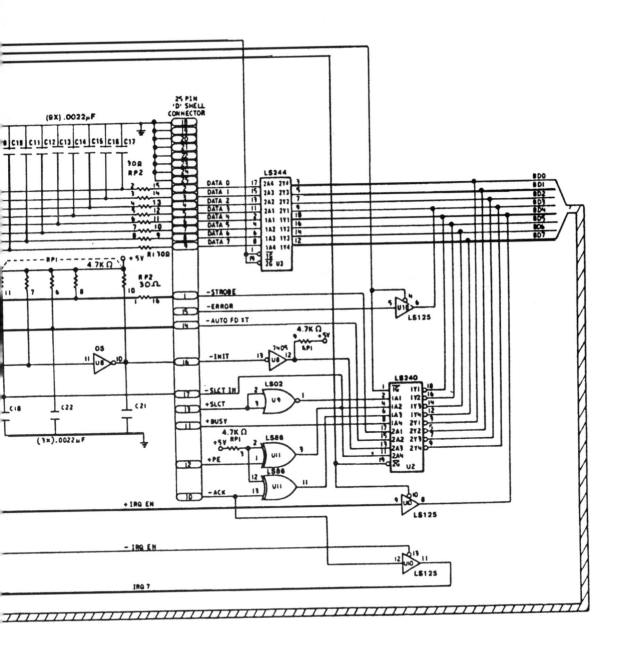

Index

Numbers in boldface type refer to figures. Numbers in italics refer to tables. Numbers in both italics and boldface type refer to sidebars.